TEST BANK I

TEST BANK I

JOHN BRINK
Calvin College

to accompany

David G. Myers

Psychology

Seventh Edition

WORTH PUBLISHERS

Test Bank I
by John Brink
to accompany
Myers: **Psychology**, Seventh Edition

Printed in the United States of America

ISBN: 0-7167-5291-3
0-7167- 9471-3 (Test Banks I and II package)

Printing: 5 4 3 2 1

Year: 06 05 04 03

Worth Publishers
41 Madison Avenue
New York, NY 10010
www.worthpublishers.com

Contents

Preface vii

PROLOGUE The Story of Psychology 1
Web Quiz 1 15
Web Quiz 2 18
Study Guide Questions 21

CHAPTER 1 Thinking Critically with Psychological Science 29
Web Quiz 1 61
Web Quiz 2 64
Study Guide Questions 67

CHAPTER 2 Neuroscience and Behavior 79
Web Quiz 1 108
Web Quiz 2 111
Study Guide Questions 114

CHAPTER 3 The Nature and Nurture of Behavior 125
Web Quiz 1 143
Web Quiz 2 146
Study Guide Questions 149

CHAPTER 4 The Developing Person 159
Web Quiz 1 197
Web Quiz 2 200
Study Guide Questions 203

CHAPTER 5 Sensation 217
Web Quiz 1 241
Web Quiz 2 244
Study Guide Questions 247

CHAPTER 6 Perception 257
Web Quiz 1 278
Web Quiz 2 281
Study Guide Questions 284

CHAPTER 7 States of Consciousness 295
Web Quiz 1 321
Web Quiz 2 324
Study Guide Questions 327

CHAPTER 8 Learning 337
Web Quiz 1 364
Web Quiz 2 367
Study Guide Questions 370

CHAPTER 9 Memory 381
Web Quiz 1 409
Web Quiz 2 412
Study Guide Questions 415

CHAPTER 10 Thinking and Language 427
Web Quiz 1 447
Web Quiz 2 450
Study Guide Questions 453

CHAPTER 11 Intelligence 465
Web Quiz 1 486
Web Quiz 2 489
Study Guide Questions 492

CHAPTER 12 Motivation and Work 503
Web Quiz 1 528
Web Quiz 2 531
Study Guide Questions 534

CHAPTER 13 Emotion 545
Web Quiz 1 567
Web Quiz 2 570
Study Guide Questions 573

CHAPTER 14 Stress and Health 583
Web Quiz 1 602
Web Quiz 2 605
Study Guide Questions 608

CHAPTER 15 Personality 619
Web Quiz 1 649
Web Quiz 2 652
Study Guide Questions 655

CHAPTER 16 Psychological Disorders 667
Web Quiz 1 689
Web Quiz 2 692
Study Guide Questions 695

CHAPTER 17 Therapy 705
Web Quiz 1 729
Web Quiz 2 732
Study Guide Questions 735

CHAPTER 18 Social Psychology 747
Web Quiz 1 776
Web Quiz 2 779
Study Guide Questions 782

Preface

Test Bank I to accompany *Psychology*, Seventh Edition, by David G. Myers is designed to gauge students' basic knowledge, to promote and evaluate their critical thinking skills, and to encourage and enhance the learning process. It includes over 2000 carefully crafted multiple-choice questions. Test Bank II contains more than 2000 additional questions, as well as questions on the PsychSim computer simulations, the PsychQuest CD-ROM modules, and *The Brain*, Second Edition, and *The Mind*, Second Edition, modules. Many of the questions in both Test Bank I and II have been newly created for the latest edition of the Myers textbook. Most notable are those associated with the new text coverage of psychology's history in the Prologue and with psychology in work settings in Chapter 12.

As a major new contribution to this latest edition of the Myers textbook, I have constructed two student self-tests for each chapter and the Prologue. Each test contains 15 multiple-choice questions; both are presented in a clearly marked section at the end of each Test Bank I chapter. They are also directly available to students and instructors as part of the Myers Psychology Web Companion (http://www.worthpublishers.com/myers). Instructors may choose to use these questions for daily quizzes or for inclusion in their regular tests as an incentive to encourage students to access the Web site testing materials. Having students take one or both of the quizzes will help prepare them for the questions that are included in Test Banks I and II. The multiple-choice questions from Richard Straub's Study Guide are also included in a clearly marked section at the end of each Test Bank I chapter.

Test Bank I also includes essay questions for each textbook chapter. These questions go well beyond a simple rephrasing of the chapter's learning objectives. They are designed to promote critical thinking by challenging students to analyze, synthesize, evaluate, and apply material contained in the textbook. Some of these questions require as little as 15 minutes to complete, others may take an entire class period. They work well as exam questions (using either a closed- or open-book format) or as homework assignments.

Preceding each multiple-choice question, the following information is provided to help you to select questions.

1. *Chapter topic:* Taken from the textbook headings and subheadings, this identification tag allows you to scan the questions and select the appropriate balance of questions from the topics you wish to cover.
2. *Textbook page number:* This provides you with a reference should students question the basis for an answer. Some instructors may wish to provide students

who answered incorrectly with this page number so that they can see the correct answer in context.

3. *Difficulty level:* Each item is rated "easy," "medium," or "difficult." You can select those that challenge your students to the extent appropriate for your course. About half the questions are in the "medium" range, 30 percent "easy," and 20 percent "difficult." As new items are added to the Test Bank, we continue to assess item difficulty in order to maintain an appropriate mix of difficulty levels.

4. *Type of question:* Either factual/definitional or conceptual.

   Factual/definitional questions test students' knowledge of information that is explicitly presented in the textbook. Specifically, they test knowledge of methods and theories, research discoveries, important people and events, and the language of psychology. More than half the questions are factual/definitional.

   Conceptual questions test students' ability to analyze or synthesize information presented in the textbook. Conceptual questions may require deduction from general principles or reasoning by analogy.

   Conceptual/application questions test students' ability to use inferential skills in applying textbook information to appropriate real-world events and experiences.

5. *Learning objectives:* Each question is keyed to one of the learning objectives listed on the first page of each chapter of this Test Bank, and also in the Instructor's Resources.

These Test Bank questions are the database for a test-generation program available on a single CD-ROM in both Windows and Macintosh formats. Instructors who adopt *Psychology*, 7/e, may obtain the electronic version of the Test Bank and test-generating software from Worth Publishers. The computerized version of the Test Bank allows instructors to select questions either manually or randomly, to edit questions, and to print multiple versions of an exam. The computerized Test Bank also includes Internet testing functionality. This will give the instructor the option of posting the test on the Internet, in addition to the standard option of creating a print or network-administered exam.

I wish to express special appreciation to Janet Sheeres for her word-processing efficiency and to Betty Shapiro Probert of The Special Projects Group for her valuable editorial help with this Test Bank. The Test Bank has also benefitted from validation information and other feedback from its users, and I welcome such information and feedback from you, plus any suggestions you may have for making the testing package more effective.

John Brink
June 2003

TEST BANK I

Prologue

The Story of Psychology

Learning Objectives

Psychology's Roots (pp. 1-9)

1. Trace the views of prescientific thinkers regarding the origins of knowledge and how the mind and body relate.

2. Discuss early psychologists' efforts to understand the structure and functions of the mind.

3. Identify the nature and scope of contemporary psychology.

Contemporary Psychology (pp. 9-16)

4. Describe psychology's concerns regarding stability and change, rationality and irrationality, nature and nurture.

5. Briefly describe the different perspectives from which psychologists examine behavior and mental processes, and explain their complementarity.

6. Identify some of the basic and applied research subfields of psychology, and differentiate the mental health professions of clinical psychology and psychiatry.

7. (Close-Up) Discuss several principles for effective learning, and explain the PRTR study methods.

Prescientific psychology, p. 2
Easy, Factual/Definitional, Objective 1, Ans: a

1. Who most clearly affirmed that the mind continues to exist after physical death?
   a. Socrates
   b. Aristotle
   c. Darwin
   d. Wundt

Prescientific psychology, p. 2
Medium, Factual/Definitional, Objective 1, Ans: d

2. Socrates emphasized the importance of ________ as a source of knowledge.
   a. experience
   b. animal spirits
   c. experimentation
   d. logic

Prescientific psychology, p. 2
Easy, Factual/Definitional, Objective 1, Ans: c

3. Plato affirmed the importance of:
   a. pragmatism.
   b. empiricism.
   c. innate ideas.
   d. natural selection.

Prescientific psychology, p. 2
Medium, Conceptual/Application, Objective 1, Ans: b

4. Professor McClure believes that young children are frequently able to make morally correct decisions because humans are endowed with an inborn knowledge of basic ethical principles. The professor's belief is most consistent with the views of:
   a. Aristotle.
   b. Plato.
   c. John Locke.
   d. Francis Bacon.

Prescientific psychology, pp. 2-3, 4
Medium, Conceptual, Objective 1, Ans: c

5. Which philosopher would have been most enthusiastic about modern empiricism?
   a. Plato
   b. Socrates
   c. Aristotle
   d. Descartes

Prescientific psychology, p. 3
Easy, Factual/Definitional, Objective 1, Ans: d

6. Who suggested that animal spirits flow through the nerves so as to produce movements of the body?
   a. Plato
   b. Aristotle
   c. John Locke
   d. René Descartes

Prescientific psychology, pp. 2, 3
Medium, Factual/Definitional, Objective 1, Ans: b

7. Both Plato and Descartes believed that:
   a. the mind is a blank slate at birth.
   b. mind and body are distinct and separable.
   c. true knowledge originates in sensory experience.
   d. mental processes reflect evolutionary change.

Prescientific psychology, pp. 3-4
Medium, Factual/Definitional, Objective 1, Ans: a

8. Francis Bacon was an early advocate of what came to be known as:
   a. empiricism.
   b. natural selection.
   c. structuralism.
   d. pragmatism.

Prescientific psychology, p. 4
Easy, Factual/Definitional, Objective 1, Ans: c

9. Who suggested that the mind at birth is a blank slate upon which experience writes?
   a. Charles Darwin
   b. René Descartes
   c. John Locke
   d. Plato

Prescientific psychology, p. 4
Medium, Conceptual/Application, Objective 1, Ans: c

10. Professor Zwier believes that children have an inborn concept of time that enables them to distinguish between the past and the present. The professor's belief is most *inconsistent* with the views of:
   a. Descartes.
   b. Socrates.
   c. Locke.
   d. Plato.

Prescientific psychology, p. 4
Easy, Factual/Definitional, Objective 1, Ans: b

11. The view that knowledge comes from experience and that science should rely on observation is called:
   a. pragmatism.
   b. empiricism.
   c. rationalism.
   d. structuralism

Prescientific psychology, pp. 2, 4
Medium, Conceptual, Objective 1, Ans: d

12. Plato's presumption of inborn knowledge most clearly contrasts with a view known as:
   a. structuralism.
   b. functionalism.
   c. rationalism.
   d. empiricism.

Prescientific psychology, pp. 2-3, 4
Difficult, Conceptual, Objective 1, Ans: c

13. Aristotle and John Locke would have been most likely to agree that:
   a. personality traits are largely inherited.
   b. the soul is separable from the body.
   c. self-concepts are heavily influenced by life experiences.
   d. observation is less important than logical reasoning.

Psychological science is born, p. 4
Medium, Factual/Definitional, Objective 2, Ans: d

14. Wilhelm Wundt's laboratory work involved experimental studies of:
 a. animal intelligence.
 b. personality development.
 c. learning and memory.
 d. reactions to sensory stimulation.

Thinking about the mind's structure, p. 4
Easy, Factual/Definitional, Objective 2, Ans: c

15. Who used the method of introspection to scientifically identify basic elements of the mind?
 a. Aristotle
 b. John Locke
 c. Edward Titchener
 d. John Watson

Thinking about the mind's structure, p. 4
Easy, Factual/Definitional, Objective 2, Ans: b

16. The self-reflective observation of one's own sensations and feeling is called:
 a. clinical psychology
 b. introspection.
 c. spaced practice.
 d. pragmatism.

Thinking about the mind's structure, p. 4
Medium, Conceptual/Application, Objective 2, Ans: e

17. Research participants were asked to monitor and report their own immediate sensory reactions to differently colored objects. This research involved a technique known as:
 a. PRTR.
 b. behavior genetics.
 c. psychoanalysis.
 d. massed practice.
 e. introspection.

Thinking about the mind's structure, p. 5
Easy, Factual/Definitional, Objective 2, Ans: a

18. The unreliability of introspection contributed to the waning popularity of:
 a. structuralism.
 b. pragmatism.
 c. empiricism.
 d. behaviorism.

Thinking about the mind's functions, p. 5
Easy, Factual/Definitional, Objective 2, Ans: c

19. William James was a prominent American:
 a. psychoanalyst.
 b. behaviorist.
 c. functionalist.
 d. structuralist.

Thinking about the mind's functions, p. 5
Easy, Factual/Definitional, Objective 2, Ans: a

20. Functionalism was a school of psychology that focused attention on the:
a. adaptive value of conscious thought.
b. component elements of sensory experience.
c. disruptive effects of unconscious motives.
d. treatment of psychological disorders.

Thinking about the mind's functions, pp. 4, 5
Medium, Conceptual, Objective 2, Ans: d

21. Edward Titchener is to ________ as William James is to ________.
a. structuralism; behaviorism
b. behaviorism; functionalism
c. functionalism; behaviorism
d. structuralism; functionalism

Thinking about the mind's functions, p. 5
Medium, Factual/Definitional, Objective 2, Ans: b

22. Which psychologist emphasized that the truth of ideas should be judged in the light of their practical consequences?
a. Freud
b. James
c. Wundt
d. Titchener

Thinking about the mind's functions, pp. 8-9
Easy, Factual/Definitional, Objective 2, Ans: c

23. Who was a student of William James and the first female president of the American Psychological Association?
a. Jean Piaget
b. Francis Bacon
c. Rosalie Raynor
d. Mary Calkins
e. René Descartes

Psychological science develops, p. 6
Easy, Factual/Definitional, Objective 3, Ans: b

24. The personality theorist, Sigmund Freud, was an Austrian:
a. chemist.
b. physician.
c. theologian.
d. politician.

Psychological science develops, p. 7
Medium, Factual/Definitional, Objective 3, Ans: d

25. In its early years, psychology focused on the study of ________, but from the 1920s into the 1960s, American psychologists emphasized the study of ________.
a. environmental influences; hereditary influences
b. maladaptive behavior; adaptive behavior
c. unconscious motives; conscious thoughts and feelings
d. mental processes; observable behavior

Psychological science develops, p. 7
Easy, Factual/Definitional, Objective 3, Ans: b

26. Behaviorists dismissed the value of:
a. science.
b. introspection.
c. empiricism.
d. psychology.

Psychological science develops, p. 7
Difficult, Conceptual, Objective 3, Ans: b

27. John Watson is to Edward Titchener as ________ is to ________.
a. heredity; environment
b. observable behavior; inner sensations
c. mental illness; psychotherapy
d. cognitive perspective; psychoanalytic perspective

Psychological science develops, p. 8
Medium, Factual/Definitional, Objective 3, Ans: c

28. Contemporary psychology is best defined as the science of:
a. conscious and unconscious mental activity.
b. observable responses to the environment.
c. behavior and mental processes.
d. thoughts, feelings, and perceptions.
e. maladaptive and adaptive behaviors.

Psychological science develops, p. 8
Difficult, Conceptual, Objective 3, Ans: b

29. Breathing is to remembering as ________ is to ________.
a. evolution; natural selection
b. behavior; mental process
c. irrationality; rationality
d. nurture; nature

Psychology's big issues, p. 9
Medium, Conceptual/Application, Objective 4, Ans: d

30. Jake acts very differently with his family than he does when he is with his friends. Jake's behavior is most directly relevant to the issue of:
a. nature versus nurture.
b. rationality versus irrationality.
c. structuralism versus functionalism.
d. stability versus change.

Psychology's big issues, p. 9
Easy, Factual/Definitional, Objective 4, Ans: d

31. Whether *homo sapiens* is an appropriate name for the human species is a question most directly relevant to the issue of:
a. stability versus change.
b. nature versus nurture.
c. structuralism versus functionalism.
d. rationality versus irrationality.

Psychology's big issues, p. 10
Easy, Factual/Definitional, Objective 4, Ans: d

32. Efforts to discover whether the intelligence of children is more heavily influenced by their genetic dispositions or by their home environments are most directly relevant to the debate regarding:
   a. structuralism versus functionalism.
   b. rationality versus irrationality.
   c. observation versus introspection.
   d. nature versus nurture.

Psychology's big issues, p. 10
Easy, Conceptual/Application, Objective 2, Ans: b

33. Lissette wonders whether personality differences between her African-American and Asian-American friends result from biological or cultural influences. In this instance, Lissette is primarily concerned with the issue of:
   a. rationality versus irrationality.
   b. nature versus nurture.
   c. behavior versus mental processes.
   d. structuralism versus functionalism.

Psychology's big issues, p. 10
Medium, Conceptual, Objective 4, Ans: c

34. Innate ability is to learned skill as ________ is to ________.
   a. Aristotle; Plato
   b. John Locke; Charles Darwin
   c. nature; nurture
   d. functionalism; structuralism

Psychology's big issues, p. 10
Medium, Factual/Definitional, Objective 4, Ans: c

35. John Locke's description of the infant mind as a blank slate is most directly relevant to the debate regarding:
   a. rationality versus irrationality.
   b. observation versus introspection.
   c. nature versus nurture.
   d. structuralism versus functionalism.

Psychology's big issues, p. 10
Difficult, Conceptual, Objective 4, Ans: a

36. In the context of debates over the origins of psychological traits, nature is to nurture as:
   a. Darwin is to Locke.
   b. Locke is to Descartes.
   c. Descartes is to Plato.
   d. Plato is to Socrates.

Psychology's big issues, p. 10
Easy, Factual/Definitional, Objective 4, Ans: b

37. The survival of organisms best suited to a particular environment is known as:
a. functionalism.
b. natural selection.
c. behavior genetics.
d. pragmatism.

Psychology's big issues, p. 10
Medium, Factual/Definitional, Objective 4, Ans: d

38. Who highlighted the reproductive advantages of environmentally adaptive traits?
a. Plato
b. Aristotle
c. John Locke
d. Charles Darwin

Psychology's perspectives, p. 11
Easy, Factual/Definitional, Objective 5, Ans: b

39. The neuroscience perspective in psychology would be most likely to emphasize that behavior is influenced by:
a. environmental circumstances.
b. blood chemistry.
c. unconscious conflicts.
d. subjective interpretations.

Psychology's perspectives, p. 11
Medium, Conceptual, Objective 5, Ans: d

40. Which perspective is most relevant to understanding the impact of strokes and brain diseases on memory?
a. evolutionary
b. behavioral
c. psychodynamic
d. neuroscience
e. behavior genetics

Psychology's perspectives, p. 11
Medium, Conceptual/Application, Objective 5, Ans: a

41. Professor Lopez believes that severe depression results primarily from an imbalanced diet and abnormal brain chemistry. Professor Lopez favors a ________ perspective on depression.
a. neuroscience
b. social-cultural
c. psychodynamic
d. behavior genetics
e. cognitive

Psychology's perspectives, p. 11
Medium, Conceptual, Objective 5, Ans: c

42. Which perspective would suggest that the facial expressions of emotion associated with lust and rage are inherited?
   a. cognitive
   b. behavioral
   c. evolutionary
   d. social-cultural

Psychology's perspectives, p. 11
Difficult, Conceptual/Application, Objective 5, Ans: d

43. Professor Crisman believes that most women prefer tall and physically strong partners because this preference enhanced the reproductive success of our female ancestors. This viewpoint best illustrates the ________ perspective.
   a. social-cultural
   b. behavioral
   c. cognitive
   d. evolutionary
   e. psychodynamic

Psychology's perspectives, p. 11
Medium, Factual/Definitional, Objective 5, Ans: c

44. Which perspective is most directly concerned with assessing the relative impact of both nature and nature on our psychological traits?
   a. evolutionary
   b. cognitive
   c. behavior genetics
   d. social-cultural
   e. psychodynamic

Psychology's perspectives, p. 11
Medium, Conceptual/Application, Objective 5, Ans: a

45. Professor Brody attempts to measure the relative impact of inborn traits and social influences on homosexual behavior. Her research efforts best illustrates the interests of the ________ perspective.
   a. behavior genetics
   b. psychodynamic
   c. behavioral
   d. cognitive

Psychology's perspectives, p. 11
Easy, Factual/Definitional, Objective 5, Ans: c

46. The distinctive feature of the psychodynamic perspective is its emphasis on:
   a. natural selection.
   b. brain chemistry.
   c. unconscious conflicts.
   d. learned behaviors.

Psychology's perspectives, p. 11
Medium, Conceptual/Application, Objective 5, Ans: c

47. Mrs. Alfieri believes that her husband's irritability toward her results from his unconscious feelings of hostility toward his own mother. Mrs. Alfieri is interpreting her husband's behavior from a(n) ________ perspective.
   a. evolutionary
   b. behavioral
   c. psychodynamic
   d. behavior genetics

Psychology's perspectives, p. 11
Easy, Factual/Definitional, Objective 5, Ans: c

48. Which perspective most clearly focuses on how we learn observable responses?
   a. evolutionary
   b. neuroscience
   c. behavioral
   d. psychodynamic
   e. behavior genetics

Psychology's perspectives, p. 11
Difficult, Conceptual, Objective 5, Ans: e

49. Mrs. Thompson believes that her son has become an excellent student because she consistently uses praise and affection to stimulate his learning efforts. Her belief best illustrates a ________ perspective.
   a. behavior genetics
   b. cognitive
   c. neuroscience
   d. psychodynamic
   e. behavioral

Psychology's perspectives, p. 11
Difficult, Conceptual, Objective 5, Ans: c

50. Nature is to nurture as the ________ perspective is to the ________ perspective.
   a. social-cultural; neuroscience
   b. neuroscience; evolutionary
   c. evolutionary; behavioral
   d. behavioral; social-cultural

Psychology's perspectives, p. 11
Easy, Factual/Definitional, Objective 5, Ans: d

51. The cognitive perspective in psychology emphasizes how:
   a. feelings are influenced by blood chemistry.
   b. people try to understand their own unconscious motives.
   c. behavior is influenced by environmental conditions.
   d. people encode, process, store, and retrieve information.

Psychology's perspectives, pp. 11-12
Medium, Factual/Definitional, Objective 5, Ans: b

52. Which perspective is most concerned with the unique ways in which individuals interpret their own life experiences?
    a. behavioral
    b. cognitive
    c. social-cultural
    d. neuroscience
    e. behavior genetics

Psychology's perspectives, pp. 11-12
Medium, Conceptual, Objective 5, Ans: a

53. Which psychological perspective is most likely to be concerned with identifying the powers and the limits of human reasoning?
    a. cognitive
    b. behavioral
    c. neuroscience
    d. social-cultural
    e. behavior genetics

Psychology's perspectives, pp. 11-12
Easy, Conceptual, Objective 5, Ans: d

54. Which perspective would be most likely to focus on the extent to which different styles of parenting are encouraged among various ethnic communities?
    a. evolutionary
    b. cognitive
    c. psychodynamic
    d. social-cultural
    e. neuroscience

Psychology's perspectives, pp. 11-12
Medium, Conceptual/Application, Objective 5, Ans: c

55. Dr. Wilson attributes the delinquent behaviors of many teens to the pressures associated with being members of street gangs. Her belief best illustrates a(n) ________ perspective.
    a. psychodynamic
    b. behavior genetics
    c. social-cultural
    d. neuroscience
    e. evolutionary

Psychology's perspectives, p. 12
Medium, Factual/Definitional, Objective 5, Ans: d

56. The various theoretical perspectives employed by psychologists:
    a. have little value for applied research.
    b. typically contradict common sense.
    c. are generally impossible to test scientifically.
    d. often complement one another.

Psychology's subfields, p. 13
Easy, Conceptual/Application, Objective 6, Ans: c

57. Dr. Robinson conducts basic research on the relationship between brain chemistry and intellectual functioning. Which psychological specialty does Dr. Robinson's research best represent?
    a. social psychology
    b. clinical psychology
    c. biological psychology
    d. industrial/organizational psychology

Psychology's subfields, p. 13
Easy, Conceptual/Application, Objective 6, Ans: c

58. Dr. Santaniello conducts basic research on how children's moral thinking changes as they grow older. It is most likely that Dr. Santaniello is a(n) ________ psychologist.
    a. social
    b. clinical
    c. developmental
    d. industrial/organizational

Psychology's subfields, p. 13
Medium, Conceptual/Application, Objective 6, Ans: a

59. Dr. Caleigh conducts basic research on the relationship between adults' language skills and their capacity to solve mathematical problems. Dr. Caleigh is most likely a(n) ________ psychologist.
    a. cognitive
    b. biological
    c. clinical
    d. social

Psychology's subfields, p. 13
Easy, Conceptual, Objective 6, Ans: d

60. Dr. Roberts engages in basic research involving the construction and validation of tests designed to assess individual differences in traits such as anxiety and self-esteem. Which specialty area does her research best represent?
    a. social psychology
    b. biological psychology
    c. industrial/organizational psychology
    d. personality psychology

Psychology's subfields, p. 13
Easy, Conceptual/Application, Objective 6, Ans: b

61. Dr. Mills engages in basic research on why individuals conform to the behaviors and opinions of others. Which specialty area does his research best represent?
    a. cognitive psychology
    b. social psychology
    c. developmental psychology
    d. clinical psychology

Psychology's subfields, p. 13
Easy, Factual/Definitional, Objective 6, Ans: a

62. Which psychological specialists are most likely to be involved in applied research?
 a. industrial/organizational psychologists
 b. developmental psychologists
 c. personality psychologists
 d. biological psychologists

Psychology's subfields, p. 13
Medium, Conceptual/Application, Objective 6, Ans: e

63. Dr. Lipka is involved in an applied research study of customer satisfaction with a newly developed line of facial cosmetics and other beauty aids. Dr. Lipka is most likely a(n) ________ psychologist.
 a. clinical
 b. developmental
 c. biological
 d. personality
 e. industrial/organizational

Psychology's subfields, p. 14
Medium, Factual/Definitional, Objective 6, Ans: c

64. Clinical psychologists are most likely to be involved in:
 a. assessing the linkages between biology and behavior.
 b. the experimental study of motivation and emotion.
 c. providing therapy to troubled people.
 d. the systematic study of how people are influenced by enduring personality traits.

Psychology's subfields, p. 14
Medium, Conceptual/Application, Objective 6, Ans: b

65. For no apparent reason, Adam has recently begun to feel so tense and anxious that he frequently stays home from work. It would be most beneficial for Adam to contact a(n) ________ psychologist.
 a. industrial/organizational
 b. clinical
 c. personality
 d. biological

Psychology's subfields, p. 14
Easy, Factual/Definitional, Objective 6, Ans: d

66. The specialist most likely to have a medical degree is a(n):
 a. clinical psychologist.
 b. industrial/organizational psychologist.
 c. developmental psychologist.
 d. psychiatrist.

(Close-Up) Your study of psychology, pp. 15-16
Easy, Factual/Definitional, Objective 7, Ans: c

67. The PRTR study method emphasizes the importance of:
   a. massed practice.
   b. rote memory.
   c. thinking critically.
   d. role modeling.

(Close-Up) Your study of psychology, p. 16
Medium, Factual/Definitional, Objective 7, Ans: d

68. In answering multiple-choice test items, smart test-takers are best advised to:
   a. check off as correct the first answer they read that seems to be right.
   b. choose the "all the above" option if it is available.
   c. carefully imagine how each of the alternative answers might be correct.
   d. recall the correct answer to each question before reading the alternative answers.

Essay Questions

1. Tom believes that children are born with neither good nor bad thoughts, desires, or character traits. He suggests, instead, that parents and culture shape individual minds and hearts in virtuous or harmful directions.

   For Plato, John Locke, and Charles Darwin, note whether that philosopher would agree or disagree with Tom's claims; in each case, explain why they would agree or disagree with Tom. Explain also why you would agree or disagree with Tom.

2. Julie, a physics major, has difficulty believing that psychology is a science, because people cannot observe other people's thoughts and sensations. Explain how Wilhelm Wundt and John Watson would have responded to Julie's skepticism regarding psychology's scientific status.

3. Jack is a second-grade student. He seems to have no interest in learning, often daydreaming in class and frequently disrupting the class by throwing objects at other students. Using the major theoretical perspectives employed by psychologists, give three alternative explanations for Jack's classroom behavior. In light of these explanations, what steps could be taken to reduce Jack's disruptive behavior?

4. Kathy does not want to become a psychologist because she has no interest in analyzing emotionally disturbed people. Use your knowledge of psychology's subfields and perspectives to expand Kathy's limited understanding of career opportunities for psychologists.

Web Quiz 1

Ans: c

1. Which philosopher most clearly rejected the idea that the mind is separable from the body?
   a. Plato
   b. Socrates
   c. Aristotle
   d. Descartes.

Ans: b

2. Professor Schroeder argues that children have an innate concept of justice that enables them to make distinctions between fair and unfair rules. This argument is most consistent with the views of:
   a. Aristotle.
   b. Socrates.
   c. John Locke.
   d. Francis Bacon.

Ans: d

3. In the context of debates over the origins of knowledge, nature is to nurture as ________ is to ________.
   a. Socrates; Plato
   b. Plato; Descartes
   c. Locke; Darwin
   d. Descartes; Locke

Ans: a

4. Edward Titchener was concerned primarily with the study of:
   a. sensory experiences.
   b. maladaptive behaviors.
   c. inherited traits.
   d. social relationships.

Ans: c

5. The early school of psychology that employed the method of introspection was known as:
   a. pragmatism.
   b. behaviorism.
   c. naturalism.
   d. structuralism.

Ans: d

6. Who was the pragmatic philosopher and author of a major textbook for the emerging discipline of psychology?
   a. Wundt
   b. Watson
   c. Titchener
   d. James

Ans: a

7. Ivan Pavlov pioneered the study of:
a. learning.
b. perception.
c. personality.
d. mental illness.

Ans: d

8. Compared with the structuralists, early behaviorists were much less likely to focus on the study of:
a. smiling.
b. screaming.
c. fighting.
d. thinking.

Ans: c

9. Experience is to genes as ________ is to _______.
a. stability; change
b. functionalism; structuralism
c. nurture; nature
d. Plato; Aristotle

Ans: a

10. Debates as to whether alcohol abuse is biologically determined or culturally influenced are most relevant to the issue of:
a. nature versus nurture.
b. rationality versus irrationality.
c. behavior versus mental processes.
d. structuralism versus functionalism.

Ans: c

11. Understanding why the fear of darkness may have contributed to the survival of our human ancestors is most relevant to the ________ perspective.
a. behavioral
b. cognitive
c. evolutionary
d. psychodynamic

Ans: b

12. Inherited traits are to learned habits as the ________ perspective is to the ________ perspective.
a. behavioral; social-cultural
b. evolutionary; behavioral
c. social-cultural; neuroscience
d. neuroscience; evolutionary

Ans: c

13. Which perspective would be most relevant to understanding the role of spaced practice on long-term memory of information.
    a. psychodynamic
    b. social-cultural
    c. cognitive
    d. behavior genetics

Ans: b

14. Basic research on persistent human traits like optimism and pessimism is most characteristic of the specialty known as ________ psychology.
    a. biological
    b. personality
    c. social
    d. developmental

Ans: b

15. Professor Thurstone conducts basic research to investigate whether a teacher's negative perceptions of some students can affect the students' subsequent academic performance. Professor Thurstone is most likely a ________ psychologist.
    a. clinical
    b. social
    c. biological
    d. personality

Web Quiz 2

Ans: a

1. Who emphasized that mental processes could exist independently of physical states?
   a. Descartes
   b. Aristotle
   c. Wundt
   d. Watson

Ans: b

2. In debating the origins of knowledge, Plato and Aristotle disagreed about the relative importance of:
   a. basic and applied research.
   b. nature and nurture.
   c. behavior and mental processes.
   d. structuralism and functionalism.

Ans: a

3. Professor Boyd suggests that children in every culture can distinguish between costs and benefits because humans have an inborn understanding of economics. The professor's suggestion is most consistent with the views of:
   a. Plato.
   b. Aristotle.
   c. Francis Bacon.
   d. John Locke.

Ans: c

4. Edward Titchener used the research method known as:
   a. PRTR.
   b. psychoanalysis.
   c. introspection.
   d. massed practice.
   e. natural selection.

Ans: b

5. Which research method was introduced by structuralists to identify basic elements of sensory experience?
   a. psychoanalysis
   b. introspection
   c. behavior genetics
   d. PRTR

Ans: d

6. Which school of psychology was most clearly concerned with the adaptive value of complex mental processes?
   a. structuralism
   b. behaviorism
   c. psychoanalysis
   d. functionalism

Ans: b

7. Wilhelm Wundt was both a:
   a. psychoanalyst and psychiatrist.
   b. physiologist and philosopher.
   c. sociologist and psychiatrist.
   d. theologian and philosopher.

Ans: c

8. The suggestion that psychology is less a set of facts than a method of evaluating ideas best highlights the ________ character of psychology.
   a. naturalistic
   b. humanistic
   c. scientific
   d. introspective

Ans: a

9. In the context of debates over the origins of knowledge, René Descartes is to John Locke as ________ is to _______.
   a. nature; nurture
   b. rationality; irrationality
   c. structuralism; functionalism
   d. observation; introspection

Ans: b

10. The importance of inherited behavioral traits was most clearly highlighted by:
   a. John Locke.
   b. Darwin.
   c. Watson.
   d. B. F. Skinner.

Ans: d

11. Which perspective is most relevant to understanding the linkages between hormone levels and sexual motivation?
   a. behavioral
   b. cognitive
   c. psychodynamic
   d. neuroscience

Ans: c

12. Understanding the extent to which personality is influenced by motives outside of one's own awareness is most relevant to the ________ perspective.
   a. neuroscience
   b. behavioral
   c. psychodynamic
   d. social-cultural

Ans: b

13. A focus on the different marriage rituals practiced by members of different ethnic groups is of most relevance to the _______ perspective.
    a. evolutionary
    b. social-cultural
    c. psychodynamic
    d. cognitive

Ans: d

14. Professor Helms conducts basic research on the progressive changes in infants' perceptual skills during the first year of life. Professor Helms is most likely a ________ psychologist.
    a. social
    b. clinical
    c. personality
    d. developmental

Ans: c

15. Dr. Stevens provides psychotherapy to people who suffer from excessive anxiety. Dr. Stevens is most likely a ________ psychologist.
    a. social
    b. developmental
    c. clinical
    d. cognitive

Study Guide Questions

Ans: b, p. 2

1. The Greek philosopher who believed that intelligence was inherited was:
   a. Aristotle.
   b. Plato.
   c. Descartes.
   d. Simonides.

Ans: d, p. 3

2. The fourth-century scholar who anticipated health psychology's focus on mind-body interactions was:
   a. Confucius.
   b. Buddha.
   c. Locke.
   d. Augustine.

Ans: c, p. 3

3. Which seventeenth-century philosopher believed that some ideas are innate?
   a. Aristotle
   b. Plato
   c. Descartes
   d. Locke

Ans: b, pp. 3, 4

4. The philosophical views of John Locke are to those of René Descartes as ________ is to ________.
   a. nature; nurture
   b. nurture; nature
   c. rationality; irrationality
   d. irrationality; rationality

Ans: c, pp. 3-4

5. Francis Bacon's ideas led most directly to the scholarly view known as:
   a. functionalism.
   b. structuralism.
   c. empiricism.
   d. introspection.

Ans: d, p. 4

6. The seventeenth-century philosopher who believed that the mind is blank at birth and that most knowledge comes through sensory experience is:
   a. Plato.
   b. Aristotle.
   c. Descartes.
   d. Locke.

Ans: b, p. 4

7. Psychology is defined as the "science of behavior and mental processes." Wilhelm Wundt would have omitted which of the following words from this definition?
   a. science
   b. behavior and
   c. and mental processes
   d. Wundt would have agreed with the definition as stated.

Ans: a, p. 4

8. The first psychology laboratory was established by ________ in the year ________.
   a. Wundt; 1879
   b. James; 1890
   c. Freud; 1900
   d. Watson; 1913

Ans: a, p. 4

9. Who would be most likely to agree with the statement, "Psychology is the science of mental life"?
   a. Wilhelm Wundt
   b. John Watson
   c. Ivan Pavlov
   d. virtually any American psychologist during the 1960s

Ans: c, p. 4

10. Jawan believes that psychologists should go back to using introspection as a research tool. This technique is based on:
   a. survey methodology.
   b. experimentation.
   c. self-examination of mental processes.
   d. the study of observable behavior.

Ans: a, p. 4

11. Who introduced the early school of structuralism?
   a. Edward Titchener
   b. Wilhelm Wundt
   c. William James
   d. Mary Whiton Calkins

Ans: d, pp. 4, 5

12. The psychological views of William James are to those of Edward Titchener as ________ is to ________.
   a. nature; nurture
   b. nurture; nature
   c. structuralism; functionalism
   d. functionalism; structuralism

Ans: c, p. 6

13. Two historical roots of psychology are the disciplines of:
    a. philosophy and chemistry.
    b. physiology and chemistry.
    c. philosophy and biology.
    d. philosophy and physics.

Ans: d, p. 6

14. Who wrote an important 1890 psychology textbook?
    a. Wilhelm Wundt
    b. Ivan Pavlov
    c. Jean Piaget
    d. William James
    e. Sigmund Freud

Ans: a, p. 7

15. In its earliest days, psychology was defined as the:
    a. science of mental life.
    b. study of conscious and unconscious activity.
    c. science of observable behavior.
    d. science of behavior and mental processes.

Ans: c, p. 7

16. Who would be most likely to agree with the statement, "Psychology should investigate only behaviors that can be observed"?
    a. Wilhelm Wundt
    b. Sigmund Freud
    c. John B. Watson
    d. William James

Ans: d, pp. 7-8

17. Dharma's term paper on the history of American psychology notes that:
    a. psychology began as the science of mental life.
    b. from the 1920s into the 1960s, psychology was defined as the science of observable behavior.
    c. contemporary psychologists study both overt behavior and covert thoughts.
    d. all of the above are true.

Ans: b, p. 8

18. In psychology, "behavior" is best defined as:
    a. anything a person says, does, or feels.
    b. any action we can observe and record.
    c. any action, whether observable or not.
    d. anything we can infer from a person's actions.

Ans: a, p. 8

19. In defining psychology, the text notes that psychology is most accurately described as a:
    a. way of asking and answering questions.
    b. field engaged in solving applied problems.
    c. set of findings related to behavior and mental processes.
    d. nonscientific approach to the study of mental disorders.

Ans: d, p. 8
20. Today, psychology is defined as the:
a. study of mental phenomena.
b. study of conscious and unconscious activity.
c. study of behavior.
d. science of behavior and mental processes.

Ans: b, p. 8
21. Sensations, dreams, beliefs, and feelings are:
a. examples of behavior.
b. examples of subjective experiences.
c. not considered appropriate subject matter for psychology today.
d. b. and c.

Ans: b, p. 8
22. To say that "psychology is a science" means that:
a. psychologists study only observable behaviors.
b. psychologists approach the study of thoughts and actions with careful observation and rigorous analysis.
c. psychological research should be free of value judgments.
d. all of the above are true.

Ans: a, p. 9
23. Dr. Ramirez is studying whether emotionally reactive infants tend to become emotionally reactive adults. Dr. Ramirez's research illustrates the ________ issue in psychology.
a. stability versus change
b. rationality versus irrationality
c. nature-nurture
d. internal-external

Ans: c, pp. 9-10
24. Which of the following is *not* a major issue in psychology?
a. stability versus change
b. rationality versus irrationality
c. top-down versus bottom-up processing
d. nature versus nurture

Ans: a, p. 10
25. Which of the following exemplifies the issue of the relative importance of nature and nurture on our behavior?
a. the issue of the relative influence of biology and experience on behavior
b. the issue of the relative influence of rewards and punishments on behavior
c. the debate as to the relative importance of heredity and instinct in determining behavior
d. the debate as to whether mental processes are a legitimate area of scientific study

Ans: d, p. 11

26. In concluding her report on the “nature-nurture debate in contemporary psychology,” Karen notes that:
   a. most psychologists believe that nature is a more important influence on the development of most human traits.
   b. most psychologists believe that nurture is more influential.
   c. the issue is more heatedly debated than ever before.
   d. nurture works on what nature endows.

Ans: a, p. 11

27. Which perspective emphasizes the learning of observable responses?
   a. behavioral
   b. social-cultural
   c. neuroscience
   d. cognitive

Ans: a, p. 11

28. The psychological perspective that places the *most* emphasis on how observable responses are learned is the ________ perspective.
   a. behavioral
   b. cognitive
   c. behavior genetics
   d. evolutionary

Ans: c, p. 11

29. Psychologists who study the degree to which genes influence our personality are working within the ________ perspective.
   a. behavioral
   b. evolutionary
   c. behavior genetics
   d. neuroscience
   e. cognitive

Ans: a, p. 11

30. Which psychological perspective emphasizes the interaction of the brain and body in behavior?
   a. neuroscience perspective
   b. cognitive
   c. behavioral
   d. behavior genetics
   e. evolutionary

Ans: a, pp. 11-12

31. During a dinner conversation, a friend says that the cognitive and behavioral perspectives are quite similar. You disagree and point out that the cognitive perspective emphasizes ________, whereas the behavioral perspective emphasizes ________.
   a. conscious processes; observable responses
   b. unconscious processes; conscious processes
   c. overt behaviors; covert behaviors
   d. introspection; experimentation

Ans: d, p. 12

32. A psychologist who explores how Asian and North American definitions of attractiveness differ is working within the ________ perspective.
    a. behavioral
    b. evolutionary
    c. cognitive
    d. social-cultural

Ans: e, p. 12

33. The way the mind encodes, processes, stores, and retrieves information is the primary concern of the ________ perspective.
    a. neuroscience
    b. evolutionary
    c. social-cultural
    d. behavioral
    e. cognitive

Ans: c, p. 12

34. Dr. Ernst explains behavior in terms of different situations. Dr. Ernst is working within the ________ perspective.
    a. behavioral
    b. evolutionary
    c. social-cultural
    d. cognitive

Ans: c, p. 12

35. Dr. Waung investigates how a person's interpretation of a situation affects his or her reaction. Evidently, Dr. Waung is working within the ________ perspective.
    a. neuroscience
    b. behavioral
    c. cognitive
    d. social-cultural

Ans: c, p. 12

36. Concerning the major psychological perspectives on behavior, the text author suggests that:
    a. researchers should work within the framework of only one of the perspectives.
    b. only those perspectives that emphasize objective measurement of behavior are useful.
    c. the different perspectives often complement one another; together, they provide a fuller understanding of behavior than provided by any single perspective.
    d. psychologists should avoid all of these traditional perspectives.

Ans: c, p. 13

37. Dr. Aswad is studying people's enduring inner traits. Dr. Aswad is most likely a(n):
    a. clinical psychologist.
    b. psychiatrist.
    c. personality psychologist.
    d. industrial-organizational psychologist.

Ans: a, p. 13

38. A psychologist who studies how worker productivity might be increased by changing office layout is engaged in ________ research.
    a. applied
    b. basic
    c. clinical
    d. developmental

Ans: d, p. 13

39. Dr. Jones' research centers on the relationship between changes in our thinking over the life span and changes in moral reasoning. Dr. Jones is most likely a:
    a. clinical psychologist.
    b. personality psychologist.
    c. psychiatrist.
    d. developmental psychologist.

Ans: c, p. 13

40. Which subfield is most directly concerned with studying human behavior in the workplace?
    a. clinical psychology
    b. personality psychology
    c. industrial-organizational psychology
    d. psychiatry

Ans: a, p. 13

41. A psychologist who conducts experiments solely intended to build psychology's knowledge base is engaged in:
    a. basic research.
    b. applied research.
    c. industrial-organizational research.
    d. clinical research.

Ans: c, p. 14

42. Which of the following individuals is also a physician?
    a. clinical psychologist
    b. experimental psychologist
    c. psychiatrist
    d. biological psychologist

Ans: c, p. 14

43. Psychologists who study, assess, and treat troubled people are called:
    a. basic researchers.
    b. applied psychologists.
    c. clinical psychologists.
    d. psychiatrists.

Ans: a, p. 14

44. Today, psychology is a discipline that:
    a. connects with a diversity of other fields.
    b. is largely independent of other disciplines.
    c. is focused primarily on basic research.
    d. is focused primarily on applied research.

Ans: c, p. 15

45. In order, the sequence of steps in the PRTR method is:
   a. preview, review, think critically, read.
   b. plan, read, take notes, review.
   c. preview, read, think critically, review.
   d. plan, review, take notes, read.

Ans: a, p. 15

46. A major principle underlying the PRTR study method is that:
   a. people learn and remember material best when they actively process it.
   b. many students overestimate their mastery of text and lecture material.
   c. study time should be spaced over time rather than crammed into one session.
   d. "overlearning" disrupts efficient retention.

Ans: c, p. 16

47. Your roommate announces that her schedule permits her to devote three hours to studying for an upcoming quiz. You advise her to:
   a. spend most of her time reading and rereading the text material.
   b. focus primarily on her lecture notes.
   c. space study time over several short sessions.
   d. cram for three hours just before the quiz.

Ans: d, p. 16

48. A fraternity brother rationalizes the fact that he spends very little time studying by saying that he "doesn't want to peak too soon and have the test material become stale." You tell him that:
   a. he is probably overestimating his knowledge of the material.
   b. if he devotes extra time to studying, his retention of the material will be improved.
   c. the more often students review material, the better their exam scores.
   d. all of the above are true.

CHAPTER **1**

Thinking Critically with Psychological Science

Learning Objectives

The Need for Psychological Science (pp. 19-26)

1. Describe the hindsight bias and explain how it often leads us to perceive psychological research as merely common sense.

2. Discuss how overconfidence contaminates our everyday judgments.

3. Explain how the scientific attitude encourages critical thinking.

4. Describe the relationship between psychological theories and scientific research.

Description (pp. 26-30)

5. Compare and contrast case studies, surveys, and naturalistic observation, and explain the importance of proper sampling.

Correlation (pp. 30-37)

6. Describe both positive and negative correlations, and explain how correlational measures can aid the process of prediction.

7. Explain why correlational research fails to provide evidence of cause-effect relationships.

8. Discuss how people form illusory correlations and perceive order in random sequences.

Experimentation (pp. 37-41)

9. Identify the basic elements of an experiment, and discuss how experimental control contributes to causal explanation.

Statistical Reasoning (pp. 42-46)

10. Explain how bar graphs can be designed to make a small difference appear to be large.

11. Describe the three measures of central tendency and the two measures of variation.

12. Discuss three important principles in making generalizations from samples, and describe how psychologists make inferences about differences between groups.

Frequently Asked Questions About Psychology (pp. 46-53)

13. Explain the value of artificially simplified laboratory conditions in learning about principles of behavior, and discuss the generalizability of psychological research in terms of culture and gender.

14. Explain why psychologists study animals, and discuss the ethics of experimentation with both animals and humans.

15. Describe how personal values can influence psychologists' research and its application, and discuss the possibility for misuse of research findings.

Did we know it all along?, p. 20
Easy, Factual/Definitional, Objective 1, Ans: c

1. The hindsight bias refers to people's tendency to:
   a. dismiss the value of replication.
   b. reject any ideas that can't be scientifically tested.
   c. exaggerate their ability to have foreseen the outcome of past events.
   d. assume that correlation proves causation.
   e. overestimate the extent to which others share their opinions.

Did we know it all along?, p. 20
Medium, Factual/Definitional, Objective 1, Ans: b

2. The perception that psychological research findings merely verify our common-sense understanding is most clearly facilitated by:
   a. illusory correlations.
   b. the hindsight bias.
   c. the false consensus effect.
   d. the placebo effect.

Did we know it all along?, p. 20
Easy, Factual/Definitional, Objective 1, Ans: c

3. Giving half the members of a group some purported psychological finding and the other half an opposite result is an easy way to demonstrate the impact of:
   a. the false consensus effect.
   b. illusory correlation.
   c. the hindsight bias.
   d. random sampling.
   e. the double-blind procedure.

Did we know it all along?, p. 20
Medium, Conceptual/Application, Objective 1, Ans: c

4. Professor Smith told one class that alcohol consumption has been found to increase sexual desire. He informed another class that alcohol consumption has been found to reduce sexual appetite. The fact that neither class was surprised by the information they received best illustrates the power of:
a. illusory correlation.
b. the false consensus effect.
c. the hindsight bias.
d. the double-blind procedure.
e. the placebo effect.

Did we know it all along?, p. 20
Easy, Conceptual/Application, Objective 1, Ans: d

5. Several weeks after a political election, voters often exaggerate their ability to have predicted the election outcome. This best illustrates:
a. the placebo effect.
b. the false consensus effect.
c. illusory correlation.
d. the hindsight bias.

Did we know it all along?, p. 20
Easy, Conceptual, Objective 1, Ans: a

6. Mike Crampton's stockbroker has informed him of substantial investment losses. When Mike tells his wife, she angrily responds, "I could have told you that your investment plan would fail!" Her comment best illustrates:
a. the hindsight bias.
b. illusory correlation.
c. the placebo effect.
d. the false consensus effect.

Did we know it all along?, pp. 21, 24-25
Difficult, Conceptual, Objective 1, Ans: b

7. Formulating testable hypotheses before conducting research is most directly useful for restraining a thinking error known as:
a. random sampling.
b. the hindsight bias.
c. the false consensus effect.
d. illusory correlation.
e. random assignment.

Did we know it all along?, pp. 20-21, 23
Difficult, Conceptual, Objective 1, Ans: a

8. The scientific attitude of humility is most likely to be undermined by:
a. the hindsight bias.
b. correlational evidence.
c. random assignment.
d. operational definitions.
e. naturalistic observation.

Overconfidence, p. 22
Easy, Conceptual, Objective 2, Ans: c

9. Government experts who are convinced of the correctness of their own mistaken political predictions most clearly demonstrate:
   a. illusory correlation.
   b. the false consensus effect.
   c. overconfidence.
   d. the placebo effect.

Overconfidence, p. 22
Medium, Conceptual, Objective 2, Ans: d

10. Overconfidence is best described as:
   a. a placebo.
   b. critical thinking.
   c. an illusory correlation.
   d. intellectual conceit.

Overconfidence, p. 22
Medium, Conceptual/Application, Objective 2, Ans: e

11. Megan was certain that she would never live far away from her family. However, in order to develop her career, she decided to move. Megan's experience best illustrates:
   a. the hindsight bias.
   b. illusory correlation.
   c. random assignment.
   d. the false consensus effect.
   e. overconfidence.

The scientific attitude, p. 23
Easy, Factual/Definitional, Objective 3, Ans: d

12. Two fundamental characteristics of the scientific attitude are:
   a. pride and enthusiasm.
   b. ingenuity and practicality.
   c. creativity and patience.
   d. skepticism and humility.

The scientific attitude, p. 23
Medium, Conceptual/Application, Objective 3, Ans: b

13. Alicia insists that Dr. Phillip's theory of aggression be checked against observable evidence. She is demonstrating the scientific attitude of:
   a. pride.
   b. skepticism.
   c. practicality.
   d. enthusiasm.

The scientific attitude, p. 23
Easy, Factual/Definitional, Objective 3, Ans: c

14. The scientific attitude requires an open-minded humility because it involves a willingness to:
   a. perceive order in random events.
   b. reject any ideas that can't be scientifically tested.
   c. recognize the errors in our own theories.
   d. respect any religious beliefs that contradict our own.

The scientific attitude, p. 23
Easy, Factual/Definitional, Objective 3, Ans: b

15. A questioning attitude regarding psychologists' assumptions and hidden values best illustrates:
    a. the false consensus effect.
    b. critical thinking.
    c. the hindsight bias.
    d. overconfidence.
    e. illusory correlation.

The scientific attitude, p. 23
Easy, Factual/Definitional, Objective 3, Ans: d

16. A hard-headed curiosity that questions truth claims and demands evidence most clearly facilitates:
    a. an illusion of control.
    b. hindsight bias.
    c. the false consensus effect.
    d. critical thinking.
    e. overconfidence.

The scientific method, p. 23
Medium, Conceptual, Objective 3, Ans: e

17. Questioning the generalizability of anecdotal evidence best illustrates:
    a. overconfidence.
    b. the false consensus effect.
    c. the hindsight bias.
    d. random assignment.
    e. critical thinking.

The scientific method, p. 24
Medium, Conceptual/Application, Objective 3, Ans: a

18. Professor Shalet contends that parents and children have similar levels of intelligence largely because they share common genes. His idea is best described as a(n):
    a. theory.
    b. replication.
    c. naturalistic observation.
    d. illusory correlation.
    e. hindsight bias.

The scientific method, p. 24
Medium, Factual/Definitional, Objective 4, Ans: c

19. The explanatory power of a scientific theory is most closely linked to its capacity to generate testable:
    a. assumptions.
    b. correlations.
    c. predictions.
    d. variables.

The scientific method, pp. 24-25
Easy, Factual/Definitional, Objective 4, Ans: b

20. A hypothesis is a(n):
    a. observable relationship between specific independent and dependent variables.
    b. testable prediction that gives direction to research.
    c. set of principles that organizes and explains newly discovered facts.
    d. unprovable assumption about the unobservable processes that underlie psychological functioning.

The scientific method, pp. 24-25
Medium, Conceptual/Application, Objective 4, Ans: c

21. Professor Delano suggests that because people are especially attracted to those who are good-looking, handsome men will be more successful than average-looking men in securing employment. The professor's prediction regarding employment success exemplifies:
    a. the hindsight bias.
    b. the false consensus effect.
    c. an hypothesis.
    d. illusory correlation.

The scientific method, p. 25
Easy, Factual/Definitional, Objective 4, Ans: d

22. A specification of how a researcher measures a research variable is known as a(n):
    a. standard deviation.
    b. control condition.
    c. replication.
    d. operational definition.
    e. case study.

The scientific method, p. 25
Medium, Conceptual/Application, Objective 4, Ans: c

23. In a written report of their research, psychologists specify exactly how anxiety is assessed, thus providing their readers with a(n):
    a. hypothesis.
    b. independent variable.
    c. operational definition.
    d. standard deviation.

The scientific method, p. 25
Medium, Factual/Definitional, Objective 4, Ans: d

24. The process of replication is most likely to be facilitated by:
    a. the hindsight bias.
    b. the false consensus effect.
    c. illusory correlation.
    d. operational definitions.
    e. the placebo effect.

The scientific method, p. 25
Medium, Factual/Definitional, Objective 4, Ans: a

25. Which technique involves repeating the essence of an earlier research study with different participants and in different circumstances?
a. replication
b. correlational research
c. random sampling
d. naturalistic observation
e. random assignment

The scientific method, p. 25
Difficult, Conceptual/Application, Objective 4, Ans: b

26. Professor Saxton was very skeptical about the findings of a recently reported experiment on the effects of sleep deprivation. Which process would best enable her to assess the reliability of these findings?
a. naturalistic observation
b. replication
c. random sampling
d. the case study

The case study, p. 26
Easy, Factual/Definitional, Objective 5, Ans: a

27. The case study is a research method in which:
a. a single individual is studied in great depth.
b. a representative sample of people are questioned regarding their opinions or behaviors.
c. organisms are carefully observed in a laboratory environment.
d. an investigator manipulates one or more variables that might affect behavior.

The case study, p. 26
Medium, Conceptual/Application, Objective 5, Ans: b

28. In order to understand the unusual behavior of an adult client, a clinical psychologist has carefully investigated the client's current life situation and his physical, social, and educational history. Which research method has the psychologist employed?
a. the survey
b. the case study
c. experimentation
d. naturalistic observation

The case study, p. 27
Medium, Factual/Definitional, Objective 5, Ans: b

29. The biggest danger of relying on case-study evidence is that it:
a. is based on naturalistic observation.
b. may be unrepresentative of what is generally true.
c. is unusually easy to explain in hindsight.
d. leads us to underestimate the causal relationships between events.

The survey, p. 27
Easy, Factual/Definitional, Objective 5, Ans: b

30. In which type of research is a representative random sample of people asked to answer questions about their behaviors or opinions?
    a. experimentation
    b. the survey
    c. the case study
    d. naturalistic observation

The survey, p. 27
Medium, Conceptual/Application, Objective 5, Ans: a

31. Which research method would be most appropriate for investigating the relationship between the religious beliefs of Americans and their attitudes toward abortion?
    a. the survey
    b. naturalistic observation
    c. the case study
    d. experimentation

The survey, p. 27
Easy, Factual/Definitional, Objective 5, Ans: b

32. Surveys indicate that people are much less likely to support "welfare" than "aid to the needy." These somewhat paradoxical survey results best illustrate the importance of:
    a. random sampling.
    b. wording effects.
    c. hindsight bias.
    d. the false consensus effect.
    e. naturalistic observation.

The survey, p. 28
Easy, Factual/Definitional, Objective 5, Ans: b

33. The tendency to overestimate the extent to which others share our own attitudes is known as:
    a. the hindsight bias.
    b. the false consensus effect.
    c. illusory correlation.
    d. an illusion of control.

The survey, p. 28
Easy, Factual/Definitional, Objective 5, Ans: c

34. Conservatives are more likely than liberals to perceive high levels of popular support for conservative views. This best illustrates:
    a. an illusion of control.
    b. illusory correlation.
    c. the false consensus effect.
    d. the hindsight bias.

The survey, p. 28
Medium, Conceptual/Application, Objective 5, Ans: a

35. Jeff mistakenly assumes that everybody around him enjoys listening to country music just as much as he does. Jeff best illustrates:
 a. the false consensus effect.
 b. the hindsight bias.
 c. an illusion of control.
 d. the placebo effect.

The survey, p. 28
Medium, Factual/Definitional, Objective 5, Ans: c

36. When conducting a survey, gathering representative samples is most directly useful for restraining a thinking error known as:
 a. the hindsight bias.
 b. an illusion of control.
 c. the false consensus effect.
 d. the placebo effect.

The survey, p. 28
Medium, Conceptual/Application, Objective 5, Ans: a

37. In order to learn about the TV viewing habits of all the children attending Oakbridge School, Professor DeVries randomly selected and interviewed 50 of the school's students. In this instance, all the children attending the school are considered to be a(n):
 a. population.
 b. representative sample.
 c. case study.
 d. independent variable.
 e. control condition.

The survey, p. 28
Medium, Conceptual/Application, Objective 5, Ans: e

38. In order to assess reactions to a proposed tuition hike at her college, Ariana sent a questionnaire to every fifteenth person in the college registrar's alphabetical listing of all currently enrolled students. Ariana employed the technique of:
 a. random assignment.
 b. naturalistic observation.
 c. replication.
 d. correlation.
 e. random sampling.

The survey, p. 28
Difficult, Factual/Definitional, Objective 5, Ans: a

39. Psychologists select a random sample of research participants in order to ensure that:
 a. the participants are representative of the population they are interested in studying.
 b. there will be a large number of participants in the research study.
 c. the study will not be influenced by the researcher's personal values.
 d. the same number of participants will be assigned to each of the experimental conditions.

The survey, p. 28
Medium, Factual/Definitional, Objective 5, Ans: c

40. Which of the following scientific procedures is most useful for helping researchers avoid false generalizations?
    a. the case study
    b. naturalistic observation
    c. random sampling
    d. operational definitions

The survey, p. 28
Difficult, Conceptual/Application, Objective 5, Ans: b

41. The sight of large, enthusiastic crowds at all of his political rallies led Governor Donavan to become overconfident about his chances of winning the upcoming election. In this instance, the governor needs to be alerted to the value of:
    a. replication.
    b. random sampling.
    c. experimental control.
    d. naturalistic observation.

The survey, p. 28
Easy, Factual/Definitional, Objective 5, Ans: b

42. People often fail to make accurate generalizations because they are unduly influenced by ________ cases.
    a. randomly selected
    b. vivid
    c. representative
    d. the most frequently occurring

The survey, p. 28
Difficult, Conceptual, Objective 5, Ans: d

43. After noting that a majority of professional basketball players are African-American, Ervin concluded that African-Americans are better athletes than members of other racial groups. Ervin's conclusion best illustrates the danger of:
    a. replication.
    b. the hindsight bias.
    c. the false consensus effect.
    d. generalizing from vivid cases.

Naturalistic observation, p. 29
Easy, Factual/Definitional, Objective 5, Ans: c

44. Psychologists who carefully watch the behavior of chimpanzee societies in the jungle are using a research method known as:
    a. the survey.
    b. experimentation.
    c. naturalistic observation.
    d. the case study.
    e. random sampling.

Naturalistic observation, p. 29
Medium, Conceptual, Objective 5, Ans: b

45. Professor Ober carefully monitors and records the behaviors of children in their classrooms in order to track the development of their social and intellectual skills. Professor Ober is most clearly engaged in:
    a. survey research.
    b. naturalistic observation.
    c. experimentation.
    d. replication.

Naturalist observation, p. 30
Difficult, Factual/Definitional, Objective 5, Ans: b

46. In order to compare the pace of life in different countries, investigators measured the speed with which postal clerks completed a simple request. This best illustrates the use of a research method known as:
    a. the case study.
    b. naturalistic observation.
    c. random assignment.
    d. the double-blind procedure.
    e. the survey.

Correlation, p. 30
Easy, Factual/Definitional, Objective 6, Ans: c

47. A statistical measure that indicates the extent to which changes in one factor are accompanied by changes in another is called a(n):
    a. standard deviation.
    b. independent variable.
    c. correlation coefficient.
    d. mean.

Correlation, p. 30
Medium, Factual/Definitional, Objective 6, Ans: b

48. Correlational research is most useful for purposes of:
    a. explanation.
    b. prediction.
    c. control.
    d. replication.

Correlation, p. 30
Medium, Factual/Definitional, Objective 6, Ans: a

49. Which of the following is a statistical measure of both the direction and the strength of a relationship between two variables?
    a. correlation coefficient
    b. standard deviation
    c. range
    d. mean

Correlation, pp. 30-31
Easy, Conceptual/Application, Objective 6, Ans: b

50. In order to determine whether the strength of people's self-esteem is related to their income levels, researchers would most likely make use of:
a. case studies.
b. correlational research.
c. experimentation.
d. naturalistic observation.

Correlation, pp. 30-31
Medium, Conceptual/Application, Objective 6, Ans: c

51. In order to discover the extent to which economic status can be used to predict political preferences, researchers are most likely to employ:
a. the case study approach.
b. naturalistic observation.
c. correlational measures.
d. experimental research.

Correlation, p. 31
Easy, Factual/Definitional, Objective 6, Ans: b

52. In order to represent graphically the correlation between two variables, researchers often construct a:
a. skewed distribution.
b. scatterplot.
c. standard deviation.
d. bar graph.

Correlation, p. 31
Difficult, Conceptual/Application, Objective 6, Ans: a

53. A researcher would be most likely to discover a positive correlation between:
a. intelligence and academic success.
b. financial poverty and physical health.
c. self-esteem and depression.
d. school grades and school absences.

Correlation, p. 31
Medium, Conceptual/Application, Objective 6, Ans: b

54. If psychologists discovered that wealthy people are less satisfied with their marriages than poor people are, this would indicate that wealth and marital satisfaction are:
a. causally related.
b. negatively correlated.
c. independent variables.
d. dependent variables.
e. positively correlated.

Correlation, p. 31
Medium, Conceptual/Application, Objective 6, Ans: c

55. If the correlation between the physical weight and reading ability of elementary school students is +.85, this would indicate that:
   a. the relationship between weight and reading ability among elementary school students is not statistically significant.
   b. low body weight has a negative effect on the reading abilities of elementary school children.
   c. better reading ability is associated with greater physical weight among elementary school students.
   d. body weight has no causal influence on the reading abilities of elementary school children.

Correlation, p. 31
Medium, Factual/Definitional, Objective 6, Ans: c

56. If the points on a scatterplot are clustered in a pattern that extends from the upper left to the lower right, this would suggest that the two variables depicted are:
   a. normally distributed.
   b. positively correlated.
   c. negatively correlated.
   d. not correlated.

Correlation, p. 31
Difficult, Conceptual/Application, Objective 6, Ans: d

57. A correlation between physical attractiveness and dating frequency of +.60 would indicate that:
   a. physical attractiveness has no causal influence on dating frequency.
   b. more frequent dating is associated with lower levels of physical attractiveness.
   c. it is impossible to predict levels of physical attractiveness based on knowledge of dating frequency.
   d. less frequent dating is associated with lower levels of physical attractiveness.

Correlation, p. 31
Medium, Conceptual/Application, Objective 6, Ans: a

58. Which of the following correlations between self-esteem and body weight would enable you to most accurately predict body weight from knowledge of self-esteem level?
   a. +.60
   b. +.01
   c. –.10
   d. –.06
   e. .00

Correlation, p. 31
Medium, Conceptual, Objective 6, Ans: a

59. Which of the following correlation coefficients expresses the weakest degree of relationship between two variables?
   a. –.12
   b. +1.00
   c. –.99
   d. +.25
   e. –.50

Correlation and causation, p. 32
Easy, Factual/Definitional, Objective 7, Ans: b

60. If those who watch a lot of TV violence are also particularly likely to behave aggressively, this would *not* necessarily indicate that watching TV violence influences aggressive behavior because:
    a. random sequences often don't look random.
    b. correlation does not prove causation.
    c. sampling extreme cases leads to false generalizations.
    d. events often seem more probable in hindsight.

Correlation and causation, p. 32
Difficult, Conceptual/Application, Objective 7, Ans: e

61. An extensive survey revealed that children with relatively high self-esteem tend to picture God as kind and loving, whereas those with lower self-esteem tend to perceive God as angry. The researchers concluded that the children's self-esteem had apparently influenced their views of God. This conclusion best illustrates the danger of:
    a. perceiving order in random events.
    b. generalizing from extreme examples.
    c. randomly sampling children's views.
    d. exaggerating the extent to which others share our beliefs.
    e. assuming that correlation proves causation.

Correlation and causation, p. 32
Difficult, Conceptual/Application, Objective 7, Ans: c

62. If psychologists discovered that intelligent parents have smarter children than unintelligent parents, this would demonstrate that:
    a. intelligence is inherited.
    b. intelligent parents provide their children with greater educational opportunities than do unintelligent parents.
    c. the intelligence of parents and children is positively correlated.
    d. all the above are true.

Correlation and causation, p. 32
Difficult, Conceptual, Objective 7, Ans: b

63. A negative correlation between degree of wealth and likelihood of suffering from a psychological disorder would indicate that:
    a. poverty makes people vulnerable to psychological disorders.
    b. the poor are more likely to have a psychological disorder than the wealthy.
    c. psychological disorders usually prevent people from accumulating wealth.
    d. all the above are true.

Illusory correlations, p. 33
Medium, Conceptual/Application, Objective 8, Ans: b

64. Statistical measurement is most directly useful for restraining a thinking error known as:
    a. the hindsight bias.
    b. illusory correlation.
    c. overconfidence.
    d. the placebo effect.
    e. random sampling.

Illusory correlations, p. 33
Easy, Factual/Definitional, Objective 8, Ans: a

65. Illusory correlation refers to:
    a. the perception of a relationship between two variables that does *not* actually exist.
    b. a correlation that exceeds the value of +1.00.
    c. a cluster of points on a scatterplot that suggests a correlation between two variables.
    d. a correlation that is not statistically significant.

Illusory correlations, p. 33
Difficult, Conceptual/Application, Objective 8, Ans: d

66. Karen erroneously believes that her test grades are negatively correlated with the amount of time she studies for her tests. Research on illusory correlation suggests that she is especially likely to notice instances in which:
    a. poor grades follow either brief study or lengthy study.
    b. either poor grades or good grades follow lengthy study.
    c. good grades follow lengthy study and poor grades follow brief study.
    d. poor grades follow lengthy study and good grades follow brief study.

Illusory correlations, p. 33
Medium, Factual/Definitional, Objective 8, Ans: c

67. The perception that seemingly infertile couples who adopt a child are subsequently more likely to conceive a child themselves best illustrates:
    a. the process of replication.
    b. random assignment.
    c. an illusory correlation.
    d. the placebo effect.

Illusory correlations, p. 34
Easy, Factual/Definitional, Objective 8, Ans: b

68. Our tendency to notice and remember instances in which a premonition of an unlikely phone call is actually followed by the call most clearly contributes to:
    a. the false consensus effect.
    b. an illusory correlation.
    c. replication.
    d. the placebo effect.

Illusory correlations, p. 34
Medium, Conceptual, Objective 8, Ans: b

69. Adelle dreamed that a handsome young man she had met the previous day asked her for a date. When he actually did call for a date several days later, Adelle concluded that dreams accurately predict future events. Her belief best illustrates:
    a. the placebo effect.
    b. illusory correlation.
    c. random assignment.
    d. the false consensus effect.

Perceiving order in random events, p. 34
Difficult, Conceptual/Application, Objective 8, Ans: d

70. If the total number of boys and girls born each year is exactly equal, which of the following would be the most likely sequence of boys (B) and girls (G) for the next six births?
 a. G G G G G G
 b. G G G B B B
 c. G B G B B G
 d. All the above would be equally likely.

Perceiving order in random events, p. 34
Difficult, Factual/Definitional, Objective 8, Ans: d

71. For randomly generated sequences of numbers, people tend to ________ the sequential repetition of any particular digit.
 a. radically overestimate
 b. slightly overestimate
 c. accurately estimate
 d. underestimate

Perceiving order in random events, pp. 34-35
Medium, Conceptual/Application, Objective 8, Ans: d

72. On a series of coin tosses, Oleg has correctly predicted heads or tails seven times in a row. In this instance, it is reasonable to conclude that Oleg's predictive accuracy:
 a. defies the laws of statistical probability.
 b. illustrates the phenomenon of illusory correlation.
 c. is inconsistent with the false consensus effect.
 d. is a random and coincidental occurrence.

Perceiving order in random events, pp. 34-35
Medium, Conceptual/Application, Objective 8, Ans: a

73. Six of the children in Mr. Myer's second-grade classroom were born on exactly the same day. This strikes him as astonishing and improbable. In this instance, he should be reminded that:
 a. random sequences of events often don't look random.
 b. events often seem more probable in hindsight.
 c. sampling extreme cases leads to false generalizations.
 d. the tendency to seek confirming evidence promotes overconfidence.

Thinking critically about hot and cold streaks (Box), p. 36
Medium, Factual/Definitional, Objective 8, Ans: a

74. The illusion of streak shooting in basketball best illustrates the need to recognize that:
 a. random sequences of events often don't look random.
 b. sampling extreme cases leads to false generalizations.
 c. events often seem more probable in hindsight.
 d. correlation does not prove causation.

Thinking critically about hot and cold streaks (Box), p. 36
Difficult, Conceptual, Objective 8, Ans: c

75. The fact that some basketball fans believe the outcome of a player's last few shots is a predictor of the outcome of that person's next shot best illustrates:
a. the hindsight bias.
b. random sampling.
c. illusory correlation.
d. the false consensus effect.

Experimentation, p. 38
Easy, Factual/Definitional, Objective 9, Ans: b

76. Which of the following methods is most helpful for revealing cause-effect relationships?
a. the survey
b. the experiment
c. correlational research
d. naturalistic observation

Experimentation, p. 38
Medium, Factual/Definitional, Objective 9, Ans: b

77. Researchers use experiments rather than other research methods in order to distinguish between:
a. facts and theories.
b. causes and effects.
c. case studies and surveys.
d. random samples and representative samples.

Experimentation, p. 38
Easy, Factual/Definitional, Objective 9, Ans: d

78. The most accurate way of assessing the impact of breast milk feedings on the intellectual development of children is by means of:
a. case studies.
b. surveys.
c. naturalistic observations.
d. experiments.

Experimentation, p. 38
Medium, Conceptual/Application, Objective 9, Ans: d

79. Which research method provides the best way of assessing whether cigarette smoking boosts mental alertness?
a. the case study
b. the survey
c. naturalistic observation
d. the experiment

Experimentation, pp. 30, 38
Medium, Conceptual/Application, Objective 9, Ans: a

80. Prediction is to ________ as explanation is to ________.
   a. correlation; experimentation
   b. case study; survey
   c. random assignment; random sampling
   d. independent variable; dependent variable
   e. the hindsight bias; false consensus

Experimentation, p. 38
Easy, Factual/Definitional, Objective 9, Ans: c

81. In which type of research would an investigator manipulate one factor in order to observe its effect on some behavior or mental process?
   a. the survey
   b. the case study
   c. experimentation
   d. naturalistic observation

Experimentation, p. 38
Medium, Conceptual/Application, Objective 9, Ans: d

82. In a test of the effects of sleep deprivation on problem-solving skills, research participants are allowed to sleep either 4 or 8 hours on each of three consecutive nights. This research is an example of:
   a. naturalistic observation.
   b. survey research.
   c. a case study.
   d. an experiment.
   e. correlational research.

Experimentation, p. 38
Easy, Factual/Definitional, Objective 9, Ans: e

83. The most foolproof way of testing the true effectiveness of a newly introduced method of psychological therapy is by means of:
   a. survey research.
   b. case study research.
   c. naturalistic observation.
   d. correlational research.
   e. experimental research.

Experimentation, p. 38
Easy, Factual/Definitional, Objective 9, Ans: d

84. Participants in an experiment are said to be "blind" if they are uninformed about:
   a. what experimental hypothesis is being tested.
   b. whether the experimental findings will be statistically significant.
   c. how the dependent variable is measured.
   d. which experimental treatment, if any, they are receiving.

Experimentation, p. 38
Easy, Factual/Definitional, Objective 9, Ans: a

85. An inert substance that may be administered instead of a drug to see if it produces any of the same effects as the drug is called a:
a. placebo.
b. median.
c. case study.
d. replication.

Experimentation, p. 38
Medium, Conceptual/Application, Objective 9, Ans: c

86. In a study of the effects of alcohol consumption, some participants drank a nonalcoholic beverage that actually smelled and tasted like alcohol. This nonalcoholic drink was a:
a. dependent variable.
b. replication.
c. placebo.
d. random sample.
e. double blind.

Experimentation, p. 39
Easy, Factual/Definitional, Objective 9, Ans: d

87. The relief of pain following the ingestion of an inert substance that is presumed to have medicinal benefits illustrates:
a. random assignment.
b. the hindsight bias.
c. the false consensus effect.
d. the placebo effect.
e. illusory correlation.

Experimentation, p. 39
Medium, Conceptual/Application, Objective 9, Ans: c

88. The placebo effect best illustrates the effect of ________ on feelings and behaviors.
a. critical thinking
b. random sampling
c. positive expectations
d. random assignment

Experimentation, p. 39
Easy, Factual/Definitional, Objective 9, Ans: d

89. Both the researchers and the participants in a drug-evaluation study are ignorant about which participants have actually received an experimental drug and which have received a placebo. This investigation involves the use of:
a. the false consensus effect.
b. the hindsight bias.
c. random sampling.
d. the double-blind procedure.
e. replication.

Experimentation, p. 39
Medium, Factual/Definitional, Objective 9, Ans: b

90. To minimize the extent to which outcome differences between experimental and control conditions can be attributed to placebo effects, researchers make use of:
a. random sampling.
b. the double-blind procedure.
c. random assignment.
d. operational definitions.
e. replication.

Experimentation, p. 39
Easy, Factual/Definitional, Objective 9, Ans: d

91. In the control condition of an experiment the:
a. experimenter exerts the greatest influence on participants' behavior.
b. research participants are exposed to all the different experimental treatments.
c. research participants are exposed to the most favorable levels of experimental treatment.
d. experimental treatment is absent.

Experimentation, p. 39
Medium, Conceptual/Application, Objective 9, Ans: c

92. In order to study the effects of loud noise on worker productivity, Dr. McDuffee had one group of research participants work in a noisy room and a second group work in a quiet room. Those who worked in the quiet room were exposed to the ________ condition.
a. experimental
b. survey
c. control
d. correlational

Experimentation, p. 39
Medium, Factual/Definitional, Objective 9, Ans: d

93. In an experimental study, men with symptoms of impotence received either Viagra or a placebo. Those who received Viagra participated in the ________ condition.
a. correlational
b. control
c. survey
d. experimental

Experimentation, p. 39
Easy, Factual/Definitional, Objective 9, Ans: a

94. Being randomly assigned to the experimental condition in a research project involves being assigned:
a. to that condition by chance.
b. to the condition in which participants are representative of people in general.
c. in a fashion that ensures that the independent variable will have a strong effect on the dependent variable.
d. to the condition in which participants are all very similar in personality characteristics.

Experimentation, p. 39
Medium, Factual/Definitional, Objective 9, Ans: a

95. To accurately infer cause and effect, experimenters should use:
a. random assignment.
b. naturalistic observation.
c. standard deviations.
d. case studies.
e. scatterplots.

Experimentation, p. 39
Medium, Conceptual/Application, Objective 9, Ans: a

96. To assess the effect of televised violence on aggression, researchers plan to expose one group of children to violent movie scenes and another group to nonviolent scenes. In order to reduce the chance that the children in one group have more aggressive personalities than those in the other group, the researchers should make use of:
a. random assignment.
b. the double-blind procedure.
c. naturalistic observations.
d. operational definitions.
e. replication.

Experimentation, p. 39
Medium, Factual/Definitional, Objective 9, Ans: c

97. Research participants are randomly assigned to different conditions in an experiment in order to:
a. reduce the likelihood that participants within any condition know each other.
b. increase the likelihood that research participants are representative of people in general.
c. reduce the likelihood of any preexisting differences between the groups of participants assigned to the different conditions.
d. increase the likelihood that the different experimental conditions have the same number of participants.

Experimentation, p. 39
Medium, Factual/Definitional, Objective 9, Ans: c

98. Correlational evidence suggested that postmenopausal women receiving hormone replacement therapy had _______ health problems than those not receiving such treatment. Experimental evidence revealed that women receiving replacement hormones subsequently experienced ________ health problems than did nontreated women.
a. fewer; fewer
b. more; more
c. fewer; more
d. more; fewer

Experimentation, p. 39
Easy, Factual/Definitional, Objective 9, Ans: b

99. In a psychological experiment, the potentially causal factor that is manipulated by the investigator is called the ________ variable.
a. dependent
b. independent
c. control
d. experimental

Experimentation, p. 39
Medium, Conceptual/Application, Objective 9, Ans: d

100. In an experimental study of the effects of anxiety on self-esteem, anxiety would be the ________ variable.
   a. experimental
   b. dependent
   c. correlational
   d. independent

Experimentation, p. 39
Easy, Factual/Definitional, Objective 9, Ans: a

101. In a psychological experiment, the factor that may be influenced by the manipulated experimental treatment is called the ________ variable.
   a. dependent
   b. experimental
   c. control
   d. independent

Experimentation, p. 39
Difficult, Conceptual/Application, Objective 9, Ans: c

102. In order to assess the influence of self-esteem on interpersonal attraction, researchers either insulted or complimented college students about their physical appearance just before they went on a blind date. In this research, the dependent variable consisted of:
   a. insults or compliments.
   b. physical appearance.
   c. interpersonal attraction.
   d. feelings of self-esteem.

Experimentation, p. 39
Difficult, Conceptual, Objective 9, Ans: a

103. Cause is to effect as ________ is to ________.
   a. independent variable; dependent variable
   b. correlation; experimentation
   c. control condition; experimental condition
   d. prediction; explanation
   e. observation; replication

Experimentation, pp. 40-41
Medium, Factual/Definitional, Objective 9, Ans: c

104. Greenwald and colleagues observed that students who listened to subliminal tapes designed to improve self-esteem subsequently demonstrated ________ in their self-esteem test scores.
   a. dramatic improvement
   b. moderate improvement
   c. no improvement
   d. dramatic deterioration

Experimentation, p. 41
Easy, Factual/Definitional, Objective 9, Ans: b

105. Many survey respondents thought it would be more reasonable to observe the reactions of 1000 individuals receiving an untested drug than to give the drug to only 500 people and compare their reactions to the other 500 who received no drug. These survey respondents most clearly failed to recognize the value of:
a. testing a random sample.
b. creating a control condition.
c. replicating others' observations.
d. operationally defining research procedures.

Describing data, p. 42
Medium, Factual/Definitional, Objective 10, Ans: d

106. When you read a bar graph, it is most important for you to:
a. understand the concept of the false consensus effect.
b. mentally transform the data into a scatterplot.
c. identify the value of the standard deviation.
d. note the range and size of the scale values.
e. remember that correlation facilitates prediction.

Measures of central tendency, p. 43
Medium, Factual/Definitional, Objective 11, Ans: a

107. The most frequently occurring score in a distribution of scores is the:
a. mode.
b. median.
c. standard deviation.
d. mean.

Measures of central tendency, p. 43
Medium, Conceptual/Application, Objective 11, Ans: a

108. In a group of five individuals, two report annual incomes of $10,000, and the other three report incomes of $14,000, $15,000, and $31,000, respectively. The mode of this group's distribution of annual incomes is:
a. $10,000.
b. $15,000.
c. $16,000.
d. $31,000.
e. $80,000.

Measures of central tendency, p. 43
Easy, Factual/Definitional, Objective 11, Ans: b

109. The mean of a distribution of scores is the:
a. most frequently occurring score.
b. arithmetic average of all the scores.
c. least frequently occurring score.
d. score exceeded by 50 percent of all the scores.

Measures of central tendency, p. 43
Medium, Conceptual/Application, Objective 11, Ans: c

110. Which measure of central tendency is used to calculate your grade-point average?
    a. standard deviation
    b. median
    c. mean
    d. mode

Measures of central tendency, p. 43
Medium, Conceptual/Application, Objective 11, Ans: b

111. Mr. and Mrs. Klostreich have six children aged 5, 6, 6, 7, 8, and 16. The mean age of the Klostreich children is:
    a. 5.
    b. 8.
    c. 6½.
    d. 7.
    e. 6.

Measures of central tendency, p. 43
Medium, Factual/Definitional, Objective 11, Ans: d

112. The median of a distribution of scores is the:
    a. most frequently occurring score.
    b. difference between the highest and lowest scores.
    c. arithmetic average of all the scores.
    d. score exceeded by 50 percent of all the scores.

Measures of central tendency, p. 43
Medium, Conceptual/Application, Objective 11, Ans: e

113. During the past year, Zara and Ivan each read 2 books, but George read 9, Ali read 12, and Marsha read 25. The median number of books read by these individuals was:
    a. 2.
    b. 50.
    c. 10.
    d. 12.
    e. 9.

Measures of central tendency, p. 43
Medium, Factual/Definitional, Objective 11, Ans: b

114. When a statistical average is reported in the news, it is most important for readers to:
    a. determine whether it is statistically significant.
    b. consider whether it is distorted by a few extreme cases.
    c. be sure that it describes a truly random sample.
    d. recognize the potential for illusory correlation.

Measures of central tendency, p. 43
Medium, Conceptual/Application, Objective 11, Ans: a

115. When Mr. Adams calculated his students' algebra test scores, he noticed that two students had extremely low scores. Which measure of central tendency is affected most by the scores of these two students?
   a. mean
   b. standard deviation
   c. mode
   d. median
   e. range

Measures of central tendency, p. 43
Difficult, Factual/Definitional, Objective 11, Ans: a

116. The 50th percentile of a skewed distribution of scores cannot be equal to:
   a. the mode.
   b. the median.
   c. the mean.
   d. any of the above.

Measures of central tendency, p. 43
Difficult, Conceptual, Objective 11, Ans: e

117. The mean of a skewed distribution of scores is *always*:
   a. larger than the mode.
   b. smaller than the mode.
   c. larger than the median.
   d. smaller than the median.
   e. larger or smaller than the median.

Measures of central tendency, p. 43
Difficult, Conceptual/Application, Objective 11, Ans: d

118. Seven members of a boys' club reported the following individual earnings from their sale of cookies: $2, $9, $8, $10, $4, $9, and $7. In this distribution of individual earnings, the median is ________ the mean and ________ the mode.
   a. greater than; greater than
   b. less than; less than
   c. equal to; equal to
   d. greater than; less than
   e. less than; greater than

Measures of central tendency, p. 43
Difficult, Conceptual/Application, Objective 11, Ans: e

119. Seven members of a Girl Scout troop report the following individual earnings from their sale of candy: $4, $1, $7, $6, $8, $2, and $7. In this distribution of individual earnings, the mean is ________ the mode and ________ the median.
   a. equal to; equal to
   b. less than; equal to
   c. equal to; greater than
   d. greater than; greater than
   e. less than; less than

Measures of central tendency, p. 43
Difficult, Conceptual, Objective 11, Ans: b

120. For which of the following distributions of scores would the median most clearly be a more appropriate measure of central tendency than the mean?
a. 9, 8, 9, 8, 7
b. 10, 22, 8, 9, 6
c. 12, 6, 8, 5, 4
d. 12, 15, 12, 9, 12
e. 23, 7, 3, 27, 16

Central tendency and variation, p. 43
Medium, Conceptual, Objective 11, Ans: d

121. Median is to range as ________ is to ________.
a. frequency distribution; bar graph
b. mean; mode
c. scatterplot; correlation
d. central tendency; variation

Central tendency and variation, pp. 43-44
Medium, Conceptual, Objective 11, Ans: c

122. Central tendency is to variation as ________ is to ________.
a. scatterplot; correlation
b. range; normal curve
c. mean; standard deviation
d. median; mode

Measures of variation, p. 43
Easy, Factual/Definitional, Objective 11, Ans: b

123. The difference between the highest and lowest scores in a distribution is the:
a. mean.
b. range.
c. median.
d. standard deviation.
e. percentile rank.

Measures of variation, p. 43
Easy, Conceptual/Application, Objective 11, Ans: d

124. During the last Central High School basketball game, the starting five players scored 11, 7, 21, 14, and 7 points, respectively. For this distribution of scores, the range is:
a. 7.
b. 11.
c. 12.
d. 14.
e. 21.

Measures of variation, p. 43
Medium, Factual/Definitional, Objective 11, Ans: e

125. Which measure of variation is affected most by a few extreme scores?
    a. mode
    b. standard deviation
    c. mean
    d. median
    e. range

Measures of variation, p. 44
Easy, Factual/Definitional, Objective 11, Ans: c

126. Which of the following is a measure of the degree of variation among a set of events?
    a. mean
    b. scatterplot
    c. standard deviation
    d. normal distribution
    e. correlation coefficient

Measures of variation, p. 44
Medium, Conceptual/Application, Objective 11, Ans: d

127. Evelyn wants to know how consistent her bowling scores have been during the past season. Which of the following measures would be most relevant to this specific concern?
    a. mean
    b. median
    c. scatterplot
    d. standard deviation
    e. correlation coefficient

Measures of variation, p. 44
Difficult, Conceptual/Application, Objective 11, Ans: b

128. The intelligence scores of college students have a ________ standard deviation than those of high school students and a ________ standard deviation than those of graduate school students.
    a. smaller; smaller
    b. smaller; larger
    c. larger; smaller
    d. larger; larger

Making inferences, p. 44
Medium, Conceptual, Objective 12, Ans: c

129. Statistical reasoning can help us to generalize correctly from a ________ to a ________.
    a. range; standard deviation
    b. standard deviation; mean
    c. sample; population
    d. scatterplot; skewed distribution

Making inferences, p. 44
Difficult, Conceptual, Objective 12, Ans: b

130. The precision with which a sample average approximates a population average increases as the ________ of the sample ________.
    a. standard deviation; increases
    b. standard deviation; decreases
    c. mean; increases
    d. mean; decreases

Making inferences, p. 44
Easy, Factual/Definitional, Objective 12, Ans: a

131. A sample average can be used to estimate a population average with greater precision if the sample is:
    a. large.
    b. a skewed distribution.
    c. highly variable.
    d. vivid and memorable.

Making inferences, p. 44
Difficult, Conceptual, Objective 12, Ans: a

132. Which of the following events is the most probable?
    a. flipping 6 or more heads in 10 coin flips
    b. flipping 60 or more heads in 100 coin flips
    c. flipping 600 or more heads in 1000 coin flips
    d. All the above are equally probable.

Making inferences, p. 44
Difficult, Conceptual, Objective 12, Ans: c

133. In a single day, 45 babies were born in hospital X, 65 babies in hospital Y, and 25 babies in hospital Z. At which hospital is there the greatest probability that more than 60 percent of the babies are of the same sex?
    a. hospital X
    b. hospital Y
    c. hospital Z
    d. The probability is the same at all three hospitals.

Making inferences, p. 44
Difficult, Conceptual, Objective 12, Ans: c

134. As the size of a representative sample increases, the ________ of that sample is most likely to decrease.
    a. range
    b. mean
    c. standard deviation
    d. median

Making inferences, p. 44
Easy, Factual/Definitional, Objective 12, Ans: a

135. Differences between two sample averages are most likely to be statistically significant if:
   a. the samples are large.
   b. the standard deviations of the samples are large.
   c. both samples are drawn from the same population.
   d. the sample means are larger than the sample medians.

Making inferences, p. 45
Easy, Factual/Definitional, Objective 12, Ans: d

136. In order to decide whether observed differences between samples reflect actual differences between populations, it is necessary to determine the ________ of the observed differences.
   a. mean
   b. median
   c. standard deviation
   d. statistical significance

Making inferences, p. 45
Difficult, Factual/Definitional, Objective 12, Ans: b

137. A statistically significant difference between two sample groups is *not* likely to be:
   a. a reflection of differences between the populations they represent.
   b. due to chance variation within and between the sample groups.
   c. observed more than 5 percent of the time the groups are compared.
   d. observed when the two groups are very large.

Can laboratory experiments illuminate everyday life?, p. 47
Medium, Factual/Definitional, Objective 13, Ans: c

138. The artificial and simplified reality of laboratory experiments is most helpful in enabling psychologists to:
   a. predict human behavior in a variety of situations.
   b. perceive order in completely random events.
   c. develop explanatory theories of everyday behaviors.
   d. observe random samples of human conduct.

Does behavior depend on one's culture?, pp. 47-48
Difficult, Conceptual, Objective 13, Ans: d

139. An awareness of extensive cultural differences in attitudes and values is most helpful for avoiding:
   a. replication.
   b. random assignment.
   c. the hindsight bias.
   d. the false consensus effect.
   e. operational definitions.

Does behavior vary with gender?, p. 48
Medium, Factual/Definitional, Objective 13, Ans: e

140. Psychological differences between the genders are:
 a. of little interest to contemporary psychologists.
 b. simply reflections of biological differences between the sexes.
 c. no longer evident in contemporary Western societies.
 d. of little relevance to real life.
 e. far outweighed by gender similarities.

Why do psychologists study animals?, p. 49
Medium, Factual/Definitional, Objective 14, Ans: d

141. Psychologists study animals because:
 a. animal behavior is just as complex as human behavior.
 b. experiments on people are generally considered to be unethical.
 c. the ethical treatment of animals is not mandated by professional guidelines.
 d. similar processes often underlie animal and human behavior.

Is it ethical to experiment on animals?, p. 49
Easy, Factual/Definitional, Objective 14, Ans: e

142. Coile and Miller's analysis of animal research published during a five-year period in American Psychological Association journals revealed that psychologists:
 a. shocked animals with extremely painful shocks that caused them to die.
 b. allowed animals to die slowly from hunger and thirst.
 c. placed animals in isolation chambers until they were driven insane.
 d. did all the above.
 e. did none of the above.

Is it ethical to experiment on animals? p. 49
Medium, Factual/Definitional, Objective 14, Ans: b

143. Animal protection organizations are more likely to support the use of animals in research involving ________ than in research involving ________.
 a. experimentation; replication
 b. naturalistic observation; experimentation
 c. case studies; naturalistic observation
 d. random assignment; case studies

Is it ethical to experiment on people?, p. 50
Difficult, Factual/Definitional, Objective 14, Ans: c

144. In an effort to prevent participants in an experiment from trying to confirm the researchers' predictions, psychologists sometimes:
 a. obtain written promises from participants to respond honestly.
 b. treat information about individual participants confidentially.
 c. deceive participants about the true purpose of an experiment.
 d. allow people to decide for themselves whether they want to participate in an experiment.

Is it ethical to experiment on people? p. 51
Medium, Factual/Definitional, Objective 14, Ans: d

145. The American Psychological Association and British Psychological Society have developed ethical principles urging investigators to:
   a. avoid the use of monetary incentives in recruiting people to participate in research.
   b. forewarn potential research participants of the exact hypotheses that the research will test.
   c. avoid the manipulation of independent variables in research involving human participants.
   d. explain the research to the participants after the study has been completed.

Is psychology free of value judgments?, p. 51
Medium, Factual/Definitional, Objective 15, Ans: c

146. Psychologists' personal values and goals:
   a. are carefully tested by means of observation and experimentation.
   b. lead them to avoid experiments involving human participants.
   c. can bias their observations and interpretations.
   d. have very little influence on the process of scientific observation.

Is psychology potentially dangerous?, p. 52
Medium, Factual/Definitional, Objective 15, Ans: a

147. The study of psychology is potentially dangerous because:
   a. psychological knowledge can be used for destructive purposes.
   b. psychologists generally believe that people are not personally responsible for their actions.
   c. psychological research necessitates performing stressful experiments on people.
   d. people are highly suggestible and can be easily manipulated.

Thinking critically about the death penalty (Box), p. 52
Medium, Factual/Definitional, Objective 15, Ans: d

148. The postmodernist viewpoint suggests that science:
   a. leads to increasingly closer approximations of objective truth.
   b. has very little influence in contemporary culture.
   c. provides the best approach for making moral and legal decisions.
   d. is a reflection of cultural assumptions and personal values.

Thinking critically about the death penalty (Box), p. 53
Medium, Factual/Definitional, Objective 15, Ans: d

149. Compared to the general adult population of the United States, those who are legally eligible to serve as jurors in capital punishment cases are ________ likely to be minorities and ________ likely to be women.
   a. less; more
   b. more; less
   c. more; more
   d. less; less

Essay Questions

1. When your best friend hears that you are taking a psychology course, she asserts that psychology is simply common sense. Explain why your awareness of both the limits of everyday reasoning and the methods of psychological research would lead you to disagree with your friend's assertion.

2. The table below lists the scores of eight subjects on a test to measure anxiety, as well as the typical number of cigarettes each person smokes daily. Scores on the anxiety test can range anywhere from a low of 0 (indicating very low anxiety) to a high of 30 (indicating very high anxiety).

Subject	Anxiety Test Score	Cigarettes Smoked Daily
1	8	11
2	9	3
3	15	11
4	14	16
5	21	26
6	12	10
7	22	24
8	17	18

Construct a scatterplot to represent the correlation between smoking and anxiety. Describe the direction of the correlation and give two possible explanations for it.

3. Speaking at a college graduation ceremony, Professor Robson compared college graduates with adults who are less educated. She correctly noted that college graduates pay more taxes, vote more frequently, engage in more volunteer activities in their communities, and are less likely to go to jail than less-educated adults. The professor concluded that colleges obviously do great things for society. How might you reasonably challenge the way the professor reached her conclusion?

4. Design an experiment to test whether alcohol consumption influences people's tendency to become socially aggressive. Be sure to specify your experimental hypothesis and identify your dependent and independent variables, as well as your experimental and control conditions. Identify any experimental procedures that would help to ensure the validity of your research.

5. Five students received the following test scores: 7, 11, 5, 6, and 11. Calculate the mode, median, mean, and range of this distribution of scores. Which measure of central tendency would change the most if an additional test score of 2 was included in the distribution?

Web Quiz 1

Ans: b

1. After the horror of 9/11, many people said the CIA and FBI should obviously have foreseen the likelihood of this form of terrorism. This perception most clearly illustrates:
   a. the false consensus effect.
   b. the hindsight bias.
   c. random sampling.
   d. the placebo effect.

Ans: d

2. When Leanne heard about experimental evidence that orange juice consumption triggers hyperactivity in children, she questioned whether the tested children had been randomly assigned to experimental conditions. Leanne's reaction best illustrates:
   a. illusory correlation.
   b. an illusion of control.
   c. the hindsight bias.
   d. critical thinking.
   e. overconfidence.

Ans: a

3. Stacey suggests that because children are more impulsive than adults, they will have more difficulty controlling their anger. Stacey's prediction regarding anger management exemplifies:
   a. an hypothesis.
   b. the hindsight bias.
   c. illusory correlation.
   d. the false consensus effect.

Ans: c

4. Which research technique is most directly useful for avoiding the thinking error known as the false consensus effect?
   a. operational definition
   b. double-blind procedure
   c. random sampling
   d. experimental control
   e. case study

Ans: d

5, Professor Carter observes and records the behavior of grocery shoppers as they select items to purchase. Which type of research is Professor Carter employing?
   a. survey research
   b. case study
   c. experimentation
   d. naturalistic observation

Ans: c

6. A negative correlation between people's physical health and their marital happiness would indicate that:
   a. poor physical health has a negative impact on marital happiness.
   b. marital unhappiness promotes poor health.
   c. higher levels of marital happiness are associated with lower levels of physical health.
   d. marital happiness has no causal influence on physical health.

Ans: e

7. Mr. Brown has gathered evidence that the weight of grade school students correlates positively with their reading skill. Before he uses this evidence to conclude that body weight enhances reading ability, Mr. Brown should first be reminded that:
   a. events often seem more probable in hindsight.
   b. random sequences of events often don't look random.
   c. sampling extreme cases leads to false generalizations.
   d. we often exaggerate the extent to which others share our opinions.
   e. correlation does not prove causation.

Ans: c

8. Which method offers the most reliable way of assessing whether athletic performance is boosted by caffeine consumption?
   a. the survey
   b. the case study
   c. the experiment
   d. naturalistic observation

Ans: e

9. In drug-treatment studies, double-blind procedures minimize outcome differences between experimental and control conditions that could be attributed to:
   a. replication.
   b. random assignment.
   c. operational definitions.
   d. random sampling.
   e. placebo effects.

Ans: d

10. In an experimental study of the extent to which mental alertness is inhibited by sleep deprivation, alertness would be the
    a. control condition.
    b. independent variable.
    c. experimental condition.
    d. dependent variable.

Ans: b

11. In order to assess whether sense of humor is affected by sexual stimulation, researchers exposed married couples to either sexually stimulating or to sexually nonstimulating movie scenes prior to watching a comedy skit. In this research, the independent variable consisted of:
    a. reactions to the comedy skit.
    b. level of sexual stimulation.
    c. marital status.
    d. sense of humor.

Ans: a

12. One person in a ten-person group is ten times older than any of the other members. With respect to age, it is *most* likely that the majority of group members are younger than the group's:
    a. mode.
    b. median.
    c. mean.
    d. standard deviation.

Ans: e

13. The ________ is a measure of ________.
    a. standard deviation; central tendency
    b. mean; variation
    c. correlation coefficient; central tendency
    d. mode; variation
    e. median; central tendency

Ans: d

14. Janet has five brothers who are 4, 6, 6, 9, and 15 years of age. The mean age of Janet's brothers is:
    a. 5.
    b. 6.
    c. 7.
    d. 8.
    e. 9

Ans: b

15. Random samples provide ________ estimates of population averages if the samples have small ________.
    a. good; means
    b. good; standard deviations
    c. poor; means
    d. poor; standard deviations

Web Quiz 2

Ans: e

1. Jamie and Lynn were sure that they had answered most of the multiple-choice questions correctly because "the questions required only common sense." However, they each scored less than 60% on the exam. This best illustrates:
   a. illusory correlation.
   b. random assignment.
   c. the false consensus effect.
   d. the hindsight bias.
   e. overconfidence.

Ans: d

2. Psychological theories:
   a. organize scientific observations.
   b. explain observed facts.
   c. generate hypotheses.
   d. do all of the above.

Ans: b

3. Which research method runs the greatest risk of collecting evidence that may be unrepresentative of what is generally true?
   a. naturalistic observation
   b. the case study
   c. experimentation
   d. the survey

Ans: c

4. Every twenty-fifth person who ordered a subscription to a weekly news magazine was contacted by market researchers to complete a survey of opinions regarding the magazine's contents. The researchers were most clearly employing a technique known as:
   a. naturalistic observation.
   b. the double-blind procedure.
   c. random sampling.
   d. the case study.
   e. replication.

Ans: d

5. Surveys are most likely to indicate that reckless behavior and self-control are:
   a. independent variables.
   b. positively correlated.
   c. dependent variables.
   d. negatively correlated.

Ans: a

6. A correlation of +.70 between children's physical height and their popularity among their peers indicates that:
   a. higher levels of popularity among one's peers is associated with greater physical height in children.
   b. there is no statistically significant relationship between children's height and their popularity.
   c. being unusually short or tall has a negative impact on children's popularity.
   d. children's height has no causal impact on their popularity.

Ans: c

7 A tendency to notice and remember instances in which our premonitions of disaster are subsequently followed by harmful events is most likely to contribute to:
   a. the false consensus effect.
   b. the hindsight bias.
   c. illusory correlations.
   d. the placebo effect.

Ans: c

8. Researchers are especially likely to use experiments rather than other methods in order to achieve greater accuracy with respect to:
   a. description.
   b. prediction.
   c. explanation.
   d. replication.

Ans: a

9. Researchers control factors that might influence a dependent variable by means of:
   a. random assignment.
   b. replication.
   c. naturalistic observation.
   d. operational definitions.

Ans: b

10. In a study of factors that might affect memory, research participants were assigned to drink either an alcoholic or a nonalcoholic beverage prior to completing a memory test. Those who drank the nonalcoholic beverage participated in the ________ condition.
   a. survey
   b. control
   c. experimental
   d. correlational

Ans: b

11. In an experimental study of the effects of dieting on weight loss, dieting would be the:
   a. control condition.
   b. independent variable.
   c. operational definition.
   d. dependent variable.
   e. placebo.

Ans: a

12. The ________ can be a particularly misleading indication of what is average for a ________ distribution of scores.
   a. mean; skewed
   b. median; skewed
   c. mean; normal
   d. median; normal

Ans: c

13. The ________ is a measure of ________.
   a. median; variation
   b. range; central tendency
   c. standard deviation; variation
   d. correlation coefficient; central tendency

Ans: b

14. Ahmed has five sisters who are 3, 3, 5, 9, and 10 years of age. The number "5" represents the ________ of the sisters' ages.
   a. mode
   b. median
   c. mean
   d. range

Ans: c

15. Differences between two samples are <u>least</u> likely to be statistically significant if the samples are ________ and the standard deviations of the samples are ________.
   a. small; small
   b. large; large
   c. small; large
   d. large; small

Study Guide Questions

Ans: b, p. 20

1. Which of the following *best* describes the hindsight bias?
   a. Events seem more predictable before they have occurred.
   b. Events seem more predictable after they have occurred.
   c. A person's intuition is usually correct.
   d. A person's intuition is usually not correct.

Ans: d, p. 21

2. Juwan eagerly opened an online trading account, believing that his market savvy would allow him to pick stocks that would make him a rich day trader. This belief best illustrates:
   a. the false consensus effect.
   b. illusory correlation.
   c. hindsight bias.
   d. overconfidence.

Ans: b, p. 23

3. To say that "psychology is a science" means that:
   a. psychologists study only observable behaviors.
   b. psychologists study thoughts and actions with an attitude of skepticism and derive their conclusions from direct observations.
   c. psychological research should be free of value judgments.
   d. all of the above are true.

Ans: d, p. 23

4. The scientific attitude of humility is based on the idea that:
   a. researchers must evaluate new ideas and theories objectively rather than accept them blindly.
   b. scientific theories must be testable.
   c. simple explanations of behavior make better theories than do complex explanations.
   d. researchers must be prepared to reject their own ideas in the face of conflicting evidence.

Ans: d, p. 23

5. The scientific attitude of skepticism is based on the belief that:
   a. people are rarely candid in revealing their thoughts.
   b. mental processes can't be studied objectively.
   c. the scientist's intuition about behavior is usually correct.
   d. ideas need to be tested against observable evidence.

Ans: d, p. 24

6. Theories are defined as:
   a. testable propositions.
   b. factors that may change in response to manipulation.
   c. statistical indexes.
   d. principles that help to organize, predict, and explain facts.

Ans: b, p. 24

7. Which of the following is true, according to the text?
a. Because laboratory experiments are artificial, any principles discovered cannot be applied to everyday behaviors.
b. No psychological theory can be considered true until tested.
c. Psychology's theories reflect common sense.
d. Psychology has few ties to other disciplines.

Ans: b, p. 24

8. You decide to test your belief that men drink more soft drinks than women by finding out whether more soft drinks are consumed per day in the men's dorm than in the women's dorm. Your belief is a(n) ________, and your research prediction is a(n) ________.
a. hypothesis; theory
b. theory; hypothesis
c. independent variable; dependent variable
d. dependent variable; independent variable

Ans: b, p. 25

9. Which of the following is *not* a basic research strategy used by psychologists?
a. description
b. replication
c. experimentation
d. correlation

Ans: d, p. 25

10. To ensure that other researchers can repeat their work, psychologists use:
a. control groups.
b. random assignment.
c. double-blind procedures.
d. operational definitions.

Ans: a, p. 26

11. After detailed study of a gunshot wound victim, a psychologist concludes that the brain region destroyed is likely to be important for memory functions. Which research strategy did the psychologist use to deduce this?
a. the case study
b. a survey
c. correlation
d. experimentation

Ans: c, p. 28

12. Your roommate is conducting a survey to learn how many hours the typical college student studies each day. She plans to pass out her questionnaire to the members of her sorority. You point out that her findings will be flawed because:
a. she has not specified an independent variable.
b. she has not specified a dependent variable.
c. the sample will probably not be representative of the population of interest.
d. of all the above reasons.

Ans: a, p. 28

13. One reason researchers base their findings on representative samples is to avoid the false consensus effect, which refers to our tendency to:
    a. overestimate the extent to which others share our belief.
    b. falsely perceive a relationship between two events when none exists.
    c. underestimate errors in our judgment.
    d. make all of the above reasoning errors.

Ans: d, p. 28

14. Well-done surveys measure attitudes in a representative subset, or ________, of an entire group, or ________.
    a. population; random sample
    b. control group; experimental group
    c. experimental group; control group
    d. random sample; population

Ans: d, p. 28

15. A professor constructs a questionnaire to determine how students at the university feel about nuclear disarmament. Which of the following techniques should be used in order to survey a random sample of the student body?
    a. Every student should be sent the questionnaire.
    b. Only students majoring in psychology should be asked to complete the questionnaire.
    c. Only students living on campus should be asked to complete the questionnaire.
    d. From an alphabetical listing of all students, every tenth (or fifteenth, e.g.) student should be asked to complete the questionnaire.

Ans: d, p. 29

16. A psychologist studies the play behavior of third-grade children by watching groups during recess at school. Which research strategy is being used?
    a. correlation
    b. case study
    c. experimentation
    d. naturalistic observation

Ans: c, p. 30

17. If height and body weight are positively correlated, which of the following is true?
    a. There is a cause-effect relationship between height and weight.
    b. As height increases, weight decreases.
    c. Knowing a person's height, one can predict his or her weight.
    d. All of the above are true.

Ans: d, p. 30

18. Which type of research strategy would allow you to determine whether students' college grades accurately predict later income?
    a. case study
    b. naturalistic observation
    c. experimentation
    d. correlation

Ans: b, p. 30

19. A researcher was interested in determining whether her students' test performance could be predicted from their proximity to the front of the classroom. So she matched her students' scores on a math test with their seating position. This study is an example of:
    a. experimentation.
    b. correlational research.
    c. a survey.
    d. naturalistic observation.

Ans: d, pp. 30-32

20. If eating saturated fat and the likelihood of contracting cancer are positively correlated, which of the following is true?
    a. Saturated fat causes cancer.
    b. People who are prone to develop cancer prefer foods containing saturated fat.
    c. A separate factor links the consumption of saturated fat to cancer.
    d. None of the above is necessarily true.

Ans: b, p. 31

21. If shoe size and IQ are negatively correlated, which of the following is true?
    a. People with large feet tend to have high IQs.
    b. People with small feet tend to have high IQs.
    c. People with small feet tend to have low IQs.
    d. IQ is unpredictable based on a person's shoe size.

Ans: c, p. 33

22. Joe believes that his basketball game is always best when he wears his old gray athletic socks. Joe is a victim of the phenomenon called:
    a. statistical significance.
    b. overconfidence.
    c. illusory correlation.
    d. hindsight bias.

Ans: b, p. 33

23. Illusory correlation refers to:
    a. the perception that two negatively correlated variables are positively correlated.
    b. the perception of a correlation between two unrelated variables.
    c. an insignificant correlation.
    d. a correlation that equals –1.0.

Ans: d, p. 34

24. The strength of the relationship between two vivid events will most likely be:
    a. significant.
    b. positive.
    c. negative.
    d. overestimated.

Ans: d, p. 38

25. Which of the following research strategies would be best for determining whether alcohol impairs memory?
 a. case study
 b. naturalistic observation
 c. survey
 d. experiment

Ans: d, p. 38

26. Which of the following research methods does *not* belong with the others?
 a. case study
 b. survey
 c. naturalistic observation
 d. experiment

Ans: a, p. 38

27. Which of the following procedures is an example of the use of a placebo?
 a. In a test of the effects of a drug on memory, a participant is led to believe that a harmless pill actually contains an active drug.
 b. A participant in an experiment is led to believe that a pill, which actually contains an active drug, is harmless.
 c. Participants in an experiment are not told which treatment condition is in effect.
 d. Neither the participants nor the experimenter know which treatment condition is in effect.

Ans: c, p. 39

28. In an experiment to determine the effects of exercise on motivation, exercise is the:
 a. control condition.
 b. intervening variable.
 c. independent variable.
 d. dependent variable.

Ans: d, p. 39

29. In an experiment to determine the effects of attention on memory, memory is the:
 a. control condition.
 b. intervening variable.
 c. independent variable.
 d. dependent variable.

Ans: b, p. 39

30. The procedure designed to ensure that the experimental and control groups do *not* differ in any way that might affect the experiment's results is called:
 a. variable controlling.
 b. random assignment.
 c. representative sampling.
 d. stratification.

Ans: b, p. 39

31. In a test of the effects of air pollution, groups of students performed a reaction-time task in a polluted or an unpolluted room. To what condition were students in the unpolluted room exposed?
   a. experimental
   b. control
   c. randomly assigned
   d. dependent

Ans: b, p. 39

32. The concept of control is important in psychological research because:
   a. without control over independent and dependent variables, researchers cannot describe, predict, or explain behavior.
   b. experimental control allows researchers to study the influence of one or two independent variables on a dependent variable while holding other potential influences constant.
   c. without experimental control, results cannot be generalized from a sample to a population.
   d. of all the above reasons.

Ans: d, p. 39

33. Rashad, who is participating in a psychology experiment on the effects of alcohol on perception, is truthfully told by the experimenter that he has been assigned to the "high-dose condition." What is wrong with this experiment?
   a. There is no control condition.
   b. Rashad's expectations concerning the effects of "high doses" of alcohol on perception may influence his performance.
   c. Knowing that Rashad is in the "high-dose" condition may influence the experimenter's interpretations of Rashad's results.
   d. Both b. and c. are correct.

Ans: c, p. 39

34. Martina believes that high doses of caffeine slow a person's reaction time. In order to test this belief, she has five friends each drink three 8-ounce cups of coffee and then measures their reaction time on a learning task. What is wrong with Martina's research strategy?
   a. No independent variable is specified.
   b. No dependent variable is specified.
   c. There is no control condition.
   d. There is no provision for replication of the findings.

Ans: c, p. 39

35. In order to study the effects of lighting on mood, Dr. Cooper had students fill out questionnaires in brightly lit or dimly lit rooms. In this study, the independent variable consisted of:
   a. the number of students assigned to each group.
   b. the students' responses to the questionnaire.
   c. the room lighting.
   d. the subject matter of the questions asked.

Ans: c, p. 39

36. In order to determine the effects of a new drug on memory, one group of people is given a pill that contains the drug. A second group is given a sugar pill that does *not* contain the drug. This second group constitutes the:
   a. random sample.
   b. experimental group.
   c. control group.
   d. test group.

Ans: a, pp. 40-41

37. In the experiment on subliminal perception, students listened for five weeks to tapes they thought would enhance their memory or self-esteem. At the end of the experiment:
   a. students who thought they had a memory tape believed their memories had improved; but, in fact, there was no improvement.
   b. self-esteem, but not memory, improved.
   c. memory, but not self-esteem, improved.
   d. both self-esteem and memory improved over the course of the experiment.

Ans: c, p. 43

38. What is the mean of the following distribution of scores: 2, 3, 7, 6, 1, 4, 9, 5, 8, 2?
   a. 5
   b. 4
   c. 4.7
   d. 3.7

Ans: d, p. 43

39. What is the median of the following distribution of scores: 1, 3, 7, 7, 2, 8, 4?
   a. 1
   b. 2
   c. 3
   d. 4

Ans: b, p. 43

40. What is the mode of the following distribution: 8, 2, 1, 1, 3, 7, 6, 2, 0, 2?
   a. 1
   b. 2
   c. 3
   d. 7

Ans: a, p. 43

41. Which of the following is the measure of central tendency that would be most affected by a few extreme scores?
   a. mean
   b. range
   c. median
   d. mode

Ans: b, p. 43

42. What is the mode of the following distribution of scores: 2, 2, 4, 4, 4, 14?
   a. 2
   b. 4
   c. 5
   d. 6

Ans: c, p. 43

43. What is the mean of the following distribution of scores: 2, 5, 8, 10, 11, 4, 6, 9, 1, 4?
   a. 2
   b. 10
   c. 6
   d. 15

Ans: c, p. 43

44. Bob scored 43 out of 70 points on his psychology exam. He was worried until he discovered that most of the class earned the same score. Bob's score was equal to the:
   a. mean.
   b. median.
   c. mode.
   d. range.

Ans: a, p. 43

45. The four families on your block all have annual household incomes of $25,000. If a new family with an annual income of $75,000 moved in, which measure of central tendency would be most affected?
   a. mean
   b. median
   c. mode
   d. standard deviation

Ans: c, p. 43

46. What is the median of the following distribution: 10, 7, 5, 11, 8, 6, 9?
   a. 6
   b. 7
   c. 8
   d. 9

Ans: d, p. 43

47. Which of the following is the measure of variation that is most affected by extreme scores?
   a. mean
   b. standard deviation
   c. mode
   d. range

Ans: c, p. 43

48. A lopsided set of scores that includes a number of extreme or unusual values is said to be:
   a. symmetrical.
   b. normal.
   c. skewed.
   d. dispersed.

Ans: d, pp. 43, 44

49. Esteban refuses to be persuaded by an advertiser's claim that people using their brand of gasoline average 50 miles per gallon. His decision probably is based on:
 a. the possibility that the average is the mean, which could be artificially inflated by a few extreme scores.
 b. the absence of information about the size of the sample studied.
 c. the absence of information about the variation in sample scores.
 d. all of the above.

Ans: a, p. 44

50. In generalizing from a sample to the population, it is important that:
 a. the sample be representative.
 b. the sample be nonrandom.
 c. the sample not be too large.
 d. all of the above be true.

Ans: b, p. 44

51. The set of scores that would likely be most representative of the population from which it was drawn would be a sample with a relatively:
 a. large standard deviation.
 b. small standard deviation.
 c. large range.
 d. small range.

Ans: d, p. 44

52. In generalizing from a sample to the population, it is important that:
 a. the sample is representative of the population.
 b. the sample is large.
 c. the scores in the sample have low variability.
 d. all of the above are observed.

Ans: d, p. 44

53. The football team's punter wants to determine how consistent his punting distances have been during the past season. He should compute the:
 a. mean.
 b. median.
 c. mode.
 d. standard deviation.

Ans: b, p. 45

54. Dr. Salazar recently completed an experiment in which she compared reasoning ability in a sample of females and a sample of males. The means of the female and male samples equaled 21 and 19, respectively, on a 25-point scale. A statistical test revealed that her results were not statistically significant. What can Dr. Salazar conclude?
 a. Females have superior reasoning ability.
 b. The difference in the means of the two samples is probably due to chance variation.
 c. The difference in the means of the two samples is reliable.
 d. None of the above is true

Ans: d, p. 45

55. If a difference between two samples is not statistically significant, which of the following can be concluded?
   a. The difference is probably not a true one.
   b. The difference is probably not reliable.
   c. The difference could be due to sampling variation.
   d. All of the above can be concluded.

Ans: c, p. 45

56. When a difference between two groups is "statistically significant," this means that:
   a. the difference is statistically real but of little practical significance.
   b. the difference is probably the result of sampling variation.
   c. the difference is not likely to be due to chance variation.
   d. all of the above are true.

Ans: d, p. 47

57. Your best friend criticizes psychological research for being artificial and having no relevance to behavior in real life. In defense of psychology's use of laboratory experiments you point out that:
   a. psychologists make every attempt to avoid artificiality by setting up experiments that closely simulate real-world environments.
   b. psychologists who conduct basic research are not concerned with the applicability of their findings to the real world.
   c. most psychological research is not conducted in a laboratory environment.
   d. psychologists intentionally study behavior in simplified environments in order to gain greater control over variables and to test general principles that help to explain many behaviors.

Ans: d, pp. 47-48

58. A friend majoring in anthropology is critical of psychological research because it often ignores the influence of culture on thoughts and actions. You point out that:
   a. there is very little evidence that cultural diversity has a significant effect on specific behaviors and attitudes.
   b. most researchers assign subjects to experimental and control conditions in such a way as to fairly represent the cultural diversity of the population under study.
   c. it is impossible for psychologists to control for every possible variable that might influence research participants.
   d. even when specific thoughts and actions vary across cultures, as they often do, the underlying processes are much the same.

Ans: d, p. 49

59. Which statement about the ethics of experimentation with people and animals is *false*?
   a. Only a small percentage of animal experiments use shock.
   b. Allegations that psychologists routinely subject animals to pain, starvation, and other inhumane conditions have been proven untrue.
   c. The American Psychological Association and the British Psychological Society have set strict guidelines for the care and treatment of human and animal subjects.
   d. Animals are used as subjects in almost 25 percent of all psychology experiments.

Ans: c, p. 51

60. Psychologists' personal values:
    a. have little influence on how their experiments are conducted.
    b. do not influence the interpretation of experimental results because of the use of statistical techniques that guard against subjective bias.
    c. can bias both scientific observation and interpretation of data.
    d. have little influence on investigative methods but a significant effect on interpretation.

CHAPTER **2**

Neuroscience and Behavior

Learning Objectives

1. Explain why psychologists are concerned with human biology.

Neural Communication (pp. 58-65)

2. Describe the structure of a neuron, and explain how neural impulses are generated.

3. Describe how nerve cells communicate, and discuss the impact of neurotransmitters and drugs on human behavior.

The Nervous System (pp. 65-69)

4. Identify the major divisions of the nervous system and describe their functions, noting the three types of neurons that transmit information through the system.

5. Contrast the simplicity of the neural pathways involved in reflexes with the complexity of neural networks.

The Brain (pp. 69-94)

6. Identify and describe several techniques for studying the brain.

7. Describe the functions of the brainstem, thalamus, cerebellum, and limbic system.

8. Identify the four lobes of the cerebral cortex, and describe the sensory and motor functions of the cortex.

9. Discuss the importance of the association areas, and describe how damage to several different cortical areas can impair language functioning.

10. Discuss the capacity of the brain to reorganize following injury or illness.

11. Describe research on the split brain, and discuss what it reveals regarding normal brain functioning.

12. Discuss the relationships among brain organization, right- and left-handedness, and physical health.

The Endocrine System (pp. 94-96)

13. Describe the nature and functions of the endocrine system and its interaction with the nervous system.

Introduction, p. 57
Easy, Factual/Definitional, Objective 1, Ans: a

1. Phrenology highlighted the presumed functions of:
   a. specific brain regions.
   b. neurotransmitters.
   c. hormones.
   d. the right brain.

Introduction, p. 57
Difficult, Conceptual, Objective 1, Ans: d

2. The person most likely to suggest that the shape of a person's skull indicates the extent to which that individual is argumentative and aggressive would be a:
   a. neurologist.
   b. behavior geneticist.
   c. psychoanalyst.
   d. phrenologist.

Introduction, p. 58
Easy, Conceptual/Application, Objective 1, Ans: b

3. Dr. Wolski does research on the potential relationship between neurotransmitter deficiencies and mood states. Which psychological specialty does Dr. Wolski's research best represent?
   a. phrenology
   b. biological psychology
   c. psychoanalysis
   d. clinical psychology

Introduction, p. 58
Medium, Conceptual, Objective 1, Ans: a

4. A biological psychologist would be most interested in the relationship between:
   a. body chemistry and violent behavior.
   b. skull shape and character traits.
   c. self-esteem and popularity.
   d. brain size and cell structure.

Neurons, p. 58
Easy, Factual/Definitional, Objective 2, Ans: c

5. Dendrites are branching extensions of:
   a. neurotransmitters.
   b. endorphins.
   c. neurons.
   d. glial cells.
   e. endocrine glands.

Neurons, p. 58
Medium, Factual/Definitional, Objective 2, Ans: a

6. The function of dendrites is to:
   a. receive incoming signals from other neurons.
   b. release neurotransmitters into the spatial junctions between neurons.
   c. coordinate the activation of the parasympathetic and sympathetic nervous systems.
   d. control pain through the release of opiatelike chemicals into the brain.

Neurons, p. 58
Easy, Factual/Definitional, Objective 2, Ans: d

7. An axon is:
   a. a cell that serves as the basic building block of the nervous system.
   b. a layer of fatty tissue that encases the fibers of many neurons.
   c. an antagonist molecule that blocks neurotransmitter receptor sites.
   d. the extension of a neuron that carries messages away from the cell body.
   e. a junction between a sending and receiving neuron.

Neurons, p. 58
Easy, Factual/Definitional, Objective 2, Ans: b

8. The longest part of a motor neuron is likely to be the:
   a. dendrite.
   b. axon.
   c. cell body.
   d. synapse.

Neurons, p. 58
Medium, Factual/Definitional, Objective 2, Ans: d

9. In transmitting sensory information to the brain, an electrical signal within a single neuron travels from the:
   a. cell body to the axon to the dendrites.
   b. dendrites to the axon to the cell body.
   c. axon to the cell body to the dendrites.
   d. dendrites to the cell body to the axon.
   e. axon to the dendrites to the cell body.

Neurons, p. 58
Easy, Factual/Definitional, Objective 2, Ans: b

10. The speed at which a neural impulse travels is increased when the axon is encased by a(n):
    a. association area.
    b. myelin sheath.
    c. endocrine gland.
    d. glial cell.
    e. synaptic vesicle.

Neurons, p. 58
Medium, Factual/Definitional, Objective 2, Ans: c

11. Neural impulses may travel as rapidly as:
    a. sound waves.
    b. light waves.
    c. 200 miles per hour.
    d. electricity through a wire.

Neurons, p. 59
Easy, Factual/Definitional, Objective 2, Ans: c

12. A brief electrical charge that travels down the axon of a neuron is called the:
    a. synapse.
    b. agonist.
    c. action potential.
    d. myelin sheath.
    e. refractory period.

Neurons, p. 59
Easy, Factual/Definitional, Objective 2, Ans: a

13. The depolarization of a neural membrane creates a(n):
    a. action potential.
    b. myelin sheath.
    c. lesion.
    d. neural network.
    e. interneuron.

Neurons, p. 59
Medium, Factual/Definitional, Objective 2, Ans: d

14. An action potential is generated by the movement of:
    a. glial cells.
    b. hormones.
    c. vesicles.
    d. ions.

Neurons, p. 59
Medium, Factual/Definitional, Objective 2, Ans: b

15. The resting potential of an axon results from the fact that an axon membrane is:
    a. encased by a myelin sheath.
    b. selectively permeable.
    c. sensitive to neurotransmitter molecules.
    d. part of a larger neural network.

Neurons, p. 59
Difficult, Conceptual, Objective 2, Ans: d

16. Resting potential is to action potential as ________ is to ________.
    a. parasympathetic nervous system; sympathetic nervous system
    b. sensory neuron; motor neuron
    c. association area; neural network
    d. polarization; depolarization
    e. PET scan; MRI

Neurons, p. 59
Difficult, Factual/Definitional, Objective 2, Ans: c

17. With regard to the process of neural transmission, a refractory period refers to a time interval in which:
    a. chemical messengers traverse the synaptic gaps between neurons.
    b. a brief electrical charge travels down an axon.
    c. positively charged atoms are pumped back outside a neural membrane.
    d. an individual reflexively withdraws from a pain stimulus.

Neurons, p. 60
Easy, Factual/Definitional, Objective 2, Ans: b

18. The minimum level of stimulation required to trigger a neural impulse is called the:
    a. reflex.
    b. threshold.
    c. synapse.
    d. action potential.

Neurons, p. 60
Easy, Factual/Definitional, Objective 2, Ans: c

19. Increasing excitatory signals above the threshold for neural activation will not affect the intensity of an action potential. This indicates that a neuron's reaction is:
    a. inhibited by the myelin sheath.
    b. delayed by the refractory period.
    c. an all-or-none response.
    d. dependent on neurotransmitter molecules.

Neurons, p. 60
Difficult, Conceptual/Application, Objective 2, Ans: c

20. A slap on the back is more painful than a pat on the back because a slap triggers:
    a. faster neural impulses.
    b. more intense neural impulses.
    c. more frequent neural impulses.
    d. all the above.

How neurons communicate, p. 60
Easy, Factual/Definitional, Objective 3, Ans: c

21. Sir Charles Sherrington observed that impulses took more time to travel a neural pathway than he might have anticipated. His observation provided evidence for the existence of:
    a. association areas.
    b. glial cells.
    c. synaptic gaps.
    d. interneurons.
    e. neural networks.

How neurons communicate, p. 60
Easy, Factual/Definitional, Objective 3, Ans: d

22. A synapse is a(n):
    a. chemical messenger that triggers muscle contractions.
    b. automatic response to sensory input.
    c. neural network.
    d. junction between a sending neuron and a receiving neuron.
    e. neural cable containing many axons.

How neurons communicate, p. 61
Easy, Factual/Definitional, Objective 3, Ans: b

23. The chemical messengers released into the spatial junctions between neurons are called:
    a. hormones.
    b. neurotransmitters.
    c. synapses.
    d. genes.
    e. glial cells.

How neurons communicate, pp. 59, 61
Difficult, Conceptual, Objective 3, Ans: b

24. Neurotransmitter is to ion as ________ is to ________.
    a. agonist; antagonist
    b. molecule; atom
    c. hormone; epinephrine
    d. GABA; ACh

How neurons communicate, p. 61
Easy, Factual/Definitional, Objective 3, Ans: c

25. Neurotransmitters are released from vesicles located in knoblike terminals on the:
    a. dendrites.
    b. cell body.
    c. axon.
    d. myelin sheath.

How neurons communicate, p. 61
Easy, Factual/Definitional, Objective 3, Ans: d

26. Reuptake refers to the:
    a. movement of neurotransmitter molecules across a synaptic gap.
    b. binding of neurotransmitter molecules to dendritic receptor sites.
    c. inflow of partially charged ions through an axon membrane.
    d. reabsorption of excess neurotransmitter molecules by a sending neuron.

How neurons communicate, p. 61
Difficult, Factual/Definitional, Objective 3, Ans: b

27. Research on neurotransmitters indicates that:
    a. a single synapse generally uses several dozen neurotransmitters.
    b. neurotransmitters can inhibit neural impulse transmission.
    c. less than a dozen neurotransmitters are involved in all neural transmission.
    d. the release of endorphins causes paralysis of the muscles.

How neurotransmitters influence us (Table 2-1), p. 62
Difficult, Factual/Definitional, Objective 3, Ans: b

28. Alzheimer's disease is most closely linked to the loss of neurons that produce:
    a. dopamine.
    b. acetylcholine.
    c. epinephrine.
    d. endorphins.

How neurotransmitters influence us, pp. 62, 95
Easy, Conceptual, Objective 3, Ans: d

29. Epinephrine is to hormone as acetylcholine is to:
    a. synapse.
    b. action potential.
    c. endorphin.
    d. neurotransmitter.

How neurotransmitters influence us, p. 62
Difficult, Factual/Definitional, Objective 3, Ans: a

30. Schizophrenia is most closely linked with excess receptor activity for the neurotransmitter:
    a. dopamine.
    b. epinephrine.
    c. acetylcholine.
    d. serotonin.

How neurotransmitters influence us (Table 2.1), p. 62
Difficult, Factual/Definitional, Objective 3, Ans: d

31. An undersupply of serotonin is most closely linked to:
    a. Alzheimer's disease.
    b. schizophrenia.
    c. Parkinson's disease.
    d. depression.

How neurotransmitters influence us (Table 2.1), p. 62
Difficult, Factual/Definitional, Objective 3, Ans: b

32. GABA is to glutamate as ________ is to ________.
    a. inhibitory hormone; excitatory hormone
    b. inhibitory neurotransmitter; excitatory neurotransmitter
    c. excitatory hormone; inhibitory hormone
    d. excitatory neurotransmitter inhibitory neurotransmitter

How neurotransmitters influence us (Table 2.1), p. 62
Difficult, Factual/Definitional, Objective 3, Ans: c

33. Migraine headaches are most closely linked with an _______ of _______.
    a. oversupply; GABA
    b. undersupply; serotonin
    c. oversupply; glutamate
    d. undersupply; acetylcholine

How neurotransmitters influence us, p. 62
Medium, Conceptual, Objective 3, Ans: c

34. Transferring messages from a motor neuron to a leg muscle requires the neurotransmitter known as:
    a. dopamine.
    b. epinephrine.
    c. acetylcholine.
    d. insulin.

How neurotransmitters influence us, p. 63
Medium, Factual/Definitional, Objective 3, Ans: c

35. Botulin poisoning from improperly canned food causes paralysis by blocking the release of:
a. endorphins.
b. epinephrine.
c. acetylcholine.
d. dopamine.

How neurotransmitters influence us, p. 63
Easy, Factual/Definitional, Objective 3, Ans: a

36. Endorphins are:
a. neurotransmitters.
b. sex hormones.
c. endocrine glands.
d. morphine antagonists.

How neurotransmitters influence us, p. 63
Medium, Factual/Definitional, Objective 3, Ans: c

37. Opiate drugs occupy the same receptor sites as:
a. acetylcholine.
b. serotonin.
c. endorphins.
d. dopamine.
e. epinephrine.

How neurotransmitters influence us, p. 63
Medium, Conceptual/Application, Objective 3, Ans: d

38. José has just played a long, bruising football game but feels little fatigue or discomfort. His lack of pain is most likely caused by the release of:
a. glutamate.
b. dopamine.
c. acetylcholine.
d. endorphins.

How neurotransmitters influence us, pp. 63, 95
Difficult, Conceptual, Objective 3, Ans: e

39. Hormone is to neurotransmitter as epinephrine is to:
a. glucose.
b. estrogen.
c. steroids.
d. insulin.
e. endorphins.

How neurotransmitters influence us, p. 63
Difficult, Factual/Definitional, Objective 3, Ans: d

40. The body's natural production of endorphins is likely to be ________ by heroin use and ________ by acupuncture.
a. increased; increased
b. decreased; decreased
c. increased; decreased
d. decreased; increased

How neurotransmitters influence us, p. 63
Medium, Conceptual/Application, Objective 3, Ans: d

41. Jason's painful withdrawal symptoms following heroin use were probably due in part to a reduction in his body's normal production of:
a. dopamine.
b. epinephrine.
c. acetylcholine.
d. endorphins.

How neurotransmitters influence us, p. 63
Medium, Conceptual, Objective 3, Ans: c

42. A drug that mimics the effects of a particular neurotransmitter or blocks its reuptake is called a(n):
a. glutimate.
b. steroid.
c. agonist.
d. opiate.

How neurotransmitters influence us, p. 63
Medium, Conceptual, Objective 3, Ans: a

43. Endorphin agonists are likely to _______ one's immediate pain and endorphin antagonists are likely to _______ one's immediate pain.
a. decrease; increase
b. increase; decrease
c. increase; increase
d. decrease; decrease

How neurotransmitters influence us, pp. 62-63
Difficult, Factual/Definitional, Objective 3, Ans: c

44. Curare is a paralyzing poison that functions as an:
a. ACh agonist.
b. GABA agonist.
c. ACh antagonist.
d. GABA antagonist.

How neurotransmitters influence us, p. 64
Difficult, Factual/Definitional, Objective 3, Ans: a

45. Dopamine injections have proven ineffective in the treatment of Parkinson's disease because dopamine:
a. fails to pass through the bloodstream into the brain.
b. suppresses the brain's natural capacity to produce endorphins.
c. blocks the capacity of neurons to absorb ACh.
d. produces uncontrollable muscle spasms.

The nervous system, p. 65
Easy, Factual/Definitional, Objective 4, Ans: d

46. The two major divisions of the nervous system are the central and the ________ nervous systems.
    a. autonomic
    b. sympathetic
    c. parasympathetic
    d. peripheral

The nervous system, p. 65
Easy, Factual/Definitional, Objective 4, Ans: c

47. The central nervous system consists of:
    a. sensory and motor neurons.
    b. somatic and autonomic subsystems.
    c. the brain and the spinal cord.
    d. sympathetic and parasympathetic branches.

The nervous system, p. 65
Easy, Conceptual/Application, Objective 4, Ans: e

48. In order for you to experience the pain of a sprained ankle, ________ must first relay messages from your ankle to your central nervous system.
    a. the limbic system
    b. interneurons
    c. the reticular formation
    d. motor neurons
    e. sensory neurons

The nervous system, p. 65
Medium, Factual/Definitional, Objective 4, Ans: c

49. Sensory neurons are an important part of the:
    a. limbic system.
    b. reticular formation.
    c. peripheral nervous system.
    d. central nervous system.

The nervous system, p. 65
Easy, Factual/Definitional, Objective 4, Ans: a

50. The vast majority of cells in the body's information-processing system are:
    a. interneurons.
    b. motor neurons.
    c. sensory neurons.
    d. neurotransmitters.

The nervous system, p. 65
Easy, Factual/Definitional, Objective 4, Ans: c

51. Information is carried from the central nervous system to the body's tissues by:
    a. interneurons.
    b. sensory neurons.
    c. motor neurons.
    d. the limbic system.

The nervous system, p. 65
Easy, Factual/Definitional, Objective 4, Ans: a

52. Motor neurons transmit signals to:
    a. glands.
    b. interneurons.
    c. sensory neurons.
    d. all the above.

The nervous system, p. 65
Medium, Conceptual/Application, Objective 4, Ans: b

53. Messages are transmitted from your spinal cord to muscles in your hands by the ________ nervous system.
    a. central
    b. peripheral
    c. parasympathetic
    d. sympathetic
    e. autonomic

The nervous system, p. 65
Difficult, Conceptual, Objective 4, Ans: c

54. The peripheral nervous system is to sensory neurons as the central nervous system is to:
    a. motor neurons.
    b. neurotransmitters.
    c. interneurons.
    d. the sympathetic nervous system.

The peripheral nervous system, p. 66
Medium, Factual/Definitional, Objective 4, Ans: a

55. The somatic nervous system is a component of the ________ nervous system.
    a. peripheral
    b. autonomic
    c. central
    d. sympathetic
    e. parasympathetic

The peripheral nervous system, p. 66
Easy, Factual/Definitional, Objective 4, Ans: d

56. The part of the peripheral nervous system that controls glandular activity and the muscles of internal organs is called the:
    a. somatic nervous system.
    b. reticular formation.
    c. limbic system.
    d. autonomic nervous system.

The peripheral nervous system, p. 66
Medium, Conceptual, Objective 4, Ans: d

57. Messages are transmitted from your spinal cord to your heart muscles by the:
    a. limbic system.
    b. somatic nervous system.
    c. central nervous system.
    d. autonomic nervous system.

The peripheral nervous system, p. 66
Difficult, Factual/Definitional, Objective 4, Ans: a

58. The parasympathetic nervous system ________ digestion and ________ heartbeat.
a. accelerates; decelerates
b. decelerates; accelerates
c. accelerates; accelerates
d. decelerates; decelerates

The peripheral nervous system, p. 66
Medium, Conceptual/Application, Objective 4, Ans: b

59. You come home one night to find a burglar in your house. Your heart starts racing and you begin to perspire. These physical reactions are triggered by the:
a. somatic nervous system.
b. sympathetic nervous system.
c. parasympathetic nervous system.
d. limbic system.

The peripheral nervous system, p. 66
Medium, Conceptual/Application, Objective 4, Ans: a

60. After discovering that the shadows outside his window were only the trees in the yard, Ralph's blood pressure decreased and his heartbeat slowed. These physical reactions were most directly regulated by his:
a. parasympathetic nervous system.
b. sympathetic nervous system.
c. somatic nervous system.
d. hippocampus.

The peripheral nervous system, p. 66
Medium, Conceptual, Objective 4, Ans: d

61. Heartbeat acceleration is to heartbeat deceleration as the ________ nervous system is to the ________ nervous system.
a. somatic; autonomic
b. autonomic; somatic
c. central; peripheral
d. sympathetic; parasympathetic
e. parasympathetic; sympathetic

The central nervous system, p. 67
Easy, Factual/Definitional, Objective 4, Ans: d

62. A simple, automatic, inborn response to a sensory stimulus is called a:
a. neural network.
b. resting potential.
c. neurotransmitter.
d. reflex.

The central nervous system, p. 67
Easy, Factual/Definitional, Objective 4, Ans: b

63. The knee-jerk reflex is controlled by interneurons in the:
a. limbic system.
b. spinal cord.
c. brainstem.
d. cerebellum.

The central nervous system, p. 67
Medium, Conceptual/Application, Objective 5, Ans: d

64. In a tragic diving accident, Andrew damaged his spinal cord and consequently suffered paralysis of his legs. Andrew's injury was located in his:
a. somatic nervous system.
b. limbic system.
c. sympathetic nervous system.
d. central nervous system.

The central nervous system, p. 67
Medium, Conceptual/Application, Objective 4, Ans: b

65. Aaron consistently exhibits a knee-jerk response without having any sensations of the taps on his knees. Aaron's experience is most indicative of a:
a. split brain.
b. severed spinal cord.
c. hemispherectomy.
d. reward deficiency syndrome.

The central nervous system, p. 68
Easy, Factual/Definitional, Objective 5, Ans: c

66. The strengthening of synaptic connections facilitates the formation of:
a. interneurons.
b. endorphins.
c. neural networks.
d. glial cells.
e. lesions.

The central nervous system, p. 68
Medium, Factual/Definitional, Objective 5, Ans: b

67. Neural networks refer to:
a. the branching extensions of a neuron.
b. functionally interconnected clusters of neurons in the central nervous system.
c. neural cables containing many axons.
d. junctions between sending and receiving neurons.
e. neurons that connect the central nervous system to the rest of the body.

The central nervous system, p. 68
Difficult, Conceptual/Application, Objective 5, Ans: c

68. A football quarterback can simultaneously make calculations of receiver distances, player movements, and gravitational forces. This best illustrates the activity of multiple:
    a. endocrine glands.
    b. endorphin agonists.
    c. neural networks.
    d. endorphin antagonists.
    e. reticular formations.

The tools of discovery, p. 70
Easy, Factual/Definitional, Objective 6, Ans: d

69. Surgical destruction of brain tissue is called a(n):
    a. split brain.
    b. EEG.
    c. synapse.
    d. lesion.
    e. MRI.

The tools of discovery, p. 70
Medium, Factual/Definitional, Objective 6, Ans: b

70. An amplified recording of the waves of electrical activity that sweep across the surface of the brain is called a(n):
    a. CT scan.
    b. EEG.
    c. PET scan.
    d. MRI.

The tools of discovery, p. 71
Difficult, Conceptual, Objective 6, Ans: a

71. EEG is to CT scan as:
    a. amplified recording of brain waves is to x-ray photography.
    b. x-ray photography is to amplified recording of brain waves.
    c. radioactive emission is to amplified recording of brain waves.
    d. amplified recording of brain waves is to radioactive emission.

The tools of discovery, p. 71
Difficult, Conceptual/Application, Objective 6, Ans: b

72. In order to identify which of Lucy's brain areas was most active when she talked, neuroscientists gave her a temporarily radioactive form of glucose and a(n):
    a. CT scan.
    b. PET scan.
    c. EEG.
    d. MRI.

The tools of discovery, p. 71
Medium, Factual/Definitional, Objective 6, Ans: a

73. To identify which specific brain areas are most active during a particular mental task, researchers would be most likely to make use of a(n):
    a. PET scan.
    b. hemispherectomy.
    c. CT scan.
    d. brain lesions.

The tools of discovery, p. 71
Medium, Factual/Definitional, Objective 6, Ans: b

74. The best way to detect enlarged fluid-filled brain regions in some patients who have schizophrenia is to use a(n):
    a. EEG.
    b. MRI.
    c. PET scan.
    d. lobotomy.

Brain structures, pp. 72-76
Difficult, Conceptual, Objective 7, Ans: d

75. The sequence of brain regions from oldest to newest is:
    a. limbic system; brainstem; cerebral cortex.
    b. brainstem; cerebral cortex; limbic system.
    c. limbic system; cerebral cortex; brainstem.
    d. brainstem; limbic system; cerebral cortex.
    e. cerebral cortex; brainstem; limbic system.

The brainstem, p. 72
Medium, Factual/Definitional, Objective 7, Ans: b

76. The part of the brainstem that controls heartbeat and breathing is called the:
    a. cerebellum.
    b. medulla.
    c. reticular formation.
    d. thalamus.

The brainstem, p. 72
Difficult, Conceptual/Application, Objective 7, Ans: a

77. If your ________ is destroyed, the left side of your brain could not control the movements of your right hand.
    a. brainstem
    b. amygdala
    c. hippocampus
    d. angular gyrus
    e. corpus callosum

The brainstem, p. 72
Easy, Factual/Definitional, Objective 7, Ans: a

78. The reticular formation is located in the:
    a. brainstem.
    b. limbic system.
    c. somatosensory cortex.
    d. motor cortex.
    e. cerebellum.

The brainstem, p. 72
Medium, Factual/Definitional, Objective 7, Ans: d

79. Severing a cat's reticular formation from higher brain regions causes the cat to:
    a. become violently aggressive.
    b. cower in fear.
    c. experience convulsive seizures.
    d. lapse into a coma.
    e. become sexually preoccupied.

The brainstem, p. 72
Medium, Conceptual/Application, Objective 7, Ans: a

80. Which region of the brainstem takes you to a state of arousal when someone nearby mentions your name?
    a. reticular formation
    b. cerebellum
    c. hypothalamus
    d. amygdala
    e. medulla

The thalamus, p. 73
Easy, Factual/Definitional, Objective 7, Ans: d

81. Which brain structure receives information from all the senses except smell?
    a. hippocampus
    b. amygdala
    c. angular gyrus
    d. thalamus

The thalamus, p. 73
Medium, Conceptual, Objective 7, Ans: a

82. Which brain structure relays information from the eyes to the visual cortex?
    a. thalamus
    b. amygdala
    c. medulla
    d. hippocampus
    e. cerebellum

The thalamus, p. 73
Difficult, Factual/Definitional, Objective 7, Ans: a

83. The brain's electrical oscillations, which slow during sleep, are coordinated by the:
    a. thalamus.
    b. cerebellum.
    c. sensory cortex.
    d. pituitary gland.

The cerebellum, pp. 72-73
Medium, Factual/Definitional, Objective 7, Ans: c

84. The "little brain" attached to the rear of the brainstem is called the:
    a. limbic system.
    b. corpus callosum.
    c. cerebellum.
    d. reticular formation.

The cerebellum, p. 73
Difficult, Conceptual/Application, Objective 7, Ans: e

85. After Kato's serious motorcycle accident, doctors detected damage to his cerebellum. Kato is most likely to have difficulty:
    a. experiencing intense emotions.
    b. reading a book.
    c. understanding what others are saying.
    d. tasting the flavors of foods.
    e. playing his guitar.

The limbic system, p. 74
Easy, Factual/Definitional, Objective 7, Ans: b

86. A doughnut-shaped system of neural structures at the border of the brainstem and cerebral hemispheres is known as the:
    a. angular gyrus.
    b. limbic system.
    c. reticular formation.
    d. peripheral nervous system.

The limbic system, p. 74
Medium, Factual/Definitional, Objective 7, Ans: c

87. Which of the following is the component of the limbic system that plays an essential role in the formation of new memories?
    a. hypothalamus
    b. thalamus
    c. hippocampus
    d. medulla

The limbic system, pp. 72, 74
Medium, Conceptual, Objective 7, Ans: a

88. The brainstem is to arousal as the limbic system is to:
    a. emotion.
    b. muscular coordination.
    c. respiration.
    d. language comprehension.

The amygdala, p. 74
Medium, Conceptual, Objective 7, Ans: d

89. To demonstrate that brain stimulation can make a rat violently aggressive, a neuroscientist should electrically stimulate the rat's:
a. reticular formation.
b. cerebellum.
c. medulla.
d. amygdala.

The hypothalamus, p. 75
Medium, Conceptual/Application, Objective 7, Ans: c

90. A brain tumor caused extensive damage to Mr. Thorndike's hypothalamus. It is most likely that he may suffer a loss of:
a. visual perception.
b. muscular coordination.
c. sexual motivation.
d. language comprehension.

The hypothalamus, pp. 75, 95
Medium, Factual/Definitional, Objective 7, Ans: d

91. The brain structure that provides a major link between the nervous system and the hormone system is the:
a. cerebellum.
b. amygdala.
c. reticular formation.
d. hypothalamus.
e. medulla.

The hypothalamus, p. 75
Difficult, Factual/Definitional, Objective 7, Ans: b

92. Olds and Milner located "pleasure centers" in the brain structure known as the:
a. sensory cortex.
b. hypothalamus.
c. cerebellum.
d. medulla.
e. amygdala.

The hypothalamus, p. 76
Medium, Factual/Definitional, Objective 7, Ans: d

93. Addictive drug cravings are likely to be associated with reward centers in the:
a. thalamus.
b. cerebellum.
c. reticular formation.
d. limbic system.
e. angular gyrus.

The cerebral cortex, p. 76
Difficult, Conceptual/Application, Objective 8, Ans: e

94. Your conscious awareness of your own name and self-identity depends primarily on the normal functioning of your:
    a. cerebellum.
    b. amygdala.
    c. hypothalamus.
    d. sympathetic nervous system.
    e. cerebral cortex.

The cerebral cortex, p. 77
Medium, Factual/Definitional, Objective 8, Ans: c

95. One function of glial cells is to:
    a. control heartbeat and breathing.
    b. mimic the effects of neurotransmitters.
    c. provide nutrients to interneurons.
    d. stimulate the production of hormones.

The cerebral cortex, p. 77
Difficult, Conceptual, Objective 8, Ans: a

96. Which lobes of the brain receive the input that enables you to feel someone scratching your back?
    a. parietal
    b. temporal
    c. occipital
    d. frontal

The cerebral cortex, p. 77
Medium, Conceptual, Objective 8, Ans: c

97. The surgical removal of a large tumor from Dane's occipital lobe resulted in extensive loss of brain tissue. Dane is most likely to suffer some loss of:
    a. muscular coordination.
    b. language comprehension.
    c. visual perception.
    d. speaking ability.
    e. pain sensations.

The cerebral cortex, p. 77
Medium, Factual/Definitional, Objective 8, Ans: b

98. Auditory stimulation is first processed in the ________ lobes.
    a. occipital
    b. temporal
    c. frontal
    d. parietal

The cerebral cortex, p. 77
Difficult, Conceptual, Objective 8, Ans: d

99. The occipital lobes are to ________ as the temporal lobes are to ________.
    a. hearing; sensing movement
    b. seeing; sensing touch
    c. sensing pleasure; sensing pain
    d. seeing; hearing
    e. speaking; hearing

The cerebral cortex, p. 77
Difficult, Conceptual, Objective 8, Ans: b

100. The sense of hearing is to the ________ lobes as the sense of touch is to the ________ lobes.
    a. frontal; occipital
    b. temporal; parietal
    c. parietal; temporal
    d. occipital; frontal

The cerebral cortex, p. 78
Medium, Factual/Definitional, Objective 8, Ans: c

101. The motor cortex is located in the ________ lobes.
    a. occipital
    b. temporal
    c. frontal
    d. parietal

The cerebral cortex, p. 78
Difficult, Conceptual/Application, Objective 8, Ans: c

102. A laboratory cat could be made to twitch its whiskers by direct stimulation of the ________ lobes of its cerebral cortex.
    a. temporal
    b. occipital
    c. frontal
    d. parietal

The cerebral cortex, p. 78
Medium, Factual/Definitional, Objective 8, Ans: b

103. Which of the following body parts is associated with the greatest amount of brain tissue in the motor cortex?
    a. arms
    b. face
    c. trunk
    d. knees

The cerebral cortex, p. 79
Easy, Factual/Definitional, Objective 8, Ans: b

104. An area at the front of the parietal lobes that receives information from the movement of body parts is called the:
   a. limbic system.
   b. sensory cortex.
   c. angular gyrus.
   d. cerebellum.
   e. reticular formation.

The cerebral cortex, p. 79
Easy, Factual/Definitional, Objective 8, Ans: d

105. The sensory cortex is most critical for our sense of:
   a. taste.
   b. sight.
   c. hearing.
   d. touch.
   e. smell.

The cerebral cortex, p. 79
Medium, Conceptual, Objective 8, Ans: c

106. Which part of your brain receives information as to whether you are moving your legs?
   a. limbic system
   b. motor cortex
   c. sensory cortex
   d. Broca's area

The cerebral cortex, p. 80
Medium, Factual/Definitional, Objective 9, Ans: c

107. The experience of auditory hallucinations by people with schizophrenia is most closely linked with the activation of areas in their:
   a. motor cortex.
   b. angular gyrus.
   c. temporal lobes.
   d. hypothalamus.

The cerebral cortex, p. 80
Easy, Factual/Definitional, Objective 9, Ans: e

108. The association areas are located in the:
   a. spinal cord.
   b. brainstem.
   c. thalamus.
   d. limbic system.
   e. cerebral cortex.

The cerebral cortex, pp. 80-81
Easy, Factual/Definitional, Objective 9, Ans: e

109. The most extensive regions of the brain, which enable learning and memory, are called the:
   a. reticular formation.
   b. projection areas.
   c. sensory areas.
   d. temporal lobes.
   e. association areas.

The cerebral cortex, p. 81
Difficult, Conceptual/Application, Objective 9, Ans: d

110. After he suffered a stroke, Mr. Santore's physical coordination skills and responsiveness to sensory stimulation quickly returned to normal. Unfortunately, however, he began to experience unusual difficulty in scheduling his daily activities and solving simple problems. It is most likely that Mr. Santore suffered damage to his:
   a. cerebellum.
   b. thalamus.
   c. hypothalamus.
   d. association areas.
   e. autonomic nervous system.

The cerebral cortex, p. 81
Difficult, Conceptual, Objective 9, Ans: d

111. The process of anticipating that you will be punished for misbehaving takes place within the:
   a. limbic system.
   b. sensory cortex.
   c. reticular formation.
   d. association areas.
   e. sympathetic nervous system.

The cerebral cortex, p. 81
Medium, Factual/Definitional, Objective 9, Ans: d

112. The ability to recognize familiar faces is disturbed by damage to the right ________ lobe.
   a. frontal
   b. parietal
   c. occipital
   d. temporal

The cerebral cortex, p. 82
Easy, Factual/Definitional, Objective 9, Ans: d

113. An impaired use of language is known as:
   a. tomography.
   b. plasticity.
   c. phrenology.
   d. aphasia.

The cerebral cortex, p. 82
Easy, Factual/Definitional, Objective 9, Ans: b

114. The part of the cerebral cortex that directs the muscle movements involved in speech is known as:
a. Wernicke's area.
b. Broca's area.
c. the amygdala.
d. the angular gyrus.
e. the reticular formation.

The cerebral cortex, p. 82
Medium, Conceptual/Application, Objective 9, Ans: b

115. After Miguel's recent automobile accident, doctors detected damage to his cerebral cortex in Broca's area. It is likely that Miguel will have difficulty:
a. remembering past events.
b. speaking fluently.
c. reading.
d. understanding other people when they speak.

The cerebral cortex, p. 82
Medium, Factual/Definitional, Objective 9, Ans: c

116. Wernicke's area is typically located in the left ________ lobe.
a. parietal
b. occipital
c. temporal
d. frontal

The cerebral cortex, p. 82
Difficult, Conceptual/Application, Objective 9, Ans: c

117. After Paul's serious snow-skiing accident, doctors detected damage to his cerebral cortex in Wernicke's area. Because of the damage, Paul is most likely to experience difficulty in:
a. remembering past events.
b. pronouncing words correctly.
c. understanding what others are saying.
d. recognizing familiar faces.

The cerebral cortex, p. 82
Difficult, Conceptual, Objective 9, Ans: a

118. After a severe automobile accident, Louis lost his ability to read, even though he could see well, speak fluently, and understand whatever others said. It is likely that his cortex was damaged in:
a. the angular gyrus.
b. Wernicke's area.
c. the frontal lobe.
d. Broca's area.

Brain reorganization, p. 84
Easy, Factual/Definitional, Objective 10, Ans: e

119. The capacity of one brain area to take over the functions of another damaged brain area is known as brain:
a. tomography.
b. phrenology.
c. hemispherectomy.
d. aphasia.
e. plasticity.

Brain reorganization, p. 84
Medium, Factual/Definitional, Objective 10, Ans: a

120. PET scans have revealed that the visual cortex is activated when blind people read Braille. This best illustrates:
a. plasticity.
b. aphasia.
c. hemispherectomy.
d. phrenology.

Brain reorganization, p. 84
Difficult, Factual/Definitional, Objective 10, Ans: b

121. A person whose hand had been amputated actually felt sensations on his nonexistent fingers when his face was stroked. This best illustrates the consequences of:
a. tomography.
b. brain plasticity.
c. the alien hand syndrome.
d. hemispherectomy.
e. aphasia.

Brain reorganization, p. 85
Medium, Factual/Definitional, Objective 10, Ans: c

122. Neural regulation of a child's language functioning is transferred to the right hemisphere if speech areas in the left hemisphere are damaged. This best illustrates:
a. aphasia.
b. hemispherectomy.
c. plasticity.
d. tomography.
e. phrenology.

Brain reorganization, p. 85
Medium, Factual/Definitional, Objective 10, Ans: a

123. The benefits of brain plasticity are most clearly demonstrated in:
a. children who have had a cerebral hemisphere surgically removed.
b. individuals with Alzheimer's disease.
c. adults with aphasia.
d. elderly stroke patients.
e. people free of any disease or brain damage.

Our divided brains, p. 85
Medium, Factual/Definitional, Objective 11, Ans: a

124. Damage to the left cerebral hemisphere is most likely to reduce a person's ability to:
a. solve arithmetic problems.
b. copy drawings.
c. recognize faces.
d. recognize familiar melodies.

Splitting the brain, p. 85
Easy, Factual/Definitional, Objective 11, Ans: b

125. The corpus callosum is a wide band of neural fibers that:
a. enables the left hemisphere to control the right side of the body.
b. transmits information between the cerebral hemispheres.
c. controls the glands and muscles of the internal organs.
d. directs the muscle movements involved in speech.

Splitting the brain, p. 85
Medium, Factual/Definitional, Objective 11, Ans: b

126. Neurosurgeons have severed the corpus callosum in human patients in order to reduce:
a. aphasia.
b. epileptic seizures.
c. depression.
d. neural plasticity.
e. reward deficiency syndrome.

Splitting the brain, pp. 86-87
Medium, Conceptual, Objective 11, Ans: a

127. If a picture of a comb is briefly flashed in the left visual field of a split-brain patient, she should be able to:
a. use her left hand to draw a picture of the comb.
b. use her right hand to draw a picture of the comb.
c. orally report what she saw.
d. use her right hand to write the word "comb."

Splitting brain, p. 87
Easy, Factual/Definitional, Objective 11, Ans: b

128. Most cases of alien hand syndrome involve some damage to the:
a. reticular formation.
b. corpus callosum.
c. angular gyrus.
d. hippocampus.
e. cerebellum.

Splitting the brain, p. 88
Difficult, Conceptual/Application, Objective 11, Ans: a

129. In a recent car accident, Tamiko sustained damage to his right cerebral hemisphere. This injury is most likely to reduce Tamiko's ability to:
a. facially express emotions.
b. solve arithmetic problems.
c. understand simple verbal requests.
d. process information in an orderly sequence.

Studying hemispheric differences in the intact brain, p. 88
Medium, Factual/Definitional, Objective 11, Ans: d

130. People typically recognize ________ more rapidly and accurately when they are flashed to the left hemisphere; they typically recognize ________ more rapidly and accurately when they are flashed to the right hemisphere.
   a. letters; numbers
   b. words; numbers
   c. numbers; letters
   d. words; pictures

Studying hemispheric differences in the intact brain, p. 88
Medium, Factual/Definitional, Objective 11, Ans: b

131. Hearing-impaired people who use sign language typically:
   a. demonstrate greater mathematical competence than people without hearing impairments.
   b. process language in their left cerebral hemisphere.
   c. recognize facial expressions of emotion with their left rather than their right cerebral hemisphere.
   d. have a slightly smaller corpus callosum than people without hearing impairments.

Studying hemispheric differences in the intact brain, p. 89
Medium, Factual/Definitional, Objective 11, Ans: c

132. Babies favor the _______ side of their mouth when beginning a smile and the ______ side when babbling.
   a. left; left
   b. right; right
   c. left; right
   d. right; left

Brain organization and handedness, p. 89
Medium, Factual/Definitional, Objective 12, Ans: a

133. Research on left-handedness suggests that:
   a. genes or prenatal factors play a role in handedness.
   b. a greater proportion of women than men are left-handed.
   c. left-handers generally demonstrate less artistic competence than right-handers.
   d. most left-handers process language primarily in their right hemisphere.

Brain organization and handedness, pp. 89-90
Medium, Factual/Definitional, Objective 12, Ans: d

134. Left-handedness is ________ than normal among people with reading disabilities and ________ than normal among artists.
   a. lower; higher
   b. lower; lower
   c. higher; lower
   d. higher; higher

Brain organization and handedness, p. 89
Medium, Factual/Definitional, Objective 12, Ans: c

135. Compared with right-handers, left-handers are ________ likely to experience headaches and ________ likely to suffer from allergies.
a. more; less
b. less; more
c. more; more
d. less; less

Brain organization and handedness, p. 90
Medium, Factual/Definitional, Objective 12, Ans: a

136. How have Coren and Halpern explained the progressive decline in the percentage of left-handers among increasingly older population samples?
a. Left-handers die at younger ages than right-handers.
b. Left-handers gradually make increasing use of their right hands as they progress through adulthood.
c. Parents today are less likely to discourage left-handedness in children than were the parents of previous generations.
d. There has been a dramatic increase in the percentage of left-handed infants born in each successive decade of this century.

Thinking critically about left brain/right brain (Box), p. 92
Medium, Factual/Definitional, Objective 12, Ans: e

137. Reading a story involves brain activity in the ________ cerebral hemisphere(s). Producing a creative artistic drawing involves brain activity in the ________ cerebral hemisphere(s).
a. left; right
b. right; left
c. left; right and left
d. right and left; right
e. right and left; right and left

The endocrine system, p. 94
Easy, Factual/Definitional, Objective 13, Ans: d

138. The endocrine system consists of:
a. glial cells.
b. neural networks.
c. interneurons.
d. glands.

The endocrine system, p. 94
Easy, Factual/Definitional, Objective 13, Ans: c

139. Hormones are the chemical messengers of the:
a. cerebral cortex.
b. autonomic nervous system.
c. endocrine system.
d. limbic system.
e. reticular formation.

The endocrine system, p. 94
Medium, Factual/Definitional, Objective 13, Ans: b

140. Endocrine glands secrete hormones directly into:
    a. synaptic gaps.
    b. the bloodstream.
    c. the limbic system.
    d. sensory neurons.
    e. interneurons.

The endocrine system, p. 95
Medium, Factual/Definitional, Objective 13, Ans: b

141. The ovaries in females and the testes in males are part of the:
    a. limbic system.
    b. endocrine system.
    c. sympathetic nervous system.
    d. reticular formation.
    e. central nervous system.

The endocrine system, p. 95
Difficult, Conceptual/Application, Objective 13, Ans: d

142. If a professor accused you of cheating on a test, your adrenal glands would probably release ________ into your bloodstream.
    a. endorphins
    b. acetylcholine
    c. seratonin
    d. epinephrine
    e. insulin

The endocrine system, p. 95
Easy, Factual/Definitional, Objective 13, Ans: d

143. The master gland of the endocrine system is the:
    a. thyroid gland.
    b. hypothalamus.
    c. adrenal gland.
    d. pituitary gland.
    e. pancreas.

The endocrine system, pp. 62, 95
Difficult, Conceptual, Objective 13, Ans: c

144. Acetylcholine is to epinephrine as ________ is to ________.
    a. sympathetic nervous system; parasympathetic nervous system
    b. motor neuron; sensory neuron
    c. neurotransmitter; hormone
    d. agonist; antagonist
    e. parasympathetic nervous system; sympathetic nervous system

The endocrine system, p. 95
Difficult, Conceptual/Application, Objective 13, Ans: d

145. At the age of 22, Mrs. LaBlanc was less than 4 feet tall. Her short stature was probably influenced by the lack of a growth hormone produced by the:
a. pancreas.
b. thyroid.
c. adrenal gland.
d. pituitary gland.
e. hypothalamus.

The mind and brain as a holistic system, p. 96
Medium, Factual/Definitional, Objective 13, Ans: c

146. According to Roger Sperry, a recognition that the mind cannot be fully explained by the activity of nerve cells is important for appreciating our human capacity for:
a. information processing.
b. neural plasticity.
c. moral responsibility.
d. computed tomography.

Essay Questions

1. The ancient Greek physician Hippocrates believed that four basic body fluids (blood, black bile, yellow bile, and phlegm) influenced human behavior, emotions, and personality. Use your understanding of the body's rapid and slower chemical communication systems to support or refute Hippocrates's theory.

2. Over the last few weeks, Mr. Klein has been bothered by nausea, frequent fainting spells, and severe headaches. Describe two ways a physician might seek to determine whether Mr. Klein's symptoms result from a brain disorder or injury.

3. After a mild stroke, Mr. McGeorge showed some signs of aphasia. What pattern of symptoms would lead you to believe the damage occurred primarily in (a) Broca's area, (b) Wernicke's area, (c) the angular gyrus?

4. After Jordan brilliantly performed a challenging and emotionally vibrant violin concerto, the orchestra conductor proudly proclaimed that Jordan was obviously a right-brained personality.

   What type of explanation is the conductor giving for Jordan's artistic skills? What's wrong with his statement? Provide an alternative reason for Jordan's talent.

Web Quiz 1

Ans: d

1. Who would have been most likely to claim that a slight protrusion in a certain region of someone's skull indicated that the individual had an optimistic personality?
   a. Aristotle
   b. Carl Wernicke
   c. John Locke
   d. Franz Gall

Ans: b

2. Drugs that block the reuptake of serotonin will thereby increase the concentration of serotonin molecules in the:
   a. axon terminals.
   b. synaptic gaps.
   c. glial cells.
   d. endocrine glands.

Ans: d

3. Natural, opiatelike neurotransmitters linked to pain control are called:
   a. ACh agonists.
   b. dendrites.
   c. morphene antagonists.
   d. endorphins.
   e. glial cells.

Ans: c

4. Botox injections smooth facial wrinkles because botulin is a(n):
   a. ACh antagonist.
   b. dopamine antagonist.
   c. ACh agonist.
   d. dopamine agonist.

Ans: d

5. In stressful situations, the sympathetic nervous system ________ the arteries of the circulatory system and ________ the pupils of the eyes.
   a. contracts; dilates
   b. dilates; contracts
   c. contracts; contracts
   d. dilates; dilates

Ans: c

6. While listening to operatic solos, musicians process the lyrics and the tunes in separate brain areas. This most clearly illustrates the functioning of different:
   a. neurotransmitters.
   b. reticular formations.
   c. neural networks.
   d. limbic systems.

Ans: b

7. Which of the following would be most useful for detecting the exact location of a brain lesion?
   a. an EEG
   b. a CT scan
   c. a PET scan
   d. a hemispherectomy

Ans: c

8. After suffering an accidental brain injury, Kira has difficulty walking in a smooth and coordinated manner. It is most probable that she has suffered damage to her:
   a. amygdala.
   b. angular gyrus.
   c. cerebellum.
   d. corpus callosum.

Ans: d

9. The limbic system structure that regulates hunger is called the:
   a. thalamus.
   b. amygdala.
   c. hippocampus.
   d. hypothalamus.

Ans: b

10. Which portion of the cerebral cortex is most directly involved in making plans and formulating moral judgments?
    a. occipital lobes
    b. frontal lobes
    c. temporal lobes
    d. parietal lobes

Ans: e

11. The regions of the parietal lobes that are involved in mathematical and spatial reasoning are known as:
    a. the angular gyrus.
    b. the corpus callosum.
    c. Wernicke's areas.
    d. the reticular formation.
    e. association areas.

Ans: c

12. Due to an automobile accident, Jenny suffered damage to her cerebral cortex in Broca's area. Jenny is most likely to experience:
    a. auditory hallucinations.
    b. memory loss.
    c. aphasia.
    d. paralysis of her left limbs.
    e. reward deficiency syndrome.

Ans: c

13. The successful functioning of children who have experienced a hemispherectomy best illustrates the value of:
    a. aphasia.
    b. phrenology.
    c. plasticity.
    d. reuptake.

Ans: d

14. Jud suffered a massive stroke which resulted in damage to his corpus callosum. Sometimes, his right hand has to prevent his left hand from strangling himself. Jud's experience best illustrates:
    a. hemispherectomy.
    b. the reward deficiency syndrome.
    c. the left-hander syndrome.
    d. the alien hand syndrome.

Ans: c

15. Which of the following chemical messengers is both a neurotransmitter and a hormone?
    a. serotonin
    b. acetylcholine
    c. norepinephrine
    d. dopamine
    e. insulin

Web Quiz 2

Ans: a

1. An axon transmits messages ________ the cell body and a dendrite transmits messages ________ the cell body.
   a. away from; toward
   b. away from; away from
   c. toward; away from
   d. toward; toward

Ans: a

2. Depressed mood states are linked to ________ levels of serotonin and ________ levels of norepinephrene.
   a. low; low
   b. high; high
   c. low; high
   d. high; low

Ans: b

3. The venom of the black widow spider is to ________ as botulin is to ________.
   a. paralysis; convulsions
   b. convulsions; paralysis
   c. depression; elation
   d. elation; depression

Ans: d

4. A drug that blocks the reuptake of a particular neurotransmitter is called a(n):
   a. opiate.
   b. antagonist.
   c. glutamate.
   d. agonist.

Ans: d

5. The peripheral nervous system consists of:
   a. association areas.
   b. the spinal cord.
   c. the reticular formation.
   d. sensory and motor neurons.

Ans: c

6. The autonomic nervous system most directly controls:
   a. speech production.
   b. thinking and memory.
   c. stomach contractions.
   d. movement of the arms and legs.

Ans: c

7. Mark was paralyzed below the waist following an accident and is now genitally unresponsive to erotic sexual images. Mark has most clearly suffered damage to his:
   a. limbic system.
   b. sensory cortex.
   c. interneurons.
   d. endocrine system.
   e. motor neurons.

Ans: c

8. In order to monitor the electrical activity in the brain that is triggered by hearing one's own name, researchers would make use of a(n):
   a. MRI.
   b. PET scan.
   c. EEG.
   d. CT scan.

Ans: b

9. Research has suggested that a reward deficiency syndrome may contribute to:
   a. insomnia.
   b. alcoholism.
   c. schizophrenia.
   d. Parkinson's disease.

Ans: b

10. Which lobe of the cerebral cortex is most directly involved in speaking?
   a. occipital
   b. frontal
   c. temporal
   d. parietal

Ans: d

11. Following massive damage to his frontal lobes, Phineas Gage was most strikingly debilitated by:
   a. aphasia.
   b. memory loss.
   c. auditory hallucinations.
   d. irritability.
   e. a reward deficiency syndrome.

Ans: d

12. In which of the following parts of the brain would a lesion most likely result in aphasia?
   a. corpus callosum
   b. amygdala
   c. hypothalamus
   d. Wernicke's area
   e. cerebellum

Ans: d

13. Brain scans indicate that professional violinists have a larger-than-normal region of the motor cortex devoted to control of left finger movements. This best illustrates:
    a. hemispherectomy.
    b. tomography.
    c. aphasia.
    d. plasticity.
    e. the alien hand syndrome.

Ans: d

14. The _______ hemisphere typically excels in making subtle linguistic inferences and the _______ hemisphere typically excels in making quick, literal interpretations of language.
    a. left; left
    b. right; right
    c. left; right
    d. right; left

Ans: a

15. The release of epinephrine and norepinephrene ________ blood pressure and _______ blood sugar levels.
    a. increases; increases
    b. decreases; decreases
    c. increases; decreases
    d. decreases; increases

Study Guide Questions

Ans: b, p. 57

1. Which of the following was a major problem with phrenology?
   a. It was "ahead of its time" and no one believed it could be true.
   b. The brain is not neatly organized into structures that correspond to our categories of behavior.
   c. The brains of humans and animals are much less similar than the theory implied.
   d. All of the above were problems with phrenology.

Ans: b, p. 58

2. The axons of certain neurons are covered by a layer of fatty tissue that helps speed neural transmission. This tissue is:
   a. the glia.
   b. the myelin sheath.
   c. acetylcholine.
   d. an endorphin.

Ans: d, p. 58

3. A biological psychologist would be *more* likely to study:
   a. how you learn to express emotions.
   b. how to help people overcome emotional disorders.
   c. life-span changes in the expression of emotion.
   d. the chemical changes that accompany emotions.

Ans: d, p. 58

4. Dr. Hernandez is studying neurotransmitter abnormalities in depressed patients. She would most likely describe herself as a:
   a. psychiatrist.
   b. clinical psychologist.
   c. psychoanalyst.
   d. biological psychologist.

Ans: a, p. 58

5. The myelin sheath that is on some neurons:
   a. increases the speed of neural transmission.
   b. slows neural transmission.
   c. regulates the release of neurotransmitters.
   d. does a. and c.
   e. does b. and c.

Ans: c, p. 59

6. During an action potential, the electrical state of the axon becomes:
   a. polarized, as positively charged atoms are admitted.
   b. polarized, as negatively charged atoms are admitted.
   c. depolarized, as positively charged atoms are admitted.
   d. depolarized, as negatively charged atoms are admitted.

Ans: d, p. 59

7. In a resting state, the axon is:
   a. depolarized, with mostly negatively charged ions outside and positively charged ions inside.
   b. depolarized, with mostly positively charged ions outside and negatively charged ions inside.
   c. polarized, with mostly negatively charged ions outside and positively charged ions inside.
   d. polarized, with mostly positively charged ions outside and negatively charged ions inside.

Ans: e, pp. 58-60

8. Which is the correct sequence in the transmission of a neural impulse?
   a. axon → dendrite → cell body → synapse
   b. dendrite → axon → cell body → synapse
   c. synapse → axon → dendrite → cell body
   d. axon → synapse → cell body → dendrite
   e. dendrite → cell body → axon → synapse

Ans: c, pp. 59-60

9. A neuron will generate action potentials more often when it:
   a. remains below its threshold.
   b. receives an excitatory input.
   c. receives more excitatory than inhibitory inputs.
   d. is stimulated by a neurotransmitter.
   e. is stimulated by a hormone.

Ans: c, p. 60

10. A strong stimulus can increase the:
    a. speed of the impulse the neuron fires.
    b. intensity of the impulse the neuron fires.
    c. number of times the neuron fires.
    d. threshold that must be reached before the neuron fires.

Ans: b, pp. 62, 75

11. Since Malcolm has been taking a drug prescribed by his doctor, he no longer enjoys the little pleasures of life, such as eating and drinking. His doctor explains that this is because the drug:
    a. triggers release of dopamine.
    b. inhibits release of dopamine.
    c. triggers release of ACh.
    d. inhibits release of ACh.

Ans: b, p. 62

12. The neurotransmitter acetylcholine (ACh) is most likely to be found:
    a. at the junction between sensory neurons and muscle fibers.
    b. at the junction between motor neurons and muscle fibers.
    c. at junctions between interneurons.
    d. in all of the above locations.

Ans: b, p. 63

13. Melissa has just completed running a marathon. She is so elated that she feels little fatigue or discomfort. Her lack of pain is probably the result of the release of:
 a. ACh.
 b. endorphins.
 c. dopamine.
 d. norepinephrine.
 e. acetylcholine.

Ans: a, p. 63

14. The pain of heroin withdrawal may be attributable to the fact that:
 a. under the influence of heroin the brain ceases production of endorphins.
 b. under the influence of heroin the brain ceases production of all neurotransmitters.
 c. during withdrawal the brain's production of all neurotransmitters is greatly increased.
 d. heroin destroys endorphin receptors in the brain.

Ans: b, p. 63

15. The effect of a drug that is an agonist is to:
 a. cause the brain to stop producing certain neurotransmitters.
 b. mimic a particular neurotransmitter.
 c. block a particular neurotransmitter.
 d. disrupt a neuron's all-or-none firing pattern.

Ans: a, p. 64

16. Parkinson's disease involves:
 a. the death of nerve cells that produce a vital neurotransmitter.
 b. impaired function in the right hemisphere only.
 c. impaired function in the left hemisphere only.
 d. excess production of the neurotransmitters dopamine and acetylcholine.

Ans: b, p. 66

17. Heartbeat, digestion, and other self-regulating bodily functions are governed by the:
 a. voluntary nervous system.
 b. autonomic nervous system.
 c. sympathetic division of the autonomic nervous system.
 d. somatic nervous system.
 e. central nervous system.

Ans: b, p. 66

18. Voluntary movements, such as writing with a pencil, are directed by the:
 a. sympathetic nervous system.
 b. somatic nervous system.
 c. parasympathetic nervous system.
 d. autonomic nervous system.

Ans: b, p. 66

19. Following Jayshree's near-fatal car accident, her physician noticed that the pupillary reflex of her eyes was abnormal. This *may* indicate that Jayshree's ________ was damaged in the accident.
    a. occipital cortex
    b. autonomic nervous system
    c. left temporal lobe
    d. cerebellum
    e. brainstem

Ans: b, p. 66

20. Your brother has been taking prescription medicine and experiencing a number of unpleasant side effects, including unusually rapid heartbeat and excessive perspiration. It is likely that the medicine is exaggerating activity in the:
    a. reticular formation.
    b. sympathetic nervous system.
    c. parasympathetic nervous system.
    d. amygdala.

Ans: a, p. 66

21. When Sandy scalded her toe in a tub of hot water, the pain message was carried to her spinal cord by the ________ nervous system.
    a. somatic
    b. sympathetic
    c. parasympathetic
    d. central

Ans: c, p. 67

22. Which is the correct sequence in the transmission of a simple reflex?
    a. sensory neuron → interneuron → sensory neuron
    b. interneuron → motor neuron → sensory neuron
    c. sensory neuron → interneuron → motor neuron
    d. interneuron → sensory neuron → motor neuron

Ans: c, p. 67

23. Which of the following are/is governed by the simplest neural pathways?
    a. emotions
    b. physiological drives, such as hunger
    c. reflexes
    d. movements, such as walking
    e. balance

Ans: a, p. 67

24. You are able to pull your hand quickly away from hot water before pain is felt because:
    a. movement of the hand is a reflex that involves intervention of the spinal cord only.
    b. movement of the hand does not require intervention by the central nervous system.
    c. the brain reacts quickly to prevent severe injury.
    d. the autonomic division of the peripheral nervous system intervenes to speed contraction of the muscles of the hand.

Ans: b, p. 68

25. In the brain, learning occurs as experience strengthens certain connections in cell work groups called:
a. action potentials.
b. neural networks.
c. endocrine systems.
d. dendrites.
e. synaptic gaps.

Ans: a, p. 71

26. The brain research technique that involves monitoring the brain's usage of glucose is called (in abbreviated form) the:
a. PET scan.
b. CT scan.
c. EEG.
d. MRI.

Ans: d, p. 71

27. The technique that uses magnetic fields and radio waves to produce computer images of structures within the brain is called:
a. the EEG.
b. a CT scan.
c. a PET scan.
d. MRI.

Ans: a, p. 71

28. Which of the following is *not* a correct description of a brain research technique?
a. using a PET scan to examine the brain's structure
b. using the EEG to record the brain's electrical activity
c. using MRI to examine the brain's structure
d. using a CT scan to examine the brain's structure

Ans: c, p. 72

29. In primitive vertebrate animals, the brain primarily regulates ________; in lower mammals, the brain enables ________.
a. emotion; memory
b. memory; emotion
c. survival functions; emotion
d. reproduction; emotion
e. reproduction; memory

Ans: c, p. 72

30. Following a head injury, a person has ongoing difficulties staying awake. Most likely, the damage occurred to the:
a. thalamus.
b. corpus callosum.
c. reticular formation.
d. cerebellum.

Ans: a, p. 72

31. Moruzzi and Magoun caused a cat to lapse into a coma by severing neural connections between the cortex and the:
    a. reticular formation.
    b. hypothalamus.
    c. thalamus.
    d. cerebellum.
    e. medulla.

Ans: c, p. 72

32. The part of the human brain that is most like that of a fish is the:
    a. cortex.
    b. limbic system.
    c. brainstem.
    d. right hemisphere.
    e. corpus callosum.

Ans: d, p. 73

33. Jessica experienced difficulty keeping her balance after receiving a blow to the back of her head. It is likely that she injured her:
    a. medulla.
    b. thalamus.
    c. hypothalamus.
    d. cerebellum.
    e. cerebrum.

Ans: d, p. 73

34. Dr. Frankenstein made a mistake during neurosurgery on his monster. After the operation, the monster "saw" with his ears and "heard" with his eyes. It is likely that Dr. Frankenstein "rewired" neural connections in the monster's:
    a. hypothalamus.
    b. cerebellum.
    c. amygdala.
    d. thalamus.
    e. hippocampus.

Ans: a, p. 74

35. Though there is no single "control center" for emotions, their regulation is primarily attributed to the brain region known as the:
    a. limbic system.
    b. reticular formation.
    c. brainstem.
    d. cerebral cortex.

Ans: b, p. 74

36. A scientist from another planet wishes to study the simplest brain mechanisms underlying emotion and memory. You recommend that the scientist study the:
    a. brainstem of a frog.
    b. limbic system of a dog.
    c. cortex of a monkey.
    d. cortex of a human.
    e. brainstem of a dog.

Ans: c, p. 75

37. If Dr. Rogers wishes to conduct an experiment on the effects of stimulating the reward centers of a rat's brain, he should insert an electrode into the:
    a. thalamus.
    b. sensory cortex.
    c. hypothalamus.
    d. corpus callosum.

Ans: d, p. 77

38. Beginning at the front of the brain and working backward then down and around, which of the following is the correct order of the cortical regions?
    a. occipital lobe; temporal lobe; parietal lobe; frontal lobe
    b. temporal lobe; frontal lobe; parietal lobe; occipital lobe
    c. frontal lobe; occipital lobe; temporal lobe; parietal lobe
    d. frontal lobe; parietal lobe; occipital lobe; temporal lobe
    e. occipital lobe; parietal lobe; temporal lobe; frontal lobe

Ans: a, p. 77

39. The visual cortex is located in the:
    a. occipital lobe.
    b. temporal lobe.
    c. frontal lobe.
    d. parietal lobe.

Ans: a, p. 78

40. Raccoons have much more precise control of their paws than dogs do. You would expect that raccoons have more cortical space dedicated to "paw control" in the ________of their brains.
    a. frontal lobes
    b. parietal lobes
    c. temporal lobes
    d. occipital lobes

Ans: b, p. 78

41. Research has found that the amount of representation in the motor cortex reflects the:
    a. size of the body parts.
    b. degree of precise control required by each of the parts.
    c. sensitivity of the body region.
    d. area of the occipital lobe being stimulated by the environment.

Ans: d, p. 79

42. In order to pinpoint the location of a tumor, a neurosurgeon electrically stimulated parts of the patient's sensory cortex. If the patient was conscious during the procedure, which of the following was probably experienced?
    a. "hearing" faint sounds
    b. "seeing" random visual patterns
    c. movement of the arms or legs
    d. a sense of having the skin touched

Ans: b, p. 80

43. Cortical areas that are not primarily concerned with sensory, motor, or language functions are:
    a. called projection areas.
    b. called association areas.
    c. located mostly in the parietal lobe.
    d. located mostly in the temporal lobe.

Ans: d, p. 81

44. The increasing complexity of animals' behavior was accompanied by a(n):
    a. increase in the size of the brainstem.
    b. decrease in the ratio of brain to body weight.
    c. increase in the size of the frontal lobes.
    d. increase in the amount of association area.

Ans: d, p. 81

45. Following a gunshot wound to his head, Jack became more uninhibited, irritable, and profane. It is likely that his personality change was the result of injury to his:
    a. parietal lobe.
    b. temporal lobe.
    c. occipital lobe.
    d. frontal lobe.
    e. endocrine system.

Ans: c, p. 82

46. Damage to ________ will usually cause a person to lose the ability to comprehend language.
    a. the angular gyrus
    b. Broca's area
    c. Wernicke's area
    d. frontal lobe association areas

Ans: c, p. 85

47. Three-year-old Marco suffered damage to the speech area of the brain's left hemisphere when he fell from a swing. Research suggests that:
    a. he will never speak again.
    b. his motor abilities will improve so that he can easily use sign language.
    c. his right hemisphere will take over much of the language function.
    d. his earlier experience with speech will enable him to continue speaking.

Ans: c, p. 85

48. The nerve fibers that enable communication between the right and left cerebral hemispheres and that have been severed in split-brain patients form a structure called the:
a. reticular formation.
b. association areas.
c. corpus callosum.
d. parietal lobes.
e. limbic system.

Ans: a, p. 86

49. Dr. Johnson briefly flashed a picture of a key in the right visual field of a split-brain patient. The patient could probably:
a. verbally report that a key was seen.
b. write the word *key* using the left hand.
c. draw a picture of a key using the left hand.
d. do none of the above.

Ans: a, pp. 86-87

50. A split-brain patient has a picture of a knife flashed to her left hemisphere and that of a fork to her right hemisphere. She will be able to:
a. identify the fork using her left hand.
b. identify a knife using her left hand.
c. identify a knife using either hand.
d. identify a fork using either hand.

Ans: d, p. 88

51. Which of the following is typically controlled by the right hemisphere?
a. language
b. learned voluntary movements
c. arithmetic reasoning
d. perceptual tasks

Ans: b, p. 88

52. Anton is applying for a technician's job with a neurosurgeon. In trying to impress his potential employer with his knowledge of the brain, he says, "After my father's stroke I knew immediately that the blood clot had affected his left cerebral hemisphere because he no longer recognized a picture of his friend." Should Anton be hired?
a. Yes. Anton obviously understands brain structure and function.
b. No. The right hemisphere, not the left, specializes in picture recognition.
c. Yes. Although blood clots never form in the left hemisphere, Anton should be rewarded for recognizing the left hemisphere's role in picture recognition.
d. No. Blood clots never form in the left hemisphere, and the right hemisphere is more involved than the left in recognizing pictures.

Ans: b, p. 88

53. Which of the following is typically controlled by the left hemisphere?
a. spatial reasoning
b. word recognition
c. the left side of the body
d. perceptual skills

Ans: a, p. 89

54. Which of the following is *not* true regarding brain organization and handedness?
    a. If a person has a left-handed identical twin, odds are that he or she will also be left-handed.
    b. Right-handedness is far more common than left-handedness throughout the world.
    c. On average, right-handers live longer than left-handers.
    d. Left-handers are more common than usual among people with reading disabilities.
    e. With age, the percentage of left-handers declines dramatically.

Ans: d, p. 92

55. (Thinking Critically) Based on research, which of the following seems true about the specialized functions of the right and left hemispheres?
    a. They are more clear-cut in men than in women.
    b. They are more clear-cut in women than in men.
    c. Most complex tasks emerge from the activity of one or the other hemisphere.
    d. Most complex activities emerge from the integrated activity of both hemispheres.

Ans: c, p. 94

56. Chemical messengers produced by endocrine glands are called:
    a. agonists.
    b. neurotransmitters.
    c. hormones.
    d. enzymes.

Ans: a, p. 94

57. I am a relatively slow-acting (but long-lasting) chemical messenger carried throughout the body by the bloodstream. What am I?
    a. a hormone
    b. a neurotransmitter
    c. acetylcholine
    d. dopamine

Ans: d, p. 95

58. The gland that regulates body growth is the:
    a. adrenal.
    b. thyroid.
    c. hypothalamus.
    d. pituitary.
    e. hyperthyroid.

Ans: d, p. 95

59. Epinephrine and norepinephrine are ________ that are released by the ________ gland.
    a. neurotransmitters; pituitary
    b. hormones; pituitary
    c. neurotransmitters; adrenal
    d. hormones; adrenal
    e. hormones; thyroid

Ans: a, p. 95

60. A bodybuilder friend suddenly seems to have grown several inches in height. You suspect that your friend's growth spurt has occurred because he has been using drugs that affect the:
    a. pituitary gland.
    b. thalamus.
    c. adrenal glands.
    d. medulla.
    e. cerebellum.

CHAPTER 3

The Nature and Nurture of Behavior

Learning Objectives

Genes: Our Biological Blueprint (pp. 100-101)

1. Describe the composition and physical location of genes.

Evolutionary Psychology: Maximizing Fitness (pp. 101-107)

2. Discuss the impact of evolutionary history on genetically predisposed behavioral tendencies.

3. Identify gender differences in sexual behavior, and describe and evaluate evolutionary explanations for those differences.

Behavior Genetics: Predicting Individual Differences (pp. 108-116)

4. Describe how twin and adoption studies help us differentiate hereditary and environmental influences on human traits.

5. Discuss how differences in infant temperament illustrate the effect of heredity on development.

6. Describe how behavior geneticists estimate trait heritability, and discuss the interaction of genetic and environmental influences.

7. Discuss the potential promise and perils of molecular genetics.

Environmental Influence (pp. 116-125)

8. Explain why we should be cautious about attributing children's successes and failures to parental influence.

9. Explain how twins may experience different prenatal environments, and describe the effect of early experience on brain development.

10. Describe how development is influenced by the individual's peer group and culture.

The Nature and Nurture of Gender (pp. 126-130)

11. Explain how biological sex is determined, and describe the role of sex hormones in biological development and gender differences.

12. Discuss the importance of gender roles, and explain how social and cognitive factors contribute to gender identity and gender-typing.

Postscript: Reflections on Nature and Nurture (pp. 131-132)

13. Discuss the danger of blaming nature and nurture for our own personal failings.

Genes: Our biological blueprint, p. 100
Medium, Factual/Definitional, Objective 1, Ans: a

1. A human sperm cell contains:
   a. 23 chromosomes.
   b. 23 genes.
   c. 46 chromosomes.
   d. 46 genes.

Genes: Our biological blueprint, p. 100
Difficult, Conceptual, Objective 1, Ans: e

2. Chromosomes are contained within:
   a. brain cells.
   b. sperm cells.
   c. bone cells.
   d. blood cells.
   e. all of the above.

Genes: Our biological blueprint, p. 100
Medium, Factual/Definitional, Objective 1, Ans: a

3. A segment of DNA capable of synthesizing a specific protein is called a:
   a. gene.
   b. gender schema.
   c. chromosome.
   d. hormone.
   e. neurotransmitter.

Genes: Our biological blueprint, p. 100
Difficult, Conceptual, Objective 1, Ans: d

4. Sperm is to cell as DNA is to:
   a. nucleotide.
   b. schema.
   c. meme.
   d. molecule.

Genes: Our biological blueprint, p. 100
Medium, Factual/Definitional, Objective 1, Ans: b

5. Genes are composed of:
   a. testosterone.
   b. nucleotides.
   c. memes.
   d. schemas.
   e. synapses.

Genes: Our biological blueprint, p. 100
Difficult, Conceptual, Objective 1, Ans: d

6. Genes are to nucleotides as ________ are to ________.
   a. letters; books
   b. words; books
   c. letters; words
   d. words; letters

Genes: Our biological blueprint, p. 100
Difficult, Factual/Definitional, Objective 1, Ans: c

7. The human genome is the complete:
   a. set of human sexual characteristics regulated by the X and Y chromosomes.
   b. range of traits that contribute to reproductive success.
   c. sequence of nucleotides organized as coiled chains of DNA.
   d. cascade of interactions between genetic predispositions and surrounding environments.

Genes: Our biological blueprint, p. 101
Medium, Factual/Definitional, Objective 1, Ans: a

8. Human genetic diversity consists of the variations in the sequence of our:
   a. nucleotides.
   b. synapses.
   c. memes.
   d. gender schemas.
   e. hormones.

Evolutionary psychology, p. 101
Easy, Factual/Definitional, Objective 2, Ans: c

9. Dmitry Belyaev and Lyudmilla Trut successfully domesticated wild foxes by means of:
   a. cloning.
   b. gender typing.
   c. selective mating.
   d. gene splicing.
   e. hormone injections.

Evolutionary psychology, p. 102
Easy, Factual/Definitional, Objective 2, Ans: c

10. The reproductive advantage enjoyed by organisms best suited to a specific ecological niche is known as:
   a. heritability.
   b. behavior genetics.
   c. natural selection.
   d. temperament.

Evolutionary psychology, p. 102
Easy, Factual/Definitional, Objective 2, Ans: d

11. Evolutionary psychologists are most likely to emphasize that human adoptiveness to a variety of different environments has contributed to human:
a. heritability.
b. genetic mutations.
c. gender schemas.
d. reproductive success.

Evolutionary psychology, p. 102
Medium, Conceptual/Application, Objective 2, Ans: b

12. If a genetically based attraction to beautiful people contributes to survival, that trait will likely be passed on to subsequent generations. This best illustrates:
a. gender typing.
b. natural selection.
c. behavior genetics.
d. gender schema theory.

Evolutionary psychology, p. 102
Easy, Factual/Definitional, Objective 2, Ans: c

13. Which of the following is a major source of genetic diversity?
a. cloning
b. gender-typing
c. mutations
d. memes

Evolutionary psychology, pp. 102-103
Medium, Conceptual, Objective 2, Ans: d

14. An evolutionary psychologist would suggest that people are genetically predisposed to:
a. fear dangerous animals.
b. love their own children.
c. seek healthy-looking mates.
d. do all of the above.

Evolutionary psychology, p. 103
Easy, Factual/Definitional, Objective 2, Ans: b

15. According to evolutionary psychologists, behaviors that promote reproductive success are likely to be:
a. socially prohibited.
b. genetically predisposed.
c. ecologically disruptive.
d. disease-producing.

Evolutionary psychology, p. 103
Difficult, Conceptual, Objective 2, Ans: b

16. Evolutionary psychologists would be most likely to predict that:
a. fathers are more protective of their children than are mothers.
b. children are not likely to be abused by their biological parents.
c. people are the most romantically attracted to those who are the most genetically dissimilar to themselves.
d. genetic predispositions have little effect on our social relationships.

Evolution and sexuality, pp. 103-104
Easy, Factual/Definitional, Objective 3, Ans: d

17. Compared with women, men are more likely to:
   a. initiate sexual activity.
   b. read pornographic materials.
   c. comply with direct requests for casual sex.
   d. do all of the above.

Evolution and sexuality, p. 104
Medium, Factual/Definitional, Objective 3, Ans: d

18. Compared with men, women are ________ likely to agree to go to bed with a stranger and ________ likely to perceive simple friendliness as a sexual come-on.
   a. more; less
   b. more; more
   c. less; more
   d. less; less

Evolution and sexuality, pp. 104-105
Medium, Conceptual/Application, Objective 3, Ans: a

19. Professor Assad suggested that a cautious attitude toward sexual encounters has proven to be more reproductively advantageous to women than to men because the reproduction process is more time-consuming for women than for men. This suggestion best illustrates the logic of a(n) ________ theory of sexual behavior.
   a. evolutionary
   b. social learning
   c. Freudian
   d. gender schema

Evolution and sexuality, p. 105
Difficult, Conceptual, Objective 3, Ans: d

20. Evolutionary psychologists would be most likely to attribute gender differences in attitudes toward casual sex to the fact that men have ________ than do women.
   a. larger bodies
   b. stronger gender identity
   c. a weaker sense of empathy
   d. greater reproductive potential

Evolution and sexuality, p. 105
Medium, Factual/Definitional, Objective 3, Ans: d

21. Men judge women as especially attractive if they appear ________ and women judge men as especially attractive if they appear ________.
   a. mature; mature
   b. youthful; youthful
   c. mature; youthful
   d. youthful; mature

Evolution and sexuality, p. 105
Easy, Factual/Definitional, Objective 3, Ans: b

22. In attracting potential mates, women are more likely than men to advertise their own ________, and men are more likely than women to advertise their own ________.
a. athletic skills; parenting skills
b. good looks; wealth
c. sexual experience; sexual inexperience
d. intelligence; nurturance

Evolution and sexuality, pp. 105-106
Medium, Conceptual, Objective 3, Ans: d

23. Brittla is obsessed with her appearance and spends a lot of time and money on cosmetics and weight-loss programs. According to evolutionary psychologists, Brittla's behavior is a product of:
a. cultural norms.
b. gender-typing.
c. gender schemas.
d. genetic predispositions.

Critiquing the evolutionary explanation, p. 106
Medium, Conceptual/Application, Objective 3, Ans: b

24. Evolutionary psychologists would be least likely to predict that:
a. a man would be distressed by the sexual infidelity of his wife.
b. a woman would engage in casual sex with many male partners.
c. a woman would prefer to marry a man who is wealthier than herself.
d. a man would prefer to marry a woman who is better looking than himself.

Critiquing the evolutionary explanation, p. 107
Difficult, Factual/Definitional, Objective 3, Ans: a

25. Critics of evolutionary psychology are most likely to suggest that it:
a. inhibits progressive efforts to change common social practices.
b. overestimates the impact of genetic mutations on human personality.
c. underestimates the impact of genetic predispositions on human sexual behavior.
d. underestimates the extent to which similar gender differences are found in all cultures.

Behavior genetics, p. 108
Easy, Factual/Definitional, Objective 4, Ans: c

26. The study of the relative power of genetic and environmental influences on behavior and personality traits is known as:
a. molecular genetics.
b. evolutionary psychology.
c. behavior genetics.
d. gender-typing.
e. human cloning.

Behavior genetics, p. 108
Difficult, Conceptual, Objective 4, Ans: d

27. A behavior geneticist would be most interested in studying hereditary influences on:
   a. skin color.
   b. sexual anatomy.
   c. physical attractiveness.
   d. personality traits.

Twin studies, p. 108
Easy, Factual/Definitional, Objective 4, Ans: a

28. Identical twins originate from the fertilization of ________ egg cell(s) by ________ sperm cell(s).
   a. a single; a single
   b. two; a single
   c. a single; two
   d. two; two

Twin studies, p. 108
Easy, Factual/Definitional, Objective 4, Ans: c

29. Twin studies suggest that Alzheimer's disease is influenced by:
   a. testosterone.
   b. gender schemas.
   c. heredity.
   d. memes.

Twin studies, pp. 108-109
Medium, Factual/Definitional, Objective 4, Ans: c

30. Compared to identical twins, fraternal twins are ________ similar in neuroticism and ________ similar in attitudes toward organized religion.
   a. more; less
   b. less; more
   c. more; more
   d. less; less

Twin studies, p. 108
Medium, Factual/Definitional, Objective 4, Ans: d

31. Compared to fraternal twins, identical twins are much more similar in:
   a. extraversion.
   b. emotional instability.
   c. risk of divorce.
   d. all of the above.

Twin studies, pp. 108-109
Easy, Factual/Definitional, Objective 4, Ans: d

32. Two individuals are most likely to share similar personality traits if they are ________ twins who were reared ________.
   a. fraternal; together
   b. identical; apart
   c. fraternal; apart
   d. identical; together

Twin studies, p. 109
Difficult, Factual/Definitional, Objective 4, Ans: d

33. Environmental influences on personality traits are most clearly highlighted by comparing ________ with ________.
    a. identical twins raised apart; fraternal twins raised apart
    b. identical twins raised together; fraternal twins raised together
    c. identical twins raised apart; fraternal twins raised together
    d. identical twins raised together; identical twins raised apart

Twin studies, p. 110
Difficult, Factual/Definitional, Objective 4, Ans: c

34. Although identical twins have been shown to have some amazing psychological similarities, one should be cautious about attributing these similarities to genetic factors because:
    a. the twins may have been raised in completely different environments.
    b. genetic factors influence physical, not psychological, characteristics.
    c. any two strangers are likely to share a string of coincidental similarities.
    d. many fraternal twins have been shown to be psychologically different from each other.

Adoption studies, p. 111
Medium, Factual/Definitional, Objective 4, Ans: c

35. The personalities of adopted children:
    a. are very similar to the personalities of the other children in their adoptive families.
    b. are very similar to the personalities of their biologically related siblings.
    c. are not very similar to the personalities of their adoptive parents.
    d. are more similar to the personalities of their caregiving adoptive parents than to the personalities of their biological parents.

Adoption studies, p. 111
Medium, Factual/Definitional, Objective 4, Ans: c

36. The home environment most clearly has a greater influence on children's ________ than on their ________.
    a. temperament; political attitudes
    b. extraversion; table manners
    c. religious beliefs; personality traits
    d. gender identity; gender schemas

Adoption studies, p. 111
Medium, Factual/Definitional, Objective 4, Ans: a

37. Research most clearly suggests that personality traits are more strongly influenced by ________ than by ________.
    a. genes; home environment
    b. home environment; genes
    c. genes; peer influence
    d. home environments; peer influence

Temperament studies, p. 112
Easy, Factual/Definitional, Objective 5, Ans: c

38. An infant's temperament refers most directly to its:
a. ability to learn.
b. physical attractiveness.
c. emotional excitability.
d. physical health.
e. sense of humor.

Temperament studies, p. 112
Medium, Conceptual/Application, Objective 5, Ans: c

39. Pat is normally very restless and fidgety, whereas Shelley is usually quiet and easygoing. The two children most clearly differ in:
a. brain maturation.
b. gender schemas.
c. temperament.
d. physical health.

Temperament studies, p. 112
Difficult, Factual/Definitional, Objective 5, Ans: b

40. Babies with an intense and highly reactive temperament tend to be:
a. intelligent and imaginative.
b. irritable and unpredictable.
c. fearless and assertive.
d. extraverted and cheerful.

Temperament studies, p. 112
Difficult, Factual/Definitional, Objective 5, Ans: b

41. A child's temperament is likely to be:
a. difficult to observe.
b. stable over time.
c. a product of parenting style.
d. a reflection of their gender schemas.

Temperament studies, p. 112
Easy, Conceptual/Application, Objective 5, Ans: a

42. Who are likely to show the greatest similarity in temperament?
a. Ruth and Ramona, identical twins
b. Philip and Paul, fraternal twins
c. Larry and Laura, brother and sister
d. Vincent Sr. and Vincent Jr., father and son

Heritability, p. 112
Easy, Factual/Definitional, Objective 6, Ans: d

43. In order to estimate trait heritability, researchers are most likely to make use of:
a. cloning.
b. gender schemas.
c. gender-typing.
d. twin studies.

Heritability, p. 112
Medium, Factual/Definitional, Objective 6, Ans: c

44. Heritability refers to the extent to which:
   a. unrelated individuals share common genes.
   b. genetic mutations can be transmitted to one's offspring.
   c. trait differences among individuals are attributable to genetic variations.
   d. adult personality is determined by infant temperament.

Heritability, p. 113
Difficult, Factual/Definitional, Objective 6, Ans: c

45. The heritability of a specific trait will be greatest among genetically ________ individuals who have been raised in ________ environments.
   a. similar; similar
   b. similar; dissimilar
   c. dissimilar; similar
   d. dissimilar; dissimilar

Heritability, p. 113
Medium, Factual/Definitional, Objective 6, Ans: c

46. Gender differences in heritable personality traits are not necessarily attributable to genetic differences between males and females because:
   a. physical maturation proceeds at a different rate for males and females.
   b. variations in temperament contribute to gender differences.
   c. heritable traits can be influenced by social environments.
   d. males and females are also affected by their different sex hormones.

Gene-environment interaction, p. 114
Medium, Conceptual, Objective 6, Ans: c

47. The unique temperaments of children evoke predictable responses from their caregivers. This best illustrates the ________ of nature and nurture.
   a. plasticity
   b. evolution
   c. interaction
   d. heritability
   e. bipolarity

Gene-environment interaction, p. 114
Medium, Conceptual/Application, Objective 6, Ans: c

48. People have always responded so positively to Alyssa's good looks that she has developed a socially confident and outgoing personality. This best illustrates the:
   a. commonality of gender identity and temperament.
   b. complementarity of gender schemas and social roles.
   c. interaction of nature and nurture.
   d. reciprocal influence of norms and memes.

Molecular genetics, p. 115
Easy, Conceptual/Application, Objective 7, Ans: b

49. Assessing possible linkages between specific nucleotide sequences and bipolar disorder would be of greatest interest to a(n):
    a. evolutionary psychologist.
    b. molecular geneticist.
    c. gender schema theorist.
    d. social learning theorist.

How much credit (or blame) do parent deserve?, pp. 117-118
Medium, Factual/Definitional, Objective 8, Ans: b

50. Adopted children raised in the same family are not especially likely to have similar personality traits. This most clearly implies that we should be cautious about attributing personality to:
    a. genetic predispositions.
    b. parental influences.
    c. gender differences.
    d. peer influences.

How much credit (or blame) do parent deserve?, p. 117
Medium, Conceptual, Objective 8, Ans: c

51. An awareness that children's temperaments influence parents' child-rearing practices should inhibit our tendency to:
    a. emphasize the interaction of nature and nurture.
    b. assess the heritability of human intelligence.
    c. blame parents for our own dysfunctional characteristics.
    d. identify cultural differences in child-rearing practices.

Prenatal environment, p. 118
Easy, Factual/Definitional, Objective 9, Ans: a

52. Identical twins are most likely to share a similar prenatal environment if they share the same:
    a. placenta.
    b. reproductive capacity.
    c. memes.
    d. gender schemas.

Prenatal environment, p. 118
Medium, Conceptual/Application, Objective 9, Ans: c

53. Dante is healthier than his twin brother because he developed with a better placental barrier against viruses. This best illustrates the impact of ________ on development.
    a. temperament
    b. gender schemas
    c. early environment
    d. genetic predispositions

Experience and brain development, p. 118
Medium, Factual/Definitional, Objective 9, Ans: c

54. Compared to environmentally impoverished rats, rats housed in enriched environments experienced a dramatic increase in the number of their:
    a. brain cells.
    b. schemas.
    c. synapses.
    d. nucleotides.

Experience and brain development, p. 119
Difficult, Conceptual/Application, Objective 9, Ans: d

55. For children from impoverished environments, stimulating educational experiences during early childhood are most likely to:
    a. facilitate the development of nucleotides.
    b. decrease their emotional attachment to their own parents.
    c. have no discernable effect on subsequent academic performance.
    d. prevent the degeneration of activated connections between neurons.

Peer influence, pp. 120-121
Medium, Conceptual/Application, Objective 10, Ans: a

56. In order to prevent teens from smoking, intervention programs for youth should first pay attention to the impact of ________ on teen smoking habits.
    a. peer influence
    b. family environments
    c. genetic predispositions
    d. gender schemas

Peer influence, pp. 120-121
Medium, Conceptual, Objective 10, Ans: d

57. It has been suggested that our sensitivity to peer influence is genetically predisposed because it has facilitated the process of human mating. This suggestion best illustrates:
    a. gender schema theory.
    b. Freudian psychology.
    c. molecular genetics.
    d. an evolutionary perspective.

Peer influence, pp. 120-121
Difficult, Factual/Definitional, Objective 10, Ans: c

58. In comparison to parental influence, peer influence is ________ likely to affect a child's English accent and ________ likely to affect a child's educational success.
    a. more; more
    b. less; less
    c. more; less
    d. less; more

Culture, p. 121
Medium, Factual/Definitional, Objective 10, Ans: d

59. Cultural diversity best illustrates our:
    a. human temperaments.
    b. gene complexes.
    c. gender identities.
    d. adaptive capacities.

Culture, p. 121
Easy, Factual/Definitional, Objective 10, Ans: d

60. The enduring traditions, ideas, attitudes, and behaviors shared by a large group of people and transmitted from one generation to the next define their:
    a. temperament.
    b. roles.
    c. racial identity.
    d. culture.

Culture, p. 122
Easy, Factual/Definitional, Objective 10, Ans: d

61. Those who study cultural influences on behavior are most likely to highlight the importance of:
    a. natural selection.
    b. temperament.
    c. schemas.
    d. norms.

Culture, p. 122
Medium, Conceptual, Objective 10, Ans: d

62. Frans avoids talking with food in his mouth because other people think it is crude and inappropriate. This best illustrates the impact of:
    a. roles.
    b. schemas.
    c. stereotypes.
    d. norms.

Culture, p. 122
Easy, Factual/Definitional, Objective 10, Ans: b

63. Personal space refers to:
    a. our inner private thoughts and personally subjective feelings about ourselves.
    b. the distance we like to maintain between ourselves and other people.
    c. the priority we give to our own personal needs over group needs.
    d. areas of a home, such as a bedroom, where privacy is important.

Culture, p. 122
Medium, Factual/Definitional, Objective 10, Ans: a

64. Studies indicate that ________ prefer more personal space than do ________.
    a. North Americans; Latin Americans
    b. the French; the British
    c. Arabs; Scandinavians
    d. women; men

Culture, p. 123
Medium, Factual/Definitional, Objective 10, Ans: d

65. Evolutionary psychologists refer to memes as self-replicating:
a. genetic mutations.
b. gender schemas.
c. neural connections.
d. cultural mutations.

Culture, pp. 100, 123-124
Medium, Conceptual, Objective 10, Ans: b

66. Genes are to the perpetuation of individuals as memes are to the perpetuation of:
a. stereotypes.
b. cultures.
c. races.
d. schemas.

Culture, p. 123
Medium, Factual/Definitional, Objective 10, Ans: c

67. Since the 1960s, Americans have experienced a(n) ________ in rates of depression and a(n) ________ in work hours.
a. increase; decrease
b. decrease; increase
c. increase; increase
d. decrease; decrease

Culture and child-rearing, p. 124
Medium, Factual/Definitional, Objective 10, Ans: c

68. Compared with today's North American parents, many Asian and African parents are more likely to encourage their children to value:
a. civil rights.
b. racial equality.
c. social harmony.
d. nonconformity.
e. self-reliance.

Culture and child-rearing, p. 124
Medium, Factual/Definitional, Objective 10, Ans: d

69. Compared with Asian parents, North American parents today place ________ emphasis on obedience and ________ emphasis on family loyalty.
a. more; less
b. less; more
c. more; more
d. less; less

Developmental similarities across groups, p. 125
Medium, Factual/Definitional, Objective 10, Ans: a

70. Cross-cultural research on human development indicates that:
   a. person-to-person differences within cultural groups are larger than differences between groups.
   b. differences among cultural groups largely reflect genetic differences among racial groups.
   c. gender differences in behavior result from differences in biology rather than from differences in life experiences.
   d. developmental processes differ greatly among individuals raised in different cultures.

The nature of gender, p. 126
Medium, Factual/Definitional, Objective 11, Ans: c

71. A human egg contains ________ chromosome and a human sperm contains ________ chromosome.
   a. a Y; either an X or a Y
   b. either an X or a Y; an X
   c. an X; either an X or a Y
   d. either an X or a Y; a Y

The nature of gender, p. 126
Easy, Factual/Definitional, Objective 11, Ans: b

72. Female children have been observed to dress and play in ways more typical of males if they were exposed to excess ________ during their prenatal development.
   a. nucleotides
   b. testosterone
   c. endorphins
   d. estrogen

The nature of gender, p. 126
Medium, Factual/Definitional, Objective 11, Ans: d

73. Prenatal testosterone secretions exert one of their earliest influences on:
   a. genes.
   b. memes.
   c. gender schemas.
   d. brain organization.

Gender roles, p. 127
Easy, Factual/Definitional, Objective 12, Ans: b

74. A cluster of behaviors expected of those who occupy a particular social position is a:
   a. norm.
   b. role.
   c. schema.
   d. meme.

Gender roles, p. 127
Easy, Factual/Definitional, Objective 12, Ans: c

75. Gender role refers to;
    a. one's biological sex.
    b. the sense of being male or female.
    c. the set of expected behaviors for males and females.
    d. the sense of being homosexual or heterosexual.
    e. how masculine a boy is or how feminine a girl is.

Gender roles, p. 127
Medium, Conceptual/Application, Objective 12, Ans: b

76. When teased by his older sister, 9-year-old Waldo does not cry because he has learned that boys are not expected to. Waldo's behavior best illustrates the importance of:
    a. temperament.
    b. gender roles.
    c. testosterone.
    d. stereotypes.
    e. gender identity.

Gender roles, p. 127
Easy, Factual/Definitional, Objective 12, Ans: c

77. The social roles assigned to women and men:
    a. are virtually the same in all cultures.
    b. have been virtually the same in all historical time periods.
    c. differ widely across cultures.
    d. differ widely across historical time periods but not across cultures.

Gender roles, p. 128
Medium, Conceptual/Application, Objective 12, Ans: a

78. On extended visits to foreign countries, you would be most likely to observe:
    a. more men than women in leadership positions.
    b. women earning approximately the same amount of money as men.
    c. men and women equally involved in child care.
    d. men and women equally involved in violent crime.

Gender and child-rearing, p. 128
Easy, Factual/Definitional, Objective 12, Ans: b

79. Gender identity refers to:
    a. one's biological sex.
    b. the sense of being male or female.
    c. the set of expected behaviors for males and for females.
    d. how masculine a boy is or how feminine a girl is.
    e. a person's identification with the parent of the opposite sex.

Gender and child-rearing, pp. 128-129
Easy, Factual/Definitional, Objective 12, Ans: d

80. A boy who consistently exhibits traditionally masculine interests and behavior patterns demonstrates the impact of:
 a. gene complexes.
 b. heritability.
 c. the X chromosome.
 d. gender-typing.

Gender and child-rearing, pp. 128-129
Medium, Conceptual, Objective 12, Ans: d

81. Ten-year-old Migdalia insists on wearing very feminine-looking clothes because she wants to appear ladylike. This best illustrates the impact of:
 a. natural selection.
 b. personal space.
 c. sexual orientation.
 d. gender-typing.

Gender and child-rearing, p. 129
Medium, Factual/Definitional, Objective 12, Ans: a

82. Social learning theorists emphasize that:
 a. observation and imitation play a crucial role in the gender-typing process.
 b. children will exhibit only those gender-typed behaviors for which they have been directly rewarded.
 c. children will not learn gender-typed behaviors if the same-sex parent is absent from the home.
 d. all of the above are true.

Gender and child-rearing, p. 129
Medium, Conceptual, Objective 12, Ans: b

83. Mr. Eskenazi frowns when his son cries but hugs his daughter when she cries. Mr. Eskenazi's contribution to the gender-typing of his children would most likely be highlighted by:
 a. twin studies.
 b. social learning theorists.
 c. adoption studies.
 d. evolutionary psychologists.

Gender and child-rearing, p. 130
Medium, Factual/Definitional, Objective 12, Ans: d

84. Children's tendency to classify behavior and personality traits in terms of masculine and feminine categories is of most direct relevance to:
 a. Freudian psychology.
 b. behavior genetics.
 c. evolutionary psychology.
 d. gender schema theory.

Gender and child-rearing, p. 130
Difficult, Conceptual/Application, Objective 12, Ans: c

85. When his mother offered to play leapfrog with him, Jorge protested, "I'm not going to play a girl's game!" Jorge's reaction best illustrates psychological processes highlighted by:
    a. behavior genetics.
    b. Freudian psychology.
    c. gender schema theory.
    d. natural selection.

Postscript: Reflections on nature and nurture, p. 131
Medium, Conceptual, Objective 13, Ans: b

86. Those who suggest that our choices today shape tomorrow's possibilities are emphasizing the importance of:
    a. behavior genetics.
    b. human responsibility.
    c. personal space.
    d. memes.

Essay Questions

1. Many would consider it ironic that men are more likely than women to feel comfortable about having casual sex with multiple partners and yet at the same time more likely to feel jealous rage over a mate's having sex with someone else. How would an evolutionary psychologist explain these gender differences? What are the strengths and weaknesses of this evolutionary explanation?

2. Describe one of your personality traits that you believe to be highly heritable and another trait that seems to be much less so. Provide evidence to support your answer, and explain why you would expect genetics to exert a much greater impact on some personality traits than on others.

3. Mr. Firkin is a shy and reserved person who often feels tense and nervous. In therapy, he recalled that he had an unhappy childhood, feeling that he did not receive enough attention from his mother and resenting the conservative family discipline and life style enforced by his father. He blames both parents for his current anxiety, unhappiness, and loneliness. In light of your understanding of the interactive influences of nature and nurture, explain why Mr. Firkin's complaints about his parents may be somewhat unfair and unhelpful.

4. Describe ways in which our society might change in the future—in the home, school, and workplace, for example—if all children were raised in families that discouraged traditional gender-typing and distinct gender roles. Consider the advantages or disadvantages of such changes while you develop an argument as to whether you would or would not recommend the development of that kind of society.

Web Quiz 1

Ans: d

1. An organism's complete set of genetic instructions is called the:
   a. heritability estimate.
   b. nucleotide.
   c. double helix.
   d. genome.

Ans: d

2. Bacteria that resist a hospital's antibiotics rapidly multiply as other bacteria die off. This best illustrates:
   a. gene complexes.
   b. behavior genetics.
   c. heritability.
   d. natural selection.

Ans: d

3. Compared to women, men are ________ likely to feel comfortable about having casual sex with different partners and ________ likely to feel jealous rage over a mate's having sex with someone else.
   a. less; more
   b. more; less
   c. less; less
   d. more; more

Ans: d

4. It has been suggested that men in all cultures tend to marry women younger than themselves because men are genetically predisposed to seek female features associated with youthful fertility. This suggestion best illustrates:
   a. social learning theory.
   b. behavior genetics.
   c. Freudian psychology.
   d. an evolutionary perspective.

Ans: b

5. Compared to fraternal twins, identical twins are ________ similar in their risk of developing Alzheimer's disease and ________ similar in risk of divorce.
   a. less; less
   b. more; more
   c. equally; more
   d. more; equally

Ans: a

6. Adoptive parents are least likely to influence the ________ of their adopted children.
   a. personality traits
   b. religious beliefs
   c. political attitudes
   d. moral values

Ans: b

7. Intense and reactive infants become unusually anxious and aroused when facing new or strange situations. This best illustrates the importance of:
   a. the X chromosome.
   b. temperament.
   c. personal space.
   d. natural selection.

Ans: b

8. Estimates of the heritability of personality traits are most directly associated with the research efforts of:
   a. molecular biologists.
   b. behavior geneticists.
   c. evolutionary psychologists.
   d. gender schema theorists.

Ans: d

9. In emphasizing that the behavioral effects of heredity depend on the specific environment in which one is raised, psychologists are highlighting the importance of:
   a. the double helix.
   b. gene complexes.
   c. natural selection.
   d. nature–nurture interactions.

Ans: c

10. Less than 10 percent of children's personality differences are attributable to the various ________ shared by family members.
   a. genes
   b. temperaments
   c. home environments
   d. cultural settings

Ans: c

11. Premature babies are especially likely to gain weight if stimulated by:
   a. sound and music.
   b. light and colors.
   c. touch and massage.
   d. movement and acceleration.

Ans: a

12. At a social gathering, Latin Americans may behave in a manner that North Americans consider intrusive and overly expressive. This best illustrates the importance of being sensitive to differing:
   a. norms.
   b. gene complexes.
   c. gender identities.
   d. heritability estimates.

Ans: c

13. Over the last century, Western parents have placed ________ priority on teaching children to respect and obey parents and ________ priority on teaching them loyalty to their country.
    a. decreasing; increasing
    b. increasing; decreasing
    c. decreasing; decreasing
    d. increasing; increasing

Ans: a

14. Jaquetta was exposed to excess testosterone during prenatal development. As a young girl, Jaquetta is likely to:
    a. prefer toy cars over dolls.
    b. exhibit superior verbal intelligence.
    c. develop a male gender identity.
    d. demonstrate a lack of gender schemas.

Ans: b

15. Concepts of maleness and femaleness that influence our perceptions are called gender:
    a. types.
    b. schemas.
    c. roles.
    d. complexes.

Web Quiz 2

Ans: b

1. Your complete genetic code consists of the exact sequence of ________ within your ________.
   a. memes; genome
   b. nucleotides; DNA
   c. genes; sex chromosomes
   d. synapses; nervous system

Ans: d

2. Evolutionary psychologists attribute the human tendency to fear snakes and heights to:
   a. gender schemas.
   b. the X chromosome.
   c. memes.
   d. genetic predispositions.

Ans: a

3. Compared to their female classmates, college-age men are ________ likely to engage in unsafe sexual practices and ________ likely to die in auto crashes.
   a. more; more
   b. more; less
   c. equally; more
   d. more; equally
   e. equally; equally

Ans: b

4. Evolutionary psychologists are likely to be criticized for ________ gender differences in human mate selection and for ________ the reproductive advantages of common social practices.
   a. underestimating; underestimating
   b. overestimating; overestimating
   c. underestimating; overestimating
   d. overestimating; underestimating

Ans: c

5. Two individuals are most likely to differ in intelligence if they are ________ twins who were raised ________.
   a. fraternal; together
   b. identical; apart
   c. fraternal; apart
   d. identical; together

Ans: d

6. Identical twins reared apart have ________ similar personalities than identical twins reared together and ________ similar personalities than fraternal twins reared apart.
   a. more; more
   b. less; less
   c. more; less
   d. less; more

Ans: e

7. Heritability refers to the extent to which trait variations among individuals are attributable to their differing:
   a. sex chromosomes.
   b. ethnic identities.
   c. gender roles.
   d. schemas.
   e. genes.

Ans: b

8. Identifying some of the specific genes that contribute to alcoholism would be of most direct interest to:
   a. evolutionary psychologists.
   b. molecular geneticists.
   c. gender schema theorists.
   d. Freudian psychologists.

Ans: b

9. The tendency to exaggerate the impact of parents' child-rearing practices on children's personality development has been most characteristic of:
   a. behavior geneticists.
   b. Freudian psychologists.
   c. gender schema theorists.
   d. evolutionary psychologists.

Ans: a

10. Identical twins who have separate placentas are somewhat less similar than identical twins who share a placenta. This best illustrates the influence of ________ on development.
   a. prenatal environments
   b. genetic predispositions
   c. gender schemas
   d. erotic plasticity

Ans: c

11. Teens who smoke typically have friends who smoke. In order to avoid overestimating the impact of peer pressure on teens' smoking habits, it would make the most sense to consider the impact of:
   a. natural selections on gender typing.
   b. temperament on physical health.
   c. smoking preferences.
   d. gene complexes on maturation.

Ans: d

12. The dramatic increase in Americans' premarital sexual activity over the past half-century best illustrates that sexual behavior is influenced by:
   a. temperament.
   b. natural selection.
   c. testosterone.
   d. norms.

Ans: c

13. A single ________ on the ________ chromosome plays a crucial role in the prenatal development of the testes.
 a. gene; X
 b. nucleotide; X
 c. gene; Y
 d. nucleotide; Y

Ans: e

14. The expectations that men initiate dates and that women select wedding gifts best illustrate aspects of:
 a. sexual orientation.
 b. gender identity.
 c. behavior genetics.
 d. gene complexes.
 e. gender roles.

Ans: c

15. Because he believes that worrying is a feminine trait, 14-year-old George has difficulty perceiving his own fears. His experience best illustrates dynamics highlighted by:
 a. social learning theory.
 b. behavior genetics.
 c. gender schema theory.
 d. evolutionary psychology.

Study Guide Questions

Ans: a, p. 100

1. If chromosomes are the "books" of heredity, the "words" are the ________ and the "letters" are the ________.
   a. genes; nucleotides
   b. nucleotides; genes
   c. genes; DNA
   d. DNA; genes

Ans: a, p. 100

2. Chromosomes are composed of small segments of ________ called ________.
   a. DNA; genes
   b. DNA; neurotransmitters
   c. genes; DNA
   d. DNA; enzymes

Ans: c, p. 100

3. Each cell of the human body has a total of:
   a. 23 chromosomes.
   b. 23 genes.
   c. 46 chromosomes.
   d. 46 genes.

Ans: b, p. 100

4. Genes direct our physical development by synthesizing:
   a. nucleotides.
   b. proteins.
   c. DNA.
   d. chromosomes.

Ans: d, p. 100

5. I am part of an "alphabet" that consists of only four letters, the sequence of which is nearly identical in all humans. What am I?
   a. a molecule of DNA
   b. a gene
   c. a chromosome
   d. a nucleotide

Ans: c, p. 100

6. The human genome is best defined as:
   a. a complex molecule containing genetic information that makes up the chromosomes.
   b. a segment of DNA.
   c. the complete instructions for making an organism.
   d. the four-letter genetic "alphabet."

Ans: a, p. 100

7. The sequence of the four nucleotide letters:
   a. is virtually the same in all humans.
   b. is virtually the same throughout the animal kingdom.
   c. varies from race to race.
   d. is more similar among females than among males.

Ans: d, p. 101

8. Which of the following most accurately summarizes the findings of the 40-year fox-breeding study described in the text?
   a. Wild wolves cannot be domesticated.
   b. "Survival of the fittest" seems to operate only when animals live in their natural habitats.
   c. By mating aggressive and unaggressive foxes, the researchers created a mutant species.
   d. By selecting and mating the tamest males and females, the researchers have produced affectionate, unaggressive offspring.

Ans: c, p. 101

9. Most human traits are:
   a. learned.
   b. determined by a single gene.
   c. influenced by many genes acting together.
   d. unpredictable.

Ans: a, p. 102

10. Mutations are random errors in ________ replication that lead to a change in the sequence of ________.
   a. gene; nucleotides
   b. chromosome; genes
   c. DNA; genes
   d. gene; DNA

Ans: a, p. 102

11. Responding to the argument that gender differences are often by-products of a culture's social and family structures, an evolutionary psychologist is most likely to point to:
   a. our great human capacity for learning.
   b. the tendency of cultural arguments to reinforce traditional gender inequalities.
   c. the infallibility of "hindsight" explanations.
   d. all of the above.

Ans: d, p. 102

12. When evolutionary psychologists use the word "fitness," they are specifically referring to:
   a. an animal's ability to adapt to changing environments.
   b. the diversity of a species' gene pool.
   c. the total number of members of the species currently alive.
   d. our ability to survive and reproduce.

Ans: a, p. 102

13. An evolutionary psychologist would be most interested in studying:
    a. why most parents are so passionately devoted to their children.
    b. hereditary influences on skin color.
    c. why certain diseases are more common among certain age groups.
    d. genetic differences in personality.

Ans: b, p. 102

14. Of the relatively few genetic differences among humans ________ are differences among races.
    a. less than 1 percent
    b. less than 10 percent
    c. approximately 25 percent
    d. approximately 40 to 50 percent

Ans: d, pp. 102, 105

15. A psychologist working from the evolutionary perspective is likely to suggest that people are biologically predisposed to:
    a. protect their offspring.
    b. fear heights.
    c. be attracted to fertile-appearing members of the opposite sex.
    d. do all of the above.

Ans: c, p. 103

16. Dr. Ross believes that principles of natural selection help explain why infants come to fear strangers about the time they become mobile. Dr. Ross is most likely a(n):
    a. behavior geneticist.
    b. molecular geneticist.
    c. evolutionary psychologist.
    d. molecular biologist.

Ans: d, p. 103

17. Through natural selection, the traits that are most likely to be passed on to succeeding generations are those that contribute to:
    a. reproduction.
    b. survival.
    c. aggressiveness.
    d. a. and b.
    e. a., b., and c.

Ans: a, p. 103

18. Gender refers to:
    a. the biological and social definitions of male and female.
    b. the biological definition of male and female.
    c. one's sense of being male or female.
    d. the extent to which one exhibits traditionally male or female traits.

Ans: d, p. 104

19. Which of the following is not true regarding gender and sexuality?
a. Men more often than women attribute a woman's friendliness to sexual interest.
b. Women are more likely than men to cite affection as a reason for first intercourse.
c. Men are more likely than females to initiate sexual activity.
d. Gender differences in sexuality are noticeably absent among gay men and lesbian women.

Ans: d, p. 104

20. Compared to men, women are more likely to:
a. be concerned with their partner's physical attractiveness.
b. initiate sexual activity.
c. cite "liking one another" as a justification for having sex in a new relationship.
d. be less accepting of casual sex.

Ans: b, p. 104

21. Casual hit-and-run sex is most frequent among:
a. males with high circulating levels of testosterone.
b. males with traditional masculine attitudes.
c. females and males who are weakly gender-typed.
d. females and males who are strongly gender-typed.

Ans: b, pp. 104-105

22. Evolutionary psychologists attribute gender differences in sexuality to the fact that women have:
a. greater reproductive potential than do men.
b. lower reproductive potential than do men.
c. weaker sex drives than men.
d. stronger sex drives than men.

Ans: b, p. 105

23. According to evolutionary psychology, men are drawn sexually to women who seem ________, while women are attracted to men who seem ________.
a. nurturing; youthful
b. youthful and fertile; mature and affluent
c. slender; muscular
d. exciting; dominant

Ans: d, pp. 106-107

24. Evolutionary explanations of gender differences in sexuality have been criticized because:
a. they offer "after-the-fact" explanations.
b. standards of attractiveness vary with time and place.
c. they underestimate cultural influences on sexuality.
d. of all of the above reasons.

Ans: b, p. 108

25. Unlike ________ twins, who develop from a single fertilized egg, ________ twins develop from separate fertilized eggs.
a. fraternal; identical
b. identical; fraternal
c. placental; nonplacental
d. nonplacental; placental

Ans: b, p. 108

26. If a fraternal twin becomes schizophrenic, the likelihood of the other twin developing serious mental illness is much lower than with identical twins. This suggests that:
 a. schizophrenia is caused by genes.
 b. schizophrenia is influenced by genes.
 c. environment is unimportant in the development of schizophrenia.
 d. identical twins are especially vulnerable to mental disorders.

Ans: b, p. 108

27. After comparing divorce rates among identical and fraternal twins, Dr. Alexander has concluded that genes do play a role. Dr. Alexander is most likely a(n):
 a. evolutionary psychologist.
 b. behavior geneticist.
 c. molecular geneticist.
 d. divorcee.

Ans: b, p. 108

28. My sibling and I developed from a single fertilized egg. Who are we?
 a. opposite sex identical twins.
 b. same-sex identical twins.
 c. opposite sex fraternal twins.
 d. same-sex fraternal twins.

Ans: c, p. 108

29. A person whose twin has Alzheimer's disease has ________ risk of sharing the disease if they are identical twins than if they are fraternal twins.
 a. less
 b. about the same
 c. much greater
 d. It is unpredictable.

Ans: d, p. 109

30. Of the following, the best way to separate the effects of genes and environment in research is to study:
 a. fraternal twins.
 b. identical twins.
 c. adopted children and their adoptive parents.
 d. identical twins raised in different environments.

Ans: e, p. 109

31. One of the best ways to distinguish how much genetic and environmental factors affect behavior is to compare children who have:
 a. the same genes and environments.
 b. different genes and environments.
 c. similar genes and environments.
 d. similar genes and similar families.
 e. the same genes but different environments.

Ans: b, pp. 109-110

32. Several studies of long-separated identical twins have found that these twins:
  a. have little in common, due to the different environments in which they were raised.
  b. have many similarities, in everything from medical histories to personalities.
  c. have similar personalities, but very different likes, dislikes, and lifestyles.
  d. are no more similar than fraternal twins reared apart.

Ans: b, p. 111

33. Adoption studies show that the personalities of adopted children:
  a. closely match those of their adoptive parents.
  b. bear more similarities to their biological parents than to their adoptive parents.
  c. closely match those of the biological children of their adoptive parents.
  d. closely match those of other children reared in the same home, whether or not they are biologically related.

Ans: c, p. 111

34. A pair of adopted children or identical twins reared in the same home are most likely to have similar:
  a. temperaments.
  b. personalities.
  c. religious beliefs.
  d. emotional reactivity.

Ans: a, p. 112

35. Three-year-old Jack is inhibited and shy. As an adult, Jack is likely to be:
  a. cautious and unassertive.
  b. spontaneous and fearless.
  c. socially assertive.
  d. Who knows? This aspect of personality is not very stable over the life span.

Ans: a, p. 112

36. Temperament refers to a person's characteristic:
  a. emotional reactivity and intensity.
  b. attitudes.
  c. behaviors.
  d. role-related traits.

Ans: a, p. 112

37. In a hypothetical world where all schools are of uniform quality, all families equally loving, and all neighborhoods equally healthy, the heritability of person-to-person differences would be:
  a. large.
  b. small.
  c. zero.
  d. unpredictable.

Ans: c, p. 112

38. To say that the heritability of a trait is approximately 50 percent means that:
   a. genes are responsible for 50 percent of the trait in an individual, and the environment is responsible for the rest.
   b. the trait's appearance in a person will reflect approximately equal genetic contributions from both parents.
   c. of the variation in the trait within a group of people, 50 percent can be attributed to genes.
   d. all of the above are correct.

Ans: b, p. 113

39. The heritability of a trait will be largest among genetically ________ individuals who grew up in ________ environments.
   a. dissimilar; dissimilar
   b. dissimilar; similar
   c. similar; similar
   d. similar; dissimilar

Ans: d, p. 114

40. When the effect of one factor (such as environment) depends on another (such as heredity), we say there is a(n) ________ between the two factors.
   a. norm
   b. positive correlation
   c. negative correlation
   d. interaction

Ans: c, p. 114

41. Despite growing up in the same home environment, Karen and her brother John have personalities as different from each other as two people selected randomly from the population. Why is this so?
   a. Personality is inherited. Because Karen and John are not identical twins, it is not surprising that they have very different personalities.
   b. Gender is the most important factor in personality. If Karen had a sister, the two of them would probably be much more alike.
   c. The interaction of their individual genes and nonshared experiences accounts for the common finding that children in the same family are usually very different.
   d. Their case is unusual; children in the same family usually have similar personalities.

Ans: b, p. 114

42. Which of the following is an example of an interaction?
   a. Swimmers swim fastest during competition against other swimmers.
   b. Swimmers with certain personality traits swim fastest during competition, while those with other personality traits swim fastest during solo time trials.
   c. As the average daily temperature increases, sales of ice cream decrease.
   d. As the average daily temperature increases, sales of lemonade increase.

Ans: b, p. 115

43. The subfield that studies the specific genes that influence behavior is:
   a. behavior genetics.
   b. molecular genetics.
   c. evolutionary psychology.
   d. memes analysis.

Ans: c, p. 117

44. Of the following, parents are most likely to influence their children's:
    a. temperament.
    b. personality.
    c. faith.
    d. emotional reactivity.

Ans: c, pp. 117-118

45. Which of the following most accurately expresses the extent of parental influence on personality?
    a. It is more extensive than most people believe.
    b. It is weaker today than in the past.
    c. It is more limited than popular psychology supposes.
    d. It is almost completely unpredictable.

Ans: d, p. 118

46. I am a rat whose cortex is lighter and thinner than my litter mates'. What happened to me?
    a. You were born prematurely.
    b. You suffer from fetal alcohol syndrome.
    c. You were raised in an enriched environment.
    d. You were raised in a deprived environment.
    e. You did not imprint during the critical period.

Ans: d, pp. 118-119

47. Research studies have found that when infant rats and premature human babies are regularly touched or massaged, they:
    a. gain weight more rapidly.
    b. develop faster neurologically.
    c. have more agreeable temperaments.
    d. do a. and b.
    e. do a., b., and c.

Ans: c, p. 119

48. Providing a child with a stimulating educational environment during early childhood is likely to:
    a. ensure the formation of a strong attachment with parents.
    b. foster the development of a calm, easygoing temperament.
    c. prevent neural connections from degenerating.
    d. do all of the above.

Ans: c, p. 120

49. The "selection effect" in peer influence refers to the tendency of children and youth to:
    a. naturally separate into same-sex playgroups.
    b. establish large, fluid circles of friends.
    c. seek out friends with similar interests and attitudes.
    d. do all of the above.

Ans: c, pp. 121-122

50. Which of the following is not true regarding cultural diversity?
a. Culture influences emotional expressiveness.
b. Culture influences personal space.
c. Culture does not have a strong influence on how strictly social roles are defined.
d. All cultures evolve their own norms.

Ans: b, p. 124

51. Chad, who grew up in the United States, is more likely to encourage ________ in his future children than Asian-born Hidiyaki, who is more likely to encourage ________ in his future children.
a. obedience; independence
b. independence; emotional closeness
c. emotional closeness; obedience
d. loyalty; emotional closeness

Ans: d, p. 124

52. Compared to children raised in Western societies, those raised in communal societies, such as Japan or China:
a. grow up with a stronger integration of the sense of family into their self-concepts.
b. exhibit greater shyness toward strangers.
c. exhibit greater concern for loyalty and social harmony.
d. have all of the above characteristics.
e. have none of the above characteristics.

Ans: c, p. 126

53. Genetically female children often play in "masculine" ways if they were exposed to excess ________ during prenatal development.
a. estrogen
b. DNA
c. testosterone
d. nucleotides

Ans: b, p. 126

54. The fertilized egg will develop into a boy if, at conception:
a. the sperm contributes an X chromosome.
b. the sperm contributes a Y chromosome.
c. the egg contributes an X chromosome.
d. the egg contributes a Y chromosome.

Ans: d, p. 126

55. The hormone testosterone:
a. is found only in females.
b. determines the sex of the developing person.
c. stimulates growth of the female sex organs.
d. stimulates growth of the male sex organs.

Ans: a, p. 127

56. Women and men are most likely to be attracted to strongly gender-typed mates in cultures characterized by:
   a. gender inequality.
   b. gender equality.
   c. flexible gender roles.
   d. few norms.

Ans: c, p. 129

57. Children who are raised by parents who discourage traditional gender-typing:
   a. are less likely to display gender-typed behaviors themselves.
   b. often become confused and develop an ambiguous gender identity.
   c. nevertheless organized themselves into "girl worlds" and "boy worlds."
   d. display excessively masculine and feminine traits as adults.

Ans: d, p. 129

58. When his son cries because another child has taken his favorite toy, Brandon admonishes him by saying, "Big boys don't cry." Evidently, Brandon is an advocate of ________ in accounting for the development of gender-linked behaviors.
   a. gender schema theory
   b. gender identity theory
   c. gender-typing theory
   d. social learning theory

Ans: d, p. 130

59. Which theory states that gender becomes a lens through which children view their experiences?
   a. social learning theory
   b. Vygotsky's sociocultural theory
   c. Piaget's theory
   d. gender schema theory

Ans: a, p. 130

60. The fact that after age 2, language forces children to begin organizing their worlds on the basis of gender is most consistent with which theory of how gender-linked behaviors develop?
   a. gender schema theory
   b. gender identity theory
   c. gender-typing theory
   d. social learning theory

CHAPTER **4**

The Developing Person

Learning Objectives

Prenatal Development and the Newborn (pp. 136-140)

1. Discuss the course of prenatal development and the destructive impact of teratogens.

2. Describe the capacities of the newborn and the use of habituation for assessing infant cognition.

Infancy and Childhood (pp. 140-159)

3. Describe the impact of physical maturation on infants' capacities and motor skills.

4. Describe Piaget's view of how the mind develops, and discuss his stage theory of cognitive development, noting current thinking regarding cognitive stages.

5. Discuss the effect of body contact, familiarity, and responsive parenting on infant social attachments.

6. Describe the benefits of a secure attachment and the impact of parental neglect and separation, as well as day care on childhood development.

7. Describe the early development of a self-concept and discuss possible effects of different parenting styles on children.

Adolescence (pp. 159-171)

8. Define adolescence and identify the major physical changes that occur during this period of life.

9. Describe adolescents' growing reasoning power, and discuss specific ways in which moral behavior is affected by moral reasoning, emotional intuitions, and social influences.

10. Discuss the search for identity and the development of intimate social relationships during the adolescent years.

Adulthood (pp. 172-188)

11. Identify the major physical changes that occur in middle and older adulthood.

12. Describe the impact of aging on adult memory and intelligence.

13. Explain why the path of adult development need not be tightly linked to one's chronological age.

14. Discuss the importance of family and work commitments in adult development.

15. Describe people's life satisfaction across the life span and their reactions to death or the prospect of dying.

Reflections on Two Major Developmental Issues (pp. 189-190)

16. Summarize current views regarding continuity versus stages and stability versus change in lifelong development.

The developing person, p. 135
Easy, Conceptual, Objective 1, Ans: b

1. Dr. Matsuko's major research interest is the long-term effects of child-rearing practices on the psychological adjustment of offspring. It is most likely that Dr. Matsuko is a(n) ________ psychologist.
   a. cognitive
   b. developmental
   c. biological
   d. psychodynamic
   e. educational

Conception, p. 136
Medium, Factual/Definitional, Objective 1, Ans: d

2. Human sperm cells are ________ than egg cells, and sperm cell production begins ________ in life than does the production of egg cells.
   a. larger; later
   b. smaller; earlier
   c. larger; earlier
   d. smaller; later

Prenatal development, pp. 136-137
Difficult, Factual/Definitional, Objective 1, Ans: d

3. During the course of successful prenatal development, a human organism begins as a(n) ________ and finally develops into a(n) ________.
   a. embryo; zygote
   b. zygote; embryo
   c. embryo; fetus
   d. zygote; fetus
   e. fetus; embryo

Prenatal development, p. 137
Difficult, Factual/Definitional, Objective 1, Ans: d

4. The formation of a placenta signals the onset of ________ development.
   a. ovular
   b. zygotic
   c. fetal
   d. embryonic

Prenatal development, p. 137
Medium, Factual/Definitional, Objective 1, Ans: a

5. The heart begins to beat and the liver begins to make red blood cells during the ________ period of prenatal development.
   a. embryonic
   b. fetal
   c. zygotic
   d. ovular

Prenatal development, p. 137
Easy, Factual/Definitional, Objective 1, Ans: a

6. Infants first demonstrate a preference for their mother's voice over the voices of other women by the time they are ________ old.
   a. 1 day
   b. 1 week
   c. 10 days
   d. 2 weeks

Prenatal development, p. 137
Easy, Factual/Definitional, Objective 1, Ans: d

7. A teratogen is a(n):
   a. fertilized egg that undergoes rapid cell division.
   b. unborn child with one or more physical defects or abnormalities.
   c. chromosomal abnormality.
   d. substance that can cross the placental barrier and harm an unborn child.

Prenatal development, p. 137
Medium, Conceptual/Application, Objective 1, Ans: d

8. If research suggested that a pregnant mother's use of an artificial sweetener caused harm to the fetus, the artificial sweetener would be considered a(n):
   a. FAS.
   b. form of DNA.
   c. depressant.
   d. teratogen.
   e. neurotransmitter.

Prenatal development, p. 137
Medium, Conceptual/Application, Objective 1, Ans: a

9. Darlene smoked heavily during the entire 9 months of her pregnancy. Her newborn baby will most likely be:
a. underweight.
b. autistic.
c. hyperactive.
d. hearing impaired.

Prenatal development, p. 137
Medium, Factual/Definitional, Objective 1, Ans: e

10. One of the most consistently damaging teratogens is:
a. epinephrine.
b. testosterone.
c. serotonin.
d. dopamine.
e. alcohol.

Prenatal development, p. 137
Medium, Factual/Definitional, Objective 1, Ans: b

11. The symptoms of fetal alcohol syndrome are most likely to include:
a. egocentrism.
b. mental retardation.
c. visual impairments.
d. autism.

The competent newborn, p. 138
Easy, Factual/Definitional, Objective 2, Ans: c

12. The rooting reflex refers to a baby's tendency to:
a. withdraw a limb to escape pain.
b. turn the head away from a cloth placed over the face.
c. open the mouth in search of a nipple when touched on the cheek.
d. be startled by a loud noise.
e. look longer at human faces than at inanimate objects.

The competent newborn, p. 138
Easy, Conceptual/Application, Objective 2, Ans: d

13. Mr. Hersch triggered a rooting reflex in his infant son by touching him on the:
a. foot.
b. knee.
c. arm.
d. cheek.

The competent newborn, p. 138
Medium, Factual/Definitional, Objective 2, Ans: d

14. Newborns have been observed to show the greatest visual interest in a:
a. rectangular shape.
b. circular shape.
c. bull's-eye pattern.
d. drawing of a human face.

The competent newborn, p. 138
Medium, Factual/Definitional, Objective 2, Ans: b

15. When placed close to a gauze breast pad from their nursing mothers, week-old babies are likely to:
    a. move their eyes in a visual search for their mother.
    b. turn their head toward the smell of their mother's pad.
    c. open their mouth in a vigorous search for a nipple.
    d. demonstrate signs of stranger anxiety.

Research strategies for understanding infants' thinking (Box), p. 139
Easy, Factual/Definitional, Objective 2, Ans: b

16. Habituation refers to the:
    a. awareness that things continue to exist even when not perceived.
    b. decreasing responsiveness to a stimulus to which one is repeatedly exposed.
    c. adjustment of current schemas to make sense of new information.
    d. interpretation of new information in terms of existing schemas.
    e. biological growth processes that are relatively uninfluenced by experience.

Research strategies for understanding infants' thinking (Box), p. 139
Medium, Factual/Definitional, Objective 2, Ans: c

17. In order to test whether newborns can visually discriminate between various shapes and colors, psychologists have made use of the process of:
    a. conservation.
    b. attachment.
    c. habituation.
    d. accommodation.
    e. imprinting.

Brain development, p. 141
Easy, Factual/Definitional, Objective 3, Ans: b

18. Maturation refers to:
    a. the acquisition of socially acceptable behaviors.
    b. biological growth processes that are relatively uninfluenced by experience.
    c. any learned behavior patterns that accompany personal growth and development.
    d. the physical and sexual development of early adolescence.

Brain development, p. 141
Difficult, Conceptual, Objective 3, Ans: c

19. Maturation is to education as ________ is to ________.
    a. accommodation; assimilation
    b. learning; experience
    c. nature; nurture
    d. imprinting; critical period
    e. environment; learning

Maturation and infant memory, p. 141
Easy, Factual/Definitional, Objective 3, Ans: a

20. The relative lack of neural interconnections in the brain at the time of birth most directly contributes to:
    a. poor memory for early life experiences.
    b. decreasing responsiveness with repeated stimulation.
    c. an insecure attachment to one's primary caregiver.
    d. the fear of strangers commonly displayed by infants.

Maturation and infant memory, p. 141
Medium, Conceptual/Application, Objective 3, Ans: d

21. Four-year-old Karen can't remember anything of the first few months of her life. This is best explained by the fact that:
    a. the trauma of birth interfered with the subsequent formation of memories.
    b. most brain cells do not yet exist at the time of birth.
    c. experiences shortly after birth are a meaningless blur of darkness and light.
    d. many neural connections that underlie memories are only beginning to form shortly after birth.

Maturation and infant memory, p. 141
Medium, Factual/Definitional, Objective 3, Ans: a

22. Despite their poor memories of early life experiences, 14-month-olds are still capable of:
    a. imitating actions that they observed others perform three months earlier.
    b. remembering the trauma of their own birth.
    c. retaining lifelong memories of sexual abuse.
    d. all the above.

Motor development, p. 142
Medium, Factual/Definitional, Objective 3, Ans: c

23. Infant motor development is typically characterized by individual differences in ________ of the major developmental milestones.
    a. both the sequence and the age-related timing
    b. the sequence but not the age-related timing
    c. the age-related timing but not the sequence
    d. neither the sequence nor the age-related timing

Motor development, p. 142
Medium, Conceptual/Application, Objective 3, Ans: b

24. Horace, the youngest child of a high school athletic director, was able to roll over at 3 months, crawl at 6 months, and walk at 12 months. This ordered sequence of motor development was largely due to:
    a. habituation.
    b. maturation.
    c. responsive parenting.
    d. imprinting.

Motor development, p. 142
Medium, Conceptual/Application, Objective 3, Ans: d

25. Mr. and Mrs. Batson can't wait to begin toilet training their year-old daughter. The Batsons most clearly need to be informed about the importance of:
a. imprinting.
b. habituation.
c. fluid intelligence.
d. maturation.
e. object permanence.

Cognitive development, p. 143
Easy, Factual/Definitional, Objective 4, Ans: c

26. Piaget is best known for his interest in the process of ________ development.
a. motor
b. social
c. cognitive
d. emotional
e. physical

Cognitive development, p. 143
Medium, Factual/Definitional, Objective 4, Ans: c

27. Piaget was convinced that the mind of a child:
a. is like a blank slate at birth.
b. is not heavily influenced by maturation.
c. assimilates reality differently than an adult's does.
d. is heavily dependent on the child's personality.

Cognitive development, p. 143
Medium, Factual/Definitional, Objective 4, Ans: c

28. According to Piaget, schemas are:
a. fixed sequences of cognitive developmental stages.
b. children's ways of coming to terms with their sexuality.
c. people's conceptual frameworks for understanding their experiences.
d. problem-solving strategies that are typically not developed until the formal operational stage.

Cognitive development, p. 143
Medium, Conceptual/Application, Objective 4, Ans: d

29. Rita expected all college professors to be old, bearded males. She found it difficult to recognize young Kim Lee as a legitimate professor due to her own:
a. egocentrism.
b. stranger anxiety.
c. insecure attachment.
d. rigid schema.

Cognitive development, p. 143
Easy, Factual/Definitional, Objective 4, Ans: b

30. Interpreting new experiences in terms of existing schemas is called:
    a. egocentrism.
    b. assimilation.
    c. imprinting.
    d. attachment.
    e. accommodation.

Cognitive development, p. 143
Difficult, Conceptual/Application, Objective 4, Ans: a

31. The first time that 4-year-old Sarah saw her older brother play a flute, she thought it was simply a large whistle. Sarah's initial understanding of the flute best illustrates the process of:
    a. assimilation.
    b. egocentrism.
    c. conservation.
    d. accommodation.
    e. maturation.

Cognitive development, p. 143
Easy, Factual/Definitional, Objective 4, Ans: d

32. According to Piaget, accommodation refers to:
    a. parental efforts to include new children in the existing family structure.
    b. incorporating new experiences into existing schemas.
    c. developmental changes in a child's behavior that facilitate social acceptance by family and peers.
    d. adjusting current schemas in order to make sense of new experiences.

Cognitive development, p. 143
Medium, Conceptual/Application, Objective 4, Ans: c

33. Nageeb thought all nurses were young females until a middle-aged male nurse took care of him. Nageeb's altered conception of a "nurse" illustrates the process of:
    a. habituation.
    b. assimilation.
    c. accommodation.
    d. attachment.
    e. imprinting.

Cognitive development, p. 143
Medium, Conceptual, Objective 4, Ans: e

34. Incorporating new information into existing theories is to ________ as modifying existing theories in light of new information is to ________.
    a. conservation; habituation
    b. imprinting; maturation
    c. object permanence; insecure attachment
    d. sensorimotor stage; preoperational stage
    e. assimilation; accommodation

Piaget's theory and current thinking (Table 4.1), p. 144
Easy, Factual/Definitional, Objective 4, Ans: c

35. Which of the following represents the correct order of Piaget's stages of cognitive development?
   a. preoperational, concrete operational, formal operational, sensorimotor
   b. sensorimotor, preoperational, formal operational, concrete operational
   c. sensorimotor, preoperational, concrete operational, formal operational
   d. preoperational, sensorimotor, concrete operational, formal operational
   e. concrete operational, sensorimotor, preoperational, formal operational

Piaget's theory and current thinking, p. 144
Easy, Conceptual/Application, Objective 4, Ans: c

36. Olivia understands her world primarily by grasping and sucking easily available objects. Olivia is clearly in Piaget's ________ stage.
   a. preoperational
   b. concrete operational
   c. sensorimotor
   d. formal operational

Piaget's theory and current thinking, p. 144
Medium, Factual/Definitional, Objective 4, Ans: a

37. During which of Piaget's stages does a person develop an awareness that things continue to exist even when they are not perceived?
   a. sensorimotor
   b. preoperational
   c. concrete operational
   d. formal operational

Piaget's theory and current thinking, p. 144
Medium, Conceptual/Application, Objective 4, Ans: a

38. When Tommy's mother hides his favorite toy under a blanket, he acts as though it no longer exists and makes no attempt to retrieve it. Tommy is clearly in Piaget's ________ stage.
   a. sensorimotor
   b. formal operational
   c. concrete operational
   d. preoperational

Piaget's theory and current thinking, pp. 145-146
Medium, Factual/Definitional, Objective 4, Ans: a

39. When researcher Karen Wynn (1992, 1995) showed 5-month-old infants a numerically impossible outcome, the infants:
   a. stared longer at the outcome.
   b. displayed rapid habituation.
   c. demonstrated an obvious lack of object permanence.
   d. showed signs of formal operational reasoning.

Piaget's theory and current thinking, p. 146
Difficult, Factual/Definitional, Objective 4, Ans: b

40. Babies accustomed to a puppet jumping three times on stage show surprise if the puppet jumps only twice. This suggests that Piaget:
a. overestimated the continuity of cognitive development.
b. underestimated the cognitive capacities of infants.
c. overestimated the impact of culture on infant intelligence.
d. underestimated the impact of object permanence on infant attachment.

Piaget's theory and current thinking, p. 146
Medium, Factual/Definitional, Objective 4, Ans: d

41. According to Piaget, a child can represent things with words and images but cannot reason with logic during the ________ stage.
a. concrete operational
b. sensorimotor
c. formal operational
d. preoperational

Piaget's theory and current thinking, p. 146
Medium, Factual/Definitional, Objective 4, Ans: c

42. If children cannot grasp the principle of conservation, they are unable to:
a. deal with the discipline of toilet training.
b. see things from the point of view of another person.
c. recognize that the quantity of a substance remains the same despite changes in its shape.
d. retain earlier schemas when confronted by new experiences.

Piaget's theory and current thinking, p. 146
Difficult, Conceptual/Application, Objective 4, Ans: b

43. Mrs. Pearson cut Judy's hot dog into eight pieces and Sylvia's into six pieces. Sylvia cried because she felt she wasn't getting as much hot dog as Judy. Piaget would say that Sylvia doesn't understand the principle of:
a. object permanence.
b. conservation.
c. assimilation.
d. egocentrism.
e. accommodation.

Piaget's theory and current thinking, p. 146
Easy, Factual/Definitional, Objective 4, Ans: c

44. The egocentrism of preschoolers was most strongly emphasized by:
a. Haidt's social intuitionist theory.
b. Kohlberg's moral development theory.
c. Piaget's cognitive development theory.
d. Erikson's psychosocial development theory.

Piaget's theory and current thinking, p. 146
Easy, Factual/Definitional, Objective 4, Ans: c

45. According to Piaget, egocentrism refers to:
   a. a sensorimotor need for self-stimulation, as evidenced in thumb sucking.
   b. young children's exaggerated interest in themselves and their own pleasure.
   c. the inability to perceive things from another person's point of view.
   d. the inability to realize that things continue to exist even when they are not visible.

Piaget's theory and current thinking, p. 146
Difficult, Conceptual/Application, Objective 4, Ans: e

46. Four-year-old Jennifer mistakenly believes that her mother would like to receive a toy doll as a Christmas present. This best illustrates Piaget's concept of:
   a. accommodation.
   b. attachment.
   c. object permanence.
   d. conservation.
   e. egocentrism.

Piaget's theory and current thinking, p. 146
Difficult, Conceptual, Objective 4, Ans: a

47. A tendency to exaggerate the extent to which our own opinions are shared by others best illustrates:
   a. egocentrism.
   b. habituation.
   c. conservation.
   d. accommodation.

Piaget's theory and current thinking, p. 147
Difficult, Conceptual, Objective 4, Ans: b

48. Preschoolers' acquisition of a theory of mind suggests that Piaget overestimated young children's:
   a. accommodation.
   b. egocentrism.
   c. habituation.
   d. stranger anxiety.
   e. sense of object permanence.

Piaget's theory and current thinking, p. 147
Easy, Factual/Definitional, Objective 4, Ans: c

49. Five-year-olds who were surprised to discover that a Band-Aids box contained pencils subsequently delighted in anticipating their friend's false belief about the contents of the box. This best illustrates that the children had developed a(n):
   a. secure attachment.
   b. conventional morality.
   c. theory of mind.
   d. concept of conservation.

Piaget's theory and current thinking, p. 147
Medium, Conceptual/Application, Objective 4, Ans: d

50. Chloe can clearly sense when her sister's teasing is intended to be friendly fun or a hostile put-down. This best illustrates that Chloe has developed a(n):
    a. sense of object permanence.
    b. insecure attachment.
    c. concept of conservation.
    d. theory of mind.

Piaget's theory and current thinking, p. 147
Easy, Factual/Definitional/Application, Objective 4, Ans: e

51. An impaired theory of mind is most closely associated with:
    a. fetal alcohol syndrome.
    b. crystallized intelligence.
    c. concrete operational thought.
    d. role confusion.
    e. autism.

Piaget's theory and current thinking, p. 148
Difficult, Factual/Definitional, Objective 4, Ans: c

52. The Russian psychologist Vygotsky suggested that children's ability to solve problems is enhanced by:
    a. basic trust.
    b. egocentrism.
    c. inner speech.
    d. conservation.
    e. imprinting.

Piaget's theory and current thinking, pp. 144, 148
Medium, Factual/Definitional, Objective 4, Ans: c

53. According to Piaget, the ability to think logically about events first develops during the ________ stage.
    a. sensorimotor
    b. formal operational
    c. concrete operational
    d. preoperational

Piaget's theory and current thinking, p. 148
Medium, Factual/Definitional, Objective 4, Ans: c

54. According to Piaget, children come to understand that the volume of a substance remains constant despite changes in its shape during the ________ stage.
    a. sensorimotor
    b. preoperational
    c. concrete operational
    d. formal operational

Piaget's theory and current thinking, pp. 144, 148
Difficult, Conceptual, Objective 4, Ans: e

55. According to Piaget, egocentrism is to conservation as the ________ stage is to the ________ stage.
   a. preoperational; sensorimotor
   b. concrete operational; preoperational
   c. sensorimotor; preoperational
   d. concrete operational; formal operational
   e. preoperational; concrete operational

Piaget's theory and current thinking, p. 148
Medium, Conceptual, Objective 4, Ans: b

56. According to Piaget, a person first comprehends that division is the reverse of multiplication during the ________ stage.
   a. preoperational
   b. concrete operational
   c. formal operational
   d. sensorimotor

Piaget's theory and current thinking, pp. 144, 148
Easy, Factual/Definitional, Objective 4, Ans: a

57. According to Piaget, during the formal operational stage people begin to:
   a. reason abstractly.
   b. adhere to social norms.
   c. distinguish between good and bad behaviors.
   d. become aware of the positive and negative consequences of their own behaviors.

Piaget's theory and current thinking, p. 149
Difficult, Conceptual, Objective 4, Ans: c

58. Four-year-olds are not completely egocentric and 5-year-olds can exhibit some understanding of conservation. This indicates that Piaget may have underestimated the:
   a. importance of critical periods in early life.
   b. role of motivation in cognitive development.
   c. continuity of cognitive development.
   d. importance of early attachment experiences.

Social development, p. 150
Difficult, Conceptual/Application, Objective 5, Ans: c

59. Lilianne is beginning to develop a fear of strangers and will reach for her mother when she sees someone who is unfamiliar. It is likely that Lilianne has just:
   a. mastered the principle of conservation.
   b. overcome the limitation of egocentrism.
   c. developed a sense of object permanence.
   d. lost her sense of secure attachment.

Social development, p. 150
Easy, Factual/Definitional, Objective 5, Ans: a

60. The powerful survival impulse that leads infants to seek closeness to their caregivers is called:
    a. attachment.
    b. imprinting.
    c. habituation.
    d. assimilation.
    e. the rooting reflex.

Social development, p. 150
Medium, Conceptual/Application, Objective 5, Ans: b

61. Little Karen will approach and play with unfamiliar animals only if her mother first reassures her that it is safe to do so. This best illustrates the adaptive value of:
    a. conservation.
    b. attachment.
    c. habituation.
    d. egocentrism.
    e. imprinting.

Origins of attachment: body contact, p. 151
Medium, Factual/Definitional, Objective 5, Ans: b

62. Studies of monkeys raised with artificial mothers suggest that mother-infant emotional bonds result primarily from mothers providing infants with:
    a. adequate nourishment.
    b. body contact.
    c. the opportunity to explore.
    d. protection from harm.
    e. self-esteem.

Origins of attachment: body contact, p. 151
Easy, Factual/Definitional, Objective 5, Ans: d

63. Providing children with a safe haven in times of stress contributes most directly to:
    a. habituation.
    b. stranger anxiety.
    c. object permanence.
    d. secure attachment.
    e. egocentrism.

Origins of attachment: familiarity, p. 151
Medium, Factual/Definitional, Objective 5, Ans: d

64. A critical period is a phase during which:
    a. children frequently disobey and resist their parents.
    b. children become able to think hypothetically and reason abstractly.
    c. parents frequently show impatience with a child's slowness in becoming toilet trained.
    d. certain events have a particularly strong impact on development.

Origins of attachment, p. 151
Easy, Factual/Definitional, Objective 5, Ans: a

65. The process of imprinting involves the formation of a(n):
   a. attachment.
   b. identity.
   c. theory of mind.
   d. primary sex characteristic.

Origins of attachment: familiarity, p. 151
Medium, Conceptual/Application, Objective 5, Ans: c

66. Which of the following is an example of imprinting?
   a. A 2-year-old poodle approaches a stranger who calls it.
   b. A 4-year-old boy imitates aggression he sees on television.
   c. A duckling demonstrates attachment to a bouncing ball.
   d. A 3-year-old girl is simultaneously learning two different languages.

Origins of attachment: familiarity, pp. 151-152
Difficult, Conceptual/Application, Objective 5, Ans: a

67. Carol is distressed because post-childbirth complications prevented her from being in close physical contact with her child during its first few hours of life. Carol should be told that:
   a. human infants do not have well-defined critical periods for the formation of a mother-infant attachment.
   b. physical contact with her infant immediately after birth would not contribute to the development of mother-infant attachment.
   c. infants should be left physically undisturbed during the first few hours of life so they can rest.
   d. as long as she can breast-feed her baby, no lasting damage will be done.

Origins of attachment: responsive parenting, p. 152
Easy, Conceptual/Application, Objective 5, Ans: c

68. One-year-old Eunice is not overly fearful of strangers but she clearly prefers being held by her mother than by anyone else. Her behavior best illustrates:
   a. habituation.
   b. the rooting reflex.
   c. secure attachment.
   d. conservation.
   e. egocentrism.

Origins of attachment: responsive parenting, p. 152
Medium, Conceptual, Objective 5, Ans: c

69. Instead of happily exploring the attractive toys located in the pediatrician's waiting room, little Sandra tenaciously clings to her mother's skirt. Sandra most clearly shows signs of:
   a. habituation.
   b. egocentrism.
   c. insecure attachment.
   d. the rooting reflex.
   e. object permanence.

Origins of attachment: responsive parenting, p. 152
Medium, Conceptual/Application, Objective 5, Ans: e

70. Aaron was extremely upset when his mother left him in the infant nursery at church and he was not reassured or comforted by her return a short while later. Aaron showed signs of:
 a. egocentrism.
 b. habituation.
 c. conservation.
 d. assimilation.
 e. insecure attachment.

Origins of attachment: responsive parenting, p. 152
Medium, Factual/Definitional, Objective 5, Ans: b

71. In a pleasant but unfamiliar setting, infants with a secure maternal attachment are most likely to:
 a. act as though their mothers are of little importance to them.
 b. use their mothers as a base from which to explore the new surroundings.
 c. cling to their mothers and ignore the new surroundings.
 d. show hostility when their mothers approach them after a brief absence.

Origins of attachment: responsive parenting, pp. 135, 152
Difficult, Conceptual, Objective 5, Ans: d

72. Nature is to nurture as ________ is to ________.
 a. secure attachment; imprinting
 b. heredity; maturation
 c. accommodation; assimilation
 d. temperament; responsive parenting

Origins of attachment: responsive parenting, p. 152
Medium, Factual/Definitional, Objective 5, Ans: b

73. Which of the following factors contributes most positively to the development of secure attachment between human infants and their mothers?
 a. breast-feeding
 b. responsive parenting
 c. family planning
 d. authoritarian discipline

Origins of attachment: responsive parenting, p. 152
Difficult, Conceptual, Objective 5, Ans: b

74. Some mothers feed their infants when they show signs of hunger, whereas others fail to respond predictably to their infants' demands for food. These different maternal feeding practices are most likely to contribute to differences in infant:
 a. habituation.
 b. attachment.
 c. conservation.
 d. maturation.
 e. egocentrism.

Origins of attachment: responsive parenting, p. 152
Easy, Factual/Definitional, Objective 5, Ans: c

75. A mother who is slow in responding to her infant's cries of distress is most likely to encourage:
   a. habituation.
   b. conservation.
   c. insecure attachment.
   d. object permanence.
   e. egocentrism.

Origins of attachment: responsive parenting, pp. 152, 154
Easy, Conceptual, Objective 5, Ans: c

76. Children's sense that their parents are trustworthy and dependable is most indicative of:
   a. maturation.
   b. accommodation.
   c. secure attachment.
   d. object permanence.
   e. habituation.

Origins of attachment: responsive parenting, p. 152
Medium, Conceptual/Application, Objective 5, Ans: e

77. Two-year-old Anna perceives her parents as cold and rejecting. This is most indicative of:
   a. habituation.
   b. egocentrism.
   c. accommodation.
   d. crystallized intelligence.
   e. insecure attachment.

Origins of attachment: responsive parenting, p. 152
Medium, Conceptual, Objective 5, Ans: a

78. When placed in strange situations without their artificial mothers, Harlow's infant monkeys demonstrated signs of:
   a. insecure attachment.
   b. egocentrism.
   c. basic trust.
   d. curiosity.

Effects of attachment, p. 154
Medium, Conceptual, Objective 6, Ans: d

79. Three-year-old Angela has a history of being securely attached to her mother. It is most likely that Angela is:
   a. unusually intelligent but also highly anxious.
   b. easily frustrated and irritable when her mother is absent.
   c. preoccupied with maintaining close physical contact with her mother.
   d. outgoing and responsive in her interactions with other children.

Effects of attachment, p. 154
Easy, Conceptual/Application, Objective 6, Ans: a

80. Marlys is a sensitive, responsive parent who consistently satisfies the needs of Sara, her infant daughter. According to Erikson, Sara is likely to:
   a. form a lifelong attitude of basic trust toward the world.
   b. encounter some difficulty in overcoming the limitation of egocentrism.
   c. encounter some difficulty in forming an attachment to her father.
   d. achieve formal operational intelligence more quickly than the average child.

Deprivation of attachment, p. 154
Medium, Factual/Definitional, Objective 6, Ans: b

81. Harlow observed that most monkeys raised in total isolation:
   a. were totally apathetic and indifferent to the first monkeys they encountered.
   b. were incapable of mating upon reaching sexual maturity.
   c. showed slower social development but more rapid cognitive development.
   d. showed no lasting adverse effects when placed in a socially enriched environment.

Deprivation of attachment, p. 154
Difficult, Conceptual/Application, Objective 6, Ans: c

82. Edith abuses both her 3-year-old and 1-year-old daughters. Her behavior is most likely related to a lack of:
   a. childhood experience with younger brothers and sisters.
   b. maturation.
   c. an early and secure attachment to her own parents.
   d. formal operational intelligence.
   e. object permanence.

Deprivation of attachment, p. 155
Medium, Factual/Definitional, Objective 6, Ans: b

83. When golden hamsters were repeatedly threatened and attacked while young, they suffered long-term changes in:
   a. object permanence.
   b. brain chemistry.
   c. the rooting reflex.
   d. maturation.
   e. habituation.

Disruption of attachment, p. 155
Difficult, Factual/Definitional, Objective 6, Ans: b

84. When infants between 6 and 16 months of age are removed from their foster mothers and placed in stable adoptive homes, they typically show:
   a. initial distress in infancy and subsequent maladjustment at age 10.
   b. initial distress in infancy but no subsequent maladjustment at age 10.
   c. no initial distress in infancy but subsequent maladjustment at age 10.
   d. neither initial distress in infancy nor subsequent maladjustment at age 10.

Disruption of attachment, p. 155
Easy, Conceptual/Application, Objective 6, Ans: e

85. For several months following a sudden and unexpected divorce, Henry was excessively preoccupied with thoughts of his ex-wife. His reaction resulted from the disruption of:
a. a critical period.
b. habituation.
c. accommodation.
d. object permanence.
e. attachment.

Does day care affect attachment?, p. 155
Medium, Conceptual/Application, Objective 6, Ans: c

86. In considering day-care opportunities for their four children, Mr. and Mrs. Taylor should be most concerned about whether the experience will influence:
a. egocentrism in their 3-year-old son, James.
b. object permanence in their 2-year-old son, Billy.
c. secure attachment in their 6-month-old daughter, Julia.
d. maturation in their 4-year-old daughter, Sandra.

Self-concept, p. 156
Medium, Conceptual/Application, Objective 7, Ans: a

87. Mrs. Carmichael secretly dabs some lipstick on the nose of her 2-year-old son and then allows him to see his face in a mirror. The child is most likely to:
a. touch his own nose.
b. touch the mirror at the point where the lipstick shows.
c. wave at his mirror image as if it were another child.
d. assimilate the lipstick mark into his existing self-concept.

Self-concept, p. 157
Difficult, Factual/Definitional, Objective 7, Ans: c

88. Compared to others their own age, children who form a positive self-concept are more likely to be:
a. obedient.
b. egocentric.
c. sociable.
d. habituated.

Child-rearing practices, p. 157
Medium, Conceptual, Objective 7, Ans: c

89. Authoritarian parents demonstrate ________ levels of parental control and ________ levels of parental responsiveness.
a. high; high
b. low; low
c. high; low
d. low; high

Child-rearing practices, p. 157
Easy, Conceptual/Application, Objective 7, Ans: a

90. The McDougals use harsh discipline on their children and demand unquestioning obedience. Psychologists are likely to characterize the McDougals as ________ parents.
a. authoritarian
b. egocentric
c. disengaged
d. authoritative

Child-rearing practices, p. 157
Easy, Factual/Definitional, Objective 7, Ans: e

91. Parents who are demanding and yet sensitively responsive to their children are said to be:
a. authoritarian.
b. accommodating.
c. egocentric.
d. permissive.
e. authoritative.

Child-rearing practices, p. 157
Medium, Factual/Definitional, Objective 7, Ans: b

92. Authoritative parents are likely to have children who:
a. are obedient but have low self-esteem.
b. have high self-esteem and are self-reliant.
c. have high self-esteem but are somewhat dependent.
d. are rebellious and have low self-esteem.

Child-rearing practices, p. 157
Medium, Conceptual, Objective 7, Ans: d

93. At age 12, Sean is happy, self-reliant, and has a positive self-image. It is most likely that Sean's parents are:
a. permissive.
b. conservative.
c. authoritarian.
d. authoritative.

Child-rearing practices, pp. 157-158
Medium, Factual/Definitional, Objective 7, Ans: d

94. Children are likely to experience the greatest sense of personal control over their lives if their parents are:
a. permissive.
b. disengaged.
c. authoritarian.
d. authoritative.

Child-rearing practices, p. 158
Medium, Factual/Definitional, Objective 7, Ans: c

95. Compared to authoritarian parents, authoritative parents are likely to be:
a. more conservative.
b. less educated.
c. more responsive.
d. less trusting.

Adolescence, p. 159
Easy, Factual/Definitional, Objective 8, Ans: c

96. Adolescence extends from:
   a. the beginning of concrete operations to the end of formal operations.
   b. 12 to 15 years of age.
   c. the beginnings of sexual maturity to independent adulthood.
   d. the beginning to the end of the growth spurt.

Adolescence, p. 159
Medium, Factual/Definitional, Objective 8, Ans: b

97. Early puberty is especially likely among ________ girls in ________ homes.
   a. underweight; father-absent.
   b. overweight; father-absent
   c. underweight; father-present
   d. overweight; father-present

Adolescence, p. 160
Medium, Factual/Definitional, Objective 8, Ans: c

98. In contemporary industrialized societies, adolescence typically begins ________ in life and ends ________ in life than it did in previous centuries.
   a. earlier; earlier
   b. later; earlier
   c. earlier; later
   d. later; later

Adolescent physical development, p. 161
Easy, Factual/Definitional, Objective 8, Ans: b

99. People experience surging physical growth and sexual maturation during:
   a. late adolescence.
   b. puberty.
   c. the preoperational stage.
   d. late childhood.

Adolescent physical development, p. 161
Easy, Factual/Definitional, Objective 8, Ans: a

100. The body structures that enable reproduction are the:
   a. primary sex characteristics.
   b. secondary sex characteristics.
   c. teratogens.
   d. sex-linked genes.
   e. gender schemas.

Adolescent physical development, p. 161
Easy, Factual/Definitional, Objective 8, Ans: b

101. Which of the following is an example of a secondary sex characteristic?
   a. female ovaries
   b. male facial hair
   c. the male grip
   d. female height

Adolescent physical development, pp. 161-162
Difficult, Conceptual, Objective 8, Ans: b

102. Primary sex characteristics are to ________ as secondary sex characteristics are to ________.
   a. male testes; adrenal glands
   b. female ovaries; deepened male voice
   c. female breasts; deepened male voice
   d. male testes; female ovaries
   e. adrenal glands; underarm hair

Adolescent physical development, p. 162
Easy, Factual/Definitional, Objective 8, Ans: c

103. Compared to "late bloomers," boys who mature sexually at an early age tend to be more:
   a. physically uncoordinated.
   b. sexually inhibited.
   c. popular and self-assured.
   d. academically successful.

Adolescent physical development, p. 162
Medium, Conceptual/Application, Objective 8, Ans: d

104. Ten-year-old Heidi is maturing early and already towers over all the girls and most of the boys in her fifth-grade class. Heidi is likely to be:
   a. the most popular student in class.
   b. self-assured and independent.
   c. challenging her teacher's authority.
   d. the object of some teasing.

Adolescent physical development, p. 163
Easy, Factual/Definitional, Objective 8, Ans: b

105. Puberty is most closely related to the onset of:
   a. menopause.
   b. menarche.
   c. crystallized intelligence.
   d. conventional morality.
   e. dementia.

Adolescent physical development, p. 163
Easy, Conceptual, Objective 8, Ans: d

106. The first ejaculation is to an adolescent boy as ________ is to an adolescent girl.
   a. sexual intercourse
   b. puberty
   c. the first kiss
   d. menarche
   e. secure attachment

Developing reasoning power, p. 163
Easy, Factual/Definitional, Objective 9, Ans: d

107. The ability to think logically about hypothetical situations is indicative of the ________ stage of development.
   a. conventional
   b. preconventional
   c. preoperational
   d. formal operational

Developing reasoning power, p. 163
Medium, Conceptual/Application, Objective 9, Ans: d

108. Fourteen-year-old Lisa was asked, "What would happen if everyone in the world suddenly went blind?" She responded, "Those who had previously been blind would become leaders." Lisa's answer indicates she is in the ________ stage of development.
   a. concrete operational
   b. preconventional
   c. postconventional
   d. formal operational
   e. preoperational

Developing morality, p. 164
Easy, Conceptual, Objective 9, Ans: c

109. Piaget is to cognitive development as Kohlberg is to ________ development.
   a. emotional
   b. physical
   c. moral
   d. social

Developing morality, p. 164
Medium, Factual/Definitional, Objective 9, Ans: c

110. According to Kohlberg, morality based on the avoidance of punishment and the attainment of concrete rewards represents a(n) ________ morality.
   a. egocentric
   b. conventional
   c. preconventional
   d. concrete operational
   e. postconventional

Developing morality, p. 164
Difficult, Conceptual/Application, Objective 9, Ans: c

111. A person who thinks it's wrong to drive over the speed limit simply because one might get punished for doing so is demonstrating Kohlberg's ________ stage of morality.
   a. conventional
   b. postconventional
   c. preconventional
   d. preoperational
   e. formal operational

Developing morality, p. 164
Medium, Factual/Definitional, Objective 9, Ans: a

112. Even though smoking marijuana would reduce the pain associated with her chronic medical condition, Juanita believes it would be morally wrong because it is prohibited by the laws of her state. Kohlberg would suggest that Juanita demonstrates a(n) _______ morality.
a. conventional
b. unconventional
c. preconventional
d. postconventional

Developing morality, p. 164
Medium, Factual/Definitional, Objective 9, Ans: b

113. According to Kohlberg, postconventional morality involves:
a. behavior based on self-interest.
b. affirmation of self-defined ethical principles.
c. strong concern for social approval.
d. unquestioning obedience to authority figures.

Developing morality, p. 164
Medium, Conceptual, Objective 9, Ans: a

114. Despite huge legal costs and social disapproval, Mr. Lambers refuses to pay income taxes because his conscience will not allow him to support a government that spends billions of dollars on military weapons. Mr. Lambers's reasoning best illustrates Kohlberg's ________ stage.
a. postconventional
b. concrete operational
c. preconventional
d. egocentric
e. conventional

Developing morality, p. 164
Difficult, Conceptual, Objective 9, Ans: e

115. Avoiding physical punishment is to ________ morality as respecting the laws of society is to ________ morality.
a. conventional; postconventional
b. preconventional; postconventional
c. postconventional; conventional
d. conventional; preconventional
e. preconventional; conventional

Developing morality, pp. 164-165
Easy, Factual/Definitional, Objective 9, Ans: c

116. Kohlberg emphasized that human behavior becomes less selfish as we mature due to:
a. social development.
b. physical development.
c. cognitive development.
d. economic development.

Developing morality, p. 165
Difficult, Factual/Definitional, Objective 9, Ans: b

117. Compared with adults from Western cultures that favor individualism, those from communal societies are *less* likely to develop ________ morality.
a. preconventional
b. postconventional
c. concrete operational
d. conventional
e. preoperational

Developing morality, p. 165
Medium, Factual/Definitional, Objective 9, Ans: a

118. Critics of Kohlberg's theory of moral development have suggested that postconventional morality is more characteristic of ________ than of ________.
a. men; women
b. Democrats; Republicans
c. socialists; capitalists
d. African Americans; white Americans
e. Catholics; Protestants

Developing morality, p. 165
Medium, Factual/Definitional, Objective 9, Ans: d

119. Haidt's social intuitionist account highlights the impact of automatic gut-level feelings on:
a. attachment.
b. habituation.
c. egocentrism.
d. moral judgments.
e. stranger anxiety.

Developing morality, p. 165
Difficult, Conceptual, Objective 9, Ans: c

120. Many people would find it more morally repulsive to kill someone by thrusting a knife into his or her body than by shooting him or her with a gun from a distance. This is best explained in terms of:
a. Erikson's psychosocial development theory.
b. Piaget's cognitive development theory.
c. Haidt's social intuitionist theory.
d. Kohlberg's moral development theory.

Developing morality, p. 165
Difficult, Factual/Definitional, Objective 9, Ans: a

121. The corrupt behavior of many ordinary people who served as Nazi concentration camp guards best illustrates that immorality often results from:
a. social influence.
b. crystallized intelligence.
c. abnormal cognitive development.
d. postconventional moral thinking.

Social development, p. 166
Medium, Conceptual, Objective 10, Ans: e

122. According to Erikson, trust is to ________ as identity is to ________.
   a. infancy; childhood
   b. childhood; adolescence
   c. adulthood; childhood
   d. adolescence; adulthood
   e. infancy; adolescence

Social development, p. 166
Medium, Conceptual, Objective 10, Ans: e

123. According to Erikson, isolation is to intimacy as role confusion is to:
   a. mistrust.
   b. guilt.
   c. competence.
   d. inferiority.
   e. identity.

Social development, pp. 166-167
Easy, Factual/Definitional, Objective 10, Ans: d

124. According to Erikson, achieving a sense of identity is the special task of the:
   a. toddler.
   b. preschooler.
   c. elementary school child.
   d. adolescent.

Forming an identity, p. 167
Difficult, Conceptual, Objective 10, Ans: c

125. Erikson would have suggested that adolescents can most effectively develop a sense of identity by:
   a. seeking a lifelong romantic relationship.
   b. severing the emotional ties between themselves and their childhood friends.
   c. investigating the personal suitability of various occupational and social roles.
   d. adopting whatever values and expectations their parents recommend.

Forming an identity, p. 167
Medium, Conceptual/Application, Objective 10, Ans: b

126. Sixteen-year-old Brenda questions her parents' values but does not fully accept her friends' standards either. Her confusion about what she really wants and values in life suggests that Brenda is struggling with the problem of:
   a. autonomy.
   b. identity.
   c. initiative.
   d. integrity.

Forming an identity, p. 167
Difficult, Conceptual, Objective 10, Ans: c

127. Branden is so apathetic about his occupational future that within two years of his high school graduation he had already been fired by four different employers. According to Erikson, Branden best illustrates:
   a. crystallized intelligence.
   b. preconventional morality.
   c. role confusion.
   d. egocentrism.

Forming an identity, p. 167
Easy, Factual/Definitional, Objective 10, Ans: b

128. The self-esteem of young Americans tends to _______ while progressing through the early teen years and _______ while progressing through the late teen years.
   a. rise; fall
   b. fall; rise
   c. rise; rise
   d. fall; fall

Developing intimacy, p. 168
Medium, Factual/Definitional, Objective 10, Ans: b

129. Erikson suggested that the adolescent search for identity is followed by a developing capacity for:
   a. competence.
   b. intimacy.
   c. autonomy.
   d. trust.

Developing intimacy, p. 168
Easy, Factual/Definitional, Objective 10, Ans: b

130. Compared with males, females are more likely to base their sense of personal identity on their:
   a. gender.
   b. social relationships.
   c. educational accomplishments.
   d. socially distinctive personality traits.

Developing intimacy, p. 168
Medium, Factual/Definitional, Objective 10, Ans: d

131. Girls typically play in ________ groups than do boys and, during their teens, girls spend ________ time with friends than do boys.
   a. larger; more
   b. smaller; less
   c. larger; less
   d. smaller; more

Developing intimacy, p. 168
Difficult, Conceptual, Objective 10, Ans: c

132. The "male answer syndrome" suggests that males are less likely than females to demonstrate:
   a. fluid intelligence.
   b. stranger anxiety.
   c. intellectual humility.
   d. conventional morality.

Developing intimacy, p. 168
Easy, Factual/Definitional, Objective 10, Ans: e

133. Women are more likely than men to:
   a. criticize and insult their marital partner.
   b. stare at people who make them angry.
   c. interrupt others while they are talking.
   d. misperceive simple friendliness as a sexual come-on.
   e. engage in intimate conversations with others.

Developing intimacy, p. 169
Medium, Factual/Definitional, Objective 10, Ans: c

134. When looking for someone to whom they can confide their personal worries, women usually turn to ________ and men usually turn to ________.
   a. men; men
   b. women; men
   c. women; women
   d. men; women

Developing intimacy, p. 169
Medium, Factual/Definitional, Objective 10, Ans: d

135. As teenagers progress through adolescence, girls become ________ assertive and boys become ________ assertive.
   a. more; more
   b. less; less
   c. more; less
   d. less; more

Separating from parents, p. 170
Difficult, Factual/Definitional, Objective 10, Ans: a

136. Research indicates that the high school girls who have the most affectionate relationships with their mothers also tend to:
   a. have the most intimate relationships with girlfriends.
   b. have somewhat less intimate relationships with girlfriends.
   c. take longer than normal to establish their own independence and separate identity.
   d. have difficulty forming intimate relationships with boys.

Separating from parents, p. 171
Difficult, Factual/Definitional, Objective 10, Ans: b

137. Compared with Americans 40 years ago, Americans today are likely to:
   a. establish their adult careers at an earlier age.
   b. marry for the first time at a later age.
   c. live separately from their parents at an earlier age.
   d. experience their first menstrual period at a later age.

Physical changes in middle adulthood, p. 172
Easy, Factual/Definitional, Objective 11, Ans: b

138. Physical abilities such as muscular strength, reaction time, sensory keenness, and cardiac output reach their peak during:
   a. late adolescence.
   b. early adulthood.
   c. puberty.
   d. middle adulthood.

Physical changes in middle adulthood, p. 173
Easy, Factual/Definitional, Objective 11, Ans: a

139. Menopause refers to:
   a. the cessation of menstruation.
   b. the loss of male sexual potency.
   c. irregular timing of menstrual periods.
   d. the loss of sexual interest in late adulthood.

Physical changes in middle adulthood, p. 173
Medium, Conceptual/Application, Objective 11, Ans: d

140. Fifty-two-year-old Jasmine is beginning menopause. If she is like many North American women, she will experience:
   a. a significant loss of sexual desire.
   b. a period of significant depression.
   c. a dramatic loss of physical energy.
   d. occasional hot flashes.

Physical changes in middle adulthood, pp. 173-174
Medium, Factual/Definitional, Objective 11, Ans: b

141. When asked if it is true that after menopause "women generally feel better than they have for years," most premenopausal women under age 45 said ________ and most older women who had already experienced menopause said ________.
   a. yes; yes
   b. no; yes
   c. yes; no
   d. no; no

Physical changes in middle adulthood, p. 174
Medium, Factual/Definitional, Objective 11, Ans: d

142. Testosterone replacement therapy may be used for the treatment of:
   a. depression.
   b. sexual impotence.
   c. physical weakness.
   d. all of the above.

Physical changes in middle adulthood, p. 174
Easy, Factual/Definitional, Objective 11, Ans: d

143. As men advance through middle adulthood they experience a gradual decline in:
 a. testosterone level.
 b. sperm count.
 c. ejaculation speed.
 d. all of the above.

Physical changes in later life, p. 175
Easy, Factual/Definitional, Objective 11, Ans: a

144. The ratio of males to females first begins declining during:
 a. prenatal development.
 b. infancy.
 c. childhood.
 d. adolescence.
 e. adulthood.

Physical changes in later life, pp. 175-176
Easy, Conceptual, Objective 11, Ans: a

145. Lewis is a 70-year-old retired college professor. In contrast to when he was 30, he now probably:
 a. does not hear as well.
 b. is more susceptible to catching the flu.
 c. has significantly fewer neural connections.
 d. has all of the above problems.

Physical changes in later life, p. 176
Easy, Factual/Definitional, Objective 11, Ans: c

146. Elderly people are *not* increasingly susceptible to:
 a. pneumonia.
 b. Parkinson's disease.
 c. common cold viruses.
 d. dementia.

Physical changes in later life, p. 176
Medium, Factual/Definitional, Objective 11, Ans: a

147. Most Americans over 65 years of age believe that:
 a. they suffer fewer health problems than do other people their age.
 b. they do not have enough money to live on.
 c. their hearing and vision are just as good as when they were young adults.
 d. their lives are less satisfying now than when they were adolescents.

Physical changes in later life, p. 177
Difficult, Factual/Definitional, Objective 11, Ans: b

148. Research on the elderly has shown that:
 a. they grow increasingly fearful of death.
 b. they become increasingly prone to car accidents.
 c. most eventually become senile.
 d. they experience less life satisfaction than younger adults.

Dementia and Alzheimer's disease, pp. 177-178
Medium, Factual/Definitional, Objective 11, Ans: c

149. Dementia is most commonly associated with:
 a. menopause.
 b. role confusion.
 c. Alzheimer's disease.
 d. crystallized intelligence.

Dementia and Alzheimer's disease, p. 178
Easy, Conceptual/Application, Objective 11, Ans: d

150. During the last few years, 75-year-old Mrs. Yamaguchi has gradually become so mentally disoriented that she can't find her way around her own house and often fails to recognize her husband. It is most likely that Mrs. Yamaguchi is suffering the effects of:
 a. crystallized intelligence.
 b. menopause.
 c. habituation.
 d. Alzheimer's disease.

Dementia and Alzheimer's disease, p. 178
Easy, Factual/Definitional, Objective 11, Ans: c

151. Alzheimer's disease involves a deterioration of neurons that produce:
 a. dopamine.
 b. estrogen.
 c. acetylcholine.
 d. epinephrine.

Aging and memory, p. 179
Medium, Factual/Definitional, Objective 12, Ans: c

152. When adults of varying ages were tested for their memory of a recently learned list of 24 words, the older adults demonstrated:
 a. no decline in either recall or recognition.
 b. a decline in recognition but not in recall.
 c. a decline in recall but not in recognition.
 d. a decline in both recognition and recall.

Aging and memory, p. 180
Difficult, Factual/Definitional, Objective 12, Ans: a

153. On which of the following tasks is a 20-year-old most likely to outperform a 70-year-old?
 a. recalling previously presented nonsense syllables
 b. recognizing previously presented foreign-language words
 c. recalling previously presented names of cities
 d. recognizing previously presented names of fruits and vegetables

Aging and intelligence, p. 180
Easy, Factual/Definitional, Objective 12, Ans: b

154. A cross-sectional study is one in which:
 a. the same people are retested over a period of years.
 b. different age groups are tested at the same time.
 c. different characteristics of a given individual are assessed at the same time.
 d. the behavior of a group is assessed by different researchers.

Aging and intelligence, p. 180
Medium, Factual/Definitional, Objective 12, Ans: b

155. Cross-sectional research indicated that during early and middle adulthood, aging is associated with ________ levels of intelligence. Longitudinal research indicated that during this same period of life, aging is associated with ________ levels of intelligence.
   a. increasing; declining
   b. declining; increasing
   c. increasing; increasing
   d. declining; declining

Aging and memory, pp. 180, 181
Difficult, Conceptual, Objective 12, Ans: b

156. Older people's capacity to learn and remember meaningful material does not decline as much as their capacity to learn and remember meaningless material. This best illustrates the value of:
   a. concrete operational thought.
   b. crystallized intelligence.
   c. formal operational thought.
   d. fluid intelligence.

Aging and intelligence, p. 181
Easy, Factual/Definitional, Objective 12, Ans: d

157. Which of the following terms refers to a person's accumulated knowledge and verbal skills?
   a. fluid intelligence
   b. concrete operational intelligence
   c. formal operational intelligence
   d. crystallized intelligence

Aging and intelligence, p. 181
Easy, Factual/Definitional, Objective 12, Ans: b

158. Fluid intelligence refers most directly to a person's:
   a. accumulated knowledge.
   b. ability to reason speedily and abstractly.
   c. ability to assume the perspective of others.
   d. ability to solve practical problems effectively and efficiently.

Aging and intelligence, pp. 181-182
Medium, Conceptual, Objective 12, Ans: c

159. The development of expertise in specific academic disciplines most clearly illustrates:
   a. autonomy.
   b. maturation.
   c. crystallized intelligence.
   d. concrete operational thought.

Aging and intelligence, pp. 181-182
Difficult, Conceptual/Application, Objective 12, Ans: c

160. In order to qualify for the office manager's job, 55-year-old Mariel's must take a series of psychological tests. Her performance on the test of ________ is likely to be poorer than if she had taken it as a 25-year-old.
   a. general knowledge
   b. spelling
   c. abstract reasoning
   d. vocabulary
   e. verbal comprehension

Aging and intelligence, p. 182
Difficult, Conceptual/Application, Objective 12, Ans: d

161. The ability to learn a new computer software program is to ________ as knowledge of state capitals is to ________.
   a. concrete operations; formal operations
   b. formal operations; concrete operations
   c. crystallized intelligence; fluid intelligence
   d. fluid intelligence; crystallized intelligence

Aging and intelligence, p. 182
Difficult, Factual/Definitional, Objective 12, Ans: d

162. Explaining why the best work of scientists is often produced in early adulthood while that of novelists often originates during middle adulthood requires a distinction between:
   a. initiative and generativity.
   b. concrete and formal operations.
   c. cross-sectional and longitudinal studies.
   d. fluid and crystallized intelligence.
   e. conventional and postconventional morality.

Adulthood's ages and stages, p. 182
Easy, Factual/Definitional, Objective 13, Ans: d

163. Researchers have discovered that the transition phase between early and middle adulthood is characterized by unusually high levels of:
   a. job dissatisfaction and career change.
   b. marital dissatisfaction and divorce.
   c. anxiety and emotional instability.
   d. none of the above.

Adulthood's ages and stages, p. 183
Easy, Conceptual/Application, Objective 13, Ans: a

164. The age at which people are expected to leave home, get a job, and marry has changed dramatically in Wallonia over the past 50 years. Developmentalists would say that the country's ________ has been altered.
   a. social clock
   b. developmental norm
   c. maturation cycle
   d. family calendar

Adulthood's ages and stages, p. 183
Medium, Factual/Definitional, Objective 13, Ans: e

165. Those who criticize theories of age-linked adult developmental stages are most likely to emphasize the importance of ________ on adult development.
   a. fluid intelligence
   b. genetic predispositions
   c. secondary sex characteristics
   d. formal operational thought
   e. the social clock

Adulthood's ages and stages, p. 183
Medium, Factual/Definitional, Objective 13, Ans: d

166. Identical twins with similar values and preferences are not very strongly attracted to one another's fiancés. This fact has been used to suggest that romantic attraction is influenced by:
   a. fluid intelligence.
   b. the social clock.
   c. secondary sex characteristics.
   d. chance encounters.
   e. basic trust.

Adulthood's commitments, p. 184
Easy, Factual/Definitional, Objective 14, Ans: c

167. Compared to 40 years ago, American men today are marrying at a(n) ________ age and American women are marrying at a(n) ________ age.
   a. younger; older
   b. older; younger
   c. older; older
   d. younger; younger

Adulthood's commitments, p. 184
Medium, Conceptual/Application, Objective 14, Ans: d

168. After living together for a year, Sylvia and Yefim have decided to marry. Research on premarital cohabitation most strongly suggests that:
   a. they have more positive attitudes toward the institution of marriage than the average couple.
   b. their marriage will have a higher-than-average probability of being successful.
   c. most of their college friends and acquaintances have viewed their cohabitation negatively.
   d. their marriage will have a higher-than-average probability of ending in divorce.

Adulthood's commitments, p. 184
Medium, Factual/Definitional, Objective 14, Ans: a

169. People whose first marriage ends in divorce typically:
   a. enter a second marriage.
   b. experience unhappiness if they ever remarry.
   c. maintain a very friendly relationship with their former spouse.
   d. are happier after divorce than couples who remain in their first marriage.

Adulthood's commitments, p. 184
Easy, Factual/Definitional, Objective 14, Ans: c

170. The best predictor of a couple's marital satisfaction is the:
   a. frequency of their sexual intimacy.
   b. intensity of their passionate feelings.
   c. ratio of their positive to negative interactions with each other.
   d. experience or nonexperience of a prior marriage.

Adulthood's commitments, p. 185
Easy, Factual/Definitional, Objective 14, Ans: c

171. When children grow up and leave home, mothers most frequently report feeling:
   a. depressed.
   b. bored.
   c. happy.
   d. anxious.

Adulthood's commitments, p. 185
Medium, Factual/Definitional, Objective 14, Ans: b

172. Among employed women, the task of raising children is especially likely to be associated with ________ marital satisfaction. The departure of mature children from the home is typically associated with ________ marital satisfaction.
   a. increasing; decreasing
   b. decreasing; increasing
   c. increasing; further increasing
   d. decreasing; further decreasing

Adulthood's commitments, p. 185
Difficult, Factual/Definitional, Objective 14, Ans: a

173. The feelings of life satisfaction and happiness of married American women:
   a. are not strongly related to whether or not they are employed outside the home.
   b. increase dramatically in the years following the birth of children.
   c. decrease dramatically when their grown-up children leave the home.
   d. are lower than those of unmarried women of comparable age.

Well-being across the life span, p. 186
Medium, Factual/Definitional, Objective 15, Ans: b

174. Compared to middle-aged adults, adolescents express ________ levels of life satisfaction and the elderly express ________ levels of life satisfaction.
   a. lower; lower
   b. similar; similar
   c. higher; lower
   d. lower; higher

Well-being across the life span, p. 186
Medium, Factual/Definitional, Objective 15, Ans: d

175. Compared to middle-aged adults, elderly people are ________ likely to experience intensely positive emotions and ________ likely to experience intensely negative emotions.
  a. more; less
  b. less; more
  c. more; more
  d. less; less
  e. equally; equally

Well-being across the life span, p. 186
Medium, Factual/Definitional, Objective 15, Ans: a

176. Compared to when she was an adolescent, elderly Mrs. Packer is likely to experience a happy mood with ________ intensity and for a ________ period of time.
  a. less; longer
  b. more; shorter
  c. less; shorter
  d. more; longer

Death and dying, p. 187
Medium, Factual/Definitional, Objective 15, Ans: c

177. During the grieving period following the death of one's spouse:
  a. the expression of intense grief contributes to a more rapid recovery from sadness.
  b. those who talk frequently with others are unusually likely to prolong their own feelings of depression.
  c. grieving men are at greater risk for ill health than are grieving women.
  d. both men and women go through predictable stages of denial followed by anger.

Death and dying, p. 187
Medium, Conceptual, Objective 15, Ans: a

178. According to Erikson, adolescence is to identity as late adulthood is to:
  a. integrity.
  b. autonomy.
  c. generativity.
  d. intimacy.

Death and dying, p. 187
Difficult, Conceptual/Application, Objective 15, Ans: d

179. Abner, a 70-year-old retired teacher, feels that his life has not been of any real value or significance. According to Erikson, Abner has failed to achieve a sense of:
  a. basic trust.
  b. intimacy.
  c. autonomy.
  d. integrity.

Continuity and stages, p. 189
Medium, Conceptual/Application, Objective 16, Ans: c

180. Mary believes that cognitive development is a matter of gradual and almost imperceptible changes over time. Her viewpoint is most directly relevant to the issue of:
   a. nature or nurture.
   b. behavior or mental processes.
   c. continuity or stages.
   d. rationality or irrationality.

Continuity and stages, p. 189
Difficult, Factual/Definitional, Objective 16, Ans: b

181. Psychologists who view the developmental process as a sequence of distinct stages generally believe that ________ is(are) the same for everyone.
   a. both the order and the timing of the stages
   b. the order but not the timing of the stages
   c. the timing but not the order of the stages
   d. neither the order nor the timing of the stages

Continuity and stages, p. 189
Medium, Factual/Definitional, Objective 16, Ans: a

182. Theories of human development have been most susceptible to criticism for overemphasizing:
   a. discrete age-linked stages.
   b. the interaction of nature and nurture.
   c. maturation during adolescent development.
   d. cognitive changes during adulthood development.

Stability and change, pp. 189-190
Medium, Conceptual, Objective 16, Ans: b

183. A belief that adult personality is completely determined in early childhood years would be most relevant to the issue of:
   a. continuity or stages.
   b. stability or change.
   c. fluid or crystallized intelligence.
   d. conventional or postconventional morality.
   e. cross-sectional or longitudinal studies.

Stability and change, p. 190
Medium, Conceptual, Objective 16, Ans: b

184. Questions about whether anxious children will grow up to be either fearful or relaxed adults most directly highlight the issue of:
   a. continuity of stages.
   b. stability or change.
   c. rationality or irrationality.
   d. nature or nurture.

Stability and change, p. 190
Medium, Conceptual, Objective 16, Ans: d

185. The fact that many happy and well-adjusted adults were once rebellious and unhappy as adolescents is most relevant to the issue of:
    a. continuity or stages.
    b. preconventional or postconventional morality.
    c. fluid or crystallized intelligence.
    d. stability or change.
    e. nature or nurture.

Stability and change, p. 190
Medium, Factual/Definitional, Objective 16, Ans: c

186. The stability of personality traits is greater among ________ than among ________.
    a. boys; girls
    b. men; women
    c. adults; children
    d. preschoolers; adolescents

Essay Questions

1. Three-year-old Ivan frequently takes other children's toys from them, showing little concern for their feelings, even when they cry. When he does this, his mother tells him to "imagine how other kids feel when they lose their toys." Use your understanding of cognitive development to explain Ivan's antisocial behavior. Why is his mother's comment unlikely to influence his behavior? How would you encourage Raul to stop behaving this way?

2. Mrs. Karina spends a lot of time stroking, cuddling, and rocking her infant son and seems to be highly aware of the baby's actions and needs. Mr. Karina worries that his wife's interactions with the baby may eventually lead the child to (a) cry easily when frustrated, (b) fearfully cling to his mother, (c) become unfriendly toward other people, and (d) become withdrawn and uninterested in his surroundings. Describe research on social development that supports or refutes each of the father's concerns.

3. Mr. and Mrs. McDonald believe in the importance of stern discipline; they impose strict rules which they expect their children to obey without question. They penalize misbehavior harshly, frequently with a spanking. Mr. and Mrs. Reynolds use milder forms of punishment to enforce their rules. They also have regular family meetings in which their children help them to establish household rules and penalties for breaking them. What do you see as the advantages and disadvantages of these two disciplinary approaches? Explain the reasons for your answer.

4. Thirteen-year-old Philip has begun to challenge many of his parents' values and to express his own set of highly idealistic standards. Compare and contrast the explanations for Philip's behavior that would be given by Kohlberg and by Erikson.

5. As Brianna begins experiencing symptoms of menopause, she worries about the loss of (a) health and vitality, (b) intellectual capacity, and (c) life satisfaction. Describe research that would serve to justify or minimize each of Brianna's concerns.

Web Quiz 1

Ans: d

1. Nutrients and oxygen are transferred from a mother to her developing fetus through the:
   a. embryo.
   b. ovaries.
   c. teratogens.
   d. placenta.

Ans: c

2. The most immediate and direct function of the rooting reflex is the facilitation of:
   a. identity.
   b. object permanence.
   c. food consumption.
   d. visual development.

Ans: e

3. Infants' tendency to gaze longer at novel stimuli than at familiar ones provides compelling evidence regarding their:
   a. self-concepts.
   b. egocentrism.
   c. basic trust.
   d. stranger anxiety.
   e. memory capacities.

Ans: b

4. The importance of schemas was most clearly highlighted by:
   a. Erikson's psychosocial development theory.
   b. Piaget's cognitive development theory.
   c. Haidt's social intuitionist theory.
   d. Kohlberg's moral development theory.

Ans: b

5. Two closed, pyramid-shaped beakers containing clearly identical amounts of a liquid are suddenly judged by a child to hold different amounts after one of the beakers is inverted. The child apparently lacks a:
   a. sense of object permanence.
   b. concept of conservation.
   c. capacity for habituation.
   d. secure attachment.

Ans: c

6. A child's realization that others may have beliefs which the child knows to be false best illustrates the development of:
   a. object permanence.
   b. egocentrism.
   c. a theory of mind.
   d. stranger anxiety.
   e. menarche.

Ans: e

7. The process of imprinting occurs during a brief developmental phase known as:
   a. menarche.
   b. puberty.
   c. menopause.
   d. habituation.
   e. a critical period.

Ans: a

8. Although 3-year-old Adam happily explores the attractive toys located in the dentist's waiting room, he periodically returns to his mother's side for brief moments. Adam most clearly displays signs of:
   a. secure attachment.
   b. object permanence.
   c. egocentrism.
   d. conservation.
   e. stranger anxiety.

Ans: d

9. "I don't care whether you want to wash the dishes, you will do so because I said so!" This statement is most representative of a(n) ________ parenting style.
   a. preconventional
   b. authoritative
   c. formal operational
   d. authoritarian

Ans: c

10. Female breasts are to ________ as male testes are to ________.
   a. menarche; menopause
   b. menopause; menarche
   c. secondary sex characteristics; primary sex characteristics
   d. primary sex characteristics; secondary sex characteristics

Ans: d

11. Mark believes that choosing to violate government laws is morally justifiable if it is done to protect the lives of innocent people. Kohlberg would suggest that this illustrates ________ morality.
   a. conventional
   b. unconventional
   c. preconventional
   d. postconventional

Ans: d

12. Adolescent females spend _______ time alone and _______ time praying than do adolescent males.
   a. more; more
   b. less; less
   c. more; less
   d. less; more

Ans: b

13. A reduction in estrogen levels is most closely associated with:
    a. puberty.
    b. menopause.
    c. Alzheimer's disease.
    d. fetal alcohol syndrome.

Ans: d

14. People differ the most in their learning and memory abilities during:
    a. late adolescence.
    b. early adulthood.
    c. middle adulthood.
    d. later adulthood.

Ans: a

15. A researcher who administers a personality test to the same children every 3 years as they progress through school is conducting a(n) ________ study.
    a. longitudinal
    b. experimental
    c. cross-sectional
    d. chronological

Web Quiz 2

Ans: c

1. For the unborn children of mothers who smoke heavily, nicotine is a(n):
   a. agonist.
   b. depressant.
   c. teratogen.
   d. hallucinogen.

Ans: b

2. Immediately after birth, infants are able to distinguish between their mothers' and strangers':
   a. faces.
   b. voices.
   c. body odors.
   d. tender touches.

Ans: a

3. Newborns habituate more rapidly to a ________ than to a ________.
   a. solid disk; facelike image
   b. facelike image; bull's-eye pattern
   c. bull's-eye pattern; solid disk
   d. facelike image; solid disk

Ans: e

4. After Nadia learned that penguins can't fly, she had to modify her existing concept of birds. This best illustrates the process of:
   a. conservation.
   b. attachment.
   c. assimilation.
   d. habituation.
   e. accommodation.

Ans: c

5. During Piaget's sensorimotor stage, children acquire a:
   a. theory of mind.
   b. concept of conservation.
   c. sense of object permanence.
   d. capacity for abstract reasoning.

Ans: a

6. Deficient social interaction and an impaired understanding of others' states of mind is most characteristic of:
   a. autism.
   b. menarche.
   c. crystallized intelligence.
   d. object permanence.
   e. an insecure attachment.

Ans: c

7. Marissa resents the burden and constraints of caring for her infant daughter and frequently ignores her cries for attention. As a consequence, her daughter is most likely to display signs of:

a. egocentrism.
b. accommodation.
c. insecure attachment.
d. habituation.
e. conservation.

Ans: d

8. Many researchers believe that people's styles of romantic love in adulthood reflect their childhood:

a. habituation.
b. egocentrism.
c. theory of mind.
d. attachment experiences.

Ans: d

9. Compared to the children with authoritarian parents, the children of authoritative parents are ________ likely to develop a sense of self-reliance and _______ likely to demonstrate a postconventional morality.

a. less; more
b. more; less
c. less; less
d. more; more

Ans: c

10. Jarrud thinks he should obey his teachers only if they are carefully watching him. Kohlberg would suggest that Jarrud demonstrates a(n) ________ morality.

a. conventional
b. unconventional
c. preconventional
d. postconventional

Ans: d

11. The sexual abuse of a very young child is so emotionally repulsive to most people that they immediately recognize it as shamefully immoral. This best illustrates that moral judgments may reflect:

a. habituation.
b. fluid intelligence.
c. insecure attachments.
d. gut-level intuitions.
e. concrete operational thought.

Ans: a

12. The process of developing a sense of identity during adolescence was highlighted by:
    a. Erikson's psychosocial development theory.
    b. Piaget's cognitive development theory.
    c. Kohlberg's moral development theory.
    d. Harlow's attachment theory.

Ans: b

13. A series of small strokes that progressively damage an elderly person's brain is most likely to produce:
    a. menarche.
    b. dementia.
    c. crystallized intelligence.
    d. Alzheimer's disease.
    e. autism.

Ans: b

14. As adults age, they show the greatest declines in _______ intelligence and in the memory capacities needed to _______ recently presented information.
    a. fluid; recognize
    b. fluid; recall
    c. crystallized; recognize
    d. crystallized; recall

Ans: a

15. Research on developmental stability and change indicates that:
    a. at the age of 1 or 2, adult personality traits are still largely unpredictable.
    b. development is almost completely dominated by discontinuity over time.
    c. temperament is a particularly unstable trait.
    d. all of the above are true.

Study Guide Questions

Ans: c, p. 135

1. Dr. Joan Goodman is studying how memory changes as people get older. She is most likely a(n) ________ psychologist.
   a. social
   b. cognitive
   c. developmental
   d. experimental

Ans: b, pp. 136-137

2. Which is the correct order of stages of prenatal development?
   a. zygote, fetus, embryo
   b. zygote, embryo, fetus
   c. embryo, zygote, fetus
   d. embryo, fetus, zygote
   e. fetus, embryo, zygote

Ans: a, p. 137

3. A child can be born a drug addict because:
   a. drugs used by the mother will pass into the child's bloodstream.
   b. addiction is an inherited personality trait.
   c. drugs used by the mother create genetic defects in her chromosomes.
   d. the fetus's blood has not yet developed a resistance to drugs.

Ans: c, p. 137

4. A child whose mother drank heavily when she was pregnant is at heightened risk of:
   a. being emotionally excitable during childhood.
   b. becoming insecurely attached.
   c. being born with the physical and cognitive abnormalities of fetal alcohol syndrome.
   d. addiction to a range of drugs throughout life.

Ans: b, p. 138

5. The rooting reflex occurs when a:
   a. newborn's foot is tickled.
   b. newborn's cheek is touched.
   c. newborn hears a loud noise.
   d. newborn makes eye contact with his or her caregiver.
   e. newborn hears his or her mother's voice.

Ans: c, p. 141

6. When psychologists discuss maturation, they are referring to stages of growth that are not influenced by:
   a. conservation.
   b. nature.
   c. nurture.
   d. continuity.

Ans: d, p. 141

7. Most people's earliest memories do not predate ________ of age.
   a. 6 months
   b. 1 year
   c. 2 years
   d. 3 years
   e. 4 years

Ans: b, p. 142

8. Calvin, who is trying to impress his psychology professor with his knowledge of infant motor development, asks why some infants learn to roll over before they lift their heads from a prone position, while others develop these skills in the opposite order. What should Calvin's professor conclude from this question?
   a. Calvin clearly understands that the sequence of motor development is not the same for all infants.
   b. Calvin doesn't know what he's talking about. Although some infants reach these developmental milestones ahead of others, the order is the same for all infants.
   c. Calvin needs to be reminded that rolling over is an inherited reflex, not a learned skill.
   d. Calvin understands an important principle: motor development is unpredictable.

Ans: b, p. 142

9. Research findings on infant motor development are consistent with the idea that:
   a. cognitive development lags significantly behind motor skills development.
   b. maturation of physical skills is relatively unaffected by experience.
   c. in the absence of relevant earlier learning experiences, the emergence of motor skills will be slowed.
   d. in humans, the process of maturation may be significantly altered by cultural factors.

Ans: a, p. 143

10. Before Piaget, people were more likely to believe that:
   a. the child's mind is a miniature model of the adult's.
   b. children think about the world in radically different ways from adults.
   c. the child's mind develops through a series of stages.
   d. children interpret their experiences in terms of their current understandings.

Ans: a, p. 144

11. Which is the correct sequence of stages in Piaget's theory of cognitive development?
   a. sensorimotor, preoperational, concrete operational, formal operational
   b. sensorimotor, preoperational, formal operational, concrete operational
   c. preoperational, sensorimotor, concrete operational, formal operational
   d. preoperational, sensorimotor, formal operational, concrete operational
   e. sensorimotor, concrete operational, preoperational, formal operational

Ans: a, p. 144

12. I am 14 months old and fearful of strangers. I am in Piaget's ________ stage of cognitive development.
   a. sensorimotor
   b. preoperational
   c. concrete operational
   d. formal operational

Ans: a, p. 144

13. During which stage of cognitive development do children acquire object permanence?
  a. sensorimotor
  b. preoperational
  c. concrete operational
  d. formal operational

Ans: c, p. 146

14. As a child observes, liquid is transferred from a tall, thin tube into a short, wide jar. The child is asked if there is now less liquid in order to determine if she has mastered:
  a. the schema for liquids.
  b. the concept of object permanence.
  c. the concept of conservation.
  d. the ability to reason abstractly.

Ans: b, p. 146

15. Piaget held that egocentrism is characteristic of the:
  a. sensorimotor stage.
  b. preoperational stage.
  c. concrete operational stage.
  d. formal operational stage.

Ans: b, p. 146

16. I am 3 years old, can use language, and have trouble taking another person's perspective. I am in Piaget's ________ stage of cognitive development.
  a. sensorimotor
  b. preoperational
  c. concrete operational
  d. formal operational

Ans: c, p. 146

17. Four-year-old Jamail has a younger sister. When asked if he has a sister, he is likely to answer ________; when asked if his sister has a brother, Jamail is likely to answer ________.
  a. yes; yes
  b. no; no
  c. yes; no
  d. no; yes

Ans: d, pp. 146, 148

18. In Piaget's theory, conservation is to egocentrism as the ________ stage is to the ________ stage.
  a. sensorimotor; formal operational
  b. formal operational; sensorimotor
  c. preoperational; sensorimotor
  d. concrete operational; preoperational

Ans: d, p. 147

19. Compared to when he was younger, 4-year-old Antonio is better able to empathize with his friend's feelings. This growing ability to take another's perspective indicates that Antonio is acquiring a:
   a. self-concept.
   b. schema.
   c. temperament.
   d. theory of mind.

Ans: a, p. 148

20. In Piaget's stage of concrete operational intelligence, the child acquires an understanding of the principle of:
   a. conservation.
   b. deduction.
   c. attachment.
   d. object permanence.

Ans: c, p. 148

21. Thirteen-year-old Irene has no trouble defeating her 11-year-old brother at a detective game that requires following clues in order to deduce the perpetrator of a crime. How might Piaget explain Irene's superiority at the game?
   a. Being older, Irene has had more years of schooling.
   b. Girls develop intellectually at a faster rate than boys.
   c. Being an adolescent, Irene is beginning to develop abstract reasoning skills.
   d. Girls typically have more experience than boys at playing games.

Ans: c, p. 149

22. According to Piaget, the ability to think logically about abstract propositions is indicative of the stage of:
   a. preoperational thought.
   b. concrete operations.
   c. formal operations.
   d. fluid intelligence.

Ans: d, p. 150

23. Stranger anxiety develops soon after:
   a. the concept of conservation.
   b. egocentrism.
   c. a theory of mind.
   d. the concept of object permanence.

Ans: b, p. 151

24. Harlow's studies of attachment in monkeys showed that:
   a. provision of nourishment was the single most important factor motivating attachment.
   b. a cloth mother produced the greatest attachment response.
   c. whether a cloth or wire mother was present mattered less than the presence or absence of other infants.
   d. attachment in monkeys is based on imprinting.

Ans: b, p. 151

25. In a 1998 movie, a young girl finds that a gaggle of geese follows her wherever she goes because she was the first "object" they saw after they were born. This is an example of:
    a. conservation.
    b. imprinting.
    c. egocentrism.
    d. basic trust.

Ans: d, p. 151

26. The term *critical period* refers to:
    a. prenatal development.
    b. the initial 2 hours after a child's birth.
    c. the preoperational stage.
    d. a restricted time for learning.

Ans: c, p. 152

27. Insecurely attached infants who are left by their mothers in an unfamiliar setting often will:
    a. hold fast to their mothers on their return.
    b. explore the new surroundings confidently.
    c. be indifferent toward their mothers on their return.
    d. display little emotion at any time.

Ans: a, p. 154

28. Joshua and Ann Bishop have a 13-month-old boy. According to Erikson, the Bishops' sensitive, loving care of their child contributes to:
    a. the child's sense of basic trust.
    b. the child's secure attachment.
    c. the child's sense of control.
    d. a. and b. only.

Ans: e, p. 154

29. The developmental theorist who suggested that securely attached children develop an attitude of basic trust is:
    a. Piaget.
    b. Harlow.
    c. Vygotsky.
    d. Freud.
    e. Erikson.

Ans: c, p. 154

30. Children who in infancy formed secure attachments to their parents are more likely than other children to:
    a. prefer the company of adults to that of other children.
    b. become permissive parents.
    c. show a great deal of social competence.
    d. be less achievement oriented.

Ans: c, p. 154

31. Which of the following was not found by Harlow in socially deprived monkeys?
    a. They had difficulty mating.
    b. They showed extreme fear or aggression when first seeing other monkeys.
    c. They showed abnormal physical development.
    d. The females were abusive mothers.

Ans: d, p. 161

32. Adolescence is marked by the onset of:
    a. an identity crisis.
    b. parent-child conflict.
    c. the concrete operational stage.
    d. puberty.

Ans: b, p. 161

33. The average age at which puberty begins is ________ in boys; in girls, it is ________.
    a. 14; 13
    b. 13; 11
    c. 11; 10
    d. 10; 9

Ans: c, p. 162

34. Among the hallmarks of growing up are a boy's first ejaculation and a girl's first menstrual period, which is also called:
    a. puberty
    b. menopause.
    c. menarche.
    d. generativity.

Ans: c, p. 162

35. Based on the text discussion of maturation and popularity, who among the following is probably the most popular sixth grader?
    a. Jessica, the most physically mature girl in the class
    b. Roger, the most intellectually mature boy in the class
    c. Rob, the tallest, most physically mature boy in the class
    d. Cindy, who is average in physical development and is on the school debating team

Ans: d, p. 162

36. Which of the following is correct?
    a. Early maturation places both boys and girls at a distinct social advantage.
    b. Early-maturing girls are more popular and self-assured than girls who mature late.
    c. Early maturation places both boys and girls at a distinct social disadvantage.
    d. Early-maturing boys are more popular and self-assured than boys who mature late.

Ans: d, p. 164

37. Whose stage theory of moral development was based on how people reasoned about ethical dilemmas?
    a. Erikson
    b. Piaget
    c. Levinson
    d. Kohlberg
    e. Kübler-Ross

Ans: c, p. 164

38. To which of Kohlberg's levels would moral reasoning based on the existence of fundamental human rights pertain?
    a. preconventional morality
    b. conventional morality
    c. postconventional morality
    d. generative morality

Ans: b, p. 164

39. Sam, a junior in high school, regularly attends church because his family and friends think he should. Which stage of moral reasoning is Sam in?
    a. preconventional
    b. conventional
    c. postconventional
    d. too little information to tell

Ans: c, p. 164

40. In preconventional morality, the person:
    a. obeys out of a sense of social duty.
    b. conforms to gain social approval.
    c. obeys to avoid punishment or to gain concrete rewards.
    d. follows the dictates of his or her conscience.

Ans: a, p. 165

41. Which of the following was not mentioned in the text as a criticism of Kohlberg's theory of moral development?
    a. It does not account for the fact that the development of moral reasoning is culture-specific.
    b. Postconventional morality appears mostly in educated, middle-class persons.
    c. The theory is biased against the moral reasoning of people in communal societies such as China.
    d. The theory is biased in favor of moral reasoning in men.

Ans: a, p. 166

42. According to Erikson, the central psychological challenges pertaining to adolescence, young adulthood, and middle age, respectively, are:
    a. identity formation; intimacy; generativity.
    b. intimacy; identity formation; generativity.
    c. generativity; intimacy; identity formation.
    d. intimacy; generativity; identity formation.
    e. identity formation; generativity; intimacy.

Ans: c, p. 167

43. After puberty, the self-concept usually becomes:
 a. more positive in boys.
 b. more positive in girls.
 c. more positive in both boys and girls.
 d. more negative in both boys and girls.

Ans: a, pp. 167-168

44. In Erikson's theory, individuals generally focus on developing ________ during adolescence and then ________ during young adulthood.
 a. identity; intimacy
 b. intimacy; identity
 c. basic trust; identity
 d. identity; basic trust

Ans: c, p. 168

45. After a series of unfulfilling relationships, 30-year-old Carlos tells a friend that he doesn't want to marry because he is afraid of losing his freedom and independence. Erikson would say that Carlos is having difficulty with the psychosocial task of:
 a. trust versus mistrust.
 b. autonomy versus doubt.
 c. intimacy versus isolation.
 d. identity versus role confusion.
 e. generativity versus stagnation.

Ans: c, p. 168

46. Compared with her teenage brother, 14-year-old Samantha is likely to play in groups that are:
 a. larger and less competitive.
 b. larger and more competitive.
 c. smaller and less competitive.
 d. smaller and more competitive.

Ans: c, p. 168

47. Compared with men, women:
 a. use conversation to communicate solutions.
 b. emphasize freedom and self-reliance.
 c. talk more openly.
 d. do all of the above.

Ans: d, p. 170

48. Fourteen-year-old Cassandra feels freer and more open with her friends than with her family. Knowing this is the case, Cassandra's parents should:
 a. be concerned, because deteriorating parent-adolescent relationships, such as this one, are often followed by a range of problem behaviors.
 b. encourage Cassandra to find new friends.
 c. seek family counseling.
 d. not worry, since adolescence is typically a time of growing peer influence and diminishing parental influence.
 e. ask their friends to suggest ways to communicate with Cassandra.

Ans: b, p. 170

49. Research on social relationships between parents and their adolescent children shows that:
 a. parental influence on children increases during adolescence.
 b. high school girls who have the most affectionate relationships with their mothers tend to enjoy the most intimate friendships with girlfriends.
 c. high school boys who have the most affectionate relationships with their fathers tend to enjoy the most intimate friendships with friends.
 d. most teens are strongly influenced by parents in matters of personal taste.
 e. parent-adolescent conflict is most common between mothers and daughters.

Ans: b, p. 173

50. The end of menstruation is called:
 a. menarche.
 b. menopause.
 c. the midlife crisis.
 d. generativity.

Ans: e, pp. 173-174

51. After menopause, most women:
 a. experience anxiety and a sense of worthlessness.
 b. lose interest in sex.
 c. secrete unusually high levels of estrogen.
 d. gain a lot of weight.
 e. feel a new sense of freedom.

Ans: a, p. 176

52. In terms of incidence, susceptibility to short-term illnesses ________ with age and susceptibility to long-term ailments ________ with age.
 a. decreases; increases
 b. increases; decreases
 c. increases; increases
 d. decreases; decreases

Ans: d, p. 177

53. Of the following, which is a possible cause of dementia?
 a. stroke
 b. brain tumor
 c. alcoholism
 d. all of the above are possible causes

Ans: d, p. 177

54. Which of the following statements concerning the effects of aging is true?
 a. Aging almost inevitably leads to dementia if the individual lives long enough.
 b. Aging increases susceptibility to short-term ailments such as the flu.
 c. Significant increases in life satisfaction are associated with aging.
 d. The aging process can be significantly affected by the individual's activity patterns.

Ans: d, p. 178

55. Underlying Alzheimer's disease is a deterioration in neurons that produce:
    a. epinephrine.
    b. norepinephrine.
    c. serotonin.
    d. acetylcholine.
    e. dopamine.

Ans: a, pp. 178-179

56. The cognitive ability that has been shown to decline during adulthood is the ability to:
    a. recall new information.
    b. recognize new information.
    c. learn meaningful new material.
    d. use judgment in dealing with daily life problems.

Ans: e, p. 179

57. Which statement illustrates cognitive development during the course of adult life?
    a. Adults in their forties have better recognition memory than do adults in their seventies.
    b. Recall and recognition memory both remain strong throughout life.
    c. Recognition memory decreases sharply at midlife.
    d. Recall memory remains strong until very late in life.
    e. Adults in their forties have better recall memory than do adults in their seventies.

Ans: a, p. 180

58. The cross-sectional method:
    a. compares people of different ages with one another.
    b. studies the same group of people at different times.
    c. tends to paint too favorable a picture of the effects of aging on intelligence.
    d. is more appropriate than the longitudinal method for studying intellectual change over the life span.

Ans: b, p. 180

59. Longitudinal tests:
    a. compare people of different ages.
    b. study the same people at different times.
    c. usually involve a larger sample than do cross-sectional tests.
    d. usually involve a smaller sample than do cross-sectional tests.
    e. are less informative than cross-sectional tests.

Ans: c, p. 180

60. Cross-sectional studies of intelligence are potentially misleading because:
    a. they are typically based on a very small and unrepresentative sample of people.
    b. retesting the same people over a period of years allows test performance to be influenced by practice.
    c. they compare people who are not only different in age, but of different eras, education levels, and affluence.
    d. of all of the above reasons.

Ans: b, p. 181

61. A person's general ability to think abstractly is called ________ intelligence. This ability generally ________ with age.
    a. fluid; increases
    b. fluid; decreases
    c. crystallized; decreases
    d. crystallized; increases

Ans: d, p. 181

62. A person's accumulation of stored information, called ________ intelligence, generally ________ with age.
    a. fluid; decreases
    b. fluid; increases
    c. crystallized; decreases
    d. crystallized; increases

Ans: c, p. 181

63. Sixty-five-year-old Calvin cannot reason as well as he could when he was younger. More than likely, Calvin's ________ intelligence has declined.
    a. analytic
    b. crystallized
    c. fluid
    d. both b. and c.

Ans: a, p. 182

64. Notable achievements in fields such as ________ are often made by younger adults in their late twenties or early thirties, when ________ intelligence is at its peak.
    a. mathematics; fluid
    b. philosophy; fluid
    c. science; crystallized
    d. literature; crystallized
    e. history; crystallized

Ans: a, p. 182

65. Deborah is a mathematician and Willie is a philosopher. Considering their professions:
    a. Deborah will make her most significant career accomplishments at an earlier age than Willie will.
    b. Deborah will make her most significant career accomplishments at a later age than Willie will.
    c. Deborah will make her most significant career accomplishments at about the same time as Willie.
    d. there is still not enough information for predicting such accomplishments.

Ans: d, pp. 182-183

66. Stage theories have been criticized because they fail to consider that development may be significantly affected by:
    a. variations in the social clock.
    b. each individual's experiences.
    c. each individual's historical and cultural setting.
    d. all of the above.

Ans: c, p. 183

67. The social clock refers to:
a. an individual or society's distribution of work and leisure time.
b. adulthood responsibilities.
c. typical ages for starting a career, marrying, and so on.
d. age-related changes in one's circle of friends.

Ans: d, p. 184

68. Research on the American family indicates that:
a. fewer than 23 percent of unmarried adults, but nearly 40 percent of married adults, report being "very happy" with life.
b. the divorce rate is now one-half the marriage rate.
c. of those who divorce, 75 percent remarry.
d. all of the above are true.

Ans: d, p. 185

69. Research on the relationship between self-reported happiness and employment in American women has revealed that:
a. women who work tend to be happier.
b. women who do not work tend to be happier.
c. women today are happier than in the past, whether they are working or not.
d. the quality of a woman's experience in her various roles is more predictive of happiness than the presence or absence of a given role.

Ans: d, p. 185

70. After their grown children have left home, most couples experience:
a. the distress of the "empty nest syndrome."
b. increased strain in their marital relationship.
c. both a. and b.
d. greater happiness and enjoyment in their relationship.

Ans: e, p. 186

71. Given the text discussion of life satisfaction patterns, which of the following people is likely to report the greatest life satisfaction?
a. Billy, a 7-year-old second-grader
b. Kathy, a 17-year-old high-school senior
c. Alan, a 30-year-old accountant
d. Mildred, a 70-year-old retired teacher
e. too little information to tell

Ans: e, p. 187

72. An elderly person who can look back on life with satisfaction and reminisce with a sense of completion has attained Erikson's stage of:
a. generativity.
b. intimacy.
c. isolation.
d. acceptance.
e. integrity.

Ans: d, p. 187

73. The popular idea that terminally ill and bereaved people go through predictable stages, such as denial, anger, and so forth:
   a. is widely supported by research.
   b. more accurately describes grieving in some cultures than others.
   c. is true of women but not men.
   d. is not supported by research studies.

Ans: c, pp. 189-190

74. Most contemporary developmental psychologists believe that:
   a. personality is essentially formed by the end of infancy.
   b. personality continues to be formed until adolescence.
   c. the shaping of personality continues during adolescence and well beyond.
   d. adolescent development has very little impact on adult personality.

Ans: c, p. 190

75. Which of the following statements is consistent with the current thinking of developmental psychologists?
   a. Development occurs in a series of sharply defined stages.
   b. The first two years are the most crucial in determining the individual's personality.
   c. The consistency of personality in most people tends to increase over the life span.
   d. Social and emotional style are among the characteristics that show the least stability over the life span.

CHAPTER **5**

Sensation

Learning Objectives

Sensing the World: Some Basic Principles (pp. 194-199)

1. Contrast the processes of sensation and perception.

2. Distinguish between absolute and difference thresholds, and discuss research findings on subliminal stimulation.

3. Describe the phenomenon of sensory adaptation, and explain its functional value.

Vision (pp. 199-211)

4. Explain the visual process, including the stimulus input, the structure of the eye, and the transduction of light energy.

5. Discuss the different levels of visual information processing and the value of parallel processing.

6. Explain the Young-Helmholtz and opponent-process theories of color vision, and describe the nature of color constancy.

Hearing (pp. 212-219)

7. Explain the auditory process, including the stimulus input and the structure and function of the ear.

8. Explain the place and frequency theories of pitch perception, and describe how we locate sounds.

9. Discuss the nature and causes of hearing loss, and describe the effects of noise on hearing and behavior.

The Other Senses (pp. 219-228)

10. Describe the sense of touch, and explain the basis of pain.

11. Describe the senses of taste and smell, and comment on the nature of sensory interaction.

12. Distinguish between kinesthesis and the vestibular sense.

Sensation and perception, p. 193
Easy, Factual/Definitional, Objective 1, Ans: e

1. The detection and encoding of stimulus energies by the nervous system is called:
a. signal detection.
b. sensory interaction.
c. subliminal perception.
d. accommodation.
e. sensation.

Sensation and perception, p. 193
Easy, Factual/Definitional, Objective 1, Ans: c

2. Perception is the process by which:
a. stimulus energies are detected.
b. stimulus energies are transformed into neural activity.
c. sensory input is selected, organized, and interpreted.
d. nerve cells respond to specific features of a stimulus.

Sensation and perception, p. 193
Medium, Conceptual, Objective 1, Ans: b

3. Sensation is to ________ as perception is to ________.
a. encoding; detection
b. detection; interpretation
c. interpretation; organization
d. organization; adaptation

Sensation and perception, p. 193
Difficult, Conceptual, Objective 1, Ans: e

4. Hearing a sequence of sounds of different pitches is to ________ as recognizing the sound sequence as a familiar melody is to ________.
a. the just noticeable difference; accommodation
b. absolute threshold; difference threshold
c. sensory interaction; feature detection
d. feature detection; sensory interaction
e. sensation; perception

Sensation and perception, p. 193
Medium, Conceptual/Application, Objective 1, Ans: e

5. Patients' negative expectations about the outcome of a surgical procedure can increase their postoperative experience of pain. This best illustrates the importance of:
a. transduction.
b. accommodation.
c. sensory adaptation.
d. difference thresholds.
e. top-down processing.

Sensation and perception, p. 193
Difficult, Conceptual/Application, Objective 1, Ans: c

6. Berdine has developed cataracts in both eyes, preventing her from being able to identify even her mother's face. Berdine most clearly suffers a deficiency in:
   a. the optic nerve.
   b. accommodation.
   c. bottom-up processing.
   d. kinesthesis.

Sensation and perception, p. 193
Medium, Factual/Definitional, Objective 1, Ans: b

7. Complete sensation in the absence of complete perception is best illustrated by:
   a. Weber's law.
   b. prosopagnosia.
   c. conduction deafness.
   d. color constancy.
   e. sensory interaction.

Thresholds, p. 194
Difficult, Conceptual/Application, Objective 2, Ans: d

8. A psychophysicist would be most directly concerned with:
   a. our psychological reactions to physical stress.
   b. the effects of physical diseases on sensory receptor cells.
   c. the automatic effect of bright lights on the contraction of the pupils.
   d. the relation between the wavelength of light and the experience of color.

Absolute thresholds, p. 195
Easy, Factual/Definitional, Objective 2, Ans: d

9. The minimum amount of stimulation a person needs to detect a stimulus 50 percent of the time is called the:
   a. sensory adaptation threshold.
   b. difference threshold.
   c. subliminal threshold.
   d. absolute threshold.

Absolute thresholds, p. 195
Easy, Conceptual/Application, Objective 2, Ans: b

10. During a hearing test, many sounds were presented at such a low level of intensity that Mr. Antall could hardly ever detect them. These sounds were below Mr. Antall's:
   a. subliminal threshold.
   b. absolute threshold.
   c. sensory adaptation threshold.
   d. difference threshold.

Absolute thresholds, p. 195
Difficult, Conceptual/Application, Objective 2, Ans: d

11. If a partially deaf person's hearing ability ________, his or her absolute threshold for sound ________.
    a. improves; remains unchanged
    b. worsens; decreases
    c. worsens; remains unchanged
    d. improves; decreases

Signal detection, p. 195
Medium, Factual/Definitional, Objective 2, Ans: a

12. Which theory emphasizes that personal expectations and motivations influence the level of absolute thresholds?
    a. signal detection theory
    b. frequency theory
    c. opponent-process theory
    d. feature detection theory

Signal detection, p. 195
Difficult, Conceptual, Objective 2, Ans: d

13. Which theory would suggest that watching a horror movie late at night could lower your absolute threshold for sound as you subsequently tried to fall asleep?
    a. sensory adaptation theory
    b. opponent-process theory
    c. frequency theory
    d. signal detection theory

Subliminal stimulation, p. 195
Easy, Factual/Definitional, Objective 2, Ans: e

14. News about the supposed effects of briefly presented messages on moviegoers' consumption of popcorn and Coca-Cola involved false claims regarding:
    a. parallel processing.
    b. difference thresholds.
    c. kinesthesis.
    d. sensory interaction.
    e. subliminal stimulation.

Subliminal stimulation, p. 195
Medium, Conceptual/Application, Objective 2, Ans: a

15. Which of the following strategies best illustrates the use of subliminal stimulation?
    a. A store plays a musical soundtrack in which a faint and imperceptible verbal warning against shoplifting is repeated frequently.
    b. The laughter of a studio audience is dubbed into the soundtrack of a televised situation comedy.
    c. A radio advertiser repeatedly smacks her lips before biting into a candy bar.
    d. An unseen television narrator repeatedly suggests that you are thirsty while a cold drink is visually displayed on the screen.

Subliminal stimulation, p. 196
Difficult, Conceptual, Objective 2, Ans: a

16. Subliminally presented stimuli:
    a. can sometimes be consciously perceived.
    b. effectively influence purchases of consumer goods.
    c. increase our absolute thresholds for visual images.
    d. are usually mentally processed as completely as any other stimuli.

Subliminal stimulation, p. 196
Medium, Factual/Definitional, Objective 2, Ans: a

17. People's response to subliminal stimulation indicates that:
    a. they are capable of processing information without any conscious awareness of doing so.
    b. their subconscious minds are incapable of resisting subliminally presented suggestions.
    c. they are more sensitive to subliminal sounds than to subliminal sights.
    d. they experience a sense of discomfort whenever they are exposed to subliminal stimuli.

Subliminal stimulation, p. 197
Difficult, Factual/Definitional, Objective 2, Ans: d

18. When informed that a brief imperceptible message would be flashed repeatedly during a popular TV program, many viewers reported feeling strangely hungry or thirsty during the show. Since the imperceptible message had nothing to do with hunger or thirst, viewers' strange reactions best illustrate:
    a. the McGurk effect.
    b. sensory adaptation.
    c. the volley principle.
    d. a placebo effect.
    e. accommodation.

Difference thresholds, p. 197
Medium, Conceptual/Application, Objective 2, Ans: d

19. Jennifer can tune her guitar more effectively than Maria because Jennifer is better at detecting whether specific strings are playing too sharp or too flat. With respect to tone sensitivity, Maria apparently has a ________ threshold than does Jennifer.
    a. lower absolute
    b. higher absolute
    c. smaller difference
    d. larger difference

Difference thresholds, p. 197
Easy, Factual/Definitional, Objective 2, Ans: b

20. The principle that two stimuli must differ by a constant proportion for their difference to be perceived is known as:
    a. the opponent-process theory.
    b. Weber's law.
    c. feature detection.
    d. frequency theory.

Difference thresholds, p. 197
Medium, Conceptual/Application, Objective 2, Ans: e

21. Giulio's bag of marbles is twice as heavy as Jim's. If it takes 5 extra marbles to make Jim's bag feel heavier, it will take 10 extra marbles to make Giulio's bag feel heavier. This best illustrates:
   a. the opponent-process theory.
   b. accommodation.
   c. frequency theory.
   d. sensory adaptation.
   e. Weber's law.

Difference thresholds, p. 197
Difficult, Factual/Definitional, Objective 2, Ans: d

22. Difference thresholds are smaller for the ________ than for the ________.
   a. brightness of lights; pitch of sounds
   b. weight of objects; pitch of sounds
   c. brightness of lights; weight of objects
   d. pitch of sounds; brightness of lights

Sensory adaptation, p. 198
Easy, Factual/Definitional, Objective 3, Ans: b

23. Sensory adaptation refers to:
   a. the process by which stimulus energies are changed into neural impulses.
   b. diminishing sensitivity to an unchanging stimulus.
   c. the process of selecting, organizing, and interpreting sensory information.
   d. changes in the shape of the lens as it focuses on objects.

Sensory adaptation, p. 198
Medium, Conceptual/Application, Objective 3, Ans: c

24. After listening to your high-volume car stereo for 15 minutes, you fail to realize how loudly the music is blasting. This best illustrates:
   a. Weber's law.
   b. accommodation.
   c. sensory adaptation.
   d. the volley principle.
   e. conduction hearing loss.

Sensory adaptation, p. 198
Difficult, Factual/Definitional, Objective 3, Ans: c

25. The constant quivering movements of our eyes are necessary in order to:
   a. facilitate the process of accommodation.
   b. illuminate the entire retina.
   c. minimize sensory adaptation.
   d. do all of the above.

Sensory adaptation, p. 198
Difficult, Conceptual, Objective 3, Ans: b

26. When stabilized retinal images of an initially presented word disappear, new words made up of parts of the initial word will subsequently appear and then vanish. This best illustrates the impact of:
a. subliminal stimulation.
b. top-down processing.
c. sensory interaction.
d. accommodation.

Vision, p. 199
Easy, Factual/Definitional, Objective 4, Ans: c

27. The process by which our sensory systems convert stimulus energies into neural messages is called:
a. accommodation.
b. sensory adaptation.
c. transduction.
d. parallel processing.
e. sensory interaction.

Vision, p. 199
Medium, Conceptual/Application, Objective 4, Ans: d

28. The local fire department sounds the 12 o'clock whistle. The process by which your ears convert the sound waves from the siren into neural impulses is an example of:
a. sensory adaptation.
b. accommodation.
c. parallel processing.
d. transduction.
e. sensory interaction.

The stimulus input: light energy (Figure 5.3), p. 200
Medium, Factual/Definitional, Objective 4, Ans: d

29. Humans experience the longest visible electromagnetic waves as the color ________ and the shortest visible waves as ________.
a. blue-violet; red
b. red; green
c. blue; yellow
d. red; blue-violet
e. black; white

The stimulus input: light energy, p. 200
Medium, Conceptual, Objective 4, Ans: e

30. Brightness is to intensity as hue is to:
a. amplitude.
b. timbre.
c. color.
d. pitch.
e. wavelength.

The stimulus input: light energy, pp. 200, 212
Difficult, Conceptual, Objective 4, Ans: a

31. Loudness is to pitch as brightness is to:
    a. hue.
    b. light.
    c. intensity.
    d. frequency.
    e. amplitude.

The stimulus input: light energy (Figure 5.4), p. 200
Difficult, Conceptual, Objective 4, Ans: a

32. Low-pitched sounds are to high-pitched sounds as ________ colors are to ________ colors.
    a. red; blue
    b. yellow; red
    c. purple; green
    d. green; orange
    e. purple; red

The eye, p. 201
Easy, Factual/Definitional, Objective 4, Ans: c

33. Which process allows more light to reach the periphery of the retina?
    a. accommodation of the lens
    b. transduction of the cones
    c. dilation of the pupils
    d. sensory adaptation of feature detectors

The eye, p. 201
Easy, Factual/Definitional, Objective 4, Ans: b

34. The amount of light entering the eye is regulated by the:
    a. lens.
    b. iris.
    c. retina.
    d. optic nerve.
    e. feature detectors.

The eye, p. 201
Easy, Factual/Definitional, Objective 4, Ans: e

35. Accommodation refers to the:
    a. diminishing sensitivity to an unchanging stimulus.
    b. system for sensing the position and movement of muscles, tendons, and joints.
    c. quivering eye movements that enable the retina to detect continuous stimulation.
    d. process by which stimulus energies are changed into neural messages.
    e. process by which the lens changes shape in order to focus images on the retina.

The eye, pp. 201, 202
Medium, Conceptual, Objective 4, Ans: c

36. Rod is to transduction as ________ is to accommodation.
   a. pupil
   b. cone
   c. lens
   d. cornea
   e. iris

The eye, pp. 201, 213
Medium, Conceptual, Objective 4, Ans: b

37. The cochlea is to the ear as the ________ is to the eye.
   a. pupil
   b. retina
   c. lens
   d. cornea
   e. optic nerve

The eye, p. 201
Easy, Factual/Definitional, Objective 4, Ans: b

38. If images of distant objects are typically focused at a point in front of the retina, a person will:
   a. have a larger-than-normal blindspot.
   b. be nearsighted.
   c. have unusually good visual acuity.
   d. be farsighted.

The eye, p. 201
Medium, Conceptual/Application, Objective 4, Ans: a

39. Henry can easily read distant road signs, but words on a page appear blurred to him. Henry probably has:
   a. shorter-than-normal eyeballs.
   b. smaller-than-normal feature detectors.
   c. longer-than-normal eyeballs.
   d. larger-than-normal feature detectors.

The retina, pp. 202, 213
Medium, Conceptual, Objective 4, Ans: a

40. Hair cells are to audition as ________ are to vision.
   a. rods and cones
   b. optic nerves
   c. pupils
   d. bipolar cells
   e. feature detectors

The retina, p. 202
Medium, Factual/Definitional, Objective 4, Ans: c

41. Which cells are located closest to the back of the retina?
   a. ganglion cells
   b. bipolar cells
   c. rods and cones
   d. feature detectors

The retina, p. 203
Easy, Factual/Definitional, Objective 4, Ans: c

42. The blind spot is located in the area of the retina:
   a. called the fovea.
   b. that contains rods but no cones.
   c. where the optic nerve leaves the eye.
   d. where bipolar cells connect with ganglion cells.

The retina, p. 203
Difficult, Factual/Definitional, Objective 4, Ans: d

43. Because several rods share a single bipolar cell, rods are less sensitive to ________ than are cones.
   a. color
   b. bright light
   c. dim light
   d. fine detail

The retina, p. 203
Easy, Factual/Definitional, Objective 4, Ans: b

44. Which receptor cells most directly enable us to distinguish different wavelengths of light?
   a. rods
   b. cones
   c. bipolar cells
   d. feature detectors

The retina, p. 203
Medium, Factual/Definitional, Objective 4, Ans: c

45. Rods are ________ light-sensitive and ________ color-sensitive than are cones.
   a. more; more
   b. less; less
   c. more; less
   d. less; more

The retina, p. 203
Difficult, Conceptual, Objective 4, Ans: c

46. Damage to the fovea would probably have the *least* effect on visual sensitivity to ________ stimuli.
   a. brilliantly colored
   b. finely detailed
   c. dimly illuminated
   d. highly familiar

The retina, p. 203
Medium, Factual/Definitional, Objective 4, Ans: d

47. Compared to humans, cats have ________ visual acuity and ________ color vision.
   a. better; worse
   b. worse; better
   c. better; better
   d. worse; worse

Feature detection, p. 204
Difficult, Factual/Definitional, Objective 5, Ans: b

48. Visual information is processed by ________ before it is processed by _______.
    a. feature detectors; rods and cones
    b. ganglion cells; feature detectors
    c. bipolar cells; rods and cones
    d. feature detectors; bipolar cells
    e. the optic nerve; ganglion cells

Feature detection, pp. 204-205
Medium, Conceptual/Application, Objective 5, Ans: b

49. When looking at the hands of a clock signifying 8 o'clock, certain brain cells in the visual cortex are more responsive than if the hands signify 10 o'clock. This is most indicative of:
    a. sensory interaction.
    b. feature detection.
    c. parallel processing.
    d. sensory interaction.
    e. accommodation.

Feature detection, pp. 204-205
Easy, Factual/Definitional, Objective 5, Ans: b

50. The feature detectors identified by Hubel and Weisel respond to specific aspects of ________ stimulation.
    a. taste
    b. visual
    c. auditory
    d. olfactory
    e. kinesthetic

Feature detection, p. 204
Medium, Factual/Definitional, Objective 5, Ans: a

51. The feature detectors identified by Hubel and Weisel consist of:
    a. nerve cells in the brain.
    b. rods and cones.
    c. bipolar cells.
    d. ganglion cells.

Feature detection, p. 205
Medium, Factual/Definitional, Objective 5, Ans: c

52. The activation of some feature detectors in response to visual stimulation depends on our assumptions and interpretations of the sensory input. This best illustrates the importance of:
    a. difference thresholds.
    b. sensory adaptation.
    c. top-down processing.
    d. sensory interaction.
    e. accommodation.

Parallel processing, p. 206
Medium, Conceptual/Application, Objective 5, Ans: e

53. The ability to simultaneously process the pitch, loudness, melody, and meaning of a song best illustrates:
a. sensory interaction.
b. kinesthesis.
c. accommodation.
d. subliminal perception.
e. parallel processing.

Parallel processing, p. 206
Medium, Factual/Definitional, Objective 5, Ans: e

54. The human ability to outperform computers in speedily recognizing familiar objects best illustrates the value of:
a. accommodation.
b. kinesthesis.
c. subliminal stimulation.
d. sensory interaction.
e. parallel processing.

Parallel processing, pp. 206-207
Medium, Conceptual/Application, Objective 5, Ans: d

55. Ms. Shields, a recent stroke victim, cannot consciously perceive the large book on the coffee table in front of her. Yet, when urged to identify the book, she correctly reads aloud the printed title on the book cover. Her response best illustrates:
a. subliminal perception.
b. sensory adaptation.
c. the volley principle.
d. blindsight.
e. sensory interaction.

Parallel processing, pp. 206-207
Medium, Factual/Definitional, Objective 5, Ans: e

56. People who demonstrate blindsight have most likely suffered damage to their:
a. cornea.
b. lens.
c. fovea.
d. optic nerve.
e. visual cortex.

Parallel processing, p. 207
Medium, Factual/Definitional, Objective 5, Ans: e

57. The process of integrating information processed simultaneously by multiple neural networks can be detected as a pattern of:
a. sequential opponent processes.
b. concurrent transduction activity.
c. trichromatic feature detection.
d. parallel difference thresholds.
e. synchronized brain waves.

Color vision, p. 209
Medium, Factual/Definitional, Objective 6, Ans: b

58. Evidence that some cones are especially sensitive to red light, others to green light, and still others to blue light is most directly supportive of the ________ theory.
   a. frequency
   b. Young-Helmholtz
   c. gate-control
   d. opponent-process
   e. signal detection

Color vision, pp. 209, 215
Medium, Conceptual, Objective 6, Ans: c

59. Frequency theory is to pitch as the Young-Helmholtz theory is to:
   a. pain.
   b. amplitude.
   c. hue.
   d. kinesthesis.
   e. brightness.

Color vision, p. 209
Medium, Factual/Definitional, Objective 6, Ans: b

60. According to the Young-Helmholtz theory, when both red- and green-sensitive cones are stimulated simultaneously, a person should see:
   a. red.
   b. yellow.
   c. blue.
   d. green.

Color vision, p. 209
Medium, Factual/Definitional, Objective 6, Ans: b

61. In additive color mixing, the combination of red, green, and blue creates ________; in subtractive color mixing, the combination of red, yellow, and blue creates ________.
   a. white; white
   b. white; black
   c. yellow; green
   d. black; white
   e. black; black

Color vision, p. 209
Medium, Conceptual/Application, Objective 6, Ans: a

62. When most people stare first at a blue circle and then shift their eyes to a white surface, the afterimage of the circle appears:
   a. yellow.
   b. red.
   c. green.
   d. blue.

Color vision, p. 209
Medium, Factual/Definitional, Objective 6, Ans: e

63. The fact that people who are colorblind to red and green may still see yellow is most easily explained by:
    a. the Young-Helmholtz theory.
    b. the gate-control theory.
    c. place theory.
    d. frequency theory.
    e. the opponent-process theory.

Color vision, pp. 209-210
Medium, Factual/Definitional, Objective 6, Ans: c

64. According to the opponent-process theory, cells that are stimulated by exposure to ________ light are inhibited by exposure to ________ light.
    a. green; blue
    b. yellow; red
    c. green; red
    d. red; blue
    e. yellow; green

Color vision, p. 210
Medium, Factual/Definitional, Objective 6, Ans: a

65. Opponent-process cells have been located in the:
    a. thalamus.
    b. cochlea.
    c. spinal cord.
    d. visual cortex.
    e. semicircular canals.

Color constancy, p. 210
Easy, Factual/Definitional, Objective 6, Ans: b

66. Color constancy refers to the fact that:
    a. light waves reflected by an object remain constant despite changes in lighting.
    b. objects are perceived to be the same color even if the light they reflect changes.
    c. the perceived color of an object has a constant relation to its brightness.
    d. the frequency of light waves is directly proportional to the light's wavelength.

Color constancy, p. 210
Medium, Factual/Definitional, Objective 6, Ans: d

67. In order to experience color constancy it is helpful to view things:
    a. from very short distances.
    b. for long periods of time.
    c. under low levels of illumination.
    d. in relation to surrounding objects.

The stimulus input: sound waves, p. 212
Medium, Conceptual/Application, Objective 7, Ans: d

68. Long sound waves are to short sound waves as a ________ voice is to a ________ voice.
a. loud; soft
b. soprano; bass
c. soft; loud
d. bass; soprano

The stimulus input: sound waves, pp. 200, 212
Difficult, Conceptual/Application, Objective 7, Ans: d

69. Red light is to blue light as ________ sounds are to ________ sounds.
a. loud; soft
b. soft; loud
c. high-pitched; low-pitched
d. low-pitched; high-pitched

The stimulus input: sound waves, p. 212
Medium, Conceptual, Objective 7, Ans: d

70. Loudness is to amplitude as pitch is to:
a. brightness.
b. hue.
c. timbre.
d. frequency.

The stimulus input: sound waves, pp. 200, 212
Medium, Conceptual, Objective 7, Ans: b

71. Brightness is to light as ________ is to sound.
a. pitch
b. loudness
c. frequency
d. amplitude
e. wavelength

The stimulus input: sound waves, p. 212
Difficult, Conceptual/Application, Objective 7, Ans: d

72. An 80-decibel sound is ________ times louder than a 60-decibel sound.
a. 2
b. 10
c. 20
d. 100
e. 200

The ear, p. 213
Easy, Factual/Definitional, Objective 7, Ans: e

73. The vibrations of the eardrum are amplified by three tiny bones located in the:
a. eustachian tube.
b. semicircular canals.
c. inner ear.
d. cochlea.
e. middle ear.

The ear, p. 213
Easy, Factual/Definitional, Objective 7, Ans: a

74. The cochlea is a:
  a. fluid-filled tube in which sound waves trigger nerve impulses.
  b. fluid-filled tube that provides a sense of upright body position.
  c. fluid-filled tube that provides a sense of body movement.
  d. set of three tiny bones that amplify the vibrations of the eardrum.

The ear, p. 213
Easy, Factual/Definitional, Objective 7, Ans: a

75. The basilar membrane is lined with:
  a. hair cells.
  b. olfactory receptors.
  c. bipolar cells.
  d. feature detectors.

The ear, pp. 202, 213
Medium, Conceptual, Objective 7, Ans: d

76. Cones are to vision as ________ are to audition.
  a. eardrums
  b. cochleas
  c. oval windows
  d. hair cells
  e. semicircular canals

The ear, p. 214
Medium, Factual/Definitional, Objective 7, Ans: a

77. Many hard-of-hearing people like sound compressed because they are still sensitive to ________ sounds.
  a. loud
  b. high-pitched
  c. prolonged
  d. unpredictable

Noise (Close-up), p. 214
Medium, Conceptual/Application, Objective 9, Ans: c

78. The noise level at Sherry's place of work sometimes becomes quite intense. This is most likely to disrupt her ability to work efficiently if the noise:
  a. occurs primarily during her first hour at work each day.
  b. comes from the chattering of her coworkers.
  c. is experienced at unpredictable intervals throughout the day.
  d. is a repetitious, low-pitched, droning sound.

How do we perceive pitch?, p. 215
Easy, Factual/Definitional, Objective 8, Ans: d

79. Place theory suggests that:
    a. structures in the inner ear provide us with a sense of the position of our bodies in space.
    b. we have a system for sensing the position and movement of the various parts of our body.
    c. we can locate the place from which a sound is emitted because of the distance between our ears.
    d. the pitch we hear is related to the place where the cochlea's basilar membrane is stimulated.

How do we perceive pitch?, p. 215
Medium, Conceptual/Application, Objective 8, Ans: e

80. After a small section of his basilar membrane was damaged, Jason experienced a noticeable loss of hearing for high-pitched sounds only. Jason's hearing loss is best explained by the ________ theory.
    a. gate-control
    b. frequency
    c. Young-Helmholtz
    d. opponent-process
    e. place

How do we perceive pitch?, p. 215
Difficult, Factual/Definitional, Objective 8, Ans: d

81. According to place theory, the perception of ________ sounds is associated with large vibrations of the ________ closest to the oval window.
    a. low-pitched; eardrum
    b. high-pitched; eardrum
    c. low-pitched; basilar membrane
    d. high-pitched; basilar membrane

How do we perceive pitch?, p. 215
Medium, Factual/Definitional, Objective 8, Ans: c

82. Which theory best explains how we perceive low-pitched sounds?
    a. place theory
    b. opponent-process theory
    c. frequency theory
    d. the Young-Helmholtz theory

How do we perceive pitch?, p. 215
Difficult, Factual/Definitional, Objective 8, Ans: e

83. The volley principle is most directly relevant to our perception of:
    a. loudness.
    b. color.
    c. brightness.
    d. pain.
    e. pitch.

How do we locate sounds?, p. 215
Easy, Factual/Definitional, Objective 8, Ans: a

84. A time lag between left and right auditory stimulation is important for accurately:
   a. locating sounds.
   b. detecting pitch.
   c. identifying timbre.
   d. judging amplitude.

How do we locate sounds?, p. 215
Medium, Conceptual, Objective 8, Ans: d

85. Cocking your head would be most useful for detecting the ______ of a sound.
   a. timbre
   b. pitch
   c. loudness
   d. location
   e. amplitude

How do we locate sounds?, p. 215
Medium, Conceptual/Application, Objective 8, Ans: c

86. The barn owl's right ear opens slightly upward while its left ear opens slightly downward. This asymmetry is most useful for enabling the owl to detect the ________ of a sound.
   a. pitch
   b. timbre
   c. location
   d. loudness
   e. amplitude

Hearing loss, p. 216
Medium, Conceptual/Application, Objective 9, Ans: b

87. Joe Wilson, age 55, has been told by experts that a hearing aid would restore his lost sense of hearing. It is likely that Joe's hearing loss involves problems within the:
   a. inner ear.
   b. middle ear.
   c. auditory nerve.
   d. basilar membrane.

Hearing loss, p. 216
Medium, Factual/Definitional, Objective 9, Ans: e

88. Damage to the basilar membrane is most likely to result in:
   a. loss of the sense of movement.
   b. loss of the sense of position.
   c. conduction hearing loss.
   d. loss of the sense of balance.
   e. nerve deafness.

Hearing loss, p. 216
Difficult, Conceptual/Application, Objective 9, Ans: d

89. As a rock musician who has experienced prolonged exposure to high-amplitude music, Rodney is beginning to lose his hearing. It is most likely that this hearing loss involves problems in the:
  a. auditory canal.
  b. eardrum.
  c. tiny bones of the middle ear.
  d. cochlea.

Hearing loss (text and Figure 5.23), p. 216
Difficult, Conceptual/Application, Objective 9, Ans: c

90. Mrs. Acheube is just beginning to experience sensorineural hearing loss. She is likely to have the greatest difficulty hearing sounds of ________ frequency and ________ amplitude.
  a. low; low
  b. low; high
  c. high; low
  d. high; high

Hearing loss, p. 217
Medium, Factual/Definitional, Objective 9, Ans: a

91. Deaf culture advocates are most likely to object to the use of cochlear implants for:
  a. children who have been deaf from birth.
  b. adults who have experienced a loss of both vision and hearing.
  c. children who have never learned sign language.
  d. adults whose hearing becomes impaired later in their lives.

Living in a silent world (Close-up), p. 218
Medium, Factual/Definitional, Objective 9, Ans: b

92. Deaf children typically do not:
  a. withdraw from social interaction with their hearing peers.
  b. suffer an inability to learn language.
  c. attend either special education classes in public schools or residential schools for the deaf.
  d. benefit psychologically from being raised in a household that uses sign language.

Touch, p. 220
Easy, Factual/Definitional, Objective 10, Ans: d

93. The sense of touch includes the four basic sensations of:
  a. pleasure, pain, warmth, and cold.
  b. pain, pressure, hot, and cold.
  c. wetness, pain, hot, and cold.
  d. pressure, pain, warmth, and cold.

Touch, p. 220
Medium, Factual/Definitional, Objective 10, Ans: a

94. Of the four distinct skin senses, specialized receptor cells have been identified for the sense of:
  a. pressure.
  b. pain.
  c. warmth.
  d. cold.

Touch, p. 220
Easy, Factual/Definitional, Objective 10, Ans: c

95. The sensation of hot results from the simultaneous stimulation of adjacent ________ spots on the skin.
 a. warmth and pain
 b. pain and cold
 c. cold and warmth
 d. warmth and pressure

Pain, p. 221
Medium, Factual/Definitional, Objective 10, Ans: a

96. Which of the following best illustrates the impact of central nervous system activity in the absence of normal sensory input?
 a. tinnitus
 b. kinesthesis
 c. transduction
 d. accommodation

Pain, pp. 210, 221
Medium, Conceptual, Objective 10, Ans: e

97. The opponent-process theory is to our sense of color as the gate-control theory is to our sense of:
 a. pitch.
 b. smell.
 c. equilibrium.
 d. kinesthesis.
 e. pain.

Pain, p. 221
Medium, Conceptual/Application, Objective 10, Ans: b

98. According to the gate-control theory, a back massage would most likely reduce your physical aches and pains by causing the:
 a. release of pain-killing endorphins in your brain.
 b. activation of specific neural fibers in your spinal cord.
 c. arousal of your autonomic nervous system and the release of adrenaline into your bloodstream.
 d. deactivation of the pain receptors on the surface of your skin.

Pain, p. 222
Difficult, Factual/Definitional, Objective 10, Ans: b

99. People's memories of the pain involved in a previously experienced medical procedure are dominated by the:
 a. pain experienced during the first moments of the procedure.
 b. pain experienced during the final moments of the procedure.
 c. total duration of the pain associated with the procedure.
 d. total duration of the procedure itself.

Pain, p. 222
Easy, Factual/Definitional, Objective 10, Ans: e

100. Which of the following pain control techniques is emphasized in the Lamaze method of childbirth training?
   a. accommodation
   b. acupuncture
   c. subliminal stimulation
   d. kinesthesis
   e. distraction

Thinking critically about firewalking (Box), p. 223
Easy, Factual/Definitional, Objective 10, Ans: b

101. Firewalking without the experience of severe pain results from the:
   a. distraction of attention away from one's feet.
   b. poor heat conductivity of hot wood coals.
   c. activation of nerves in the spinal cord that block transmission of pain signals.
   d. alteration of body chemistry induced by a state of meditation.

Taste, p. 224
Medium, Factual/Definitional, Objective 11, Ans: d

102. Taste receptors are located:
   a. on the top of the tongue.
   b. on the sides of the tongue.
   c. on the roof of the mouth.
   d. in all of the above places.

Taste, p. 224
Easy, Factual/Definitional, Objective 11, Ans: c

103. Receptor cells for our sense of ________ reproduce themselves every week or two.
   a. vision
   b. hearing
   c. taste
   d. equilibrium

Taste, p. 224
Easy, Factual/Definitional, Objective 11, Ans: d

104. Your sensitivity to taste will decline if you:
   a. smoke heavily.
   b. consume large amounts of alcohol.
   c. grow older.
   d. do any of the above.

Taste, p. 224
Medium, Conceptual/Application, Objective 11, Ans: b

105. During the months when there is a large amount of pollen in the air, your hay fever severely affects your sense of smell. At the same time your food all seems to taste the same. This illustrates the importance of:
a. accommodation.
b. sensory interaction.
c. kinesthesis.
d. serial processing.
e. sensory adaptation.

Taste, pp. 224-225
Difficult, Factual/Definitional, Objective 11, Ans: d

106. The McGurk effect best illustrates:
a. phantom limb sensations.
b. subliminal priming.
c. the volley principle.
d. sensory interaction.
e. color constancy.

Smell, p. 225
Easy, Factual/Definitional, Objective 11, Ans: e

107. Which of the following senses is best described as a chemical sense?
a. touch
b. kinesthesis
c. audition
d. vision
e. smell

Smell, p. 225
Medium, Conceptual/Application, Objective 11, Ans: c

108. Which of the following would play a role in quickly alerting you to a gas leak in your home?
a. vestibular sacs
b. bipolar cells
c. olfactory receptors
d. feature detectors
e. basilar membrane

Smell, pp. 226-227
Medium, Factual/Definitional, Objective 11, Ans: c

109. Pleasant memories are most likely to be evoked by exposure to:
a. bright colors.
b. soft touches.
c. fragrant odors.
d. loud sounds.

Smell, p. 227
Difficult, Factual/Definitional, Objective 11, Ans: d

110. The olfactory cortex is located within the:
   a. frontal lobes.
   b. parietal lobes.
   c. occipital lobes.
   d. temporal lobes.

Body position and movement, p. 227
Easy, Factual/Definitional, Objective 12, Ans: c

111. Our sense of the position and movement of individual body parts is called:
   a. feature detection.
   b. accommodation.
   c. kinesthesis.
   d. sensory interaction.
   e. the vestibular sense.

Body position and movement, p. 227
Medium, Factual/Definitional, Objective 12, Ans: c

112. Receptor cells for kinesthesis are located in the:
   a. fovea.
   b. inner ear.
   c. muscles, tendons, and joints.
   d. olfactory epithelium.
   e. auditory cortex.

Body position and movement, p. 227
Medium, Factual/Definitional, Objective 12, Ans: c

113. The semicircular canals are most directly relevant to:
   a. hearing.
   b. kinesthesis.
   c. the vestibular sense.
   d. parallel processing.
   e. accommodation.

Body position and movement, p. 228
Medium, Conceptual/Application, Objective 12, Ans: e

114. Which of the following play the biggest role in our feeling dizzy and unbalanced after a thrilling roller coaster ride?
   a. olfactory receptors
   b. feature detectors
   c. basilar membranes
   d. bipolar cells
   e. semicircular canals

Essay Questions

1. Use your understanding of absolute thresholds, sensory adaptation, and pain control to argue that sensation is often influenced by our motives, expectations, and psychological states of mind.

2. You are the president of a corporation that owns several large department stores. A board member has a plan for preventing shoplifting: In each store play musical soundtracks containing subaudible and consciously imperceptible verbal messages such as "don't steal" and "shoplifting is a crime."

   Carefully discuss your reasons for supporting or rejecting this proposal to engage in subliminal persuasion.

3. In what sense is there a correspondence between the experiences of hue and pitch? Discuss how the Young-Helmholtz theory of color vision and the place theory of pitch perception are conceptually similar or different.

4. A friend believes that the five human senses—seeing, hearing, tasting, smelling, and feeling—are distinct and independent. Explain what is wrong with your friend's belief.

Web Quiz 1

Ans: b

1. Experiencing sudden pain is to _______ as recognizing that you are suffering a heart attack is to ________.
   a. transduction; accommodation
   b. sensation; perception
   c. absolute threshold; difference threshold
   d. gate-control theory; the volley principle

Ans: a

2. The impact of boredom and fatigue on people's absolute thresholds is highlighted by:
   a. signal detection theory.
   b. opponent-process theory.
   c. Weber's law.
   d. frequency theory.
   e. the Young-Helmholtz theory.

Ans: c

3. If a visual image is first presented subliminally, the chance of a person later recognizing the same briefly presented image is improved. This best illustrates:
   a. the pervasive impact of sensory interaction.
   b. the difference between signal detection and feature detectors.
   c. that information can be processed outside of conscious awareness.
   d. that the process of accommodation takes place over a period of time.

Ans: c

4. If you move your watchband up your wrist an inch or so, you will feel it for only a few moments. This best illustrates:
   a. parallel processing.
   b. accommodation.
   c. sensory adaptation.
   d. Weber's law.

Ans: a

5. Visible lights have ________ wavelengths than radio waves and _______ wavelengths than X-rays.
   a. shorter; longer
   b. longer; shorter
   c. shorter; shorter
   d. longer; longer

Ans: e

6. The central focal point in the retina where cones are heavily concentrated is known as the:
   a. pupil.
   b. lens.
   c. optic nerve.
   d. cornea.
   e. fovea.

Ans: d

7. Visual information is processed by ganglion cells ________ it is processed by rods and cones and ________ it is processed by bipolar cells.
   a. before; after
   b. after; before
   c. before; before
   d. after; after

Ans: b

8. Some stroke victims lose the capacity to perceive motion but retain the capacity to perceive shapes and colors. Others lose the capacity to perceive colors but retain the capacity to perceive movement and form. These peculiar visual disabilities best illustrate our normal capacity for:
   a. sensory adaptation.
   b. parallel processing.
   c. sensory interaction.
   d. accommodation.
   e. prosopagnosia.

Ans: e

9. The opponent-process theory is most useful for explaining one of the characteristics of:
   a. phantom limb sensations.
   b. prosopagnosia.
   c. nearsightedness.
   d. accommodation.
   e. afterimages.

Ans: b

10. Damage to the basilar membrane is most likely to affect one's:
   a. vision.
   b. audition.
   c. sense of smell.
   d. sense of taste.
   e. vestibular sense.

Ans: d

11. Digital hearing aids produce ________ sound by restricting the range of sound _______.
   a. stereophonic; frequencies
   b. stereophonic; amplitudes
   c. compressed; frequencies
   d. compressed; amplitudes

Ans: c

12. The volley principle is most relevant to understanding how we sense:
   a. pain.
   b. color.
   c. pitch.
   d. taste.
   e. body movement.

Ans: c

13. Infant rats deprived of their mothers' grooming touch produce ________ growth hormone and have a ________ metabolic rate.
    a. less; higher
    b. more; lower
    c. less, lower
    d. more; higher

Ans: a

14. The absolute threshold for taste sensations is relatively _______ among people who smoke and relatively ________ among people who abuse alcohol.
    a. high; high
    b. low; low
    c. high; low
    d. low; high

Ans: b

15. Receptor cells for the vestibular sense send messages to the:
    a. fovea.
    b. cerebellum.
    c. olfactory cortex.
    d. frontal lobes.
    e. limbic system.

Web Quiz 2

Ans: b

1. Interpreting new sensory information within the framework of a past memory illustrates:
   a. accommodation.
   b. top-down processing.
   c. Weber's law.
   d. sensory adaptation.

Ans: d

2. Damage to a region of the temporal lobe essential to recognizing faces results in a condition known as:
   a. the McGurk effect.
   b. Young-Helmholtz syndrome.
   c. kinesthesis.
   d. prosopagnosia.
   e. tinnitus.

Ans: c

3. Which of the following is most notable for its short-term effects on thinking?
   a. sensory interaction
   b. bottom-up processing
   c. subliminal stimulation
   d. top-down processing
   e. serial processing

Ans: c

4. The size of the difference threshold is greater for heavier objects than for lighter ones. This best illustrates:
   a. sensory interaction.
   b. the volley principle.
   c. Weber's law.
   d. parallel processing.
   e. the opponent-process theory.

Ans: d

5. The ring of muscle tissue that controls the pupil's size is called the:
   a. cornea.
   b. fovea.
   c. lens.
   d. iris.

Ans: d

6. Which of the following activities most clearly takes place in the rods and cones?
   a. accommodation
   b. sensory interaction
   c. top-down processing
   d. sensory transduction

Ans: c

7. The phenomenon of blindsight best illustrates that visual information can be processed without:
   a. sensory transduction.
   b. parallel processing.
   c. conscious awareness.
   d. feature detectors.

Ans: d

8. Even with sunglasses on, grass appears equally as green as it does without glasses. This best illustrates:
   a. Weber's law.
   b. sensory interaction.
   c. accommodation.
   d. color constancy.

Ans: a

9. The number of complete sound waves that strike one's eardrum in a given second determines the _______ of the sound.
   a. pitch
   b. transduction
   c. decibel level
   d. difference threshold

Ans: b

10. The hammer, anvil, and stirrup are three tiny bones that transmit vibrations to the:
   a. vestibular sacs.
   b. oval window.
   c. eardrum.
   d. semicircular canal.
   e. olfactory receptors.

Ans: c

11. Herman von Helmholtz developed both a(n) ________ theory of color discrimination and a ________ theory of pitch discrimination.
   a. trichromatic; frequency
   b. opponent-process; frequency
   c. trichromatic; place
   d. opponent process; place

Ans: c

12. Elderly people typically have an especially _______ absolute threshold for _______ pitched sounds.
   a. high; low
   b. low; high
   c. high; high
   d. low; low

Ans: b

13. Tinnitus is a phantom ______ sensation.
    a. visual
    b. auditory
    c. taste
    d. touch
    e. kinesthetic

Ans: e

14. A drink's strawberry odor enhances our perception of its sweetness. This best illustrates:
    a. the volley principle.
    b. accommodation.
    c. sensory adaptation.
    d. Weber's law.
    e. sensory interaction.

Ans: e

15. The sensory experience of bending one's knees or raising one's arms exemplifies:
    a. the vestibular sense.
    b. top-down processing.
    c. sensory interaction.
    d. parallel processing.
    e. kinesthesis.

Study Guide Questions

Ans: c, p. 193

1. Superman's eyes used ________, while his brain used ________.
   a. perception; sensation
   b. top-down processing; bottom-up processing
   c. bottom-up processing; top-down processing
   d. sensory adaptation; subliminal perception

Ans: b, p. 193

2. Sensation is to ________ as perception is to ________.
   a. recognizing a stimulus; interpreting a stimulus
   b. detecting a stimulus; recognizing a stimulus
   c. interpreting a stimulus; detecting a stimulus
   d. seeing; hearing

Ans: c, p. 194

3. Given normal sensory ability, a person standing atop a mountain on a dark, clear night can see a candle flame atop a mountain 30 miles away. This is a description of vision's:
   a. difference threshold.
   b. jnd.
   c. absolute threshold.
   d. signal detection.

Ans: b, p. 195

4. Which of the following is true?
   a. The absolute threshold for any stimulus is a constant.
   b. The absolute threshold for any stimulus varies somewhat.
   c. The absolute threshold is defined as the minimum amount of stimulation necessary for a stimulus to be detected 75 percent of the time.
   d. The absolute threshold is defined as the minimum amount of stimulation necessary for a stimulus to be detected 60 percent of the time.

Ans: d, pp. 196-197

5. Concerning the evidence for subliminal stimulation, which of the following is the best answer?
   a. The brain processes some information without our awareness.
   b. Stimuli too weak to cross our thresholds for awareness may trigger a response in our sense receptors.
   c. Because the "absolute" threshold is a statistical average, we are able to detect weaker stimuli some of the time.
   d. All of the above are true.

Ans: c, p. 197

6. If you can just notice the difference between 10- and 11-pound weights, which of the following weights could you differentiate from a 100-pound weight?
   a. 101-pound weight
   b. 105-pound weight
   c. 110-pound weight
   d. there is no basis for prediction

Ans: d, p. 197

7. In shopping for a new stereo, you discover that you cannot differentiate between the sounds of models X and Y. The difference between X and Y is below your:
   a. absolute threshold.
   b. signal detection.
   c. receptor threshold.
   d. difference threshold.

Ans: d, p. 197

8. Weber's law states that:
   a. the absolute threshold for any stimulus is a constant.
   b. the jnd for any stimulus is a constant.
   c. the absolute threshold for any stimulus is a constant proportion.
   d. the jnd for any stimulus is a constant proportion.

Ans: a, p. 198

9. When admiring the texture of a piece of fabric, Calvin usually runs his fingertips over the cloth's surface. He does this because:
   a. if the cloth were held motionless, sensory adaptation to its feel would quickly occur.
   b. the sense of touch does not adapt.
   c. a relatively small amount of brain tissue is devoted to processing touch from the fingertips.
   d. of all of the above reasons.

Ans: c, p. 198

10. A decrease in sensory responsiveness accompanying an unchanging stimulus is called:
   a. sensory fatigue.
   b. accommodation.
   c. sensory adaptation.
   d. sensory interaction.

Ans: a, p. 198

11. Which of the following is an example of sensory adaptation?
   a. finding the cold water of a swimming pool warmer after you have been in it for a while
   b. developing an increased sensitivity to salt the more you use it in foods
   c. becoming very irritated at the continuing sound of a dripping faucet
   d. all of the above are examples

Ans: d, p. 199

12. The process by which sensory information is converted into neural energy is:
   a. sensory adaptation.
   b. feature detection.
   c. signal detection.
   d. transduction.
   e. parallel processing.

Ans: a, p. 200

13. Wavelength is to ________ as ________ is to brightness.
   a. hue; intensity
   b. intensity; hue
   c. frequency; amplitude
   d. brightness; hue

Ans: a, p. 200

14. One light may appear reddish and another greenish if they differ in:
    a. wavelength.
    b. amplitude.
    c. opponent processes.
    d. brightness.

Ans: c, p. 201

15. Nearsightedness is a condition in which the:
    a. lens has become inflexible.
    b. lens is too thin.
    c. eyeball is longer than normal.
    d. eyeball is shorter than normal.

Ans: d, p. 201

16. The size of the pupil is controlled by the:
    a. lens.
    b. retina.
    c. cornea.
    d. iris.

Ans: d, p. 201

17. In comparing the human eye to a camera, the film would be analogous to the eye's:
    a. pupil.
    b. lens.
    c. cornea.
    d. retina.

Ans: e, p. 201

18. Which of the following is the correct order of the structures through which light passes after entering the eye?
    a. lens, pupil, cornea, retina
    b. pupil, cornea, lens, retina
    c. pupil, lens, cornea, retina
    d. cornea, retina, pupil, lens
    e. cornea, pupil, lens, retina

Ans: a, p. 201

19. The process by which the lens changes its curvature is:
    a. accommodation.
    b. sensory adaptation.
    c. focusing.
    d. transduction.

Ans: b, pp. 201-202

20. The transduction of light energy into nerve impulses takes place in the:
    a. iris.
    b. retina.
    c. lens.
    d. optic nerve.
    e. rods.

Ans: d, p. 203

21. One reason that your ability to detect fine visual details is greatest when scenes are focused on the fovea of your retina is that:
   a. there are more feature detectors in the fovea than in the peripheral regions of the retina.
   b. cones in the fovea are nearer to the optic nerve than those in peripheral regions of the retina.
   c. many rods, which are clustered in the fovea, have individual bipolar cells to relay their information to the cortex.
   d. many cones, which are clustered in the fovea, have individual bipolar cells to relay their information to the cortex.

Ans: d, p. 203

22. Which of the following is not true of cones?
   a. Cones enable color vision.
   b. Cones are highly concentrated in the foveal region of the retina.
   c. Cones have a higher absolute threshold for brightness than rods.
   d. Each cone has its own bipolar cell.

Ans: b, p. 203

23. Assuming that the visual systems of humans and other mammals function similarly, you would expect that the retina of a nocturnal mammal (one active only at night) would contain:
   a. mostly cones.
   b. mostly rods.
   c. an equal number of rods and cones.
   d. more bipolar cells than an animal active only during the day.

Ans: b, p. 203

24. As the football game continued into the night, LeVar noticed that he was having difficulty distinguishing the colors of the players' uniforms. This is because the ________, which enable color vision, have a ________ absolute threshold for brightness than the available light intensity.
   a. rods; higher
   b. cones; higher
   c. rods; lower
   d. cones; lower

Ans: d, p. 203

25. In order to maximize your sensitivity to fine visual detail you should:
   a. stare off to one side of the object you are attempting to see.
   b. close one eye.
   c. decrease the intensity of the light falling upon the object.
   d. stare directly at the object.

Ans: e, p. 203

26. The receptor of the eye that functions best in dim light is the:
   a. fovea.
   b. ganglion cell.
   c. cone.
   d. bipolar cell.
   e. rod.

Ans: d, p. 204

27. Hubel and Wiesel discovered feature detectors in the visual:
    a. fovea.
    b. optic nerve.
    c. iris.
    d. cortex.
    e. retina.

Ans: b, p. 206

28. The brain breaks vision into separate dimensions such as color, depth, movement, and form, and works on each aspect simultaneously. This is called:
    a. feature detection.
    b. parallel processing.
    c. accommodation.
    d. opponent processing.

Ans: a, p. 209

29. Most color-deficient people will probably:
    a. lack functioning red- or green-sensitive cones.
    b. see the world in only black and white.
    c. also suffer from poor vision.
    d. have above-average vision to compensate for the deficit.

Ans: a, p. 209

30. The Young-Helmholtz theory proposes that:
    a. there are three different types of color-sensitive cones.
    b. retinal cells are excited by one color and inhibited by its complementary color.
    c. there are four different types of cones.
    d. rod, not cone, vision accounts for our ability to detect fine visual detail.

Ans: c, p. 210

31. According to the opponent-process theory:
    a. there are three types of color-sensitive cones.
    b. the process of color vision begins in the cortex.
    c. neurons involved in color vision are stimulated by one color's wavelength and inhibited by another's.
    d. all of the above are true.

Ans: c, p. 210

32. Which of the following is the most accurate description of how we process color?
    a. Throughout the visual system, color processing is divided into separate red, green, and blue systems.
    b. Red-green, blue-yellow, and black-white opponent processes operate throughout the visual system.
    c. Color processing occurs in two stages: (1) a three-color system in the retina and (2) opponent-process cells en route to the visual cortex.
    d. Color processing occurs in two stages: (1) an opponent-process system in the retina and (2) a three-color system en route to the visual cortex.

Ans: a, p. 210

33. In the opponent-process theory, the three pairs of processes are:
  a. red-green, blue-yellow, black-white.
  b. red-blue, green-yellow, black-white.
  c. red-yellow, blue-green, black-white.
  d. dependent upon the individual's past experience.

Ans: c, p. 210

34. After staring at a very intense red stimulus for a few minutes, Carrie shifted her gaze to a beige wall and "saw" the color ________. Carrie's experience provides support for the ________ theory.
  a. green; trichromatic
  b. blue; opponent-process
  c. green; opponent-process
  d. blue; trichromatic

Ans: d, p. 210

35. I am a cell in the thalamus that is excited by red and inhibited by green. I am a(n):
  a. feature detector.
  b. cone.
  c. bipolar cell.
  d. opponent-process cell.
  e. rod.

Ans: d, p. 210

36. Which of the following explains why a rose appears equally red in bright and dim light?
  a. the Young-Helmholtz theory
  b. the opponent-process theory
  c. feature detection
  d. color constancy

Ans: b, p. 212

37. Frequency is to pitch as ________ is to ________.
  a. wavelength; loudness
  b. amplitude; loudness
  c. wavelength; intensity
  d. amplitude; intensity

Ans: a, p. 213

38. Which of the following correctly lists the order of structures through which sound travels after entering the ear?
  a. auditory canal, eardrum, middle ear, cochlea
  b. eardrum, auditory canal, middle ear, cochlea
  c. eardrum, middle ear, cochlea, auditory canal
  d. cochlea, eardrum, middle ear, auditory canal
  e. auditory canal, middle ear, eardrum, cochlea

Ans: d, p. 213

39. Dr. Frankenstein has forgotten to give his monster an important part; as a result, the monster cannot transduce sound. Dr. Frankenstein omitted the:
 a. eardrum.
 b. middle ear.
 c. semicircular canals.
 d. basilar membrane.

Ans: c, p. 213

40. The receptors for hearing are located in:
 a. the outer ear.
 b. the middle ear.
 c. the inner ear.
 d. all parts of the ear.

Ans: c, pp. 213, 227

41. The inner ear contains receptors for:
 a. audition and kinesthesis.
 b. kinesthesis and the vestibular sense.
 c. audition and the vestibular sense.
 d. audition, kinesthesis, and the vestibular sense.

Ans: a, p. 215

42. The place theory of pitch perception cannot account for how we hear:
 a. low-pitched sounds.
 b. middle-pitched sounds.
 c. high-pitched sounds.
 d. chords (three or more pitches simultaneously).

Ans: c, p. 215

43. Which of the following is the most accurate explanation of how we discriminate pitch?
 a. For all audible frequencies, pitch is coded according to the place of maximum vibration on the cochlea's basilar membrane.
 b. For all audible frequencies, the rate of neural activity in the auditory nerve matches the frequency of the sound wave.
 c. For very high frequencies, pitch is coded according to place of vibration on the basilar membrane; for lower pitches, the rate of neural activity in the auditory nerve matches the sound's frequency.
 d. For very high frequencies, the rate of neural activity in the auditory nerve matches the frequency of the sound wave; for lower frequencies, pitch is coded according to the place of vibration on the basilar membrane.

Ans: a, p. 215

44. The frequency theory of hearing is better than place theory at explaining our sensation of:
 a. the lowest pitches.
 b. pitches of intermediate range.
 c. the highest pitches.
 d. all of the above.

Ans: d, p. 215

45. Seventy-five-year-old Claude has difficulty hearing high-pitched sounds. Most likely his hearing problem involves:
   a. his eardrum.
   b. his auditory canal.
   c. the bones of his middle ear.
   d. the hair cells of his inner ear.

Ans: c, p. 216

46. The hearing losses that occur with age are especially pronounced for:
   a. low-pitched sounds.
   b. middle-pitched sounds.
   c. high-pitched sounds.
   d. chords.

Ans: d, p. 216

47. Nerve deafness is caused by:
   a. wax buildup in the outer ear.
   b. damage to the eardrum.
   c. blockage in the middle ear because of infection.
   d. damage to the cochlea.
   e. a puncture to the eardrum.

Ans: c, p. 220

48. Of the four distinct skin senses, the only one that has definable receptors is:
   a. warmth.
   b. cold.
   c. pressure.
   d. pain.

Ans: d, p. 221

49. According to the gate-control theory, a way to alleviate chronic pain would be to stimulate the ________ nerve fibers that ________ the spinal gate.
   a. small; open
   b. small; close
   c. large; open
   d. large; close

Ans: c, p. 221

50. The phantom limb sensation indicates that:
   a. pain is a purely sensory phenomenon.
   b. the central nervous system plays only a minor role in the experience of pain.
   c. pain involves the brain's interpretation of neural activity.
   d. all of the above are true.

Ans: d, pp. 221-222

51. How does pain differ from other senses?
   a. It has no identifiable receptors.
   b. It has no single stimulus.
   c. It is influenced by both physical and psychological phenomena.
   d. All of the above are true.

Ans: a, pp. 221-222

52. While competing in the Olympic trials, marathoner Kirsten O'Brien suffered a stress fracture in her left leg. That she did not experience significant pain until the race was over is probably attributable to the fact that during the race:
   a. the pain gate in her spinal cord was closed by information coming from her brain.
   b. her body's production of endorphins decreased.
   c. an increase in the activity of small pain fibers closed the pain gate.
   d. a decrease in the activity of large pain fibers closed the pain gate.
   e. a decrease in the activity of large pain fibers opened the pain gate.

Ans: a, p. 224

53. The receptors for taste are located in the:
   a. taste buds.
   b. cochlea.
   c. fovea.
   d. cortex.

Ans: c, p. 224

54. Tamiko hates the bitter taste of her cough syrup. Which of the following would she find most helpful in minimizing the syrup's bad taste?
   a. tasting something very sweet before taking the cough syrup
   b. keeping the syrup in her mouth for several seconds before swallowing it
   c. holding her nose while taking the cough syrup
   d. gulping the cough syrup so that it misses her tongue

Ans: d, p. 224

55. The principle that one sense may influence another is:
   a. transduction.
   b. sensory adaptation.
   c. Weber's law.
   d. sensory interaction.

Ans: c, p. 224

56. Elderly Mrs. Martinez finds that she must spice her food heavily or she cannot taste it. Unfortunately, her son often finds her cooking inedible because it is so spicy. What is the likely explanation for their taste differences?
   a. Women have higher taste thresholds than men.
   b. Men have higher taste thresholds than women.
   c. Being elderly, Mrs. Martinez probably has fewer taste buds than her son.
   d. All of the above are likely explanations.

Ans: d, p. 224

57. Which of the following is an example of sensory interaction?
   a. finding that despite its delicious aroma, a weird-looking meal tastes awful
   b. finding that food tastes bland when you have a bad cold
   c. finding it difficult to maintain your balance when you have an ear infection
   d. all of the above are examples

Ans: d, p. 224

58. Which of the following is not one of the basic tastes?
    a. sweet
    b. salty
    c. umami
    d. bland
    e. sour

Ans: b, p. 227

59. Kinesthesis involves:
    a. the bones of the middle ear.
    b. information from the muscles, tendons, and joints.
    c. membranes within the cochlea.
    d. the body's sense of balance.

Ans: b, p. 227

60. What enables you to feel yourself wiggling your toes even with your eyes closed?
    a. vestibular sense
    b. sense of kinesthesis
    c. the skin senses
    d. sensory interaction

CHAPTER 6

Perception

Learning Objectives

Selective Attention and Perceptual Illusions (pp. 231-236)

1. Describe how the process of perception is directed and limited by selective attention.

2. Explain how illusions help us to understand perception.

Perceptual Organization (pp. 236-248)

3. Discuss Gestalt psychology's contribution to our understanding of perception.

4. Explain the figure-ground relationship, and identify principles of perceptual grouping in form perception.

5. Discuss research on depth perception involving the use of the visual cliff, and describe the binocular and monocular cues in depth perception.

6. Describe stroboscopic movement and the phi phenomenon.

7. Describe the perceptual constancies, and show how the perceived size-distance relationship operates in visual illusions.

Perceptual Interpretation (pp. 248-257)

8. Describe the debate over the role of nature and nurture in perception, and discuss what research findings on sensory deprivation and restored vision have contributed to this debate.

9. Explain what the use of distorting goggles indicates regarding the adaptability of perception.

10. Discuss the effects of experiences, assumptions, expectations, and context on our perceptions.

11. Describe the efforts of human factors psychologists to help design machines that are best suited to our perceptual capabilities.

Is There Extrasensory Perception? (pp. 257-262)

12. State the claims of ESP, and explain why most research psychologists remain skeptical.

Selective attention, p. 231
Easy, Factual/Definitional, Objective 1, Ans: a

1. Our inability to consciously perceive all the sensory information available to us at any single point in time best illustrates the necessity of:
   a. selective attention.
   b. perceptual adaptation.
   c. retinal disparity.
   d. perceptual constancy.
   e. the phi phenomenon.

Selective attention, p. 231
Easy, Conceptual/Application, Objective 1, Ans: c

2. While reading a novel, Raoul isn't easily distracted by the sounds of the TV or even by his brothers' loud arguments. This best illustrates:
   a. interposition.
   b. perceptual adaptation.
   c. selective attention.
   d. perceptual constancy.
   e. the cocktail party effect.

Selective attention, p. 231
Medium, Conceptual/Application, Objective 1, Ans: d

3. A bank teller was so distracted by the sight of a bank robber's weapon that she failed to perceive important features of the criminal's physical appearance. This best illustrates:
   a. visual capture.
   b. perceptual set.
   c. retinal disparity.
   d. selective attention.
   e. the phi phenomenon.

Selective attention, p. 232
Easy, Factual/Definitional, Objective 1, Ans: c

4. The cocktail party effect provides an example of:
   a. perceptual constancy.
   b. perceptual set.
   c. selective attention.
   d. the phi phenomenon.
   e. perceptual adaptation.

Selective attention, p. 232
Easy, Factual/Definitional, Objective 1, Ans: e

5. In one experiment, most of the participants who viewed a videotape of men playing basketball remained unaware of an umbrella-toting woman sauntering across the screen. This illustrated the impact of:
   a. perceptual adaptation.
   b. visual capture.
   c. retinal disparity.
   d. stroboscopic movement.
   e. selective attention.

Selective attention (text and Figure 6.2), pp. 232, 233
Easy, Factual/Definitional, Objective 1, Ans: e

6. While a student provided directions to a construction worker, two experimenters rudely interrupted by passing between them carrying a door. The student's failure to notice that the construction worker was replaced by a different person during this interruption illustrates:
   a. retinal disparity.
   b. visual capture.
   c. stroboscopic movement.
   d. perceptual adaptation.
   e. change blindness.

Perceptual illusions, pp. 234-235
Medium, Factual/Definitional, Objective 2, Ans: d

7. When asked to estimate the distances of white disks under either clear or foggy conditions, people:
   a. judged the disks to be closer when viewed in the fog than when viewed in the sunshine.
   b. found it impossible to make any distance estimates under foggy conditions.
   c. judged the disks to be the same distance away whether viewed under clear or foggy conditions.
   d. judged the disks to be farther away when viewed in the fog than when viewed in the sunshine.

Perceptual illusions, p. 236
Easy, Factual/Definitional, Objective 2, Ans: b

8. When there is a conflict between bits of information received by two or more senses, which sense tends to dominate the others?
   a. hearing
   b. vision
   c. smell
   d. touch
   e. none of the above; the senses work together as equal partners

Perceptual illusions, p. 236
Easy, Factual/Definitional, Objective 2, Ans: e

9. When the soundtrack for a movie is played in the back of a classroom, students tend to perceive the sound as originating from the picture screen in the front of the room. This best illustrates:
   a. location constancy.
   b. the phi phenomenon.
   c. selective attention.
   d. perceptual adaptation.
   e. visual capture.

Perceptual illusions, p. 236
Difficult, Conceptual/Application, Objective 2, Ans: c

10. Janice experienced motion sickness simply from watching a movie scene of a thrilling motorcycle chase. Her experience best illustrates the impact of:
a. retinal disparity.
b. location constancy.
c. visual capture.
d. perceptual adaptation.
e. relative motion.

Perceptual illusions, p. 236
Medium, Conceptual/Application, Objective 3, Ans: b

11. The tendency to hear the steady drip of a leaky sink faucet as if it were a repeating rhythm of two or more beats best illustrates:
a. perceptual constancy.
b. perceptual organization.
c. the phi phenomenon.
d. perceptual adaptation.

Perceptual organization, p. 236
Easy, Factual/Definitional, Objective 3, Ans: d

12. A gestalt is best described as a(n):
a. binocular cue.
b. texture gradient.
c. perceptual adaptation.
d. organized whole.
e. perceptual set.

Perceptual organization, p. 236
Medium, Factual/Definitional, Objective 3, Ans: c

13. Gestalt psychologists emphasize that:
a. perception is the same as sensation.
b. we learn to perceive the world through experience.
c. the whole is more than the sum of its parts.
d. sensation has no effect on perception.

Perceptual organization, pp. 235, 236
Difficult, Conceptual, Objective 3, Ans: e

14. In the ripple illusion, people perceive a flat two-dimensional drawing as three-dimensional. This best illustrates that:
a. binocular cues provide more information than monocular cues.
b. perception can occur apart from sensory input.
c. visual information is especially likely to capture our attention.
d. we readily adjust to an artificially displaced visual field.
e. perception involves top-down processing.

Perceptual organization, p. 236
Difficult, Factual/Definitional, Objective 3, Ans: c

15. The organizational principles identified by Gestalt psychologists best illustrate the importance of:
   a. perceptual constancy.
   b. retinal disparity.
   c. top-down processing.
   d. perceptual adaptation.
   e. visual capture.

Perceptual organization, p. 236
Difficult, Factual/Definitional, Objective 3, Ans: c

16. Monkeys have feature-detecting brain cells that respond to illusory contours. This best illustrates that:
   a. binocular cues are more informative than monocular cues.
   b. the right and left eyes receive slightly different images of the same object.
   c. sensation and perception blend into one continuous process.
   d. sensory information may not be consciously experienced.
   e. animals readily adjust to artificially inverted visual fields.

Figure and ground, p. 237
Easy, Factual/Definitional, Objective 4, Ans: c

17. The perception of an object as distinct from its surroundings is called:
   a. perceptual set.
   b. perceptual constancy.
   c. figure-ground perception.
   d. the phi phenomenon.

Figure and ground, p. 237
Easy, Conceptual/Application, Objective 4, Ans: c

18. As the airplane descended for a landing, the pilot saw several beautiful islands that appeared to float in a vast expanse of blue ocean water. In this instance, the ocean is a:
   a. figure.
   b. gestalt.
   c. ground.
   d. perceptual set.

Figure and ground, p. 237
Medium, Conceptual, Objective 4, Ans: d

19. Figure is to ground as ________ is to ________.
   a. form; substance
   b. up; down
   c. summer; winter
   d. moon; sky
   e. perception; sensation

Grouping, p. 237
Medium, Factual/Definitional, Objective 4, Ans: a

20. The principles of connectedness and closure best illustrate that:
    a. sensations are organized into meaningful patterns.
    b. perception is the direct product of sensation.
    c. cultural experiences shape perception.
    d. visual information is especially likely to capture our attention.

Grouping, p. 237
Medium, Conceptual/Application, Objective 4, Ans: a

21. Because Carmella, Jorge, and Gail were all sitting behind the same bowling lane, Ruth perceived that they were all members of the same bowling team. This best illustrates the organizational principle of:
    a. proximity.
    b. convergence.
    c. closure.
    d. continuity.
    e. connectedness.

Grouping, p. 237
Medium, Conceptual/Application, Objective 4, Ans: d

22. Because the two teams wore different-colored uniforms, Cheri perceived the ten basketball players as two distinct groups. This best illustrates the principle of:
    a. proximity.
    b. color constancy.
    c. closure.
    d. similarity.
    e. convergence.

Grouping, p. 237
Medium, Conceptual/Application, Objective 4, Ans: d

23. The perception of the letter "t" as two intersecting lines rather than as four nonintersecting lines illustrates the principle of:
    a. convergence.
    b. proximity.
    c. closure.
    d. continuity.
    e. similarity.

Grouping, p. 237
Difficult, Conceptual/Application, Objective 4, Ans: d

24. The principle of connectedness would most likely lead you to perceive all the ________ as parts of a single unit.
    a. words in a sentence
    b. clouds in the sky
    c. letters in the alphabet
    d. rungs in a ladder
    e. fish in the sea

Grouping, p. 237
Easy, Factual/Definitional, Objective 4, Ans: c

25. The perceptual tendency to fill in gaps in order to perceive disconnected parts as a whole object is called:
    a. interposition.
    b. constancy.
    c. closure.
    d. continuity.
    e. convergence.

Grouping, p. 237
Medium, Conceptual, Objective 4, Ans: c

26. Although a few keys on the piano were broken, Shana couldn't prevent herself from mentally filling in the missing notes of the familiar melodies. This best illustrates the principle of:
    a. proximity.
    b. continuity.
    c. closure.
    d. convergence.
    e. interposition.

Depth perception, p. 238
Easy, Factual/Definitional, Objective 5, Ans: c

27. The visual cliff is a laboratory device for testing ________ in infants.
    a. size constancy
    b. selective attention
    c. depth perception
    d. perceptual adaptation
    e. figure-ground perception

Depth perception, p. 238
Medium, Factual/Definitional, Objective 5, Ans: c

28. Infants who were exposed to the visual cliff:
    a. tried to climb up the cliff if their mothers were at the top.
    b. gave no evidence that they could perceive depth.
    c. refused to cross over the "deep" side to their mothers.
    d. eagerly crossed to their mothers by means of the "bridge" provided.

Depth perception, p. 239
Medium, Factual/Definitional, Objective 5, Ans: a

29. Infants are especially likely to avoid crawling over the edge of a visual cliff if they:
    a. have a lot of previous crawling experience.
    b. have little previous experience with heights.
    c. lack a capacity for psychokinesis.
    d. lack vision in one eye.

Depth perception, pp. 238-239, 248
Difficult, Conceptual, Objective 5, Ans: b

30. The ability of newly hatched chicks to perceive depth best serves to support the views of:
    a. Locke.
    b. Kant.
    c. Freud.
    d. Aristotle.

Depth perception: binocular cues, p. 239
Easy, Factual/Definitional, Objective 5, Ans: c

31. Retinal disparity refers to the:
    a. tendency to see parallel lines as coming together in the distance.
    b. tendency to see stimuli that are near each other as parts of a unified object.
    c. somewhat different images our two eyes receive of the same object.
    d. extent to which our eyes turn toward each other when looking at an object.

Depth perception: binocular cues (Figure 6.8), p. 239
Medium, Factual/Definitional, Objective 5, Ans: c

32. Holding two index fingers in front of the eyes can create the perception of a floating finger sausage. This best illustrates the effect of:
    a. convergence.
    b. relative clarity.
    c. retinal disparity.
    d. interposition.
    e. visual capture.

Depth perception: binocular cues, pp. 239, 240
Difficult, Conceptual/Application, Objective 5, Ans: d

33. As Dick carefully watches his dog running away from him, it is likely that he will experience a(n) ________ in retinal disparity and a(n) ________ in convergence.
    a. decrease; increase
    b. increase; decrease
    c. increase; increase
    d. decrease; decrease

Depth perception: binocular cues (Figure 6.9), p. 240
Easy, Factual/Definitional, Objective 5, Ans: c

34. The ability to perceive the Greek letter psi in the textbook stereogram illustrates the importance of:
    a. convergence.
    b. interposition.
    c. retinal disparity.
    d. texture gradient.
    e. perceptual adaptation.

Depth perception: binocular cues, p. 240
Medium, Factual/Definitional, Objective 5, Ans: b

35. Which of the following is a binocular cue for the perception of distance?
a. interposition
b. convergence
c. closure
d. linear perspective
e. texture gradient

Depth perception: monocular cues, p. 240
Easy, Factual/Definitional, Objective 5, Ans: c

36. If two objects are assumed to be the same size, the object that casts the smaller retinal image is perceived to be:
a. more coarsely textured.
b. less hazy.
c. more distant.
d. closer.

Depth perception: monocular cues, p. 240
Easy, Factual/Definitional, Objective 5, Ans: a

37. The monocular depth cue in which an object blocking another object is perceived as closer is:
a. interposition.
b. relative height.
c. relative clarity.
d. linear perspective.

Depth perception: monocular cues, p. 240
Medium, Factual/Definitional, Objective 5, Ans: d

38. Relative clarity is a cue for depth perception in which closer objects:
a. create larger retinal images than do distant objects.
b. obstruct our view of distant objects.
c. appear lower in the horizontal plane than do distant objects.
d. appear clearer and more distinct than do distant objects.

Depth perception: monocular cues, p. 240
Difficult, Conceptual/Application, Objective 5, Ans: b

39. Although the mountains were over 30 miles away, the morning sky was so clear that Showana thought they were only half the distance. This best illustrates the importance of:
a. lightness constancy.
b. relative clarity.
c. relative height.
d. texture gradient.
e. relative size.

Depth perception: monocular cues, p. 240
Easy, Factual/Definitional, Objective 5, Ans: c

40. Which of the following cues do artists use to convey depth on a flat canvas?
a. convergence
b. continuity
c. interposition
d. closure
e. all of the above

Depth perception: monocular cues, p. 241
Difficult, Conceptual, Objective 5, Ans: a

41. Which of the following cues is most essential to the perception of depth in the visual cliff?
a. texture gradient
b. interposition
c. stroboscopic movement
d. connectedness

Depth perception: monocular cues, p. 241
Easy, Factual/Definitional, Objective 5, Ans: b

42. Relative height is a cue involving our perception of objects higher in our field of vision as:
a. brighter.
b. farther away.
c. hazier.
d. smaller.

Depth perception: monocular cues, p. 241
Difficult, Conceptual/Application, Objective 5, Ans: d

43. If you stared at a house as you walked down a street, the trees in front of the house would appear to be moving in the ________ direction as you, and the trees behind the house would appear to be moving in the ________ direction as you.
a. opposite; opposite
b. same; opposite
c. same; same
d. opposite; same

Depth perception: monocular cues, pp. 241, 242
Medium, Conceptual/Application, Objective 5, Ans: c

44. Distant trees were located closer to the top of the artist's canvas than were the nearby flowers. The artist was clearly using the distance cue known as:
a. linear perspective.
b. texture gradient.
c. relative height.
d. relative clarity.
e. interposition.

Depth perception: monocular cues, pp. 241, 242
Medium, Factual/Definitional, Objective 5, Ans: c

45. We perceive bright objects as ________ than dim objects and vertical lines as ________ than identical horizontal lines.
   a. closer; shorter
   b. farther away; longer
   c. closer; longer
   d. farther away; shorter

Depth perception: monocular cues, p. 242
Medium, Conceptual/Application, Objective 5, Ans: b

46. As the farmer looked across her field, the parallel rows of young corn plants appeared to converge in the distance. This provided her with a distance cue known as:
   a. proximity.
   b. linear perspective.
   c. closure.
   d. continuity.
   e. interposition.

Motion perception, p. 243
Medium, Factual/Definitional, Objective 6, Ans: c

47. The steadily increasing size of the retinal image of an approaching object is especially important for perceiving the object's:
   a. shape.
   b. relative clarity.
   c. motion.
   d. height.
   e. weight.

Motion perception, p. 243
Easy, Factual/Definitional, Objective 6, Ans: c

48. The quick succession of briefly flashed images in a motion picture produces:
   a. retinal disparity.
   b. the Ponzo illusion.
   c. stroboscopic movement.
   d. convergence.
   e. subliminal persuasion.

Motion perception, p. 243
Easy, Factual/Definitional, Objective 6, Ans: b

49. The phi phenomenon refers to:
   a. the tendency for visual information to dominate other types of sensory information.
   b. the perception of movement created by the successive blinking on and off of adjacent lights.
   c. the ability to adjust to an artificially displaced visual field.
   d. the tendency to fill in gaps so as to perceive disconnected parts as a whole object.

Motion perception, p. 243
Medium, Conceptual/Application, Objective 6, Ans: c

50. The sequentially flashing Christmas tree lights appeared to generate pulsating waves of motion. This best illustrates:
a. relative motion.
b. retinal disparity.
c. the phi phenomenon.
d. visual capture.
e. perceptual adaptation.

Perceptual constancy, p. 244
Medium, Conceptual/Application, Objective 7, Ans: d

51. Although college textbooks frequently cast a trapezoidal image on the retina, students typically perceive the books as rectangular objects. This illustrates the importance of:
a. interposition.
b. size constancy.
c. linear perspective.
d. shape constancy.
e. binocular cues.

Perceptual constancy, p. 244
Easy, Conceptual/Application, Objective 7, Ans: b

52. As the retinal image of a horse galloping toward you becomes larger, it is unlikely that the horse will appear to grow larger. This best illustrates the phenomenon of:
a. visual capture.
b. size constancy.
c. closure.
d. convergence.
e. linear perspective.

Size-distance relationship, p. 244
Easy, Factual/Definitional, Objective 7, Ans: c

53. The perceived size of an object is most strongly influenced by that object's perceived:
a. shape.
b. color.
c. distance.
d. motion.

Size-distance relationship, p. 244
Difficult, Factual/Definitional, Objective 7, Ans: b

54. If two objects cast retinal images of the same size, the object that appears to be closer is perceived as ________ the object that appears to be more distant.
a. overlapping
b. smaller than
c. larger than
d. the same size as

Size-distance relationship, p. 244
Medium, Conceptual/Application, Objective 7, Ans: b

55. Because she mistakenly thought she was much closer to the mountain than she actually was, Fiona perceived the mountain to be ________ than it actually was.
   a. higher
   b. smaller
   c. more richly colorful
   d. larger

Size-distance relationship, p. 244
Medium, Factual/Definitional, Objective 7, Ans: c

56. When the moon is near the horizon, it appears larger than when it is high in the sky. This effect is primarily a result of:
   a. the slightly dimmer appearance of the horizon moon.
   b. the scattering of the horizon moon's light waves, which penetrate the atmosphere at an angle.
   c. distance cues, which make the horizon moon seem farther away.
   d. the brighter appearance of the horizon moon.

Size-distance relationship (Figure 6.13), pp. 244-245
Difficult, Factual/Definitional, Objective 7, Ans: c

57. Of two identical horizontal bars in the Ponzo illusion, the bar that is ________ in the visual field appears to be ________ because it appears to be farther away.
   a. higher; shorter
   b. lower; shorter
   c. higher; longer
   d. lower; longer

Size-distance relationship, p. 245
Difficult, Factual/Definitional, Objective 7, Ans: d

58. It has been suggested that experience with the corners of buildings and the rectangular shapes of a carpentered world may contribute to:
   a. the Ponzo illusion.
   b. shape constancy.
   c. the moon illusion.
   d. the Müller-Lyer illusion.
   e. size constancy.

Size-distance relationship, pp. 244-245
Difficult, Factual/Definitional, Objective 7, Ans: d

59. Knowing about the effects of the perceived distance of objects on their perceived size helps us to understand:
   a. the moon illusion.
   b. the Müller-Lyer illusion.
   c. the Ponzo illusion.
   d. all of the above.

Lightness constancy, p. 246
Medium, Conceptual/Application, Objective 7, Ans: d

60. Jody's horse looks just as black in the brilliant sunlight as it does in the dim light of the stable. This illustrates what is known as:
a. perceptual set.
b. perceptual adaptation.
c. sensory interaction.
d. lightness constancy.
e. the phi phenomenon.

Lightness constancy, p. 246
Medium, Factual/Definitional, Objective 7, Ans: c

61. Lightness constancy is most clearly facilitated by:
a. visual capture.
b. interposition.
c. relative luminance.
d. retinal disparity.
e. the phi phenomenon.

Perceptual interpretation, p. 248
Medium, Factual/Definitional, Objective 8, Ans: a

62. Who emphasized that perceptual understanding comes from inborn ways of organizing sensory experience?
a. Kant
b. Aristotle
c. Locke
d. Freud

Perceptual interpretation, p. 248
Easy, Factual/Definitional, Objective 8, Ans: a

63. The philosopher John Locke believed that people:
a. learn to perceive the world through experience.
b. are endowed at birth with perceptual skills.
c. experience the whole as different from the sum of its parts.
d. should be unable to adapt to an inverted visual world.

Perceptual interpretation, p. 248
Difficult, Conceptual, Objective 8, Ans: c

64. John Locke is to Immanuel Kant as ________ is to ________.
a. figure; ground
b. perception; sensation
c. nurture; nature
d. experience; learning
e. perceptual constancy; perceptual adaptation

Sensory deprivation and restored vision, p. 248
Difficult, Conceptual/Application, Objective 8, Ans: a

65. Lenore had been blind from birth. Immediately after corrective eye surgery, she could visually perceive figure-ground relationships. This fact would serve to support the position advanced by:
    a. Kant.
    b. parapsychologists.
    c. Aristotle.
    d. Locke.

Sensory deprivation and restored vision, p. 248
Medium, Conceptual, Objective 8, Ans: a

66. If an adult who was blind from birth gains the ability to see, that person would have the greatest difficulty visually distinguishing:
    a. circles from squares.
    b. the sun from the moon.
    c. red from green.
    d. a white cloud from the blue sky.

Sensory deprivation and restored vision, p. 249
Medium, Factual/Definitional, Objective 8, Ans: d

67. Research on visual restriction indicates that:
    a. when adults who were blind from birth gain the ability to see, they have little trouble visually distinguishing familiar shapes.
    b. the effects of visual restriction on visual perception are very different for kittens than for humans.
    c. those who have cataracts during a period of adulthood endure permanent loss of depth perception.
    d. visual restriction during infancy has a more lasting effect than the same restriction in adulthood.

Sensory deprivation and restored vision, p. 249
Medium, Conceptual/Application, Objective 8, Ans: c

68. Rebecca was born with cataracts that were not surgically removed until she was 3 years old. As a result, Rebecca is most likely to:
    a. have lost visual receptor cells in her eyes.
    b. be unable to perceive figure-ground relationships.
    c. have inadequate neural connections in her visual cortex.
    d. be unable to selectively attend to visual information.

Sensory deprivation and restored vision, p. 249
Easy, Factual/Definitional, Objective 8, Ans: d

69. Blakemore and Cooper found that kittens had difficulty perceiving vertical rods if they had previously:
    a. worn goggles through which only diffuse, unpatterned light could be seen.
    b. worn goggles that inverted what they saw.
    c. been restricted to a visual environment consisting solely of vertical stripes.
    d. been restricted to a visual environment consisting solely of horizontal stripes.

Perceptual adaptation, p. 249
Easy, Factual/Definitional, Objective 9, Ans: c

70. The ability to adjust to an artificially displaced or even inverted visual field is called:
    a. perceptual set.
    b. selective attention.
    c. perceptual adaptation.
    d. visual capture.
    e. shape constancy.

Perceptual adaptation, pp. 248, 249-250
Medium, Conceptual, Objective 9, Ans: a

71. Research with distorting goggles best supports the view of human perception advanced by:
    a. Locke.
    b. Freud.
    c. Kant.
    d. Aristotle.

Perceptual adaptation, p. 249
Difficult, Conceptual/Application, Objective 9, Ans: c

72. After a period of adjustment to special lenses that turn the visual field upside down:
    a. a frog could accurately retrieve flies with its tongue.
    b. a pigeon could easily fly over a very low fence.
    c. a person could successfully read a book.
    d. all of the above could occur.

Perceptual adaptation, pp. 249-250
Medium, Conceptual/Application, Objective 9, Ans: e

73. Although he was wearing a pair of glasses that shifted the apparent location of objects 20 degrees to his right, Lars was still able to play tennis very effectively. This best illustrates the value of:
    a. retinal disparity.
    b. perceptual set.
    c. shape constancy.
    d. visual capture.
    e. perceptual adaptation.

Perceptual set, pp. 250-251
Medium, Conceptual/Application, Objective 10, Ans: e

74. The news headline read "Local Prostitutes Appeal to City Mayor." Most readers immediately recognized that this was not a reference to the mayor's sexual desires. This best illustrates the value of:
    a. relative clarity.
    b. visual capture.
    c. bottom-up processing.
    d. linear perspective.
    e. perceptual set.

Perceptual set, pp. 250-251
Medium, Conceptual, Objective 10, Ans: d

75. Stereotypes are mental conceptions that can strongly influence the way we interpret the behaviors of individuals belonging to specific racial or ethnic groups. A stereotype is most similar to a:
a. feature detector.
b. stereogram.
c. perceptual adaptation.
d. perceptual set.
e. texture gradient.

Perceptual set, p. 251
Medium, Conceptual/Application, Objective 10, Ans: d

76. After hearing rumors about the outbreak of an infectious disease, Alyosha began to perceive his normal aches and pains as disease-related symptoms. His reaction best illustrates the impact of:
a. bottom-up processing.
b. the cocktail party effect.
c. stroboscopic movement.
d. perceptual set.
e. relative clarity.

Perceptual set, p. 251
Medium, Factual/Definitional, Objective 10, Ans: e

77. When listening to rock music played backward, people often perceive an evil message only if specifically forewarned what to listen for. This best illustrates the dangers of:
a. bottom-up processing.
b. feature detection.
c. the phi phenomenon.
d. relative clarity.
e. perceptual set.

Perceptual set, p. 252
Medium, Factual/Definitional, Objective 10, Ans: d

78. The tendency to perceive a moving light in the late evening sky as belonging to an airplane rather than a UFO best illustrates the impact of:
a. visual capture.
b. relative clarity.
c. feature detection.
d. perceptual set.
e. the phi phenomenon.

Perceptual set, p. 252
Easy, Factual/Definitional, Objective 10, Ans: b

79. A concept that helps us to interpret ambiguous sensations is called a:
a. gestalt.
b. schema.
c. stereogram.
d. perceptual constancy.
e. perceptual adaptation.

Perceptual set, pp. 236, 252
Medium, Conceptual, Objective 10, Ans: b

80. The influence of schemas on our interpretations of ambiguous sensations best illustrates:
   a. shape constancy.
   b. top-down processing.
   c. visual capture.
   d. the phi phenomenon.
   e. extrasensory perception.

Perceptual set, p. 252
Medium, Factual/Definitional, Objective 10, Ans: d

81. Young children tend to draw human figures in a rather unrealistic way. This reflects their:
   a. selective attention to monocular cues.
   b. selective attention to legs and feet.
   c. linear perspective.
   d. perceptual schemas.
   e. perceptual adaptations.

Context effects, pp. 237, 253
Difficult, Conceptual, Objective 11, Ans: d

82. When hearing the words "eel is on the wagon," you would likely perceive the first word as "wheel." Given "eel is on the orange," you would likely perceive the first word as "peel." This context effect best illustrates the organizational principle of:
   a. proximity.
   b. continuity.
   c. interposition.
   d. closure.
   e. convergence.

Context effects, p. 253
Easy, Factual/Definitional, Objective 10, Ans: b

83. The presence and location of two curious rabbits influence our perceptions of the "magician's cabinet" pictured in the textbook. This provides an illustration of:
   a. visual capture.
   b. context effects.
   c. the Ponzo illusion.
   d. perceptual adaptation.
   e. stroboscopic movement.

Context effects, p. 254
Medium, Conceptual/Application, Objective 10, Ans: b

84. Although Sue Yen sees her chemistry professor several times each week, she had difficulty recognizing the professor when she happened to see her in the grocery store. This best illustrates the importance of:
   a. visual capture.
   b. context effects.
   c. proximity.
   d. relative clarity.
   e. perceptual adaptation.

Context effects, p. 254
Medium, Conceptual/Application, Objective 10, Ans: d

85. When Rick learned that many students had received a failing grade on the midterm exam, he was no longer disappointed by his C grade. His experience best illustrates the importance of:
   a. perceptual adaptation.
   b. bottom-up processing.
   c. relative clarity.
   d. context effects.
   e. interposition.

Context effects, pp. 245, 254
Difficult, Conceptual, Objective 10, Ans: d

86. The horizon moon appears to shrink in size if it is viewed through a narrow tube that eliminates the perception of distance cues. This best illustrates the importance of:
   a. relative clarity.
   b. stroboscopic movement.
   c. perceptual adaptation.
   d. context effects.
   e. visual capture.

Perception and the human factor, p. 255
Easy, Factual/Definitional, Objective 11, Ans: d

87. Using natural mapping to design stove controls that require no labels would be of special interest to:
   a. Gestalt psychologists.
   b. evolutionary psychologists.
   c. parapsychologists.
   d. human factors psychologists.

Perception and the human factor, p. 255
Medium, Conceptual, Objective 11, Ans: a

88. Human factors psychologists would be most likely to aid in the design of:
   a. computer keyboards.
   b. weight-reduction programs.
   c. protective clothing.
   d. classroom management techniques.

Is there extrasensory perception?, p. 258
Easy, Factual/Definitional, Objective 12, Ans: a

89. Parapsychology refers to the:
   a. study of phenomena such as telepathy or clairvoyance.
   b. perception of remote events.
   c. perception of future events.
   d. direct transmission of thoughts from one mind to another.

Is there extrasensory perception?, p. 258
Medium, Factual/Definitional, Objective 12, Ans: a

90. The existence of convincing scientific evidence that ESP is possible would pose the greatest challenge to the:
   a. contemporary scientific understanding of human nature.
   b. continued existence of parapsychology.
   c. continuation of research on the processes that underlie ordinary forms of sensation and perception.
   d. ordinary belief systems of most Americans.

Claims of ESP, p. 258
Medium, Factual/Definitional, Objective 12, Ans: a

91. Telepathy refers to the:
   a. extrasensory transmission of thoughts from one mind to another.
   b. extrasensory perception of events that occur at places remote to the perceiver.
   c. perception of future events, such as a person's fate.
   d. ability to understand and share the emotions of another person.

Claims of ESP, p. 258
Medium, Conceptual/Application, Objective 12, Ans: d

92. Jamal claims that his special psychic powers enable him to perceive exactly where the body of a recent murder victim is secretly buried. Jamal is claiming to possess the power of:
   a. psychokinesis.
   b. precognition.
   c. telepathy.
   d. clairvoyance.

Claims of ESP, p. 258
Difficult, Conceptual/Application, Objective 12, Ans: d

93. The extrasensory ability to perceive an automobile accident taking place in a distant location is to ________ as the extrasensory ability to know at any moment exactly what your best friend is thinking is to ________.
   a. telepathy; precognition
   b. precognition; psychokinesis
   c. psychokinesis; clairvoyance
   d. clairvoyance; telepathy

Claims of ESP, p. 258
Easy, Conceptual/Application, Objective 12, Ans: c

94. Margo insists that her dreams frequently enable her to perceive and predict future events. Margo is claiming to possess the power of:
   a. telepathy.
   b. clairvoyance.
   c. precognition.
   d. psychokinesis.

Claims of ESP, p. 258
Medium, Conceptual/Application, Objective 12, Ans: d

95. Andre claims that he can make a broken watch begin to run again simply by entering a state of intense mental concentration. Andre is claiming to possess the power of:
    a. precognition.
    b. telepathy.
    c. clairvoyance.
    d. psychokinesis.

Claims of ESP, p. 259
Easy, Factual/Definitional, Objective 12, Ans: e

96. Psychics who have worked with police departments in an effort to solve difficult crimes have demonstrated the value of:
    a. clairvoyance.
    b. telepathy.
    c. precognition.
    d. all of the above.
    e. none of the above.

Claims of ESP, p. 260
Medium, Factual/Definitional, Objective 12, Ans: b

97. The greatest difficulty facing contemporary parapsychology is the:
    a. inability to subject claims of ESP to scientific testing.
    b. lack of a reproducible ESP phenomenon.
    c. willingness of most parapsychologists to knowingly accept fraudulent evidence.
    d. difficulty of persuading many people that there really is such a thing as ESP.

Claims of ESP, p. 260
Difficult, Factual/Definitional, Objective 12, Ans: c

98. Psychologists are skeptical about the existence of ESP because:
    a. ESP researchers frequently accept evidence that they know is fraudulent.
    b. there is no way to scientifically test claims of ESP.
    c. many apparent demonstrations of ESP have been shown to be a hoax.
    d. all of the above are true.

Essay Questions

1. You have been asked to paint a picture that includes buildings, fields, a river, and a mountain. Describe how you would use at least five monocular cues to give your painting a sense of depth.

2. The moon typically appears larger near the horizon than when high in the sky. The height of the Gateway Arch in St. Louis typically appears greater than its width. Explain these two perceptual illusions and show how your explanations for both illusions are similar.

3. Explain how research on size constancy, restored vision, perceptual adaptation, and perceptual sets serves to support and/or refute John Locke's emphasis on the importance of learning in perception.

4. Last night one of your mother's best friends had a car accident. Your mother feels guilty because three days ago she dreamt of such an accident but failed to warn her friend. How would you explain your mother's experience? What advice would you give her?

Web Quiz 1

Ans: c

1. Drivers have been observed to detect traffic signals more slowly if they are also conversing on a cell phone. This best illustrates the impact of:
a. visual capture.
b. retinal disparity.
c. selective attention.
d. stroboscopic movement.
e. perceptual adaptation.

Ans: a

2. The fact that perceptions involve more than the sum of our sensations best illustrates the importance of:
a. top-down processing.
b. relative clarity.
c. retinal disparity.
d. visual capture.
e. the ganzfeld procedure.

Ans: b

3. The way in which you quickly group the individual letters in this test item into separate words best illustrates the principle of:
a. closure.
b. proximity.
c. interposition.
d. convergence.
e. continuity.

Ans: c

4. Monocular cue is to _______ as binocular cue is to ________.
a. proximity; continuity
b. relative size; relative motion
c. texture gradient; convergence
d. the moon illusion; the Ponzo illusion

Ans: e

5. The lights along the runway were shrouded in such a thick fog that the pilot of an incoming plane nearly overshot the runway. The pilot was most likely misled by the distance cue known as:
a. interposition.
b. lightness constancy.
c. convergence.
d. linear perspective.
e. relative clarity.

Ans: b

6. Drivers sometimes overestimate the distance between their own vehicle and pedestrians who are short because they rely on the distance cue known as:
a. linear perspective.
b. relative size.
c. interposition.
d. convergence.

Ans: d

7. The fact that we recognize objects as having a consistent form regardless of changing viewing angles illustrates:
a. interposition.
b. change blindness.
c. the phi phenomenon.
d. perceptual constancy.
e. convergence.

Ans: b

8. The ability to accurately perceive distances most clearly underlies our capacity for:
a. closure.
b. size constancy.
c. perceptual adaptation.
d. extrasensory perception.

Ans: a

9. The moon illusion refers to our tendency to perceive the moon as unusually ________ when it is ________.
a. large; near the horizon
b. large; high in the sky
c. bright; near the horizon
d. bright; high in the sky

Ans: a

10. Immanuel Kant and John Locke would have been most likely to disagree about the extent to which perception is influenced by:
a. cultural experience.
b. retinal disparity.
c. change blindness.
d. relative luminance.

Ans: e

11. Goggles that allow animals to see only diffuse, unpatterned light have inhibiting effects on perceptual development similar to the effects of:
a. interposition.
b. change blindness.
c. motion parallax.
d. visual capture.
e. cataracts.

Ans: c

12. People perceive an adult-child pair as looking more alike when told they are parent and child. This best illustrates the effect of:
    a. bottom-up processing.
    b. visual capture.
    c. perceptual set.
    d. shape constancy.
    e. interposition.

Ans: d

13. Once we have formed a wrong idea about reality, we have more difficulty seeing the truth. This best illustrates the impact of:
    a. change blindness.
    b. relative clarity.
    c. the phi phenomenon.
    d. top-down processing.
    e. visual capture.

Ans: d

14. ATM machines are more complex than VCRs but are easier to operate thanks to the efforts of:
    a. parapsychologists.
    b. Gestalt psychologists.
    c. evolutionary psychologists.
    d. human factors psychologists.

Ans: c

15. Psychics are unable to make millions of dollars betting on horse races. This undermines their claims to possess the power of:
    a. clairvoyance.
    b. interposition.
    c. precognition.
    d. telepathy.

Web Quiz 2

Ans: d

1. Selective attention is best illustrated by:
   a. the moon illusion.
   b. perceptual constancy.
   c. the phi phenomenon.
   d. change blindness.
   e. retinal disparity.

Ans: c

2. Perceiving the voice of a ventriloquist as originating from the mouth of a dummy best illustrates:
   a. convergence.
   b. interposition.
   c. visual capture.
   d. stroboscopic movement.
   e. the cocktail party effect.

Ans: e

3. Racial and ethnic stereotypes can sometimes bias our perceptions of others' behaviors. This best illustrates the impact of:
   a. retinal disparity.
   b. relative clarity.
   c. change blindness.
   d. perceptual adaptation.
   e. top-down processing.

Ans: c

4. Rules for organizing stimuli into coherent groups were first identified by:
   a. evolutionary psychologists.
   b. human factors psychologists.
   c. Gestalt psychologists.
   d. parapsychologists.

Ans: a

5. When your psychology textbook presents readers with a series of short blue lines, they perceive an illusory glowing blue worm. This best illustrates the principle of:
   a. closure.
   b. convergence.
   c. linear perspective.
   d. perceptual constancy.
   e. interposition.

Ans: b

6. Pedro recognized that his son was closer to him than his daughter because his son partially obstructed his view of his daughter. Pedro's perception was most clearly influenced by a distance cue known as:
   a. proximity.
   b. interposition.
   c. convergence.
   d. relative clarity.
   e. retinal disparity.

Ans: a

7. Railroad tracks appear to converge in the distance. This provides a cue for depth perception known as:
   a. linear perspective.
   b. interposition.
   c. connectedness.
   d. continuity.
   e. closure.

Ans: d

8. A door casts an increasingly trapezoidal image on our retinas as it opens, yet we still perceive it as rectangular. This illustrates:
   a. convergence.
   b. interposition.
   c. stroboscopic movement.
   d. shape constancy.
   e. motion parallax.

Ans: d

9. The specific perceptual processes that underlie the moon illusion also contribute to:
   a. clairvoyance.
   b. retinal disparity.
   c. change blindness.
   d. the Ponzo illusion.
   e. the phi phenomenon.

Ans: c

10. Relative luminance most clearly contributes to:
    a. the phi phenomenon.
    b. perceptual adaptation.
    c. lightness constancy.
    d. the moon illusion.
    e. change blindness.

Ans: b

11. Which philosopher would have predicted that an extended period of sensory deprivation would inhibit the development of one's perceptual capacities?
    a. Plato
    b. Locke
    c. Descartes
    d. Kant

Ans: e

12. After hearing that Bryce had served a prison sentence, Janet began to perceive his friendly behavior as insincere and manipulative. This best illustrates the impact of:
    a. interposition.
    b. visual capture.
    c. bottom-up processing.
    d. the phi phenomenon.
    e. perceptual set.

Ans: d

13. A neutral facial expression may be perceived as sadder at a funeral than at a circus. This best illustrates:
    a. interposition.
    b. visual capture.
    c. the Ponzo illusion.
    d. a context effect.
    e. bottom-up processing.

Ans: c

14. Jordan claims that with intense mental concentration, he can make objects float in mid-air. Jordan is claiming to possess the power of:
    a. telepathy.
    b. interposition.
    c. psychokinesis.
    d. clairvoyance.
    e. precognition.

Ans: d

15. The distance between our right and left eyes functions to provide us with a cue for depth perception known as:
    a. proximity.
    b. interposition.
    c. visual capture.
    d. retinal disparity.
    e. linear perspective.

Study Guide Questions

Ans: d, p. 231

1. The study of perception is primarily concerned with how we:
   a. detect sights, sounds, and other stimuli.
   b. sense environmental stimuli.
   c. develop sensitivity to illusions.
   d. interpret sensory stimuli.

Ans: c, pp. 234, 241

2. The illusion that the St. Louis Gateway arch appears taller than it is wide (even though its height and width are equal) is based on our sensitivity to which monocular depth cue?
   a. relative size
   b. interposition
   c. relative height
   d. retinal disparity

Ans: b, pp. 235, 240-241

3. People asked to judge the distances of white disks under either clear or foggy conditions:
   a. estimated the disks to be more distant when viewed under clear conditions.
   b. estimated the disks to be nearer when viewed under clear conditions.
   c. took atmospheric conditions into consideration and judged the disks to be equally distant under the two viewing conditions.
   d. were much less accurate under foggy conditions.

Ans: d, p. 236

4. The historical movement associated with the statement "The whole may exceed the sum of its parts" is:
   a. parapsychology.
   b. behavioral psychology.
   c. functional psychology.
   d. Gestalt psychology.

Ans: d, p. 236

5. Which of the following illustrates the principle of visual capture?
   a. We tend to form first impressions of other people on the basis of appearance.
   b. Because visual processing is automatic, we can pay attention to a visual image and any other sensation at the same time.
   c. We cannot simultaneously attend to a visual image and another sensation.
   d. When there is a conflict between visual information and that from another sense, vision tends to dominate.

Ans: c, p. 236

6. Which of the following statements is consistent with the Gestalt theory of perception?
   a. Perception develops largely through learning.
   b. Perception is the product of heredity.
   c. The mind organizes sensations into meaningful perceptions.
   d. Perception results directly from sensation.

Ans: d, p. 236

7. The term gestalt means:
   a. grouping.
   b. sensation.
   c. perception.
   d. whole.
   e. visual capture.

Ans: c, p. 236

8. When the traffic light changed from red to green, the drivers on both sides of Leon's vehicle pulled quickly forward, giving Leon the disorienting feeling that his car was rolling backward. Which principle explains Leon's misperception?
   a. relative motion
   b. continuity
   c. visual capture
   d. proximity

Ans: b, p. 236

9. ________ processing refers to how the physical characteristics of stimuli influence their interpretation.
   a. Top-down
   b. Bottom-up
   c. Parapsychological
   d. Human factors

Ans: a, p. 236

10. ________ processing refers to how our knowledge and expectations influence perception.
    a. Top-down
    b. Bottom-up
    c. Parapsychological
    d. Human factors

Ans: d, p. 236

11. Concluding her presentation on sensation and perception, Kelly notes that:
    a. sensation is bottom-up processing.
    b. perception is top-down processing.
    c. a. and b. are both true.
    d. sensation and perception blend into one continuous process.

Ans: c, p. 237

12. The figure-ground relationship has demonstrated that:
    a. perception is largely innate.
    b. perception is simply a point-for-point representation of sensation.
    c. the same stimulus can trigger more than one perception.
    d. different people see different things when viewing a scene.

Ans: c, p. 237

13. Figure is to ground as ________ is to ________.
 a. night; day
 b. top; bottom
 c. cloud; sky
 d. sensation; perception

Ans: e, p. 237

14. All of the following are laws of perceptual organization except:
 a. proximity.
 b. closure.
 c. continuity.
 d. connectedness.
 e. simplicity.

Ans: e, p. 237

15. Figures tend to be perceived as whole, complete objects, even if spaces or gaps exist in the representation, thus demonstrating the principle of:
 a. connectedness.
 b. similarity.
 c. continuity.
 d. proximity.
 e. closure.

Ans: b, p. 237

16. The tendency to organize stimuli into smooth, uninterrupted patterns is called:
 a. closure.
 b. continuity.
 c. similarity.
 d. proximity.
 e. connectedness.

Ans: c, p. 237

17. Studying the road map before her trip, Colleen had no trouble following the route of the highway she planned to travel. Colleen's ability illustrates the principle of:
 a. closure.
 b. similarity.
 c. continuity.
 d. proximity.
 e. connectedness.

Ans: a, pp. 238-239

18. Studies of the visual cliff have provided evidence that much of depth perception is:
 a. innate.
 b. learned.
 c. innate in lower animals, learned in humans.
 d. innate in humans, learned in lower animals.

Ans: d, pp. 238, 241
19. Which of the following depth cues creates the impression of a visual cliff?
a. interposition
b. relative height
c. linear perspective
d. texture gradient
e. relative clarity

Ans: d, p. 239
20. When we stare at an object, each eye receives a slightly different image, providing a depth cue known as:
a. convergence.
b. linear perspective.
c. relative motion.
d. retinal disparity.

Ans: c, pp. 239-241
21. Which of the following is not a monocular depth cue?
a. texture gradient
b. relative height
c. retinal disparity
d. interposition
e. light and shadow

Ans: d, p. 240
22. The tendency to perceive hazy objects as being at a distance is known as ________. This is a ________ depth cue.
a. linear perspective; binocular
b. linear perspective; monocular
c. relative clarity; binocular
d. relative clarity; monocular

Ans: b, p. 240
23. When two familiar objects of equal size cast unequal retinal images, the object that casts the smaller retinal image will be perceived as being:
a. closer than the other object.
b. more distant than the other object.
c. larger than the other object.
d. smaller than the other object.

Ans: e, p. 240
24. If you slowly bring your finger toward your face until it eventually touches your nose, eye-muscle cues called ________ convey depth information to your brain.
a. retinal disparity
b. interposition
c. continuity
d. proximity
e. convergence

Ans: b, p. 240

25. How do we perceive a pole that partially covers a bush?
    a. as farther away
    b. as nearer
    c. as larger
    d. there is not enough information to determine the object's size or distance

Ans: c, p. 241

26. Objects higher in our field of vision are perceived as ________ due to the principle of ________.
    a. nearer; relative height
    b. nearer; linear perspective
    c. farther away; relative height
    d. farther away; linear perspective

Ans: d, p. 241

27. The depth cue that occurs when we watch stable objects at different distances as we are moving is:
    a. convergence.
    b. interposition.
    c. relative clarity.
    d. relative motion.

Ans: d, p. 241

28. Because the flowers in the foreground appeared coarse and grainy, the photographer decided that the picture was taken too near the subject. This conclusion was based on which depth cue?
    a. relative size
    b. interposition
    c. retinal disparity
    d. texture gradient

Ans: a, p. 242

29. Which of the following is a monocular depth cue?
    a. light and shadow
    b. convergence
    c. retinal disparity
    d. all of the above are monocular depth cues

Ans: c, p. 242

30. An artist paints a tree orchard so that the parallel rows of trees converge at the top of the canvas. Which cue has the artist used to convey distance?
    a. interposition
    b. relative clarity
    c. linear perspective
    d. texture gradient

Ans: d, p. 242

31. According to the principle of light and shadow, if one of two identical objects reflects more light to your eyes it will be perceived as:
   a. larger.
   b. smaller.
   c. farther away.
   d. nearer.

Ans: a, p. 243

32. As we move, viewed objects cast changing shapes on our retinas, although we do not perceive the objects as changing. This is part of the phenomenon of:
   a. perceptual constancy.
   b. relative motion.
   c. linear perspective.
   d. continuity.

Ans: c, p. 243

33. Each time you see your car, it projects a different image on the retinas of your eyes, yet you do not perceive it as changing. This is because of:
   a. perceptual set.
   b. retinal disparity.
   c. perceptual constancy.
   d. convergence.

Ans: b, p. 244

34. The phenomenon of size constancy is based upon the close connection between an object's perceived ________ and its perceived ________.
   a. size; shape
   b. size; distance
   c. size; brightness
   d. shape; distance
   e. shape; brightness

Ans: a, p. 244

35. In the absence of perceptual constancy:
   a. objects would appear to change size as their distance from us changed.
   b. depth perception would be based exclusively on monocular cues.
   c. depth perception would be based exclusively on binocular cues.
   d. depth perception would be impossible.

Ans: d, p. 244

36. As her friend Milo walks toward her, Noriko perceives his size as remaining constant because his perceived distance ________ at the same time that her retinal image of him ________.
   a. increases; decreases
   b. increases; increases
   c. decreases; decreases
   d. decreases; increases

Ans: c, p. 244

37. Your friend tosses you a frisbee. You know that it is getting closer instead of larger because of:
   a. shape constancy.
   b. relative motion.
   c. size constancy.
   d. all of the above.

Ans: a, pp. 244-245

38. The moon illusion occurs in part because distance cues at the horizon make the moon seem:
   a. farther away and therefore larger.
   b. closer and therefore larger.
   c. farther away and therefore smaller.
   d. closer and therefore smaller.

Ans: a, pp. 245-246

39. Which explanation of the Müller-Lyer illusion is offered by the text?
   a. The corners in our carpentered world teach us to interpret outward- or inward-pointing arrowheads at the end of a line as a cue to the line's distance from us and so to its length.
   b. The drawing's violation of linear perspective makes one line seem longer.
   c. Top-down processing of the illusion is prevented because of the stimuli's ambiguity.
   d. All of the above were offered as explanations.

Ans: c, p. 246

40. The insensitivity of many rural Africans to the Müller-Lyer illusion proves that perception:
   a. is largely a "bottom-up" phenomenon.
   b. is unpredictable.
   c. is influenced by cultural experience.
   d. is characterized by all of the above.

Ans: d, p. 246

41. The fact that a white object under dim illumination appears lighter than a gray object under bright illumination is called:
   a. relative luminance.
   b. perceptual adaptation.
   c. color contrast.
   d. lightness constancy.

Ans: b, p. 248

42. Adults who are born blind but later have their vision restored:
   a. are almost immediately able to recognize familiar objects.
   b. typically fail to recognize familiar objects.
   c. are unable to follow moving objects with their eyes.
   d. have excellent eye-hand coordination.

Ans: b, p. 248

43. Which philosopher maintained that knowledge comes from inborn ways of organizing our sensory experiences?
    a. Locke
    b. Kant
    c. Gibson
    d. Walk
    e. Neisser

Ans: a, p. 248

44. According to the philosopher ________, we learn to perceive the world.
    a. Locke
    b. Kant
    c. Gibson
    d. Walk
    e. Neisser

Ans: d, pp. 248-253

45. Which of the following influences perception?
    a. biological maturation
    b. the context in which stimuli are perceived
    c. expectations
    d. all of the above

Ans: c, p. 249

46. Which of the following statements best describes the effects of sensory restriction?
    a. It produces functional blindness when experienced for any length of time at any age.
    b. It has greater effects on humans than on animals.
    c. It has more damaging effects when experienced during infancy.
    d. It has greater effects on adults than on children.

Ans: c, p. 249

47. Kittens reared seeing only horizontal lines:
    a. later had difficulty perceiving both horizontal and vertical lines.
    b. later had difficulty perceiving vertical lines, but eventually regained normal sensitivity.
    c. later had difficulty perceiving vertical lines, and never regained normal sensitivity.
    d. showed no impairment in perception, indicating that neural feature detectors develop even in the absence of normal sensory experiences.

Ans: c, p. 250

48. Experiments with distorted visual environments demonstrate that:
    a. adaptation rarely takes place.
    b. animals adapt readily, but humans do not.
    c. humans adapt readily, while lower animals typically do not.
    d. adaptation is possible during a critical period in infancy but not thereafter.

Ans: d, p. 250

49. Although carpenter Smith perceived a briefly viewed object as a screwdriver, police officer Wesson perceived the same object as a knife. This illustrates that perception is guided by:
a. linear perspective.
b. shape constancy.
c. retinal disparity.
d. perceptual set.
e. convergence.

Ans: a, p. 250

50. The phenomenon that refers to the ways in which an individual's expectations influence perception is called:
a. perceptual set.
b. retinal disparity.
c. convergence.
d. visual capture.

Ans: b, p. 255

51. Thanks to ______, TiVo has solved the TV recording problem caused by the complexity of VCRs.
a. parapsychologists.
b. human factors psychologists.
c. psychokineticists.
d. Gestalt psychologists.

Ans: c, p. 255

52. Dr. Martin is using natural mapping to redesign the instrument gauges of automobiles to be more "user friendly." Dr. Martin is evidently a(n):
a. psychophysicist.
b. cognitive psychologist.
c. human factors psychologist.
d. experimental psychologist.

Ans: d, p. 258

53. A person claiming to be able to read another's mind is claiming to have the ESP ability of:
a. psychokinesis.
b. precognition.
c. clairvoyance.
d. telepathy.

Ans: c, p. 258

54. Psychologists who study ESP are called:
a. clairvoyants.
b. telepaths.
c. parapsychologists.
d. levitators.

Ans: c, p. 258

55. Jack claims that he often has dreams that predict future events. He claims to have the power of:
    a. telepathy.
    b. clairvoyance.
    c. precognition.
    d. psychokinesis.

Ans: d, p. 258

56. Regina claims that she can bend spoons, levitate furniture, and perform many other "mind over matter" feats. Regina apparently believes she has the power of:
    a. telepathy.
    b. clairvoyance.
    c. precognition.
    d. psychokinesis.

Ans: d, pp. 258-259

57. The predictions of leading psychics are:
    a. often ambiguous prophecies later interpreted to match actual events.
    b. no more accurate than guesses made by others.
    c. nearly always inaccurate.
    d. all of the above.

Ans: c, p. 260

58. Which of the following statements concerning ESP is true?
    a. Most ESP researchers are quacks.
    b. There have been a large number of reliable demonstrations of ESP.
    c. Most research psychologists are skeptical of the claims of defenders of ESP.
    d. There have been reliable laboratory demonstrations of ESP, but the results are no different from those that would occur by chance.

Ans: d, p. 261

59. Using the ganzfeld procedure to investigate telepathy, researchers have found that:
    a. when external distractions are reduced, both the "sender" and the "receiver" become much more accurate in demonstrating ESP.
    b. Only "senders" become much more accurate.
    c. Only "receivers" become much more accurate.
    d. Over many studies, none of the above occur.

CHAPTER 7

States of Consciousness

Learning Objectives

Waking Consciousness (pp. 265-268)

1. Discuss the nature of consciousness and its significance in the history of psychology.

2. Contrast conscious and subconscious information processing.

3. Discuss the content and potential functions of daydreams and fantasies.

Sleep and Dreams (pp. 269-285)

4. Discuss the importance of seasonal, monthly, and daily biological rhythms.

5. Describe the cyclical nature and possible functions of sleep.

6. Identify the major sleep disorders.

7. Discuss the content and possible functions of dreams.

Hypnosis (pp. 285-293)

8. Discuss hypnosis, noting the behavior of hypnotized people and claims regarding its uses.

9. Discuss the controversy over whether hypnosis is an altered state of consciousness.

Drugs and Consciousness (pp. 294-304)

10. Discuss the nature of drug dependence, and identify some common misconceptions about addiction.

11. Describe the physiological and psychological effects of depressants, stimulants, and hallucinogens.

12. Discuss the factors that contribute to drug use.

Near-Death Experiences (pp. 305-306)

13. Describe the near-death experience and the controversy over whether it provides evidence for a mind-body dualism.

Waking consciousness, p. 265
Easy, Factual/Definitional, Objective 1, Ans: b

1. The school of thought in psychology that systematically avoided the study of consciousness during the first half of this century was:
   a. psychoanalysis.
   b. behaviorism.
   c. functionalism.
   d. structuralism.
   e. Gestalt psychology.

Waking consciousness, p. 266
Easy, Factual/Definitional, Objective 1, Ans: e

2. Consciousness is:
   a. the ability to solve problems, reason, and remember.
   b. the sudden and often novel realization of the solution to a problem.
   c. the process of organizing and interpreting sensory information.
   d. effortless encoding of incidental information into memory.
   e. our awareness of ourselves and our environment.

Levels of information processing, pp. 266-267
Medium, Factual/Definitional, Objective 2, Ans: c

3. The ability to simultaneously monitor the shape as well as the color of an object best illustrates the value of:
   a. dualism.
   b. dissociation.
   c. parallel processing.
   d. conscious awareness.
   e. posthypnotic suggestion.

Levels of information processing, p. 267
Medium, Factual/Definitional, Objective 2, Ans: b

4. Compared to subconscious information processing, conscious information processing is relatively ________ and especially effective for solving ________ problems.
   a. fast; novel
   b. slow; novel
   c. fast; routine
   d. slow; routine

Levels of information processing, p. 267
Medium, Conceptual, Objective 2, Ans: b

5. Consciousness is to subconsciousness as ________ is to ________.
   a. monism; dualism
   b. serial processing; parallel processing
   c. narcolepsy; sleep apnea
   d. latent content; manifest content
   e. delta wave; alpha wave

Daydreams and fantasies, p. 267
Easy, Factual/Definitional, Objective 3, Ans: b

6. Research indicates that young adults spend ________ time daydreaming and admit to ________ sexual fantasies than do older adults.
   a. more; fewer
   b. more; more
   c. less; more
   d. less; fewer

Daydreams and fantasies, p. 268
Medium, Factual/Definitional, Objective 3, Ans: d

7. Studies of daydreaming indicate that:
   a. for most people, daydreaming is a rare occurrence.
   b. older adults spend more time daydreaming than do younger adults.
   c. among college students, women's daydreams have more athletic content than do men's.
   d. individuals who are prone to violence, delinquency, and drug usage have fewer vivid fantasies.

Sleep and dreams, p. 269
Medium, Factual/Definitional, Objective 4, Ans: e

8. Research on sleep and dreams indicates that:
   a. older adults sleep more than young adults.
   b. when people dream of performing some activity, their limbs often move in concert with the dream.
   c. sleepwalkers are acting out their dreams.
   d. the circadian rhythm has no influence on our patterns of sleep.
   e. none of the above are true.

Biological rhythms, p. 269
Easy, Factual/Definitional, Objective 4, Ans: d

9. Those who emphasize that mood fluctuations may be indicative of seasonal affective disorder are highlighting the importance of:
   a. the menstrual cycle.
   b. dissociation.
   c. REM sleep.
   d. biological rhythms.
   e. narcolepsy.

Circadian rhythm, p. 269
Easy, Factual/Definitional, Objective 4, Ans: b

10. Circadian rhythm refers to:
    a. the pattern of emotional ups and downs we routinely experience.
    b. a pattern of biological functioning that occurs on a roughly 24-hour cycle.
    c. the experience of jet lag following an extensive transoceanic flight.
    d. the cycle of five distinct stages that we experience during a normal night's sleep.

Circadian rhythm, pp. 269-270
Easy, Factual/Definitional, Objective 4, Ans: b

11. With the approach of night, our body temperatures begin to drop. This best illustrates the dynamics of the:
    a. hypnogogic state.
    b. circadian rhythm.
    c. alpha wave pattern.
    d. REM rebound.
    e. menstrual cycle.

Thinking Critically about PMS (Box), p. 270
Difficult, Factual/Definitional, Objective 4, Ans: c

12. Women are most likely to overestimate the negative impact of the menstrual cycle on their mood because:
    a. men typically underestimate women's menstrual discomfort.
    b. premenstrual distress heightens one's sense of gender identity.
    c. evidence that confirms one's preconceptions is easily remembered.
    d. PMS is a socially acceptable excuse for substandard work performance.

Thinking Critically about PMS (Box), p. 270
Medium, Factual/Definitional, Objective 4, Ans: c

13. When comparing women's day-to-day self-reports of their moods with their later recall of these same daily moods, negative emotions are most pronounced in the:
    a. day-to-day reports of premenstrual mood.
    b. day-to-day reports of postmenstrual mood.
    c. later recall of premenstrual mood.
    d. later recall of postmenstrual mood.

Circadian rhythm, p. 271
Easy, Conceptual/Application, Objective 4, Ans: b

14. After flying from California to New York, Arthur experienced a restless, sleepless night. His problem was most likely caused by a disruption of his normal:
    a. REM sleep.
    b. circadian rhythm.
    c. hypnogogic sensations.
    d. alpha wave pattern.

Circadian rhythm, p. 271
Medium, Factual/Definitional, Objective 4, Ans: d

15. Exposure to bright light causes the ________ gland to ________ the production of melatonin.
   a. thyroid; increase
   b. thyroid; decrease
   c. pineal; increase
   d. pineal; decrease

Circadian rhythm, p. 271
Medium, Conceptual, Objective 5, Ans: c

16. Our resistance to going to bed as early as we had planned is most likely a reflection of:
   a. dissociation.
   b. narcolepsy.
   c. the circadian rhythm.
   d. night terrors.
   e. sleep apnea.

Sleep stages, p. 272
Easy, Conceptual/Application, Objective 5, Ans: b

17. Jordanna has decided to go to bed early. Although her eyes are closed and she's very relaxed, she has not yet fallen asleep. An EEG is most likely to indicate the presence of:
   a. delta waves.
   b. alpha waves.
   c. sleep spindles.
   d. rapid eye movements.

Sleep stages, p. 273
Easy, Factual/Definitional, Objective 5, Ans: e

18. False sensory experiences that occur in the absence of appropriate sensory stimulation are called:
   a. night terrors.
   b. dreams.
   c. psychedelics.
   d. dissociations.
   e. hallucinations.

Sleep stages, p. 273
Medium, Factual/Definitional, Objective 5, Ans: a

19. Sensations of falling or floating weightlessly (hypnogogic sensations) are most closely associated with ________ sleep.
   a. Stage 1
   b. Stage 2
   c. Stage 3
   d. Stage 4

Sleep stages, p. 273
Easy, Factual/Definitional, Objective 5, Ans: c

20. The rhythmic bursts of brain activity that occur during Stage 2 sleep are called:
    a. alpha waves.
    b. paradoxical sleep.
    c. sleep spindles.
    d. delta waves.

Sleep stages, p. 273
Difficult, Factual/Definitional, Objective 5, Ans: c

21. Bedwetting is most likely to occur during ________ sleep.
    a. Stage 1
    b. Stage 2
    c. slow-wave
    d. paradoxical

Sleep stages, p. 273
Difficult, Conceptual/Application, Objective 5, Ans: d

22. At 1:00 a.m, Luis gets out of bed and begins to sleepwalk. An EEG of his brain activity is most likely to indicate the presence of:
    a. alpha waves.
    b. sleep spindles.
    c. REM sleep.
    d. delta waves.

Sleep stages, p. 273
Medium, Factual/Definitional, Objective 5, Ans: a

23. The brain waves associated with REM sleep are most similar to those of:
    a. Stage 1 sleep.
    b. Stage 2 sleep.
    c. Stage 3 sleep.
    d. Stage 4 sleep.

Sleep stages, pp. 273-274
Medium, Factual/Definitional, Objective 5, Ans: b

24. Genital arousal is most likely to be associated with:
    a. sleep apnea.
    b. paradoxical sleep.
    c. Stage 4 sleep.
    d. sleep spindles.

Sleep stages, p. 274
Difficult, Factual/Definitional, Objective 5, Ans: b

25. During the course of a full night's sleep, people are most likely to spend more time in ________ sleep than in ________ sleep.
    a. Stage 4; Stage 2
    b. REM; Stage 4
    c. Stage 3; REM
    d. REM; Stage 2

Sleep stages, p. 274
Medium, Factual/Definitional, Objective 5, Ans: c

26. REM sleep is called paradoxical sleep because:
    a. our heart rate is slow and steady, while our breathing is highly irregular.
    b. we are deeply asleep but can be awakened easily.
    c. our nervous system is highly active, while our voluntary muscles hardly move.
    d. it leads to highly imaginative dreams that are perceived as colorless images.

Sleep stages, p. 274
Medium, Conceptual/Application, Objective 5, Ans: e

27. After sleeping for about an hour, José enters a phase of paradoxical sleep. He is likely to:
    a. be easily awakened.
    b. have slower, more regular breathing.
    c. have slower brain waves.
    d. talk in his sleep.
    e. have very relaxed muscles.

Sleep stages, p. 274
Easy, Conceptual/Application, Objective 5, Ans: a

28. Three hours after going to sleep, Shoshanna's heart rate increases, her breathing becomes more rapid, and her eyes move rapidly under her closed lids. Research suggests that Shoshanna is:
    a. dreaming.
    b. entering the third stage of sleep.
    c. ready to sleepwalk.
    d. exhibiting a sleep spindle.
    e. experiencing a night terror.

Sleep stages, p. 275
Easy, Conceptual/Application, Objective 5, Ans: b

29. Forty-year-old Lance insists that he never dreams. Research suggests that he probably:
    a. experiences very little REM sleep.
    b. would report a vivid dream if he were awakened during REM sleep.
    c. dreams during Stage 4 rather than during REM sleep.
    d. experiences more Stage 4 sleep than most people.
    e. passes through the sleep cycle much more rapidly than most people.

Sleep stages, pp. 273, 275
Medium, Conceptual/Application, Objective 5, Ans: d

30. At 3 o'clock in the morning, John has already slept for 4 hours. As long as his sleep continues, we can expect an increasing occurrence of:
    a. sleeptalking.
    b. slower, more regular breathing.
    c. muscle tension.
    d. genital arousal.
    e. Stage 4 sleep.

Sleep stages, p. 275
Medium, Factual/Definitional, Objective 5, Ans: b

31. The human sleep cycle repeats itself about every:
    a. 30 minutes.
    b. 90 minutes.
    c. 2 1/2 hours.
    d. 4 hours.

Why do we sleep?, p. 275
Medium, Factual/Definitional, Objective 5, Ans: e

32. Research on sleep patterns indicates that:
    a. the elderly and newborns have very similar sleep patterns.
    b. different sleep patterns reflect significant personality differences.
    c. the duration and pattern of sleep among fraternal twins is strikingly similar.
    d. everyone needs a minimum of 6 1/2 hours of sleep per night to function well.
    e. sleep patterns may be genetically influenced.

Why do we sleep?, pp. 276-277
Medium, Factual/Definitional, Objective 5, Ans: c

33. Traffic accident rates have been found to ________ after the spring change to daylight savings time and to ________ after the fall change back to standard time.
    a. increase; increase
    b. decrease; decrease
    c. increase; decrease
    d. decrease; increase

Why do we sleep?, p. 277
Medium, Factual/Definitional, Objective 5, Ans: c

34. Sleep deprivation has been shown to:
    a. increase attentiveness to highly motivating tasks.
    b. reduce hypertension.
    c. diminish immunity to disease.
    d. do all of the above.

Why do we sleep?, p. 277
Easy, Factual/Definitional, Objective 5, Ans: c

35. Chronic sleep deprivation is likely to ________ obesity and ________ memory.
    a. promote; facilitate
    b. inhibit; impair
    c. promote; impair
    d. inhibit; facilitate

Why do we sleep?, p. 278
Difficult, Factual/Definitional, Objective 5, Ans: a

36. The chemical adenosine is most likely to reduce:
    a. alertness.
    b. Stage 4 sleep.
    c. narcolepsy.
    d. REM sleep.

Why do we sleep?, p. 278
Medium, Factual/Definitional, Objective 5, Ans: c

37. The pituitary gland is particularly likely to release a growth hormone during:
    a. Stage 2 sleep.
    b. Stage 1 sleep.
    c. slow-wave sleep.
    d. paradoxical sleep.

Why do we sleep?, p. 278
Medium, Factual/Definitional, Objective 5, Ans: a

38. Compared to when they were only 20 years old, 60-year-olds:
    a. spend less time in deep sleep.
    b. spend less time in Stage 1 sleep.
    c. spend more time in paradoxical sleep.
    d. complete the sleep cycle more slowly.

Sleep disorders, p. 279
Difficult, Factual/Definitional, Objective 6, Ans: a

39. REM sleep is ________ by alcohol and ________ by sleeping pills.
    a. inhibited; inhibited
    b. facilitated; inhibited
    c. inhibited; facilitated
    d. facilitated; facilitated

Sleep disorders, p. 279
Medium, Factual/Definitional, Objective 6, Ans: a

40. Which of the following is the best advice for a person concerned about occasional insomnia?
    a. Relax and drink a glass of milk before bedtime.
    b. Eat a big dinner late in the evening so you'll feel drowsy at bedtime.
    c. Relax with a drink of your favorite alcoholic beverage just before bedtime.
    d. Engage in some form of vigorous physical exercise shortly before bedtime.
    e. Be sure to sleep later than usual once you do get to sleep.

Sleep disorders, p. 279
Difficult, Conceptual, Objective 6, Ans: d

41. Which of the following is bad advice for a person trying to overcome insomnia?
    a. Awaken at the same time every day even if you have had a restless night.
    b. Drink a glass of milk 15 minutes before bedtime.
    c. Avoid taking short naps during the day.
    d. Drink a glass of wine 15 minutes before bedtime.
    e. Don't engage in strenuous physical exercise just before bedtime.

Sleep disorders, p. 279
Easy, Factual/Definitional, Objective 6, Ans: c

42. Narcolepsy is a disorder involving:
    a. the temporary cessation of breathing during sleep.
    b. sudden uncontrollable seizures.
    c. periodic uncontrollable attacks of overwhelming sleepiness.
    d. difficulty falling and staying asleep.

Sleep disorders, p. 279
Medium, Conceptual/Application, Objective 6, Ans: a

43. During a heated argument with his teenage daughter, Mr. Reid suddenly lapsed into a state of REM sleep. Mr. Reid apparently suffers from:
a. narcolepsy.
b. insomnia.
c. sleep apnea.
d. REM rebound.

Sleep Disorders, p. 280
Difficult, Factual/Definitional, Objective 6, Ans: c

44. The absence of a hypothalamic neural center that produces hypocretin has been linked to:
a. insomnia.
b. sleep apnea.
c. narcolepsy.
d. night terrors.

Sleep disorders, p. 280
Easy, Factual/Definitional, Objective 6, Ans: b

45. Which of the following disorders is characterized by the temporary cessation of breathing while asleep?
a. narcolepsy
b. sleep apnea
c. night terror
d. insomnia

Sleep disorders, p. 280
Medium, Conceptual/Application, Objective 6, Ans: a

46. Mr. Oates always sleeps restlessly, snorting and gasping throughout the night. It is most likely that Mr. Oates suffers from:
a. sleep apnea.
b. narcolepsy.
c. night terror.
d. insomnia.

Sleep disorders, p. 280
Difficult, Factual/Definitional, Objective 6, Ans: b

47. Night terrors:
a. typically occur during REM sleep.
b. usually occur during the first few hours after falling asleep.
c. are nightmares that occur only in children.
d. are often accompanied by the temporary cessation of breathing.
e. are vividly recalled the next morning.

Sleep disorders, p. 280
Medium, Conceptual, Objective 6, Ans: a

48. Nightmares are to ________ as night terrors are to ________.
   a. REM sleep; Stage 4 sleep
   b. narcolepsy; sleep apnea
   c. delta waves; alpha waves
   d. Stage 4 sleep; Stage 1 sleep
   e. Stage 1 sleep; REM sleep

Sleep disorders, p. 280
Easy, Factual/Definitional, Objective 6, Ans: d

49. Compared to adults, children are ________ likely to experience night terrors and ________ likely to experience sleepwalking.
   a. more; less
   b. less; more
   c. less; less
   d. more; more

What do we dream?, p. 281
Difficult, Factual/Definitional, Objective 7, Ans: c

50. Research studies of the content of dreams indicate that:
   a. men are less likely than women to report dreams with sexual overtones.
   b. the genital arousal that occurs during sleep is typically related to sexual dreams.
   c. people are more likely to dream of failure than of success.
   d. most dreams are pleasant, exotic, and unrelated to ordinary daily life.

What do we dream?, p. 281
Medium, Factual/Definitional, Objective 7, Ans: d

51. Compared to young women, young men are ________ likely to report dreams involving sexual imagery, and they are ________ likely to dream about members of the same sex.
   a. less; more
   b. more; less
   c. less; less
   d. more; more

What do we dream?, p. 281
Medium, Conceptual/Application, Objective 7, Ans: b

52. As Inge recalled her dream, she was dancing with a tall, dark gentleman when suddenly the music shifted to loud rock and the man disappeared. According to Freud, Inge's account represents the ________ content of her dream.
   a. paradoxical
   b. manifest
   c. latent
   d. dissociated
   e. delusional

What do we dream?, p. 282
Medium, Factual/Definitional, Objective 7, Ans: c

53. While soundly asleep people cannot:
   a. talk and dream at the same time.
   b. incorporate environmental changes into the manifest content of their dreams.
   c. learn tape-recorded messages to which they are repeatedly exposed.
   d. do any of the above.

Why do we dream?, p. 282
Medium, Factual/Definitional, Objective 7, Ans: d

54. According to Freud, the latent content of a dream refers to:
   a. its accompanying brain-wave pattern.
   b. the previous day's events that prompted the dream.
   c. the sensory stimuli in the sleeping environment that are incorporated into the dream.
   d. its underlying but censored meaning.

Why do we dream?, p. 282
Medium, Conceptual/Application, Objective 7, Ans: c

55. Greg remembered a recent dream in which his girlfriend suddenly grabbed the wheel of his speeding car to prevent him from driving off the edge of a cliff. Greg's therapist suggested that the dream might be a representation of the girlfriend's frantic efforts to save the couple from sexual disaster. According to Freud, the therapist was attempting to reveal the ________ of Greg's dream.
   a. REM content
   b. circadian rhythm
   c. latent content
   d. manifest content

Why do we dream?, p. 282
Easy, Factual/Definitional, Objective 7, Ans: a

56. According to Freud, the dreams of adults can be traced back to:
   a. erotic wishes.
   b. stressful life events.
   c. physiological needs for brain stimulation.
   d. random bursts of neural activity.

Why do we dream?, pp. 282-283
Easy, Factual/Definitional, Objective 7, Ans: d

57. Evidence suggests that we consolidate our memories of recent life events through:
   a. dissociation.
   b. sleep apnea.
   c. night terrors.
   d. REM sleep.

Why do we dream?, pp. 282-283
Difficult, Factual/Definitional, Objective 7, Ans: d

58. The theory that dreams help to solidify our memories of daytime experiences is supported by the finding that:
    a. with increasing age and experience, people spend progressively more of their sleep time in REM sleep.
    b. dreams are triggered by neural activity that originates in the higher learning centers of the cerebral cortex.
    c. the manifest content of our dreams usually reflects the events of the previous day.
    d. people deprived of REM sleep remember less of certain pre-sleep information than people deprived of other sleep stages.

Why do we dream? (text and Figure 7.9), p. 283
Easy, Factual/Definitional, Objective 7, Ans: b

59. Research indicates that the percentage of total sleep spent in REM sleep is higher in ________ than in ________.
    a. artists; scientists
    b. infants; adults
    c. females; males
    d. the elderly; adolescents

Why do we dream?, p. 283
Medium, Factual/Definitional, Objective 7, Ans: c

60. Which theory suggests that dreams are mental responses to random bursts of neural stimulation?
    a. dissociation theory
    b. social influence theory
    c. activation-synthesis theory
    d. Freud's dream theory

Why do we dream?, p. 283
Medium, Conceptual, Objective 7, Ans: d

61. Vivid dreams often involve sudden and surprising changes in scene. This best serves to support the theory that dreams:
    a. strengthen our memories of the preceding day's events.
    b. are expressions of erotic feelings and desires.
    c. help to prepare us for the stress and challenges of the following day.
    d. are triggered by random bursts of neural activity.

Why do we dream?, p. 284
Easy, Factual/Definitional, Objective 7, Ans: d

62. REM rebound involves the:
    a. tendency for REM sleep periods to become increasingly longer and more frequent as a normal night of sleep progresses.
    b. increase in REM sleep that characteristically follows intense learning episodes or stressful daytime experiences.
    c. unusual symptoms of tiredness and irritability that follow periods of REM sleep deprivation.
    d. tendency for REM sleep to increase following REM sleep deprivation.

Why do we dream?, p. 284
Difficult, Factual/Definitional, Objective 7, Ans: c

63. The best indication that dreaming serves a necessary biological function is provided by the fact that:
   a. most dreams are psychologically meaningless.
   b. the disruption of REM sleep leads to narcolepsy.
   c. most mammals experience REM rebound.
   d. sexual tension is naturally discharged during REM sleep.

Hypnosis, p. 286
Easy, Conceptual, Objective 8, Ans: b

64. While under hypnosis, Juanita describes her experience of being kidnapped at age 5. In suggesting that she will soon forget this traumatic event, the hypnotist is encouraging Juanita to experience:
   a. posthypnotic regression.
   b. posthypnotic amnesia.
   c. temporal dissociation.
   d. narcolepsy.
   e. insomnia.

Hypnosis, pp. 281, 286
Medium, Conceptual, Objective 8, Ans: c

65. Freud is to ________ as Mesmer is to ________.
   a. narcolepsy; hypnosis
   b. slow-wave sleep; paradoxical sleep
   c. dream interpretation; animal magnetism
   d. posthypnotic suggestion; sleep apnea
   e. hallucinations; REM rebound

Can anyone experience hypnosis?, p. 287
Easy, Factual/Definitional, Objective 8, Ans: d

66. Research on susceptibility to hypnosis indicates that:
   a. very few people can actually be hypnotized.
   b. people who are most easily hypnotized usually have difficulty paying attention to their own personal thoughts and feelings.
   c. how well a person responds to hypnotic suggestion depends primarily on the skill and experience of the hypnotist.
   d. people who are highly responsive to hypnotic suggestion tend to have rich fantasy lives.

Can anyone experience hypnosis?, p. 287
Medium, Conceptual/Application, Objective 8, Ans: b

67. A stage hypnotist can best increase the hypnotizability of select audience members by first providing them with a:
   a. memory quiz that encourages them to recall their own early life experiences.
   b. convincing demonstration of his or her hypnotic induction skills.
   c. caffeinated beverage that temporarily boosts mental alertness.
   d. simple promise that they will not be publicly humiliated.

Can hypnosis enhance recall of forgotten events?, p. 287
Medium, Conceptual/Application, Objective 8, Ans: b

68. Twenty-eight-year-old Theodore has an irrational fear of dogs. His therapist hypnotizes him and asks him to mentally relive his earliest childhood experience with a dog. The therapist is making use of:
    a. posthypnotic amnesia.
    b. age regression.
    c. retrograde amnesia.
    d. temporal dissociation.
    e. the hidden observer.

Can hypnosis enhance recall of forgotten events?, pp. 287-288
Medium, Factual/Definitional, Objective 8, Ans: b

69. Researchers are most likely to question the value of hypnosis for:
    a. reducing fear.
    b. enhancing memory.
    c. relieving pain.
    d. facilitating relaxation.

Can hypnosis force people to act against their will?, p. 288
Medium, Factual/Definitional, Objective 8, Ans: b

70. In one study, both hypnotized and unhypnotized subjects were told to throw acid in a research assistant's face. In this experiment, hypnotized people:
    a. usually refused to engage in antisocial behavior.
    b. behaved in the same fashion as unhypnotized individuals.
    c. were easily influenced to act against their own will.
    d. experienced a heightened sense of personal responsibility for their actions.

Can hypnosis force people to act against their will?, pp. 288, 290
Difficult, Conceptual, Objective 8, Ans: c

71. Experiments in which hypnotized individuals have been encouraged to perform apparently dangerous acts best illustrate that:
    a. hypnosis is a special state of dissociated consciousness.
    b. information processing during hypnosis occurs only at a subconscious level.
    c. people are surprisingly susceptible to destructive social influence.
    d. the use of hypnosis as a form of entertainment is clearly inappropriate.

Thinking critically about hypnotic age regression (Box), p. 289
Difficult, Factual/Definitional, Objective 8, Ans: b

72. In Robert True's study, hypnotized subjects correctly reported the day of the week on which their fourth, seventh, and tenth birthdays occurred. This experiment illustrated that:
    a. hypnosis can promote accurate recall of forgotten material.
    b. hypnotists can subtly influence the memories of their subjects.
    c. every experience a person has ever had is recorded in the brain.
    d. hypnosis involves a state of dissociated consciousness.

Can hypnosis be therapeutic?, p. 290
Easy, Conceptual, Objective 8, Ans: b

73. Just prior to awakening Chinua from a hypnotic state, the therapist told him that during the next few days he would feel nauseous whenever he reached for a cigarette. Chinua's therapist was attempting to make use of:
a. age regression.
b. posthypnotic suggestion.
c. a hidden observer.
d. posthypnotic amnesia.
e. REM rebound.

Can hypnosis be therapeutic?, p. 290
Medium, Factual/Definitional, Objective 8, Ans: d

74. Psychologists who are critical of hypnotherapy are most likely to question whether its benefits are:
a. outweighed by the dangers of dissociation.
b. restricted to superficial problems.
c. retained beyond the hypnotic session itself.
d. produced by the hypnosis itself.

Can hypnosis alleviate pain?, p. 290
Medium, Factual/Definitional, Objective 8, Ans: d

75. People can be hypnotically induced to:
a. surpass their normal waking levels of physical strength and stamina.
b. perform dangerous acts that they would not perform in a normal state.
c. recall correctly almost anything that has ever happened to them.
d. report significant relief from the pain of placing their arms in ice water.

Can hypnosis alleviate pain?, p. 290
Easy, Factual/Definitional, Objective 8, Ans: b

76. A split in consciousness in which some thoughts occur simultaneously with and yet separately from other thoughts is called:
a. narcolepsy.
b. dissociation.
c. paradoxical sleep.
d. posthypnotic amnesia.

Can hypnosis alleviate pain?, p. 290
Medium, Factual/Definitional, Objective 8, Ans: a

77. One plausible theory suggests that hypnosis relieves pain by:
a. distracting attention.
b. blocking sensory input.
c. speeding up the circadian rhythm.
d. eliciting delta waves characteristic of deep sleep.

Hypnosis as a social phenomenon, p. 291
Medium, Factual/Definitional, Objective 9, Ans: d

78. The claim that hypnotic phenomena are regulated by normal conscious control processes is associated with the theory that hypnosis involves:
    a. paradoxical sleep.
    b. dissociation.
    c. slow-wave sleep.
    d. role playing.

Hypnosis as a social phenomenon, p. 291
Medium, Conceptual/Application, Objective 9, Ans: b

79. Hypnotized people who have been age regressed are no more genuinely childlike than unhypnotized people who are asked to feign childlike behavior. This fact most clearly supports:
    a. Freud's dream theory.
    b. social influence theory.
    c. the activation-synthesis theory.
    d. dissociation theory.

Hypnosis as a social phenomenon, pp. 288, 291-292
Difficult, Conceptual, Objective 9, Ans: d

80. Orne and Evans discovered that unhypnotized subjects performed the same dangerous acts as hypnotized subjects. This finding is most consistent with the theory that hypnosis involves:
    a. age regression.
    b. dissociation.
    c. paradoxical sleep.
    d. conscious role playing.

Hypnosis as divided consciousness, p. 292
Medium, Factual/Definitional, Objective 9, Ans: b

81. The claim that hypnotic phenomena are regulated by control processes outside our normal awareness is associated with the theory that hypnosis involves:
    a. slow-wave sleep.
    b. dissociation.
    c. paradoxical sleep.
    d. role playing.

Hypnosis as divided consciousness, pp. 292-293
Difficult, Conceptual/Application, Objective 9, Ans: a

82. Evidence that highly hypnotizable people are no more successful than others at simultaneously reading a book and listening to music would most clearly challenge:
    a. dissociation theory.
    b. the activation-synthesis theory.
    c. Freud's dream theory.
    d. social influence theory.

Hypnosis as divided consciousness, pp. 292-293
Difficult, Factual/Definitional, Objective 9, Ans: d

83. In Hilgard's studies of pain sensitivity, the hidden observer reported experiences typically associated with:
   a. the Freudian unconscious.
   b. paradoxical sleep.
   c. slow-wave sleep.
   d. normal consciousness.

Hypnosis as divided consciousness, pp. 292-293
Difficult, Conceptual/Application, Objective 9, Ans: a

84. When hypnosis is used to induce deafness, the hidden observer is likely to be ______ to auditory stimulation. When hypnosis is used to induce blindness, the hidden observer is likely to be ______ to visual stimulation.
   a. sensitive; sensitive
   b. insensitive; sensitive
   c. sensitive; insensitive
   d. insensitive; insensitive

Hypnosis as divided consciousness, pp. 292-293
Medium, Factual/Definitional, Objective 9, Ans: d

85. The divided-consciousness theory of hypnosis receives support from evidence that:
   a. hypnosis can block sensory input.
   b. hypnosis can affect voluntary but not involuntary behaviors.
   c. hypnotized people often seem to play the role of "good hypnotic subjects."
   d. hypnotized people can be aware of pain sensation without experiencing emotional distress.

Hypnosis as divided consciousness, pp. 292-293
Difficult, Conceptual/Application, Objective 9, Ans: d

86. Joan's dentist used hypnosis when he filled a deep cavity. Joan insisted that she felt no pain, but when the dentist asked her to raise her hand if some part of her could feel the pain, she raised her hand. This supports the theory that hypnosis involves:
   a. paradoxical sleep.
   b. role playing.
   c. motivational conflict.
   d. dissociation.

Dependence and addiction, p. 294
Easy, Factual/Definitional, Objective 10, Ans: d

87. The need to take larger and larger doses of a drug in order to experience its effects is an indication of:
   a. withdrawal.
   b. dissociation.
   c. resistance.
   d. tolerance.
   e. narcolepsy.

Dependence and addiction, p. 294
Easy, Factual/Definitional, Objective 10, Ans: c

88. The discomfort and distress that follow the discontinued use of certain drugs is called:
a. intolerance.
b. narcolepsy.
c. withdrawal.
d. retraction.
e. dissociation.

Dependence and addiction, p. 294
Easy, Conceptual/Application, Objective 10, Ans: d

89. When Celeste was unable to obtain her regular supply of heroin, she began to develop tremors, fever, and an intense craving for the drug. Celeste was experiencing symptoms of:
a. narcolepsy.
b. dissociation.
c. insomnia.
d. withdrawal.

Dependence and addiction, p. 294
Easy, Factual/Definitional, Objective 10, Ans: d

90. Unpleasant withdrawal symptoms are indicative of:
a. insomnia.
b. narcolepsy.
c. dissociation.
d. physical dependence.
e. REM rebound.

Misconceptions about addiction, pp. 294-295
Difficult, Factual/Definitional, Objective 10, Ans: c

91. Research on the use of addictive drugs indicates that:
a. an occasional cigarette smoker almost always becomes a heavy smoker.
b. regular marijuana smokers typically experience an irresistible craving for THC.
c. many people are able to stop using morphine without professional help.
d. individuals who receive morphine from physicians for pain relief usually develop the irresistible cravings of an addict.

Misconceptions about addiction, p. 295
Medium, Factual/Definitional, Objective 10, Ans: c

92. The greatest danger of viewing drug addiction as a disease is that this may lead drug addicts to:
a. feel increased feelings of shame.
b. hide the drug abuse from public view.
c. feel powerless to overcome the addiction.
d. become victims of social hostility and prejudice.

Depressants, p. 296
Easy, Factual/Definitional, Objective 11, Ans: e

93. In large doses, alcohol is a ________; in small amounts, it is a ________.
a. depressant; stimulant
b. stimulant; depressant
c. hallucinogen; depressant
d. stimulant; stimulant
e. depressant; depressant

Depressants, p. 296
Medium, Factual/Definitional, Objective 11, Ans: a

94. Under the influence of alcohol, men on dates are ________ likely to be sexually coercive than they would otherwise be and restaurant patrons are ________ likely to tip generously than they otherwise would.
a. more; more
b. less; less
c. more; less
d. less; more

Depressants, p. 296
Medium, Factual/Definitional, Objective 11, Ans: d

95. Alcohol consumption is most likely to make people more:
a. fearful.
b. self-conscious.
c. sexually inhibited.
d. self-disclosing.

Depressants, p. 296
Difficult, Conceptual/Application, Objective 11, Ans: b

96. After a stressful day at the office, Arthur has five or six drinks at a local bar before going home for dinner. Research suggests that Arthur's heavy drinking will have the most adverse effect on his ability to remember:
a. at the time he is drinking the names of the people he has just met.
b. the next day the names of the people he talked to and what he said while drinking.
c. at the time he is drinking the name of his employer and his own home address.
d. the next day the names of the business associates he talked to before going to the bar.

Depressants, pp. 296-297
Medium, Factual/Definitional, Objective 11, Ans: d

97. Alcohol consumption tends to ________ self-awareness and ________ feelings of guilt.
a. decrease; increase
b. increase; decrease
c. increase; increase
d. decrease; decrease

Depressants, p. 297
Medium, Factual/Definitional, Objective 11, Ans: d

98. University men were shown an erotic movie clip. Compared with those who thought they had recently consumed a nonalcoholic beverage, men who believed they had recently consumed an alcoholic beverage were ________ likely to report having strong sexual fantasies and ________ likely to report having feelings of guilt.
   a. more; more
   b. less; less
   c. less; more
   d. more; less

Depressants, p. 297
Easy, Factual/Definitional, Objective 11, Ans: b

99. Which drugs are most likely to be prescribed as tranquilizers?
   a. amphetamines
   b. barbiturates
   c. hallucinogens
   d. opiates

Depressants, p. 297
Medium, Factual/Definitional, Objective 11, Ans: c

100. The use of barbiturates ________ anxiety and ________ sympathetic nervous system activity.
   a. increases; decreases
   b. decreases; increases
   c. decreases; decreases
   d. increases; increases

Depressants, p. 297
Difficult, Conceptual, Objective 11, Ans: c

101. The most rapid increase in drug tolerance is likely to be experienced by the regular user of:
   a. marijuana.
   b. caffeine.
   c. heroin.
   d. barbiturates.

Depressants, p. 298
Medium, Factual/Definitional, Objective 11, Ans: a

102. Repeated use of an opiate:
   a. decreases the brain's production of endorphins.
   b. increases heart and breathing rates.
   c. does not seem to be followed by serious withdrawal symptoms.
   d. triggers auditory as well as visual hallucinations.

Depressants and stimulants, pp. 297, 298
Medium, Conceptual, Objective 11, Ans: b

103. Amphetamines are to ________ as barbiturates are to ________.
   a. hallucinogens; depressants
   b. stimulants; depressants
   c. hallucinogens; stimulants
   d. stimulants; hallucinogens

Stimulants, p. 298
Medium, Conceptual/Application, Objective 11, Ans: c

104. François was dismayed to discover that some of his football teammates were using drugs to enhance their footwork and endurance on the playing field. Which of the following drugs were the players most likely using?
   a. morphine derivatives
   b. marijuana
   c. amphetamines
   d. barbiturates

Stimulants, p. 298
Medium, Factual/Definitional, Objective 11, Ans: a

105. Amphetamines ________ appetite and ________ self-confidence.
   a. decrease; increase
   b. increase; decrease
   c. increase; increase
   d. decrease; decrease

Stimulants, p. 298
Difficult, Conceptual, Objective 11, Ans: b

106. Soon after taking a psychoactive drug, Zachary experienced a diminished appetite, an increased pulse rate, dilated pupils, and feelings of self-confidence and euphoria. Zachary most likely experienced the effects of:
   a. heroin.
   b. cocaine.
   c. LSD.
   d. marijuana.

Stimulants, p. 298
Difficult, Factual/Definitional, Objective 11, Ans: b

107. When cocaine is snorted, free-based, or injected, it produces a rush of euphoria by:
   a. depleting the brain's supply of serotonin.
   b. blocking the reuptake of dopamine.
   c. stimulating the release of excess norepinephrine.
   d. triggering a state of dissociation.

Stimulants, p. 299
Medium, Factual/Definitional, Objective 11, Ans: b

108. Caged rats respond to foot shocks with unusually high levels of aggression after ingesting:
   a. heroin.
   b. cocaine.
   c. marijuana.
   d. barbiturates.

Stimulants, p. 299
Medium, Factual/Definitional, Objective 11, Ans: c

109. Which of the following is an amphetamine derivative that acts as a mild hallucinogen?
   a. marijuana
   b. Nembutal
   c. ecstasy
   d. heroin
   e. LSD

Stimulants, p. 299
Difficult, Factual/Definitional, Objective 11, Ans: b

110. One of the immediate effects of ecstasy is:
   a. increased appetite.
   b. dehydration.
   c. lethargy.
   d. pupil constriction.
   e. decreased blood pressure.

Hallucinogens, p. 299
Medium, Factual/Definitional, Objective 11, Ans: a

111. Which of the following is a psychedelic drug?
   a. LSD
   b. cocaine
   c. heroin
   d. caffeine
   e. nicotine

Hallucinogens, p. 299
Easy, Conceptual, Objective 11, Ans: b

112. After ingesting a small dose of a psychoactive drug, Laqueta experienced vivid visual hallucinations and felt as if she were separated from her own body. Laqueta most likely experienced the effects of:
   a. cocaine.
   b. LSD.
   c. heroin.
   d. marijuana.

Hallucinogens, p. 300
Easy, Factual/Definitional, Objective 11, Ans: a

113. THC, the active ingredient in ________, is classified as a ________.
   a. marijuana; hallucinogen
   b. marijuana; stimulant
   c. cocaine; stimulant
   d. cocaine; hallucinogen
   e. heroin; depressant

Hallucinogens, p. 300
Easy, Conceptual/Application, Objective 11, Ans: c

114. Mrs. Roberts, who suffers from AIDS, has been given an ordinarily illegal drug at the university hospital. Considering her specific medical condition, it is likely that she has received:
   a. LSD.
   b. cocaine.
   c. marijuana.
   d. heroin.

Hallucinogens, p. 301
Medium, Factual/Definitional, Objective 11, Ans: c

115. Symptoms of drug withdrawal are likely to be ________ severe among those with ________ levels of drug tolerance.
   a. most; low
   b. most; moderate
   c. most; high
   d. equally; low, moderate, or high

Influences on drug use, p. 302
Easy, Factual/Definitional, Objective 12, Ans: d

116. Boys who tend to be fearless and impulsive at age 6 are ________ likely to smoke and ________ likely to drink alcohol as teens.
   a. less; more
   b. more; less
   c. less; less
   d. more; more

Influences on drug use, p. 302
Medium, Factual/Definitional, Objective 12, Ans: c

117. Which of the following has been presented as evidence that alcoholism is genetically influenced?
   a. Alcohol abuse is positively correlated with depression.
   b. Alcohol abusers are typically not aware that they are addicted to the drug.
   c. Children whose parents abuse alcohol have a relatively high tolerance for alcohol.
   d. Alcohol abusers are unable to stop using alcohol without professional help.

Influences on drug use, p. 303
Medium, Factual/Definitional, Objective 12, Ans: c

118. Compared to their white counterparts, African-American teens report ________ rates of alcohol use and ________ rates of cocaine use.
   a. lower; higher
   b. higher; lower
   c. lower; lower
   d. higher; higher

Influences on drug use, p. 303
Easy, Conceptual/Application, Objective 12, Ans: c

119. Sixteen-year-old Bethany is becoming increasingly concerned about her use of marijuana on weekends. In order to reduce her use of this drug Bethany should:
   a. recognize that life is stressful and often beyond control.
   b. be warned that marijuana interferes with female sexual functioning.
   c. stop associating with friends who use marijuana.
   d. recognize that drug use results from her own lack of social skills.

Near-death experiences, p. 305
Medium, Factual/Definitional, Objective 13, Ans: b

120. Near-death experiences are:
   a. typically recalled as very scary and unpleasant.
   b. quite similar to drug-induced hallucinogenic experiences.
   c. recalled by nearly all who have been revived from a cardiac arrest.
   d. explained from a dualist perspective by most scientists today.

Near-death experiences, p. 306
Medium, Factual/Definitional, Objective 13, Ans: e

121. The belief that death involves the liberation of the soul from a bodily prison illustrates:
   a. reincarnation.
   b. monism.
   c. dissociation.
   d. narcolepsy.
   e. dualism.

Near-death experiences, p. 306
Medium, Factual/Definitional, Objective 13, Ans: d

122. Monism refers to the presumption that:
   a. hypnosis and REM sleep are identical states of consciousness.
   b. near-death experiences provide scientific evidence for life after death.
   c. different psychological theories offer complementary rather than contradictory perspectives.
   d. mind and body are different aspects of the same thing.

Essay Questions

1. Because he has difficulty falling asleep at night, Professor Hogan doesn't go to bed until very late. Before he retires, he tries to wear himself out by running around the block several times. Then he treats himself to a beer and perhaps a pizza while preparing his lecture for the next day's early morning classes. What specific advice would you give the professor to help him fall asleep?

2. Franco studied all evening for a chemistry test the following morning. That night he dreamt that he copied test answers from a female classmate sitting nearby. Compare and contrast a Freudian and an information-processing explanation of Franco's dream.

3. A good friend of yours hopes that hypnosis will improve his memory and help him study longer and more effectively. He worries, however, that he might not be easily hypnotized. Your mother hopes that hypnosis will help relieve her arthritis pain but fears that under hypnosis she might do something embarrassing. Discuss the extent to which the hopes and fears of your friend and your mother are realistic. Where appropriate, use research evidence to support your conclusions.

4. A classmate believes that alcohol, marijuana, and cocaine all have similar effects on behavior and that therefore all three drugs ought to be legalized. Carefully evaluate the strengths and weaknesses of your classmate's position.

Web Quiz 1

Ans: a

1. If asked to press a button when they are tapped, people can respond in 1/10th of a second. This best illustrates the importance of:
   a. subconscious information processing.
   b. biological rhythms.
   c. dissociation.
   d. hypnogogic sensations.

Ans: c

2. Staying up especially late on weekends is most likely to have an influence on:
   a. narcolepsy.
   b. sleep apnea.
   c. the circadian rhythm.
   d. seasonal affective disorder.

Ans: b

3. The different brain wave patterns that accompany various sleep stages are recorded by means of a(n):
   a. REM.
   b. EEG.
   c. EMG.
   d. PET scan.

Ans: d

4. Sleepwalking is most likely to be associated with ________ sleep.
   a. Stage 1.
   b. Stage 2.
   c. Stage 3.
   d. Stage 4.
   e. REM.

Ans: e

5. A recurring sleep stage during which most vivid dreams commonly occur is known as ________ sleep.
   a. Stage 1.
   b. Stage 2.
   c. Stage 3.
   d. Stage 4.
   e. REM.

Ans: d

6. Sleep is _______ by adenosine and _______ by serotonin.
   a. inhibited; facilitated
   b. facilitated; inhibited
   c. inhibited; inhibited
   d. facilitated; facilitated

Ans: d

7. Which of the following sleep disorders is most strongly associated with obesity?
   a. narcolepsy
   b. insomnia
   c. night terrors
   d. sleep apnea

Ans: c

8. The distinction between manifest content and latent content is central to ________ theory of dreams.
   a. the activation-synthesis
   b. the memory consolidation
   c. Freud's wish-fulfillment
   d. Hilgard's dissociation

Ans: a

9. The social influence theory of hypnosis receives support from evidence that:
   a. behaviors produced through hypnotic procedures can also be produced without them.
   b. hypnotized subjects have a hidden observer.
   c. easily hypnotized individuals have difficulty focusing attention on their own thoughts and feelings.
   d. very few people are at all responsive to hypnotic suggestions.

Ans: b

10. Research most clearly disputes claims of:
   a. REM rebound.
   b. age regression.
   c. circadian rhythms.
   d. hypnogogic sensations.

Ans: a

11. Those who are highly hypnotizable are especially at risk for:
   a. false memories.
   b. sleep apnea.
   c. drug abuse.
   d. narcolepsy.

Ans: c

12. Dissociation has been used as an explanation for:
   a. narcolepsy.
   b. paradoxical sleep.
   c. hypnotic pain relief.
   d. the near-death experience.

Ans: b

13. Research on addictive drugs most clearly indicates that:
   a. the medical use of morphine to control pain typically leads to addictive drug cravings.
   b. most of America's ex-smokers were able to overcome their nicotine addiction without professional treatment.
   c. addictions to narcotic drugs can't be overcome without professional treatment programs.
   d. relationship dependencies have the same addictive characteristics as drug dependencies.

Ans: d

14. Cocaine is to ________ as marijuana is to ________.
    a. depressants; stimulants
    b. stimulants; depressants
    c. hallucinogens; depressants
    d. stimulants; hallucinogens

Ans: a

15. The experience of vivid geometric images and dreamlike scenes is most likely to be triggered by:
    a. LSD.
    b. heroin.
    c. Nembutal.
    d. amphetamines.

Web Quiz 2

Ans: e

1. A car driver's ability to navigate a familiar route while carrying on an animated conversation with passengers best illustrates the importance of:
   a. dualism.
   b. REM rebound.
   c. the hidden observer.
   d. biological rhythms.
   e. parallel processing.

Ans: d

2. The five-stage sleep cycle provides an example of:
   a. sleep apnea.
   b. dissociation.
   c. serial processing.
   d. biological rhythms.
   e. latent content.

Ans: a

3. Bright light inhibits our feelings of sleepiness by influencing the production of:
   a. melatonin.
   b. dopamine.
   c. MDMA.
   d. THC.

Ans: b

4. The large, slow brain waves associated with Stage 4 sleep are called:
   a. sleep spindles.
   b. delta waves.
   c. alpha waves.
   d. REMs.

Ans: d

5. The visual and auditory areas of the brain are most active during ________ sleep.
   a. Stage 1.
   b. Stage 2.
   c. slow-wave.
   d. paradoxical.

Ans: b

6. Those who complain of insomnia typically _______ how long it actually takes them to fall asleep and ________ how long they actually slept.
   a. underestimate; overestimate
   b. overestimate; underestimate
   c. underestimate; underestimate
   d. overestimate; overestimate

Ans: b

7. Which sleep disorder is most likely to be accompanied by sleepwalking and sleeptalking?
   a. narcolepsy
   b. night terrors
   c. sleep apnea
   d. insomnia

Ans: a

8. The activation-synthesis theory provides a physiological explanation for:
   a. dreaming.
   b. sleep apnea.
   c. narcolepsy.
   d. posthypnotic amnesia.

Ans: d

9. An Austrian physician's so-called "animal magnetism" best illustrated the dynamics of:
   a. biological rhythms.
   b. REM rebound.
   c. psychoactive drugs.
   d. hypnosis.
   e. narcolepsy.

Ans: c

10. In order to help patients control their undesired symptoms or unhealthy behaviors, clinicians would be most likely to make use of:
    a. dissociation.
    b. REM rebound.
    c. posthypnotic suggestion.
    d. hypnogogic sensations.

Ans: c

11. In an experiment, hypnotized subjects are told to scratch their ear if they hear the word "psychology" mentioned later. The fact that they do so only if they think the experiment is still under way most clearly supports the theory that hypnosis involves:
    a. dissociation.
    b. psychological dependence.
    c. role playing.
    d. hypnogogic sensations.

Ans: b

12. The experience of insomnia following discontinued use of a psychoactive drug best illustrates:
    a. narcolepsy.
    b. withdrawal.
    c. REM rebound.
    d. dissociation.
    e. sleep apnea.

Ans: c

13. Which of the following psychoactive drugs produces the quickest and most powerful rush of euphoria?
a. alcohol
b. marijuana
c. cocaine
d. barbiturates

Ans: d

14. Recent studies indicate that sixth graders ________ their friends' use of marijuana and college students ________ their classmates' enthusiasm for alcohol.
a. underestimate; overestimate
b. overestimate; underestimate
c. underestimate; underestimate
d. overestimate; overestimate

Ans: a

15. Hallucinations similar to those that accompany the near-death experience can be produced by:
a. oxygen deprivation.
b. dehydration.
c. narcolepsy.
d. dissociation.
e. cocaine use.

Study Guide Questions

Ans: b, p. 265

1. At its beginning, psychology focused on the study of:
   a. observable behavior.
   b. consciousness.
   c. abnormal behavior.
   d. all of the above.

Ans: d, p. 265

2. As defined by the text, consciousness includes which of the following?
   a. daydreaming
   b. sleeping
   c. hypnosis
   d. all of the above

Ans: e, p. 266

3. "Consciousness" is defined in the text as:
   a. mental life.
   b. selective attention to ongoing perceptions, thoughts, and feelings.
   c. information processing.
   d. a vague concept no longer useful to contemporary psychologists.
   e. our awareness of ourselves and our environment.

Ans: c, pp. 266-267

4. Concluding his presentation on levels of information processing, Miguel states that:
   a. humans process both conscious and subconscious information in parallel.
   b. conscious processing occurs in parallel, while subconscious processing is serial.
   c. conscious processing is serial, while subconscious processing is parallel.
   d. all information processing is serial in nature.

Ans: b, p. 267

5. Which of the following statements concerning daydreaming is true?
   a. People prone to violence or drug use tend to have more frequent vivid daydreams.
   b. Most daydreaming involves the familiar details of our everyday lives.
   c. Psychologists consider children's daydreams to be unhealthy.
   d. All of the above are true.

Ans: e, p. 267

6. Which of the following groups tends to daydream the most?
   a. elderly men
   b. elderly women
   c. middle-aged women
   d. middle-aged men
   e. young adults

Ans: c, p. 269

7. Circadian rhythms are the:
   a. brain waves that occur during Stage 4 sleep.
   b. muscular tremors that occur during opiate withdrawal.
   c. regular body cycles that occur on a 24-hour schedule.
   d. brain waves that are indicative of Stage 2 sleep.

Ans: e, p. 269

8. Which of the following is not an example of a biological rhythm?
   a. feeling depressed during the winter months
   b. the female menstrual cycle
   c. the five sleep stages
   d. the peaking of body temperature during the day
   e. sudden sleep attacks during the day

Ans: c, p. 271

9. The sleep-waking cycles of people who stay up too late typically are ________ hours in duration.
   a. 23
   b. 24
   c. 25
   d. 26

Ans: c, p. 271

10. When our ________ is disrupted, we experience jet lag.
    a. daydreaming
    b. REM sleep
    c. circadian rhythm
    d. Stage 4 sleep
    e. Stage 1 sleep

Ans: e, p. 272

11. A person whose EEG shows a high proportion of alpha waves is most likely:
    a. dreaming.
    b. in Stage 2 sleep.
    c. in Stage 3 sleep.
    d. in Stage 4 sleep.
    e. awake and relaxed.

Ans: a, p. 273

12. Sleep spindles predominate during which stage of sleep?
    a. Stage 2
    b. Stage 3
    c. Stage 4
    d. REM sleep

Ans: d, p. 273

13. During which stage of sleep does the body experience increased heart rate, rapid breathing, and genital arousal?
    a. Stage 2
    b. Stage 3
    c. Stage 4
    d. REM sleep

Ans: a, p. 273

14. Which of the following is characteristic of REM sleep?
    a. genital arousal
    b. increased muscular tension
    c. night terrors
    d. slow, regular breathing
    e. alpha waves

Ans: d, p. 273

15. Although her eyes are closed, Adele's brain is generating bursts of electrical activity. It is likely that Adele is:
    a. under the influence of a depressant.
    b. under the influence of an opiate.
    c. in NREM sleep.
    d. in REM sleep.
    e. having a near-death experience.

Ans: b, p. 274

16. REM sleep is referred to as "paradoxical sleep" because:
    a. studies of people deprived of REM sleep indicate that REM sleep is unnecessary.
    b. the body's muscles remain relaxed while the brain and eyes are active.
    c. it is very easy to awaken a person from REM sleep.
    d. the body's muscles are very tense while the brain is in a nearly meditative state.
    e. erection during REM sleep indicates sexual arousal.

Ans: c, p. 274

17. A PET scan of a sleeping person's brain reveals increased activity in the visual and auditory areas. This most likely indicates that the sleeper:
    a. has a neurological disorder.
    b. is not truly asleep.
    c. is in REM sleep.
    d. suffers from narcolepsy.

Ans: d, p. 275

18. The sleep cycle is approximately ________ minutes.
    a. 30
    b. 50
    c. 75
    d. 90

Ans: e, pp. 276-277

19. The effects of chronic sleep deprivation include:
    a. suppression of the immune system.
    b. altered metabolic and hormonal functioning.
    c. impaired creativity.
    d. increased accident proneness.
    e. all of the above.

Ans: b, p. 279

20. A person who falls asleep in the midst of a heated argument probably suffers from:
    a. sleep apnea.
    b. narcolepsy.
    c. night terrors.
    d. insomnia.

Ans: a, p. 279

21. One effect of sleeping pills is to:
    a. decrease REM sleep.
    b. increase REM sleep.
    c. decrease Stage 2 sleep.
    d. increase Stage 2 sleep.

Ans: a, p. 282

22. According to Freud, dreams are:
    a. a symbolic fulfillment of erotic wishes.
    b. the result of random neural activity in the brainstem.
    c. the brain's mechanism for self-stimulation.
    d. transparent representations of the individual's conflicts.

Ans: b, p. 282

23. Jill dreams that her boyfriend pushes her in front of an oncoming car. Her psychoanalyst suggests that the dream might symbolize her fear that her boyfriend is rushing her into sexual activity prematurely. The analyst is evidently attempting to interpret the ________ content of Jill's dream.
    a. manifest
    b. latent
    c. dissociated
    d. overt

Ans: c, p. 282

24. People who heard unusual phrases prior to sleep were awakened each time they began REM sleep. The fact that they remembered less the next morning provides support for the ________ theory of dreaming.
    a. manifest content
    b. physiological
    c. information-processing
    d. activation-synthesis
    e. latent content

Ans: d, pp. 282-284

25. Which of the following is not a theory of dreaming mentioned in the text?
   a. Dreams facilitate information processing.
   b. Dreaming stimulates the developing brain.
   c. Dreams result from random neural activity originating in the brainstem.
   d. Dreaming is an attempt to escape from social stimulation.

Ans: a, p. 283

26. According to the activation-synthesis theory, dreaming represents:
   a. the brain's efforts to integrate unrelated bursts of activity in brain areas that process visual images with emotional tone provided by activity in the limbic system.
   b. a mechanism for coping with the stresses of daily life.
   c. a symbolic depiction of a person's unfulfilled wishes.
   d. an information-processing mechanism for converting the day's experiences into long-term memory.

Ans: d, p. 284

27. Barry has just spent four nights as a subject in a sleep study in which he was awakened each time he entered REM sleep. Now that the experiment is over, which of the following can be expected to occur?
   a. Barry will be extremely irritable until his body has made up the lost REM sleep.
   b. Barry will sleep so deeply for several nights that dreaming will be minimal.
   c. There will be an increase in sleep Stages 1–4.
   d. There will be an increase in Barry's REM sleep.

Ans: b, p. 284

28. Which of the following statements regarding REM sleep is true?
   a. Adults spend more time than infants in REM sleep.
   b. REM sleep deprivation results in a REM rebound.
   c. People deprived of REM sleep adapt easily.
   d. Sleeping medications tend to increase REM sleep.
   e. REM sleep periods become shorter as the night progresses.

Ans: b, p. 286

29. The modern discovery of hypnosis is generally attributed to:
   a. Freud.
   b. Mesmer.
   c. Spanos.
   d. Hilgard.

Ans: b, p. 287

30. Of the following individuals, who is likely to be the most hypnotically suggestible?
   a. Bill, a reality-oriented stockbroker
   b. Janice, an actress with a rich imagination
   c. Megan, a sixth-grader who has trouble focusing her attention on a task
   d. Darren, who has never been able to really "get involved" in movies or novels

Ans: d, p. 287

31. Hypnotic responsiveness is:
    a. the same in all people.
    b. generally greater in women than men.
    c. generally greater in men than women.
    d. greater when people are led to expect it.

Ans: a, pp. 287-288

32. An attorney wants to know if the details and accuracy of an eyewitness's memory for a crime would be improved under hypnosis. Given the results of relevant research, what should you tell the attorney?
    a. Most hypnotically retrieved memories are either false or contaminated.
    b. Hypnotically retrieved memories are usually more accurate than conscious memories.
    c. Hypnotically retrieved memories are purely the product of the subject's imagination.
    d. Hypnosis only improves memory of anxiety-provoking childhood events.

Ans: b, p. 290

33. As a form of therapy for relieving problems such as warts, hypnosis is:
    a. ineffective.
    b. no more effective than positive suggestions given without hypnosis.
    c. highly effective.
    d. more effective with adults than children.

Ans: d, p. 290

34. Research studies of the effectiveness of hypnosis as a form of therapy have demonstrated that:
    a. for problems of self-control, such as smoking, hypnosis is equally effective with subjects who can be deeply hypnotized and those who cannot.
    b. posthypnotic suggestions have helped alleviate headaches, asthma, warts, and stress-related skin disorders.
    c. positive suggestions given without hypnosis are often as effective as hypnosis as a form of therapy.
    d. all of the above are true.

Ans: c, p. 291

35. Which of the following statements concerning hypnosis is true?
    a. People will do anything under hypnosis.
    b. Hypnosis is the same as sleeping.
    c. Hypnosis is not associated with a distinct physiological state.
    d. Hypnosis improves memory recall.

Ans: c, p. 291

36. Those who consider hypnosis a social phenomenon contend that:
    a. hypnosis is an altered state of consciousness.
    b. hypnotic phenomena are unique to hypnosis.
    c. if a hypnotist eliminates the motivation for acting, hypnotized subjects become unresponsive.
    d. all of the above are true.

Ans: b, p. 291

37. Those who believe that hypnosis is a social phenomenon argue that "hypnotized" individuals are:
    a. consciously faking their behavior.
    b. merely acting out a role.
    c. underachievers striving to please the hypnotist.
    d. all of the above.

Ans: d, p. 292

38. According to Hilgard, hypnosis is:
    a. no different from a state of heightened motivation.
    b. a hoax perpetrated by frauds.
    c. the same as dreaming.
    d. a dissociation between different levels of consciousness.
    e. a type of "animal magnetism."

Ans: a, p. 294

39. A person who requires increasing amounts of a drug in order to feel its effect is said to have developed:
    a. tolerance.
    b. physical dependency.
    c. psychological dependency.
    d. resistance.
    e. withdrawal symptoms.

Ans: e, p. 294

40. Dan has recently begun using an addictive, euphoria-producing drug. Which of the following will probably occur if he repeatedly uses this drug?
    a. As his tolerance to the drug develops, Dan will experience increasingly pleasurable "highs."
    b. The dosage needed to produce the desired effect will increase.
    c. After each use, he will become more and more depressed.
    d. Dependence will become less of a problem.
    e. Both b. and c. will occur.

Ans: c, pp. 294-295

41. Which of the following is not a common misconception about addiction?
    a. To overcome an addiction a person almost always needs professional therapy.
    b. Psychoactive and medicinal drugs very quickly lead to addiction.
    c. Biological factors place some individuals at increased risk for addiction.
    d. Many other repetitive, pleasure-seeking behaviors fit the drug-addiction-as-disease-needing-treatment model.

Ans: c, p. 295

42. Psychoactive drugs affect behavior and perception through:
    a. the power of suggestion.
    b. the placebo effect.
    c. alteration of neural activity in the brain.
    d. psychological, not physiological, influences.

Ans: a, p. 296

43. Alcohol has the most profound effect on:
    a. the transfer of experiences to long-term memory.
    b. immediate memory.
    c. previously established long-term memories.
    d. all of the above.

Ans: d, p. 296

44. Which of the following is classified as a depressant?
    a. amphetamines
    b. LSD
    c. marijuana
    d. alcohol
    e. MDMA

Ans: e, pp. 296-297

45. Roberto is moderately intoxicated by alcohol. Which of the following changes in his behavior is likely to occur?
    a. If angered, he is more likely to become aggressive than when he is sober.
    b. He will be less self-conscious about his behavior.
    c. If sexually aroused, he will be less inhibited about engaging in sexual activity.
    d. The next day he may be unable to remember what happened while he was drinking.
    e. All of the above are likely.

Ans: d, p. 298

46. Which of the following is not a stimulant?
    a. amphetamines
    b. caffeine
    c. nicotine
    d. alcohol

Ans: c, p. 298

47. Cocaine and crack produce a euphoric rush by:
    a. blocking the actions of serotonin.
    b. depressing neural activity in the brain.
    c. blocking the reuptake of dopamine in brain cells.
    d. stimulating the brain's production of endorphins.
    e. preventing the body from producing endorphins.

Ans: b, p. 299

48. I am a synthetic stimulant and mild hallucinogen that produces euphoria and social intimacy by triggering the release of dopamine and serotonin. What am I?
    a. LSD
    b. MDMA
    c. THC
    d. cocaine

Ans: c, p. 300

49. THC is the major active ingredient in:
    a. nicotine.
    b. MDMA.
    c. marijuana.
    d. cocaine.
    e. amphetamine.

Ans: a, p. 300

50. Which of the following statements concerning marijuana is not true?
    a. The by-products of marijuana are cleared from the body more quickly than are the by-products of alcohol.
    b. Regular users may achieve a high with smaller amounts of the drug than occasional users would need to get the same effect.
    c. Marijuana is not as addictive as nicotine or cocaine.
    d. Large doses of marijuana hasten the loss of brain cells.

Ans: a, p. 302

51. Which of the following was not cited in the text as evidence that heredity influences alcohol use?
    a. Children whose parents abuse alcohol have a lower tolerance for multiple alcoholic drinks taken over a short period of time.
    b. Boys who are impulsive and fearless at age 6 are more likely to drink as teenagers.
    c. Laboratory mice have been selectively bred to prefer alcohol to water.
    d. Adopted children are more susceptible if one or both of their biological parents has a history of alcoholism.

Ans: a, p. 302

52. Which of the following statements concerning alcoholism is not true?
    a. Adopted individuals are more susceptible to alcoholism if they had an adoptive parent with alcoholism.
    b. Having an identical twin with alcoholism puts a person at increased risk for alcohol problems.
    c. Compared to children of parents who do not drink, children of parents with alcoholism have a higher tolerance for multiple alcoholic drinks.
    d. Researchers have bred rats that prefer alcohol to water.

Ans: d, pp. 302-303

53. How a particular psychoactive drug affects a person depends on:
    a. the dosage and form in which the drug is taken.
    b. the user's expectations and personality.
    c. the situation in which the drug is taken.
    d. all of the above.

Ans: c, p. 303

54. The lowest rates of drug use among high school seniors is reported by:
    a. white males.
    b. white females.
    c. black males.
    d. Latinos.

Ans: d, p. 303

55. Which of the following is usually the most powerful determinant of whether teenagers begin using drugs?
   a. family strength
   b. religiosity
   c. school adjustment
   d. peer influence

Ans: d, pp. 303-304

56. Which of the following statements concerning the roots of drug use is not true?
   a. Heavy users of alcohol, marijuana, and cocaine often are depressed.
   b. If an adolescent's friends use drugs, odds are that he or she will, too.
   c. Teenagers who come from happy families and do well in school seldom use drugs.
   d. It is nearly impossible to predict whether or not a particular adolescent will experiment with drugs.

Ans: d, p. 304

57. Which of the following was not suggested by the text as an important aspect of drug prevention and treatment programs?
   a. education about the long-term costs of a drug's temporary pleasures
   b. efforts to boost people's self-esteem and purpose in life
   c. attempts to modify peer associations
   d. "scare tactics" that frighten prepubescent children into avoiding drug experimentation

Ans: b, p. 305

58. Which of the following statements concerning near-death experiences is true?
   a. Fewer than 1 percent of patients who come close to dying report having them.
   b. They typically consist of fantastic, mystical imagery.
   c. They are more commonly experienced by females than by males.
   d. They are more commonly experienced by males than by females.

Ans: c, p. 306

59. Which theorists believe that the mind and the body are separate entities?
   a. the behaviorists
   b. the monists
   c. the dualists
   d. the Freudians

Ans: b, p. 306

60. Levar believes that once the body has died, the mind also ceases to exist. Evidently, Levar is a(n):
   a. behaviorist.
   b. monist.
   c. dualist.
   d. atheist.
   e. mesmerist.

CHAPTER **8**

Learning

Learning Objectives

Introduction to Learning (pp. 309-312)

1. Discuss the importance of learning and the process of learning associations.

Classical Conditioning (pp. 312-322)

2. Describe the general process of classical conditioning as demonstrated by Pavlov's experiments.

3. Explain the processes of acquisition, extinction, spontaneous recovery, generalization, and discrimination.

4. Discuss the importance of cognitive processes and biological predispositions in classical conditioning.

5. Explain the importance of Pavlov's work, and describe how it might apply to an understanding of human health and well-being.

Operant Conditioning (pp. 322-335)

6. Describe the process of operant conditioning, including the procedure of shaping, as demonstrated by Skinner's experiments.

7. Identify the different types of reinforcers, and describe the major schedules of partial reinforcement.

8. Discuss the effects of punishment on behavior.

9. Discuss the importance of cognitive processes and biological predispositions in operant conditioning.

10. Explain why Skinner's ideas were controversial, and describe some major applications of operant conditioning.

Learning by Observation (pp. 336-340)

11. Describe the process of observational learning as demonstrated by Bandura's experiments, and discuss the impact of antisocial and prosocial modeling.

Introduction to learning, p. 309
Medium, Factual/Definitional, Objective 1, Ans: c

1. According to the text, learning:
   a. always produces an improvement in behavior.
   b. requires the ability to think abstractly.
   c. enables us to adapt to our environment.
   d. does not occur in simple animals.

Introduction to learning, p. 310
Medium, Factual/Definitional, Objective 1, Ans: b

2. When people pressed their arms upward rather than downward while observing unfamiliar Chinese symbols, they subsequently rated these stimuli more positively. This best illustrates the impact of:
   a. the overjustification effect.
   b. associative learning.
   c. latent learning.
   d. generalization.
   e. shaping.

Introduction to learning, p. 311
Easy, Conceptual, Objective 1, Ans: c

3. Response-stimulus associations are to ________ as stimulus-stimulus associations are to ________.
   a. latent learning; observational learning
   b. generalization; discrimination
   c. operant conditioning; classical conditioning
   d. secondary reinforcement; primary reinforcement
   e. acquisition; extinction

Introduction to learning, pp. 309, 311
Easy, Factual/Definitional, Objective 1, Ans: c

4. By learning to associate a squirt of water with an electric shock, sea snails demonstrate the process of:
   a. habituation.
   b. spontaneous recovery.
   c. classical conditioning.
   d. observational learning.
   e. operant conditioning.

Introduction to learning, p. 311
Easy, Factual/Definitional, Objective 1, Ans: d

5. By pushing vending machine buttons, children often learn that this action is associated with the delivery of a candy bar. This best illustrates the process underlying:
   a. latent learning.
   b. respondent behavior.
   c. spontaneous recovery.
   d. operant conditioning.
   e. habituation.

Classical conditioning, p. 312
Easy, Factual/Definitional, Objective 2, Ans: d

6. The first experimental studies of associative learning were conducted by:
   a. Watson.
   b. Skinner.
   c. Bandura.
   d. Pavlov.
   e. Wundt.

Classical conditioning, p. 312
Easy, Factual/Definitional, Objective 2, Ans: c

7. John B. Watson considered himself to be a(n):
   a. physiological psychologist.
   b. cognitive psychologist.
   c. behaviorist.
   d. psychoanalyst.
   e. operant conditioner.

Classical conditioning, p. 312
Medium, Factual/Definitional, Objective 2, Ans: a

8. John B. Watson believed that psychology should be the science of:
   a. observable behavior.
   b. cognitive processes.
   c. genetic predispositions.
   d. all of the above.

Classical conditioning, p. 312
Difficult, Conceptual/Application, Objective 2, Ans: c

9. John B. Watson would have expressed the greatest disapproval of attempts to scientifically study whether:
   a. consumer buying habits are influenced by newspaper advertisements.
   b. worker productivity is influenced by hourly wage rates.
   c. academic achievement is influenced by a positive self-concept.
   d. aggressive behavior is influenced by threats of punishment.

Pavlov's experiments, p. 312
Medium, Conceptual/Application, Objective 2, Ans: b

10. Last year, Dr. Moritano cleaned Natacha's skin with rubbing alcohol prior to administering each of a series of painful rabies vaccination shots. Which of the following processes accounts for the fact that Natacha currently becomes fearful every time she smells rubbing alcohol?
   a. observational learning
   b. classical conditioning
   c. the overjustification effect
   d. operant conditioning
   e. latent learning

Pavlov's experiments, p. 313
Difficult, Conceptual, Objective 2, Ans: c

11. The "psychic secretions" that interfered with Pavlov's experiments on digestion were:
   a. unconditioned responses.
   b. primary reinforcers.
   c. conditioned responses.
   d. conditioned stimuli.
   e. conditioned reinforcers.

Pavlov's experiments, p. 313
Difficult, Conceptual/Application, Objective 2, Ans: c

12. Which of the following is an unconditioned response?
   a. playing jump rope
   b. running through a maze to get a food reward
   c. sweating in hot weather
   d. clapping after a thrilling concert performance

Pavlov's experiments, p. 313
Easy, Factual/Definitional, Objective 2, Ans: c

13. In Pavlov's experiments on the salivary conditioning of dogs, the UCS was:
   a. a tone.
   b. salivation to the sound of a tone.
   c. the presentation of food in the dog's mouth.
   d. salivation to the food in the mouth.

Pavlov's experiments, p. 313
Medium, Conceptual/Application, Objective 2, Ans: a

14. In Aldous Huxley's *Brave New World*, infants develop a fear of books after books are repeatedly presented with a loud noise. In this fictional example, the loud noise is a(n):
   a. unconditioned stimulus.
   b. unconditioned response.
   c. conditioned stimulus.
   d. conditioned response.

Pavlov's experiments, p. 313
Easy, Factual/Definitional, Objective 2, Ans: b

15. In Pavlov's experiments, the dog's salivation triggered by the taste of food was a(n):
    a. conditioned response.
    b. unconditioned response.
    c. unconditioned stimulus.
    d. conditioned stimulus.

Pavlov's experiments, p. 314
Easy, Factual/Definitional, Objective 2, Ans: a

16. In Pavlov's experiments, the dog's salivation triggered by the sound of the tone was a(n):
    a. conditioned response.
    b. unconditioned stimulus.
    c. unconditioned response.
    d. conditioned stimulus.

Pavlov's experiments, p. 314
Medium, Conceptual, Objective 2, Ans: c

17. Male Japanese quail became sexually aroused by a red light that was repeatedly associated with the presentation of a female quail. The sexual arousal elicited by the red light was a:
    a. UCR.
    b. UCS.
    c. CR.
    d. CS.

Pavlov's experiments, p. 314
Difficult, Conceptual/Application, Objective 2, Ans: a

18. A child's fear at the sight of a hypodermic needle is a(n):
    a. conditioned response.
    b. unconditioned stimulus.
    c. conditioned stimulus.
    d. unconditioned response.

Pavlov's experiments, p. 314
Easy, Factual/Definitional, Objective 2, Ans: c

19. If a tone causes a dog to salivate because it has regularly been associated with the presentation of food, the tone is called a(n):
    a. unconditioned stimulus.
    b. primary reinforcer.
    c. conditioned stimulus.
    d. immediate reinforcer.

Pavlov's experiments, p. 314
Difficult, Conceptual/Application, Objective 2, Ans: b

20. A real estate agent showed Gavin several pictures of lakeshore property while they were eating a delicious, mouth-watering meal. Later, when Gavin was given a tour of the property, he drooled with delight. For Gavin, the lakeshore property was a:
    a. UCS.
    b. CS.
    c. UCR.
    d. CR.

Classical conditioning: acquisition, p. 314
Easy, Conceptual/Application, Objective 3, Ans: b

21. Researchers condition a flatworm to contract its body to a light by repeatedly pairing the light with electric shock. The stage in which the flatworm's contraction response to light is established and gradually strengthened is called:
a. shaping.
b. acquisition.
c. generalization.
d. spontaneous recovery.
e. latent learning.

Classical conditioning: acquisition, p. 314
Medium, Factual/Definitional, Objective 3, Ans: c

22. In classical conditioning, the ________ signals the impending occurrence of the ________.
a. UCS; CS
b. UCR; CR
c. CS; UCS
d. CR; UCR
e. UCS; CR

Classical conditioning: acquisition, p. 315
Difficult, Conceptual/Application, Objective 3, Ans: d

23. A geometric figure is most likely to become sexually arousing if presented shortly ________ an appropriate ________.
a. after; UCR
b. after; UCS
c. before; UCR
d. before; UCS
e. after; CS

Classical conditioning: extinction and spontaneous recovery, p. 316
Medium, Factual/Definitional, Objective 3, Ans: d

24. Extinction occurs when a ________ is no longer paired with a ________.
a. UCR; CR
b. CS; UCR
c. UCS; UCR
d. CS; UCS
e. UCS; CR

Classical conditioning: extinction and spontaneous recovery, p. 316
Medium, Conceptual/Application, Objective 3, Ans: b

25. Makayla developed an intense fear of flying five years ago when she was in a plane crash. The fact that today she can again fly without distress indicates that her fear has undergone:
a. spontaneous recovery.
b. extinction.
c. generalization.
d. discrimination.

Classical conditioning: extinction and spontaneous recovery, p. 316
Easy, Factual/Definitional, Objective 3, Ans: d

26. Spontaneous recovery refers to the:
    a. expression of learning that had occurred earlier but had not been expressed because of lack of incentive.
    b. organism's tendency to respond spontaneously to stimuli similar to the CS as though they were the CS.
    c. return of a response after punishment has been terminated.
    d. reappearance, after a rest pause, of an extinguished conditioned response.

Classical conditioning: extinction and spontaneous recovery, p. 316
Easy, Factual/Definitional, Objective 3, Ans: d

27. The occurrence of spontaneous recovery suggests that during extinction the ________ is ________.
    a. CS; eliminated
    b. CR; eliminated
    c. CS; suppressed
    d. CR; suppressed

Classical conditioning: generalization, p. 316
Easy, Factual/Definitional, Objective 3, Ans: a

28. Toddlers taught to fear speeding cars may also begin to fear speeding trucks and motorcycles. This best illustrates:
    a. generalization.
    b. secondary reinforcement.
    c. shaping.
    d. latent learning.
    e. spontaneous recovery.

Classical conditioning: generalization (Figure 8.8), p. 316
Difficult, Factual/Definitional, Objective 3, Ans: d

29. Pavlov attached miniature vibrators to various parts of a dog's body in order to demonstrate the process of:
    a. spontaneous recovery.
    b. continuous reinforcement.
    c. latent learning.
    d. generalization.
    e. habituation.

Classical conditioning: generalization, p. 316
Medium, Conceptual/Application, Objective 3, Ans: c

30. Monica's psychotherapist reminds her so much of her own father that she has many of the same mixed emotional reactions to him that she has to her own dad. Her reactions to her therapist best illustrate the importance of:
    a. habituation.
    b. latent learning.
    c. generalization.
    d. delayed reinforcement.
    e. shaping.

Classical conditioning: generalization, p. 316
Difficult, Conceptual, Objective 3, Ans: b

31. Because of the discomfort and embarrassment associated with his childhood bedwetting, Andrew becomes nervous whenever he has the urge to urinate. If genital arousal subsequently makes Andrew unusually anxious, this would best illustrate:
   a. shaping.
   b. generalization.
   c. latent learning.
   d. secondary reinforcement.
   e. the overjustification effect.

Classical conditioning: discrimination, p. 317
Easy, Factual/Definitional, Objective 3, Ans: c

32. The ability to distinguish between a conditioned stimulus and similar stimuli that do not signal an unconditioned stimulus is called:
   a. shaping.
   b. acquisition.
   c. discrimination.
   d. generalization.
   e. latent learning.

Classical conditioning: discrimination, p. 317
Difficult, Conceptual/Application, Objective 3, Ans: d

33. Jacqueline is sexually aroused by the sight of her handsome boyfriend but not by the sight of her equally handsome brother. This best illustrates the value of:
   a. latent learning.
   b. shaping.
   c. intermittent reinforcement.
   d. discrimination.
   e. extinction.

Updating Pavlov's understanding: cognitive processes, p. 317
Medium, Factual/Definitional, Objective 4, Ans: d

34. The predictability rather than the frequency of CS-UCS associations appears to be crucial for classical conditioning. This highlights the importance of ________ in conditioning.
   a. shaping
   b. discrimination
   c. generalization
   d. cognitive processes
   e. intermittent reinforcement

Updating Pavlov's understanding: cognitive processes, p. 317
Medium, Conceptual/Application, Objective 4, Ans: b

35. Nikki has learned to expect the sound of thunder whenever she sees a flash of lightning. This suggests that associative learning involves:
   a. the overjustification effect.
   b. cognitive processes.
   c. spontaneous recovery.
   d. continuous reinforcement.
   e. shaping.

Updating Pavlov's understanding: cognitive processes, p. 317
Difficult, Conceptual, Objective 4, Ans: d

36. A person adhering to the cognitive perspective would be likely to emphasize that classical conditioning depends on:
   a. an organism's active behavioral responses to environmental stimulation.
   b. the amount of time between the presentation of the CS and the UCS.
   c. how frequently an organism is exposed to an association of a CS and a UCS.
   d. an organism's expectation that a UCS will follow a CS.

Updating Pavlov's understanding: biological predispositions, p. 318
Easy, Factual/Definitional, Objective 4, Ans: c

37. Rats easily learn to associate nausea-producing radiation treatments with:
   a. loud sounds.
   b. bright lights.
   c. novel tastes.
   d. high-pitched sounds.
   e. any of the above.

Updating Pavlov's understanding: biological predispositions, p. 318
Medium, Factual/Definitional, Objective 4, Ans: a

38. The idea that any perceivable neutral stimulus can serve as a CS was challenged by:
   a. Garcia and Koelling's findings on taste aversion in rats.
   b. Pavlov's findings on the conditioned salivary response.
   c. Watson and Rayner's findings on fear conditioning in infants.
   d. Bandura's findings on observational learning and aggression in children.

Updating Pavlov's understanding: biological predispositions, p. 318
Medium, Factual/Definitional, Objective 4, Ans: b

39. Garcia and Koelling's studies of taste aversion in rats demonstrated that classical conditioning is constrained by:
   a. cognitive processes.
   b. biological predispositions.
   c. environmental factors.
   d. continuous reinforcement.
   e. latent learning.

Updating Pavlov's understanding: biological predispositions, p. 318
Medium, Factual/Definitional, Objective 4, Ans: b

40. Humans most easily develop a conditioned aversion to alcohol if its taste is associated with a(n):
   a. anger-producing punishment.
   b. nausea-producing food.
   c. pain-producing accident.
   d. fear-producing threat.

Updating Pavlov's understanding: biological predispositions, p. 318
Medium, Conceptual/Application, Objective 4, Ans: e

41. Children learn to fear spiders more easily than they learn to fear butterflies. This best illustrates the impact of ________ on learning.
   a. spontaneous recovery
   b. conditioned reinforcers
   c. shaping
   d. cognitive processes
   e. biological predispositions

Pavlov's legacy, p. 319
Medium, Factual/Definitional, Objective 5, Ans: b

42. Pavlov's research on classical conditioning was important because:
   a. it highlighted the role of cognitive processes in learning.
   b. so many different species of animals, including humans, can be classically conditioned.
   c. it demonstrated an essential difference between animal and human learning.
   d. of all the above reasons.

Applications of classical conditioning, p. 320
Difficult, Conceptual/Application, Objective 5, Ans: c

43. In order to assess whether Mrs. Webster had Alzheimer's disease, researchers conditioned her to blink in response to a sound that signaled the delivery of a puff of air directed toward her face. In this application of classical conditioning, the sound was a:
   a. UCS.
   b. UCR.
   c. CS.
   d. CR.

Applications of classical conditioning, pp. 320-321
Medium, Factual/Definitional, Objective 5, Ans: d

44. Watson and Rayner's study of Little Albert demonstrated how specific fears:
   a. can interfere with the process of learning.
   b. can be used as negative reinforcers.
   c. are acquired through observational learning.
   d. may be produced through classical conditioning.

Applications of classical conditioning, pp. 316, 321
Medium, Factual/Definitional, Objective 5, Ans: b

45. After learning to fear a white rat, Little Albert responded with fear to the sight of a rabbit. This best illustrates the process of:
   a. secondary reinforcement.
   b. generalization.
   c. shaping.
   d. latent learning.
   e. spontaneous recovery.

Rape as classical conditioning (Close-up), p. 321
Medium, Conceptual/Application, Objective 5, Ans: d

46. Months after she was raped, Courtney's heart pounds with fear merely at the sight of the place in which she was attacked. This best illustrates:
    a. shaping.
    b. generalization.
    c. delayed reinforcement.
    d. associative learning.
    e. latent learning.

Applications of classical conditioning, pp. 320-321
Difficult, Conceptual/Application, Objective 5, Ans: d

47. After he was spanked on several occasions by his mother for spilling his milk, Colin developed a strong fear of his mother. In this case, spanking is a(n) ________ for Colin's fear.
    a. negative reinforcer
    b. conditioned stimulus
    c. secondary reinforcer
    d. unconditioned stimulus

Operant conditioning, p. 323
Easy, Factual/Definitional, Objective 6, Ans: c

48. In which form of learning is behavior said to be influenced by its consequences?
    a. observational learning
    b. classical conditioning
    c. operant conditioning
    d. latent learning

Operant conditioning, p. 323
Difficult, Conceptual/Application, Objective 6, Ans: e

49. Laurie's thumbsucking has become habitual because she begins to feel less anxious whenever she sucks her thumb. This best illustrates the process of:
    a. generalization.
    b. extinction.
    c. classical conditioning.
    d. latent learning.
    e. operant conditioning.

Classical and operant conditioning, pp. 312, 323
Medium, Conceptual, Objectives 2 & 6, Ans: a

50. The study of respondent behavior is to ________ as the study of operant behavior is to ________.
    a. Pavlov; Skinner
    b. Bandura; Skinner
    c. Skinner; Bandura
    d. Bandura; Pavlov

Classical and operant conditioning, p. 323
Difficult, Conceptual, Objectives 2 & 6, Ans: c

51. Operant behavior is to ________ associations as respondent behavior is to ________ associations.
   a. stimulus-stimulus; response-response
   b. stimulus-response; response-stimulus
   c. response-stimulus; stimulus-stimulus
   d. response-response; stimulus-stimulus

Skinner's experiments, p. 323
Difficult, Factual/Definitional, Objective 6, Ans: d

52. B. F. Skinner's work elaborated what E. L. Thorndike had called:
   a. shaping.
   b. behaviorism.
   c. observational learning.
   d. the law of effect.
   e. latent learning.

Skinner's experiments, p. 323
Medium, Factual/Definitional, Objective 6, Ans: d

53. A Skinner box is a(n):
   a. soundproofed cubicle in which organisms are classically conditioned in the absence of distracting noise.
   b. aversive or punishing event that decreases the occurrence of certain undesirable behaviors.
   c. special "slot machine" that is used to study the effects of partial reinforcement on gambling behavior.
   d. chamber containing a bar or key that an animal can manipulate to obtain a reward.
   e. television projection device designed for use in laboratory studies of observational learning.

Shaping behavior, p. 324
Medium, Conceptual/Application, Objective 6, Ans: d

54. You would be most likely to use operant conditioning to teach a dog to:
   a. fear cars in the street.
   b. dislike the taste of dead birds.
   c. wag its tail whenever it is emotionally excited.
   d. retrieve sticks and balls.

Shaping behavior, p. 324
Easy, Conceptual/Application, Objective 6, Ans: a

55. An animal trainer is teaching a miniature poodle to balance on a ball. Initially, he gives the poodle a treat for approaching the ball, then only for placing its front paws on the ball, and finally only for climbing on the ball. The trainer is using the method of:
   a. successive approximations.
   b. delayed reinforcement.
   c. latent learning.
   d. classical conditioning.
   e. secondary reinforcement.

Shaping behavior, p. 324
Easy, Conceptual/Application, Objective 6, Ans: e

56. Five-year-old Trevor is emotionally disturbed and refuses to communicate with anyone. To get him to speak, his teacher initially gives him candy for any utterance, then only for a clearly spoken word, and finally only for a complete sentence. The teacher is using the method of:
a. latent learning.
b. modeling.
c. delayed reinforcement.
d. spontaneous recovery.
e. shaping.

Shaping behavior, p. 324
Medium, Conceptual, Objective 6, Ans: c

57. Because Mr. Baron demonstrates appreciation only for classroom performance that is flawless, his students have become poor and unmotivated learners. Mr. Baron most clearly needs to be informed of the value of:
a. generalization.
b. modeling.
c. shaping.
d. latent learning.
e. spontaneous recovery.

Principles of reinforcement, p. 325
Easy, Factual/Definitional, Objective 7, Ans: d

58. An event that increases the frequency of the behavior that it follows is a(n):
a. conditioned stimulus.
b. respondent.
c. unconditioned stimulus.
d. reinforcer.
e. operant.

Principles of reinforcement, p. 325
Difficult, Conceptual/Application, Objective 7, Ans: a

59. Every Saturday morning Arnold quickly washes the family's breakfast dishes so that his father will allow him to wash his car. In this instance, washing the car is a(n):
a. positive reinforcer.
b. unconditioned response.
c. conditioned response.
d. negative reinforcer.

Principles of reinforcement, p. 325
Medium, Conceptual/Application, Objective 7, Ans: a

60. Receiving delicious food is to escaping electric shock as ________ is to ________.
a. positive reinforcer; negative reinforcer
b. primary reinforcer; secondary reinforcer
c. immediate reinforcer; delayed reinforcer
d. reinforcement; punishment
e. partial reinforcement; continuous reinforcement

Principles of reinforcement, p. 325
Medium, Factual/Definitional, Objective 7, Ans: c

61. Positive reinforcers ________ the rate of operant responding and negative reinforcers ________ the rate of operant responding.
    a. decrease; increase
    b. increase; decrease
    c. increase; increase
    d. have no effect on; decrease
    e. increase; have no effect on

Principles of reinforcement, p. 325
Difficult, Conceptual/Application, Objective 7, Ans: b

62. Mason, a stockbroker, runs two miles every day after work because it reduces his level of stress. Mason's running habit is maintained by a ________ reinforcer.
    a. positive
    b. negative
    c. conditioned
    d. partial

Primary and conditioned reinforcers, p. 325
Easy, Factual/Definitional, Objective 7, Ans: c

63. The taste of food and the termination of painful electric shock are both ________ reinforcers.
    a. positive
    b. negative
    c. primary
    d. conditioned

Primary and conditioned reinforcers, p. 325
Easy, Factual/Definitional, Objective 7, Ans: d

64. A stimulus that acquires reinforcing power by association with another reinforcer is called a ________ reinforcer.
    a. negative
    b. primary
    c. partial
    d. conditioned
    e. positive

Primary and conditioned reinforcers, p. 325
Medium, Conceptual/Application, Objective 7, Ans: a

65. Which of the following is the best example of a conditioned reinforcer?
    a. applause for an excellent piano recital
    b. a spanking for eating cookies before dinner
    c. a cold root beer for mowing the lawn on a hot day
    d. termination of shock after removing one's finger from a live electric wire

Primary and conditioned reinforcers, p. 325
Difficult, Conceptual/Application, Objective 7, Ans: b

66. The removal of electric shock is to good grades as ________ is to ________.
   a. delayed reinforcer; immediate reinforcer
   b. primary reinforcer; conditioned reinforcer
   c. discrimination; generalization
   d. partial reinforcement; continuous reinforcement
   e. operant conditioning; classical conditioning

Immediate and delayed reinforcers, p. 325
Medium, Conceptual/Application, Objective 7, Ans: d

67. In order to quickly teach a dog to roll over on command, you would be best advised to use ________ rather than ________.
   a. classical conditioning; operant conditioning
   b. partial reinforcement; continuous reinforcement
   c. latent learning; shaping
   d. immediate reinforcers; delayed reinforcers
   e. negative reinforcers; positive reinforcers

Immediate and delayed reinforcers, p. 326
Difficult, Conceptual, Objective 7, Ans: c

68. As people near the completion of a lucrative task, they typically become increasingly less likely to give up and discontinue their work. This best illustrates that operant behavior is most effectively influenced by ________ reinforcers.
   a. primary
   b. negative
   c. immediate
   d. partial

Immediate and delayed reinforcers, p. 326
Difficult, Factual/Definitional, Objective 7, Ans: d

69. Smoking, excessive drinking, and drug abuse demonstrate our greater responsiveness to ________ reinforcement than to ________ reinforcement.
   a. negative; positive
   b. primary; secondary
   c. partial; continuous
   d. immediate; delayed

Reinforcement schedules, p. 326
Easy, Factual/Definitional, Objective 7, Ans: b

70. Resistance to extinction is most strongly encouraged by ________ reinforcement.
   a. delayed
   b. intermittent
   c. conditioned
   d. negative

Reinforcement schedules, p. 326
Medium, Factual/Definitional, Objective 7, Ans: a

71. A response is learned most rapidly and is most resistant to extinction if it is acquired under conditions of ________ reinforcement followed by ________ reinforcement.
   a. continuous; partial
   b. primary; secondary
   c. partial; continuous
   d. secondary; primary

Reinforcement schedules, p. 326
Difficult, Conceptual/Application, Objective 7, Ans: c

72. Four-year-old Della asks her mother for a special treat every time they go to the grocery store. Although at one time her mother granted every request, she now does so less consistently. Research suggests that Della will:
   a. soon give up asking for a treat entirely.
   b. come to ask for a treat only occasionally.
   c. continue to ask for a treat nearly every time she goes to the store.
   d. ask for a treat every time her mother takes her out, even if they don't go to the grocery store.

Reinforcement schedules, p. 327
Easy, Factual/Definitional, Objective 7, Ans: c

73. A fixed-ratio schedule of reinforcement is one in which a response is reinforced only after a(n):
   a. specified time period has elapsed.
   b. unpredictable time period has elapsed.
   c. specified number of responses have been made.
   d. unpredictable number of responses have been made.

Reinforcement schedules, p. 327
Difficult, Conceptual/Application, Objective 7, Ans: a

74. Blake is a carpet installer who wants to be paid for each square foot of carpet he lays rather than with an hourly wage. Blake prefers working on a ________ schedule of reinforcement.
   a. fixed-ratio
   b. fixed-interval
   c. variable-interval
   d. variable-ratio

Reinforcement schedules, p. 327
Difficult, Conceptual/Application, Objective 7, Ans: b

75. Paul and Michael sell magazine subscriptions by telephone. Paul is paid $1.00 for every five calls he makes, while Michael is paid $1.00 for every subscription he sells, regardless of the number of calls he makes. Paul's telephoning is reinforced on a ________ schedule, whereas Michael's is reinforced on a ________ schedule.
   a. variable-ratio; fixed-ratio
   b. fixed-ratio; variable-ratio
   c. fixed-ratio; variable-interval
   d. fixed-interval; variable-ratio

Reinforcement schedules, p. 327
Medium, Factual/Definitional, Objective 7, Ans: d

76. Purchasing state lottery tickets is reinforced with monetary winnings on a ________ schedule.
   a. fixed-interval
   b. variable-interval
   c. fixed-ratio
   d. variable-ratio

Reinforcement schedules, p. 327
Medium, Conceptual/Application, Objective 7, Ans: d

77. Asking women for dates is most likely to be reinforced on a ________ schedule.
   a. fixed-interval
   b. fixed-ratio
   c. variable-interval
   d. variable-ratio

Reinforcement schedules, p. 327
Easy, Factual/Definitional, Objective 7, Ans: b

78. A fixed-interval schedule of reinforcement is one in which a response is reinforced only after a(n):
   a. unpredictable time period has elapsed.
   b. specified time period has elapsed.
   c. specified number of responses has been made.
   d. unpredictable number of responses has been made.

Reinforcement schedules, p. 327
Medium, Conceptual/Application, Objective 7, Ans: a

79. An executive in a computer software firm works with his office door closed. At the same time every hour he opens the door to see what his employees are doing. The employees have learned to work especially hard during the five minutes before and while the door is open. Their work pattern is typical of responses that are reinforced on a ________ schedule.
   a. fixed-interval
   b. fixed-ratio
   c. variable-ratio
   d. variable-interval

Reinforcement schedules, p. 327
Medium, Conceptual/Application, Objective 7, Ans: c

80. On the first day of class Professor Wallace tells her geography students that pop quizzes will be given at unpredictable times throughout the semester. Clearly, studying for Professor Wallace's surprise quizzes will be reinforced on a ________ schedule.
   a. fixed-interval
   b. fixed-ratio
   c. variable-interval
   d. variable-ratio

Reinforcement schedules, p. 327
Medium, Conceptual/Application, Objective 7, Ans: c

81. Watching the night sky for shooting stars is likely to be reinforced on a ________ schedule.
a. fixed-interval
b. fixed-ratio
c. variable-interval
d. variable-ratio

Reinforcement schedules, p. 327
Difficult, Factual/Definitional, Objective 7, Ans: d

82. Rates of operant responding are ________ for fixed-ratio than for fixed-interval schedules; they are ________ for variable-ratio than for variable-interval schedules.
a. lower; higher
b. higher; lower
c. lower; lower
d. higher; higher

Punishment, p. 328
Easy, Factual/Definitional, Objective 8, Ans: b

83. An aversive consequence that decreases the recurrence of the behavior that precedes it is a:
a. negative reinforcer.
b. punishment.
c. conditioned stimulus.
d. delayed reinforcer.
e. conditioned reinforcer.

Punishment, pp. 325, 328
Medium, Conceptual, Objective 8, Ans: c

84. The introduction of a pleasant stimulus is to ________ as the withdrawal of a pleasant stimulus is to ________.
a. positive reinforcer; negative reinforcer
b. acquisition; extinction
c. reinforcement; punishment
d. generalization; discrimination
e. primary reinforcer; secondary reinforcer

Punishment, p. 328
Medium, Conceptual/Application, Objective 8, Ans: e

85. Myron quit gambling after he lost over a thousand dollars betting on horse races. This best illustrates the effects of:
a. negative reinforcers.
b. primary reinforcers.
c. secondary reinforcers.
d. intermittent reinforcement.
e. punishment.

Punishment, pp. 325, 328
Medium, Factual/Definitional, Objective 8, Ans: a

86. Negative reinforcers ________ the rate of operant responding, and punishments ________ the rate of operant responding.
   a. increase; decrease
   b. decrease; increase
   c. decrease; decrease
   d. have no effect on; decrease
   e. decrease; have no effect on

Punishment, p. 328
Medium, Factual/Definitional, Objective 8, Ans: b

87. For purposes of effective child-rearing, most psychologists favor the use of ________ over ________.
   a. shaping; modeling
   b. reinforcement; punishment
   c. spontaneous recovery; extinction
   d. classical conditioning; operant conditioning
   e. primary reinforcers; secondary reinforcers

Punishment, pp. 328-329
Medium, Factual/Definitional, Objective 8, Ans: d

88. The use of physical punishment may:
   a. lead to the suppression but not the forgetting of undesirable behavior.
   b. demonstrate that aggression is a way of coping with problems.
   c. lead people to fear and avoid the punishing agent.
   d. do all of the above.

Updating Skinner's understanding: cognition, p. 329
Medium, Conceptual, Objective 9, Ans: b

89. Operant response rates remain highest when individuals anticipate that their behavior will actually lead to further reinforcement. This best illustrates the importance of ________ in operant conditioning.
   a. secondary reinforcers
   b. cognitive processes
   c. biological predispositions
   d. the overjustification effect
   e. spontaneous recovery

Updating Skinner's understanding: cognition, p. 329
Difficult, Conceptual/Application, Objective 9, Ans: e

90. Megan fails to see any connection between how hard she works and the size of her annual pay raises. Consequently, she puts little effort into her job even though she strongly desires sizeable pay increases. This best illustrates the importance of ________ in the operant conditioning of work habits.
   a. primary reinforcers
   b. the overjustification effect
   c. biological predispositions
   d. spontaneous recovery
   e. cognitive processes

Updating Skinner's understanding: cognition, p. 329
Easy, Conceptual/Application, Objective 9, Ans: a

91. After a week at college, Su-Chuan has formed a mental representation of the layout of the campus and no longer gets lost. Su-Chuan has developed a:
a. cognitive map.
b. discriminative survey.
c. perceptual delineation.
d. geographical heuristic.
e. fixed-interval schedule.

Updating Skinner's understanding: cognition, p. 330
Medium, Factual/Definitional, Objective 9, Ans: b

92. If rats are allowed to wander through a complicated maze, they will subsequently run the maze with few errors when a food reward is placed at the end. Their good performance demonstrates:
a. shaping.
b. latent learning.
c. delayed reinforcement.
d. spontaneous recovery.
e. modeling.

Updating Skinner's understanding: cognition, p. 330
Easy, Factual/Definitional, Objective 9, Ans: b

93. The fact that learning can occur without reinforcement is most clearly demonstrated by studies of:
a. shaping.
b. latent learning.
c. spontaneous recovery.
d. computer-assisted instruction.

Updating Skinner's understanding: cognition, p. 330
Medium, Conceptual, Objective 9, Ans: d

94. Studies of latent learning highlight the importance of:
a. primary reinforcers.
b. respondent behavior.
c. spontaneous recovery.
d. cognitive processes.
e. conditioned reinforcers.

Updating Skinner's understanding: overjustification, p. 330
Easy, Factual/Definitional, Objective 9, Ans: e

95. Experiments have shown that children who are promised a payoff for playing with an interesting toy subsequently lose interest in the toy. These experiments provide an example of:
a. spontaneous recovery.
b. respondent behavior.
c. observational learning.
d. negative reinforcement.
e. the overjustification effect.

Updating Skinner's understanding: overjustification, p. 330
Medium, Conceptual/Application, Objective 9, Ans: a

96. For several years Ruth played softball for the sheer enjoyment of the game. Her loss of intrinsic interest in playing after being recruited by a professional team for $100 a game best illustrates:
   a. the overjustification effect.
   b. spontaneous recovery.
   c. intermittent reinforcement.
   d. latent learning.
   e. respondent behavior.

Updating Skinner's understanding: overjustification, p. 330
Medium, Conceptual, Objective 9, Ans: d

97. Which of the following is the best example of the overjustification effect?
   a. Zeke loses interest in playing baseball after the coach suspends him for a throwing error.
   b. Bill dislikes doing homework even more after his father eliminates his allowance because he received an "F" in geometry.
   c. Phyllis enjoys babysitting more after her hourly wage is tripled.
   d. Phoebe loses her former interest in playing the violin after her mother promises to pay her 3 dollars for each hour of practice.

Updating Skinner's understanding: overjustification, p. 330
Easy, Factual/Definitional, Objective 9, Ans: b

98. The desire to perform a behavior due to promised rewards or threats of punishment involves:
   a. latent learning.
   b. extrinsic motivation.
   c. partial reinforcement.
   d. delayed reinforcers.

Updating Skinner's understanding: overjustification, p. 330
Easy, Factual/Definitional, Objective 9, Ans: e

99. Using rewards to bribe people to engage in an activity they already enjoy is most likely to inhibit:
   a. respondent behavior.
   b. continuous reinforcement.
   c. latent learning.
   d. spontaneous recovery.
   e. intrinsic motivation.

Updating Skinner's understanding: overjustification, p. 330
Easy, Conceptual/Application, Objective 9, Ans: b

100. Because Yuri was curious about human behavior, he enrolled in an introductory psychology course. George registered because he heard it was an easy course that would boost his grade point average. In this instance, Yuri's behavior was a reflection of ________, whereas George's behavior was a reflection of ________.
   a. operant conditioning; classical conditioning
   b. intrinsic motivation; extrinsic motivation
   c. an unconditioned response; a conditioned response
   d. a fixed-interval schedule; a variable interval schedule

Updating Skinner's understanding: biological predispositions, p. 331
Medium, Factual/Definitional, Objective 9, Ans: d

101. It's easier to train a pigeon to peck a disk for a food reward than to flap its wings for a food reward. This illustrates the importance of ________ in learning.
   a. primary reinforcers
   b. stimulus generalization
   c. spontaneous recovery
   d. biological predispositions
   e. shaping

Updating Skinner's understanding: biological predispositions, pp. 331-332
Medium, Factual/Definitional, Objective 9, Ans: e

102. After pigs learned to pick up and deposit wooden coins in a piggy bank, the pigs subsequently dropped the coins repeatedly and pushed them with their snouts. This best illustrates the importance of ________ in operant conditioning.
   a. primary reinforcement
   b. spontaneous recovery
   c. latent learning
   d. generalization
   e. biological predispositions

Skinner's legacy, p. 332
Medium, Factual/Definitional, Objective 10, Ans: b

103. According to B. F. Skinner, human behavior is controlled primarily by:
   a. biological predispositions.
   b. external influences.
   c. emotions.
   d. unconscious motives.
   e. conscious intentions.

Skinner's legacy, p. 332
Difficult, Conceptual/Application, Objective 10, Ans: c

104. In explaining juvenile delinquency, B. F. Skinner would most likely have emphasized:
   a. inherited predispositions.
   b. fear and greed.
   c. faulty child-rearing practices.
   d. a lack of moral values in contemporary society.

Skinner's legacy, p. 332
Medium, Factual/Definitional, Objective 10, Ans: a

105. B. F. Skinner's critics have claimed that he neglected the importance of the individual's:
   a. personal freedom.
   b. early childhood experiences.
   c. pleasure-seeking tendencies.
   d. cultural background.

Applications of operant conditioning, p. 332
Difficult, Factual/Definitional, Objective 10, Ans: d

106. B. F. Skinner believed that teaching machines could promote effective learning because they allow for both:
a. continuous reinforcement and latent learning.
b. positive reinforcement and punishment.
c. classical and operant conditioning.
d. shaping and immediate reinforcement.
e. observational learning and spontaneous recovery.

Applications of operant conditioning, p. 332
Medium, Conceptual, Objective 10, Ans: a

107. Which of the following is *least* likely to be considered an important component of effective student instruction involving the use of interactive software?
a. respondent behavior
b. immediate reinforcement
c. operant behavior
d. shaping

Applications of operant conditioning, p. 333
Medium, Conceptual/Application, Objective 10, Ans: c

108. Two years ago, the de Castellane Manufacturing Company included its employees in a profit-sharing plan in which workers receive semi-annual pay bonuses based on the company's profits. Since this plan was initiated, worker productivity at de Castellane has nearly doubled. This productivity increase is best explained in terms of:
a. observational learning.
b. latent learning.
c. operant conditioning.
d. classical conditioning.
e. spontaneous recovery.

Applications of operant conditioning, p. 333
Medium, Factual/Definitional, Objective 10, Ans: a

109. Compared with apartment dwellers whose landlords pay their energy costs, those apartment dwellers who pay their own energy costs use less energy. This most clearly illustrates that consumer energy usage is influenced by:
a. operant conditioning.
b. classical conditioning.
c. observational learning.
d. spontaneous recovery.
e. latent learning.

Applications of operant conditioning, pp. 333-334
Medium, Conceptual, Objective 10, Ans: c

110. When grocery shopping with his mother, 4-year-old Hakim sometimes throws temper tantrums if his mother refuses his requests for a particular snack food. Parent training experts would suggest that his mother should:
a. threaten to punish Hakim if he continues his tantrums.
b. offer to buy the snack food Hakim wants only if he quiets down and behaves himself.
c. continue shopping while ignoring Hakim's tantrums.
d. return any snack foods that are already in her cart to the store shelves.

Learning by observation, p. 336
Easy, Factual/Definitional, Objective 11, Ans: d

111. Our ability to learn by witnessing and imitating the behavior of others best illustrates:
   a. respondent behavior.
   b. prosocial behavior.
   c. operant conditioning.
   d. observational learning.

Learning by observation, p. 336
Easy, Conceptual/Application, Objective 11, Ans: d

112. Jeremy wears his baseball cap backward because he noticed his older brother does so. This illustrates the importance of:
   a. respondent behavior.
   b. immediate reinforcement.
   c. spontaneous recovery.
   d. modeling.
   e. shaping.

Learning by observation, p. 336
Difficult, Factual/Definitional, Objective 11, Ans: c

113. Rhesus macaque monkeys are more likely to reconcile after a fight if they grow up with forgiving older stumptail macaque monkeys. This best illustrates the impact of:
   a. immediate reinforcement.
   b. spontaneous recovery.
   c. observational learning.
   d. respondent behavior.
   e. shaping.

Learning by observation, p. 336
Easy, Factual/Definitional, Objective 11, Ans: c

114. Mirror neurons provide a biological basis for:
   a. the overjustification effect.
   b. spontaneous recovery.
   c. observational learning.
   d. extrinsic motivation.

Learning by observation, p. 336
Medium, Factual/Definitional, Objective 11, Ans: c

115. We find it harder to frown when viewing a smile than when viewing a frown. This can most clearly be attributed to:
   a. the overjustification effect.
   b. spontaneous recovery.
   c. mirror neurons.
   d. extrinsic motivation.

Bandura's experiments, p. 337
Easy, Factual/Definitional, Objective 11, Ans: b

116. Who highlighted the importance of observational learning?
   a. Watson
   b. Bandura
   c. Skinner
   d. Pavlov

Bandura's experiments, pp. 336-337
Easy, Factual/Definitional, Objective 11, Ans: d

117. In a well-known experiment, preschool children pounded and kicked a large inflated Bobo doll that an adult had just beaten on. This experiment served to illustrate the importance of:
   a. negative reinforcement.
   b. operant conditioning.
   c. respondent behavior.
   d. observational learning.
   e. spontaneous recovery.

Bandura's experiments, p. 337
Medium, Conceptual, Objective 11, Ans: d

118. Skinner is to shaping as Bandura is to:
   a. punishing.
   b. extinguishing.
   c. discriminating.
   d. modeling.
   e. generalizing.

Applications of observational learning, p. 337
Medium, Conceptual/Application, Objective 11, Ans: c

119. Dan and Joel, both 4-year-olds, have been watching reruns of "Superman" on television. Joel's mother recently found the boys standing on the garage roof, ready to try flying. What best accounts for the boys' behavior?
   a. shaping
   b. delayed reinforcement
   c. observational learning
   d. immediate reinforcement
   e. classical conditioning

Applications of observational learning, p. 337
Easy, Factual/Definitional, Objective 11, Ans: c

120. Children of abusive parents often learn to be aggressive by imitating their parents. This illustrates the importance of:
   a. delayed reinforcement.
   b. spontaneous recovery.
   c. observational learning.
   d. respondent behavior.
   e. shaping.

Applications of observational learning, p. 337
Difficult, Conceptual/Application, Objective 11, Ans: d

121. Mr. Schneider frequently tells his children that it is important to wash their hands before meals, but he rarely does so himself. Experiments suggest that his children will learn to:
a. practice and preach the virtues of cleanliness.
b. practice cleanliness but not preach its virtues.
c. neither practice nor preach the virtues of cleanliness.
d. preach the virtues of cleanliness but not practice cleanliness.

Applications of observational learning, p. 338
Medium, Conceptual/Application, Objective 11, Ans: b

122. The frequent observation of television violence is most likely to lead 9-year-old Fred to:
a. react with a sense of distress at the sight of two children fighting on the school playground.
b. overestimate the percentage of crimes that involve violent acts.
c. be more inhibited about personally starting a fight on the school playground.
d. overestimate the pain and injury experienced by victims of violent crime.

Applications of observational learning, p. 338
Difficult, Factual/Definitional, Objective 11, Ans: a

123. Children are especially likely to behave aggressively after viewing TV violence in which an attractive person commits ________ violence that causes ________ visible pain or harm.
a. justified; no
b. unjustified; no
c. justified; a lot of
d. unjustified; a lot of

Applications of observational learning, pp. 339-340
Easy, Factual/Definitional, Objective 11, Ans: e

124. A dramatic increase in children's violent play immediately after they viewed a video of the "Power Rangers" illustrates the role of television as a source of:
a. respondent behavior.
b. the overjustification effect.
c. spontaneous recovery.
d. negative reinforcement.
e. observational learning.

Essay Questions

1. (a) How would you classically condition an adventuresome 2-year-old to be more fearful of running across a busy street near her house?

(b) How would you classically condition a preschool child who is afraid of dogs to enjoy playing with a neighbor's friendly dog?

Be sure to identify the UCS, CS, UCR, and CR in both answers.

2. (a) Several days after drinking an excessive amount of alcohol, Karen becomes nauseated simply by the smell of liquor. The sight of the half-empty liquor bottle from which she drank does not, however, upset her. What does Karen's pattern of response indicate about the limits of associative learning?

   (b) If George is spanked immediately *after* his baby sister cries, he is likely to become fearful every time she cries. If Ken is spanked immediately *before* his baby sister cries, he is not likely to become fearful when she cries. What do the different reactions of George and Ken suggest about the role of cognitive processes in associative learning?

3. Mr. Byrne can't understand why scolding his seventh-grade students for disruptive classroom behaviors makes them more unruly. Explain Mr. Byrne's predicament in terms of operant conditioning principles. Show how he could use operant conditioning techniques to (a) reduce disruptive behaviors and (b) increase cooperative behaviors.

4. For Vina, cigarettes reduce feelings of tension and anxiety. Because of her heavy smoking, however, she has a bad morning cough and breathing difficulties.

   How can the principles of operant conditioning help to explain the development and continuation of Vina's self-defeating smoking habit? Explain the extent to which the reinforcement for Vina's habit is positive or negative, primary or conditioned, immediate or delayed, partial or continuous.

5. Although Mr. Wright often tells his children about the importance of donating time and money to charitable causes, he rarely does so himself. He believes that this hypocrisy will not rub off on his children, however, as long as he has plausible excuses for his lack of charity. Use your understanding of learning processes to explain how Mr. Wright's children are likely to be affected by their father's behavior. What advice would you give to Mr. Wright?

Web Quiz 1

Ans: e

1. Through direct experience with animals, we come to anticipate that dogs will bark and that birds will chirp. This best illustrates:
   a. the law of effect.
   b. spontaneous recovery.
   c. respondent behavior.
   d. the overjustification effect.
   e. associative learning.

Ans: d

2. Pavlov noticed that dogs began salivating at the mere sight of the person who regularly brought food to them. For the dogs, the sight of this person was a(n):
   a. primary reinforcer.
   b. unconditional stimulus.
   c. immediate reinforcer.
   d. conditioned stimulus.

Ans: a

3. Blinking in response to a puff of air directed to your eye is a(n):
   a. UCR.
   b. UCS.
   c. CR.
   d. CS.

Ans: a

4. Conditioning seldom occurs when a(n) ________ comes after a(n) _____.
   a. CS; UCS
   b. UCR; CS
   c. secondary reinforcer; operant behavior
   d. negative reinforcer; operant behavior

Ans: b

5. Long after her conditioned fear of spiders had been extinguished, Marcy experienced an unexpected surge of nervousness when first shown her cousin's new pet tarantula. Her unexpected nervousness best illustrates:
   a. latent learning.
   b. spontaneous recovery.
   c. delayed reinforcement.
   d. the overjustification effect.
   e. shaping.

Ans: d

6. A year after surviving a classroom shooting incident, Matthew Birnie still responded with terror at the sight of toy guns and to the sound of balloons popping. This reaction best illustrates:
   a. an unconditioned response.
   b. operant conditioning.
   c. latent learning.
   d. generalization.
   e. extinction.

Ans: c

7. The predictability of an association between a CS and a UCS facilitates an organism's ability to anticipate the occurrence of the UCS. This fact is most likely to be highlighted by a(n) ________ perspective.
   a. evolutionary
   b. behaviorist
   c. cognitive
   d. neuroscience

Ans: c

8. The law of effect was most clearly highlighted by:
   a. Pavlov's studies of conditioned salivation.
   b. Garcia and Koelling's research on taste aversion.
   c. Skinner's experiments on reinforcement.
   d. Bandura's studies of observational learning.
   e. Watson and Raynor's findings on fear conditioning.

Ans: e

9. In teaching her son to play basketball, Mrs. Richards initially reinforces him with praise for simply dribbling while standing still, then only for walking while dribbling, and finally only for running while dribbling. She is using a procedure known as:
   a. generalization.
   b. partial reinforcement.
   c. spontaneous recovery.
   d. secondary reinforcement.
   e. shaping.

Ans: d

10. If the onset of a light reliably signals the onset of food, a rat in a Skinner box will work to turn on the light. In this case, the light is a ________ reinforcer.
    a. partial
    b. primary
    c. negative
    d. conditioned
    e. delayed

Ans: d

11. Amos plays the slot machine for hours at a time. The monetary winnings dispensed to him by the machine provide an example of ________ reinforcement.
   a. negative
   b. primary
   c. delayed
   d. partial

Ans: c

12. Airline frequent flyer programs that reward customers with a free flight after every 25,000 miles of travel illustrate the use of a ________ schedule of reinforcement.
   a. fixed-interval
   b. variable-interval
   c. fixed-ratio
   d. variable-ratio

Ans: b

13. Because she has oversight responsibility for the servicing and repair of her company's fleet of cars, Rhonda frequently calls the garage mechanic to inquire whether service on various cars has been completed. She is likely to be reinforced with positive responses to her inquiries on a ________ schedule.
   a. fixed-interval
   b. variable-interval
   c. fixed-ratio
   d. variable-ratio

Ans: d

14. The overjustification effect involves the loss of:
   a. continuous reinforcement.
   b. primary reinforcers.
   c. spontaneous recovery.
   d. intrinsic motivation.
   e. immediate reinforcers.

Ans: b

15. If one chimpanzee watches a second chimp solve a puzzle for a food reward, the first chimp may thereby learn how to solve the puzzle. This best illustrates:
   a. operant conditioning.
   b. observational learning.
   c. respondent behavior.
   d. spontaneous recovery.
   e. classical conditioning.

Web Quiz 2

Ans: d

1. If you have frightening experience immediately after hearing a strange sound, your fear may be aroused when you hear that sound again. This best illustrates:
   a. generalization.
   b. spontaneous recovery.
   c. the overjustification effect.
   d. classical conditioning.
   e. the law of effect.

Ans: d

2. Researchers condition a flatworm to contract when exposed to light by repeatedly pairing the light with electric shock. The electric shock is a(n):
   a. negative reinforcer.
   b. conditioned stimulus.
   c. conditioned reinforcer.
   d. unconditioned stimulus.

Ans: c

3. You repeatedly hear a tone just before having a puff of air directed to your eye. Blinking to the tone presented without an air puff is a(n):
   a. UCR.
   b. UCS.
   c. CR.
   d. CS

Ans: a

4. People have been observed to form negative attitudes toward Pokémon characters who were repeatedly shown with negative words and images next to them. This best illustrates the impact of:
   a. classical conditioning.
   b. the law of effect.
   c. negative reinforcers.
   d. the overjustification effect.
   e. delayed reinforcers.

Ans: b

5. One psychologist recalled that the smell of onion breath no longer to trigged sexual arousal after the smell was no longer paired with his girlfriend's kisses. This best illustrates:
   a. acquisition.
   b. extinction.
   c. generalization.
   d. discrimination.
   e. the law of effect.

Ans: b

6. After being bitten by his neighbor's dog, Miguel experienced fear at the sight of that dog but not at the sight of other dogs. This best illustrates the process of:
   a. extinction.
   b. discrimination.
   c. conditioned reinforcement.
   d. latent learning.
   e. shaping.

Ans: c

7. If you get violently ill a couple of hours after eating contaminated food, you will probably develop an aversion to the taste of that food but not to the sight of the restaurant where you ate or to the sound of the music you heard there. This best illustrates that associative learning is constrained by:
   a. intrinsic motivation.
   b. spontaneous recovery.
   c. biological predispositions.
   d. conditioned reinforcers.
   e. the law of effect.

Ans: c

8. If children get attention from their parents for doing cartwheels, they will repeat the trick in anticipation of more attention. This best illustrates:
   a. spontaneous recovery.
   b. respondent behavior.
   c. operant conditioning.
   d. latent learning.
   e. habituation.

Ans: b

9. Matt regularly buckles his seat belt simply because it turns off the car's irritating warning buzzer. This best illustrates the value of:
   a. respondent behavior.
   b. negative reinforcement.
   c. generalization.
   d. secondary reinforcement.
   e. spontaneous recovery.

Ans: e

10. A word of praise is to a soothing backrub as ________ is to ________.
   a. delayed reinforcer; immediate reinforcer
   b. operant conditioning; classical conditioning
   c. partial reinforcement; continuous reinforcement
   d. observational learning; latent learning
   e. conditioned reinforcer; primary reinforcer

Ans: d

11. For professional baseball players, swinging at a pitched ball is reinforced with a home run on a ________ schedule.
    a. fixed-interval
    b. variable-interval
    c. fixed-ratio
    d. variable-ratio

Ans: a

12. During a typical morning, Colin checks the clock frequently before being reinforced with confirmation that the time for his regularly scheduled lunch break has arrived. In this case, Colin's behavior is reinforced on a ________ schedule.
    a. fixed-interval
    b. variable-interval
    c. fixed-ratio
    d. variable-ratio

Ans: e

13. For some children who bite themselves or bang their heads, squirting water into their faces when they hurt themselves has been observed to decrease the frequency of these self-abusive behaviors. This best illustrates the potential value of:
    a. latent learning.
    b. conditioned reinforcers.
    c. negative reinforcers.
    d. primary reinforcers.
    e. punishment.

Ans: c

14. Laurie lost some of her intrinsic interest in caring for her baby sister when her mother began promising to pay her money to look after her sister. Laurie's experience best illustrates:
    a. respondent behavior.
    b. latent learning.
    c. the overjustification effect.
    d. spontaneous recovery.
    e. negative reinforcement.

Ans: b

15. Which pioneering learning researcher highlighted the antisocial effects of aggressive models on children's behavior?
    a. Watson
    b. Bandura
    c. Pavlov
    d. Skinner

Study Guide Questions

Ans: c, p. 309

1. Learning is best defined as:
   a. any behavior emitted by an organism without being elicited.
   b. a change in the behavior of an organism.
   c. a relatively permanent change in the behavior of an organism due to experience.
   d. behavior based on operant rather than respondent conditioning.

Ans: d, p. 311

2. Which of the following is a form of associative learning?
   a. classical conditioning
   b. operant conditioning
   c. observational learning
   d. all of the above

Ans: d, pp. 312, 323

3. Operant conditioning is to ________ classical conditioning is to ________.
   a. Pavlov; Watson
   b. Skinner; Bandura
   c. Pavlov; Skinner
   d. Skinner; Pavlov

Ans: a, p. 313

4. As a child, you were playing in the yard one day when a neighbor's cat wandered over. Your mother (who has a terrible fear of animals) screamed and snatched you into her arms. Her behavior caused you to cry. You now have a fear of cats. Identify the UCS.
   a. your mother's behavior
   b. your crying
   c. the cat
   d. your fear today

Ans: c, p. 313

5. In Pavlov's original experiment with dogs, the meat served as a(n):
   a. CS.
   b. CR.
   c. UCS.
   d. UCR.

Ans: b, p. 313

6. As a child, you were playing in the yard one day when a neighbor's cat wandered over. Your mother (who has a terrible fear of animals) screamed and snatched you into her arms. Her behavior caused you to cry. You now have a fear of cats. Identify the UCR.
   a. your mother's behavior
   b. your crying
   c. the cat
   d. your fear today

Ans: d, p. 313

7. In Pavlov's original experiment with dogs, salivation to meat was the:
   a. CS.
   b. CR.
   c. UCS.
   d. UCR.

Ans: a, pp. 313-314

8. You always rattle the box of dog biscuits before giving your dog a treat. As you do so, your dog salivates. Rattling the box is a(n) ________; your dog's salivation is a(n) ________.
   a. CS; CR
   b. CS; UCR
   c. UCS; CR
   d. UCS; UCR

Ans: b, pp. 313-314

9. In Pavlov's original experiment with dogs, the tone was initially a(n) ________ stimulus; after it was paired with meat, it became a(n) ________ stimulus.
   a. conditioned; neutral
   b. neutral; conditioned
   c. conditioned; unconditioned
   d. unconditioned; conditioned

Ans: d, p. 314

10. As a child, you were playing in the yard one day when a neighbor's cat wandered over. Your mother (who has a terrible fear of animals) screamed and snatched you into her arms. Her behavior caused you to cry. You now have a fear of cats. Identify the CR.
    a. your mother's behavior
    b. your crying
    c. the cat
    d. your fear today

Ans: a, p. 314

11. Two groups of rats receive classical conditioning trials in which a tone and electric shock are presented. For Group 1 the electric shock always follows the tone. For Group 2 the tone and shock occur randomly. Which of the following is likely to result?
    a. The tone will become a CS for Group 1 but not for Group 2.
    b. The tone will become a CS for Group 2 but not for Group 1.
    c. The tone will become a CS for both groups.
    d. The tone will not become a CS for either group.

Ans: c, p. 314

12. As a child, you were playing in the yard one day when a neighbor's cat wandered over. Your mother (who has a terrible fear of animals) screamed and snatched you into her arms. Her behavior caused you to cry. You now have a fear of cats. Identify the CS.
    a. your mother's behavior
    b. your crying
    c. the cat
    d. your fear today

Ans: b, p. 314

13. For the most rapid conditioning, a CS should be presented:
    a. about 1 second after the UCS.
    b. about a half-second before the UCS.
    c. about 15 seconds before the UCS.
    d. at the same time as the UCS.

Ans: c, p. 316

14. During extinction, the ________ is omitted; as a result, the ________ seems to disappear.
    a. UCS; UCR
    b. CS; CR
    c. UCS; CR
    d. CS; UCR

Ans: c, p. 316

15. In Pavlov's studies of classical conditioning of a dog's salivary responses, spontaneous recovery occurred:
    a. during acquisition, when the CS was first paired with the UCS.
    b. during extinction, when the CS was first presented by itself.
    c. when the CS was reintroduced following extinction of the CR and a rest period.
    d. during discrimination training, when several conditioned stimuli were introduced.

Ans: c, p. 316

16. When a conditioned stimulus is presented without an accompanying unconditioned stimulus, ________ will soon take place.
    a. generalization
    b. discrimination
    c. extinction
    d. aversion
    e. spontaneous recovery

Ans: b, p. 316

17. Bill once had a blue car that was in the shop more than it was out. Since then he will not even consider owning blue- or green-colored cars. Bill's aversion to green cars is an example of:
    a. discrimination.
    b. generalization.
    c. latent learning.
    d. the overjustification effect.

Ans: e, p. 317

18. In order to obtain a reward, a monkey learns to press a lever when a 1000-Hz tone is on but not when a 1200-Hz tone is on. What kind of training is this?
    a. extinction
    b. generalization
    c. classical conditioning
    d. spontaneous recovery
    e. discrimination

Ans: c, p. 317

19. Classical conditioning experiments by Rescorla and Wagner demonstrate that an important factor in conditioning is:
    a. the subject's age.
    b. the strength of the stimuli.
    c. the predictability of an association.
    d. the similarity of stimuli.
    e. all of the above.

Ans: b, pp. 317, 329

20. Cognitive processes are:
    a. unimportant in classical and operant conditioning.
    b. important in both classical and operant conditioning.
    c. more important in classical than in operant conditioning.
    d. more important in operant than in classical conditioning.

Ans: c, pp. 318-319

21. In Garcia and Koelling's studies of taste-aversion learning, rats learned to associate:
    a. taste with electric shock.
    b. sights and sounds with sickness.
    c. taste with sickness.
    d. taste and sounds with electric shock.
    e. taste and sounds with electric shock, then sickness.

Ans: a, pp. 318-319

22. Experiments on taste-aversion learning demonstrate that:
    a. for the conditioning of certain stimuli, the UCS need not immediately follow the CS.
    b. any perceivable stimulus can become a CS.
    c. all animals are biologically primed to associate illness with the taste of a tainted food.
    d. all of the above are true.

Ans: b, p. 319

23. Last evening May-ling ate her first cheeseburger and french fries at an American fast-food restaurant. A few hours later she became ill. It can be expected that:
    a. May-ling will develop an aversion to the sight of a cheeseburger and french fries.
    b. May-ling will develop an aversion to the taste of a cheeseburger and french fries.
    c. May-ling will not associate her illness with the food she ate.
    d. May-ling will associate her sickness with something she experienced immediately before she became ill.

Ans: e, p. 320

24. In which of the following may classical conditioning play a role?
    a. emotional problems
    b. the body's immune response
    c. how animals adapt to the environment
    d. helping drug addicts
    e. all of the above

Ans: b, pp. 320-321

25. In Watson and Rayner's experiment, the loud noise was the ________ and the white rat was the ________.
    a. CS; CR
    b. UCS; CS
    c. CS; UCS
    d. UCS; CR
    e. UCR; CR

Ans: c, p. 322

26. One difference between classical and operant conditioning is that:
    a. in classical conditioning the responses operate on the environment to produce rewarding or punishing stimuli.
    b. in operant conditioning the responses are triggered by preceding stimuli.
    c. in classical conditioning the responses are automatically elicited by stimuli.
    d. in operant conditioning the responses are reflexive.

Ans: d, pp. 323, 325

27. Reggie's mother tells him that he can watch TV after he cleans his room. Evidently, Reggie's mother is attempting to use ________ to increase room cleaning.
    a. operant conditioning
    b. secondary reinforcement
    c. positive reinforcement
    d. all of the above

Ans: a, p. 323

28. You teach your dog to fetch the paper by giving him a cookie each time he does so. This is an example of:
    a. operant conditioning.
    b. classical conditioning.
    c. conditioned reinforcement.
    d. partial reinforcement.

Ans: b, p. 323

29. The type of learning associated with Skinner is:
    a. classical conditioning.
    b. operant conditioning.
    c. respondent conditioning.
    d. observational learning.

Ans: a, p. 323

30. Shaping is a(n) ________ technique for ________ a behavior.
    a. operant; establishing
    b. operant; suppressing
    c. respondent; establishing
    d. respondent; suppressing

Ans: a, pp. 323, 325

31. Online testing systems and interactive software are applications of the operant conditioning principles of:
    a. shaping and immediate reinforcement.
    b. immediate reinforcement and punishment.
    c. shaping and primary reinforcement.
    d. continuous reinforcement and punishment.

Ans: c, p. 324

32. Which of the following is an example of shaping?
    a. A dog learns to salivate at the sight of a box of dog biscuits.
    b. A new driver learns to stop at an intersection when the light changes to red.
    c. A parrot is rewarded first for making any sound, then for making a sound similar to "Laura," and then for "speaking" its owner's name.
    d. A psychology student reinforces a laboratory rat only occasionally, to make its behavior more resistant to extinction.

Ans: b, p. 325

33. A response that leads to the removal of an unpleasant stimulus is one being:
    a. positively reinforced.
    b. negatively reinforced.
    c. punished.
    d. extinguished.

Ans: c, p. 325

34. Putting on your coat when it is cold outside is a behavior that is maintained by:
    a. discrimination learning.
    b. punishment.
    c. negative reinforcement.
    d. classical conditioning.
    e. positive reinforcement.

Ans: b, p. 325

35. Jack finally takes out the garbage in order to get his father to stop pestering him. Jack's behavior is being influenced by:
    a. positive reinforcement.
    b. negative reinforcement.
    c. a primary reinforcer.
    d. punishment.

Ans: d, p. 325

36. Which of the following is the best example of a conditioned reinforcer?
    a. putting on a coat on a cold day
    b. relief from pain after the dentist stops drilling your teeth
    c. receiving a cool drink after washing your mother's car on a hot day
    d. receiving an approving nod from the boss for a job well done
    e. having a big meal after going without food all day

Ans: d, p. 325

37. Which of the following is an example of reinforcement?
    a. presenting a positive stimulus after a response
    b. removing an unpleasant stimulus after a response
    c. being told that you have done a good job
    d. all of the above are examples

Ans: b, pp. 325-326

38. For operant conditioning to be most effective, when should the reinforcers be presented in relation to the desired response?
    a. immediately before
    b. immediately after
    c. at the same time as
    d. at least a half hour before
    e. in any of the above sequences

Ans: d, pp. 325, 328

39. In distinguishing between negative reinforcers and punishment, we note that:
    a. punishment, but not negative reinforcement, involves use of an aversive stimulus.
    b. in contrast to punishment, negative reinforcement decreases the likelihood of a response by the presentation of an aversive stimulus.
    c. in contrast to punishment, negative reinforcement increases the likelihood of a response by the presentation of an aversive stimulus.
    d. in contrast to punishment, negative reinforcement increases the likelihood of a response by the termination of an aversive stimulus.

Ans: b, p. 326

40. Which of the following statements concerning reinforcement is correct?
    a. Learning is most rapid with intermittent reinforcement, but continuous reinforcement produces the greatest resistance to extinction.
    b. Learning is most rapid with continuous reinforcement, but intermittent reinforcement produces the greatest resistance to extinction.
    c. Learning is fastest and resistance to extinction is greatest after continuous reinforcement.
    d. Learning is fastest and resistance to extinction is greatest following intermittent reinforcement.

Ans: d, p. 326

41. On an intermittent reinforcement schedule, reinforcement is given:
    a. in very small amounts.
    b. randomly.
    c. for successive approximations of a desired behavior.
    d. only some of the time.

Ans: c, p. 327

42. You are expecting an important letter in the mail. As the regular delivery time approaches you glance more and more frequently out the window, searching for the letter carrier. Your behavior in this situation typifies that associated with which schedule of reinforcement?
    a. fixed-ratio
    b. variable-ratio
    c. fixed-interval
    d. variable-interval

Ans: c, p. 327

43. Gambling is reinforced according to which schedule?
    a. fixed-interval
    b. fixed-ratio
    c. variable-interval
    d. variable-ratio

Ans: a, p. 327

44. From a casino owner's viewpoint, which of the following jackpot payout schedules would be the most desirable for reinforcing customer use of a slot machine?
    a. variable-ratio
    b. fixed-ratio
    c. variable-interval
    d. fixed-interval

Ans: c, p. 327

45. The "piecework," or commission, method of payment is an example of which reinforcement schedule?
    a. fixed-interval
    b. variable-interval
    c. fixed-ratio
    d. variable-ratio

Ans: c, p. 327

46. Lars, a shoe salesman, is paid every two weeks, whereas Tom receives a commission for each pair of shoes he sells. Evidently, Lars is paid on a ________ schedule of reinforcement, and Tom on a ________ schedule of reinforcement.
    a. fixed-ratio; fixed-interval
    b. continuous; intermittent
    c. fixed-interval; fixed-ratio
    d. variable-interval; variable-ratio
    e. variable-ratio; variable-interval

Ans: c, p. 327

47. Leon's psychology instructor has scheduled an exam every third week of the term. Leon will probably study the most just before an exam and the least just after an exam. This is because the schedule of exams is reinforcing studying according to which schedule?
    a. fixed-ratio
    b. variable-ratio
    c. fixed-interval
    d. variable-interval

Ans: b, p. 327

48. The highest and most consistent rate of response is produced by a ________ schedule.
    a. fixed-ratio
    b. variable-ratio
    c. fixed-interval
    d. variable-interval

Ans: d, pp. 328-329

49. Punishment is a controversial way of controlling behavior because:
    a. behavior is not forgotten and may return.
    b. punishing stimuli often create fear.
    c. punishment often increases aggressiveness.
    d. of all of the above reasons.

Ans: d, p. 329

50. After discovering that her usual route home was closed due to road repairs, Sharetta used her knowledge of the city and sense of direction to find an alternate route. This is an example of:
    a. latent learning.
    b. observational learning.
    c. shaping.
    d. using a cognitive map.
    e. discrimination.

Ans: a, p. 329

51. A cognitive map is a(n):
    a. mental representation of one's environment.
    b. sequence of thought processes leading from one idea to another.
    c. set of instructions detailing the most effective means of teaching a particular concept.
    d. biological predisposition to learn a particular skill.
    e. educational tool based on operant conditioning techniques.

Ans: d, p. 330

52. After exploring a complicated maze for several days, a rat subsequently ran the maze with very few errors when food was placed in the goal box for the first time. This performance illustrates:
    a. classical conditioning.
    b. discrimination learning.
    c. observational learning.
    d. latent learning.

Ans: b, p. 330

53. Which of the following would be most likely to result in the overjustification effect?
    a. Each day that her son fails to clean his room, Mrs. Shih adds an additional chore he must complete.
    b. Kim's mother decides to reward her daughter's enjoyment of karate by paying her 75 cents for each hour that she practices.
    c. The manager of a shoe store decides to give a bonus to the employee who sells the most shoes each week.
    d. After her soccer team's poor performance, the coach scolds the players.
    e. Greg's father "pays" himself $2.00 a day for not smoking.

Ans: b, p. 330

54. When people are paid for performing tasks they enjoy, their self-motivation may decrease. This is called:
    a. latent learning.
    b. the overjustification effect.
    c. primary reinforcement.
    d. modeling.
    e. negative reinforcement.

Ans: b, p. 330

55. Nancy decided to take introductory psychology because she has always been interested in human behavior. Jack enrolled in the same course because he thought it would be easy. Nancy's behavior was motivated by ________, Jack's by ________.
    a. extrinsic motivation; intrinsic motivation
    b. intrinsic motivation; extrinsic motivation
    c. drives; incentives
    d. incentives; drives

Ans: a, p. 331

56. A pigeon can easily be taught to flap its wings in order to avoid shock but not for food reinforcement. According to the text, this is most likely so because:
    a. pigeons are biologically predisposed to flap their wings in order to escape aversive events and to use their beaks to obtain food.
    b. shock is a more motivating stimulus for birds than food is.
    c. hungry animals have difficulty delaying their eating long enough to learn *any* new skill.
    d. of all of the above reasons.

Ans: c, p. 333

57. The manager of a manufacturing plant wishes to use positive reinforcement to increase the productivity of workers. Which of the following procedures would probably be the most effective?
    a. Deserving employees are given a general merit bonus at the end of each fiscal year.
    b. A productivity goal that seems attainable, yet is unrealistic, is set for each employee.
    c. Employees are given immediate bonuses for specific behaviors related to productivity.
    d. Employees who fail to meet standards of productivity receive pay cuts.

Ans: b, p. 336

58. After watching coverage of the Olympics on television recently, Lynn and Susan have been staging their own "summer games." Which of the following best accounts for their behavior?
    a. classical conditioning
    b. observational learning
    c. latent learning
    d. shaping
    e. discrimination

Ans: a, p. 336

59. Mirror neurons are found in the brain's ________ and are believed to be the neural basis for ________.
   a. frontal lobe; observational learning
   b. frontal lobe; classical conditioning
   c. temporal lobe; operant conditioning
   d. temporal lobe; observational learning

Ans: b, p. 336

60. Learning by imitating others' behaviors is called ________ learning. The researcher best known for studying this type of learning is ________.
   a. secondary; Skinner
   b. observational; Bandura
   c. secondary; Pavlov
   d. observational; Watson

Ans: d, p. 337

61. In promoting observational learning, the most effective models are those that we perceive as:
   a. similar to ourselves.
   b. respected and admired.
   c. successful.
   d. any of the above.

Ans: c, p. 337

62. Mrs. Ramirez often tells her children that it is important to buckle their seat belts while riding in the car, but she rarely does so herself. Her children will probably learn to:
   a. use their seat belts and tell others it is important to do so.
   b. use their seat belts but not tell others it is important to do so.
   c. tell others it is important to use seat belts but rarely use them themselves.
   d. neither tell others that seat belts are important nor use them.

Ans: c, p. 339

63. Regarding the impact of television violence on children, most researchers believe that:
   a. aggressive children simply prefer violent programs.
   b. television simply reflects, rather than contributes to, violent social trends.
   c. violence on television leads to aggressive behavior.
   d. there is only a weak correlation between exposure to violence and aggressive behavior.

CHAPTER 9

Memory

Learning Objectives

The Phenomenon of Memory (pp. 344-346)

1. Describe memory in terms of information processing, and distinguish among sensory memory, short-term memory, and long-term memory.

Encoding: Getting Information In (pp. 347-354)

2. Distinguish between automatic and effortful processing, and discuss the importance of rehearsal.

3. Explain the importance of meaning, imagery, and organization in the encoding process.

Storage: Retaining Information (pp. 354-361)

4. Describe the limited nature of sensory memory and short-term memory.

5. Describe the capacity and duration of long-term memory, and discuss the biological changes that may underlie memory formation and storage.

6. Distinguish between implicit and explicit memory, and identify the different brain structures associated with each.

Retrieval: Getting Information Out (pp. 361-365)

7. Contrast recall, recognition, and relearning measures of memory.

8. Describe the importance of retrieval cues and the impact of environmental contexts and internal emotional states on retrieval.

Forgetting (pp. 365-371)

9. Explain why the capacity to forget can be beneficial, and discuss the role of encoding failure and storage decay in the process of forgetting.

10. Explain what is meant by retrieval failure, and discuss the effects of interference and motivated forgetting on retrieval.

Memory Construction (pp. 372-381)

11. Describe the evidence for the constructive nature of memory and the impact of imagination and leading questions on eyewitness recall.

12. Describe the difficulties in discerning true memories from false ones and the reliability of children's eyewitness recall.

13. Discuss the controversy over reports of repressed and recovered memories of childhood sexual abuse.

Improving Memory (pp. 381-382)

14. Explain how an understanding of memory can contribute to effective study techniques.

Information processing, p. 345
Easy, Factual/Definitional, Objective 1, Ans: c

1. The process of encoding refers to:
   a. the persistence of learning over time.
   b. the recall of information previously learned.
   c. getting information into memory.
   d. the motivated forgetting of painful memories.
   e. a clear memory of an emotionally significant event.

Information processing, p. 345
Medium, Conceptual, Objective 1, Ans: d

2. Storage is to encoding as ________ is to ________.
   a. recognition; recall
   b. imagery; mnemonics
   c. rehearsal; retrieval
   d. retention; acquisition
   e. priming; relearning

Information processing, p. 345
Easy, Factual/Definitional, Objective 1, Ans: d

3. The process of getting information out of memory storage is called:
   a. priming.
   b. encoding.
   c. relearning.
   d. retrieval.
   e. rehearsal.

Information processing, p. 346
Easy, Factual/Definitional, Objective 1, Ans: a

4. Your consciously activated but limited-capacity memory is called ________ memory.
   a. short-term
   b. implicit
   c. mood-congruent
   d. explicit
   e. automatic

Information processing, pp. 345, 346
Difficult, Conceptual, Objective 1, Ans: e

5. A flashbulb memory would typically be stored in ________ memory.
   a. iconic
   b. implicit
   c. short-term
   d. state-dependent
   e. long-term

Information processing, p. 346
Difficult, Factual/Definitional, Objective 1, Ans: e

6. The integration of new incoming information with knowledge retrieved from long-term storage necessarily involves the activity of:
   a. automatic processing.
   b. implicit memory.
   c. semantic encoding.
   d. proactive interference.
   e. working memory.

Encoding: getting information in, p. 347
Easy, Factual/Definitional, Objective 2, Ans: a

7. Automatic and effortful processing involve two types of:
   a. encoding.
   b. retrieval.
   c. interference.
   d. storage.
   e. repression.

Automatic processing, p. 347
Easy, Factual/Definitional, Objective 2, Ans: c

8. Automatic processing occurs without:
   a. visual imagery.
   b. semantic encoding.
   c. conscious awareness.
   d. sensory memory.

Automatic processing, p. 347
Medium, Factual/Definitional, Objective 2, Ans: d

9. Our ability to perform two or more complex encoding tasks simultaneously best illustrates the value of:
   a. source amnesia.
   b. flashbulb memory.
   c. state-dependent memory.
   d. automatic processing.
   e. the spacing effect.

Automatic processing, p. 347
Medium, Conceptual/Application, Objective 2, Ans: a

10. During her psychology test, Kelsey could not remember the meaning of the term "proactive interference." Surprisingly, however, she accurately remembered that the term appeared on the fourth line of a left-hand page in her textbook. Her memory of this incidental information is best explained in terms of:
    a. automatic processing.
    b. the serial position effect.
    c. the spacing effect.
    d. the method of loci.
    e. the next-in-line effect.

Automatic processing, p. 347
Medium, Factual/Definitional, Objective 2, Ans: c

11. The effortful processing of information:
    a. typically interferes with the capacity to think creatively.
    b. cannot easily be suppressed and inhibited.
    c. can become automatic through practice.
    d. occurs less frequently among adults than children.

Effortful processing, p. 347
Easy, Factual/Definitional, Objective 2, Ans: b

12. The conscious repetition of information in order to maintain it in memory is called:
    a. automatic processing.
    b. rehearsal.
    c. priming.
    d. chunking.

Effortful processing, p. 347
Easy, Conceptual/Application, Objective 2, Ans: b

13. In an effort to remember how to spell "rhinoceros," Samantha writes the word 30 times. She is using a technique known as:
    a. priming.
    b. rehearsal.
    c. the "peg-word" system.
    d. chunking.
    e. the method of loci.

Effortful processing, pp. 347, 362
Difficult, Conceptual, Objective 2, Ans: a

14. Priming is to retrieval as rehearsal is to:
    a. encoding.
    b. chunking.
    c. imagery.
    d. repression.
    e. automatic processing.

Effortful processing, p. 348
Medium, Factual/Definitional, Objective 2, Ans: a

15. Ebbinghaus's use of nonsense syllables to study memory led to the discovery that:
    a. the amount remembered depends on the time spent learning.
    b. what is learned in one mood is most easily retrieved in that same mood.
    c. information that is automatically processed is rarely forgotten.
    d. our sensory memory capacity is essentially unlimited.

Effortful processing, p. 348
Difficult, Conceptual, Objective 2, Ans: e

16. Immediately after participants at a business seminar took turns introducing themselves, Anne remembered everybody's name except for the person who introduced himself just before she did. This best illustrates that memory is influenced by:
    a. the spacing effect.
    b. long-term potentiation.
    c. the serial position effect.
    d. retrieval failure.
    e. rehearsal.

Effortful processing, p. 348
Medium, Factual/Definitional, Objective 2, Ans: d

17. Our inability to remember information presented in the seconds just before we fall asleep is most likely due to:
    a. motivated forgetting.
    b. the misinformation effect.
    c. retroactive interference.
    d. encoding failure.
    e. long-term potentiation.

Effortful processing, p. 348
Medium, Conceptual/Application, Objective 2, Ans: a

18. Jamille performs better on foreign language vocabulary tests if she studies the material 15 minutes every day for 8 days than if she crams for 2 hours the night before the test. This illustrates what is known as:
    a. the spacing effect.
    b. the serial position effect.
    c. mood-congruent memory.
    d. chunking.
    e. automatic processing.

Effortful processing, p. 348
Medium, Factual/Definitional, Objective 2, Ans: d

19. Students who restudy course material in order to pass a comprehensive examination are especially likely to demonstrate long-term retention of the course material. This best illustrates:
    a. implicit memory.
    b. the serial position effect.
    c. the method of loci.
    d. the spacing effect.
    e. chunking.

Effortful processing, p. 349
Easy, Factual/Definitional, Objective 2, Ans: a

20. The tendency to immediately recall the first and last items in a list better than the middle items is known as the ________ effect.
    a. serial position
    b. misinformation
    c. next-in-line
    d. priming
    e. spacing

Effortful processing, p. 349
Medium, Conceptual/Application, Objective 2, Ans: c

21. One day after Usha hears her mother's list of 12 grocery items, Usha is most likely to remember the items ________ of the list.
    a. at the beginning and end
    b. at the end
    c. at the beginning
    d. in the middle

Effortful processing, p. 349
Difficult, Conceptual/Application, Objective 2, Ans: c

22. The day after Kirsten was introduced to 13 people at a business luncheon, she could recall the names of only the first 4 people to whom she had been introduced. Her effective recall of these particular names best illustrates the benefits of:
    a. automatic processing.
    b. the next-in-line effect.
    c. rehearsal.
    d. flashbulb memory.
    e. the method of loci.

Encoding meaning, pp. 350-351
Medium, Factual/Definitional, Objective 3, Ans: b

23. The fact that our preconceived ideas contribute to our ability to process new information best illustrates the importance of:
    a. the serial position effect.
    b. semantic encoding.
    c. retroactive interference.
    d. iconic memory.
    e. repression.

Encoding meaning, p. 350
Medium, Factual/Definitional, Objective 3, Ans: b

24. Semantic encoding refers to the processing of:
    a. sounds.
    b. meanings.
    c. visual images.
    d. unfamiliar units.

Encoding meaning, pp. 350-351
Difficult, Conceptual/Application, Objective 3, Ans: c

25. When people are asked to recall a list of words they had earlier memorized, they often substitute synonyms for some of the words on the original list. This best illustrates the effects of:
    a. implicit memory.
    b. source amnesia.
    c. semantic encoding.
    d. memory decay.
    e. state-dependent memory.

Encoding meaning, p. 350
Medium, Conceptual/Application, Objective 3, Ans: e

26. Superior memory for rap lyrics that include the most rhymes best illustrates the value of:
    a. the next-in-line effect.
    b. the spacing effect.
    c. mood-congruent memory.
    d. the serial position effect.
    e. acoustic encoding.

Encoding meaning, p. 350
Difficult, Factual/Definitional, Objective 3, Ans: d

27. Craik and Tulving experimentally demonstrated that people effectively remember seeing a specific word after they decide whether that word fits into an incomplete sentence. This research highlighted the effectiveness of:
    a. the method of loci.
    b. the "peg-word" system.
    c. automatic processing.
    d. semantic encoding.
    e. the next-in-line effect.

Encoding meaning, pp. 350-351
Medium, Conceptual, Objective 3, Ans: b

28. Children can better remember an ancient Latin verse if the definition of each unfamiliar Latin word is carefully explained to them. This best illustrates the value of:
    a. iconic memory.
    b. semantic encoding.
    c. the method of loci.
    d. automatic processing.
    e. the "peg-word" system.

Encoding meaning, p. 351
Medium, Conceptual, Objective 3, Ans: b

29. In order to remember the information presented in her psychology textbook, Susan often relates it to her own life experiences. Susan's strategy is an effective memory aid because it facilitates:
    a. iconic memory.
    b. semantic encoding.
    c. automatic processing.
    d. proactive interference.
    e. the serial position effect.

Encoding meaning, p. 351
Medium, Conceptual, Objective 3, Ans: a

30. Which of the following questions about the word *depressed* would best prepare you to correctly remember tomorrow that you had seen the word on today's test?
a. How well does the word describe you?
b. Does the word consist of ten letters?
c. Is the word written in capital letters?
d. Does the word rhyme with *obsessed*?

Encoding imagery, p. 351
Medium, Factual/Definitional, Objective 3, Ans: c

31. We are more likely to remember the words "typewriter, cigarette, and fire" than the words "void, process, and inherent." This best illustrates the value of:
a. long-term potentiation.
b. flashbulb memory.
c. visual encoding.
d. iconic memory.

Encoding imagery, p. 351
Medium, Conceptual/Application, Objective 3, Ans: d

32. Elaine recalls last year's Paris vacation more positively than she evaluated it when it occurred. This best illustrates:
a. the self-reference effect.
b. source amnesia.
c. proactive interference.
d. rosy retrospection.
e. the spacing effect.

Encoding imagery, p. 351
Easy, Factual/Definitional, Objective 3, Ans: d

33. A mnemonic device is a:
a. mental picture.
b. test or measure of memory.
c. technique for encoding language sounds.
d. memory aid.
e. word, event, or place that triggers a memory of the past.

Encoding imagery, p. 351
Easy, Factual/Definitional, Objective 3, Ans: d

34. As an aid to memorizing lengthy speeches, ancient Greek orators would visualize themselves moving through familiar locations. They were making use of:
a. the serial position effect.
b. the next-in-line effect.
c. implicit memory.
d. the method of loci.
e. the spacing effect.

Encoding imagery, pp. 351, 352
Difficult, Conceptual, Objective 3, Ans: a

35. Acronyms are to chunking as the method of loci is to:
    a. imagery.
    b. rehearsal.
    c. acoustic encoding.
    d. automatic processing.
    e. the "peg-word" system.

Organizing information for encoding, pp. 351, 352
Difficult, Conceptual, Objective 3, Ans: c

36. The method of loci is to imagery as acronyms are to:
    a. priming.
    b. rehearsal.
    c. chunking.
    d. the "peg-word" system.

Organizing information for encoding, p. 352
Easy, Factual/Definitional, Objective 3, Ans: d

37. Chunking refers to:
    a. getting information into memory through the use of visual imagery.
    b. the effortless processing of familiar information to get it into long-term memory storage.
    c. the combined use of automatic and effortful processing to ensure the retention of unfamiliar information.
    d. the organization of information into meaningful units.

Organizing information for encoding, p. 352
Medium, Factual/Definitional, Objective 3, Ans: b

38. Chess masters can recall the exact positions of most pieces after a brief glance at the game board. This ability is best explained in terms of:
    a. flashbulb memory.
    b. chunking.
    c. iconic memory.
    d. the serial position effect.
    e. the method of loci.

Organizing information for encoding, p. 352
Medium, Conceptual/Application, Objective 3, Ans: a

39. In order to remember to buy sugar, ham, oranges, and potatoes the next time he goes grocery shopping, Hakeen forms the word "shop" with the first letter of each item. He is using a memory aid known as:
    a. chunking.
    b. the spacing effect.
    c. the serial position effect.
    d. the method of loci.
    e. the next-in-line effect.

Organizing information for encoding, p. 352
Medium, Conceptual, Objective 3, Ans: b

40. George has learned the sentence "My Very Earnest Mother Just Showed Us Nine Planets" as a way to remember the names of the nine planets. This illustrates the use of:
a. the method of loci.
b. mnemonics.
c. the spacing effect.
d. the "peg-word" system.
e. automatic processing.

Organizing information for encoding, p. 353
Difficult, Conceptual/Application, Objective 3, Ans: b

41. Sabrina went to the store for furniture polish, carrots, pencils, ham, sponges, celery, notebook paper, and salami. She remembered to buy all these items by reminding herself that she needed food products that included meats and vegetables and that she needed nonfood products that included school supplies and cleaning aids. Sabrina made effective use of:
a. the spacing effect.
b. hierarchical organization.
c. automatic processing.
d. the "peg-word" system.
e. the method of loci.

Sensory memory, p. 354
Difficult, Factual/Definitional, Objective 4, Ans: c

42. When Sperling visually displayed three rows of three letters each for only one twentieth of a second, experimental participants:
a. recalled only half the letters because they had insufficient time to see all of them.
b. recalled only about seven of the letters due to memory storage limitations.
c. had a momentary photographic memory of all nine letters.
d. recalled all the letters in any particular row when given a special recall signal several seconds after the letters had disappeared.

Sensory memory, p. 354
Easy, Factual/Definitional, Objective 4, Ans: c

43. A momentary sensory memory of visual stimuli is called ________ memory.
a. echoic
b. implicit
c. iconic
d. flashbulb

Sensory memory, p. 354
Medium, Conceptual/Application, Objective 4, Ans: a

44. The address for obtaining tickets to a popular quiz show flashes on the TV screen, but the image disappears before Sergei has had a chance to write down the complete address. To his surprise, however, he has retained a momentary mental image of the five-digit zip code. His experience best illustrates ________ memory.
a. iconic
b. flashbulb
c. implicit
d. echoic
e. state-dependent

Sensory memory, pp. 354, 359
Difficult, Conceptual, Objective 4, Ans: a

45. Explicit memory is to long-term memory as iconic memory is to ________ memory.
   a. sensory
   b. short-term
   c. flashbulb
   d. implicit
   e. state-dependent

Sensory memory, p. 355
Easy, Factual/Definitional, Objective 4, Ans: d

46. Echoic memory refers to:
   a. the encoded meanings of words and events in long-term memory.
   b. a vivid memory of an emotionally significant event.
   c. the automatic retention of incidental information about the timing and frequency of events.
   d. a momentary sensory memory of auditory stimuli.

Sensory memory, p. 355
Medium, Conceptual/Application, Objective 4, Ans: e

47. For a moment after hearing his dog's high-pitched bark, Mr. Silvers has a vivid auditory impression of the dog's yelp. His experience most clearly illustrates ________ memory.
   a. short-term
   b. iconic
   c. mood-congruent
   d. implicit
   e. echoic

Sensory and short-term memories, p. 355
Easy, Factual/Definitional, Objective 4, Ans: a

48. Some of the information in our ________ memory is encoded into ________ memory.
   a. iconic; short-term
   b. short-term; sensory
   c. flashbulb; short-term
   d. long-term; iconic

Short-term memory, p. 355
Difficult, Factual/Definitional, Objective 4, Ans: b

49. Peterson and Peterson demonstrated that unrehearsed short-term memories for three consonants almost completely decay in as short a time as:
   a. 1 second.
   b. 12 seconds.
   c. 1 minute.
   d. 12 minutes.
   e. 1 hour.

Short-term memory, p. 355
Medium, Factual/Definitional, Objective 4, Ans: e

50. After being asked to remember three consonants, subjects in a study by Peterson and Peterson counted aloud backward by threes in order to prevent:
   a. source amnesia.
   b. retroactive interference.
   c. proactive interference.
   d. encoding failure.
   e. rehearsal.

Short-term memory, p. 355
Easy, Factual/Definitional, Objective 4, Ans: a

51. "The magical number seven, plus or minus two" refers to the storage capacity of ________ memory.
   a. short-term
   b. explicit
   c. flashbulb
   d. implicit
   e. sensory

Short-term memory, p. 355
Difficult, Factual Definitional, Objective 4, Ans: a

52. Short-term memory is slightly better:
   a. for random digits than for random letters.
   b. for visual information than for auditory information.
   c. in children than in adults.
   d. in females than in males.

Long-term memory, p. 356
Easy, Factual/Definitional, Objective 5, Ans: c

53. Which type of memory has an essentially unlimited storage capacity?
   a. echoic memory
   b. short-term memory
   c. long-term memory
   d. state-dependent memory

Storing memories in the brain, p. 356
Medium, Factual/Definitional, Objective 5, Ans: d

54. Walter Penfield observed that electrical stimulation of the brains of wide-awake patients sometimes led them to report vivid recollections. Penfield incorrectly assumed that:
   a. his patients were inventing false memories.
   b. the brain's total storage capacity is very limited.
   c. the brain's physical memory trace decays gradually over time.
   d. the stimulation activated permanently stored memories.

Storing memories in the brain, pp. 356-357
Medium, Factual/Definitional, Objective 5, Ans: d

55. After hamsters learned whether to turn right or left in a maze in order to find food, their body temperature was lowered until the electrical activity in their brains ceased. When the hamsters were revived, they still remembered what they had learned prior to the "blackout." The hamsters' directional memory was apparently a(n) ________ memory.
a. sensory
b. repressed
c. state-dependent
d. long-term
e. implicit

Storing memories in the brain: synaptic changes, p. 357
Medium, Factual/Definitional, Objective 5, Ans: b

56. Research by Kandel and Schwartz on sea snails indicates that memory formation is associated with the:
a. structure of DNA molecules.
b. release of certain neurotransmitters.
c. activity level of the hippocampus.
d. development of the cerebellum.

Storing memories in the brain: synaptic changes, p. 357
Medium, Factual/Definitional, Objective 5, Ans: d

57. Long-term potentiation is a(n):
a. elimination of anxiety-producing thoughts from conscious awareness.
b. disruptive effect of prior learning on recall of new information.
c. process of getting information out of memory storage.
d. neural basis for memory.

Storing memories in the brain: synaptic changes, p. 357
Easy, Factual/Definitional, Objective 5, Ans: c

58. Passing an electric current through the brain during electroconvulsive therapy is most likely to disrupt ________ memory.
a. implicit
b. mood-congruent
c. short-term
d. flashbulb

Stress hormones and memory, p. 358
Difficult, Conceptual, Objective 5, Ans: d

59. The temporary release of stress hormones into the bloodstream facilitates:
a. repression.
b. source amnesia.
c. retroactive interference.
d. long-term potentiation.

Stress hormones and memory, p. 358
Difficult, Conceptual, Objective 5, Ans: d

60. Which of the following substances is most likely to facilitate the formation of new memories?
   a. alcohol, which often makes people feel relaxed and uninhibited
   b. Valium, a prescription drug that reduces tension and anxiety
   c. marijuana, which sometimes produces feelings of euphoria
   d. epinephrine, a physically and emotionally arousing hormone

Stress hormones and memory, p. 358
Medium, Factual/Definitional, Objective 5, Ans: c

61. By shrinking the hippocampus, prolonged stress is most likely to inhibit the process of:
   a. source misattribution.
   b. proactive interference.
   c. long-term memory storage.
   d. repression.

Storing implicit and explicit memories, p. 359
Medium, Factual/Definitional, Objective 6, Ans: d

62. The ability to learn something without any conscious memory of having learned it suggests the need to distinguish between:
   a. proactive and retroactive interference.
   b. short-term and long-term memory.
   c. recognition and recall.
   d. explicit and implicit memory.

Storing implicit and explicit memories, p. 359
Easy, Factual/Definitional, Objective 6, Ans: e

63. A retention of skills and dispositions without conscious recollection is known as ________ memory.
   a. state-dependent
   b. flashbulb
   c. short-term
   d. sensory
   e. implicit

Storing implicit and explicit memories, p. 359
Medium, Factual/Definitional, Objective 6, Ans: d

64. Remembering how to solve a jigsaw puzzle without any conscious recollection that one can do so best illustrates ________ memory.
   a. short-term
   b. explicit
   c. flashbulb
   d. implicit
   e. sensory

Storing implicit and explicit memories, p. 359
Medium, Conceptual, Objective 6, Ans: b

65. Memory of facts is to ________ as memory of skills is to ________.
 a. brainstem; hippocampus
 b. explicit memory; implicit memory
 c. automatic processing; effortful processing
 d. short-term memory; long-term memory

Storing implicit and explicit memories, p. 360
Easy, Factual/Definitional, Objective 6, Ans: b

66. The hippocampus plays a critical role in ________ memory.
 a. iconic
 b. explicit
 c. echoic
 d. implicit

Storing implicit and explicit memories, p. 360
Medium, Factual/Definitional, Objective 6, Ans: b

67. Damage to the ________ is most likely to interfere with explicit memories of newly learned verbal information. Damage to the ________ is most likely to interfere with explicit memories of newly learned visual designs.
 a. right hippocampus; left hippocampus
 b. left hippocampus; right hippocampus
 c. left hippocampus; right cerebellum
 d. right cerebellum; left cerebellum
 e. left cerebellum; right cerebellum

Storing implicit and explicit memories, p. 360
Medium, Conceptual/Application, Objective 6, Ans: c

68. Although Faustina can learn and remember how to read reversed mirror-image writing, she is unable to learn and remember the names of people to whom she has been introduced. Faustina is most likely to have suffered damage to her:
 a. hypothalamus.
 b. brainstem.
 c. hippocampus.
 d. cerebellum.

Storing implicit and explicit memories, p. 360
Medium, Factual/Definitional, Objective 6, Ans: e

69. Studies of the conditioned eye-blink response in rabbits suggest that implicit memories are stored in the:
 a. hypothalamus.
 b. association areas.
 c. motor cortex.
 d. hippocampus.
 e. cerebellum.

Storing implicit and explicit memories, p. 360
Medium, Conceptual, Objective 6, Ans: c

70. Cerebellum is to ________ memory as hippocampus is to ________ memory.
a. short-term; long-term
b. long-term; short-term
c. implicit; explicit
d. explicit; implicit
e. iconic; echoic

Storing implicit and explicit memories, p. 361
Difficult, Factual/Definitional, Objective 6, Ans: e

71. An understanding of the different brain circuits involved in implicit and explicit memories is most helpful for explaining:
a. the serial position effect.
b. the spacing effect.
c. repression.
d. state-dependent memory.
e. infantile amnesia.

Retrieval: getting information out, p. 361
Medium, Conceptual/Application, Objective 7, Ans: d

72. When an eyewitness to an auto accident is asked to describe what happened, which test of memory is being utilized?
a. reconstruction
b. recognition
c. rehearsal
d. recall
e. relearning

Retrieval: getting information out, p. 362
Medium, Conceptual/Application, Objective 7, Ans: b

73. Which memory test would most effectively reveal that Mr. Quintano, at age 55, still remembers many of his high school classmates?
a. recall
b. recognition
c. rehearsal
d. reconstruction

Retrieval: getting information out, pp. 361-362
Difficult, Conceptual, Objective 7, Ans: b

74. Which test of memory typically provides the fewest retrieval cues?
a. recognition
b. recall
c. relearning
d. rehearsal

Retrieval cues, p. 362
Easy, Factual/Definitional, Objective 8, Ans: a

75. Words, events, places, and emotions that trigger our memory of the past are called:
a. retrieval cues.
b. déjà vu.
c. iconic traces.
d. context effects.
e. schemas.

Retrieval cues, p. 362
Easy, Conceptual/Application, Objective 8, Ans: d

76. When 80-year-old Ida looked at her old wedding pictures, she was flooded with vivid memories of her parents, her husband, and the early years of her marriage. The pictures served as powerful:
a. encoding devices.
b. iconic memories.
c. automatic processing devices.
d. retrieval cues.

Retrieval cues, p. 362
Easy, Factual/Definitional, Objective 8, Ans: b

77. Memories are primed by:
a. repression.
b. retrieval cues.
c. retroactive interference.
d. the serial position effect.
e. source amnesia.

Retrieval cues, p. 362
Medium, Factual/Definitional, Objective 8, Ans: e

78. Hearing the word "rabbit" may lead people to spell the spoken word "hair" as "h-a-r-e." This best illustrates the outcome of a process known as:
a. chunking.
b. retroactive interference.
c. the method of loci.
d. repression.
e. priming.

Retrieval cues, p. 362
Difficult, Conceptual/Application, Objective 8, Ans: e

79. Watching a TV soap opera involving marital conflict and divorce led Andrea to recall several instances in which her husband had mistreated her. The effect of the TV program on Andrea's recall provides an example of:
a. the spacing effect.
b. repression.
c. the serial position effect.
d. automatic processing.
e. priming.

Context effects, p. 363
Medium, Factual/Definitional, Objective 8, Ans: b

80. After learning that kicking would move a crib mobile, infants showed that they recalled this learning best if they were tested in the same crib. This best illustrates the effect of ________ on recall.
    a. the serial position effect
    b. retrieval cues
    c. state-dependent memory
    d. the spacing effect
    e. the method of loci

Context effects, p. 363
Easy, Factual/Definitional, Objective 8, Ans: d

81. Déjà vu refers to the:
    a. emotional arousal produced by events that prime us to recall associated events.
    b. tendency to remember experiences that are consistent with one's current mood.
    c. unconscious activation of particular associations in memory.
    d. eerie sense of having previously experienced a situation or event.

Moods and memories, p. 364
Medium, Conceptual, Objective 8, Ans: e

82. After his last drinking spree, Fakim hid a half-empty liquor bottle. He couldn't remember where he hid it until he started drinking again. Fakim's pattern of recall best illustrates:
    a. the spacing effect.
    b. proactive interference.
    c. the serial position effect.
    d. motivated forgetting.
    e. state-dependent memory.

Moods and memories, p. 364
Medium, Factual/Definitional, Objective 8, Ans: d

83. Mood-congruent memory refers to the effect of emotional states on the process of:
    a. repression.
    b. encoding.
    c. storage.
    d. retrieval.
    e. relearning.

Moods and memories, p. 364
Medium, Factual/Definitional, Objective 8, Ans: e

84. Negative associations primed by distressing emotions most clearly illustrate:
    a. repression.
    b. retroactive interference.
    c. the misinformation effect.
    d. proactive interference.
    e. mood-congruent memory.

Moods and memories, p. 364
Medium, Conceptual/Application, Objective 8, Ans: c

85. Whenever he feels sexually jealous, David is flooded with painful recollections of the rare occasions in which he had observed his girlfriend flirting with other men. David's experience best illustrates:
a. source misattribution.
b. retroactive interference.
c. mood-congruent memory.
d. the misinformation effect.
e. repression.

Moods and memories, p. 364
Medium, Factual/Definitional, Objective 8, Ans: b

86. The effect of moods on our interpretation of new information suggests that our emotional states influence the process of:
a. repression.
b. encoding.
c. storage.
d. retrieval.
e. priming.

Forgetting, p. 365
Medium, Factual/Definitional, Objective 9, Ans: c

87. A person who has trouble forgetting information, such as the Russian memory whiz S, often seems to have a limited capacity for:
a. implicit memory.
b. explicit memory.
c. abstract thinking.
d. visual imagery.

Forgetting, p. 365
Easy, Factual/Definitional, Objective 9, Ans: c

88. In describing what he calls the seven sins of memory, Daniel Schacter suggests that storage decay contributes to:
a. absent-mindedness.
b. repression.
c. transience.
d. implicit memory.

Forgetting, p. 365
Medium, Conceptual, Objective 9, Ans: b

89. In considering the seven sins of memory, misattribution is to the sin of ________ as blocking is to the sin of ________.
a. retroactive interference; proactive interference
b. distortion; forgetting
c. proactive interference; retroactive interference
d. intrusion; distortion

Encoding failure, p. 366
Difficult, Factual/Definitional, Objective 9, Ans: a

90. The inability to recall which numbers on a telephone dial are not accompanied by letters is most likely due to:
a. encoding failure.
b. retrieval failure.
c. the spacing effect.
d. retroactive interference.
e. proactive interference.

Encoding failure, p. 366
Easy, Factual/Definitional, Objective 9, Ans: a

91. The inability to remember how Lincoln's head appears on a penny is most likely due to a failure in:
a. encoding.
b. storage.
c. retrieval.
d. implicit memory.
e. iconic memory.

Storage decay, p. 367
Medium, Factual/Definitional, Objective 9, Ans: a

92. The famous Ebbinghaus "forgetting curve" indicates that how well we remember information depends on:
a. how long ago we learned that information.
b. the nature of our mood during encoding and retrieval.
c. whether the information is part of our implicit or explicit memory.
d. whether the information was acoustically or visually encoded.

Storage decay, p. 367
Difficult, Factual/Definitional, Objective 9, Ans: d

93. Ebbinghaus discovered that the rate at which we forget newly learned information is initially ________ and subsequently ________.
a. slow; stays slow
b. slow; speeds up
c. rapid; stays rapid
d. rapid; slows down

Retrieval failure, p. 368
Medium, Conceptual/Application, Objective 10, Ans: d

94. Judy is embarrassed because she suddenly cannot remember a friend's name. Judy's poor memory most likely results from a failure in:
a. storage.
b. encoding.
c. rehearsal.
d. retrieval.
e. automatic processing.

Retrieval failure, p. 368
Medium, Conceptual/Application, Objective 10, Ans: d

95. The title of a song is on the tip of Gerard's tongue, but he cannot recall it until someone mentions the songwriter's name. Gerard's initial inability to recall the title was most likely caused by:
    a. a physical decay of stored memory.
    b. encoding failure.
    c. state-dependent memory.
    d. retrieval failure.
    e. repression.

Retrieval failure, p. 368
Medium, Factual/Definitional, Objective 10, Ans: d

96. The fact that elderly people are often less able than younger adults to recall previously learned information can be best explained in terms of the greater difficulty older people have with:
    a. automatic processing.
    b. iconic memory.
    c. state-dependent memory.
    d. retrieval.
    e. implicit memory.

Interference, p. 368
Easy, Factual/Definitional, Objective 10, Ans: e

97. The disruptive effect of prior learning on the recall of new information is called:
    a. state-dependent memory.
    b. retroactive interference.
    c. the serial position effect.
    d. the spacing effect.
    e. proactive interference.

Interference, p. 368
Medium, Conceptual/Application, Objective 10, Ans: d

98. Arnold so easily remembers his old girlfriend's telephone number that he finds it difficult to recall his new girlfriend's number. Arnold's difficulty best illustrates:
    a. retroactive interference.
    b. the next-in-line effect.
    c. source amnesia.
    d. proactive interference.
    e. repression.

Interference, p. 368
Medium, Conceptual/Application, Objective 10, Ans: c

99. After learning the combination for his new locker at school, Milton is unable to remember the combination for his year-old bicycle lock. Milton is experiencing the effects of:
    a. encoding failure.
    b. source amnesia.
    c. retroactive interference.
    d. proactive interference.
    e. automatic processing.

Interference, p. 368
Medium, Factual/Definitional, Objective 10, Ans: c

100. Retroactive interference involves the disruption of:
a. encoding.
b. storage.
c. retrieval.
d. all of the above.

Interference, pp. 368-369
Easy, Factual/Definitional, Objective 10, Ans: e

101. The finding that people who sleep after learning a list of nonsense syllables forget less than people who stay awake provides evidence that forgetting may involve:
a. encoding failure.
b. repression.
c. implicit memory loss.
d. the hippocampus.
e. interference.

Motivated forgetting, p. 370
Medium, Conceptual/Application, Objective 10, Ans: d

102. Compulsive gamblers frequently recall losing less money than is actually the case. Their memory failure best illustrates:
a. source amnesia.
b. proactive interference.
c. the serial position effect.
d. motivated forgetting.
e. the next-in-line effect.

Motivated forgetting, p. 370
Difficult, Factual/Definitional, Objective 10, Ans: c

103. Michael Ross and his colleagues observed that people exposed to very convincing arguments about the desirability of frequent toothbrushing tended to:
a. quickly forget the arguments if they were in the habit of brushing frequently.
b. quickly forget the arguments if they were not in the habit of brushing frequently.
c. exaggerate how frequently they had brushed their teeth in the past.
d. exaggerate how infrequently they had brushed their teeth in the past.

Motivated forgetting, p. 370
Easy, Factual/Definitional, Objective 10, Ans: d

104. A type of motivated forgetting in which painful memories are blocked from conscious awareness is:
a. retroactive interference.
b. proactive interference.
c. the spacing effect.
d. repression.
e. priming.

Motivated forgetting, p. 370
Medium, Conceptual, Objective 10, Ans: d

105. Sigmund Freud emphasized that the forgetting of painful experiences is caused by a process that involves:
  a. source amnesia.
  b. retroactive interference.
  c. memory decay.
  d. retrieval failure.
  e. long-term potentiation.

Memory construction, p. 372
Medium, Factual/Definitional, Objective 11, Ans: b

106. Research on memory construction indicates that memories of past experiences are likely to be:
  a. difficult to retrieve but never completely lost.
  b. distorted by our current assumptions.
  c. much more vivid if they are seldom rehearsed.
  d. retrieved in the very same form and detail as they were originally encoded.

Memory construction, p. 372
Difficult, Factual/Definitional, Objective 11, Ans: c

107. Our schemas often influence the form in which information is retrieved from long-term memory. This fact is most relevant to appreciating the importance of:
  a. long-term potentiation.
  b. automatic processing.
  c. memory construction.
  d. the spacing effect.
  e. visual encoding.

Misinformation and imagination effects, p. 372
Medium, Factual/Definitional, Objective 11, Ans: d

108. Many of the experimental participants who were asked how fast two cars in a filmed traffic accident were going when they smashed into each other subsequently recalled seeing broken glass at the scene of the accident. This experiment best illustrated:
  a. proactive interference.
  b. the self-reference effect.
  c. the spacing effect.
  d. the misinformation effect.
  e. state-dependent memory.

Misinformation and imagination effects, p. 372
Difficult, Factual/Definitional, Objective 11, Ans: a

109. Loftus and Palmer asked two groups of observers how fast two cars had been going in a filmed traffic accident. Observers who heard the vividly descriptive word "smashed" in relation to the accident later recalled:
  a. broken glass at the scene of the accident.
  b. that the drivers of the vehicles were intoxicated.
  c. that the drivers of the vehicles were males.
  d. the details of the accident with vivid accuracy.

Misinformation and imagination effects, p. 372
Medium, Conceptual/Application, Objective 11, Ans: e

110. After reading a newspaper report suggesting that drunken driving might have contributed to a recent auto accident, several people who actually witnessed the accident began to remember the driver involved as traveling at a greater speed than was actually the case. This provides an example of:
   a. proactive interference.
   b. the serial position effect.
   c. state-dependent memory.
   d. the self-reference effect.
   e. the misinformation effect.

Misinformation and imagination effects, p. 372
Medium, Factual/Definitional, Objective 11, Ans: b

111. The misinformation effect best illustrates the dynamics of:
   a. automatic processing.
   b. memory construction.
   c. repression.
   d. proactive interference.
   e. mood-congruent memory.

Misinformation and imagination effects, pp. 372-373
Medium, Factual/Definitional, Objective 11, Ans: a

112. Research on the misinformation effect indicates that:
   a. events from the distant past are especially vulnerable to memory distortion.
   b. people can easily distinguish between their own true and false memories.
   c. hypnotic suggestion is an effective technique for accurate memory retrieval.
   d. it is very difficult to lead people to construct memories of events that never happened.

Source amnesia, p. 374
Medium, Factual/Definitional, Objective 11, Ans: c

113. The psychologist Jean Piaget constructed a vivid, detailed memory of being kidnapped after hearing his nursemaid's false reports of such an event. His experience best illustrates:
   a. implicit memory.
   b. proactive interference.
   c. source amnesia.
   d. mood-congruent memory.
   e. the self-reference effect.

Source amnesia, p. 374
Medium, Conceptual/Application, Objective 11, Ans: e

114. After attending group therapy sessions for adult survivors of childhood sexual abuse, Karen mistakenly remembered details from others' traumatic life stories as part of her own life history. This best illustrates the dangers of:
   a. proactive interference.
   b. mood-congruent memory.
   c. the self-reference effect.
   d. implicit memory.
   e. source amnesia.

Source amnesia, p. 374
Medium, Conceptual/Application, Objective 11, Ans: e

115. As a child, Andre experienced a vivid dream in which he was chased and attacked by a ferocious dog. Many years later, he mistakenly recalled that this had actually happened to him. Andre's false recollection best illustrates:
a. the self-reference effect.
b. mood-congruent memory.
c. proactive interference.
d. implicit memory.
e. source amnesia.

Discerning true and false memories, p. 375
Difficult, Factual/Definitional, Objective 12, Ans: c

116. We often cannot reliably distinguish between true and false memories because:
a. false memories activate the identical brain regions as true ones.
b. false memories contain the same level of detail as true ones.
c. false memories are often just as durable as true ones.
d. all of the above are true.

Discerning true and false memories, p. 375
Difficult, Factual/Definitional, Objective 12, Ans: d

117. PET scans reveal that the ________ is equally active whether an individual falsely or correctly remembers that specific words were read to him or her.
a. cerebral cortex
b. left temporal lobe
c. cerebellum
d. hippocampus

Discerning true and false memories, pp. 375-376
Medium, Conceptual/Application, Objective 12, Ans: b

118. Karl and Dee had a joyful wedding ceremony. After their painful divorce, however, they began to remember the wedding as a somewhat hectic, unpleasant, and frightening event. Their recollections best illustrate the nature of:
a. proactive interference.
b. memory construction.
c. the spacing effect.
d. the serial position effect.
e. repression.

Discerning true and false memories, p. 376
Medium, Factual/Definitional, Objective 12, Ans: a

119. When asked to recall their attitudes of 10 years ago regarding marijuana use, people offer recollections closer to their current view than they actually reported a decade earlier. This best illustrates:
a. memory construction.
b. proactive interference.
c. the self-reference effect.
d. mood-congruent memory.
e. repression.

Discerning true and false memories, p. 376
Medium, Factual/Definitional, Objective 12, Ans: b

120. Police interrogators have been trained to ask less suggestive and more effective questions in order to avoid:
   a. long-term potentiation.
   b. the misinformation effect.
   c. mood-congruent memory.
   d. proactive interference.
   e. the next-in-line effect.

Children's eyewitness recall, p. 376
Easy, Factual/Definitional, Objective 12, Ans: c

121. Which of the following poses the greatest threat to the credibility of children's recollections of sexual abuse?
   a. the serial position effect
   b. the spacing effect
   c. the misinformation effect
   d. long-term potentiation
   e. the next-in-line effect

Children's eyewitness recall, p. 376
Difficult, Factual/Definitional, Objective 12, Ans: d

122. When children are officially interviewed about their recollections of possible sexual abuse, their reports are especially credible if:
   a. they are asked specific, detailed questions about the issue rather than more general, open-ended questions.
   b. after responding to an interviewer, they are repeatedly asked the same question they just answered.
   c. they use anatomically correct dolls to indicate if and where they had been physically touched.
   d. involved adults have not discussed the issue with them prior to the interview.

Children's eyewitness recall, p. 377
Medium, Factual/Definitional, Objective 12, Ans: c

123. Research on young children's false eyewitness recollections has indicated that:
   a. children are less susceptible to source amnesia than adults.
   b. children are no more susceptible to the misinformation effect than adults.
   c. it is surprisingly difficult for both children and professional interviewers to reliably separate the children's true memories from false memories.
   d. all of the above are true.

Repressed or constructed memories of abuse?, pp. 377-378
Medium, Conceptual/Application, Objective 13, Ans: e

124. Incest survivors who lack conscious memories of their sexual abuse are sometimes told that they are simply in a stage of "denial." This explanation for their lack of abuse memories emphasizes:
   a. proactive interference.
   b. encoding failure.
   c. the misinformation effect.
   d. source amnesia.
   e. retrieval failure.

Repressed or constructed memories of abuse?, pp. 378-379
Easy, Factual/Definitional, Objective 13, Ans: d

125. Which of the following techniques used by professional therapists are highly likely to promote the construction of false memories?
   a. hypnosis
   b. dream analysis
   c. imagination-enhancing exercises
   d. all of the above

Repressed or constructed memories of abuse?, p. 379
Difficult, Factual/Definitional, Objective 13, Ans: d

126. Adults with symptoms of distress commonly experienced by incest survivors have often been advised and encouraged to recover memories of sexual abuse that they might have experienced in childhood. A major shortcoming of this advice is that:
   a. most extremely stressful life experiences are never encoded into long-term memory.
   b. it is very difficult to retrieve stored memories that have not been recalled for a long period of time.
   c. by the time one experiences the symptoms of distress that result from abuse, there is very little one can do to find relief.
   d. people experience these symptoms of distress for a variety of reasons other than sexual abuse.

Repressed or constructed memories of abuse?, p. 379
Medium, Factual/Definitional, Objective 13, Ans: e

127. With respect to the controversy regarding reports of repressed memories of sexual abuse, statements by major psychological and psychiatric associations suggest that:
   a. the accumulated experiences of our lives are all preserved somewhere in our minds.
   b. the more stressful an experience is, the more quickly it will be consciously forgotten.
   c. repression is the most common mechanism underlying the failure to recall early childhood abuse.
   d. professional therapists can reliably distinguish between their clients' true and false childhood memories.
   e. adult memories of experiences happening before age 3 are unreliable.

Repressed or constructed memories of abuse?, p. 380
Medium, Conceptual, Objective 13, Ans: d

128. When memory researcher Elizabeth Loftus was an adolescent, her uncle incorrectly insisted that as a child she had found her own mother's drowned body. Loftus herself later falsely recollected finding the body. This best illustrates:
   a. proactive interference.
   b. implicit memory.
   c. the self-reference effect.
   d. the misinformation effect.
   e. mood-congruent memory.

Repressed or constructed memories of abuse?, p. 380
Medium, Factual/Definitional, Objective 13, Ans: d

129. Memory experts who express skepticism regarding reports of repressed and recovered memories are most likely to emphasize that:
   a. people rarely recall memories of long-forgotten events.
   b. most extremely traumatic life experiences are never encoded into long-term memory.
   c. only those memories that are recovered with the help of a professional psychotherapist are likely to be reliable.
   d. extremely stressful life experiences are especially likely to be well remembered.

Improving memory, p. 381
Easy, Factual/Definitional, Objective 14, Ans: e

130. Speed-reading complex material yields little long-term retention because it inhibits:
   a. the serial position effect.
   b. retroactive interference.
   c. the next-in-line effect.
   d. proactive interference.
   e. rehearsal.

Essay Questions

1. A friend claims that the faster you read, the more you remember. Use your knowledge of effortful processing and effective encoding strategies to refute your friend's claim.

2. Describe three mnemonic devices that would enable you to remember the following list of grocery items: milk, eggs, margarine, oranges, rhubarb, ice cream, eggplant, and sausage. Explain why each would be effective.

3. Although you genuinely enjoyed studying hard for a biology exam, during the test you are feeling frustrated and irritable because you can't recall the answer to a series of fairly easy factual questions. What techniques could you use to effectively remember the information previously learned?

4. Professor Markus is a brilliant mathematician who is 70 years old and still enjoys teaching. Over the past few years she has experienced increasing difficulty remembering the names of her students. Suggest several possible explanations for the professor's increasing memory failure.

5. During the process of psychotherapy, Elaine accurately recovered some long-forgotten and painful memories from her childhood. This experience led her to conclude that these memories must have been repressed for many years. Use your understanding of the nature of memory to refute Elaine's conclusion.

Web Quiz 1

Ans: c

1. After suffering a brain injury in a motorcycle accident, Adam cannot form new memories. He can, however, remember his life experiences before the accident. Adam's memory difficulty most clearly illustrates:
   a. repression.
   b. retroactive interference.
   c. encoding failure.
   d. source amnesia.
   e. motivated forgetting.

Ans: d

2. The extensive rehearsal necessary to encode nonsense syllables best illustrates:
   a. the spacing effect.
   b. implicit memory.
   c. the serial position effect.
   d. effortful processing.
   e. chunking.

Ans: e

3. At a block party, Cyndi is introduced to eight new neighbors. Moments later, she can only remember the names of the first three and last two neighbors. Her experience illustrates:
   a. source amnesia.
   b. the next-in-line effect.
   c. the spacing effect.
   d. implicit memory.
   e. the serial position effect.

Ans: b

4. Although Jordan could not recall the exact words of a poem he had recently heard, he clearly remembered the meaning of the poem. This best illustrates the importance of:
   a. implicit memory.
   b. semantic encoding.
   c. mood-congruent memory.
   d. the serial position effect.
   e. the method of loci.

Ans: c

5. It is easier to remember "what sobriety conceals, alcohol reveals" than to recall "what sobriety conceals, alcohol unmasks." This best illustrates the value of:
   a. the serial position effect.
   b. mood-congruent memory.
   c. acoustic encoding.
   d. the spacing effect.
   e. implicit memory.

Ans: d

6. Employing the single word "HOMES" to remember the names of North America's five Great Lakes best illustrates the use of:
   a. the "peg-word" system.
   b. the method of loci.
   c. the serial position effect.
   d. a mnemonic device.
   e. implicit memory.

Ans: e

7. Which of the following is believed to be the biological basis for learning and memory?
   a. priming
   b. chunking
   c. semantic encoding
   d. proactive interference
   e. long-term potentiation

Ans: c

8. Mr. Nydam suffers amnesia and is unable to remember playing golf on a particular course. Yet the more he plays the course, the more his game improves. His experience illustrates the need to distinguish between:
   a. short-term and long-term memory.
   b. proactive and retroactive interference.
   c. explicit and implicit memory.
   d. recognition and recall.

Ans: a

9. Memories of emotional events are especially likely to be facilitated by activation of the:
   a. amygdala.
   b. hypothalamus.
   c. sensory cortex.
   d. motor cortex.

Ans: c

10. A measure of your memory in which you need to pick the correctly learned answer from a displayed list of options is known as a measure of:
   a. recall.
   b. rehearsal.
   c. recognition.
   d. reconstruction.
   e. relearning.

Ans: a

11. The happier Judie is, the more readily she recalls her teachers as warm and generous. This best illustrates that emotional states can be:
   a. retrieval cues.
   b. short-term memories.
   c. visually encoded.
   d. sensory memories.
   e. flashbulb memories.

Ans: b

12. During her evening Spanish language exam, Janica so easily remembers the French vocabulary she studied that morning that she finds it difficult to recall the Spanish vocabulary she rehearsed that afternoon. Her difficulty best illustrates:
    a. the spacing effect.
    b. proactive interference.
    c. source amnesia.
    d. state-dependent memory.
    e. retroactive interference.

Ans: e

13. Mrs. McBride can't remember how frequently she criticizes her children because it would be too embarrassing for her. Sigmund Freud would have suggested that her poor memory illustrates:
    a. source amnesia.
    b. proactive interference.
    c. the self-reference effect.
    d. automatic processing.
    e. repression.

Ans: c

14. When 6-year-old Teresa reported that she had been verbally threatened by a stranger in a passing car, her mother asked her what color car the man was driving. Several hours later Teresa mistakenly recalled that she had been threatened by a male driver rather than by a female passenger. Teresa's experience best illustrates:
    a. implicit memory.
    b. proactive interference.
    c. the misinformation effect.
    d. state-dependent memory.
    e. the serial position effect.

Ans: d

15. Recalling something that you had once merely imagined happening as something you had directly experienced best illustrates:
    a. the self-reference effect.
    b. mood-congruent memory.
    c. proactive interference
    d. source amnesia.
    e. implicit memory

Web Quiz 2

Ans: b

1. Many people can easily recall exactly what they were doing when they heard the news of the 9/11 terrorist tragedy. This best illustrates ________ memory.
   a. echoic
   b. flashbulb
   c. implicit
   d. iconic
   e. state-dependent

Ans: c

2. When you hear familiar words in your native language, it is virtually impossible not to register the meanings of the words. This best illustrates the importance of:
   a. chunking.
   b. flashbulb memory.
   c. automatic processing.
   d. iconic memory.
   e. the spacing effect.

Ans: a

3. An understanding of the spacing effect provides insight into effective strategies for:
   a. encoding.
   b. echoic memory.
   c. chunking.
   d. state-dependent memory.
   e. automatic processing.

Ans: d

4. Ebbinghaus observed that it is much easier to learn meaningful material than to learn nonsense material. This best illustrates the advantage of:
   a. the "peg-word" system.
   b. the spacing effect.
   c. mood-congruent memory.
   d. semantic encoding.
   e. implicit memory.

Ans: a

5. The method of loci relies heavily on the use of:
   a. visual encoding.
   b. implicit memory.
   c. the spacing effect.
   d. the self-reference effect.
   e. mood-congruent memory.

Ans: e

6. The combination of individual letters into familiar words enables you to remember more of the letters in this sentence. This best illustrates the value of:
   a. the spacing effect.
   b. iconic memory.
   c. the "peg-word" system.
   d. the method of loci.
   e. chunking.

Ans: c

7. When you have to make a long-distance call, dialing an unfamiliar area code plus a seven-digit number, you are likely to have trouble retaining the just-looked-up number. This best illustrates the limited capacity of ________ memory.
   a. long-term
   b. implicit
   c. short-term
   d. explicit
   e. flashbulb

Ans: a

8 Certain amnesic patients are incapable of recalling activities, yet they can be conditioned to blink their eyes in response to a specific sound. They have most likely suffered damage to the:
   a. hippocampus.
   b. cerebellum.
   c. hypothalamus.
   d. amygdala.

Ans: c

9 Which of the following is most likely to be stored as an implicit memory?
   a. a mental image of one's best friend
   b. the date of one's own birth
   c. a conditioned fear of guns
   d. one's own name

Ans: e

10. In an effort to recall his early life experiences, Aaron formed vivid mental images of the various rooms in his childhood home. Aaron was engaging in the process of:
   a. automatic processing.
   b. implicit memory.
   c. semantic encoding.
   d. iconic memory.
   e. priming.

Ans: b

11. Whenever Valerie experiences intense feelings of fear, she is overwhelmed with childhood memories of her abusive parents. Valerie's experience best illustrates:
   a. repression.
   b. mood-congruent memory.
   c. retroactive interference.
   d. the misinformation effect.
   e. implicit memory.

Ans: e

12. While taking the final exam in her American history class, Marie was surprised and frustrated by her momentary inability to remember the name of the first president of the United States. Her difficulty most clearly illustrates:
    a. source amnesia.
    b. state-dependent memory.
    c. the serial position effect.
    d. the self-reference effect.
    e. retrieval failure.

Ans: b

13. Although Ron typically smokes two packs of cigarettes a day, he recalls smoking little more than a pack a day. This poor memory best illustrates:
    a. the misinformation effect.
    b. motivated forgetting.
    c. the spacing effect.
    d. source amnesia.
    e. the self-reference effect.

Ans: d

14. The surprising ease with which people form false memories best illustrates that the processes of encoding and retrieval involve:
    a. implicit memory.
    b. automatic processing.
    c. long-term potentiation.
    d. memory construction.
    e. repression.

Ans: c

15. Several months after watching a science fiction movie about spaceship travel and alien abductions, Steve began to remember that he had been abducted by aliens and personally subjected to many of the horrors portrayed in the movie. His mistaken recall best illustrates:
    a. implicit memory.
    b. the spacing effect.
    c. source amnesia.
    d. mood-congruent memory.
    e. repression.

Study Guide Questions

Ans: d, p. 345

1. The three steps in memory information processing are:
   a. input, processing, output.
   b. input, storage, output.
   c. input, storage, retrieval.
   d. encoding, storage, retrieval.
   e. encoding, retrieval, storage.

Ans: b, p. 345

2. The process of getting information out of memory storage is called:
   a. encoding.
   b. retrieval.
   c. rehearsal.
   d. storage.

Ans: d, p. 345

3. Which of the following is the best example of a flashbulb memory?
   a. suddenly remembering to buy bread while standing in the checkout line at the grocery store
   b. recalling the name of someone from high school while looking at his or her yearbook snapshot
   c. remembering to make an important phone call
   d. remembering what you were doing on September 11, 2001, when terrorists crashed planes into the World Trade Center towers

Ans: a, pp. 345-346

4. The three-stage processing model of memory was proposed by:
   a. Atkinson and Shifrin.
   b. Herman Ebbinghaus.
   c. Loftus and Palmer.
   d. George Sperling.

Ans: b, p. 346

5. The concept of working memory is analogous to a computer's:
   a. read-only memory (ROM).
   b. random-access memory (RAM).
   c. mouse.
   d. keyboard.

Ans: a, p. 347

6. The first thing Karen did when she discovered that she had misplaced her keys was to re-create in her mind the day's events. That she had little difficulty in doing so illustrates:
   a. automatic processing.
   b. effortful processing.
   c. state-dependent memory.
   d. priming.

Ans: b, p. 347
7. Information is maintained in short-term memory only briefly unless it is:
a. encoded.
b. rehearsed.
c. iconic or echoic.
d. retrieved.

Ans: b, pp. 347, 350
8. Although you can't recall the answer to a question on your psychology midterm, you have a clear mental image of the textbook page on which it appears. Evidently, your ________ encoding of the answer was ________.
a. semantic; automatic
b. visual; automatic
c. semantic; effortful
d. visual; effortful

Ans: a, p. 348
9. The spacing effect means that:
a. distributed study yields better retention than cramming.
b. retention is improved when encoding and retrieval are separated by no more than one hour.
c. learning causes a reduction in the size of the synaptic gap between certain neurons.
d. delaying retrieval until memory has consolidated improves recall.

Ans: e, p. 349
10. According to the serial position effect, when recalling a list of words you should have the greatest difficulty with those:
a. at the beginning of the list.
b. at the end of the list.
c. at the end and in the middle of the list.
d. at the beginning and end of the list.
e. in the middle of the list.

Ans: a, p. 349
11. Experimenters gave people a list of words to be recalled. When the participants were tested after a delay, the items that were best recalled were those:
a. at the beginning of the list.
b. in the middle of the list.
c. at the end of the list.
d. at the beginning and the end of the list.

Ans: d, p. 350
12. Darren was asked to memorize a list of letters that included *v*, *q*, *y*, and *j*. He later recalled these letters as *e*, *u*, *i*, and *k*, suggesting that the original letters had been encoded:
a. automatically.
b. visually.
c. semantically.
d. acoustically.

Ans: c, p. 350

13. Craik and Tulving had research participants process words visually, acoustically, or semantically. In a subsequent recall test, which type of processing resulted in the greatest retention?
    a. visual
    b. acoustic
    c. semantic
    d. acoustic and semantic processing were equally beneficial

Ans: d, p. 351

14. Memory techniques such as the method of loci, acronyms, and the peg-word system are called:
    a. consolidation devices.
    b. imagery techniques.
    c. encoding strategies.
    d. mnemonic devices.

Ans: c, p. 351

15. To help him remember the order of ingredients in difficult recipes, master chef Giulio often associates them with the route he walks to work each day. Giulio is using which mnemonic technique?
    a. peg-word system
    b. acronyms
    c. the method of loci
    d. chunking

Ans: e, p. 352

16. One way to increase the amount of information in memory is to group it into larger, familiar units. This process is referred to as:
    a. consolidating.
    b. organization.
    c. memory construction.
    d. encoding.
    e. chunking.

Ans: c, p. 353

17. Textbook chapters are often organized into ________ in order to facilitate information processing.
    a. mnemonic devices
    b. chunks
    c. hierarchies
    d. recognizable units

Ans: b, p. 353

18. When Gordon Bower presented words grouped by category or in random order, recall was:
    a. the same for all words.
    b. better for the categorized words.
    c. better for the random words.
    d. improved when participants developed their own mnemonic devices.

Ans: a, p. 354

19. Visual sensory memory is referred to as:
    a. iconic memory.
    b. echoic memory.
    c. photomemory.
    d. semantic memory.

Ans: d, p. 354

20. In Sperling's memory experiment, research participants were shown three rows of three letters, followed immediately by a low-, medium-, or high-pitched tone. The participants were able to report:
    a. all three rows with perfect accuracy.
    b. only the top row of letters.
    c. only the middle row of letters.
    d. any one of the three rows of letters.

Ans: e, p. 355

21. Echoic memories fade after approximately:
    a. 1 hour.
    b. 1 minute.
    c. 30 seconds.
    d. 1 second.
    e. 3 to 4 seconds.

Ans: c, p. 355

22. It is easier to recall information that has just been presented when the information:
    a. consists of random letters rather than words.
    b. is seen rather than heard.
    c. is heard rather than seen.
    d. is experienced in an unusual context.

Ans: c, p. 355

23. Our short-term memory span is approximately ________ items.
    a. 2
    b. 5
    c. 7
    d. 10

Ans: a, p. 355

24. Brenda has trouble remembering her new five-digit zip plus four-digit address code. What is the most likely explanation for the difficulty Brenda is having?
    a. Nine digits are at or above the upper limit of most people's short-term memory capacity.
    b. Nine digits are at or above the upper limit of most people's iconic memory capacity.
    c. The extra four digits cannot be organized into easily remembered chunks.
    d. Brenda evidently has an impaired implicit memory.

Ans: d, p. 356

25. Lashley's studies, in which rats learned a maze and then had various parts of their brains surgically removed, showed that the memory:
 a. was lost when surgery took place within 1 hour of learning.
 b. was lost when surgery took place within 24 hours of learning.
 c. was lost when any region of the brain was removed.
 d. remained no matter which area of the brain was tampered with.

Ans: c, p. 357

26. Studies demonstrate that learning causes permanent neural changes in the ________ of animals' neurons.
 a. myelin
 b. cell bodies
 c. synapses
 d. all of the above

Ans: c, p. 357

27. Kandel and Schwartz have found that when learning occurs, more of the neurotransmitter ________ is released into synapses.
 a. ACh
 b. dopamine
 c. serotonin
 d. noradrenaline

Ans: a, p. 357

28. The disruption of memory that occurs when football players have been knocked out provides evidence for the importance of:
 a. consolidation in the formation of new memories.
 b. consolidation in the retrieval of long-term memories.
 c. nutrition in normal neural functioning.
 d. all of the above.

Ans: d, p. 357

29. *Long-term potentiation* refers to:
 a. the disruptive influence of old memories on the formation of new memories.
 b. the disruptive influence of recent memories on the retrieval of old memories.
 c. our tendency to recall experiences that are consistent with our current mood.
 d. the increased efficiency of synaptic transmission between certain neurons following learning.
 e. our increased ability to recall long-ago events as we grow older.

Ans: c, pp. 357-358

30. During basketball practice, Jan's head was painfully elbowed. If the trauma to her brain disrupts her memory, we would expect that Jan would be most likely to forget:
 a. the name of her teammates.
 b. her telephone number.
 c. the name of the play during which she was elbowed.
 d. the details of events that happened shortly after the incident.

Ans: d, p. 359

31. Memory for skills is called:
    a. explicit memory.
    b. declarative memory.
    c. episodic memory.
    d. implicit memory.

Ans: b, p. 359

32. Studies of amnesia victims suggest that:
    a. memory is a single, unified system.
    b. there are two distinct types of memory.
    c. there are three distinct types of memory.
    d. memory losses following brain trauma are unpredictable.
    e. brain trauma eliminates the ability to learn.

Ans: c, p. 359

33. Elderly Mr. Flanagan can easily recall his high school graduation, but he cannot remember the name of the president of the United States. Evidently, Mr. Flanagan's ________ memory is better than his ________ memory.
    a. implicit; explicit
    b. explicit; implicit
    c. episodic; semantic
    d. semantic; episodic

Ans: b, p. 359

34. Amnesia patients typically experience disruption of:
    a. implicit memories.
    b. explicit memories.
    c. iconic memories.
    d. echoic memories.

Ans: c, p. 360

35. After suffering damage to the hippocampus, a person would probably:
    a. lose memory for skills such as bicycle riding.
    b. be incapable of being classically conditioned.
    c. lose the ability to store new facts.
    d. experience all of the above changes.

Ans: d, p. 360

36. Amnesia victims typically have experienced damage to the ________ of the brain.
    a. frontal lobes
    b. cerebellum
    c. thalamus
    d. hippocampus
    e. cortex

Ans: b, pp. 360-361

37. Which area of the brain is most important in the processing of implicit memories?
    a. hippocampus
    b. cerebellum
    c. hypothalamus
    d. amygdala

Ans: a, p. 361

38. Which of the following has been proposed as a neurophysiological explanation of infantile amnesia?
    a. The slow maturation of the hippocampus leaves the infant's brain unable to store images and events.
    b. The deficient supply of serotonin until about age 3 makes encoding very limited.
    c. The limited availability of association areas of the cortex until about age 3 impairs encoding and storage.
    d. All of the above explanations have been proposed.

Ans: a, p. 361

39. Which of the following measures of retention is the least sensitive in triggering retrieval?
    a. recall
    b. recognition
    c. relearning
    d. déjà vu

Ans: d, pp. 361-362

40. Which of the following is *not* a measure of retention?
    a. recall
    b. recognition
    c. relearning
    d. retrieval

Ans: d, pp. 361-362

41. Complete this analogy: Fill-in-the-blank test questions are to multiple-choice questions as:
    a. encoding is to storage.
    b. storage is to encoding.
    c. recognition is to recall.
    d. recall is to recognition.
    e. encoding is to recall.

Ans: a, p. 362

42. In an effort to remember the name of the classmate who sat behind her in fifth grade, Martina mentally recited the names of other classmates who sat near her. Martina's effort to refresh her memory by activating related associations is an example of:
    a. priming.
    b. déjà vu.
    c. encoding.
    d. relearning.

Ans: d, p. 363

43. In a study on context cues, people learned words while on land or when they were underwater. In a later test of recall, those with the best retention had:
 a. learned the words on land, that is, in the more familiar context.
 b. learned the words underwater, that is, in the more exotic context.
 c. learned the words and been tested on them in different contexts.
 d. learned the words and been tested on them in the same context.

Ans: b, p. 363

44. Walking through the halls of his high school 10 years after graduation, Tom experienced a flood of old memories. Tom's experience showed the role of:
 a. state-dependent memory.
 b. context effects.
 c. retroactive interference.
 d. echoic memory.
 e. iconic memory.

Ans: d, p. 363

45. The eerie feeling of having been somewhere before is an example of:
 a. state dependency.
 b. encoding failure.
 c. priming.
 d. déjà vu.

Ans: c, p. 364

46. Being in a bad mood after a hard day of work, Susan could think of nothing positive in her life. This is best explained as an example of:
 a. priming.
 b. memory construction.
 c. mood-congruent memory.
 d. retrieval failure.
 e. repression.

Ans: d, p. 365

47. When he was 8 years old, Frank was questioned by the police about a summer camp counselor suspected of molesting children. Even though he was not, in fact, molested by the counselor, today 19-year-old Frank "remembers" the counselor touching him inappropriately. Frank's false memory is an example of which "sin" of memory?
 a. blocking
 b. transience
 c. misattribution
 d. suggestibility

Ans: d, p. 365

48. According to memory researcher Daniel Schacter, blocking occurs when:
 a. our inattention to details produces encoding failure.
 b. we confuse the source of information.
 c. our beliefs influence our recollections.
 d. information is on the tip of our tongue, but we can't get it out.

Ans: b, p. 365

49. Which of the following terms does *not* belong with the others?
a. misattribution
b. blocking
c. suggestibility
d. bias

Ans: c, p. 367

50. Which of the following best describes the typical forgetting curve?
a. a steady, slow decline in retention over time
b. a steady, rapid decline in retention over time
c. a rapid initial decline in retention becoming stable thereafter
d. a slow initial decline in retention becoming rapid thereafter

Ans: c, p. 368

51. At your high school reunion you cannot remember the last name of your homeroom teacher. Your failure to remember is most likely the result of:
a. encoding failure.
b. storage failure.
c. retrieval failure.
d. state-dependent memory.

Ans: a, p. 368

52. When Carlos was promoted, he moved into a new office with a new phone extension. Every time he is asked for his phone number, Carlos first thinks of his old extension, illustrating the effects of:
a. proactive interference.
b. retroactive interference.
c. encoding failure.
d. storage failure.

Ans: b, p. 368

53. After finding her old combination lock, Janice can't remember its combination because she keeps confusing it with the combination of her new lock. She is experiencing:
a. proactive interference.
b. retroactive interference.
c. encoding failure.
d. storage failure.
e. repression.

Ans: d, pp. 369-370

54. Jenkins and Dallenbach found that memory was better in subjects who were ________ during the retention interval, presumably because ________ was reduced.
a. awake; decay
b. asleep; decay
c. awake; interference
d. asleep; interference

Ans: b, pp. 369-370

55. Which of the following sequences would be best to follow if you wanted to minimize interference-induced forgetting in order to improve your recall on the psychology midterm?
   a. study, eat, test
   b. study, sleep, test
   c. study, listen to music, test
   d. study, exercise, test

Ans: c, p. 370

56. Repression is an example of:
   a. encoding failure.
   b. memory decay.
   c. motivated forgetting.
   d. all of the above.

Ans: a, p. 370

57. Lewis cannot remember the details of the torture he experienced as a prisoner of war. According to Freud, Lewis's failure to remember these painful memories is an example of:
   a. repression.
   b. retrieval failure.
   c. state-dependent memory.
   d. flashbulb memory.
   e. implicit memory.

Ans: d, p. 372

58. Studies by Loftus and Palmer, in which people were quizzed about a film of an accident, indicate that:
   a. when quizzed immediately, people can recall very little, due to the stress of witnessing an accident.
   b. when questioned as little as one day later, their memory was very inaccurate.
   c. most people had very accurate memories as much as six months later.
   d. people's recall may easily be affected by misleading information.

Ans: d, p. 372

59. Which of the following illustrates the constructive nature of memory?
   a. Janice keeps calling her new boyfriend by her old boyfriend's name.
   b. After studying all afternoon and then getting drunk in the evening, Don can't remember the material he studied.
   c. After getting some good news, elated Kareem has a flood of good memories from his younger years.
   d. Although elderly Mrs. Harvey, who has Alzheimer's disease, has many gaps in her memory, she invents sensible accounts of her activities so that her family will not worry.

Ans: c, pp. 372-373

60. The misinformation effect provides evidence that memory:
   a. is constructed during encoding.
   b. is unchanging once established.
   c. may be reconstructed during recall according to how questions are framed.
   d. is highly resistant to misleading information.

Ans: b, pp. 372-373

61. Research on memory construction reveals that memories:
    a. are stored as exact copies of experience.
    b. reflect a person's biases and assumptions.
    c. may be chemically transferred from one organism to another.
    d. even if long term, usually decay within about five years.

Ans: b, p. 375

62. PET scans taken when a person is truly or falsely recalling a word reveal different patterns of activity in an area of the:
    a. hippocampus.
    b. left temporal lobe.
    c. cerebellum.
    d. thalamus.

Ans: d, pp. 375-376

63. Hypnotically "refreshed" memories may prove inaccurate—especially if the hypnotist asks leading questions—because of:
    a. encoding failure.
    b. state-dependent memory.
    c. proactive interference.
    d. memory construction.

Ans: d, pp. 378-379

64. Memory researchers are suspicious of long-repressed memories of traumatic events that are "recovered" with the aid of drugs or hypnosis because:
    a. such experiences usually are vividly remembered.
    b. such memories are unreliable and easily influenced by misinformation.
    c. memories of events happening before about age 3 are especially unreliable.
    d. of all of the above reasons.

Ans: c, p. 381-382

65. Which of the following was *not* recommended as a strategy for improving memory?
    a. active rehearsal
    b. distributed study
    c. speed-reading
    d. encoding meaningful associations
    e. use of mnemonic devices

CHAPTER **10**

Thinking and Language

Learning Objectives

Thinking (pp. 385-400)

1. Describe the nature of concepts and the role of prototypes in concept formation.

2. Discuss how we use trial and error, algorithms, heuristics, and insight to solve problems.

3. Describe how the confirmation bias and fixation can interfere with effective problem solving.

4. Explain how the representativeness and availability heuristics influence our judgments.

5. Describe the effects that overconfidence and framing can have on our judgments and decisions.

6. Discuss how our beliefs distort logical reasoning, and describe the belief perseverance phenomenon.

7. Describe artificial intelligence, and contrast the human mind and the computer as information processors.

Language (pp. 401-408)

8. Describe the structure of language in terms of sounds, meanings, and grammar.

9. Trace the course of language acquisition from the babbling stage through the two-word stage.

10. Explain how the nature-nurture debate is illustrated in theories of language development.

Thinking and Language (pp. 409-412)

11. Discuss Whorf's linguistic relativity hypothesis and the relationship between thought and language.

Animal Thinking and Language (pp. 413-417)

12. Describe the research on animal cognition and communication, and discuss the controversy over whether animals can use language.

Thinking, p. 385
Easy, Factual/Definitional, Objective 1, Ans: d

1. Which psychological specialty is most directly concerned with the systematic study of problem solving, decision making, concept formation, and forming judgments?
   a. developmental psychology
   b. social psychology
   c. clinical psychology
   d. cognitive psychology
   e. personality psychology

Thinking, p. 385
Medium, Conceptual/Application, Objective 1, Ans: d

2. Professor Pegler's research efforts focus on how the use of heuristics influences people's assessments of financial risks. Which specialty area does his research best represent?
   a. developmental psychology
   b. biological psychology
   c. clinical psychology
   d. cognitive psychology
   e. personality psychology

Concepts, p. 386
Medium, Conceptual/Application, Objective 1, Ans: c

3. When we use the word "automobile" to refer to a category of transport vehicles, we are using this word as a(n):
   a. phoneme.
   b. heuristic.
   c. concept.
   d. algorithm.

Concepts, p. 386
Medium, Factual/Definitional, Objective 1, Ans: a

4. Pigeons can reliably discriminate pictures of cars from pictures of chairs. This best illustrates their capacity to develop:
   a. concepts.
   b. syntax.
   c. heuristics.
   d. mental sets.
   e. algorithms.

Concepts, p. 386
Easy, Factual/Definitional, Objective 1, Ans: c

5. A prototype is a:
   a. mental grouping of similar objects, events, or people.
   b. step-by-step procedure for solving problems.
   c. best example of a particular category.
   d. rule-of-thumb strategy for solving problems efficiently.

Concepts, p. 386
Medium, Factual/Definitional, Objective 1, Ans: c

6. In the process of classifying objects, people are especially likely to make use of:
   a. algorithms.
   b. phonemes.
   c. prototypes.
   d. mental sets.

Concepts, p. 386
Difficult, Conceptual, Objective 1, Ans: a

7. Prototype is to category as ________ is to ________.
   a. rose; flower
   b. rock; mountain
   c. man; woman
   d. rope; weapon

Concepts, p. 386
Medium, Factual/Definitional, Objective 1, Ans: c

8. With which of the following statements will people typically agree most quickly?
   a. A penguin is a bird.
   b. A goose is a bird.
   c. A robin is a bird.
   d. An ostrich is a bird.

Concepts, p. 386
Medium, Conceptual/Application, Objective 1, Ans: d

9. Eva had difficulty recognizing that a sea horse was a fish because it did not closely resemble her ________ of a fish.
   a. mental set
   b. heuristic
   c. algorithm
   d. prototype

Concepts, p. 386
Medium, Conceptual/Application, Objective 1, Ans: b

10. People are likely to take less time to recognize a woman as a nurse than a man as a nurse because a woman more closely resembles their ________ of a nurse.
   a. heuristic
   b. prototype
   c. algorithm
   d. mental set

Solving problems, p. 387
Medium, Conceptual/Application, Objective 2, Ans: e

11. Myron didn't know whether the boy's locker room was located down the hallway to his right or the one to his left. Crossing his fingers, he decided to try the left hallway. Myron's strategy for finding the locker room best illustrates the use of:
    a. the belief perseverance phenomenon.
    b. the confirmation bias.
    c. the representativeness heuristic.
    d. the framing effect.
    e. trial and error.

Solving problems, p. 387
Easy, Factual/Definitional, Objective 2, Ans: d

12. An algorithm is a:
    a. simple strategy for solving problems quickly and efficiently.
    b. method of hypothesis testing involving trial and error.
    c. best example of a particular category.
    d. methodical step-by-step procedure for solving problems.

Solving problems, p. 387
Medium, Conceptual/Application, Objective 2, Ans: c

13. A chess-playing computer program that routinely calculates all possible outcomes of all possible game moves best illustrates problem solving by means of:
    a. the availability heuristic.
    b. belief perseverance.
    c. an algorithm.
    d. the representativeness heuristic.
    e. functional fixedness.

Solving problems, p. 387
Easy, Factual/Definitional, Objective 2, Ans: b

14. Simple thinking strategies that allow us to solve problems and make judgments efficiently are called:
    a. semantics.
    b. heuristics.
    c. prototypes.
    d. algorithms.
    e. fixations.

Solving problems, p. 387
Medium, Factual/Definitional, Objective 2, Ans: a

15. The use of heuristics rather than algorithms is most likely to:
    a. save time in arriving at solutions to problems.
    b. yield more accurate solutions to problems.
    c. minimize the overconfidence phenomenon.
    d. involve greater reliance on language skills.

Solving problems, p. 387
Medium, Conceptual/Application, Objective 2, Ans: e

16. As he attempted to spell the word "receive," Tim reminded himself "i before e except after c." Tim's self-reminder best illustrates the use of:
    a. a prototype.
    b. trial and error.
    c. insight.
    d. an algorithm.
    e. a heuristic.

Solving problems, p. 387
Medium, Conceptual/Application, Objective 2, Ans: c

17. After spending two hours trying to solve an engineering problem, Amira finally gave up. As she was trying to fall asleep that night, a solution to the problem popped into her head. Amira's experience best illustrates:
    a. the belief perseverance phenomenon.
    b. the availability heuristic.
    c. insight.
    d. the framing effect.
    e. confirmation bias.

Confirmation bias, p. 388
Easy, Factual/Definitional, Objective 3, Ans: a

18. The confirmation bias refers to the tendency to:
    a. search for information consistent with our preconceptions.
    b. judge the likelihood of events on the basis of how easily we can remember examples of them.
    c. overestimate the accuracy of our beliefs and judgments.
    d. overestimate the degree to which other people will confirm our beliefs.

Confirmation bias, p. 388
Medium, Conceptual/Application, Objective 3, Ans: b

19. Because she believes that boys are naughtier than girls, Mrs. Zumpano, a second-grade teacher, watches boys more closely than she watches girls for any signs of misbehavior. Mrs. Zumpano's surveillance strategy best illustrates:
    a. the availability heuristic.
    b. confirmation bias.
    c. functional fixedness.
    d. the representativeness heuristic.
    e. the framing effect.

Confirmation bias, p. 388
Medium, Factual/Definitional, Objective 3, Ans: d

20. When Peter Wason asked people to guess the rule he had used to devise a sequence of three numbers, they typically guessed incorrectly. Their errors best illustrated the effect of:
    a. functional fixedness.
    b. the availability heuristic.
    c. framing.
    d. confirmation bias.
    e. the representativeness heuristic.

Confirmation bias, p. 388
Difficult, Conceptual, Objective 3, Ans: d

21. Scientists are trained to carefully observe and record any research outcomes that are inconsistent with their hypotheses. This practice most directly serves to inhibit:
a. the framing effect.
b. artificial intelligence.
c. functional fixedness.
d. confirmation bias.
e. naturalistic observation.

Fixation, p. 388
Easy, Factual/Definitional, Objective 3, Ans: b

22. The inability to take a new perspective on a problem is called a:
a. confirmation bias.
b. fixation.
c. heuristic.
d. framing effect.
e. prototype.

Fixation, pp. 388-389, 390
Medium, Factual/Definitional, Objective 3, Ans: a

23. Some people are unable to arrange six matches to form four equilateral triangles because they fail to consider a three-dimensional arrangement. This best illustrates the hazards of:
a. fixations.
b. heuristics.
c. algorithms.
d. framing.
e. overconfidence.

Fixation, p. 389
Easy, Conceptual, Objective 3, Ans: c

24. A mental set is most likely to inhibit:
a. confirmation bias.
b. overconfidence.
c. creativity.
d. belief perseverance.

Fixation, p. 389
Difficult, Conceptual/Application, Objective 3, Ans: b

25. Throughout his elementary and high school years, Charlie got away with copying his test answers from classmates. Because the college's test proctors are very observant, Charlie spends as many hours devising new ways to cheat as it would take him to study and perform well in an honest fashion. Charlie's strategy for passing tests illustrates the consequences of:
a. functional fixedness.
b. a mental set.
c. confirmation bias.
d. the availability heuristic.
e. the framing effect.

Fixation, p. 389
Easy, Factual/Definitional, Objective 3, Ans: a

26. The tendency to think of objects only in terms of their normal uses is called:
a. functional fixedness.
b. the availability heuristic.
c. confirmation bias.
d. belief perseverance.
e. the representativeness heuristic.

Fixation, p. 389
Medium, Conceptual/Application, Objective 3, Ans: c

27. Marlene forgot to bring a pillow on the camping trip, so she spent a very uncomfortable and restless night. Unfortunately, she never thought of using her down-filled jacket as a pillow. Marlene's oversight best illustrates:
a. confirmation bias.
b. belief perseverance.
c. functional fixedness.
d. the availability heuristic.
e. overconfidence.

The representativeness heuristic, p. 389
Medium, Factual/Definitional, Objective 4, Ans: a

28. The representativeness heuristic refers to our tendency to:
a. judge the likelihood of category membership by how closely an object or event resembles a particular prototype.
b. judge the likelihood of an event in terms of how readily instances of its occurrence are remembered.
c. search for information that is consistent with our preconceptions.
d. cling to our initial conceptions, even though they have been discredited.

The representativeness heuristic, p. 390
Difficult, Factual/Definitional, Objective 4, Ans: c

29. The danger of using the representativeness heuristic is that it may lead us to:
a. make judgments in a very inefficient, time-consuming fashion.
b. judge event likelihood solely on the basis of event memorability.
c. disregard probability information that is relevant to our judgments.
d. judge objects only in terms of their functional utility.

The representativeness heuristic, p. 390
Medium, Conceptual/Application, Objective 4, Ans: c

30. Miss Jan De Jong is orderly, neat, fairly quiet, and shy. She enjoys reading in her spare time and belongs to a social club that includes three librarians, nine real estate agents, and eight social workers. A tendency to conclude that Jan must be one of the three librarians would illustrate the powerful influence of:
a. confirmation bias.
b. the framing effect.
c. the representativeness heuristic.
d. the belief perseverance phenomenon.
e. the availability heuristic.

The representativeness heuristic, p. 390
Difficult, Conceptual/Application, Objective 4, Ans: d

31. Mistakenly concluding that the forgetful acts of an elderly person must be indicative of Alzheimer's disease best illustrates the impact of:
a. functional fixedness.
b. belief perseverance.
c. confirmation bias.
d. the representativeness heuristic.
e. framing.

The representativeness heuristic, p. 390
Difficult, Conceptual/Application, Objective 4, Ans: c

32. Jacquelyn suffered symptoms so similar to those associated with pregnancy-induced morning sickness that she erroneously concluded that she was pregnant. Jacquelyn's conclusion best illustrates the influence of:
a. confirmation bias.
b. the availability heuristic.
c. the representativeness heuristic.
d. functional fixedness.

The availability heuristic, p. 390
Easy, Factual/Definitional, Objective 4, Ans: e

33. Our tendency to judge the likelihood of an event on the basis of how readily we can remember instances of its occurrence is called the:
a. framing effect.
b. belief perseverance phenomenon.
c. confirmation bias.
d. representativeness heuristic.
e. availability heuristic.

The availability heuristic, p. 390
Easy, Conceptual/Application, Objective 4, Ans: e

34. Dean overestimates the proportion of family chores for which he takes sole responsibility because it's easier for him to recall what he has done than to recall what other family members have done. This best illustrates the impact of:
a. overconfidence.
b. functional fixedness.
c. the representativeness heuristic.
d. confirmation bias.
e. the availability heuristic.

The availability heuristic, p. 391
Medium, Conceptual/Application, Objective 4, Ans: d

35. By encouraging people to imagine their homes being destroyed by a fire, insurance salespeople are especially successful at selling large homeowners' policies. They are most clearly exploiting the influence of:
a. belief perseverance.
b. the representativeness heuristic.
c. overconfidence.
d. the availability heuristic.
e. functional fixedness.

The availability heuristic, p. 391
Medium, Factual/Definitional, Objective 4, Ans: e

36. A single, memorable case of welfare fraud has a greater impact on estimates of the frequency of welfare abuse than do statistics showing that this case is actually the exception to the rule. This illustrates that judgments are influenced by the:
a. confirmation bias.
b. representativeness heuristic.
c. belief perseverance phenomenon.
d. framing effect.
e. availability heuristic.

The availability heuristic, p. 391
Medium, Conceptual/Application, Objective 4, Ans: e

37. A televised image of a starving child had a greater impact on Mr. White's perception of the extensiveness of world hunger than did a statistical chart summarizing the tremendous scope of the problem. This suggests that his assessment of the world hunger problem is influenced by:
a. the belief perseverance phenomenon.
b. the representativeness heuristic.
c. confirmation bias.
d. fixations.
e. the availability heuristic.

Risks-Do we fear the right things?, (Box), p. 392
Easy, Factual/Definitional, Objective 4, Ans: c

38. The indelible memories of the 9/11 terrorist tragedy unduly inflated many people's estimates of the risks associated with air travel. This best illustrates the importance of:
a. functional fixedness.
b. the representativeness heuristic.
c. the availability heuristic.
d. confirmation bias.
e. framing.

Overconfidence, p. 391
Easy, Factual/Definitional, Objective 5, Ans: c

39. The overconfidence phenomenon refers to the tendency to:
a. cling to our initial conceptions, even though they have been discredited.
b. search for information consistent with our preconceptions.
c. underestimate the extent to which our beliefs and judgments are erroneous.
d. judge the likelihood of an event in terms of how readily instances of its occurrence are remembered.

Overconfidence, pp. 392-393
Easy, Factual/Definitional, Objective 5, Ans: e

40. Stockbrokers often believe that their own expertise will enable them to select stocks that will outperform the market average. This belief best illustrates:
a. functional fixedness.
b. confirmation bias.
c. the framing effect.
d. the availability heuristic.
e. overconfidence.

Overconfidence, pp. 392-393
Easy, Conceptual/Application, Objective 5, Ans: c

41. When Larina started college, she was certain that she had the willpower to never smoke marijuana. By the end of her freshman year, however, Larina had used this drug on three different occasions. Larina's experience best illustrates:
   a. the availability heuristic.
   b. confirmation bias.
   c. overconfidence.
   d. the framing effect.
   e. the belief perseverance phenomenon.

Overconfidence, p. 394
Easy, Factual/Definitional, Objective 5, Ans: e

42. College students routinely underestimate how much time it will take them to complete assigned course projects. This best illustrates the impact of:
   a. framing.
   b. functional fixedness.
   c. the availability heuristic.
   d. the representativeness heuristic.
   e. overconfidence.

Framing decisions, p. 394
Medium, Factual/Definitional, Objective 5, Ans: e

43. Consumers respond more positively to ground beef advertised as "75 percent lean" than to ground beef described as "25 percent fat." This illustrates that consumer reactions are influenced by:
   a. the representativeness heuristic.
   b. the belief perseverance phenomenon.
   c. confirmation bias.
   d. the availability heuristic.
   e. framing.

Framing decisions, p. 394
Difficult, Conceptual/Application, Objective 5, Ans: e

44. On Monday, the meteorologist forecast a 20 percent chance of rain, so Sheryl took her umbrella to work. On Friday, he reported an 80 percent chance that it would not rain, so Sheryl left her umbrella at home. Sheryl's behavior illustrates:
   a. confirmation bias.
   b. the belief perseverance phenomenon.
   c. overconfidence.
   d. the representativeness heuristic.
   e. the framing effect.

Framing decisions, p. 395
Difficult, Factual/Definitional, Objective 5, Ans: c

45. People asked to forfeit an early payment discount are less upset than when they are asked to bear a late payment surcharge. This best illustrates the importance of:
   a. belief perseverance.
   b. confirmation bias.
   c. framing.
   d. functional fixedness.
   e. the representativeness heuristic.

Belief bias, p. 395
Medium, Factual/Definitional, Objective 6, Ans: a

46. The tendency for one's preexisting opinions to distort logical reasoning is known as:
   a. belief bias.
   b. functional fixedness.
   c. framing.
   d. the availability heuristic.
   e. linguistic determinism.

Belief bias, p. 395
Difficult, Conceptual/Application, Objective 6, Ans: e

47. Wu believes that some murderers truly love their own children; he also believes that all who truly love their own children are effective parents. Wu's negative attitude toward murderers is so strong, however, that he finds it very difficult to accept the logical conclusion that some murderers are effective parents. His difficulty best illustrates:
   a. overconfidence.
   b. the framing effect.
   c. confirmation bias.
   d. the availability heuristic.
   e. belief bias.

The belief perseverance phenomenon, p. 396
Medium, Factual/Definitional, Objective 6, Ans: d

48. People with opposing views of capital punishment reviewed mixed evidence regarding its effectiveness as a crime deterrent. As a result, their opposing views differed more strongly than ever. This best illustrates:
   a. the framing effect.
   b. functional fixedness.
   c. the representativeness heuristic.
   d. belief perseverance.
   e. the availability heuristic.

The belief perseverance phenomenon, p. 396
Difficult, Factual/Definitional, Objective 6, Ans: b

49. Research findings suggest that the best advice to give people who want to avoid belief perseverance is:
   a. "Try to justify your positions."
   b. "Consider the opposite."
   c. "Don't draw hasty conclusions."
   d. "Consider the objective evidence."

The belief perseverance phenomenon, p. 396
Difficult, Conceptual/Application, Objective 6, Ans: d

50. Andre first became suspicious of his roommate's honesty while trying to account for his own missing billfold. Although Andre later recalled that he had left his billfold in the glove compartment of his own car, his newly formed doubt about his roommate's honesty remained as strong as ever. Andre's irrational suspicion of his roommate best illustrates:
    a. confirmation bias.
    b. the representativeness heuristic.
    c. functional fixedness.
    d. the belief perseverance phenomenon.
    e. the framing effect.

The belief perseverance phenomenon, pp. 396-397
Difficult, Conceptual, Objective 6, Ans: c

51. The value of generating positive first impressions in your initial interactions with a new employer is best underscored by the research on:
    a. overconfidence.
    b. the framing effect.
    c. belief perseverance.
    d. functional fixedness.
    e. the representativeness heuristic.

Simulating thinking with artificial intelligence, p. 397
Difficult, Conceptual, Objective 7, Ans: c

52. Psychologists are interested in artificial intelligence because:
    a. computers have minds but not emotions that cloud judgment.
    b. computer microchips operate almost exactly like the neurons of the brain.
    c. computers can simulate some human problem-solving strategies.
    d. of all of the above reasons.

Simulating thinking with artificial intelligence, p. 398
Difficult, Conceptual/Application, Objective 7, Ans: c

53. Which of the following illustrates an application of artificial intelligence?
    a. a computer that enables apes to communicate with humans
    b. a computer-controlled system that simulates the sound of human voices
    c. a computer programmed to play chess
    d. all of the above are applications of artificial intelligence

Simulating thinking with artificial intelligence, p. 398
Medium, Factual/Definitional, Objective 7, Ans: a

54. In order to more closely mimic human thought processes than they now do, computers of the future must have the capacity for:
    a. the parallel processing of information.
    b. following precise rules of logic.
    c. using heuristics to solve problems.
    d. retrieving detailed facts from memory.
    e. using algorithms to solve problems.

Simulating thinking with artificial intelligence, p. 398
Difficult, Factual/Definitional, Objective 7, Ans: d

55. Unlike conventional computer systems, neural networks have a capacity for:
    a. following precise rules of logic.
    b. retrieving detailed facts from memory.
    c. using algorithms to solve problems.
    d. processing numerous informational units simultaneously.
    e. using heuristics to solve problems.

Language structure, p. 401
Easy, Factual/Definitional, Objective 8, Ans: d

56. The smallest distinctive sound unit of language is a:
    a. prototype.
    b. phenotype.
    c. morpheme.
    d. phoneme.

Language structure, p. 401
Medium, Conceptual/Application, Objective 8, Ans: c

57. The various vowel sounds that can be placed between a "t" and an "n" produce words such as tan, ten, tin, and ton. These various vowel sounds represent different:
    a. morphemes.
    b. prototypes.
    c. phonemes.
    d. semantics.
    e. phenotypes.

Language structure, p. 401
Difficult, Factual/Definitional, Objective 8, Ans: d

58. English words are constructed from about ________ different phonemes.
    a. 5
    b. 6
    c. 26
    d. 40

Language structure, p. 401
Easy, Factual/Definitional, Objective 8, Ans: a

59. Morphemes are:
    a. the smallest speech units that carry meaning.
    b. the best examples of particular categories of objects.
    c. the smallest distinctive sound units of a language.
    d. rules for combining words into grammatically correct sentences.

Language structure, p. 401
Difficult, Conceptual, Objective 8, Ans: d

60. The word "cats" contains ________ phoneme(s) and ________ morpheme(s).
    a. 2; 1
    b. 4; 1
    c. 2; 4
    d. 4; 2

Language structure, p. 402
Medium, Factual/Definitional, Objective 8, Ans: d

61. Semantics refers to the:
    a. logical and methodical procedures for solving problems.
    b. orderly arrangement of words into grammatically correct sentences.
    c. simple thinking strategies that facilitate quick decision making.
    d. derivation of meaning from morphemes, words, and sentences.

Language structure, p. 402
Medium, Conceptual/Application, Objective 8, Ans: b

62. The rock musician was hit with a rotten egg while performing his latest hit song. The fact that you can recognize two different meanings for the word "hit" in the preceding sentence demonstrates the importance of:
    a. syntax.
    b. semantics.
    c. morphemes.
    d. prototypes.
    e. linguistic determinism.

Language structure, p. 402
Easy, Factual/Definitional, Objective 8, Ans: b

63. In order to combine words into grammatically sensible sentences, one needs to adhere to proper rules of:
    a. semantics.
    b. syntax.
    c. nomenclature.
    d. phonics.

Language structure, p. 402
Difficult, Conceptual/Application, Objective 8, Ans: e

64. Lavonne was careful to avoid the use of dangling participles and run-on sentences in her essay because she did not want to lose points for faulty:
    a. semantics.
    b. phonemes.
    c. algorithms.
    d. morphemes.
    e. syntax.

Language structure, pp. 401, 402
Medium, Factual/Definitional, Objective 8, Ans: c

65. Consonant phonemes generally convey ________ information than do vowel phonemes, and frequently used words are generally ________ than infrequently used words.
    a. more; longer
    b. less; shorter
    c. more; shorter
    d. less; longer

Acquiring language, p. 403
Easy, Factual/Definitional, Objective 9, Ans: a

66. The earliest stage of speech development is called the ________ stage.
    a. babbling
    b. telegraphic speech
    c. one-word
    d. grammatical
    e. semantic

Acquiring language, p. 403
Medium, Factual/Definitional, Objective 9, Ans: c

67. Infants are first able to discriminate speech sounds during the ________ stage.
    a. one-word
    b. telegraphic
    c. babbling
    d. syntactic
    e. echoic

Acquiring language, p. 403
Difficult, Factual/Definitional, Objective 9, Ans: d

68. At some point during the babbling stage, infants begin to:
    a. imitate adult grammar.
    b. make speech sounds only if their hearing is unimpaired.
    c. speak in simple words that may be barely recognizable.
    d. lose their ability to discriminate sounds that they never hear.

Acquiring language, p. 403
Easy, Factual/Definitional, Objective 9, Ans: a

69. Children first begin to use sounds to communicate meaning during the ________ stage.
    a. one-word
    b. two-word
    c. echoic
    d. telegraphic
    e. babbling

Acquiring language, p. 403
Medium, Conceptual/Application, Objective 9, Ans: e

70. At the age of 15 months, Anita repeatedly cries "hoy" when she wants her mother to hold her. Anita is most likely in the ________ stage of language development.
    a. syntactic
    b. babbling
    c. telegraphic speech
    d. echoic
    e. one-word

Acquiring language, p. 404
Easy, Factual/Definitional, Objective 9, Ans: c

71. Telegraphic speech is most closely associated with the ________ stage of language development.
 a. one-word
 b. babbling
 c. two-word
 d. echoic
 e. phonetic

Acquiring language, p. 404
Difficult, Conceptual/Application, Objective 9, Ans: b

72. Which of the following would be most characteristic of a 2-year-old's telegraphic speech?
 a. "a doggy"
 b. "eat apple"
 c. "to store"
 d. "ball pretty"

Explaining language development, p. 404
Medium, Conceptual, Objective 10, Ans: d

73. With respect to the debate over the process of language development, nature is to nurture as ________ is to ________.
 a. Skinner; Whorf
 b. Whorf; Skinner
 c. Skinner; Chomsky
 d. Chomsky; Skinner

Explaining language development, p. 404
Difficult, Factual/Definitional, Objective 10, Ans: a

74. Noam Chomsky has emphasized that the acquisition of language by children is facilitated by:
 a. an inborn readiness to learn grammatical rules.
 b. their ability to imitate the words and grammar modeled by parents.
 c. the learned association of word sounds with various objects, events, actions, and qualities.
 d. the positive reinforcement that adults give children for speaking correctly.

Explaining language development, p. 405
Medium, Factual/Definitional, Objective 10, Ans: c

75. It is difficult to explain language acquisition solely in terms of imitation and reinforcement because children:
 a. acquire language even in the absence of social interaction.
 b. resent being corrected for grammatical mistakes.
 c. overgeneralize grammatical rules, producing speech errors they have never heard before.
 d. employ telegraphic speech patterns before speaking in complex sentences.

Explaining language development, p. 405
Medium, Conceptual/Application, Objective 10, Ans: d

76. When 3-year-old Rosalie complained, "Boris hitted me with a ball," she was illustrating the tendency of young children to:
a. use telegraphic speech patterns.
b. imitate the incorrect speech patterns of others.
c. receive inadequate reinforcement for correct language usage.
d. use certain grammatical rules in sentence construction.

Explaining language development, p. 406
Medium, Factual/Definitional, Objective 10, Ans: b

77. Infants can learn the difference between syllable sequences that follow an ABA pattern (such as: ga-ti-ga) and those that follow an ABB pattern (such as: wo-fe-fe). This best illustrates the infant's capacity to learn:
a. telegraphic speech.
b. statistical probabilities in speech.
c. a universal grammar underlying speech.
d. any speech system by means of operant conditioning.

Explaining language development, p. 407
Medium, Factual/Definitional, Objective 10, Ans: c

78. The best evidence that there is a critical period for language acquisition is the fact that:
a. infants babble phonemes that do not occur in their parents' native language.
b. toddlers maintain a capacity to discriminate phonemes that they have never heard.
c. people most easily master the grammar of a second language during childhood.
d. preschoolers often overgeneralize certain rules of grammatical structure.

Explaining language development, pp. 407-408
Difficult, Factual/Definitional, Objective 10, Ans: d

79. Compared to deaf adults exposed to sign language from birth, those who first learn sign language as teens are less likely to:
a. correctly imitate the signs they are shown.
b. use signs to indicate concrete objects.
c. mentally associate signs with written words.
d. comprehend grammatical subtleties of sign language.

Language influences thinking, p. 409
Easy, Factual/Definitional, Objective 11, Ans: d

80. Whorf's linguistic determinism hypothesis emphasizes that:
a. infancy is a critical period for language development.
b. all languages share a similar grammar.
c. our linguistic proficiencies influence our social status.
d. words shape the way people think.

Language influences thinking, p. 409
Medium, Factual/Definitional, Objective 11, Ans: a

81. Many bilinguals experience a different sense of self depending on which language they are using. This most clearly illustrates the implications of:
a. Whorf's linguistic determinism hypothesis.
b. Skinner's language acquisition theory.
c. Bandura's social-cognitive theory.
d. Chomsky's language acquisition theory.

Language influences thinking, p. 409
Medium, Conceptual/Application, Objective 11, Ans: c

82. It has been suggested that Eskimos' rich vocabulary for describing snow enables them to perceive differences in snow conditions that would otherwise go unnoticed. This suggestion most clearly illustrates:
a. functional fixedness.
b. the representativeness heuristic.
c. linguistic determinism.
d. the framing effect.
e. belief perseverance.

Language influences thinking, p. 409
Difficult, Conceptual/Application, Objective 11, Ans: c

83. Even though 18-month-old Ohmar has not yet learned the words for different colors, he recognizes color differences just as accurately as his 4-year-old brother, who can name the different colors. This fact would most directly challenge:
a. Chomsky's language acquisition theory.
b. Bandura's social-cognitive theory.
c. Whorf's linguistic determinism hypothesis.
d. Skinner's language acquisition theory.

Language influences thinking, pp. 409-410
Medium, Factual/Definitional, Objective 11, Ans: a

84. Research with children indicates that the use of the generic pronoun "he" tends to trigger images of:
a. a male.
b. a female about a third of the time the pronoun is used.
c. a female about half the time the pronoun is used.
d. persons who are neither obviously male nor obviously female.

Thinking without language, p. 411
Easy, Factual/Definitional, Objective 11, Ans: a

85. The fact that we can think without language is best illustrated in research on:
a. mental imagery.
b. functional fixedness.
c. the framing effect.
d. algorithms.
e. the representativeness heuristic.

Thinking without language, p. 412
Easy, Factual/Definitional, Objective 11, Ans: c

86. Our capacity for thinking without language is best illustrated by:
a. the framing effect.
b. functional fixedness.
c. unconscious information processing.
d. the representativeness heuristic.
e. the belief perseverance phenomenon.

Do animals think?, p. 413
Medium, Factual/Definitional, Objective 12, Ans: b

87. The problem-solving abilities of forest-dwelling chimpanzees are best illustrated by their naturally developed use of:
a. sign language.
b. hand tools.
c. heuristics.
d. artificial intelligence.

Do animals exhibit language?, p. 414
Medium, Factual/Definitional, Objective 12, Ans: a

88. The dance of the honeybee illustrates that animals are capable of:
a. communicating useful information.
b. learning a sign language.
c. following grammatical rules.
d. all of the above.

Do animals exhibit language?, p. 415
Medium, Factual/Definitional, Objective 12, Ans: c

89. Beatrice and Allen Gardner taught the chimpanzee Washoe to communicate by means of:
a. pictures.
b. Morse code.
c. sign language.
d. a simplified typewriter.

Do animals exhibit language?, p. 416
Medium, Factual/Definitional, Objective 12, Ans: c

90. Research on the language capabilities of apes clearly demonstrates that they have the capacity to:
a. vocalize the most common vowel sounds.
b. acquire language vocabulary as rapidly as most children.
c. communicate meaning through the use of symbols.
d. do all of the above.

Do animals exhibit language?, p. 416
Medium, Conceptual, Objective 10, Ans: c

91. Those who are skeptical with regard to claims that apes share our capacity for language are especially likely to highlight chimps' limited use of appropriate:
a. morphemes.
b. heuristics.
c. syntax.
d. phonemes.
e. neural networks.

Essay Questions

1. Describe several heuristics that you might use or that you have used when deciding whether you should (a) study especially hard for a test and (b) ask someone for a date (or accept a date). Under what circumstances are these heuristics likely to contribute to poor decision making?

2. You are the commissioner of a state lottery system that sponsors daily and weekly drawings. Lottery tickets have not been selling well over the past few months. Describe four ways you could take advantage of people's use of the availability heuristic in order to boost sales. Explain why you would judge your tactics to be fair or unfair to your customers.

3. Heike's older brother has suffered from chronic depression for several years. Unfortunately, Heike has been incorrectly informed by her parents that there is a 40 percent chance she will also suffer from depression. Explain how the availability heuristic, framing, the confirmation bias, and belief perseverance might lead Heike to conclude that she will definitely be a victim of a severe depressive disorder.

4. After returning from a shopping trip with his mother, little Tommy reported, "I goed to the store and eated candy." Why might a behaviorist such as B. F. Skinner have had some difficulty explaining Tommy's incorrect grammatical construction? What does his error suggest about the process of language acquisition?

Web Quiz 1

Ans: e

1. In her research, Professor Kyoto seeks to identify circumstances in which confirmation bias is especially likely to impede effective problem solving. Which specialty area does her research best represent?
   a. biological psychology
   b. developmental psychology
   c. personality psychology
   d. clinical psychology
   e. cognitive psychology

Ans: b

2. Arnold had difficulty recognizing that bullfighting was a sport because it failed to resemble his ________ of a sport.
   a. phoneme
   b. prototype
   c. algorithm
   d. heuristic

Ans: b

3. In attempting to solve difficult sexual assault cases, a police detective frequently reminds himself to focus investigative suspicion on the victims' friends and acquaintances. This strategy best illustrates the use of:
   a. an algorithm.
   b. a heuristic.
   c. telegraphic speech.
   d. the framing effect.

Ans: d

4. Because he erroneously believes that older workers are not as motivated as younger workers to work hard, a factory foreman is especially vigilant for any signs of laziness among his senior workers. His supervision strategy best illustrates:
   a. the framing effect.
   b. the availability heuristic.
   c. functional fixedness.
   d. confirmation bias.
   e. the representativeness heuristic.

Ans: e

5. People are often unable to come up with the simple solutions to some of the three-jugs problems presented in the text because they repeat more complicated solutions that worked in the past. This best illustrates the dynamics of:
   a. the framing effect.
   b. functional fixedness.
   c. the availability heuristic.
   d. artificial intelligence.
   e. a mental set.

Ans: d

6. A defense attorney emphasizes to a jury that her client works full-time, supports his family, and enjoys leisure-time hobbies. Although none of this information is relevant to the trial, it is designed to make the defendant appear to be a typical member of the local community. The lawyer is most clearly seeking to take advantage of:
a. confirmation bias.
b. functional fixedness.
c. belief perseverance.
d. the representativeness heuristic.

Ans: a

7. Prompt feedback regarding your performance on psychology practice tests is most likely to inhibit:
a. overconfidence.
b. the framing effect.
c. functional fixedness.
d. the representativeness heuristic.
e. the availability heuristic.

Ans: d

8. Brutus believes that men enjoy watching professional football and that women are categorically distinct from men. His gender stereotypes are so strong, however, that he mistakenly reasons from these premises the illogical conclusion that women do not enjoy watching professional football. His reasoning difficulty best illustrates:
a. confirmation bias.
b. the framing effect.
c. the availability heuristic.
d. belief bias.
e. functional fixedness.

Ans: b

9. Maintaining one's conceptions even after the basis on which they were formed has been discredited is known as:
a. the representativeness heuristic.
b. belief perseverance.
c. confirmation bias.
d. functional fixedness.
e. the availability heuristic.

Ans: a

10. The word "chimps" contains ________ phoneme(s) and ________ morpheme(s).
a. 5; 1
b. 6; 2
c. 1; 5
d. 2; 6

Ans: a

11. Adding *-ed* to the word "laugh" means that the action took place in the past. This illustrates one of the rules of English:
   a. semantics.
   b. algorithms.
   c. syntax.
   d. phonemes.

Ans: d

12. Vocal sounds that are not included in one's native language first begin to disappear from usage during the ________ stage of language development.
   a. one-word
   b. two-word
   c. telegraphic
   d. babbling

Ans: c

13. Which language theorist would have been most likely to emphasize that children master the rule for forming the past tense of regular verbs like "push" before they learn common past tense constructions of irregular verbs like "go"?
   a. Skinner
   b. Whorf
   c. Chomsky
   d. Frisch

Ans: c

14. To simulate the learning of the statistical relationships among language terms, researchers are likely to make use of:
   a. telegraphic speech.
   b. the framing effect.
   c. computer neural networks.
   d. the representativeness heuristic.

Ans: c

15. Your ability to recall which direction you turn the faucet handle in your bathroom in order to get cold water best illustrates the importance of:
   a. algorithms.
   b. the framing effect.
   c. thinking without language.
   d. the representativeness heuristic.
   e. the belief perseverance phenomenon.

Web Quiz 2

Ans: b

1. We more quickly recognize that a blue jay is a bird than that a penguin is a bird because a blue jay more closely resembles our________ of a bird.
   a. heuristic
   b. prototype
   c. algorithm
   d. phoneme

Ans: b

2. Prototype is to category as ________ is to ________.
   a. wheel; car
   b. milk; beverage
   c. waiter; restaurant
   d. comedian; laughter

Ans: c

3. To find Tabasco sauce in a large grocery store, you could systematically search every shelf in every store aisle. This best illustrates problem solving by means of:
   a. the availability heuristic.
   b. functional fixedness.
   c. an algorithm.
   d. belief perseverance.
   e. the representativeness heuristic.

Ans: a

4. Max is so used to thinking that a tough competitive style of behavior is the best way to impress others that he fails to recognize that the most effective way to impress his girlfriend is with cooperative tenderness. Max's oversight best illustrates:
   a. a fixation.
   b. the framing effect.
   c. the representativeness heuristic.
   d. functional fixedness.
   e. overconfidence.

Ans: a

5. Pablo vainly searches for a screwdriver while failing to recognize that a readily available coin in his pocket would turn the screw. His oversight best illustrates:
   a. functional fixedness.
   b. the availability heuristic.
   c. belief perseverance.
   d. the framing effect.
   e. the representativeness heuristic.

Ans: e

6. The easier it is for people to remember an instance in which they were betrayed by a friend, the more they expect such an event to recur. This best illustrates the impact of:
   a. framing.
   b. belief perseverance.
   c. the representativeness heuristic.
   d. functional fixedness.
   e. the availability heuristic.

Ans: a

7. College students are more likely to judge a condom as effective when informed that it has a 95 percent success rate than when told it has a 5 percent failure rate. This best illustrates the impact of:
   a. framing.
   b. confirmation bias.
   c. functional fixedness.
   d. belief perseverance.
   e. the representativeness heuristic.

Ans: d

8. Professor Chadwick evaluated a graduate student's research proposal negatively simply because he had heard a rumor about the student's incompetence. When later informed that the rumor had been patently false, the professor's assessment of the student's research proposal remained almost as negative as ever. This best illustrates:
   a. the representativeness heuristic.
   b. functional fixedness.
   c. the availability heuristic.
   d. belief perseverance.
   e. framing.

Ans: d

9. A computer program designed to process the information in a psychology textbook and correctly answer multiple-choice questions regarding the text contents illustrates an application of:
   a. linguistic determinism.
   b. functional fixedness.
   c. the framing effect.
   d. artificial intelligence.
   e. telegraphic speech.

Ans: c

10. In the English language, adjectives are typically placed before nouns, as in "white house." This illustrates a rule of English:
    a. semantics.
    b. algorithms.
    c. syntax.
    d. phonemes.

Ans: d

11. The two-word stage of language development typically begins at the age of ________ months.
    a. 6
    b. 10
    c. 14
    d. 24
    e. 36

Ans: a

12. The fact that children speak with an accent that is similar to their peers is best explained by ________ theory of language acquisition.
    a. Skinner's
    b. Whorf's
    c. Chomsky's
    d. Frisch's

Ans: d

13. Learning a spoken language during childhood ________ the learning of sign language during adolescence. Learning sign language during childhood _______ the learning of a spoken language during adolescence.
    a. inhibits; facilitates
    b. facilitates; inhibits
    c. inhibits; inhibits
    d. facilitates; facilitates

Ans: b

14. Using different words for two very similar objects enables people to recognize conceptual distinctions between the objects. This illustrates:
    a. telegraphic speech.
    b. linguistic determinism.
    c. functional fixedness.
    d. the representativeness heuristic.

Ans: c

15. When choosing who should retrieve food for them, humans prefer someone who has witnessed it being hidden. Chimps do not. This best illustrates that chimps have a more limited:
    a. prototype.
    b. confirmation bias.
    c. theory of mind.
    d. representativeness heuristic.

Study Guide Questions

Ans: c, p. 385

1. The text defines cognition as:
   a. silent speech.
   b. all mental activity.
   c. mental activity associated with processing, understanding, and communicating information.
   d. logical reasoning.
   e. problem solving.

Ans: a, p. 385

2. Dr. Mendoza is studying the mental strategies people use when solving problems. Dr. Mendoza is clearly a(n):
   a. cognitive psychologist.
   b. experimental psychologist.
   c. organizational psychologist.
   d. developmental psychologist.

Ans: b, p. 386

3. A mental grouping of similar things, events, or people is called a(n):
   a. prototype.
   b. concept.
   c. algorithm.
   d. heuristic.
   e. mental set.

Ans: c, p. 386

4. When forming a concept, people often develop a best example, or ________, of a category.
   a. denoter
   b. heuristic
   c. prototype
   d. algorithm

Ans: b, p. 386

5. Complete the following analogy: Rose is to flower as:
   a. concept is to prototype.
   b. prototype is to concept.
   c. concept is to hierarchy.
   d. hierarchy is to concept.

Ans: b, p. 386

6. The basic units of cognition are:
   a. phonemes.
   b. concepts.
   c. prototypes.
   d. morphemes.

Ans: b, p. 387

7. If you want to be absolutely certain that you will find the solution to a problem you know *is* solvable, you should use:
   a. a heuristic.
   b. an algorithm.
   c. insight.
   d. trial and error.

Ans: b, p. 387

8. A dessert recipe that gives you the ingredients, their amounts, and the steps to follow is an example of a(n):
   a. prototype.
   b. algorithm.
   c. heuristic.
   d. mental set.

Ans: d, p. 387

9. Which of the following is an example of the use of heuristics?
   a. trying every possible letter ordering when unscrambling a word
   b. considering each possible move when playing chess
   c. using the formula "area = length × width" to find the area of a rectangle
   d. playing chess using a defensive strategy that has often been successful for you

Ans: c, p. 387

10. Experts in a field prefer heuristics to algorithms because heuristics:
   a. guarantee solutions to problems.
   b. prevent mental sets.
   c. often save time.
   d. prevent fixation.
   e. do all of the above.

Ans: d, p. 387

11. Boris the chess master selects his next move by considering moves that would threaten his opponent's queen. His opponent, a chess-playing computer, selects its next move by considering *all* possible moves. Boris is using a(n) ________ and the computer is using a(n) ________.
   a. algorithm; heuristic
   b. prototype; mental set
   c. mental set; prototype
   d. heuristic; algorithm

Ans: d, p. 388

12. During a televised political debate, the Republican and Democratic candidates each argued that the results of a recent public opinion poll supported their party's platform regarding sexual harassment. Because both candidates saw the information as supporting their belief, it is clear that both were victims of:
   a. functional fixedness.
   b. mental set.
   c. belief bias.
   d. confirmation bias.

Ans: d, p. 388

13. Confirmation bias refers to the tendency to:
    a. allow preexisting beliefs to distort logical reasoning.
    b. cling to one's initial conceptions after the basis on which they were formed has been discredited.
    c. search randomly through alternative solutions when problem solving.
    d. look for information that is consistent with one's beliefs.

Ans: a, p. 388

14. A common problem in everyday reasoning is our tendency to:
    a. accept as logical those conclusions that agree with our own opinions.
    b. accept as logical those conclusions that disagree with our own opinions.
    c. underestimate the accuracy of our knowledge.
    d. accept as logical conclusions that involve unfamiliar concepts.

Ans: c, p. 389

15. Mental set and functional fixedness are two types of:
    a. algorithms.
    b. heuristics.
    c. fixation.
    d. insight.

Ans: d, p. 389

16. Failing to see that an article of clothing can be inflated as a life preserver is an example of:
    a. belief bias.
    b. the availability heuristic.
    c. the representativeness heuristic.
    d. functional fixedness.

Ans: b, p. 389

17. Failing to solve a problem that requires using an object in an unusual way illustrates the phenomenon of:
    a. mental set.
    b. functional fixedness.
    c. framing.
    d. belief perseverance.
    e. overconfidence.

Ans: c, p. 389

18. Marilyn was asked to solve a series of five math problems. The first four problems could only be solved by a particular sequence of operations. The fifth problem could also be solved following this sequence; however, a much simpler solution was possible. Marilyn did not realize this simpler solution and solved the problem in the way she had solved the first four. Her problem-solving strategy was hampered by:
    a. functional fixedness.
    b. the overconfidence phenomenon.
    c. mental set.
    d. her lack of a prototype for the solution.

Ans: e, p. 389

19. Rudy is 6 feet 6 inches tall, weighs 210 pounds, and is very muscular. If you think that Rudy is more likely to be a basketball player than a computer programmer, you are a victim of:
a. belief bias.
b. the availability heuristic.
c. mental set.
d. functional fixedness.
e. the representativeness heuristic.

Ans: c, p. 389

20. You hear that one of the Smith children is an outstanding Little League player and immediately conclude it's their one son rather than any of their four daughters. You reached your quite possibly erroneous conclusion as the result of:
a. the confirmation bias.
b. the availability heuristic.
c. the representativeness heuristic.
d. belief perseverance.

Ans: e, pp. 389-390

21. Representativeness and availability are examples of:
a. mental sets.
b. belief bias.
c. algorithms.
d. fixation.
e. heuristics.

Ans: b, p. 390

22. Airline reservations typically decline after a highly publicized airplane crash because people overestimate the incidence of such disasters. In such instances, people's decisions are being influenced by:
a. belief bias.
b. the availability heuristic.
c. the representativeness heuristic.
d. functional fixedness.

Ans: d, p. 390

23. Your stand on an issue such as the use of nuclear power for electricity involves personal judgment. In such a case, one memorable occurrence can weigh more heavily than a bookful of data, thus illustrating:
a. belief perseverance.
b. confirmation bias.
c. the representativeness heuristic.
d. the availability heuristic.
e. belief bias.

Ans: d, p. 390

24. Assume that Congress is considering revising its approach to welfare and to this end is hearing a range of testimony. A member of Congress who uses the availability heuristic would be most likely to:
    a. want to experiment with numerous possible approaches to see which of these seems to work best.
    b. want to cling to approaches to welfare that seem to have had some success in the past.
    c. refuse to be budged from his or her beliefs despite persuasive testimony to the contrary.
    d. base his or her ideas on the most vivid, memorable testimony given, even though many of the statistics presented run counter to this testimony.

Ans: c, p. 391

25. Most people tend to:
    a. accurately estimate the accuracy of their knowledge and judgments.
    b. underestimate the accuracy of their knowledge and judgments.
    c. overestimate the accuracy of their knowledge and judgments.
    d. lack confidence in their decision-making strategies.

Ans: a, p. 394

26. In relation to ground beef, consumers respond more positively to an ad describing it as "75 percent lean" than to one referring to its "25 percent fat" content. This is an example of:
    a. the framing effect.
    b. confirmation bias.
    c. mental set.
    d. overconfidence.

Ans: a, p. 396

27. Which of the following illustrates belief perseverance?
    a. Your belief remains intact even in the face of evidence to the contrary.
    b. You refuse to listen to arguments counter to your beliefs.
    c. You tend to become flustered and angered when your beliefs are refuted.
    d. You tend to search for information that supports your beliefs.
    e. Your beliefs tend to distort logical reasoning.

Ans: d, p. 397

28. Which of the following describes artificial intelligence?
    a. the science of low-temperature phenomena
    b. the study of animal behavior in its natural habitat
    c. the study of control processes in electronic and biological systems
    d. the science that explores human thought by attempting to model it on the computer
    e. the best example of a category

Ans: d, pp. 397-398

29. Because of their lightning speed, computers can retrieve and manipulate stored data faster than people can, but the human brain beats the computer hands down when it comes to:
    a. using heuristics.
    b. following algorithms.
    c. serial processing.
    d. simultaneous processing.

Ans: d, p. 398

30. Neural network computers:
    a. can be programmed to mimic excitatory and inhibitory neural messages.
    b. have a greater capacity than conventional computers to learn from experience.
    c. are not limited to serial processing.
    d. can do all of the above.
    e. can do none of the above.

Ans: a, p. 401

31. Phonemes are the basic units of ________ in language.
    a. sound
    b. meaning
    c. grammar
    d. semantics
    e. syntax

Ans: c, p. 401

32. The English language has approximately ________ phonemes.
    a. 25
    b. 30
    c. 40
    d. 45
    e. 50

Ans: a, p. 401

33. The word "predates" contains ________ phonemes and ________ morphemes.
    a. 7; 3
    b. 3; 7
    c. 7; 2
    d. 3; 2

Ans: b, p. 401

34. Complete the following: *-ed* is to *sh* as ________ is to ________.
    a. phoneme; morpheme
    b. morpheme; phoneme
    c. grammar; syntax
    d. syntax; grammar

Ans: d, p. 402

35. The rules most directly involved in permitting a person to derive meaning from words and sentences are rules of:
    a. syntax.
    b. grammar.
    c. phonemic structure.
    d. semantics.

Ans: d, p. 402

36. The sentence “Blue jeans wear false smiles” has correct ________ but incorrect ________.
  a. morphemes; phonemes
  b. phonemes; morphemes
  c. semantics; syntax
  d. syntax; semantics

Ans: b, p. 402

37. *Syntax* refers to the:
  a. sounds in a word.
  b. rules for grouping words into sentences.
  c. rules by which meaning is derived from sentences.
  d. overall rules of a language.

Ans: a, p. 403

38. A listener hearing a recording of Japanese, Spanish, and North American children babbling would:
  a. not be able to tell them apart.
  b. be able to tell them apart if they were older than 6 months.
  c. be able to tell them apart if they were older than 8 to 10 months.
  d. be able to tell them apart at any age.

Ans: a, p. 403

39. Which of the following is *not* true of babbling?
  a. It is imitation of adult speech.
  b. It is the same in all cultures.
  c. It typically occurs from about age 4 months to 1 year.
  d. Babbling increasingly comes to resemble a particular language.
  e. Deaf babies babble with gestures.

Ans: d, p. 403

40. One reason an English-speaking adult may have difficulty pronouncing Russian words is that:
  a. the vocal tracts of English- and Russian-speaking people develop differently in response to the demands of the two languages.
  b. although English and Russian have very similar morphemes, their phonemic inventories are very different.
  c. although English and Russian have very similar phonemes, their morphemic inventories are very different.
  d. after the babbling stage, a child who hears only English stops uttering other phonemes.

Ans: b, p. 404

41. The child who says “Milk gone” is engaging in ________. This type of utterance demonstrates that children are actively experimenting with the rules of ________.
  a. babbling; syntax
  b. telegraphic speech; syntax
  c. babbling; semantics
  d. telegraphic speech; semantics

Ans: c, p. 404

42. Telegraphic speech is typical of the ________ stage.
a. babbling
b. one-word
c. two-word
d. three-word

Ans: c, p. 404

43. Children first demonstrate a rudimentary understanding of syntax during the ________ stage.
a. babbling
b. one-word
c. two-word
d. three-word

Ans: d, p. 404

44. Skinner and other behaviorists have argued that language development is the result of:
a. imitation.
b. reinforcement.
c. association.
d. all of the above.

Ans: a, p. 405

45. Which of the following utterances is an example of overgeneralization of a grammatical rule?
a. "We goed to the store."
b. "Ball pretty."
c. "The sky is crying."
d. "We eat 'paghetti."

Ans: d, pp. 404-405

46. Which of the following is *not* cited by Chomsky as evidence that language acquisition cannot be explained by learning alone?
a. Children master the complicated rules of grammar with ease.
b. Children create sentences they have never heard.
c. Children make the kinds of mistakes that suggest they are attempting to apply rules of grammar.
d. Children raised in isolation from language spontaneously begin speaking words.

Ans: c, p. 405

47. Which of the following *best* describes Chomsky's view of language development?
a. Language is an entirely learned ability.
b. Language is an innate ability.
c. Humans have a biological predisposition to acquire language.
d. There are no cultural influences on the development of language.

Ans: b, p. 407

48. The study in which people who immigrated to the United States at various ages were compared in terms of their ability to understand English grammar found that:
   a. age of arrival had no effect on mastery of grammar.
   b. those who immigrated as children understood grammar as well as native speakers.
   c. those who immigrated as adults understood grammar as well as native speakers.
   d. whether or not English was spoken in the home was the most important factor in mastering the rules of grammar.

Ans: d, pp. 407-408

49. Deaf children who are not exposed to sign language until they are teenagers:
   a. are unable to master the basic words of sign language.
   b. learn the basic words but not how to order them.
   c. are unable to master either the basic words or syntax of sign language.
   d. never become as fluent as those who learned to sign at a younger age.

Ans: c, p. 408

50. According to the text, language acquisition is best described as:
   a. the result of conditioning and reinforcement.
   b. a biological process of maturation.
   c. an interaction between biology and experience.
   d. a mystery of which researchers have no real understanding.

Ans: c, p. 409

51. In preparing her class presentation, "Updating Chomsky's Understanding of Language Development," Britney's outline includes all of the following evidence *except* that:
   a. computer neural networks programmed to learn to form the past tense of irregular verbs can learn to do so, even without "inborn" linguistic rules.
   b. infants rapidly learn to detect subtle differences between simple sequences of syllables.
   c. infants can recognize color differences even before they can name different colors.
   d. children isolated from language during the first seven years of life never fully develop language.

Ans: d, p. 409

52. Whorf's linguistic determination hypothesis states that:
   a. language is primarily a learned ability.
   b. language is partially an innate ability.
   c. the size of a person's vocabulary reflects his or her intelligence.
   d. our language shapes our thinking.

Ans: b, p. 409

53. The linguistic determinism hypothesis is challenged by the finding that:
   a. chimps can learn to communicate spontaneously by using sign language.
   b. people with no word for a certain color can still perceive that color accurately.
   c. the Eskimo language contains a number of words for snow, whereas English has only one.
   d. infants' babbling contains many phonemes that do not occur in their own language and that they therefore cannot have heard.

Ans: c, p. 410

54. Several studies have indicated that the generic pronoun "he":
    a. tends for children and adults alike to trigger images of both males and females.
    b. tends for adults to trigger images of both males and females, but for children to trigger images of males.
    c. tends for both children and adults to trigger images of males but not females.
    d. for both children and adults triggers images of females about one-fourth of the time it is used.

Ans: b, p. 411

55. Which of the following is true regarding the relationship between thinking and language?
    a. "Real" thinking requires the use of language.
    b. People sometimes think in images rather than in words.
    c. A thought that cannot be expressed in a particular language cannot occur to speakers of that language.
    d. All of the above are true.

Ans: d, p. 412

56. Regarding the relationship between thinking and language, which of the following most accurately reflects the position taken in the text?
    a. Language determines everything about our thinking.
    b. Language determines the way we think.
    c. Thinking without language is not possible.
    d. Thinking affects our language, which then affects our thought.

Ans: e, p. 413

57. The chimpanzee Sultan used a short stick to pull a longer stick that was out of reach into his cage. He then used the longer stick to reach a piece of fruit. Researchers hypothesized that Sultan's discovery of the solution to his problem was the result of:
    a. trial and error.
    b. heuristics.
    c. functional fixedness.
    d. mental set.
    e. insight.

Ans: d, pp. 413-414

58. Researchers who are convinced that animals can think point to evidence that:
    a. monkeys demonstrate the ability to "count" by learning to touch pictures of objects in ascending numerical order.
    b. chimpanzees regularly use branches, stones, and other objects as tools in their natural habitats.
    c. chimps invent grooming and courtship customs and pass them on to their peers.
    d. all of the above occur.

Ans: a, p. 414

59. Researchers who believe that some primates possess a rudimentary theory of mind point to evidence that:
   a. chimpanzees have been observed using mirrors to inspect themselves.
   b. vervet monkeys have different alarm calls for different predators.
   c. orangutans in the wild frequently use stones as tools.
   d. honeybees communicate the direction and distance of a food source by performing an intricate dance.
   e. all of the above occur.

Ans: c, p. 414

60. Biologist Karl von Frisch shared the Nobel prize for his discovery that honeybees communicate with each other by:
   a. varying the acoustic pitch of their buzzing noises.
   b. secreting chemical odors called pheromones.
   c. performing an intricate dance.
   d. leading other worker bees on lengthy flights to find nectar.

Ans: c, p. 415

61. Researchers taught the chimpanzee Washoe and the gorilla Koko to communicate by using:
   a. various sounds.
   b. plastic symbols of various shapes and colors.
   c. sign language.
   d. all of the above.

Ans: d, pp. 415-416

62. Which of the following has been argued by critics of ape language research?
   a. Ape language is merely imitation of the trainer's behavior.
   b. There is little evidence that apes can equal even a 3-year-old's ability to order words with proper syntax.
   c. By seeing what they wish to see, trainers attribute greater linguistic ability to apes than actually exists.
   d. All of the above have been argued.

Ans: d, p. 416

63. Many psychologists are skeptical of claims that chimpanzees can acquire language because the chimps have not shown the ability to:
   a. use symbols meaningfully.
   b. acquire speech.
   c. acquire even a limited vocabulary.
   d. use syntax in communicating.

CHAPTER **11**

Intelligence

Learning Objectives

The Origins of Intelligence Testing (pp. 419-422)

1. Trace the origins of intelligence testing, and describe Stern's formula for the intelligence quotient.

What Is Intelligence? (pp. 422-432)

2. Describe the nature of intelligence, and discuss whether it should be considered a general mental ability or many specific abilities.

3. Identify the factors associated with creativity, and describe the relationship between creativity and intelligence.

4. Describe efforts to correlate intelligence with brain anatomy, brain functioning, and cognitive processing speed.

Assessing Intelligence (pp. 432-437)

5. Distinguish between aptitude and achievement tests, and describe modern tests of mental abilities such as the WAIS.

6. Describe test standardization, and explain the importance of appropriate standardization samples for effectively interpreting intelligence test scores.

7. Distinguish between the reliability and validity of intelligence tests, and explain how reliability and validity are assessed.

The Dynamics of Intelligence (pp. 437-441)

8. Discuss the stability of intelligence scores, and describe the two extremes of the normal distribution of intelligence.

Genetic and Environmental Influences on Intelligence (pp. 441-452)

9. Discuss evidence for both genetic and environmental influences on intelligence.

10. Describe group differences in intelligence test scores, and show how they can be explained in terms of environmental factors.

11. Discuss whether intelligence tests are culturally biased.

The origins of intelligence testing, p. 420
Easy, Factual/Definitional, Objective 1, Ans: c

1. Binet and Simon designed a test of intellectual abilities in order to:
   a. provide a quantitative estimate of inherited intellectual potential.
   b. distinguish between academic and practical intelligence.
   c. identify children likely to have difficulty learning in school.
   d. assess general capacity for goal-directed adaptive behavior.

The origins of intelligence testing, p. 420
Medium, Factual/Definitional, Objective 1, Ans: d

2. Binet and Simon assumed that intellectually bright children:
   a. can be identified at a very young age by measuring their physical coordination and sensory skills.
   b. have a mental age that is completely unrelated to their chronological age.
   c. are just as likely to have difficulty in regular classes as slow learners.
   d. are as intellectually developed as average children who are older than they.

The origins of intelligence testing, p. 420
Medium, Factual/Definitional, Objective 1, Ans: b

3. To assess mental age, Binet and Simon measured children's:
   a. head size.
   b. reasoning skills.
   c. muscular power.
   d. sensory acuity.
   e. all of the above.

The origins of intelligence testing, p. 420
Easy, Conceptual/Application, Objective 1, Ans: a

4. Five-year-old Wilbur performs on an intelligence test at a level characteristic of an average 4-year-old. Wilbur's mental age is:
   a. 4.
   b. 4.5.
   c. 5.
   d. 80.
   e. 125.

The origins of intelligence testing, p. 420
Difficult, Conceptual, Objective 1, Ans: b

5. Who would have been the *least* enthusiastic about a reliance on eugenics for the improvement of human intellectual functioning?
   a. Plato
   b. Binet
   c. Terman
   d. Darwin

The origins of intelligence testing, pp. 420-421
Medium, Conceptual, Objective 1, Ans: a

6. Binet and Terman would have been most likely to disagree about the:
   a. extent to which intelligence is determined by heredity.
   b. need to standardize intelligence tests.
   c. possibility of predicting people's academic success from intelligence test scores.
   d. extent to which individuals differ in their intellectual abilities.

The origins of intelligence testing, p. 421
Medium, Factual/Definitional, Objective 1, Ans: d

7. For the original version of the Stanford-Binet, IQ was defined as:
   a. mental age multiplied by 100.
   b. chronological age subtracted from mental age and multiplied by 100.
   c. chronological age divided by mental age and multiplied by 100.
   d. mental age divided by chronological age and multiplied by 100.

The origins of intelligence testing, p. 421
Medium, Conceptual/Application, Objective 1, Ans: a

8. A 12-year-old who responded to the original Stanford-Binet with the proficiency typical of an average 9-year-old was said to have an IQ of:
   a. 75.
   b. 85.
   c. 115.
   d. 125.
   e. 133.

The origins of intelligence testing, p. 421
Difficult, Conceptual/Application, Objective 1, Ans: b

9. Twelve-year-old Benjy has an IQ of 75 on the original version of the Stanford-Binet. His mental age is:
   a. 8.
   b. 9.
   c. 10.
   d. 12.
   e. 16.

The origins of intelligence testing, p. 421
Difficult, Conceptual, Objective 1, Ans: a

10. The eugenics movement would have been most likely to encourage:
   a. selective breeding of highly intelligent people.
   b. creation of special education programs for intellectually inferior children.
   c. construction of culturally and racially unbiased tests of intelligence.
   d. use of factor analysis for identification of various types of intelligence.

The origins of intelligence testing, p. 421
Medium, Factual/Definitional, Objective 1, Ans: c

11. During the World War I era, the U.S. government developed intelligence tests to evaluate newly arriving immigrants. For most proponents of the eugenics movement, inferior test scores were viewed as reflecting the immigrants':
a. educational background.
b. ignorance of American culture.
c. innate mental abilities.
d. unfamiliarity with intelligence test questions.
e. socioeconomic status.

What is intelligence?, p. 422
Difficult, Conceptual/Application, Objective 2, Ans: c

12. Joni claims that she is intellectually gifted because she "possesses" an IQ of 145. She is most clearly committing the error known as:
a. heritability.
b. the Flynn effect.
c. reification.
d. the naturalistic fallacy.
e. savant syndrome.

What is intelligence?, p. 422
Easy, Factual/Definitional, Objective 2, Ans: b

13. In considering the nature of intelligence, experts would be most likely to agree that intelligence is a(n):
a. inborn ability to perform well on standard intelligence tests.
b. ability to learn from experience.
c. general trait that underlies success on nearly any task.
d. multiple array of completely independent adaptive traits.

Is intelligence one general or several specific abilities?, p. 423
Easy, Factual/Definitional, Objective 2, Ans: d

14. Factor analysis is a statistical procedure used to:
a. derive IQ scores by comparing mental age with chronological age.
b. evaluate how accurately test items predict a criterion behavior.
c. extract test norms from a standardization sample.
d. identify clusters of closely related test items.
e. provide a quantitative estimate of heritability.

Is intelligence one general or several specific abilities?, p. 423
Medium, Factual/Definitional, Objective 2, Ans: e

15. In order to assess whether intelligence is a single trait or a collection of several distinct abilities, psychologists have made extensive use of:
a. the normal distribution.
b. criterion-based validation.
c. standardization.
d. reliability assessment.
e. factor analysis.

Is intelligence one general or several specific abilities?, p. 423
Easy, Factual/Definitional, Objective 2, Ans: c

16. Spearman's *g* factor refers to:
a. the internal consistency of an intelligence test.
b. the genetic contribution to intelligence.
c. a general intelligence that underlies success on a wide variety of tasks.
d. a highly developed skill or talent possessed by an otherwise retarded person.
e. the ability to understand and regulate emotions.

Is intelligence one general or several specific abilities?, p. 423
Difficult, Conceptual, Objective 2, Ans: b

17. Who would have been most enthusiastic about the value of a single intelligence test score as an index of an individual's mental capacities?
a. Thurstone
b. Spearman
c. Gardner
d. Sternberg

Is intelligence one general or several specific abilities?, p. 424
Medium, Conceptual/Application, Objective 2, Ans: d

18. Twenty-five-year-old Alexandra is mentally handicapped and can neither read nor write. However, after hearing lengthy, unfamiliar, and complex musical selections just once, she can reproduce them precisely on the piano. It is likely that Alexandra is:
a. gifted with a high level of Spearman's *g* factor.
b. gifted with a high level of emotional intelligence.
c. suffering from Down syndrome.
d. someone with savant syndrome.

Is intelligence one general or several specific abilities?, p. 424
Medium, Factual/Definitional, Objective 2, Ans: a

19. The characteristics of savant syndrome most directly suggest that intelligence is:
a. a diverse set of distinct abilities.
b. largely unpredictable and unmeasurable.
c. a culturally constructed concept.
d. dependent upon the speed of cognitive processing.

Is intelligence one general or several specific abilities?, p. 424
Medium, Conceptual, Objective 2, Ans: d

20. Those who define intelligence as academic aptitude are most likely to criticize:
a. Terman's concept of innate intelligence.
b. Spearman's concept of general intelligence.
c. Binet's concept of mental age.
d. Gardner's concept of multiple intelligences.
e. Stern's concept of intelligence quotient.

Is intelligence one general or several specific abilities?, p. 424
Medium, Factual/Definitional, Objective 2, Ans: b

21. Howard Gardner is most likely to agree that the concept of intelligence includes:
   a. minimizing one's negative emotions.
   b. spatially analyzing visual input.
   c. experiencing positive self-esteem.
   d. behaving morally.

Is intelligence one general or several specific abilities?, p. 425
Medium, Conceptual/Application, Objective 2, Ans: c

22. Which of the following persons best illustrates Sternberg and Wagner's concept of practical intelligence?
   a. Jamal, a college student who quickly recognizes the correct answers to multiple-choice test questions
   b. Gareth, a graduate student who generates many creative research ideas
   c. Shelley, a newspaper reporter who has a knack for making connections with very important people
   d. Cindy, a young mother who prefers playing with her children to cleaning her house

Is intelligence one general or several specific abilities?, p. 426
Easy, Factual/Definitional, Objective 2, Ans: a

23. The ability to control one's impulses and delay immediate pleasures in pursuit of long-term goals is most clearly a characteristic of:
   a. emotional intelligence.
   b. heritability.
   c. mental age.
   d. savant syndrome.
   e. the *g* factor.

Is intelligence one general or several specific abilities?, p. 426
Medium, Conceptual/Application, Objective 2, Ans: e

24. Although Nicole scored well above average on the SAT, she frequently loses her temper and needlessly antagonizes even her best friends. Her behavior best illustrates an inadequate level of:
   a. heritability.
   b. predictive validity.
   c. the *g* factor.
   d. mental age.
   e. emotional intelligence.

Intelligence and creativity, p. 428
Difficult, Factual/Definitional, Objective 4, Ans: b

25. The correlation between intelligence test scores and creativity test scores is ________ among those whose intelligence score is ________ than 120.
   a. negative; greater than
   b. positive; less than
   c. negative; less than
   d. positive; greater than

Intelligence and creativity, pp. 428-429
Medium, Conceptual/Application, Objective 4, Ans: c

26. Which of the following suggestions would be *least* helpful to a young performing artist who wants to become a highly creative ballet dancer?
   a. "Study the performances of the world's best ballet artists."
   b. "Develop friendly and supportive relationships with fellow ballet dancers."
   c. "Win competitive performances that will lead to performance arts scholarship offers."
   d. "Take time for those practice drills that you find most enjoyable."

Intelligence and creativity, p. 429
Easy, Factual/Definitional, Objective 4, Ans: b

27. Intrinsic motivation is an important component of:
   a. the intelligence quotient.
   b. creativity.
   c. the Flynn effect.
   d. savant syndrome.
   e. the *g* factor.

Intelligence and creativity, p. 429
Medium, Conceptual/Application, Objective 4, Ans: b

28. Scientists are most likely to be creative if they:
   a. investigate issues about which they have very little previous knowledge.
   b. approach problems they find intrinsically interesting and satisfying to study.
   c. think about the benefits to themselves and society that might result from their work.
   d. do all of the above.

Is intelligence neurologically measurable?, pp. 429-430
Easy, Factual/Definitional, Objective 3, Ans: d

29. There is a ________ correlation between head size and intelligence and a ________ correlation between brain size and intelligence.
   a. slightly negative; slightly positive
   b. slightly positive; slightly negative
   c. moderately positive; slightly positive
   d. slightly positive; moderately positive

Is intelligence neurologically measurable?, pp. 430, 431
Difficult, Factual/Definitional, Objective 3, Ans: c

30. Brain size (adjusted for body size) is ________ correlated with intelligence, and the speed of taking in perceptual information is ________ correlated with intelligence.
   a. positively; negatively
   b. negatively; positively
   c. positively; positively
   d. negatively; negatively

Is intelligence neurologically measurable?, pp. 430-431
Easy, Factual/Definitional, Objective 3, Ans: a

31. Precocious college students with unusually high levels of verbal intelligence are most likely to:
    a. retrieve information from memory at an unusually rapid speed.
    b. perform at only an average level on tests of mathematical aptitude.
    c. experience less loneliness and achieve happier marriages than the average college student.
    d. demonstrate unusually high levels of the practical managerial intelligence common to successful business executives.

Is intelligence neurologically measurable?, p. 431
Medium, Factual/Definitional, Objective 3, Ans: c

32. Studies suggest that there is a positive correlation between intelligence and the brain's:
    a. rate of glucose consumption.
    b. production of endorphins.
    c. neural processing speed.
    d. ability to process language in the right rather than the left hemisphere.

Modern tests of mental abilities, p. 432
Easy, Factual/Definitional, Objective 5, Ans: e

33. Tests designed to predict ability to learn new skills are called ________ tests.
    a. achievement
    b. interest
    c. reliability
    d. standardized
    e. aptitude

Modern tests of mental abilities, p. 432
Easy, Conceptual/Application, Objective 5, Ans: d

34. A test of your capacity to learn to be an automobile mechanic would be considered a(n) ________ test.
    a. reliability
    b. interest
    c. achievement
    d. aptitude
    e. intelligence

Modern tests of mental abilities, p. 432
Easy, Factual/Definitional, Objective 5, Ans: d

35. Achievement tests are designed to:
    a. measure desire and potential capacity to successfully meet challenges.
    b. assess ability to produce novel and valuable ideas.
    c. compare an individual's personality with those of highly successful people.
    d. assess learned knowledge or skills.

Modern tests of mental abilities, p. 432
Medium, Conceptual/Application, Objective 5, Ans: a

36. The written exam for a driver's license would most likely be considered a(n) ________ test.
    a. achievement
    b. reliability
    c. interest
    d. aptitude
    e. intelligence

Modern tests of mental abilities, p. 432
Medium, Conceptual, Objective 5, Ans: d

37. Aptitude tests are to ________ as achievement tests are to ________.
    a. current interests; past competence
    b. past competence; current interests
    c. current competence; future performance
    d. future performance; current competence

Modern tests of mental abilities, p. 433
Difficult, Factual/Definitional, Objective 5, Ans: d

38. The WAIS consists of separate ________ subtests.
    a. intelligence and creativity
    b. aptitude and achievement
    c. validity and reliability
    d. verbal and performance

Modern tests of mental abilities, p. 433
Medium, Factual/Definitional, Objective 5, Ans: a

39. Object assembly, picture arrangement, and block design are three subtests of the:
    a. WAIS.
    b. MEIS.
    c. Stanford-Binet.
    d. GRE.

Standardization, p. 434
Easy, Factual/Definitional, Objective 6, Ans: b

40. If a test is standardized, this means that:
    a. it accurately measures what it is intended to measure.
    b. a person's test performance can be compared with that of a pretested group.
    c. most test scores will cluster near the average.
    d. the test will yield consistent results when administered on different occasions.

Standardization, p. 434
Medium, Conceptual/Application, Objective 6, Ans: a

41. When Brandon was told that he correctly answered 80 percent of the items on a mathematical achievement test, he asked how his performance compared with that of the average test taker. Brandon's concern was directly related to the issue of:
    a. standardization.
    b. predictive validity.
    c. reliability.
    d. content validity.

Standardization, p. 434
Difficult, Factual/Definitional, Objective 6, Ans: a

42. Unlike today's most widely used intelligence tests, the original Stanford-Binet can be most clearly criticized with respect to its:
   a. standardization sample.
   b. reliability.
   c. factor analysis.
   d. predictive validity.
   e. heritability.

Standardization, p. 434
Easy, Factual/Definitional, Objective 6, Ans: d

43. The bell-shaped pattern that represents the frequency of occurrence of intelligence test scores in the general population is called a:
   a. standardization sample.
   b. reliability coefficient.
   c. factor analysis.
   d. normal curve.
   e. savant syndrome.

Standardization (Figure 11.3), p. 434
Difficult, Factual/Definitional, Objective 6, Ans: c

44. About ________ percent of WAIS scores fall between 85 and 115.
   a. 30
   b. 50
   c. 68
   d. 96

Standardization, pp. 434-435
Difficult, Conceptual/Application, Objective 6, Ans: c

45. The normal curve would represent the distribution of:
   a. the American population in terms of gender.
   b. American schoolchildren in terms of their ages.
   c. American women in terms of their physical heights.
   d. all of the above.

Standardization, p. 435
Medium, Factual/Definitional, Objective 6, Ans: c

46. Comparing the average performance of the initial WAIS standardization sample with the average performance of the most recent WAIS standardization sample provides convincing evidence of:
   a. heritability.
   b. the *g* factor.
   c. the Flynn effect.
   d. emotional intelligence.
   e. savant syndrome.

Standardization, p. 435
Medium, Factual/Definitional, Objective 6, Ans: b

47. During the 1960s and 1970s, performance on the WAIS ________ and performance on college entrance aptitude tests ________.
    a. declined; declined
    b. improved; declined
    c. declined; improved
    d. improved; improved

Standardization, p. 435
Medium, Factual/Definitional, Objective 6, Ans: a

48. The decline in college aptitude test scores during the 1960s and 1970s was due in part to:
    a. the increasing academic diversity of students taking these tests.
    b. the standardization of college aptitude tests on more representative samples of the population.
    c. the introduction of new and increasingly difficult aptitude test questions.
    d. today's students' inexperience with standardized tests.

Standardization, p. 435
Medium, Factual/Definitional, Objective 6, Ans: b

49. It would be most reasonable to suggest that the Flynn effect is due in part to:
    a. the deteriorating quality of parental involvement in children's education.
    b. increasingly improved childhood health and nutrition.
    c. the decreasing reliance on a single test score as an index of mental aptitudes.
    d. the failure to restandardize existing intelligence tests.

Reliability, p. 435
Medium, Factual/Definitional, Objective 7, Ans: c

50. If a test yields consistent results every time it is used, it has a high degree of:
    a. standardization.
    b. predictive validity.
    c. reliability.
    d. content validity.
    e. heritability.

Reliability, p. 435
Medium, Conceptual/Application, Objective 7, Ans: b

51. Melinda completed the Computer Programming Aptitude Test when she applied for a position with Beta Electronics. Six months later, she took the same test when she applied for a position with another company. The fact that her scores were almost identical on the two occasions suggests that the test has a high degree of:
    a. content validity.
    b. reliability.
    c. predictive validity.
    d. standardization.

Reliability, p. 436
Difficult, Factual/Definitional, Objective 7, Ans: b

52. Researchers assess the correlation between scores obtained on two halves of a single test in order to measure the ________ of a test.
   a. validity
   b. reliability
   c. standardization
   d. normal distribution
   e. factor analysis

Reliability and validity, p. 436
Medium, Conceptual, Objective 7, Ans: b

53. Validity is to reliability as ________ is to ________.
   a. causation; correlation
   b. accuracy; consistency
   c. stability; change
   d. aptitude; achievement
   e. academic intelligence; emotional intelligence

Reliability and validity, p. 436
Medium, Conceptual/Application, Objective 7, Ans: c

54. A measure of intelligence based on head size is likely to have a ________ level of reliability and a ________ level of validity.
   a. low; low
   b. low; high
   c. high; low
   d. high; high

Validity, p. 436
Easy, Factual/Definitional, Objective 7, Ans: a

55. A test that measures or predicts what it is supposed to is said to have a high degree of:
   a. validity.
   b. standardization.
   c. reliability.
   d. normality.

Validity, p. 436
Easy, Conceptual/Application, Objective 7, Ans: d

56. Your psychology professor has announced that the next test will assess your understanding of sensation and perception. When you receive the test, however, you find that very few questions actually relate to these topics. In this instance, you would be most concerned about the ________ of the test.
   a. reliability
   b. factor analysis
   c. standardization
   d. validity
   e. normal distribution

Validity, p. 436
Medium, Conceptual/Application, Objective 7, Ans: b

57. If both depressed and nondepressed individuals receive similar scores on a diagnostic test for depression, it is said that the test:
   a. has not been standardized.
   b. is not valid.
   c. is not reliable.
   d. has not been factor-analyzed.
   e. does not produce scores that form a normal distribution.

Validity, p. 436
Medium, Factual/Definitional, Objective 7, Ans: e

58. Psychologists measure the correlation between aptitude test scores and school grades in order to assess the ________ of the aptitude test.
   a. reliability
   b. standardization
   c. normal distribution
   d. factor analysis
   e. validity

Validity, p. 436
Medium, Factual/Definitional, Objective 7, Ans: a

59. Intelligence test scores are most likely to predict accurately the academic success of ________ students.
   a. elementary school
   b. high school
   c. college
   d. graduate school

Validity, p. 436
Difficult, Factual/Definitional, Objective 7, Ans: c

60. Why does the predictive validity of general aptitude tests decrease as the educational level of the students who take them increases?
   a. More educated students have taken aptitude tests so frequently that for them such tests are no longer pure measures of aptitude.
   b. Comparisons of mental age with chronological age are inadequate for assessing the aptitude of older and more educated students.
   c. There is a relatively restricted range of aptitude test scores among students at higher educational levels.
   d. Among more educated students, motivation has a much greater effect on academic success than does aptitude.

Validity, p. 436
Difficult, Conceptual, Objective 7, Ans: d

61. The correlation between academic success and intelligence test scores will be highest if computed for a group of individuals whose scores range between:
   a. 55 and 100.
   b. 85 and 115.
   c. 100 and 145.
   d. 70 and 130.

The dynamics of intelligence: stability or change?, pp. 437-438
Medium, Factual/Definitional, Objective 8, Ans: c

62. The best indicator of infants' intellectual aptitude is their:
a. readiness to crawl at an early age.
b. capacity for imitating adult facial expressions.
c. tendency to quickly shift their gaze from a familiar to a novel picture.
d. ability to discriminate their mother's voice from that of a female stranger.
e. head circumference at birth in relation to their total weight.

The dynamics of intelligence: stability or change?, p. 438
Difficult, Conceptual/Application, Objective 8, Ans: c

63. In order for Mr. and Mrs. Goldberg to best predict their newborn daughter's future intellectual aptitude they should:
a. carefully assess the infant's sensory and reflexive responses.
b. observe their daughter's general level of emotional reactivity.
c. obtain information about their own levels of intelligence.
d. monitor the age at which their child first walks and talks.

The dynamics of intelligence: stability or change?, p. 438
Easy, Conceptual/Application, Objective 8, Ans: d

64. Intelligence scores are most likely to be stable over a one-year period for a ________ student whose intelligence test score is ________.
a. preschool; 80
b. second-grade; 125
c. sixth-grade; 115
d. tenth-grade; 95

The dynamics of intelligence: stability or change?, p. 438
Medium, Factual/Definitional, Objective 8, Ans: a

65. The highly positive correlations between scores received on comparable sections of the SAT and GRE provide evidence for the ________ of these test scores.
a. reliability
b. heritability
c. content validity
d. predictive validity
e. normal distribution

Extremes of intelligence, p. 439
Easy, Conceptual/Application, Objective 8, Ans: d

66. Mr. and Mrs. Linkletter are parents of a mentally retarded child. It is most likely that their child:
a. is a female rather than a male.
b. suffers obvious physical defects.
c. was born with an extra chromosome.
d. will have difficulty adapting to the normal demands of independent adult life.

Extremes of intelligence (Table 11.1), p. 439
Difficult, Conceptual/Application, Objective 8, Ans: d

67. Sasha is mildly mentally retarded. She has achieved the equivalent of a fifth-grade education and will soon begin vocational training so that she can earn a living. Sasha's intelligence score is most likely between:
a. 5 and 20.
b. 20 and 35.
c. 35 and 50.
d. 50 and 70.
e. 75 and 90.

Extremes of intelligence, p. 439
Easy, Factual/Definitional, Objective 8, Ans: d

68. Individuals with Down syndrome are:
a. unlikely to have difficulty in regular school classes.
b. mentally retarded due to neglect during infancy.
c. mentally retarded, except for one specific ability in which they excel.
d. born with an extra chromosome.

Extremes of intelligence, p. 440
Medium, Factual/Definitional, Objective 8, Ans: d

69. Grouping children in separate educational classes according to their level of intellectual aptitude tends to ________ their self-esteem and ________ their academic achievement.
a. increase; increase
b. increase; decrease
c. decrease; decrease
d. decrease; have little effect on
e. increase; have little effect on

Extremes of intelligence, p. 440
Difficult, Factual/Definitional, Objective 8, Ans: b

70. "Gifted child" education programs are most likely to be criticized for:
a. overemphasizing the genetic determinants of giftedness.
b. limiting the concept of giftedness to superior academic aptitude.
c. claiming that intelligence test scores can predict children's academic success.
d. underestimating the extent to which a *g* factor underlies success in a wide variety of tasks.

Genetic and environmental influences on intelligence, p. 442
Easy, Factual/Definitional, Objective 9, Ans: d

71. The similarity between the intelligence test scores of identical twins raised apart is:
a. less than that between children and their biological parents.
b. equal to that between identical twins reared together.
c. equal to that between fraternal twins reared together.
d. greater than that between ordinary siblings reared together.

Genetic and environmental influences on intelligence, p. 442
Difficult, Factual/Definitional, Objective 9, Ans: d

72. Which of the following observations provides the best evidence that intelligence test scores are influenced by heredity?
   a. Japanese children have higher average intelligence scores than American children.
   b. Fraternal twins are more similar in their intelligence scores than are ordinary siblings.
   c. The intelligence scores of children are positively correlated with the intelligence scores of their parents.
   d. Identical twins reared separately are more similar in their intelligence scores than fraternal twins reared together.

Genetic and environmental influences on intelligence, p. 443
Medium, Conceptual/Application, Objective 9, Ans: a

73. Which pair of individuals is most likely to receive similar intelligence test scores?
   a. opposite-sex fraternal twins
   b. ordinary siblings of the same sex
   c. a mother and daughter
   d. a father and daughter

Genetic and environmental influences on intelligence, p. 443
Medium, Factual/Definitional, Objective 9, Ans: d

74. The intelligence test scores of adopted children are *least* likely to be positively correlated with the scores of their adoptive siblings during:
   a. middle childhood.
   b. early adolescence.
   c. middle adolescence.
   d. early adulthood.

Genetic and environmental influences on intelligence, p. 443
Difficult, Factual/Definitional, Objective 9, Ans: d

75. With increasing age, adopted children's intelligence test scores become ________ positively correlated with their adoptive parents' scores and ________ positively correlated with their biological parent's scores.
   a. more; more
   b. less; less
   c. more; less
   d. less; more

Genetic and environmental influences on intelligence, p. 443
Medium, Factual/Definitional, Objective 9, Ans: b

76. The heritability of intelligence refers to:
   a. the extent to which an individual's intelligence is attributable to genetic factors.
   b. the percentage of variation in intelligence within a group that is attributable to genetic factors.
   c. the extent to which a group's intelligence is attributable to genetic factors.
   d. a general underlying intelligence factor that is measured by every task on an intelligence test.

Genetic and environmental influences on intelligence, pp. 443-444
Medium, Conceptual/Application, Objective 9, Ans: a

77. If 10 genetically identical individuals were all raised in different homes, the heritability of intelligence for this group would be ________ percent.
    a. 0
    b. 10
    c. 50
    d. 100

Genetic and environmental influences on intelligence, pp. 443-444
Difficult, Factual/Definitional, Objective 9, Ans: c

78. The heritability of intelligence is lowest among genetically ________ individuals who have been raised in ________ environments.
    a. similar; similar
    b. dissimilar; similar
    c. similar; dissimilar
    d. dissimilar; dissimilar

Genetic and environmental influences on intelligence, pp. 443-445
Medium, Factual/Definitional, Objective 9, Ans: d

79. The importance of environmental influences on intelligence is provided by evidence that:
    a. fraternal twins have more similar intelligence test scores than ordinary siblings.
    b. intellectual development of neglected children in impoverished environments is often retarded.
    c. Head Start programs for disadvantaged children can decrease the likelihood of their having to repeat a grade in school.
    d. all of the above are true.

Genetic and environmental influences on intelligence, p. 445
Medium, Factual/Definitional, Objective 9, Ans: c

80. Research indicates that Head Start programs:
    a. contribute to dramatic and enduring gains in the participants' intelligence test scores.
    b. yield the greatest benefits for participants coming from intellectually stimulating home environments.
    c. reduce the likelihood that participants will repeat grades or require special education.
    d. do all of the above.

Genetic and environmental influences on intelligence, p. 445
Easy, Factual/Definitional, Objective 9, Ans: b

81. Increasing years of schooling over the last half century have most likely contributed to:
    a. the eugenics movement.
    b. the Flynn effect.
    c. the normal curve.
    d. savant syndrome.

Ethnic similarities and differences, pp. 446-447
Medium, Conceptual/Application, Objective 10, Ans: d

82. Disproportionately more Whites than Blacks would be admitted into American colleges if performance scores on ________ were the only criterion for college admissions.
    a. the Stanford-Binet
    b. the WAIS
    c. the SAT
    d. any of the above

Ethnic similarities and differences, pp. 446-447
Difficult, Conceptual/Application, Objective 10, Ans: d

83. On average, the intelligence test scores of the Wallonians are much higher than those of the Danasians. The difference in the average test scores of the two groups might be a product of:
    a. genetic differences between two groups with similar environments.
    b. environmental differences between two groups with similar genetics.
    c. genetic and environmental differences between the two groups.
    d. any of the above.

Ethnic similarities and differences, p. 447
Medium, Factual/Definitional, Objective 10, Ans: b

84. Research on racial and ethnic differences in intelligence indicates that:
    a. desegregation has actually decreased the academic achievement of black American children.
    b. the average mathematics achievement test scores of Asian children are notably higher than those of North American children.
    c. among American Blacks, those with African ancestry receive the highest intelligence test scores.
    d. the Black-White difference in SAT scores has increased since 1979.
    e. all of the above are true.

Ethnic similarities and differences, p. 448
Medium, Factual/Definitional, Objective 10, Ans: b

85. The average difference in intellectual aptitude scores of white and black college graduates has been observed to be greatest when these individuals were:
    a. eighth graders.
    b. high school juniors.
    c. college sophomores.
    d. college seniors.

Gender similarities and differences, p. 448
Easy, Factual/Definitional, Objective 10, Ans: a

86. Girls are most likely to outperform boys in a(n):
    a. spelling bee.
    b. math test.
    c. computer programming contest.
    d. chess tournament.

Gender similarities and differences, p. 448
Medium, Factual/Definitional, Objective 10, Ans: d

87. Boys outnumber girls at the ________ levels of reading ability and at the ________ levels of mathematical problem-solving ability.
   a. high; low
   b. low; low
   c. high; high
   d. low; high

Gender similarities and differences, p. 448
Easy, Conceptual, Objective 10, Ans: c

88. Boys are most likely to outnumber girls in a class designed for students gifted in:
   a. reading.
   b. speech.
   c. mathematics.
   d. a foreign language.

Gender similarities and differences, p. 449
Medium, Factual/Definitional, Objective 10, Ans: b

89. Boys are most likely to outperform girls in a(n):
   a. essay contest.
   b. chess tournament.
   c. speed-reading tournament.
   d. spelling bee.
   e. speech-giving contest.

Gender similarities and differences, p. 449
Medium, Factual/Definitional, Objective 10, Ans: c

90. Exposure to high levels of male sex hormones during prenatal development is most likely to facilitate the subsequent development of:
   a. the *g* factor.
   b. savant syndrome.
   c. spatial abilities.
   d. Down syndrome.
   e. emotional intelligence.

Gender similarities and differences, p. 449
Easy, Factual/Definitional, Objective 10, Ans: c

91. Research on gender and emotional intelligence suggests that women are more skilled than men at:
   a. avoiding the experience of emotional ambivalence.
   b. preventing emotions from distorting reasoning.
   c. interpreting others’ facial expressions of emotion.
   d. delaying emotional gratification in pursuit of long-term goals.

The question of bias, p. 450
Easy, Factual/Definitional, Objective 11, Ans: a

92. Most experts would agree that intelligence tests are "biased" in the sense that:
   a. test performance is influenced by cultural experiences.
   b. the reliability of intelligence tests is close to zero.
   c. the heritability of intelligence is 100 percent.
   d. numerical scores of intelligence serve to dehumanize individuals.

The question of bias, pp. 450-451
Difficult, Conceptual, Objective 11, Ans: c

93. Experts who defend intelligence tests against the charge of being culturally biased and discriminatory would be most likely to highlight the ________ of intelligence tests.
   a. normal distribution
   b. content validity
   c. predictive validity
   d. reliability
   e. standardization

The question of bias, p. 451
Medium, Conceptual/Application, Objective 11, Ans: c

94. When completing a verbal aptitude test, members of an ethnic minority group are particularly likely to perform below their true ability levels if they believe that the test:
   a. is a measure of emotional intelligence as well as academic intelligence.
   b. assesses their interests as well as their abilities.
   c. is biased against members of their own ethnic group.
   d. results in a distribution of scores that form a bell-shaped curve.

The question of bias, p. 451
Medium, Factual/Definitional, Objective 11, Ans: b

95. Intelligence tests have effectively reduced discrimination in the sense that they have:
   a. avoided questions that require familiarity with any specific culture.
   b. helped limit reliance on educators' subjectively biased judgments of students' academic potential.
   c. provided an objective measure of teaching effectiveness in different public school systems.
   d. done all of the above.

Essay Questions

1. You have been hired by a large public school system to construct a musical aptitude test. Describe how you would standardize your test and assess its reliability and validity. Explain why it might be more difficult to develop a valid musical aptitude test than a reliable one.

2. Although Susan is a brilliant pianist and highly acclaimed ballet dancer, her high school intelligence test scores were only average. What does Susan's experience suggest regarding (a) the reliability and validity of intelligence tests, (b) the nature of intelligence, and (c) the desirability of currently popular "gifted child" education programs?

3. A classmate makes the following claim: “Despite numerous federally funded Head Start programs and nationwide efforts to desegregate public schools, Blacks continue to lag behind their White counterparts in intelligence and academic achievement. Clearly, Black Americans must be genetically inferior to White Americans.”

   Use research evidence and logical arguments to intelligently refute your classmate’s statement.

4. Juan is the oldest son of Mexican parents who immigrated to the United States less than five years ago. Juan’s high school teachers perceive him to be fairly intelligent, but his SAT scores are low and he is having trouble getting into college. Juan’s mother angrily claims that “intelligence tests are biased against Hispanics.” Juan’s father sadly counters, “It’s not the tests that are biased; it’s American education that is biased.”

   Carefully explain why you would agree or disagree with the comments made by each of the parents.

Web Quiz 1

Ans: c

1. The widely used American revision of Alfred Binet's original intelligence test was developed by:
   a. Charles Spearman.
   b. Howard Gardner.
   c. Lewis Terman.
   d. Robert Sternberg.
   e. William James.

Ans: d

2. An 8-year-old who responded to the original Stanford-Binet with the proficiency of an average 10-year-old was said to have an IQ of:
   a. 80.
   b. 100.
   c. 110.
   d. 125.
   e. 150.

Ans: e

3. Which procedure is used to identify different dimensions of performance that underlie people's intelligence test scores?
   a. standardization
   b. validation
   c. reification
   d. heritability estimates
   e. factor analysis

Ans: d

4. When Phoebe strongly disagrees with her sister's opinion, she effectively controls her own anger and responds with empathy to her sister's frustration regarding their dispute. Her behavior best illustrates:
   a. factor analysis.
   b. analytic intelligence.
   c. predictive validity.
   d. emotional intelligence.
   e. savant syndrome.

Ans: c

5. Managers who want to foster innovation in the workplace should seek to facilitate the ________ of their employees.
   a. standardization
   b. factor analysis
   c. intrinsic motivation
   d. emotional intelligence

Ans: a

6. Compared to others, people who are highly intelligent exhibit ________ neural plasticity and ________ brain-wave responses to simple stimuli.
a. more; faster
b. less; slower
c. more; slower
d. less; faster

Ans: e

7. A test designed to assess whether aspiring physicians should be granted the legal right to practice medicine would most likely be considered a(n) ________ test.
a. *g*-factor
b. aptitude
c. factor analysis
d. reliability
e. achievement

Ans: a

8. Before publishing her test of musical aptitude, Professor Reed first administered the test to a representative sample of people. This was most clearly necessary for test:
a. standardization.
b. reliability.
c. heritability.
d. validity.

Ans: a

9. When retested on the WAIS, people's second scores generally match their first scores quite closely. This indicates that the test has a high degree of:
a. reliability.
b. content validity.
c. heritability.
d. predictive validity.

Ans: b

10. If course exams assess a student's mastery of a representative sample of course material, they are said to:
a. be reliable.
b. have content validity.
c. be standardized.
d. have predictive validity.

Ans: b

11. Mark experiences severe mental retardation. Although he speaks very little, he has been trained to put on his own clothes and perform simple tasks under close supervision. Mark's intelligence test score is most likely between:
a. 0 and 15.
b. 20 and 35.
c. 40 and 55.
d. 60 and 75.
e. 80 and 95.

Ans: d

12. Comparing the academic accomplishments of those who score extremely low with those who score extremely high on intelligence tests is an effective way to highlight the tests':
   a. standardization.
   b. heritability.
   c. reliability.
   d. validity.

Ans: c

13. The similarity between the intelligence test scores of nontwin siblings reared together is:
   a. greater than that between identical twins reared apart.
   b. equal to that between fraternal twins reared together.
   c. greater than that between unrelated adoptive siblings reared together.
   d. less than that between children and their biological parents.

Ans: d

14. With his concern for "mental orthopedics," Alfred Binet would have been most enthusiastic about:
   a. eugenics.
   b. factor analysis.
   c. predictive validity.
   d. Head Start programs.
   e. the normal curve.

Ans: a

15. Stereotype threat is most likely to depress female students' performance on a difficult ________ test and to depress male students' performance on a difficult ________ test.
   a. math problem solving; verbal fluency
   b. verbal fluency; math problem solving
   c. spatial abilities; athletic abilities
   d. athletic abilities; spatial abilities

Web Quiz 2

Ans: c

1. The first modern test of intelligence was developed in:
   a. Germany.
   b. Britain.
   c. France.
   d. the United States.

Ans: e

2. An 8-year-old who responded to the original Stanford-Binet with the proficiency typical of an average 10-year-old was said to have a mental age of:
   a. 8.
   b. 8.5.
   c. 9.
   d. 9.5.
   e. 10.

Ans: d

3. Although diagnosed with autism and hardly able to speak coherently, 18-year-old Andrew can produce intricate and detailed drawings of scenes he has viewed only once. Andrew illustrates a condition known as:
   a. *g* factor.
   b. Down syndrome.
   c. emotional intelligence.
   d. savant syndrome.

Ans: a

4. Superior performance on the WAIS is most likely to be indicative of:
   a. Sternberg's concept of analytical intelligence.
   b. Gardner's concept of athletic intelligence.
   c. Cantor and Kihlstrom's concept of social intelligence.
   d. Salovey and Mayer's concept of emotional intelligence.

Ans: b

5. College students who focus on the interest and challenge of their school work rather than on simply meeting deadlines and securing good grades are especially likely to demonstrate:
   a. emotional intelligence.
   b. creativity.
   c. reliability.
   d. factor analysis.
   e. the *g* factor.

Ans: a

6. A high school counselor gave Amy a test designed to predict whether she could learn to become a successful architect. Amy most likely received a(n) ________ test.
   a. aptitude
   b. *g* factor
   c. emotional intelligence
   d. factor analysis

Ans: d

7. A performance score on the WAIS that is higher than all but 2 percent of all scores earns an intelligence score of:
   a. 98.
   b. 115.
   c. 120.
   d. 130.
   e. 145.

Ans: e

8. Some hereditarians have been fearful that higher twentieth-century birth rates among those with lower intelligence scores would shove average intelligence scores progressively downward. This fear has been most directly alleviated by the discovery of:
   a. the normal curve.
   b. savant syndrome.
   c. the *g* factor.
   d. emotional intelligence.
   e. the Flynn effect.

Ans: b

9. Mary's bathroom scale always overstates people's actual weight by exactly six pounds. The scale has ________ reliability and ________ validity.
   a. low; high
   b. high; low
   c. low; low
   d. high; high

Ans: d

10. College grades are the criterion for the ________ of the SAT.
   a. heritability
   b. reliability
   c. standardization
   d. predictive validity

Ans: d

11. Children at 20 months of age who spoke sentences typical of 3-year-olds ________ especially likely to be reading by age 4-and-a-half. Eight-graders who outperform most high schoolers on a college aptitude test ________ especially likely to be reading by age 5.
   a. were; were
   b. were not; were not
   c. were; were not
   d. were not; were

Ans: d

12. The largest segment of persons with mental retardation achieve intelligence test scores between:
   a. 0 and 10.
   b. 10 and 30.
   c. 30 and 50.
   d. 50 and 70.
   e. 70 and 90.

Ans: c

13. The heritability of intelligence scores among children of less-educated parents tends to be relatively ________ due to the relatively ________ variability among their family environments.
    a. low; low
    b. high; high
    c. low; high
    d. high; low

Ans: c

14. Compared to North American students, Asian students perform ________ on math aptitude and achievements tests and they spend ________ time studying math.
    a. better; less
    b. no better; less
    c. better; more
    d. no better; more

Ans: e

15. Women have been found to score lower on math tests when they are tested alongside of men. This best illustrates the impact of:
    a. the Flynn effect.
    b. savant syndrome.
    c. standardization.
    d. emotional intelligence.
    e. stereotype threat.

Study Guide Questions

Ans: d, p. 420

1. A 6-year-old child has a mental age of 9. The child's IQ is:
   a. 96.
   b. 100.
   c. 125.
   d. 150.
   e. 166.

Ans: c, p. 420

2. The test created by Alfred Binet was designed specifically to:
   a. measure inborn intelligence in adults.
   b. measure inborn intelligence in children.
   c. predict school performance in children.
   d. identify mentally retarded children so that they could be institutionalized.
   e. do all of the above.

Ans: b, p. 421

3. If asked to guess the intelligence score of a stranger, your best guess would be:
   a. 75.
   b. 100.
   c. 125.
   d. "I don't know; intelligence scores vary too widely."

Ans: d, p. 421

4. Benito was born in 1937. In 1947, he scored 130 on an intelligence test. What was Benito's mental age when he took the test?
   a. 9
   b. 10
   c. 11
   d. 13
   e. It cannot be determined from the information provided.

Ans: a, p. 421

5. Originally, IQ was defined as:
   a. mental age divided by chronological age and multiplied by 100.
   b. chronological age divided by mental age and multiplied by 100.
   c. mental age subtracted from chronological age and multiplied by 100.
   d. chronological age subtracted from mental age and multiplied by 100.

Ans: e, p. 421

6. The formula for the intelligence quotient was devised by:
   a. Sternberg.
   b. Gall.
   c. Binet.
   d. Terman.
   e. Stern.

Ans: c, p. 421

7. Current intelligence tests compute an individual's intelligence score as:
   a. the ratio of mental age to chronological age multiplied by 100.
   b. the ratio of chronological age to mental age multiplied by 100.
   c. the amount by which the test-taker's performance deviates from the average performance of others the same age.
   d. the ratio of the test-taker's verbal intelligence score to his or her nonverbal intelligence score.

Ans: c, p. 421

8. According to the text, what can be concluded from early intelligence testing in the United States?
   a. Most European immigrants were "feeble-minded."
   b. Army recruits of other than West European heritage were intellectually deficient.
   c. The tests were biased against people who did not share the culture assumed by the test.
   d. Both a. and b. could be concluded.

Ans: c, p. 422

9. Most experts view intelligence as a person's:
   a. ability to perform well on intelligence tests.
   b. innate mental capacity.
   c. ability to learn from experience, solve problems, and adapt to new situations.
   d. diverse skills acquired throughout life.

Ans: d, pp. 422, 440

10. By creating a label such as "gifted," we begin to act as if all children are naturally divided into two categories, gifted and nongifted. This logical error is referred to as:
   a. rationalization.
   b. nominalizing.
   c. factor analysis.
   d. reification.
   e. heritability.

Ans: a, p. 423

11. The concept of a *g* factor implies that intelligence:
   a. is a single overall ability.
   b. is several specific abilities.
   c. cannot be defined or measured.
   d. is both a. and c.
   e. is a dynamic rather than stable phenomenon.

Ans: c, p. 424

12. Melvin has been diagnosed as having savant syndrome, which means that he:
   a. has an IQ of 120 or higher.
   b. would score high on a test of analytical intelligence.
   c. is mentally retarded but has one exceptional ability.
   d. was exposed to high levels of testosterone during prenatal development.

Ans: d, p. 424

13. The existence of ________ reinforces the generally accepted notion that intelligence is a multidimensional quality.
    a. adaptive skills
    b. mental retardation
    c. general intelligence
    d. savant syndrome

Ans: d, p. 425

14. Don's intelligence scores were only average, but he has been enormously successful as a corporate manager. Psychologists Sternberg and Wagner would probably suggest that Don's ________ intelligence exceeds his ________ intelligence.
    a. verbal; performance
    b. performance; verbal
    c. academic; practical
    d. practical; academic

Ans: d, p. 426

15. Gerardeen has superb social skills, manages conflicts well, and has great empathy for her friends and co-workers. Peter Salovey and John Mayer would probably say that Gerardeen possesses a high degree of:
    a. *g*.
    b. social intelligence.
    c. practical intelligence.
    d. emotional intelligence.

Ans: c, p. 427

16. Amelia recently took a test that assessed her ability to perceive, understand, and regulate her emotions. The test she took was the:
    a. WAIS.
    b. WISC.
    c. MEIS.
    d. SAT.

Ans: c, p. 428

17. Studies of 2- to 7-month-old babies show that babies who quickly become bored with a picture:
    a. often develop learning disabilities later on.
    b. score lower on infant intelligence tests.
    c. score higher on intelligence tests several years later.
    d. score very low on intelligence tests several years later.

Ans: d, p. 428

18. Which of the following best describes the relationship between creativity and intelligence?
    a. Creativity appears to depend on the ability to think imaginatively and has little if any relationship to intelligence.
    b. Creativity is best understood as a certain kind of intelligence.
    c. The more intelligent a person is, the greater his or her creativity.
    d. A certain level of intelligence is necessary but not sufficient for creativity.

Ans: c, p. 429

19. Vanessa is a very creative sculptress. We would expect that Vanessa also:
    a. has an exceptionally high intelligence score.
    b. is quite introverted.
    c. has a venturesome personality and is intrinsically motivated.
    d. lacks expertise in most other skills.
    e. is more successful than other sculptors.

Ans: d, pp. 430-431

20. When performing a task, the brains of highly skilled people:
    a. retrieve information from memory more quickly.
    b. register simple stimuli more quickly.
    c. demonstrate a more complex brain-wave response to stimuli.
    d. do all of the above.

Ans: a, p. 432

21. Before becoming attorneys, law students must pass a special licensing exam, which is an ________ test. Before entering college, high school students must take the SAT, which is an ________ test.
    a. achievement; aptitude
    b. aptitude; achievement
    c. achievement; achievement
    d. aptitude; aptitude

Ans: b, p. 432

22. Tests of ________ measure what an individual can do now, whereas tests of ________ predict what an individual will be able to do later.
    a. aptitude; achievement
    b. achievement; aptitude
    c. reliability; validity
    d. validity; reliability

Ans: b, p. 434

23. If you wanted to develop a test of musical aptitude in North American children, which would be the appropriate standardization group?
    a. children all over the world
    b. North American children
    c. children of musical parents
    d. children with known musical ability

Ans: d, p. 434

24. The bell-shaped distribution of intelligence scores in the general population is called a:
    a. *g* distribution.
    b. standardization curve.
    c. bimodal distribution.
    d. normal distribution.

Ans: b, p. 434

25. Standardization refers to the process of:
 a. determining the accuracy with which a test measures what it is supposed to.
 b. defining meaningful scores relative to a representative pretested group.
 c. determining the consistency of test scores obtained by retesting people.
 d. measuring the success with which a test predicts the behavior it is designed to predict.

Ans: c, p. 435

26. The Flynn effect refers to the fact that:
 a. White and Black infants score equally well on measures of infant intelligence.
 b. Asian students outperform North American students on math achievement tests.
 c. The IQ scores of today's better fed and educated population exceed that of the 1930s population.
 d. Individual differences within a race are much greater than between-race differences.

Ans: d, p. 435

27. Over the past 80 years, college aptitude test scores have ________ and WAIS scores have ________.
 a. declined; remained stable
 b. remained stable; declined
 c. risen; declined
 d. declined; risen

Ans: b, p. 435

28. Jack takes the same test of mechanical reasoning on several different days and gets virtually identical scores. This suggests that the test has:
 a. high content validity.
 b. high reliability.
 c. high predictive validity.
 d. been standardized.
 e. all of the above qualities.

Ans: c, pp. 434-436

29. Which of the following is *not* a requirement of a good test?
 a. reliability
 b. standardization
 c. reification
 d. validity
 e. criterion

Ans: d, p. 436

30. Which of the following is true of people who score high on aptitude tests?
 a. They achieve greater career success.
 b. They are likely to be happier.
 c. They always do well in college.
 d. None of the above is true.
 e. All of the above are true.

Ans: b, p. 436

31. A school psychologist found that 85 percent of those who scored above 115 on an aptitude test were "A" students and 75 percent of those who scored below 85 on the test were "D" students. The psychologist concluded that the test had high ________ validity because scores on it correlated highly with the ________ behavior.
   a. content; criterion
   b. predictive; criterion
   c. content; target
   d. predictive; target

Ans: c, p. 436

32. If a test designed to indicate which applicants are likely to perform the best on the job fails to do so, the test has:
   a. low reliability.
   b. low content validity.
   c. low predictive validity.
   d. not been standardized.

Ans: a, p. 436

33. Which of the following statements is true?
   a. The predictive validity of intelligence tests is not as high as their reliability.
   b. The reliability of intelligence tests is not as high as their predictive validity.
   c. Modern intelligence tests have extremely high predictive validity and reliability.
   d. The predictive validity and reliability of most intelligence tests is very low.

Ans: d, p. 436

34. You would not use a test of hearing acuity as an intelligence test because it would lack:
   a. content reliability.
   b. predictive reliability.
   c. predictive validity.
   d. content validity.

Ans: b, p. 438

35. At age 16, Angel's intelligence score was 110. What will her score probably be at age 32?
   a. 105
   b. 110
   c. 115
   d. There is no basis for predicting an individual's future IQ.

Ans: d, p. 438

36. A high-school psychologist who is looking at a student's intelligence score finds a jump of 30 points between the earliest score at age 2 and the most recent at age 17. The psychologist's knowledge of testing would probably lead her to conclude that such a jump:
   a. indicates that different tests were used, creating an apparent change in intelligence level, although it actually remained stable.
   b. signals a significant improvement in the child's environment over this period.
   c. is unsurprising, since intelligence scores do not become stable until late adolescence.
   d. is mainly the result of the age at which the first test was taken.

Ans: d, p. 438

37. By what age does a child's performance on an intelligence test become stable?
    a. 2
    b. 4
    c. 6
    d. 7
    e. 12

Ans: b, p. 438

38. Before about age ________, intelligence tests generally do not predict future scores.
    a. 1
    b. 4
    c. 5
    d. 10
    e. 15

Ans: c, p. 439

39. Twenty-two-year-old Dan has an intelligence score of 63 and the academic skills of a fourth-grader, and is unable to live independently. Dan *probably*:
    a. has Down syndrome.
    b. has savant syndrome.
    c. is mentally retarded.
    d. will eventually achieve self-supporting social and vocational skills.

Ans: a, p. 439

40. Down syndrome is normally caused by:
    a. an extra chromosome in the person's genetic makeup.
    b. a missing chromosome in the person's genetic makeup.
    c. malnutrition during the first few months of life.
    d. prenatal exposure to an addictive drug.

Ans: e, p. 439

41. Which of the following statements is true?
    a. About 1 percent of the population is mentally retarded.
    b. More males than females are mentally retarded.
    c. A majority of the mentally retarded can learn academic skills.
    d. Many of the mentally retarded are mainstreamed into regular classrooms.
    e. All of the above are true.

Ans: c, pp. 439-440

42. In his study of children with high intelligence scores, Terman found that:
    a. the children were more emotional and less healthy than a control group.
    b. the children were ostracized by classmates.
    c. the children were healthy and well-adjusted, and did well academically.
    d. later, as adults, they nearly all achieved great vocational success.

Ans: e, p. 440

43. Sorting children into gifted and nongifted educational groups:
    a. presumes that giftedness is a single trait.
    b. does not result in higher academic achievement scores.
    c. promotes racial segregation and prejudice.
    d. sometimes creates self-fulfilling prophecies.
    e. has all of the above effects.

Ans: a, p. 442

44. Which of the following provides the strongest evidence of the role of heredity in determining intelligence?
    a. The IQ scores of identical twins raised separately are very similar.
    b. The intelligence scores of fraternal twins are more similar than those of ordinary siblings.
    c. The intelligence scores of identical twins raised together are more similar than those of identical twins raised apart.
    d. The intelligence scores of adopted children show relatively weak correlations with scores of adoptive as well as biological parents.

Ans: c, p. 442

45. Current estimates are that ________ percent of the total variation among intelligence scores can be attributed to genetic factors.
    a. less than 10
    b. approximately 25
    c. between 50 and 75
    d. over 75

Ans: a, p. 443

46. If you compare the same trait in people of similar heredity who live in very different environments, heritability for that trait will be ________; heritability for the trait is most likely to be ________ among people of very different heredities who live in similar environments.
    a. low; high
    b. high; low
    c. environmental; genetic
    d. genetic; environmental

Ans: c, p. 443

47. To say that the heritability of a trait is approximately 50 percent means:
    a. that genes are responsible for 50 percent of the trait in an individual, and the environment is responsible for the rest.
    b. that the trait's appearance in a person will reflect approximately equal genetic contributions from both parents.
    c. that of the variation in the trait within a group of people, 50 percent can be attributed to heredity.
    d. all of the above.

Ans: a, p. 443

48. Studies of adopted children and their biological and adoptive families demonstrate that with age, genetic influences on intelligence:
    a. become more apparent.
    b. become less apparent.
    c. become more difficult to entangle from environmental influences.
    d. become easier to entangle from environmental influences.

Ans: c, p. 444

49. Which of the following provides the strongest evidence of environment's role in intelligence?
    a. Adopted children's intelligence scores are more like their adoptive parents' scores than their biological parents'.
    b. Children's intelligence scores are more strongly related to their mothers' scores than to their fathers'.
    c. Children moved from a deprived environment into an intellectually enriched one show gains in intellectual development.
    d. The intelligence scores of identical twins raised separately are no more alike than those of siblings.

Ans: c, p. 444

50. Which of the following statements most accurately reflects the text's position regarding the relative contribution of genes and environment in determining intelligence?
    a. Except in cases of a neglectful early environment, each individual's basic intelligence is largely the product of heredity.
    b. With the exception of those with genetic disorders such as Down syndrome, intelligence is primarily the product of environmental experiences.
    c. Both genes and life experiences significantly influence performance on intelligence tests.
    d. Because intelligence tests have such low predictive validity, the question cannot be addressed until psychologists agree on a more valid test of intelligence.

Ans: c, p. 444

51. J. McVicker Hunt found that institutionalized children given "tutored human enrichment":
    a. showed no change in intelligence test performance compared with institutionalized children who did not receive such enrichment.
    b. responded so negatively as a result of their impoverished early experiences that he felt it necessary to disband the program.
    c. thrived intellectually and socially on the benefits of positive caregiving.
    d. actually developed greater intelligence than control subjects who had lived in foster homes since birth.

Ans: d, pp. 444-445

52. First-time parents Geena and Brad want to give their baby's intelligence a jump-start by providing a super-enriched learning environment. Experts would suggest that the new parents should:
    a. pipe stimulating classical music into the baby's room.
    b. hang colorful mobiles and artwork over the baby's crib.
    c. take the child to one of the new "superbaby" preschools that specialize in infant enrichment.
    d. relax, since there is no surefire environmental recipe for giving a child a superior intellect.

Ans: a, p. 445

53. Which of the following is *not* cited as evidence of the reciprocal relationship between schooling and intelligence?
   a. Neither education level nor intelligence scores accurately predict income.
   b. Intelligence scores tend to rise during the school year.
   c. High school graduates have higher intelligence scores than do those who drop out early.
   d. High intelligence is conducive to prolonged schooling.

Ans: d, p. 445

54. Research on the effectiveness of Head Start suggests that enrichment programs:
   a. produce permanent gains in intelligence scores.
   b. improve school readiness, but have no measurable impact on intelligence scores.
   c. improve intelligence scores but not school readiness.
   d. produce temporary gains in intelligence scores.

Ans: d, p. 447

55. Hiroko's math achievement score is considerably higher than that of most American students her age. Which of the following is true regarding this difference between Asian and North American students:
   a. It is a recent phenomenon.
   b. It may be due to the fact that Asian students have a longer school year.
   c. It holds only for girls.
   d. Both a. and b. are true.
   e. a., b., and c. are true.

Ans: c, pp. 447-448

56. Most psychologists believe that racial gaps in test scores:
   a. have been exaggerated when they are, in fact, insignificant.
   b. indicate that intelligence is in large measure inherited.
   c. are in large measure caused by environmental factors.
   d. are increasing.

Ans: d, pp. 447-448

57. Reported racial gaps in average intelligence scores are most likely attributable to:
   a. the use of biased tests of intelligence.
   b. the use of unreliable tests of intelligence.
   c. genetic factors.
   d. environmental factors.

Ans: d, pp. 447-448

58. The contribution of environmental factors to racial gaps in intelligence scores is indicated by:
   a. evidence that individual differences within a race are much greater than differences between races.
   b. evidence that White and Black infants score equally well on certain measures of infant intelligence.
   c. the fact that Asian students outperform North American students on math achievement and aptitude tests.
   d. all of the above.

Ans: b, p. 449

59. Which of the following is *not* true?
    a. In math grades, the average girl typically equals or surpasses the average boy.
    b. The gender gap in math and science scores is increasing.
    c. Women are better than men at detecting emotions.
    d. Males score higher than females on tests of spatial abilities.

Ans: b, p. 449

60. High levels of male hormones during prenatal development may enhance:
    a. verbal reasoning.
    b. spatial abilities.
    c. overall intelligence.
    d. all of the above.

CHAPTER **12**

Motivation and Work

Learning Objectives

Motivational Concepts (pp. 456-459)

1. Define motivation, and identify several theories of motivated behavior.

2. Describe Maslow's hierarchy of motives.

Hunger (pp. 459-467)

3. Describe the physiological determinants of hunger.

4. Discuss psychological and cultural influences on hunger, and describe the symptoms of anorexia nervosa and bulimia nervosa.

Sexual Motivation (pp. 467-482)

5. Describe how researchers have attempted to assess common sexual practices.

6. Describe the human sexual response cycle, and discuss the impact of both hormones and psychological factors on sexual motivation and behavior.

7. Identify factors contributing to increased rates of pregnancy and sexually transmitted infection among today's adolescents.

8. Describe research findings on the nature and dynamics of sexual orientation, and discuss the place of values in sex research.

The Need to Belong (pp. 483-485)

9. Describe the adaptive value of social attachments, and identify both healthy and unhealthy consequences of our need to belong.

Motivation at Work (pp. 485-496)

10. Discuss the importance of various motives for working, and identify the aims of industrial-organizational psychology.

11. Describe how personnel psychologists seek to facilitate employee selection, work placement, and performance appraisal.

12. Define achievement motivation, and discuss the impact of employee satisfaction and engagement on organizational success.

13. Describe how effective managers seek to build upon their employees' strengths, set specific goals, and utilize an appropriate leadership style.

Motivation, p. 455
Easy, Factual/Definitional, Objective 1, Ans: c

1. Motivation is defined by psychologists as:
   a. an impulse to accomplish something of significance.
   b. rigidly patterned behavior characteristic of all people.
   c. a need or desire that energizes and directs behavior toward a goal.
   d. the cause of behavior.

Instincts and evolutionary psychology, p. 456
Easy, Factual/Definitional, Objective 1, Ans: c

2. Rigid patterns of behavior characteristic of a species and developed without practice are called:
   a. set points.
   b. drives.
   c. instincts.
   d. needs.
   e. incentives.

Instincts and evolutionary psychology, p. 456
Medium, Factual/Definitional, Objective 1, Ans: d

3. Instinctive behavior is:
   a. designed to reduce drives.
   b. triggered by a biological need.
   c. extrinsically motivated.
   d. unlearned.

Instincts and evolutionary psychology, p. 456
Medium, Conceptual/Application, Objective 1, Ans: b

4. It is characteristic of bears to hibernate. This behavior is an example of:
   a. a refractory period.
   b. an instinct.
   c. homeostasis.
   d. an incentive.
   e. a drive.

Instincts and evolutionary psychology, p. 456
Medium, Conceptual/Application, Objective 1, Ans: c

5. Mr. Porter believes that aggression is an unlearned behavior characteristic of all children. He obviously believes that aggression is a(n):
a. incentive.
b. homeostatic mechanism.
c. instinct.
d. drive.

Instincts and evolutionary psychology, p. 456
Easy, Factual/Definitional, Objective 1, Ans: b

6. Which theory of motivation most clearly emphasizes the importance of genetic predispositions?
a. Theory X
b. instinct theory
c. Theory Y
d. arousal theory

Drives and incentives, p. 457
Medium, Factual/Definitional, Objective 1, Ans: a

7. A need refers to:
a. a physiological state that usually triggers motivational arousal.
b. an aroused or activated state that is often triggered by a psychological need.
c. anything that is perceived as having positive or negative value in motivating behavior.
d. a desire to perform a behavior due to rewards or threats of punishment.
e. a rigidly patterned behavioral urge characteristic of all people.

Drives and incentives, p. 457
Easy, Factual/Definitional, Objective 1, Ans: c

8. An aroused or activated state that is often triggered by physiological need is called a(n):
a. instinct.
b. incentive.
c. drive.
d. set point.

Drives and incentives, p. 457
Easy, Conceptual, Objective 1, Ans: b

9. For a thirsty person, drinking water serves to reduce:
a. homeostasis.
b. a drive.
c. an instinct.
d. the refractory period.
e. metabolic rate.

Drives and incentives, p. 457
Difficult, Conceptual, Objective 1, Ans: c

10. Food deprivation is to hunger as ________ is to ________.
   a. homeostasis; thirst
   b. incentive; instinct
   c. need; drive
   d. motivation; emotion
   e. pornography; lust

Drives and incentives, p. 457
Medium, Conceptual, Objective 1, Ans: c

11. Needs are ________ correlated with ________.
   a. positively; incentives
   b. negatively; incentives
   c. positively; drives
   d. negatively; drives

Drives and incentives, p. 457
Medium, Factual/Definitional, Objective 1, Ans: c

12. Homeostasis refers to:
   a. a rigidly patterned behavior characteristic of an entire species.
   b. an aroused or activated state that is often triggered by a physiological need.
   c. the body's tendency to maintain a constant internal state.
   d. a physical need that usually triggers motivational arousal.

Drives and incentives, p. 457
Medium, Conceptual/Application, Objective 1, Ans: c

13. For a hungry person, the consumption of food serves to:
   a. lower the set point.
   b. shorten the refractory period.
   c. maintain homeostasis.
   d. reduce an instinct.

Drives and incentives, p. 457
Easy, Factual/Definitional, Objective 1, Ans: b

14. Positive and negative environmental stimuli that motivate behavior are called:
   a. needs.
   b. incentives.
   c. goals.
   d. drives.

Drives and incentives, p. 457
Difficult, Conceptual/Application, Objective 1, Ans: e

15. Which of the following is clearly *not* an example of an incentive?
   a. $1000
   b. threat of punishment
   c. electric shock
   d. smell of popcorn
   e. lack of bodily fluids

Drives and incentives, p. 457
Medium, Conceptual/Application, Objective 1, Ans: c

16. On some college football teams, players are rewarded for outstanding performance with a gold star on their helmets. This practice best illustrates the use of:
    a. set points.
    b. 360-degree feedback.
    c. incentives.
    d. participative management.

Drives and incentives, p. 457
Medium, Factual/Definitional, Objective 1, Ans: d

17. The importance of learning in motivation is most obvious from the influence of:
    a. instincts.
    b. homeostasis.
    c. arousal.
    d. incentives.

Drives and incentives, p. 457
Difficult, Conceptual, Objective 1, Ans: a

18. A lack of bodily fluids is to cold water as ________ is to ________.
    a. need; incentive
    b. drive; incentive
    c. need; drive
    d. instinct; set point
    e. homeostasis; refractory period

Optimum arousal, p. 457
Easy, Conceptual/Application, Objective 1, Ans: d

19. Which theory would be most helpful for explaining why people are motivated to watch horror movies?
    a. instinct theory
    b. drive-reduction theory
    c. Theory X
    d. arousal theory

Optimum arousal, p. 457
Medium, Conceptual/Application, Objective 1, Ans: a

20. Which theory would be most likely to predict that rats are motivated to explore precisely those areas of an experimental maze where they receive mild electrical shocks?
    a. arousal theory
    b. Theory X
    c. instinct theory
    d. drive-reduction theory

Optimum arousal, p. 457
Difficult, Factual/Definitional, Objective 1, Ans: d

21. The arousal theory of motivation would be most useful for understanding the aversive effects of:
    a. refractory periods.
    b. sexual disorders.
    c. hunger.
    d. boredom.
    e. anorexia nervosa.

A hierarchy of motives, p. 458
Easy, Factual/Definitional, Objective 2, Ans: d

22. The most basic or lowest-level need in Maslow's hierarchy of human motives includes the need for:
    a. self-esteem.
    b. love and friendship.
    c. religious fulfillment.
    d. food and drink.
    e. achievement.

A hierarchy of motives, p. 458
Medium, Factual/Definitional, Objective 2, Ans: b

23. According to Maslow, our need for ________ must be met before we are preoccupied with satisfying our need for ________.
    a. love; food
    b. adequate clothing; self-esteem
    c. religious fulfillment; adequate housing
    d. self-actualization; friendship
    e. political freedom; economic security

A hierarchy of motives, p. 458
Difficult, Conceptual/Application, Objective 2, Ans: d

24. On the basis of Maslow's hierarchy of needs, one would be least likely to predict that a:
    a. starving person might sell his child to obtain food.
    b. teacher with high self-esteem might seek a career change to use his abilities more fully.
    c. successful business executive might show greater concern for his family relationships than for becoming president of his corporation.
    d. prisoner might choose to die rather than betray his country.

A hierarchy of motives, p. 458
Difficult, Factual/Definitional, Objective 2, Ans: d

25. Financial satisfaction is more strongly predictive of subjective well-being in poor nations than in wealthy ones. This fact would most clearly be anticipated by:
    a. Freud's instinct theory.
    b. Adler's social psychological theory.
    c. Darwin's evolutionary theory.
    d. Maslow's theory of motivational priorities.

Hunger, pp. 459-460
Medium, Factual/Definitional, Objective 3, Ans: c

26. Ancel Keys and his colleagues observed that men on a semistarvation diet:
    a. became apathetic and lost interest in food.
    b. remained interested in food but avoided talking or thinking about it.
    c. lost interest in sex and social activities.
    d. became increasingly preoccupied with political and religious issues.

The physiology of hunger, p. 461
Easy, Factual/Definitional, Objective 3, Ans: b

27. Research on the physiological basis of hunger has indicated that:
    a. there is no relationship between stomach contractions and the experience of hunger.
    b. hunger continues in humans whose cancerous stomachs have been removed.
    c. rats whose stomachs have been removed must be force-fed to prevent starvation.
    d. a full stomach necessarily prevents hunger.

The physiology of hunger: body chemistry, p. 461
Medium, Factual/Definitional, Objective 3, Ans: b

28. Increases in insulin increase hunger indirectly by:
    a. increasing leptin levels.
    b. decreasing blood glucose levels.
    c. increasing PYY levels.
    d. decreasing orexin levels.

The physiology of hunger: body chemistry, p. 461
Difficult, Factual/Definitional, Objective 3, Ans: a

29. Increases in ________ increase hunger, whereas increases in ________ decrease hunger.
    a. insulin; blood glucose
    b. blood glucose; leptin
    c. leptin; orexin
    d. orexin; insulin

The physiology of hunger: body chemistry, p. 461
Difficult, Conceptual/Application, Objective 3, Ans: b

30. After two days without eating, Myra is very hungry. At this time it is likely that her blood glucose level is ________ and her blood insulin level is ________.
    a. low; low
    b. low; high
    c. high; high
    d. high; low

The physiology of hunger: the brain, p. 461
Medium, Conceptual/Application, Objective 3, Ans: a

31. Dr. Milosz electrically stimulates the lateral hypothalamus of a well-fed laboratory rat. This procedure is likely to:
    a. cause the rat to begin eating.
    b. decrease the rat's basal metabolic rate.
    c. facilitate conversion of the rat's blood glucose to fat.
    d. permanently lower the rat's set point.

The physiology of hunger: the brain, p. 461
Difficult, Factual/Definitional, Objective 3, Ans: b

32. When a rat's blood sugar level decreases, the ________ hypothalamus releases the hunger-triggering hormone ________.
a. lateral; leptin
b. lateral; orexin
c. ventromedial; leptin
d. ventromedial; orexin

The physiology of hunger: the brain, p. 461
Difficult, Conceptual, Objective 3, Ans: b

33. Arousal of hunger is to inhibition of hunger as ________ is to ________.
a. a high blood insulin level; a low blood glucose level
b. stimulation of the lateral hypothalamus; stimulation of the ventromedial hypothalamus
c. a low blood insulin level; a high blood glucose level
d. stimulation of the ventromedial hypothalamus; stimulation of the lateral hypothalamus

The physiology of hunger: the brain, p. 461
Difficult, Factual/Definitional, Objective 3, Ans: d

34. Destruction of the ventromedial hypothalamus of a rat is most likely to:
a. lower its set point for body weight.
b. cause it to stop eating.
c. lower its blood insulin level.
d. facilitate conversion of its blood glucose to fat.

The physiology of hunger: the brain, p. 462
Difficult, Factual/Definitional, Objective 3, Ans: a

35. Mice are most likely to eat less when they experience ________ levels of ________.
a. elevated; leptin
b. reduced; glucose
c. elevated; orexin
d. reduced; ghrelin

The physiology of hunger: the brain, p. 462
Medium, Factual/Definitional, Objective 3, Ans: c

36. The secretion of ghrelin ________ appetite, and the secretion of PYY ________ appetite.
a. stimulates; stimulates
b. suppresses; suppresses
c. stimulates; suppresses
d. suppresses; stimulates

The physiology of hunger: the brain, p. 462
Easy, Factual/Definitional, Objective 3, Ans: d

37. The set point is:
a. the stage of the sexual response cycle that occurs just before orgasm.
b. the body temperature of a healthy organism, for example, 98.6 degrees F in humans.
c. the point at which energy expenditures from exercise and from metabolism are equal.
d. the specific body weight maintained automatically by most adults over long periods of time.

The physiology of hunger: the brain, p. 462
Medium, Conceptual, Objective 3, Ans: b

38. An explanation of motivation in terms of homeostasis is best illustrated by the concept of:
a. instinct.
b. set point.
c. refractory period.
d. incentive.

The physiology of hunger: the brain, p. 462
Difficult, Factual/Definitional, Objective 3, Ans: c

39. When an organism's weight rises above its set point, the organism is likely to experience a(n):
a. decrease in both hunger and basal metabolic rate.
b. increase in hunger and a decrease in basal metabolic rate.
c. decrease in hunger and an increase in basal metabolic rate.
d. increase in both hunger and basal metabolic rate.

Taste preference: biology or culture?, p. 463
Difficult, Factual/Definitional, Objective 4, Ans: d

40. The level of serotonin in the brain is ________ by a diet high in ________.
a. decreased; sugar
b. decreased; salt
c. increased; protein
d. increased; carbohydrates

Taste preference: biology or culture?, p. 463
Medium, Factual/Definitional, Objective 4, Ans: c

41. People are most likely to dislike the taste of ________ foods.
a. salty
b. starchy
c. novel
d. familiar

Taste preference: biology or culture?, p. 464
Easy, Factual/Definitional, Objective 4, Ans: a

42. The recipes commonly used in countries with hot climates are more likely to include ________ than those in countries with colder climates.
a. spices
b. carbohydrates
c. fats
d. proteins

Eating disorders, p. 464
Easy, Factual/Definitional, Objective 4, Ans: d

43. Anorexia nervosa is typically characterized by:
a. an unusually high rate of metabolism.
b. cyclical fluctuations between extreme thinness and obesity.
c. frequent migraine headaches.
d. an obsessive fear of becoming obese.

Eating disorders, p. 464
Medium, Conceptual/Application, Objective 4, Ans: e

44. About eight months ago, 14-year-old Shelley went on a drastic weight-loss diet that caused her to drop from 110 to 80 pounds. Although she is now dangerously underweight and undernourished, she continues to think she looks fat. Her frustrated father recently forced her to eat a peanut butter sandwich, but Shelley immediately went to the bathroom and threw it all up. Shelley most clearly suffers from:
a. excess leptin.
b. an abnormally low set point.
c. bulimia nervosa.
d. hypermetabolism.
e. anorexia nervosa.

Eating disorders, p. 464
Medium, Conceptual/Application, Objective 4, Ans: a

45. Twenty-two-year-old Tawana is slightly overweight and loves to eat, particularly snack foods and rich desserts. Fearful of becoming overweight, she frequently takes a laxative following episodes of binge eating. Tawana most clearly suffers from:
a. bulimia nervosa.
b. anorexia nervosa.
c. excess PYY.
d. an abnormally high set point.
e. hypermetabolism.

Eating disorders, pp. 464-465
Difficult, Factual/Definitional, Objective 4, Ans: b

46. Anorexia patients are most likely to have parents who:
a. have physically or sexually abused their children.
b. are high-achieving and protective.
c. have been recently separated or divorced.
d. are unconcerned about physical appearance and body weight.

Eating disorders, p. 465
Easy, Factual/Definitional, Objective 4, Ans: d

47. Over the past 50 years, American women have expressed ________ satisfaction with their physical appearance and have experienced a(n) ________ incidence of serious eating disorders.
a. increasing; decreasing
b. increasing; increasing
c. decreasing; decreasing
d. decreasing; increasing

Eating disorders, p. 465
Easy, Factual/Definitional, Objective 4, Ans: c

48. In a British survey of bank and university staff, men were ________ likely to be overweight than were women, and men were ________ likely to perceive themselves as overweight than were women.
a. more; more
b. less; less
c. more; less
d. less; more

Eating disorders, p. 465
Medium, Conceptual/Application, Objective 4, Ans: c

49. If Mary Ann is a typical college student, it is most probable that she:
    a. thinks she weighs less than she would like to weigh.
    b. thinks she weighs less than what men actually prefer her to weigh.
    c. thinks men prefer her to weigh less than they actually prefer.
    d. thinks men prefer her to weigh less than she would like to weigh.

Describing sexual behavior, p. 468
Difficult, Factual/Definitional, Objective 5, Ans: b

50. With regard to the incidence of premarital sexual intercourse among Americans during the 1940s, Alfred Kinsey found that:
    a. nearly all men and most women reported having premarital sexual intercourse.
    b. most men and nearly half the women reported having premarital sexual intercourse.
    c. most men but very few women reported having premarital sexual intercourse.
    d. very few individuals of either sex admitted having premarital sexual intercourse.

Describing sexual behavior, p. 468
Medium, Conceptual, Objective 5, Ans: d

51. If researchers wanted to improve upon the scientific accuracy of Alfred Kinsey's research on American sexual practices, their first concern should involve:
    a. using telephone rather than face-to-face interviews.
    b. interviewing a larger number of people.
    c. having females rather than males interview the female respondents.
    d. interviewing a more representative sample of the American population.

Describing sexual behavior, p. 468
Medium, Factual/Definitional, Objective 5, Ans: c

52. Recent surveys of American sexual practices suggest that:
    a. pregnancy rates among unwed teens have declined dramatically during the past several years.
    b. public school sex education programs have actually discouraged use of contraceptives.
    c. less than 5 percent of married people engaged in extramarital sex during the past year.
    d. a majority of American men approve of extramarital sex.
    e. concern over the AIDS virus has not affected the sexual practices of unmarried Americans.

The sexual response cycle, p. 469
Medium, Factual/Definitional, Objective 6, Ans: c

53. Research on the sexual response cycle indicates that:
    a. males and females experience a similar refractory period following orgasm.
    b. women undergo a decrease in physiological arousal more slowly if they have experienced orgasm than if they have not.
    c. enough sperm may be released prior to male orgasm to enable conception.
    d. during the resolution phase, sexual excitement increases in females but decreases in males.

The sexual response cycle, p. 469
Difficult, Factual/Definitional, Objective 6, Ans: a

54. During the resolution phase of the sexual response cycle:
   a. women undergo a decrease in physiological arousal more rapidly if they have just experienced orgasm than if they have not.
   b. women are less likely than men to be aroused to yet another orgasm.
   c. men undergo a decrease in physiological arousal less rapidly if they have just experienced orgasm than if they have not.
   d. women generally return to an unaroused physiological state more rapidly than do men.

The sexual response cycle, p. 469
Medium, Factual/Definitional, Objective 6, Ans: d

55. The refractory period is:
   a. the moment before orgasm during which sexual arousal is maintained at a fairly high level.
   b. the stage of the sexual response cycle during which sexual excitation reaches its climax.
   c. the span of the monthly female reproductive cycle during which ovulation occurs.
   d. the time span after orgasm during which a male cannot be aroused to another orgasm.

The sexual response cycle, p. 469
Medium, Conceptual/Application, Objective 6, Ans: e

56. Kamil, a 33-year-old lawyer, experiences premature ejaculation. Research suggests that his disorder can be minimized by:
   a. engaging in sexual activity less frequently.
   b. eliminating his high level of sexual guilt.
   c. uncovering the unconscious fears that underlie his problem.
   d. providing therapy designed to raise his self-esteem.
   e. learning ways to control his urge to ejaculate.

Hormones and sexual behavior, pp. 469-470
Easy, Factual/Definitional, Objective 6, Ans: d

57. In most mammals, female sexual receptivity is greatest when:
   a. testosterone levels are lowest.
   b. testosterone levels are highest.
   c. estrogen levels are lowest.
   d. estrogen levels are highest.

Hormones and sexual behavior, p. 470
Medium, Factual/Definitional, Objective 6, Ans: a

58. Research on sex hormones and human sexual behavior indicates that:
   a. women's sexual interests are not closely linked to the phases of their menstrual cycles.
   b. adult men who have been castrated show virtually no reduction in sex drive.
   c. sexual interests are aroused by decreased testosterone levels in women and increased testosterone levels in men.
   d. imprisoned male sex offenders typically experience lower-than-normal testosterone levels.

Hormones and sexual behavior, p. 470
Easy, Factual/Definitional, Objective 6, Ans: a

59. James Dabbs and his colleagues observed that male collegians' ________ levels were especially likely to increase while they were conversing with a ________ college student.
a. testosterone; female
b. insulin; male
c. glucose; female
d. PYY; male

Hormones and sexual behavior, p. 470
Easy, Factual/Definitional, Objective 6, Ans: c

60. The brain structure that detects sex hormone levels and activates sexual arousal is the:
a. cerebellum.
b. amygdala.
c. hypothalamus.
d. medulla.
e. thalamus.

The psychology of sex, p. 471
Medium, Conceptual, Objective 6, Ans: a

61. The drive-reduction theory of motivation is more applicable to hunger than to sex because, unlike hunger, sexual desire is not a direct response to:
a. a physiological need.
b. an external incentive.
c. hypothalamic activity.
d. any of the above.

The psychology of sex: external stimuli, p. 471
Difficult, Conceptual, Objective 6, Ans: d

62. Generalizing from laboratory research, we know that husbands and wives who want to heighten their level of sexual arousal will benefit most if the husband listens to a tape having a ________ theme and the wife listens to a tape having a ________ theme.
a. sexually explicit; romantic
b. romantic; sexually explicit
c. romantic; romantic
d. sexually explicit; sexually explicit

The psychology of sex: external stimuli, p. 471
Medium, Conceptual/Application, Objective 6, Ans: c

63. Ivan just spent an evening watching pornographic movies of attractive women who actually seemed to enjoy being sexually molested. This experience is most likely to lead him to:
a. see his own girlfriend as sexually unreceptive.
b. perceive himself as sexually impotent.
c. be more willing to hurt women.
d. feel unsure about his gender identity.
e. view sexual promiscuity as morally wrong.

The psychology of sex: imagined stimuli, p. 472
Medium, Factual/Definitional, Objective 6, Ans: d

64. Compared to women, men are more likely to experience:
   a. recollections of their previous sexual interactions.
   b. dreams about members of the opposite sex.
   c. fantasies of being sexually overpowered.
   d. sexually vivid dreams that lead to orgasm.

Adolescent sexuality (Figure 12.9), p. 473
Medium, Factual/Definitional, Objective 7, Ans: c

65. The birth rate in North America over the past 40 years has ________ among married women and ________ among unmarried women.
   a. decreased; decreased
   b. decreased; remained stable
   c. decreased; increased
   d. remained stable; increased
   e. remained stable; remained stable

Adolescent sexuality, p. 473
Medium, Factual/Definitional, Objective 7, Ans: b

66. Many sexually active American adolescents fail to avoid pregnancy because:
   a. low sex guilt inhibits the careful planning of contraceptive use.
   b. they are ignorant concerning basic human reproductive functioning.
   c. sex education courses have actually discouraged contraceptive use.
   d. of all of the above reasons.

Adolescent sexuality, pp. 473-474
Easy, Factual/Definitional, Objective 7, Ans: b

67. Alcohol consumption ________ self-awareness and ________ sexual inhibitions.
   a. increases; decreases
   b. decreases; decreases
   c. increases; increases
   d. decreases; increases

Adolescent sexuality, p. 474
Easy, Factual/Definitional, Objective 7, Ans: c

68. Teens are most likely to delay becoming sexually active if they:
   a. have low self-esteem.
   b. experience refractory periods.
   c. have high rather than average intelligence test scores.
   d. are uncomfortable discussing contraception with parents and friends.
   e. are uninformed about the safe and risky phases of the menstrual cycle.

Adolescent sexuality, pp. 474-475
Difficult, Factual/Definitional, Objective 7, Ans: d

69. The proper use of condoms:
 a. completely prevents HIV infections and reduces the risk of all other STIs.
 b. dramatically reduces the risk of HIV infections and completely prevents transmission of all other STIs.
 c. fails to reduce the risk of HIV infections but completely prevents transmission of all other STIs.
 d. dramatically reduces the risk of HIV infections but fails to prevent the transmission of certain other STIs.

Sexual orientation, p. 475
Easy, Conceptual/Application, Objective 8, Ans: c

70. Isaac, a 25-year-old law student, is heterosexual; his brother Chaim, a 21-year-old college senior, is homosexual. The brothers obviously differ in their:
 a. gender identity.
 b. sexual role.
 c. sexual orientation.
 d. gender type.
 e. gender schema.

Sexual orientation, p. 475
Medium, Factual/Definitional, Objective 8, Ans: c

71. The average American ________ the percent of men who are gay and ________ the percent of women who are lesbian.
 a. overestimates; underestimates
 b. underestimates; overestimates
 c. overestimates; overestimates
 d. underestimates; underestimates

Sexual orientation, p. 475
Medium, Factual/Definitional, Objective 8, Ans: b

72. Homosexuality is ________ common than bisexuality, and male homosexuality is ________ common than female homosexuality.
 a. less; less
 b. more; more
 c. more; less
 d. less; more

Sexual orientation, p. 476
Medium, Factual/Definitional, Objective 8, Ans: c

73. A homosexual orientation is:
 a. equally likely among members of both sexes.
 b. associated with a lack of clear gender identity.
 c. very persistent and difficult to change.
 d. a result of being sexually victimized during childhood.
 e. characteristic of over 10 percent of American males.

Sexual orientation, p. 476
Medium, Factual/Definitional, Objective 8, Ans: b

74. Gender differences in erotic plasticity are best illustrated by the fact that:
    a. women experience lengthier refractory periods than do men.
    b. women's sexual orientation tends to be more changeable than men's.
    c. women are less likely than men to be equally aroused by male and female erotic stimuli.
    d. women become aware of their sexual orientation much earlier in life than do men.

Sexual orientation, p. 476
Medium, Factual/Definitional, Objective 8, Ans: c

75. Research on sexual orientation indicates that:
    a. there have always been some cultures that are predominantly homosexual.
    b. homosexuality is more common among women than men.
    c. committed long-term love relationships are more common among lesbians than among gay men.
    d. more than 10 percent of men are exclusively homosexual.

Understanding sexual orientation, p. 477
Easy, Factual/Definitional, Objective 8, Ans: e

76. Research on the environmental conditions that influence sexual orientation indicates that:
    a. homosexuals are more likely than heterosexuals to have been sexually abused during childhood.
    b. homosexuals are more likely than heterosexuals to have been overprotected by their mothers.
    c. homosexuals are more likely than heterosexuals to have been raised in a father-absent home.
    d. homosexuals are more likely than heterosexuals to have been exposed to a gay or lesbian schoolteacher.
    e. the reported backgrounds of homosexuals and heterosexuals are similar.

The brain and sexual orientation, p. 478
Difficult, Factual/Definitional, Objective 8, Ans: d

77. Simon LeVay discovered that a cluster of neural cells located in the ________ was ________ in homosexual men than in heterosexual men.
    a. cerebellum; larger
    b. hypothalamus; larger
    c. cerebellum; smaller
    d. hypothalamus; smaller

Genes and sexual orientation, p. 478
Medium, Factual/Definitional, Objective 8, Ans: c

78. The identical twin brothers of male homosexuals experience ________ rates of homosexuality. The fraternal twin brothers of male homosexuals experience ________ rates of homosexuality.
    a. above average; below average
    b. above average; average
    c. above average; above average
    d. average; average

Genes and sexual orientation, p. 478
Difficult, Factual/Definitional, Objective 8, Ans: d

79. With a single transplanted gene, scientists can now cause male ________ to display homosexual behavior.
a. rats
b. chimpanzees
c. dogs
d. fruit flies

Prenatal hormones and sexual orientation, p. 478
Medium, Factual/Definitional, Objective 8, Ans: a

80. Research has found that an animal's sexual orientation can be altered by:
a. manipulations of prenatal hormone conditions.
b. destruction of the ventromedial hypothalamus.
c. injections of sex hormones in early adulthood.
d. destruction of the amygdala.

Prenatal hormones and sexual orientation, p. 478
Easy, Factual/Definitional, Objective 8, Ans: e

81. If pregnant sheep are injected with ________ during a critical gestation period, their female offspring will show homosexual behavior.
a. estrogen
b. insulin
c. PYY
d. orexin
e. testosterone

Understanding sexual orientation, p. 480
Medium, Factual/Definitional, Objective 8, Ans: d

82. Accepting attitudes toward homosexuals are ________ common among men than women and ________ common among those who believe sexual orientation is genetically rather than environmentally determined.
a. more; more
b. less; less
c. more; less
d. less; more

Sex and human values, p. 481
Medium, Factual/Definitional, Objective 8, Ans: d

83. With respect to sex research and human values, the text suggests that:
a. sexual activity is largely a medical and biological issue, not a moral issue.
b. scientific methods prevent sex researchers from being influenced by their own personal values.
c. researchers should not reveal their sexual values because sexual standards are a matter of personal taste.
d. sex research and education should be accompanied by open consideration of sexual values.

The need to belong, p. 483
Easy, Conceptual, Objective 9, Ans: b

84. Evolutionary psychologists are most likely to suggest that almost all humans are genetically predisposed to:
    a. engage in both homosexual and heterosexual behaviors.
    b. form close enduring relationships with fellow humans.
    c. avoid eating carbohydrate-laden foods when feeling depressed.
    d. satisfy their need for political freedom before seeking emotional security.

The need to belong, p. 483
Difficult, Factual/Definitional, Objective 9, Ans: e

85. When asked what is most necessary for a happy and meaningful life, most people first mention the importance of satisfying their ________ needs.
    a. achievement
    b. self-actualization
    c. safety
    d. sexual
    e. belongingness

The need to belong, p. 483
Medium, Conceptual/Application, Objective 9, Ans: b

86. Foolish conformity to peer pressure is most likely to be motivated by ________ needs.
    a. safety
    b. belongingness
    c. achievement
    d. self-actualization
    e. sexual

The need to belong, p. 484
Medium, Factual/Definitional, Objective 9, Ans: c

87. In a series of studies, research participants were informed that personality test results indicated they were the type likely to end up alone later in life. As a result, they became ________ likely to underperform on aptitude tests and ________ likely to become aggressive toward someone who had insulted them.
    a. more; less
    b. less; more
    c. more; more
    d. less; less

The need to belong, p. 484
Easy, Factual/Definitional, Objective 9, Ans: d

88. When peoples' need to belong is fulfilled through close relationships, they are less likely to:
    a. commit suicide.
    b. contract physical illness.
    c. suffer psychological disorders.
    d. experience any of the above.

Motivation at work, p. 486
Easy, Factual/Definitional, Objective 10, Ans: c

89. Those who view their work as a necessary but personally unfulfilling way to make money are said to view work as a:
   a. flow.
   b. set point.
   c. job.
   d. refractory period.
   e. career.

Motivation at work, p. 486
Medium, Conceptual/Application, Objective 10, Ans: d

90. Andrea views her work as primarily an opportunity to climb up the corporate ladder in pursuit of increasingly better positions. Andrea apparently views her work as a:
   a. calling.
   b. job.
   c. set point.
   d. career.
   e. flow.

Motivation at work, p. 486
Medium, Conceptual, Objective 10, Ans: b

91. Work is most likely to satisfy the higher-level needs in Maslow's hierarchy for those who:
   a. work only part-time.
   b. view their work as a calling.
   c. are strongly motivated by high wages.
   d. are supervised by Theory X managers.

Motivation at work, p. 486
Medium, Factual/Definitional, Objective 10, Ans: e

92. After studying artists who would spend hour after hour painting or sculpting with enormous concentration, Csikszentmihalyi formulated the concept of:
   a. a hierarchy of motives.
   b. erotic plasticity.
   c. achievement motivation.
   d. 360-degree feedback.
   e. flow.

Motivation at work, p. 486
Medium, Factual/Definitional, Objective 10, Ans: d

93. Flow is characterized by a ________ awareness of self and a ________ awareness of the passing of time.
   a. heightened; diminished
   b. diminished; heightened
   c. heightened; heightened
   d. diminished; diminished

Motivation at work, p. 486
Easy, Factual/Definitional, Objective 10, Ans: e

94. Which profession is most directly involved in the application of psychology's principles to the workplace?
a. social psychology
b. personality psychology
c. cognitive psychology
d. developmental psychology
e. industrial-organizational psychology

I/O psychology at work (Close-up), p. 487
Medium, Factual/Definitional, Objective 10, Ans: e

95. Developing assessment tools for selecting and placing employees is of most direct relevance to:
a.. social psychology.
b. clinical psychology.
c. organizational psychology.
d. human factors psychology.
e. personnel psychology.

Harnessing strengths, pp. 487-488
Medium, Factual/Definitional, Objective 11, Ans: a

96. The longer employees have worked for an organization and the higher they climb, the less likely they are to strongly agree that:
a. their job is suited to their strengths.
b. 360-degree feedback promotes open communication.
c. their work is a calling.
d. they prefer Theory Y management strategies.

Harnessing strengths, p. 488
Easy, Conceptual/Application, Objective 11, Ans: d

97. After discovering that their company's best software developers are highly analytical, personnel psychologists focused their employment ads for additional software developers less on applicants' experience and more on their ability to engage in logical problem solving. This best illustrates their commitment to:
a. 360-degree feedback.
b. Theory Y management.
c. structured interviews.
d. a strengths-based selection system.

Discovering your strengths (Close-up), p. 488
Easy, Factual/Definitional, Objective 11, Ans: a

98. Work activities that are specifically suited to your strengths are most likely to be those associated with the experience of:
a. flow.
b. 360-degree feedback.
c. transformational leadership.
d. refractory periods.
e. homeostasis.

The interview illusion, p. 489
Easy, Conceptual/Application, Objective 11, Ans: e

99. Mr. Walters has many years of experience as a personnel officer for a large corporation. He does not review most job applicants' reference files because he is confident of his ability to predict their future work performance based on his direct face-to-face conversations with them. Mr. Walters' confidence best illustrates:
a. Theory Y management.
b. 360-degree feedback.
c. the halo error.
d. transformational leadership.
e. the interview illusion.

The interview illusion, p. 489
Easy, Factual/Definitional, Objective 11, Ans: b

100. When meeting job applicants, employers often discount the influence of varying situations on applicants' behaviors and presume that what they observe applicants do and say reflects the applicants' enduring personal traits. This most clearly contributes to:
a. severity errors.
b. the interview illusion.
c. strengths-based selection systems.
d. the experience of flow.
e. Theory Y management.

Structured interviews, p. 490
Medium, Conceptual/Application, Objective 11, Ans: a

101. Dr. Thompson is involved in scripting interview questions that will effectively predict job applicants' success in specific work positions. Her work best illustrates that of a(n) ________ psychologist.
a. personnel
b. organizational
c. human factors
d. clinical

Appraising performance, p. 491
Easy, Conceptual/Application, Objective 11, Ans: c

102. Kelsey's awareness of her own effectiveness as a customer service manger is enhanced by the performance appraisals she periodically receives from fellow managers, subordinates, customers, and her supervisor. This best illustrates the value of:
a. experiencing flow.
b. Theory X management.
c. 360-degree feedback.
d. Maslow's motivational hierarchy.
e. Theory Y management.

Appraising performance, p. 491
Easy, Conceptual/Application, Objective 11, Ans: e

103. Carlos is so friendly and likable that his job supervisors and coworkers often appraise his work skills and performance more positively than is actually warranted. This best illustrates evaluators' vulnerability to:
a. homeostasis.
b. the interview illusion.
c. intrinsic motivation.
d. the experience of flow.
e. halo errors.

Organizational psychology, p. 491
Easy, Conceptual/Application, Objective 12, Ans: d

104. Jeff, who is 14, engages in rigorous tennis drills or competitive play at least four hours every day because he wants to master the sport and play on one of the best college teams in the country. His goal and behavior best illustrate the concept of:
a. set point.
b. drive reduction.
c. human factors psychology.
d. achievement motivation.
e. homeostasis.

Organizational psychology, p. 491
Easy, Factual/Definitional, Objective 12, Ans: a

105. When researchers monitored the professional accomplishments of more than 1500 highly intelligent individuals, they found that the most successful were more ambitious, energetic, and persistent. This best illustrates the importance of:
a. drive reduction.
b. 360-degree feedback.
c. achievement motivation.
d. homeostasis.
e. set points.

Satisfaction and engagement, p. 492
Medium, Factual/Definitional, Objective 12, Ans: b

106. Organizational psychologists are most likely to be involved in:
a. matching people's strengths with specific job assignments.
b. modifying work environments in order to improve employee engagement.
c. contributing to the design of user-friendly industrial machines.
d. designing training programs to prepare unemployed persons for existing jobs.

Managing well: harnessing job-relevant strengths, pp. 494-495
Medium, Factual/Definitional, Objective 13, Ans: c

107. College administrators hoping to improve faculty productivity do not expect every full-time professor in their institution to teach the same number of courses or engage in the same amount of research because this would:
a. interfere with the practice of 360-degree feedback.
b. promote Theory Y management practices.
c. fail to adequately develop the unique strengths of each professor.
d. require an equal amount of time and effort from professors receiving very different salaries.

Managing well: setting specific challenging goals, p. 494
Easy, Factual/Definitional, Objective 13, Ans: d

108. The on-time completion of major work projects is most clearly facilitated by:
    a. establishing set points.
    b. scripting structured interviews.
    c. receiving 360-degree feedback.
    d. stating implementation intentions.

Managing well: choosing an appropriate leadership style, p. 494
Easy, Conceptual, Objective 13, Ans: c

109. Managers with a task-leadership style would be most likely to:
    a. mediate a conflict between two argumentative employees.
    b. give employees a high degree of freedom to develop their own work procedures.
    c. remind employees of the exact deadlines for the completion of work projects.
    d. avoid closely monitoring the productivity of individual employees.

Managing well: choosing an appropriate leadership style, p. 495
Easy, Factual/Definitional, Objective 13, Ans: d

110. Effective managers often demonstrate ________ levels of task leadership and ________ levels of social leadership.
    a. high; low
    b. low; high
    c. low; low
    d. high; high

Managing well: choosing an appropriate leadership style, p. 495
Medium, Factual/Definitional, Objective 13, Ans: d

111. Theory Y managers are more likely than Theory X managers to assume that employees are motivated by a:
    a. desire for higher wages.
    b. desire for safer working conditions.
    c. fear of losing their jobs.
    d. need for self-esteem.

Managing well: choosing an appropriate leadership style, p. 495
Difficult, Conceptual, Objective 13, Ans: b

112. Participative management is to _______ as directive management is to ________.
    a. leniency errors, halo errors
    b. Theory Y; Theory X
    c. task leadership; social leadership
    d. unstructured interviews; structured interviews

Managing well: choosing an appropriate leadership style, p. 495
Medium, Factual/Definitional, Objective 13, Ans: d

113. Theory X managers are more likely than Theory Y managers to:
    a. provide employees with very challenging work assignments.
    b. give employees a high degree of responsibility for developing their own work procedures.
    c. encourage employees to critically discuss controversial company policies.
    d. frequently monitor individual employees in order to make sure they are working.

Managing well: choosing an appropriate leadership style, pp. 458, 495
Difficult, Conceptual, Objective 13, Ans: d

114. In terms of Maslow's motivational hierarchy, the higher-level needs of employees are most likely to be satisfied by:
    a. Theory X managers.
    b. monetary incentives.
    c. unstructured interviews.
    d. participative management.

Managing well: choosing an appropriate leadership style, pp. 458, 495
Difficult, Conceptual, Objective 13, Ans: b

115. Maslow's lower-level needs are to ________ as Maslow's higher-level needs are to _______.
    a. social leadership; task leadership
    b. Theory X; Theory Y
    b. participative management; directive management
    d. structured interviews; unstructured interviews
    e. leniency errors; severity errors

Managing well: choosing an appropriate leadership style, p. 495
Medium, Factual/Definitional, Objective 13, Ans: c

116. Theory Y managers are more likely than Theory X managers to:
    a. frequently monitor individual employees in order to make sure they are working.
    b. discourage employees from critically discussing controversial company policies.
    c. give employees a high degree of responsibility for developing their own work procedures.
    d. remind employees of the exact deadlines for the completion of work projects.

Managing well: choosing an appropriate leadership style, p. 495
Medium, Factual/Definitional, Objective 13, Ans: a

117. In terms of Maslow's motivational hierarchy, the higher-level needs of employees are most likely to be satisfied by:
    a. Theory Y managers.
    b. monetary incentives.
    c. unstructured interviews.
    d. directive management.

Essay Questions

1. Abraham Maslow suggested that "a person who is lacking food, love, and self-esteem would most likely hunger for food more strongly than anything else." Conversely, the novelist Dostoyevski wrote, "without a firm idea of himself and the purpose of his life, man cannot live even if surrounded with bread." Give evidence that would lead you to support *both* statements.

2. Although Jan appears to be underweight, she is afraid of becoming fat and consistently restricts her food intake. Although Gene appears to be overweight, he enjoys eating and always eats as much as he wants. Explain how their different reactions to food might result from (a) differences in their inner bodily states *and* (b) differences in their reactions to external incentives.

3. The rate of teenage pregnancy in the United States has risen sharply in the last 40 years, despite the increased availability of contraceptives. Suggest how parents, teachers, religious leaders, government officials, and teenagers themselves could help remedy this situation. Include at least one concrete suggestion for *each* of these groups.

4. People often refer to homosexuals as persons rather than referring to homosexual behavior as something persons do. In fact, those who experience homosexual desires or engage in homosexual practices are often assumed to be gay or lesbian in the same sense that they are male or female. Describe the potential advantages and disadvantages of this assumption, and critically evaluate how it might influence research on the origins of differing sexual orientations.

5. Describe the contrasting effects of directive management and participative management on employee morale. Discuss these differences in terms of Maslow's hierarchy of motives. Explain why the effectiveness of each style would depend on the personality traits and cultural background of the employees.

Web Quiz 1

Ans: d

1. After spending years in the ocean, a mature salmon swims up its home river to return to its birthplace. This behavior is an example of:
   a. homeostasis.
   b. a set point.
   c. a refractory period.
   d. an instinct.
   e. flow.

Ans: a

2. Need is to drive as ________ is to _______.
   a. food deprivation; hunger
   b. motivation; incentive
   c. thirst; basal metabolic rate
   d. instinct; incentive

Ans: c

3. Insulin is to the pancreas as ghrelin is to:
   a. the hypothalamus.
   b. fat cells.
   c. the stomach.
   d. the liver.

Ans: c

4. A starving rat will lose all interest in food if its ________ is destroyed.
   a. lateral thalamus
   b. ventromedial thalamus
   c. lateral hypothalamus
   d. ventromedial hypothalamus

Ans: b

5. The secretion of leptin _________ hunger and the secretion of orexin ________ hunger.
   a. increases; decreases
   b. decreases; increases
   c. increases; increases
   d. decreases; decreases

Ans: d

6. In an attempt to lose some of the weight she has gained from binge eating, Melissa tries to compensate by using laxatives and exercising until she is exhausted. Melissa most clearly demonstrates symptoms of:
   a. anorexia nervosa.
   b. hypermetabolism.
   c. excess leptin.
   d. bulimia nervosa.
   e. a refractory period.

Ans: a

7. Over the past 50 years, the incidence of anorexia nervosa has steadily increased. This is most clearly attributable to:
a. cultural ideals of beauty that increasingly encourage thinness.
b. increasing levels of childhood sexual abuse.
c. the onset of adolescence at increasingly younger ages.
d. the decreasing emphasis on maintaining stable marriages.

Ans: b

8. During which phase of the sexual response cycle does the refractory period begin?
a. the plateau phase
b. the resolution phase
c. the excitement phase
d. orgasm

Ans: a

9. The removal of a woman's ovaries may contribute to decreasing sexual interest because her natural ________ level is _______.
a. testosterone; lowered
b. testosterone; raised
c. PYY; lowered
d. PYY; raised

Ans: d

10. A Columbia University study found that teens who took vows pledging virginity until marriage were subsequently:
a. more likely than other adolescents to suffer health problems.
b. less likely than other adolescents to experience positive self-esteem.
c. just as likely as other adolescents to have intercourse before marriage.
d. less likely than other adolescents to use contraceptives if they did have intercourse before marriage.

Ans: d

11. The fraternal birth order effect has been explained in terms of:
a. observational learning.
b. erotic plasticity.
c. refractory periods.
d. maternal immune responses.
e. drive-reduction theory.

Ans: e

12. The fraternal birth order effect refers to a factor associated with:
a. task leadership.
b. basal metabolic rate.
c. employee engagement.
d. refractory periods.
e. sexual orientation.

Ans: b

13. Work is most likely to satisfy the higher-level needs in Maslow's hierarchy if it is associated with:
    a. frequent pay raises.
    b. the experience of flow.
    c. 360-degree feedback.
    d. structured interviews.

Ans: c

14. Evaluations of job applicants based on informal interviews are ________ predictors of future job performance than handwriting analysis and ________ predictors than aptitude tests.
    a. better; better
    b. worse; worse
    c. better; worse
    d. worse; better

Ans: a

15. A tendency to assume that employees view work as a job rather than a calling is most characteristic of:
    a. Theory X managers.
    b. Theory Y mangers.
    c. task leaders.
    d. social leaders.

Web Quiz 2

Ans: b

1. By motivating us to satisfy our physical needs, hunger and thirst serve to:
   a. raise the set point.
   b. maintain homeostasis.
   c. lower blood insulin levels.
   d. shorten the refractory period.

Ans: b

2. Who emphasized that people whose needs for safety are unmet will not be preoccupied with satisfying their needs for love?
   a. Kinsey
   b. Maslow
   c. Masters and Johnson
   d. Freud
   e. Darwin

Ans: a

3. Orexin is an appetite hormone secreted by the:
   a. hypothalamus.
   b. pancreas.
   c. stomach.
   d. liver.

Ans: c

4. Destruction of the ________ causes an animal to ________.
   a. lateral hypothalamus; overeat
   b. lateral hypothalamus; start eating
   c. ventromedial hypothalamus; overeat
   d. ventromedial hypothalamus; stop eating

Ans: a

5. The concept of a set point is relevant to understanding the experience of:
   a. hunger.
   b. sexual motivation.
   c. achievement motivation.
   d. the need to belong.

Ans: d

6. Lindsey is extremely afraid of becoming obese even though she is underweight. She often checks her body in the mirror for any signs of fat and refuses to eat most foods because she insists they are fatty or high in calories. Lindsey most clearly demonstrates symptoms of:
   a. a refractory period.
   b. bulimia nervosa.
   c. an abnormally high set point.
   d. anorexia nervosa.
   e. excess PYY.

Ans: a

7. Bulimia patients are most likely to come from families with an unusually high incidence of:
a. alcoholism and depression.
b. sexual abuse.
c. religious involvement.
d. eating disorders.

Ans: d

8. The accuracy of Alfred Kinsey's survey findings regarding American sexual practices in the 1940s is highly questionable because:
a. few of his survey respondents were very well educated.
b. he used structured rather than unstructured interviews to gather information.
c. his survey respondents were paid large sums of money for participating in the research.
d. his leading questions may have encouraged false participant responses.

Ans: c

9. Sleep researchers have discovered that:
a. most dreams have explicit sexual content.
b. genital arousal seldom occurs when people are dreaming.
c. nocturnal emissions are more likely when orgasm has not occurred recently.
d. men and women are equally likely to experience orgasm in response to sexually explicit dreams.

Ans: d

10. Compared to sexual intercourse rates among teens in North America, the rates among teens are ________ in Western Europe and ________ in Asia.
a. lower; lower
b. higher; higher
c. lower; higher
d. higher; lower

Ans: b

11. Regardless of their sexual orientation, women are more likely than men to be aroused by both male and female sexual images. This best illustrates gender differences in:
a. set points.
b. erotic plasticity.
c. refractory periods.
d. basal metabolic rate.
e. the hierarchy of needs.

Ans: c

12. Which of the following is *not* true with respect to sexual orientation?
a. Virtually all cultures in all times have been predominantly heterosexual.
b. The environmental factors that influence sexual orientation are presently unknown.
c. Men who report a change from a homosexual to a heterosexual orientation typically achieve an exclusively opposite-sex attraction.
d. Homosexuality rates are higher than average among the identical twin brothers of homosexuals.

Ans: c

13. Personnel psychology is one of the main subfields of:
    a. personality psychology.
    b. clinical psychology.
    c. industrial-organizational psychology.
    d. social psychology.
    e. cognitive psychology.

Ans: e

14. For each performance review, Professor Donnell is evaluated by her students, colleagues, department chair, and research assistants. This best illustrates:
    a. homeostasis.
    b. Theory X management.
    c. the experience of flow.
    d. human factors psychology.
    e. 360-degree feedback.

Ans: c

15. Compared to ineffective managers, those who are effective are more likely to:
    a. make employees aware that their work performance is being monitored continuously.
    b. focus equal attention on the strengths and weaknesses of workers' performances.
    c. give employees positive reinforcement when they perform well.
    d. do all of the above.

Study Guide Questions

Ans: d, p. 455

1. Motivation is best understood as a state that:
   a. reduces a drive.
   b. aims at satisfying a biological need.
   c. energizes an organism to act.
   d. energizes and directs behavior.

Ans: d, p. 456

2. One shortcoming of the instinct theory of motivation is that it:
   a. places too much emphasis on environmental factors.
   b. focuses only on cognitive aspects of motivation.
   c. applies only to animal behavior.
   d. does not explain human behaviors; it simply names them.

Ans: c, p. 456

3. Few human behaviors are rigidly patterned enough to qualify as:
   a. needs.
   b. drives.
   c. instincts.
   d. incentives.

Ans: e, pp. 456-457

4. Instinct theory and drive-reduction theory both emphasize ________ factors in motivation.
   a. environmental
   b. cognitive
   c. psychological
   d. social
   e. biological

Ans: c, p. 457

5. Which of the following is *not* an example of homeostasis?
   a. perspiring in order to restore normal body temperature
   b. feeling hungry and eating to restore the level of blood glucose to normal
   c. feeling hungry at the sight of an appetizing food
   d. all of the above are examples of homeostasis

Ans: b, p. 457

6. Which of the following is a difference between a drive and a need?
   a. Needs are learned; drives are inherited.
   b. Needs are physiological states; drives are psychological states.
   c. Drives are generally stronger than needs.
   d. Needs are generally stronger than drives.

Ans: a, p. 457

7. Homeostasis refers to:
   a. the tendency to maintain a steady internal state.
   b. the tendency to seek external incentives for behavior.
   c. the setting of the body's "weight thermostat."
   d. a theory of the development of sexual orientation.

Ans: a, p. 457

8. One problem with the idea of motivation as drive reduction is that:
   a. because some motivated behaviors do not seem to be based on physiological needs, they cannot be explained in terms of drive reduction.
   b. it fails to explain any human motivation.
   c. it cannot account for homeostasis.
   d. it does not explain the hunger drive.

Ans: c, p. 457

9. Which of the following is *inconsistent* with the drive-reduction theory of motivation?
   a. When body temperature drops below 98.6° Fahrenheit, blood vessels constrict to conserve warmth.
   b. A person is driven to seek a drink when his or her cellular water level drops below its optimum point.
   c. Monkeys will work puzzles even if not given a food reward.
   d. A person becomes hungry when body weight falls below its biological set point.
   e. None of the above is inconsistent.

Ans: c, p. 457

10. Mary loves hang-gliding. It would be most difficult to explain Mary's behavior according to:
   a. incentives.
   b. achievement motivation.
   c. drive-reduction theory.
   d. Maslow's hierarchy of needs.

Ans: e, p. 458

11. For two weeks, Orlando has been on a hunger strike in order to protest his country's involvement in what he perceives as an immoral war. Orlando's willingness to starve himself in order to make a political statement conflicts with the theory of motivation advanced by:
   a. Kinsey.
   b. Murray.
   c. Keys.
   d. Masters and Johnson.
   e. Maslow.

Ans: d, p. 458

12. Beginning with the most basic needs, which of the following represents the correct sequence of needs in the hierarchy described by Maslow?
   a. safety; physiological; esteem; belongingness and love; self-fulfillment
   b. safety; physiological; belongingness and love; esteem; self-fulfillment
   c. physiological; safety; esteem; belongingness and love; self-fulfillment
   d. physiological; safety; belongingness and love; esteem; self-fulfillment
   e. physiological; safety; self-fulfillment; esteem; belongingness and love

Ans: d, p. 458

13. According to Maslow's theory:
   a. the most basic motives are based on physiological needs.
   b. needs are satisfied in a specified order.
   c. the highest motives relate to self-actualization.
   d. all of the above are true.

Ans: c, pp. 459-460

14. In his study of men on a semistarvation diet, Keys found that:
    a. the metabolic rate of the subjects increased.
    b. the subjects eventually lost interest in food.
    c. the subjects became obsessed with food.
    d. the subjects' behavior directly contradicted predictions made by Maslow's hierarchy of needs.

Ans: a, p. 461

15. Increases in insulin will:
    a. lower blood sugar and trigger hunger.
    b. raise blood sugar and trigger hunger.
    c. lower blood sugar and trigger satiety.
    d. raise blood sugar and trigger satiety.

Ans: b, p. 461

16. The brain area that when stimulated suppresses eating is the:
    a. lateral hypothalamus.
    b. ventromedial hypothalamus.
    c. lateral thalamus.
    d. ventromedial thalamus.

Ans: d, p. 461

17. Two rats have escaped from their cages in the neurophysiology lab. The technician needs your help in returning them to their proper cages. One rat is grossly overweight; the other is severely underweight. You confidently state that the overweight rat goes in the "________-lesion" cage, while the underweight rat goes in the "________-lesion" cage.
    a. hippocampus; amygdala
    b. amygdala; hippocampus
    c. lateral hypothalamus; ventromedial hypothalamus
    d. ventromedial hypothalamus; lateral hypothalamus

Ans: a, p. 461

18. Electrical stimulation of the lateral hypothalamus will cause an animal to:
    a. begin eating.
    b. stop eating.
    c. become obese.
    d. begin copulating.
    e. stop copulating.

Ans: b, p. 461

19. In animals, destruction of the lateral hypothalamus results in ________, whereas destruction of the ventromedial hypothalamus results in ________.
    a. overeating; loss of hunger
    b. loss of hunger; overeating
    c. an elevated set point; a lowered set point
    d. increased thirst; loss of thirst
    e. increased metabolic rate; weight loss

Ans: e, p. 462

20. I am a protein produced by fat cells and monitored by the hypothalamus. When in abundance, I cause the brain to increase metabolism. What am I?
    a. PYY
    b. ghrelin
    c. orexin
    d. insulin
    e. leptin

Ans: c, p. 462

21. Obese mice eat less, become more active, and lose weight after they have been injected with:
    a. insulin.
    b. glucose.
    c. leptin.
    d. estrogen.
    e. testosterone.

Ans: b, p. 462

22. Lucille has been sticking to a strict diet but can't seem to lose weight. What is the most likely explanation for her difficulty?
    a. Her body has a very low set point.
    b. Her pre-diet weight was near her body's set point.
    c. Her weight problem is actually caused by an underlying eating disorder.
    d. Lucille is an "external."

Ans: c, p. 462

23. When obese people receive leptin injections, their body weight typically:
    a. decreases slightly.
    b. decreases by a large amount.
    c. remains unchanged.
    d. increases slightly.

Ans: c, p. 463

24. Randy, who has been under a lot of stress lately, has intense cravings for sugary junk foods, which tend to make him feel more relaxed. Which of the following is the most likely explanation for his craving?
    a. Randy feels that he deserves to pamper himself with sweets because of the stress he is under.
    b. The extra sugar gives Randy the energy he needs to cope with the demands of daily life.
    c. Carbohydrates boost levels of serotonin, which has a calming effect.
    d. The extra sugar tends to lower blood insulin level, which promotes relaxation.

Ans: c, p. 463

25. Ali's parents have tried hard to minimize their son's exposure to sweet, fattening foods. If Ali has the occasion to taste sweet foods in the future, which of the following is likely:
    a. He will have a strong aversion to such foods.
    b. He will have a neutral reaction to sweet foods.
    c. He will display a preference for sweet tastes.
    d. It is impossible to predict Ali's reaction.

Ans: b, pp. 463-464

26. The text suggests that a "neophobia" for unfamiliar tastes:
    a. is more common in children than in adults.
    b. protected our ancestors from potentially toxic substances.
    c. may be an early warning sign of an eating disorder.
    d. only grows stronger with repeated exposure to those tastes.
    e. does all of the above.

Ans: d, p. 464

27. Bulimia nervosa involves:
    a. binging.
    b. purging.
    c. dramatic weight loss.
    d. a. and b.
    e. a., b., and c.

Ans: c, p. 464

28. Which of the following is *not* typical of both anorexia and bulimia?
    a. far more frequent occurrence in women than in men
    b. preoccupation with food and fear of being overweight
    c. weight significantly and noticeably outside normal ranges
    d. low self-esteem and feelings of depression

Ans: c, pp. 464-465

29. Kathy has been undergoing treatment for bulimia. There is an above-average probability that one or more members of Kathy's family have a problem with:
    a. high achievement.
    b. overprotection.
    c. alcoholism.
    d. all of the above.

Ans: b, p. 464-465

30. Of the following individuals, who might be most prone to developing an eating disorder?
    a. Jason, an adolescent boy who is somewhat overweight and is unpopular with his peers
    b. Jennifer, a teenage girl who has a poor self-image and a fear of not being able to live up to her parents' high standards
    c. Susan, a 35-year-old woman who is a "workaholic" and devotes most of her energies to her high-pressured career
    d. Bill, a 40-year-old man who has had problems with alcoholism and is seriously depressed after losing his job of 20 years

Ans: e, p. 465

31. Which of the following is true concerning eating disorders?
    a. Genetic factors may influence susceptibility.
    b. Abnormal levels of certain neurotransmitters may play a role.
    c. People with eating disorders are at risk for anxiety or depression.
    d. Family background is a significant factor.
    e. All of the above are true.

Ans: a, p. 465

32. Although the cause of eating disorders is still unknown, proposed explanations focus on all of the following *except*:
a. metabolic factors.
b. genetic factors.
c. family background factors.
d. cultural factors.

Ans: c, p. 466

33. Investigations of how men and women view body image found that:
a. men and women alike expressed significant self-dissatisfaction.
b. men and women alike accurately assessed the body weight for their own sex that the other sex preferred.
c. men tended to rate their current weight as corresponding both to their ideal weight and to women's ideal weight for men.
d. women tended to be satisfied with their current body weight but to think that men preferred a thinner body shape for women.

Ans: d, p. 468

34. Kinsey's studies of sexual behavior showed that:
a. males enjoy sex more than females.
b. females enjoy sex more than males.
c. premarital sex is less common than is popularly believed.
d. sexual behavior is enormously varied.

Ans: b, p. 469

35. The correct order of the stages of Masters and Johnson's sexual response cycle is:
a. plateau; excitement; orgasm; resolution.
b. excitement; plateau; orgasm; resolution.
c. excitement; orgasm; resolution; refractory.
d. plateau; excitement; orgasm; refractory.
e. excitement; orgasm; plateau; resolution.

Ans: d, p. 469

36. According to Masters and Johnson, the sexual response of males is most likely to differ from that of females during:
a. the excitement phase.
b. the plateau phase.
c. orgasm.
d. the resolution phase.

Ans: d, p. 469

37. Which of the following has been found to be most effective in treating sexual disorders?
a. psychoanalysis.
b. cognitive therapy.
c. drug therapy.
d. behavior therapy.

Ans: a, p. 470

38. Castration of male rats results in:
   a. reduced testosterone and sexual interest.
   b. reduced testosterone, but no change in sexual interest.
   c. reduced estrogen and sexual interest.
   d. reduced estrogen, but no change in sexual interest.

Ans: d, p. 471

39. The power of external stimuli in sexual motivation is illustrated in Julia Heiman's experiment, in which subjects' responses to various romantic, erotic, or neutral audio tapes were recorded. Which of the following was among the findings of her research?
   a. The women were more aroused by the romantic tape; the men were more aroused by the sexually explicit tape.
   b. The sexually experienced subjects reported greater arousal when the tape depicted a sexual encounter in which a woman is overpowered by a man and enjoys being dominated.
   c. Whereas the men's physical arousal was both obvious and consistent with their verbal reports, the women's verbal reports did not correspond very directly with their measured physical arousal.
   d. Both men and women were aroused most by the sexually explicit tape.

Ans: a, p. 473

40. Of the following parts of the world, teen intercourse rates are highest in:
   a. Western Europe.
   b. Canada.
   c. the United States.
   d. Asia.
   e. Arab countries.

Ans: e, pp. 473-474

41. Which of the following was *not* identified as a contributing factor in the high rate of unprotected sex among adolescents?
   a. alcohol use
   b. mass media sexual norms
   c. guilt related to sexual activity
   d. ignorance
   e. thrill-seeking

Ans: c, p. 474

42. Which of the following teens is most likely to delay the initiation of sex?
   a. Jack, who has below-average intelligence
   b. Jason, who is not religiously active
   c. Ron, who regularly volunteers his time in community service
   d. it is impossible to predict

Ans: c, p. 475

43. Which of the following is currently true regarding first-year college students' opinions of casual sex?
   a. The majority feel that sex between persons who know each other for only a short time is acceptable.
   b. The majority feel that condom use is unnecessary, because they know when the safe times are.
   c. The majority feel that sex between persons who know each other for only a short time is unacceptable.
   d. The majority feel that they will be ostracized by their peers if they don't do "what everyone else is doing."

Ans: c, p. 475

44. Sexual orientation refers to:
   a. a person's tendency to display behaviors typical of males or females.
   b. a person's sense of identity as a male or female.
   c. a person's enduring sexual attraction toward members of a particular gender.
   d. all of the above.

Ans: c, p. 476

45. Which of the following is *not* true regarding sexual orientation?
   a. Sexual orientation is neither willfully chosen nor willfully changed.
   b. Women's sexual orientation tends to be less strongly felt than men's.
   c. Men's sexual orientation is potentially more fluid and changeable than women's.
   d. Women, regardless of sexual orientation, respond to both female and male erotic stimuli.
   e. Homosexual behavior does not always indicate a homosexual orientation.

Ans: c, p. 478

46. Some scientific evidence makes a preliminary link between homosexuality and:
   a. late sexual maturation.
   b. the age of an individual's first erotic experience.
   c. atypical prenatal hormones.
   d. early problems in relationships with parents.
   e. all of the above.

Ans: b, p. 479

47. Exposure of a fetus to the hormones typical of females between ________ and ________ months after conception may predispose the developing human to become attracted to males.
   a. 1; 3
   b. 2; 5
   c. 4; 7
   d. 6; 9
   e. 9; 11

Ans: d, pp. 479-480

48. Which of the following statements concerning homosexuality is true?
   a. Homosexuals have abnormal hormone levels.
   b. As children, most homosexuals were molested by an adult homosexual.
   c. Homosexuals had a domineering opposite-sex parent.
   d. New research indicates that sexual orientation may be at least partly physiological.

Ans: d, p. 481

49. It has been said that the body's major sex organ is the brain. With regard to sex education:
    a. transmission of value-free information about the wide range of sexual behaviors should be the primary focus of the educator.
    b. transmission of technical knowledge about the biological act should be the classroom focus, free from the personal values and attitudes of researchers, teachers, and students.
    c. the home, not the school, should be the focus of all instruction about reproductive behavior.
    d. people's attitudes, values, and morals cannot be separated from the biological aspects of sexuality.

Ans: c, p. 483

50. Summarizing her report on the need to belong, Rolanda states that:
    a. "Cooperation amongst our ancestors was uncommon."
    b. "Social bonding is not in our nature; it is a learned human trait."
    c. "Because bonding with others increased our ancestors' success at reproduction and survival, it became part of our biological nature."
    d. both a. and b. are true.

Ans: c, p. 483

51. When asked what makes life meaningful, most people first mention:
    a. good health.
    b. challenging work.
    c. satisfying relationships.
    d. serving others.

Ans: d, p. 486

52. Which of the following individuals would be characterized as experiencing "flow"?
    a. Sheila, who, despite viewing her work as merely a job, performs her work conscientiously
    b. Larry, who sees his work as an artist as a calling
    c. Darren, who views his present job as merely a stepping stone in his career
    d. Montal, who often becomes so immersed in his writing that he loses all sense of self and time

Ans: c, p. 486

53. Dr. Iverson conducts research focusing on how management styles influence worker motivation. Dr. Iverson would most accurately be described as a(n):
    a. motivation psychologist.
    b. personnel psychologist.
    c. organizational psychologist.
    d. human factors psychologist.
    e. industrial-organizational psychologist.

Ans: d, p. 489

54. Which of the following was *not* identified as a contributing factor in the interviewer illusion?
    a. the fact that interviews reveal applicants' intentions but not necessarily their habitual behaviors
    b. the tendency of interviewers to think that interview behavior only reflects applicants' enduring traits
    c. the tendency of interviewers to more often follow the successful careers of applicants they hired rather than those who were not hired
    d. the tendency of most interviewers to rely on unstructured rather than structured interviews

Ans: c, p. 491

55. Which of the following is *not* an aspect of Murray's definition of achievement motivation?
 a. the desire to master skills
 b. the desire for control
 c. the desire to gain approval
 d. the desire to attain a high standard

Ans: c, p. 491

56. Because Alethea is very friendly and likable, her supervisor gives her a positive rating on her overall job performance. By generalizing from these specific traits to a biased overall evaluation, Alethea's supervisor has committed a:
 a. leniency error.
 b. severity error.
 c. halo error.
 d. recency error.

Ans: a, pp. 491-492

57. In order to predict future excellence in a young scholar, athlete, or artist, one would best examine the individual's:
 a. preparation and daily discipline.
 b. natural talent.
 c. peer group.
 d. home environment.

Ans: b, p. 494

58. For as long as she has been the plant manager, Juanita has welcomed input from employees and has delegated authority. Bill, in managing his department, takes a more authoritarian, iron-fisted approach. Juanita's style is one of ________ leadership, whereas Bill's is one of ________ leadership.
 a. task; social
 b. social; task
 c. directive; democratic
 d. democratic; participative

Ans: d, p. 494-495

59. To increase employee productivity, industrial- organizational psychologists advise managers to:
 a. adopt a directive leadership style.
 b. adopt a democratic leadership style.
 c. instill competitiveness in each employee.
 d. deal with employees according to their individual motives.

Ans: d, pp. 494-495

60. Darren, a sales clerk at a tire store, enjoys his job, not so much for the money as for its challenge and the opportunity to interact with a variety of people. The store manager asks you to recommend a strategy for increasing Darren's motivation. Which of the following is most likely to be effective?
    a. Create a competition among the salespeople so that whoever has the highest sales each week receives a bonus.
    b. Put Darren on a week-by-week employment contract, promising him continued employment only if his sales increase each week.
    c. Leave Darren alone unless his sales drop and then threaten to fire him if his performance doesn't improve.
    d. Involve Darren as much as possible in company decision making and use rewards to inform him of his successful performance.

Ans: a, p. 495

61. Theory ________ managers tend to adopt a style of ________ leadership.
    a. X; task
    b. X; social
    c. Y; autocratic
    d. Y; directive

Ans: d, p. 495

62. Because Brent believes that his employees are intrinsically motivated to work for reasons beyond money, Brent would be described as a(n) ________ manager.
    a. directive
    b. autocratic
    c. theory X
    d. theory Y

Ans: c, p. 495

63. Execuvac Company subscribes to the ________ principle that employees are happier and more productive if they are ________.
    a. Theory X; given simple tasks and monitored closely
    b. Theory Y; paid enough to fulfill basic needs for food and shelter
    c. Theory Y; allowed to participate in managerial decision making
    d. Theory X; allowed to set their own work hours

CHAPTER 13

Emotion

Learning Objectives

Theories of Emotion (pp. 500-505)

1. Identify the three components of emotions and contrast the James-Lange and Cannon-Bard theories of emotion.

2. Describe Schachter's two-factor theory of emotion, and discuss evidence suggesting that some emotional reactions involve no conscious thought.

3. Describe how emotions can be differentiated along the dimensions of valence and arousal level.

Embodied Emotion (pp. 505-510)

4. Describe the physiological changes that occur during emotional arousal, and discuss the relationship between arousal and performance.

5. Describe the relationship between physiological states and specific emotions, and discuss the effectiveness of the polygraph in detecting lies.

Expressed Emotion (pp. 510-517)

6. Describe some nonverbal indicators of emotion, and discuss the extent to which people from different cultures display and interpret facial expressions of emotion in a similar manner.

7. Describe the effects of facial expressions on emotional experience.

Experienced Emotion (pp. 518-529)

8. Discuss the significance of environmental and biological factors in the acquisition of fear.

9. Discuss the catharsis hypothesis, and identify some of the advantages and disadvantages of openly expressing anger.

10. Identify some potential causes and consequences of happiness, and describe how happiness is influenced by our prior experiences and by others' attainments.

Introduction to emotion, p. 499
Medium, Factual/Definitional, Objective 1, Ans: c

1. The basic components of emotion are:
   a. sympathetic arousal, parasympathetic inhibition, and cognitive labeling.
   b. physical gestures, facial expressions, and psychological drives.
   c. expressive behaviors, physiological arousal, and conscious experience.
   d. cognition, affect, and behavior.

The James-Lange theory, p. 500
Easy, Factual/Definitional, Objective 1, Ans: b

2. Who suggested that "we feel sorry because we cry . . . afraid because we tremble"?
   a. Stanley Schachter
   b. William James
   c. Walter Cannon
   d. Richard Lazarus
   e. Charles Darwin

The James-Lange theory, p. 500
Easy, Factual/Definitional, Objective 1, Ans: a

3. The James-Lange theory of emotion states that:
   a. to experience emotion is to be aware of one's physiological responses to an emotion-arousing event.
   b. the expression of emotion reduces one's level of physiological arousal.
   c. an emotion-arousing stimulus simultaneously triggers both physiological arousal and the subjective experience of emotion.
   d. to experience emotion one must be physically aroused and able to cognitively label the emotion.

The James-Lange theory, p. 500
Medium, Conceptual/Application, Objective 1, Ans: d

4. Cassandra's mother told her, "You know you are in love when your heart beats fast and you experience that unique trembling feeling inside." This remark best illustrates the ________ theory of emotion.
   a. Cannon-Bard
   b. two-factor
   c. catharsis
   d. James-Lange

The James-Lange theory, pp. 500, 516
Medium, Factual/Definitional, Objective 1, Ans: c

5. The fact that facial expressions of emotion tend to intensify the experience of emotion serves to support the:
   a. catharsis hypothesis.
   b. Cannon-Bard theory.
   c. James-Lange theory.
   d. adaptation-level principle.
   e. relative deprivation principle.

The James-Lange theory, pp. 500, 516
Difficult, Conceptual, Objective 1, Ans: d

6. Researchers have found that people experience cartoons as more amusing while holding a pen with their teeth than while holding it with their lips. This finding best serves to support the:
   a. relative deprivation principle.
   b. Cannon-Bard theory.
   c. adaptation-level principle.
   d. James-Lange theory.
   e. catharsis hypothesis.

The James-Lange theory, pp. 500-501
Medium, Factual/Definitional, Objective 1, Ans: c

7. Evidence that neck-level spinal cord injuries reduce the intensity with which people experience certain emotions most directly supports the:
   a. Cannon-Bard theory.
   b. adaptation-level principle.
   c. James-Lange theory.
   d. catharsis hypothesis.
   e. relative deprivation principle.

The Cannon-Bard theory, p. 500
Easy, Factual/Definitional, Objective 1, Ans: d

8. The idea that an emotion-arousing stimulus is simultaneously routed to the cortex and the sympathetic nervous system is central to the:
   a. James-Lange theory.
   b. relative deprivation principle.
   c. two-factor theory.
   d. Cannon-Bard theory.
   e. catharsis hypothesis.

The Cannon-Bard theory, p. 500
Easy, Conceptual, Objective 1, Ans: a

9. According to the Cannon-Bard theory, body arousal is to the sympathetic nervous system as subjective awareness of emotion is to the:
   a. cortex.
   b. hypothalamus.
   c. thalamus.
   d. parasympathetic nervous system.

The Cannon-Bard theory, p. 500
Difficult, Factual/Definitional, Objective 1, Ans: a

10. You would still be able to experience emotion in the absence of any sympathetic nervous system arousal according to the:
    a. Cannon-Bard theory.
    b. James-Lange theory.
    c. two-factor theory.
    d. catharsis hypothesis.
    e. adaptation-level principle.

The Cannon-Bard theory, pp. 500-501
Difficult, Conceptual/Application, Objective 1, Ans: b

11. Tranquilizing drugs that inhibit sympathetic nervous system activity often effectively reduce people's subjective experience of intense fear and anxiety. Which theory of emotion would have the greatest difficulty explaining this effect?
    a. James-Lange
    b. Cannon-Bard
    c. two-factor
    d. All of the above would have equal difficulty explaining this effect.

The James-Lange and two factor theories, p. 501
Medium, Factual/Definitional, Objective 1, Ans: a

12. The two-factor theory of emotion places more emphasis on the importance of ________ than does the James-Lange theory.
    a. cognitive activity
    b. subjective well-being
    c. physiological arousal
    d. catharsis

Schachter's two-factor theory of emotion, p. 501
Easy, Factual/Definitional, Objective 2, Ans: d

13. The two-factor theory of emotion was proposed by:
    a. Walter Cannon.
    b. Robert Zajonc.
    c. William James.
    d. Stanley Schachter.
    e. Richard Lazarus.

Schachter's two-factor theory of emotion, p. 501
Easy, Factual/Definitional, Objective 2, Ans: d

14. According to the two-factor theory, the two basic components of emotions are ________ and ________.
    a. facial expressions; cognitive labels
    b. emotion-arousing events; physical arousal
    c. physical arousal; overt behavior
    d. cognitive labels; physical arousal

Schachter's two-factor theory of emotion, p. 501
Medium, Conceptual/Application, Objective 2, Ans: c

15. Noticing that his heart was pounding and that his palms were sweaty while he was taking a difficult test, Harley concluded that he was "anxious." Noticing that his heart was pounding and that his palms were sweaty when an attractive lady asked him to dance, Dmitri concluded that he was "falling in love." The differing emotions experienced by Harley and Dmitri can best be explained by the:
    a. relative deprivation principle.
    b. James-Lange theory.
    c. two-factor theory.
    d. catharsis hypothesis.
    e. adaptation-level principle.

Schachter's two-factor theory of emotion, p. 501
Medium, Conceptual/Application, Objective 2, Ans: b

16. A therapist tells a patient who is afraid of elevators that his rapid breathing while on an elevator is not due to fear but is a natural consequence of too little oxygen in a small, enclosed space. With this new interpretation of his arousal, the patient no longer dreads elevators. The reduction in the patient's fear is best understood in terms of the:
    a. adaptation-level principle.
    b. two-factor theory.
    c. James-Lange theory.
    d. catharsis hypothesis.
    e. relative deprivation principle.

Schachter's two-factor theory of emotion, p. 502
Easy, Factual/Definitional, Objective 2, Ans: c

17. The results of the experiment in which subjects were injected with epinephrine prior to spending time with either a euphoric or an irritated person support the idea that:
    a. some emotions can be experienced apart from cognition.
    b. there are subtle but distinct physiological differences among the emotions.
    c. our experience of emotion depends on how we interpret bodily arousal.
    d. happiness is largely a function of our prior experience and of whom we compare ourselves with.

Schachter's two-factor theory of emotion, p. 502
Difficult, Factual/Definitional, Objective 2, Ans: c

18. In the Schachter and Singer experiment, subjects were injected with epinephrine prior to spending time with a person who acted either euphoric or irritated. Which individuals in this experiment were least likely to experience the emotion demonstrated by the experimenter's accomplice?
    a. those who were led to think the injection would produce no physiological arousal
    b. those who were promised a large sum of money for participating in the experiment
    c. those who were told that the injection would cause them to become physiologically aroused
    d. those who were asked to run in place after receiving the injection

Schachter's two-factor theory of emotion, pp. 502-503
Medium, Conceptual/Application, Objective 2, Ans: a

19. After being physically aroused by his daily three-mile run, Martin finds that he experiences stronger resentment if his wife asks for an unexpected favor and more intense romantic feelings if she kisses him. Martin's experience can best be explained by the:
    a. two-factor theory.
    b. James-Lange theory.
    c. Cannon-Bard theory.
    d. catharsis hypothesis.
    e. adaptation-level principle.

Schachter's two-factor theory of emotion, pp. 502-503
Medium, Conceptual/Application, Objective 2, Ans: e

20. Lee was momentarily terrified as a passing automobile nearly sideswiped his car. When one of his passengers joked that he almost had a two-color car, Lee laughed uncontrollably. Lee's emotional volatility is best explained in terms of the:
a. adaptation-level principle.
b. relative deprivation principle.
c. James-Lange theory.
d. catharsis hypothesis.
e. two-factor theory.

Schachter's two-factor theory of emotion, pp. 501-503
Difficult, Conceptual, Objective 2, Ans: c

21. The two-factor theory of emotion would have the greatest difficulty explaining why a:
a. person comes to fear snakes after he sees someone else bitten by one.
b. person's fear of snakes is reduced after she receives a calming tranquilizer.
c. person automatically fears snakes even though he thinks they are attractive and harmless.
d. person's fear of snakes is reduced after she learns that most snakes are harmless.

Must cognition precede emotion?, p. 503
Medium, Factual/Definitional, Objective 2, Ans: d

22. Evidence that people can develop an emotional preference for stimuli to which they have been unknowingly exposed has convinced Robert Zajonc that:
a. our thoughts are not influenced by our emotional states.
b. our normal feelings of love and anger are often irrational.
c. the two-factor theory of emotion is essentially correct.
d. sometimes emotions precede cognition.
e. emotional reactions bias our perceptions of the world.

Must cognition precede emotion?, p. 503
Medium, Factual/Definitional, Objective 2, Ans: e

23. Our most rapid and automatic emotional responses may result from the routing of sensory input from the thalamus directly to the:
a. hippocampus.
b. hypothalamus.
c. cerebellum.
d. brainstem.
e. amygdala.

Must cognition precede emotion?, p. 504
Medium, Factual/Definitional, Objective 2, Ans: c

24. In their dispute over the role of cognition in emotion, both Zajonc and Lazarus agree that:
a. cognitive reactions always precede emotional reactions.
b. emotional reactions always precede cognitive reactions.
c. some emotional reactions involve no conscious thinking.
d. cognitive reactions and emotional reactions always occur simultaneously.

Two dimensions of emotion, p. 504
Easy, Factual/Definitional, Objective 3, Ans: a

25. The emotion of rage is characterized by negative valence and ________ arousal.
    a. high
    b. positive
    c. low
    d. negative

Two dimensions of emotion, p. 504
Medium, Conceptual/Application, Objective 3, Ans: d

26. While completing a final exam, Karen labels her arousal as energizing, whereas Mike labels his arousal as threatening. The emotional experiences of the two test takers are likely to differ the most with respect to:
    a. duration.
    b. intensity.
    c. adaptation level.
    d. valence.

Two dimensions of emotion, p. 504
Easy, Conceptual, Objective 3, Ans: e

27. Anger is to rage as fear is to:
    a. guilt.
    b. shame.
    c. pain.
    d. disgust.
    e. terror.

Emotion and physiology, p. 506
Medium, Factual/Definitional, Objective 4, Ans: b

28. During an emergency, increasing levels of emotional arousal are likely to be accompanied by:
    a. decreases in blood sugar levels.
    b. slowing of digestion.
    c. increases in salivation.
    d. constriction of pupils to increase visual acuity.
    e. decreases in respiration rate.

Emotion and physiology, p. 506
Easy, Factual/Definitional, Objective 4, Ans: b

29. A hormone that increases heart rate, blood pressure, and blood sugar levels in times of emergency is:
    a. acetylcholine.
    b. epinephrine.
    c. testosterone.
    d. insulin.
    e. glycogen.

Emotion and physiology, p. 506
Easy, Conceptual/Application, Objective 4, Ans: a

30. As her professor distributed the mathematics test to the class, Blair's heart started to pound and her palms began to sweat. These physiological reactions were activated by her ________ nervous system.
   a. sympathetic
   b. central
   c. somatic
   d. parasympathetic

Emotion and physiology, p. 506
Difficult, Factual/Definitional, Objective 4, Ans: b

31. Activation of the sympathetic nervous system ________ respiration and ________ salivation.
   a. increases; increases
   b. increases; decreases
   c. decreases; decreases
   d. decreases; increases

Emotion and physiology, p. 506
Easy, Factual/Definitional, Objective 4, Ans: d

32. Which division of the nervous system calms the body after an emergency passes?
   a. somatic
   b. central
   c. sympathetic
   d. parasympathetic

Emotion and physiology, p. 506
Medium, Conceptual/Application, Objective 4, Ans: a

33. When her son fails to arrive home as expected, Elena fears he has been in an accident. Both her heart and respiration rate remain elevated until she sees him come safely through the door. Her body soon returns to normal due to the action of her ________ nervous system.
   a. parasympathetic
   b. sympathetic
   c. central
   d. somatic

Emotion and physiology, p. 506
Difficult, Conceptual, Objective 4, Ans: c

34. The parasympathetic nervous system is to the sympathetic nervous system as ________ is to ________.
   a. raising of blood sugar; lowering of blood sugar
   b. inhibition of digestion; activation of digestion
   c. contraction of pupils; dilation of pupils
   d. increasing blood pressure; decreasing blood pressure

Emotion and physiology, p. 506
Easy, Factual/Definitional, Objective 4, Ans: a

35. Performance of a task is typically ________ when arousal is ________.
    a. best; moderate
    b. worst; moderate
    c. best; low
    d. best; high
    e. mediocre; moderate

Emotion and physiology, p. 506
Medium, Conceptual/Application, Objective 4, Ans: e

36. Thaddeus will play a violin solo at his school tomorrow. His musical performance is likely to be ________ if his physiological arousal during the performance is ________.
    a. best; very low
    b. worst; moderate
    c. best; very high
    d. mediocre; moderate
    e. best; moderate

Emotion and physiology, p. 506
Difficult, Factual/Definitional, Objective 4, Ans: d

37. The level of arousal typically associated with optimal performance tends to be ________ on tasks that are ________.
    a. lower; frequently practiced
    b. higher; relatively difficult
    c. lower; relatively easy
    d. lower; relatively difficult

Emotion and physiology, p. 506
Difficult, Conceptual/Application, Objective 4, Ans: a

38. Relatively high levels of physiological arousal would most likely interfere with effectively:
    a. solving a crossword puzzle.
    b. repeating the alphabet.
    c. riding a bicycle.
    d. washing dishes.
    e. enjoying a televised football game.

The physiology of specific emotions, p. 507
Difficult, Factual/Definitional, Objective 5, Ans: d

39. The emotion of fear is sometimes accompanied by ________ and ________ that differ from those that accompany rage.
    a. hormone secretions; perspiration levels
    b. breathing rates; hormone secretions
    c. breathing rates; blood pressure levels
    d. hormone secretions; finger temperatures
    e. heart rates; blood pressure levels

The physiology of specific emotions, p. 507
Difficult, Factual/Definitional, Objective 5, Ans: a

40. As people experience negative emotions, the ________ frontal lobe of the brain becomes ________ electrically active.
a. right; more
b. right; less
c. left; more
d. left; less

The physiology of specific emotions, p. 507
Difficult, Conceptual, Objective 5, Ans: b

41. Increased activity in the right frontal lobe is to ________ as increased activity in the left frontal lobe is to ________.
a. anger; fear
b. disgust; joy
c. love; hate
d. elation; depression
e. love; lust

Thinking critically about lie detection (Box), p. 508
Easy, Factual/Definitional, Objective 5, Ans: e

42. For purposes of lie detection, investigators have most commonly made use of a(n):
a. electrocardiograph.
b. electroencephalograph.
c. myograph.
d. tomograph.
e. polygraph.

Thinking critically about lie detection (Box), p. 508
Medium, Conceptual/Application, Objective 5, Ans: d

43. Boyd, a suspect in a criminal investigation, has agreed to take a lie detector test. The machine used in this test is most likely to measure his:
a. blood sugar levels.
b. pupil dilation.
c. hormone secretions.
d. perspiration levels.
e. facial expressions of emotions.

Thinking critically about lie detection (Box), p. 509
Medium, Factual/Definitional, Objective 5, Ans: c

44. Research on the accuracy of lie detector tests suggests that they:
a. pose no threat to the innocent.
b. are accurate only 50 percent of the time, even when administered by experts.
c. are more likely to declare the innocent guilty than to declare the guilty innocent.
d. are more likely to declare the guilty innocent than to declare the innocent guilty.

Thinking critically about lie detection (Box), p. 509
Easy, Factual/Definitional, Objective 5, Ans: b

45. The guilty knowledge test is typically used to:
   a. provide emotionally troubled individuals with a way to safely release their aggressive urges.
   b. assess a suspect's responses to details of a crime.
   c. screen potential employees for possible past misdeeds.
   d. assure people that they are no worse than others with whom they compare themselves.

Thinking critically about lie detection (Box), p. 509
Easy, Conceptual/Application, Objective 5, Ans: c

46. A polygraph examination of a suspected murderer included an assessment of his reaction to a detailed description of the victim's clothing and death wounds—details that would be known only to a person at the scene of the crime. The investigators were using the:
   a. catharsis hypothesis.
   b. "facial feedback" effect.
   c. guilty knowledge test.
   d. adaptation-level phenomenon.
   e. relative deprivation principle.

Nonverbal communication, p. 510
Easy, Conceptual/Application, Objective 6, Ans: a

47. Chiana and her husband both want to feel and express greater warmth and affection for each other. They would be advised to spend time looking intently at one another's:
   a. eyes.
   b. lips.
   c. hand gestures.
   d. body postures.

Nonverbal communication, p. 511
Medium, Factual/Definitional, Objective 6, Ans: b

48. People are especially good at quickly detecting facial expressions of:
   a. love.
   b. anger.
   c. surprise.
   d. happiness.
   e. boredom.

Nonverbal communication, p. 511
Difficult, Factual/Definitional, Objective 6, Ans: c

49. Research on the nonverbal expression of emotion indicates that:
   a. the body movements and gestures used to express emotions are the same throughout the world.
   b. it is difficult to use nonverbal cues in order to mislead others about one's true emotions.
   c. introverts are better than extraverts at recognizing nonverbal expressions of emotion in others.
   d. accurately identifying emotional facial expressions in people from different cultures requires personal experience with those cultures.

Nonverbal communication, pp. 511, 512
Medium, Factual/Definitional, Objective 6, Ans: a

50. In terms of ability to recognize others' facial expressions of emotion, introverts do ________ than extraverts and women do ________ than men.
   a. better; better
   b. worse; better
   c. better; worse
   d. worse; worse

Nonverbal communication, p. 512
Easy, Factual/Definitional, Objective 6, Ans: c

51. Compared to men, women are ________ effective in discerning if someone is telling a lie and they are ________ effective in discerning which of two people in a photo is the other's supervisor.
   a. more; less
   b. less; more
   c. more; more
   d. less; less

Nonverbal communication, p. 513
Medium, Factual/Definitional, Objective 6, Ans: a

52. Women are especially likely to surpass men in their ability to convey nonverbal expressions of:
   a. happiness.
   b. sadness.
   c. surprise.
   d. anger.

Nonverbal communication, p. 513
Medium, Conceptual/Application, Objective 6, Ans: d

53. Eva's boyfriend says he loves her, but she wants proof. In order to obtain the most trustworthy nonverbal signals of how he really feels, Eva should carefully observe:
   a. his general body posture when he stands near her.
   b. the way he holds her hand when they walk together.
   c. how close he stands to her when they are talking.
   d. his facial expressions when they spend time together.
   e. the way he positions his legs when he sits near her.

Nonverbal communication, p. 514
Medium, Factual/Definitional, Objective 6, Ans: b

54. Specific interpretations of the emotional significance of nonverbal behaviors are risky because:
   a. there is very little relationship between cognition and emotion.
   b. specific nonverbal responses may be associated with a variety of different emotions.
   c. people typically attempt to conceal their true feelings.
   d. there is very little relationship between specific emotions and specific facial expressions.

Culture and emotional expression, p. 514
Medium, Factual/Definitional, Objective 6, Ans: d

55. People from different cultures are most likely to differ with respect to:
   a. the way they categorize basic emotions such as fear and anger.
   b. their facial expressions of different emotions such as sadness or surprise.
   c. the specific states of physiological arousal associated with their feelings of happiness or disgust.
   d. how they interpret hand gestures such as the "thumbs up" signal.

Culture and emotional expression, p. 514
Easy, Factual/Definitional, Objective 6, Ans: c

56. The universally understandable language of human emotion consists of:
   a. hand gestures.
   b. body postures.
   c. facial expressions.
   d. tone of voice.
   e. music and dance.

Culture and emotional expression, p. 515
Difficult, Factual/Definitional, Objective 6, Ans: c

57. Research on nonverbal communication indicates that:
   a. very young children's facial expressions of emotion are very difficult to interpret.
   b. children learn the facial expressions associated with emotion by observing adults.
   c. blind children who have never observed others demonstrate normal facial expressions of emotion.
   d. boys are better than girls at recognizing nonverbal expressions of emotion.
   e. children are unable to interpret facial expressions until they reach adolescence.

Culture and emotional expression, p. 515
Medium, Conceptual, Objective 6, Ans: a

58. The fact that people from widely different cultures display and interpret facial expressions of emotion in a similar manner best illustrates the impact of:
   a. human genetic similarities.
   b. the adaptation-level phenomenon.
   c. the catharsis hypothesis.
   d. the feel-good, do-good phenomenon.
   e. the worldwide distribution of American television programming.

Culture and emotional expression, p. 515
Medium, Factual/Definitional, Objective 6, Ans: a

59. It has been suggested that baring the teeth is universally associated with the expression of anger because this ability to convey threats has helped humans to survive. This suggestion best illustrates the:
   a. evolutionary perspective.
   b. relative deprivation principle.
   c. Cannon-Bard theory.
   d. two-factor theory.
   e. adaptation-level principle.

Culture and emotional expression, pp. 515-516
Medium, Factual/Definitional, Objective 6, Ans: b

60. In which country are people most likely to convey obvious facial expressions of their inner feelings?
  a. China
  b. Australia
  c. Japan
  d. India

Culture and emotional expression, p. 516
Medium, Conceptual, Objective 6, Ans: d

61. Japanese citizens are less likely than Americans to express their feelings of anger nonverbally. This cultural difference best reflects the Japanese culture's greater emphasis on:
  a. privacy.
  b. happiness.
  c. personal meditation.
  d. interdependence.
  e. verbal communication.

The effects of facial expressions, p. 516
Medium, Factual/Definitional, Objective 7, Ans: e

62. Laboratory experiments have found that as compared with frowners, students who were induced to smile:
  a. had increased blood sugar levels.
  b. were less fearful of an unfamiliar stimulus.
  c. expressed greater dislike of the experimenter.
  d. expressed more empathy for a stranger.
  e. found cartoons more humorous.

The effects of facial expressions, p. 516
Difficult, Conceptual, Objective 7, Ans: a

63. Facial expressions of anger are most likely to facilitate:
  a. sympathetic nervous system arousal.
  b. the catharsis of hostile urges.
  c. feelings of love.
  d. empathy.

The effects of facial expressions, p. 516
Difficult, Conceptual/Application, Objective 7, Ans: d

64. Repeatedly saying the word "me" puts people in a better mood than repeatedly saying "you." This best illustrates the:
  a. catharsis hypothesis.
  b. feel-good, do-good phenomenon.
  c. adaptation-level phenomenon.
  d. "facial feedback" effect.
  e. relative deprivation principle.

The effects of facial expressions, p. 517
Medium, Factual/Definitional, Objective 7, Ans: d

65. Imitating another person's facial expression of emotion is most likely to facilitate:
 a. the feel-good, do-good phenomenon.
 b. the catharsis of aggressive feelings.
 c. parasympathetic nervous system activity.
 d. empathy.

Fear, p. 519
Medium, Conceptual/Application, Objective 8, Ans: c

66. Ever since Lupe was scolded and punished by her teacher for misbehaving, Lupe has been fearful of being near the teacher. This illustrates that:
 a. fear is a biologically maladaptive response.
 b. young children are biologically predisposed to fear almost anything.
 c. fear can be learned.
 d. emotions are most negative when we are only moderately aroused.

Fear, p. 519
Medium, Conceptual/Application, Objective 8, Ans: b

67. Most young children are fearful of bees, even though they have never been stung by one. This best illustrates that fear:
 a. is a maladaptive response.
 b. can be learned through observation.
 c. is genetically determined.
 d. results from relative deprivation.

Fear, p. 519
Difficult, Factual/Definitional, Objective 8, Ans: d

68. Research suggests that monkeys reared in the wild fear snakes because they:
 a. are biologically predisposed to fear nearly all primitive forms of life.
 b. have a particularly strong nervous system reaction to snake bites.
 c. have encountered snakes near dead monkeys.
 d. have observed other monkeys' fearful reactions to snakes.
 e. frequently compete with snakes for control of territory and natural resources.

Fear, p. 519
Medium, Factual/Definitional, Objective 8, Ans: c

69. Research on human fear indicates that:
 a. fear is more often a poisonous emotion than an adaptive one.
 b. people but not animals may acquire fear through observational learning.
 c. people seem to be biologically predisposed to learn some fears more quickly than others.
 d. genetic factors are unimportant in understanding fearfulness.

Fear, p. 519
Medium, Factual/Definitional, Objective 8, Ans: b

70. Rabbits fail to react with fear to a signal of impending shock if they have suffered damage to the:
a. hippocampus.
b. amygdala.
c. thalamus.
d. hypothalamus.
e. corpus callosum.

Fear, pp. 519-520
Difficult, Factual/Definitional, Objective 8, Ans: c

71. After learning to associate a blue slide with a blaring horn, people who have suffered damage to the hippocampus ________ show a fear reaction to the blue slide, and they ________ be able to remember why they are fearful of the blue slide.
a. will; will
b. will not; will not
c. will; will not
d. will not; will

Anger, p. 521
Medium, Factual/Definitional, Objective 9, Ans: c

72. The term "catharsis" refers to emotional:
a. disturbance.
b. inhibition.
c. release.
d. adaptation.

Anger, p. 521
Easy, Factual/Definitional, Objective 9, Ans: b

73. The idea that anger is reduced through aggressive action or fantasy is known as the:
a. adaptation-level principle.
b. catharsis hypothesis.
c. feel-good, do-good phenomenon.
d. two-factor theory.
e. relative deprivation principle.

Anger, p. 521
Medium, Conceptual/Application, Objective 9, Ans: a

74. A psychotherapist suggests that Theresa can effectively reduce the anger she feels toward her ex-boyfriend by tearing pictures of him into little pieces. This suggestion illustrates the therapist's acceptance of the:
a. catharsis hypothesis.
b. adaptation-level principle.
c. James-Lange theory.
d. two-factor theory.
e. relative deprivation principle.

Anger, p. 521
Difficult, Conceptual, Objective 9, Ans: b

75. Which of the following children is most likely to calm down emotionally shortly after venting his anger?
   a. Jack, who attacks his intimidating older brother for spitting at him
   b. Jeremiah, who attacks his irritating younger brother for spitting at him
   c. Jed, who attacks his friendly older brother for no good reason at all
   d. Jason, who attacks his playful younger brother for no good reason at all

Anger, p. 521
Medium, Factual/Definitional, Objective 9, Ans: c

76. Charles Darwin's suggestion that violent gestures increase one's anger is most inconsistent with the:
   a. James-Lange theory.
   b. adaptation-level principle.
   c. catharsis hypothesis.
   d. relative deprivation principle.

Anger, p. 521
Difficult, Factual/Definitional, Objective 9, Ans: d

77. Employees who have just been laid off are asked questions that encourage them to express hostility toward their employer. Research suggests that this opportunity to vent anger will:
   a. calm their emotions and reduce their anger.
   b. improve their relationships with management by allowing an open airing of differences.
   c. rechannel their anger into constructive motivation.
   d. increase their hostility.

Anger, pp. 521-522
Medium, Conceptual/Application, Objective 9, Ans: d

78. Rosaria is upset with her husband for not putting his dirty clothes in the laundry basket. Anger experts would most likely recommend that she deal with her frustration by saying to him:
   a. "Why do you expect me to do all the work around here?"
   b. "I'm not your mother like you think. Take some responsibility."
   c. "From now on I'm going to leave my dirty clothes around for you to pick up."
   d. "I get annoyed when you leave your dirty clothes for me to pick up."
   e. "I refuse to make dinner until you do the laundry."

Anger, p. 522
Easy, Factual/Definitional, Objective 9, Ans: b

79. Mentally rehearsing one's resentments contributes to ________ perspiration levels and ________ blood pressure levels than mentally rehearsing forgiveness.
   a. lower; lower
   b. higher; higher
   c. lower; higher
   d. higher; lower

Happiness, p. 522
Easy, Factual/Definitional, Objective 10, Ans: a

80. The feel-good, do-good phenomenon refers to the fact that when people feel happy they:
a. are more willing to help others.
b. perceive the world as a safer place.
c. make decisions more effectively.
d. experience a more positive self-image.
e. report greater satisfaction with their whole lives.

Happiness, p. 522
Easy, Conceptual/Application, Objective 10, Ans: b

81. Jed wants his roommate Dante to help him study for a physics test. Dante is most likely to want to help after he has:
a. helped some friends repair a flat tire on their car.
b. received an unexpected "A" on his psychology test.
c. heard that a friend was involved in an automobile accident.
d. been caught cheating on a math test.

Happiness, pp. 522, 524
Medium, Conceptual, Objective 10, Ans: d

82. Subjective well-being is to happiness as objective well-being is to:
a. ethnic identity.
b. relative deprivation.
c. self-esteem.
d. economic status.

Happiness, pp. 523-524
Medium, Conceptual/Application, Objective 10, Ans: d

83. The loss of an arm in an automobile accident is likely to ________ a person's long-term feelings of life satisfaction. Winning first place in a national tennis tournament is likely to ________ a person's long-term feelings of life satisfaction.
a. decrease; have little effect on
b. decrease; increase
c. have little effect on; increase
d. have little effect on; have little effect on

Happiness, p. 524
Medium, Factual/Definitional, Objective 10, Ans: b

84. During the last four decades, the spendable income of Americans (adjusting for inflation) has ________ and their self-reported personal happiness has ________.
a. remained almost unchanged; decreased
b. increased; remained almost unchanged
c. remained almost unchanged; increased
d. remained almost unchanged; remained almost unchanged

Happiness (Figure 13.20), p. 525
Medium, Conceptual, Objective 10, Ans: e

85. Subjective well-being among college students is ________ with the extent to which love is valued and ________ with the extent to which money is valued.
a. positively correlated; positively correlated
b. positively correlated; uncorrelated
c. uncorrelated; positively correlated
d. uncorrelated; uncorrelated
e. positively correlated; negatively correlated

Happiness and the adaptation-level principle, p. 525
Medium, Factual/Definitional, Objective 10, Ans: b

86. The adaptation-level phenomenon refers to the:
a. perception that one is worse off than those with whom one compares oneself.
b. tendency for standards of judgment to be heavily influenced by previous experiences.
c. tendency for emotional release to reduce levels of physiological arousal.
d. tendency for evolution to favor organisms that adapt best to the environment.

Happiness and the adaptation-level principle, p. 525
Medium, Conceptual/Application, Objective 10, Ans: e

87. Rannilt was euphoric after learning of her acceptance into the medical school of her choice. After a few weeks, however, she feels hardly any emotional excitement when she thinks about her admission to medical school. This change in her feelings can best be explained in terms of the:
a. catharsis hypothesis.
b. relative deprivation principle.
c. feel-good, do-good phenomenon.
d. Cannon-Bard theory.
e. adaptation-level phenomenon.

Happiness and the adaptation-level principle, p. 526
Medium, Factual/Definitional, Objective 10, Ans: e

88. Which of the following best explains why million-dollar lottery winners and paraplegics report similar levels of happiness?
a. James-Lange theory
b. Cannon-Bard theory
c. relative deprivation principle
d. two-factor theory
e. adaptation-level phenomenon

Happiness and the relative deprivation principle, p. 526
Easy, Factual/Definitional, Objective 10, Ans: e

89. The relative deprivation principle refers to the tendency for our personal happiness to be heavily influenced by:
a. genetics.
b. previous experiences.
c. catharsis.
d. physiological arousal.
e. others' attainments.

Happiness and the relative deprivation principle, pp. 526-527
Difficult, Factual/Definitional, Objective 10, Ans: c

90. During World War II, promotion rates in the U.S. Air Corps were high, yet soldiers in this military branch were unhappy about the speed at which they were promoted. Their unhappiness is best explained in terms of the:
a. James-Lange theory.
b. adaptation-level phenomenon.
c. relative deprivation principle.
d. two-factor theory.
e. catharsis hypothesis.

Happiness and the relative deprivation principle, p. 527
Medium, Conceptual/Application, Objective 10, Ans: a

91. Haley's parents bought her a used bicycle for her birthday. She was thrilled until she learned that her best friend received a brand new bicycle to celebrate Groundhog Day. Haley's declining satisfaction illustrates the:
a. relative deprivation principle.
b. adaptation-level phenomenon.
c. catharsis hypothesis.
d. James-Lange theory.
e. two-factor theory.

Happiness and the relative deprivation principle, p. 527
Difficult, Conceptual/Application, Objective 10, Ans: d

92. Winston has a very negative academic self-concept because he attends a school where most of his classmates are academically outstanding. Winston's experience best illustrates the:
a. adaptation-level phenomenon.
b. two-factor theory.
c. catharsis hypothesis.
d. relative deprivation principle.
e. James-Lange theory.

Happiness and the relative deprivation principle, p. 527
Medium, Conceptual/Application, Objective 10, Ans: e

93. Logan is an unsuccessful businessman who feels little satisfaction with life. In order to increase his subjective well-being, Logan should:
a. imagine what his own life might be like if he became rich and famous.
b. compare himself with friends who became rich and successful.
c. identify how his own foolish decisions and lack of foresight have contributed to his unhappiness.
d. recall past moments when his life was much more pleasant than it is now.
e. imagine what his life might be like if he were suffering from a fatal disease.

Predictors of happiness, p. 527
Medium, Factual/Definitional, Objective 10, Ans: d

94. Which of the following factors has been found to be clearly related to feelings of general happiness or life satisfaction?
   a. being well educated
   b. having children
   c. being over 50 years old
   d. having a meaningful religious faith
   e. being physically attractive

Predictors of happiness, p. 527
Medium, Factual/Definitional, Objective 10, Ans: b

95. A general sense of happiness or life satisfaction is most unrelated to whether or not people:
   a. sleep well.
   b. are well educated.
   c. have a happy marriage.
   d. have a meaningful religious faith.

Predictors of happiness, p. 528
Medium, Conceptual, Objective 10, Ans: a

96. Subjective well-being is most strongly influenced by:
   a. genetic predispositions.
   b. gender identity.
   c. educational experience.
   d. physical attractiveness.

How to be happier (Close-up), p. 528
Easy, Factual/Definitional, Objective 10, Ans: b

97. In order to improve their own subjective well-being, people should:
   a. focus more attention on themselves.
   b. participate in regular aerobic exercise.
   c. overestimate how much they can accomplish.
   d. do all of the above.

Essay Questions

1. Tranquilizing drugs that inhibit sympathetic nervous system activity often effectively reduce people's subjective experience of intense fear and anxiety. Use one of the major theories of emotion to account for the emotion-reducing effects of such tranquilizers. Which theory of emotion would have the greatest difficulty explaining these effects? Why?

2. A newspaper advice columnist suggests that thinking can be voluntarily controlled and changed, but emotions are gut-level, biological reactions that can't be voluntarily controlled or modified. Use your knowledge of emotion research and theory to either support or refute the columnist's claim.

3. Idaliza is furious because her steady boyfriend spent half an hour talking with his former girlfriend at last night's school dance. A friend suggests that Idaliza ought to get the anger out of her system by repeatedly pounding her pillow while she imagines that she is hitting her boyfriend. Explain why this might be an ineffective way for Idaliza to reduce her anger. Suggest better ways.

4. Jim, a 42-year-old engineer, is unhappy about his yearly salary although it is the highest salary he has ever earned. His wife, Carla, suggests that he vividly recall how little he earned at the age of 32. She also recommends that he watch a TV program about famine victims in Africa. Use your understanding of psychological principles to explain why Carla's suggestions might help to increase Jim's feelings of economic satisfaction.

Web Quiz 1

Ans: b

1. Which theory suggests that you would not experience intense anger unless you were first aware of your racing heart or of other symptoms of physiological arousal?
   a. the relative deprivation theory
   b. the James-Lange theory
   c. the adaptation-level theory
   d. the Cannon-Bard theory

Ans: b

2. Who suggested that the physiological reactions associated with a variety of different emotions were much the same?
   a. William James
   b. Walter Cannon
   c. Robert Zajonc
   d. Charles Darwin

Ans: d

3. If people who have just been aroused by watching rock videos are insulted, their feelings of anger will be greater than those of people who have been similarly provoked but were not previously aroused. This is best explained by the:
   a. relative deprivation principle.
   b. Cannon-Bard theory.
   c. catharsis hypothesis.
   d. two-factor theory.
   e. adaptation-level principle.

Ans: c

4. Whether we feel angry or depressed in response to a low exam grade depends on whether we attribute the poor grade to an unfair test or to our own lack of academic ability. This best illustrates that emotions are influenced by:
   a. physical arousal.
   b. relative deprivation.
   c. cognitive appraisals.
   d. genetic predispositions.

Ans: a

5. The instantaneous and automatic fear response experienced when unexpectedly stumbling upon a snake illustrates the importance of the:
   a. amygdala.
   b. hypothalamus.
   c. pituitary gland.
   d. hippocampus.

Ans: d

6. Activation of the sympathetic nervous system ________ salivation and ________ blood pressure.
a. increases; increases
b. decreases; decreases
c. increases; decreases
d. decreases; increases

Ans: c

7. Julie will be competing in a basketball free throw contest. Her performance is likely to be ________ if her physiological arousal during the performance is ________.
a. best; very low
b. best; very high
c. best; moderate
d. worst; moderate
e. mediocre; moderate

Ans: d

8. A lie detector machine is used to monitor people's:
a. insulin levels.
b. stomach contraction.
c. brain activity.
d. respiration.

Ans: a

9. People who were exposed to different parts of emotion-laden faces detected anger mostly from the ________ and happiness mostly from the ________.
a. eyes; mouth
b. mouth; eyes
c. eyes; eyes
d. mouth; mouth

Ans: c

10. Who would have been most likely to suggest that the facial expression of disgust is an inherited behavioral trait that enables us to quickly eject foul-tasting and harmful food from our mouths?
a. Richard Lazarus
b. Stanley Schachter
c. Charles Darwin
d. Walter Cannon

Ans: c

11. If you mimic another person's facial expressions of emotion, you probably will feel increasing empathy for that person. This is best explained in terms of the:
a. catharsis hypothesis.
b. relative deprivation principle.
c. James-Lange theory.
d. feel-good, do-good phenomenon.
e. Cannon-Bard theory.

Ans: c

12. People ________ the long-term emotional impact of sustaining a paralyzing physical injury and they ________ the long-term emotional impact of acquiring wealth.
    a. overestimate; underestimate
    b. underestimate; overestimate
    c. overestimate; overestimate
    d. underestimate; underestimate

Ans: d

13. Luciano believes that the best way to get over the anger he feels toward one of his high school teachers is to scream shameful profanities while hitting a punching bag. His belief best illustrates the:
    a. relative deprivation principle.
    b. feel-good, do-good phenomenon.
    c. adaptation-level phenomenon.
    d. catharsis hypothesis.
    e. guilty knowledge test.

Ans: e

14. After receiving exciting news about the birth of a healthy grandson, Mr. Haney was easily persuaded to contribute a generous sum of money to a neighborhood church. This best illustrates the:
    a. two-factor theory.
    b. adaptation-level phenomenon.
    c. James-Lange theory.
    d. relative deprivation principle.
    e. feel-good, do-good phenomenon.

Ans: b

15. Professor Crane was ecstatic when he learned that one of his research studies had been approved for publication. His feelings of joy quickly dissipated, however, when he heard a colleague recently had three different research articles accepted for publication. His declining emotional satisfaction is best explained in terms of the:
    a. "facial feedback" effect.
    b. relative deprivation principle.
    c. James-Lange theory.
    d. adaptation-level phenomenon.
    e. catharsis hypothesis.

Web Quiz 2

Ans: a

1. Who suggested that we can stimulate the subjective experience of cheerfulness simply by acting as if we are already cheerful?
   a. William James
   b. Walter Cannon
   c. Stanley Schachter
   d. Richard Lazarus

Ans: d

2. The importance of autonomic nervous system arousal to our subjective experience of emotion is most clearly minimized by the:
   a. two-factor theory.
   b. James-Lange theory.
   c. catharsis hypothesis.
   d. Cannon-Bard theory.

Ans: e

3. When Mr. Morgan began to misinterpret his harmless symptoms of autonomic nervous system arousal as indicative of an impending heart attack, he suffered an unusually intense level of fear. His emotional suffering is best understood in terms of the:
   a. catharsis hypothesis.
   b. James-Lange theory.
   c. relative deprivation principle.
   d. adaptation-level principle.
   e. two-factor principle.

Ans: c

4. The physiological arousal of parents who momentarily lose their young child in a large shopping mall can actually heighten their feelings of elation shortly thereafter when the child is found. This is best explained by the:
   a. catharsis hypothesis.
   b. Cannon-Bard theory.
   c. two-factor theory.
   d. James-Lange theory.
   e. relative deprivation principle.

Ans: c

5. Evidence that emotion precedes physiological arousal would be most inconsistent with the _______. Evidence that emotion precedes mentally labeling our physiological arousal would be most inconsistent with the ________.
   a. relative deprivation principle; adaptation-level principle
   b. adaptation-level principle; relative deprivation principle
   c. James-Lange theory; two-factor theory
   d. two-factor theory; James-Lange theory

Ans: b

6. Antonio's car stalls in the middle of a railroad crossing just as a train is rapidly approaching. His emotional arousal is likely to be accompanied by:
a. a decreased blood sugar level.
b. an increased respiration rate.
c. contraction of the arteries.
d. dilation of his pupils.

Ans: b

7. Shondra, an experienced member of her high school swimming team, has just recently joined her high school debate team. A high level of physiological arousal during team competition is likely to ________ her swimming performance and ________ her debate performance.
a. enhance; enhance
b. enhance; disrupt
c. disrupt; enhance
d. disrupt; disrupt

Ans: d

8. Exuberant infants and alert, energetic adults are especially likely to show high levels of brain activity in the:
a. limbic system.
b. sensory cortex.
c. cerebellum.
d. left frontal lobe.

Ans: e

9. An approach to lie detection that assesses a suspect's physiological response to details of a crime known only to police investigators is called the:
a. relative deprivation principle.
b. catharsis hypothesis.
c. adaptation-level principle.
d. feel-good, do-good phenomenon.
e. guilty knowledge test.

Ans: c

10. Feigned smiles are initiated ________ abruptly and last for a ________ time than genuine smiles.
a. more; shorter
b. less; longer
c. more; longer
d. less; shorter

Ans: c

11. Compared to North Americans, Asians are ________ likely to display feelings of anger and ________ likely to display feelings of shame.
a. less; less
b. more; more
c. less; more
d. more; less

Ans: e

12. If people wrinkle their nose in disgust when presented with a strange-looking food, they are likely to experience an increasingly intense emotional aversion to the food. This best illustrates the:
a. Cannon-Bard theory.
b. relative deprivation principle.
c. feel-good, do-good phenomenon.
d. catharsis hypothesis.
e. "facial feedback" effect.

Ans: b

13. Ariana believes that yelling at her husband serves to calm her angry feelings toward him. Her belief is most clearly inconsistent with the:
a. adaptation-level principle.
b. James-Lange theory.
c. catharsis hypothesis.
d. relative deprivation principle.

Ans: c

14. The feel-good, do-good phenomenon refers to the impact of ________ on ________.
a. optimism; good health
b. mood; self-control
c. happiness; helpfulness
d. empathy; interpersonal conflict

Ans: d

15. A celebrity actress experiences ever-increasing levels of professional acclaim following each successful movie role. Yet with each success, she experiences no more than a temporary surge of subjective well-being. This is best explained in terms of the:
a. catharsis hypothesis.
b. James-Lange theory.
c. two-factor theory.
d. adaptation-level phenomenon.
e. relative deprivation principle.

Study Guide Questions

Ans: d, p. 499

1. Emotions are:
   a. physiological reactions.
   b. behavioral expressions.
   c. conscious feelings.
   d. all of the above.

Ans: a, p. 500

2. Two years ago Maria was in an automobile accident in which her spinal cord was severed, leaving her paralyzed from her neck down. Today, Maria finds that she experiences emotions less intensely than she did before her accident. This tends to support which theory of emotion?
   a. James-Lange theory
   b. Cannon-Bard theory
   c. adaptation-level theory
   d. relative deprivation theory

Ans: b, p. 500

3. You are on your way to school to take a big exam. Suddenly, on noticing that your pulse is racing and that you are sweating, you feel nervous. With which theory of emotion is this experience most consistent?
   a. Cannon-Bard theory
   b. James-Lange theory
   c. relative deprivation theory
   d. adaptation-level theory

Ans: a, p. 500

4. Which theory of emotion implies that every emotion is associated with a unique physiological reaction?
   a. James-Lange theory
   b. Cannon-Bard theory
   c. two-factor theory
   d. valence theory

Ans: b, p. 500

5. Which theory of emotion emphasizes the simultaneous experience of body response and emotional feeling?
   a. James-Lange theory
   b. Cannon-Bard theory
   c. two-factor theory
   d. valence theory

Ans: b, p. 500

6. The Cannon-Bard theory of emotion states that:
   a. emotions have two ingredients: physical arousal and a cognitive label.
   b. the conscious experience of an emotion occurs at the same time as the body's physical reaction.
   c. emotional experiences are based on an awareness of the body's responses to an emotion-arousing stimulus.
   d. emotional ups and downs tend to balance in the long run.

Ans: d, pp. 500-501

7. Which of the following was *not* raised as a criticism of the James-Lange theory of emotion?
   a. The body's responses are too similar to trigger the various emotions.
   b. Emotional reactions occur before the body's responses can take place.
   c. The cognitive activity of the cortex plays a role in the emotions we experience.
   d. People with spinal cord injuries at the neck typically experience less emotion.

Ans: c, p. 501

8. Schachter's two-factor theory emphasizes that emotion involves both:
   a. the sympathetic and parasympathetic divisions of the nervous system.
   b. verbal and nonverbal expression.
   c. physical arousal and a cognitive label.
   d. universal and culture-specific aspects.

Ans: c, p. 501

9. After hitting a grand-slam home run, Mike noticed that his heart was pounding. Later that evening, after nearly having a collision while driving on the freeway, Mike again noticed that his heart was pounding. That he interpreted this reaction as fear, rather than as ecstasy, can best be explained by the:
   a. James-Lange theory.
   b. Cannon-Bard theory.
   c. two-factor theory.
   d. adaptation-level theory.

Ans: c, p. 502

10. Who will probably be angrier after learning that he or she has received a parking ticket?
    a. Bob, who has just awakened from a nap
    b. Veronica, who has just finished eating a big lunch
    c. Dan, who has just completed a tennis match
    d. Alicia, who has been reading a romantic novel
    e. It cannot be determined from the information given

Ans: c, p. 502

11. In the Schachter-Singer experiment, which subjects reported feeling an emotional change in the presence of the experimenter's highly emotional confederate?
    a. those receiving epinephrine and expecting to feel physical arousal
    b. those receiving a placebo and expecting to feel physical arousal
    c. those receiving epinephrine but not expecting to feel physical arousal
    d. those receiving a placebo and not expecting to feel physical arousal

Ans: d, p. 502

12. Which of the following was *not* presented in the text as evidence that some emotional reactions involve no deliberate, rational thinking?
    a. Some of the neural pathways involved in emotion are separate from those involved in thinking and memory.
    b. Emotional reactions are sometimes quicker than our interpretations of a situation.
    c. People can develop an emotional preference for visual stimuli to which they have been unknowingly exposed.
    d. Arousal of the sympathetic nervous system will trigger an emotional reaction even when artificially induced by an injection of epinephrine.

Ans: a, pp. 502-503

13. Several studies have shown that physical arousal can intensify just about any emotion. For example, when people who have been physically aroused by exercise are insulted, they often misattribute their arousal to the insult. This finding illustrates the importance of:
a. cognitive labels of arousal in the conscious experience of emotions.
b. a minimum level of arousal in triggering emotional experiences.
c. the simultaneous occurrence of physical arousal and cognitive labeling in emotional experience.
d. all of the above.

Ans: c, p. 503

14. Evidence that changes in facial expression can directly affect people's feelings and body states has convinced Robert Zajonc that:
a. the heart is always subject to the mind.
b. emotional reactions involve deliberate rational thinking.
c. cognition is not necessary for emotion.
d. the interpretation of facial expressions is a learned skill.

Ans: c, p. 504

15. Margaret is a finalist in the U.S. Ice Skating Championship. She is very excited about the competition and is feeling energized. More than likely, the two dimensions of her current emotion would be a ________ and ________.
a. positive valence; low arousal
b. negative valence; low arousal
c. positive valence; high arousal
d. negative valence; high arousal

Ans: a, pp. 506

16. Which of the following most accurately describes emotional arousal?
a. Emotions prepare the body to fight or flee.
b. Emotions are voluntary reactions to emotion-arousing stimuli.
c. Because all emotions have the same physiological basis, emotions are primarily psychological events.
d. Emotional arousal is always accompanied by cognition.
e. All of the above are accurate descriptions.

Ans: e, p. 506

17. In an emergency situation, emotional arousal will result in:
a. increased rate of respiration.
b. increased blood sugar.
c. a slowing of digestion.
d. pupil dilation.
e. all of the above.

Ans: c, p. 506

18. A relatively high level of arousal would be most likely to facilitate:
a. remembering the lines of a play.
b. shooting free throws in basketball.
c. sprinting 100 meters.
d. taking a final exam in introductory psychology.

Ans: d, p. 506

19. Which of the following is correct regarding the relationship between arousal and performance?
 a. Generally, performance is optimal when arousal is low.
 b. Generally, performance is optimal when arousal is high.
 c. On easy tasks, performance is optimal when arousal is low.
 d. On easy tasks, performance is optimal when arousal is high.

Ans: b, p. 506

20. After Brenda scolded her brother for forgetting to pick her up from school, the physical arousal that had accompanied her anger diminished. Which division of her nervous system mediated her physical *relaxation*?
 a. sympathetic division
 b. parasympathetic division
 c. skeletal division
 d. peripheral nervous system

Ans: c, p. 506

21. Which division of the nervous system is especially involved in bringing about emotional arousal?
 a. somatic nervous system
 b. peripheral nervous system
 c. sympathetic nervous system
 d. parasympathetic nervous system
 e. central nervous system

Ans: b, p. 506

22. The body's response to danger is triggered by the release of ________ by the ________ glands.
 a. acetylcholine; adrenal
 b. epinephrine and norepinephrine; adrenal
 c. acetylcholine; pituitary
 d. epinephrine and norepinephrine; pituitary

Ans: c, p. 507

23. Concerning emotions and their accompanying body responses, which of the following appears to be true?
 a. Each emotion has its own body response and underlying brain circuit.
 b. All emotions involve the same body response as a result of the same underlying brain circuit.
 c. Many emotions involve similar body responses but have different underlying brain circuits.
 d. All emotions have the same underlying brain circuits but different body responses.

Ans: c, p. 507

24. Nine-month-old Nicole's left frontal lobe is more active than her right frontal lobe. We can expect that, all other things being equal, Nicole:
 a. may suffer from mild depression for most of her life.
 b. may have trouble "turning off" upsetting feelings later in her life.
 c. may be more cheerful than those with more active right frontal lobes.
 d. may have trouble expressing feelings later in her life.

Ans: a, p. 507

25. Julio was extremely angry when he came in for a routine EEG of his brain activity. When he later told this to the doctor, she was no longer concerned about the:
    a. increased electrical activity in Julio's right hemisphere.
    b. increased electrical activity in Julio's left hemisphere.
    c. decreased electrical activity in Julio's amygdala.
    d. increased electrical activity in Julio's amygdala.

Ans: c, p. 507

26. When the scientist electrically stimulated one area of a monkey's brain, the monkey became enraged. When another electrode was activated, the monkey cowered in fear. The electrodes were most likely implanted in the:
    a. pituitary gland.
    b. adrenal glands.
    c. limbic system.
    d. right hemisphere.

Ans: d, p. 507

27. A student participating in an experiment concerned with physical responses that accompany emotions reports that her mouth is dry, her heart is racing, and she feels flushed. What emotion is the subject experiencing?
    a. anger
    b. fear
    c. ecstasy
    d. it cannot be determined from the information given

Ans: a, p. 507

28. Electrical stimulation of which brain region can produce terror or rage in cats?
    a. limbic system
    b. hypothalamus
    c. cortex
    d. cerebellum

Ans: c, p. 507

29. In laboratory experiments, fear and joy:
    a. result in an increase in heart rate.
    b. stimulate different facial muscles.
    c. increase heart rate and stimulate different facial muscles.
    d. result in a decrease in heart rate.

Ans: b, p. 507

30. People who are exuberant and persistently cheerful show increased activity in the brain's ________, which is rich in receptors for the neurotransmitter ________.
    a. right frontal lobe; dopamine
    b. left frontal lobe; dopamine
    c. amygdala; serotonin
    d. thalamus; serotonin

Ans: d, p. 508

31. The polygraph measures:
   a. lying.
   b. brain rhythms.
   c. chemical changes in the body.
   d. physiological indexes of arousal.

Ans: e, pp. 508-509

32. As part of her job interview, Jan is asked to take a lie-detector test. Jan politely refuses and points out that:
   a. a guilty person can be found innocent by the polygraph.
   b. an innocent person can be found guilty.
   c. a liar can learn to fool a lie-detector test.
   d. these tests err one-third of the time.
   e. all of the above are true.

Ans: c, p. 509

33. Current estimates are that the polygraph is inaccurate approximately ________ of the time.
   a. three-fourths
   b. one-half
   c. one-third
   d. one-fourth
   e. one-tenth

Ans: c, p. 509

34. Psychologist David Lykken is opposed to the use of lie detectors because:
   a. they represent an invasion of a person's privacy and could easily be used for unethical purposes.
   b. there are often serious discrepancies among the various indicators such as perspiration and heart rate.
   c. polygraphs cannot distinguish the various possible causes of arousal.
   d. they are accurate only about 50 percent of the time.

Ans: c, p. 509

35. Law enforcement officials sometimes use a lie detector to assess a suspect's responses to details of the crime believed to be known only to the perpetrator. This is known as the:
   a. inductive approach.
   b. deductive approach.
   c. guilty knowledge test.
   d. screening examination.
   e. prevarication probe.

Ans: c, p. 512

36. I am an emotionally literate person who is very accurate at reading others' nonverbal behavior, detecting lies, and describing my feelings. Who am I?
   a. an introvert
   b. an extrovert
   c. a woman
   d. a man

Ans: b, pp. 514-515

37. Which of the following is true?
    a. Gestures are universal; facial expressions, culture-specific.
    b. Facial expressions are universal; gestures, culture-specific.
    c. Both gestures and facial expressions are universal.
    d. Both gestures and facial expressions are culture-specific.

Ans: b, pp. 514-515

38. Research on nonverbal communication has revealed that:
    a. it is easy to hide your emotions by controlling your facial expressions.
    b. facial expressions tend to be the same the world over, while gestures vary from culture to culture.
    c. most authentic expressions last between 7 and 10 seconds.
    d. most gestures have universal meanings; facial expressions vary from culture to culture.

Ans: d, p. 515

39. Children in New York, Nigeria, and New Zealand smile when they are happy and frown when they are sad. This suggests that:
    a. the Cannon-Bard theory is correct.
    b. some emotional expressions are learned at a very early age.
    c. the two-factor theory is correct.
    d. facial expressions of emotion are universal and biologically determined.

Ans: d, p. 515

40. Darwin believed that:
    a. the expression of emotions helped our ancestors to survive.
    b. all humans express basic emotions using similar facial expressions.
    c. human facial expressions of emotion retain elements of animals' emotional displays.
    d. all of the above are true.

Ans: d, p. 516

41. Who is the *least* likely to display negative emotions openly?
    a. Paul, a game warden in Australia
    b. Niles, a stockbroker in Belgium
    c. Deborah, a physicist in Toronto
    d. Yoko, a dentist in Japan

Ans: c, p. 516

42. In cultures that emphasize social interdependence:
    a. emotional displays are typically intense.
    b. emotional displays are typically prolonged.
    c. negative emotions are rarely displayed.
    d. all of the above are true.

Ans: b, pp. 516-517

43. The candidate stepped before the hostile audience, panic written all over his face. It is likely that the candidate's facial expression caused him to experience:
    a. a lessening of his fear.
    b. an intensification of his fear.
    c. a surge of digestive enzymes in his body.
    d. increased body temperature.

Ans: d, p. 518

44. Izard believes that there are ________ basic emotions.
   a. 3
   b. 5
   c. 7
   d. 10
   e. 12

Ans: b, p. 519

45. For which of the following fears do humans appear to be biologically prepared?
   a. fear of electricity
   b. fear of cliffs
   c. fear of flowers
   d. fear of flying
   e. fear of bombs

Ans: d, p. 519

46. Most human fears are:
   a. universal.
   b. biologically determined.
   c. present at birth.
   d. learned.

Ans: c, p. 520

47. Averill found that most people become angry:
   a. once a day.
   b. once a week.
   c. several times a week.
   d. several times a month.
   e. there is no common pattern to anger.

Ans: d, p. 521

48. Expressing anger can be adaptive when you:
   a. retaliate immediately.
   b. have mentally rehearsed all the reasons for your anger.
   c. count to 10, then blow off steam.
   d. first wait until the anger subsides, then deal with the situation in a civil manner.

Ans: d, p. 521

49. Jane was so mad at her brother that she exploded at him when he entered her room. That she felt less angry afterward is best explained by the principle of:
   a. adaptation level.
   b. physiological arousal.
   c. relative deprivation.
   d. catharsis.

Ans: a, p. 521

50. Concerning the catharsis hypothesis, which of the following is true?
    a. Expressing anger can be temporarily calming if it does not leave one feeling guilty or anxious.
    b. The arousal that accompanies unexpressed anger never dissipates.
    c. Expressing one's anger always calms one down.
    d. Psychologists agree that under no circumstances is catharsis beneficial.

Ans: c, p. 521

51. Catharsis will be most effective in reducing anger toward another person if:
    a. you wait until you are no longer angry before confronting the person.
    b. the target of your anger is someone you feel has power over you.
    c. your anger is directed specifically toward the person who angered you.
    d. the other person is able to retaliate by also expressing anger.

Ans: c, p. 522

52. As elderly Mr. Hooper crosses the busy intersection, he stumbles and drops the packages he is carrying. Which passerby is most likely to help Mr. Hooper?
    a. Drew, who has been laid off from work for three months
    b. Leon, who is on his way to work
    c. Bonnie, who graduated from college the day before
    d. Nancy, whose father recently passed away

Ans: b, p. 522

53. Research indicates that a person is most likely to be helpful to others if he or she:
    a. is feeling guilty about something.
    b. is happy.
    c. recently received help from another person.
    d. recently offered help to another person.

Ans: d, pp. 522-523

54. A graph depicting the course of positive emotions over the hours of the day since waking would:
    a. start low and rise steadily until bedtime.
    b. start high and decrease steadily until bedtime.
    c. remain at a stable, moderate level throughout the day.
    d. rise over the early hours and dissipate during the day's last several hours.
    e. vary too much from person to person to predict.

Ans: d, p. 525

55. Research suggests that people generally experience the greatest well-being when they strive for:
    a. wealth.
    b. modest income increases from year to year.
    c. slightly higher status than their friends, neighbors, and coworkers.
    d. intimacy and personal growth.

Ans: b, p. 525

56. When Professor Simon acquired a spacious new office, he was overjoyed. Six months later, however, he was taking the office for granted. His behavior illustrates the:
    a. relative deprivation principle.
    b. adaptation-level phenomenon.
    c. valence theory.
    d. optimum arousal principle.

Ans: d, p. 526

57. Cindy was happy with her promotion until she found out that Janice, who has the same amount of experience, receives a higher salary. Cindy's feelings are *best* explained according to the:
    a. adaptation-level phenomenon.
    b. valence theory.
    c. catharsis hypothesis.
    d. principle of relative deprivation.

Ans: a, pp. 526-527

58. Dermer found that students who had studied others who were worse off than themselves felt greater satisfaction with their own lives; this is the principle of:
    a. relative deprivation.
    b. adaptation level.
    c. behavioral contrast.
    d. opponent processes.

Ans: e, p. 527

59. Which of the following is true?
    a. People with more education tend to be happier.
    b. Beautiful people tend to be happier than plain people.
    c. Women tend to be happier than men.
    d. People with children tend to be happier.
    e. People who are socially outgoing or who exercise regularly tend to be happier.

Ans: d, p. 527

60. Which of these factors have researchers *not* found to correlate with happiness?
    a. a satisfying marriage or close friendship
    b. high self-esteem
    c. religious faith
    d. intelligence

CHAPTER **14**

Stress and Health

Learning Objectives

1. Identify the major concerns of health psychology.

Stress and Illness (pp. 532-546)

2. Describe the biology of the "fight or flight" response to stress and the physical characteristics and phases of the general adaptation syndrome.

3. Discuss the health consequences of catastrophes, significant life changes, and daily hassles.

4. Describe the effects of a perceived lack of control, economic inequality, and a pessimistic outlook on health.

5. Discuss the role of stress in causing coronary heart disease, and contrast Type A and Type B personalities.

6. Describe how stress increases the risk of disease by inhibiting the activities of the body's immune system.

7. Describe the impact of learning on immune system functioning.

Promoting Health (pp. 546-573)

8. Identify and discuss different strategies for coping with stress, and explain why people should be skeptical about the value of complementary and alternative medicine.

9. Explain why people smoke, and discuss ways of preventing and reducing this health hazard.

10. Discuss the relationship between nutrition and physical well-being, and describe the research findings on obesity and weight control.

Behavioral medicine and health psychology, p. 531
Easy, Factual/Definitional, Objective 1, Ans: c

1. The subfield of psychology that provides psychology's contribution to the prevention and treatment of illness is known as:
   a. medical psychology.
   b. neuropsychology.
   c. health psychology.
   d. behavioral psychology.
   e. psychobiology.

Behavioral medicine and health psychology, p. 531
Easy, Conceptual/Application, Objective 1, Ans: d

2. State University's psychology department and school of medicine are co-sponsoring a new professional program that applies behavioral and medical knowledge to health and disease. State University will clearly be offering a new degree in:
   a. medical psychology.
   b. human engineering.
   c. holistic medicine.
   d. behavioral medicine.
   e. neuropsychology.

Behavioral medicine and health psychology (Figure 14.1), p. 532
Medium, Factual/Definitional, Objective 1, Ans: d

3. In 1900, ________ was the major cause of death in the United States. Today, the major threat to life results from ________.
   a. heart disease; accidents
   b. accidents; influenza
   c. smallpox; cancer
   d. tuberculosis; heart disease

Stress and stressors, p. 532
Medium, Factual/Definitional, Objective 2, Ans: c

4. Stress is defined in the text as:
   a. a physiological reaction to any negative life event.
   b. the experience of conflicting motives that produce anxiety and tension.
   c. the process by which we appraise and cope with environmental threats and challenges.
   d. the blocking of an attempt to reach some important goal.
   e. physical, emotional, or mental exhaustion.

Stress and stressors, p. 532
Easy, Conceptual/Application, Objective 2, Ans: e

5. Rush hour traffic is to upset stomach as ________ is to ________.
   a. fight; flight
   b. Type B; Type A
   c. lymphocyte; macrophage
   d. hypertension; indigestion
   e. stressor; stress reaction

Stress and stressors, p. 533
Medium, Conceptual/Application, Objective 2, Ans: e

6. Luigi minimized the stress of testing positive for HIV by viewing this circumstance as an opportunity for a renewed religious commitment and spiritual growth. His reaction best illustrates the importance of:
   a. spontaneous remission.
   b. the general adaptation syndrome.
   c. the Type A personality.
   d. biofeedback
   e. stress appraisal.

The stress response system, p. 533
Medium, Factual/Definitional, Objective 2, Ans: a

7. In the 1920s, Walter Cannon discovered that stress produced an outpouring of ________ into the bloodstream.
   a. epinephrine and norepinephrine
   b. acetylcholine and endorphins
   c. lymphocytes and glucocorticoids
   d. estrogen and testosterone

The stress response system, p. 533
Easy, Conceptual/Application, Objective 2, Ans: b

8. As you are waiting to be interviewed for a job, your heart rate, body temperature, and breathing rate begin to increase. These physiological changes are produced by activation of the ________ nervous system.
   a. parasympathetic
   b. sympathetic
   c. somatic
   d. central

The stress response system, p. 533
Difficult, Factual/Definitional, Objective 2, Ans: a

9. In response to stress, the adrenal gland releases:
   a. cortisol.
   b. lymphocytes.
   c. uric acid.
   d. teratogens.
   e. acetylcholine.

The stress response system, p. 533
Difficult, Conceptual, Objective 2, Ans: d

10. The inner part of the adrenal gland is to ________ as the outer part of the adrenal gland is to ________.
    a. epinephrine; norepinephrine
    b. norepinephrine; epinephrine
    c. cortisol; norepinephrine
    d. epinephrine; cortisol
    e. cortisol; epinephrine

The stress response system, p. 534
Medium, Factual/Definitional, Objective 2, Ans: e

11. When Hans Selye injected rats with an ovarian hormone extract, he observed that:
   a. their right cerebral hemispheres became enlarged.
   b. the number of T lymphocytes in their body increased.
   c. their adrenal cortex shrank.
   d. their secondary sex characteristics became exaggerated.
   e. they developed bleeding ulcers.

The stress response system, p. 534
Difficult, Factual/Definitional, Objective 2, Ans: c

12. Hans Selye discovered that stressors cause the adrenal cortex to ________ in size, and the thymus gland to ________ in size.
   a. increase; increase
   b. decrease; increase
   c. increase; decrease
   d. decrease; decrease

The stress response system, p. 534
Easy, Factual/Definitional, Objective 2, Ans: c

13. The general adaptation syndrome describes stages in the:
   a. conditioning of the immune response.
   b. body's response to aerobic exercise.
   c. body's response to prolonged stress.
   d. process of biofeedback.

The stress response system, p. 534
Medium, Factual/Definitional, Objective 2, Ans: b

14. The three successive phases of the general adaptation syndrome are:
   a. attention, comprehension, and resistance.
   b. alarm reaction, resistance, and exhaustion.
   c. adrenal release, cognitive appraisal, and stomach ulceration.
   d. reactive frustration, sympathetic arousal, and parasympathetic inhibition.

The stress response system, p. 534
Medium, Conceptual/Application, Objective 2, Ans: c

15. Cameron, a 50-year-old electrician, opens his pay envelope and, to his surprise, finds a pink slip inside indicating that he has been fired from his job. Which phase of the general adaptation syndrome is John most likely experiencing?
   a. fight or flight
   b. resistance
   c. alarm reaction
   d. adjustment
   e. exhaustion

The stress response system, p. 534
Difficult, Factual/Definitional, Objective 2, Ans: b

16. Resistance to stress is greatest during ________ of the GAS.
    a. Phase 1
    b. Phase 2
    c. Phase 3
    d. Phase 4

The stress response system, pp. 534, 542
Difficult, Conceptual, Objective 2, Ans: c

17. The threat to one's immune system is greatest during ________ of the GAS.
    a. Phase 1
    b. Phase 2
    c. Phase 3
    d. Phase 4

The stress response system, p. 535
Difficult, Factual/Definitional, Objective 2, Ans: a

18. Prolonged stress due to sustained military combat is associated with a decrease in the size of a brain structure vital to:
    a. memory.
    b. sexual behavior.
    c. motor reflexes.
    d. speech production.

Stressful life events, p. 536
Medium, Factual/Definitional, Objective 3, Ans: b

19. Research on stressful life events indicates that:
    a. those who live a relatively peaceful, monastic life actually suffer a higher-than-average rate of heart attacks.
    b. those who have been recently widowed or divorced are more vulnerable to disease and death.
    c. survivors of a natural disaster are immunized against stress and have fewer long-term health problems.
    d. all of the above are true.

Stressful life events, p. 536
Easy, Factual/Definitional, Objective 3, Ans: d

20. Residents of urban ghettos are especially likely to experience:
    a. enlargement of the thymus gland.
    b. shrinkage of the adrenal cortex.
    c. the proliferation of lymphocytes.
    d. hypertension.

Stress and perceived control, p. 537
Medium, Factual/Definitional, Objective 4, Ans: d

21. Rats that received electric shocks were unlikely to develop ulcers if the:
    a. shocks were systematically associated with the delivery of appetizing food.
    b. shocks were quickly terminated by the experimenter.
    c. rats didn't anticipate the shocks ahead of time.
    d. rats could control the termination of the shocks.
    e. shocks became a routine part of the rats' daily life.

Stress and perceived control, p. 537
Easy, Factual/Definitional, Objective 4, Ans: b

22. British civil service workers in executive positions live longer than those in clerical positions. This best illustrates the value of:
    a. spontaneous remission.
    b. perceived control.
    c. the general adaptation syndrome.
    d. alternative medicine.

Stress and perceived control, pp. 537-538
Medium, Factual/Definitional, Objective 4, Ans: c

23. Life expectancy is ________ correlated with wealth and ________ correlated with income inequality.
    a. positively; positively
    b. negatively; negatively
    c. positively; negatively
    d. negatively; positively

Stress and perceived control, pp. 537-538
Easy, Conceptual/Application, Objective 4, Ans: c

24. Adina wants advice on how to cope with the stress of college life. She would be best advised to approach college with a sense of personal:
    a. skepticism and humility.
    b. ambition and competitiveness.
    c. control and optimism.
    d. urgency and time-consciousness.

Stress and perceived control, p. 539
Medium, Factual/Definitional, Objective 4, Ans: b

25. A loss of perceived control tends to result in:
    a. the proliferation of lymphocytes.
    b. the suppression of immune responses.
    c. a reduction in the release of cortisol.
    d. all of the above.

Stress and the heart, p. 539
Easy, Factual/Definitional, Objective 5, Ans: d

26. The risk of heart disease is increased by:
    a. smoking.
    b. lack of exercise.
    c. hypertension.
    d. all of the above.

Stress and the heart, p. 539
Medium, Conceptual/Application, Objective 5, Ans: a

27. Ben is a self-employed accountant who works overtime during the first two weeks of April to finish his clients' tax forms before the filing deadline. During this time, Ben is most likely to show a(n):
a. elevated blood cholesterol level.
b. reduction in the release of epinephrine.
c. reduction in the release of cortisol.
d. proliferation of lymphocytes.

Stress and the heart, p. 539
Easy, Factual/Definitional, Objective 5, Ans: d

28. Friedman and Rosenman referred to competitive, hard-driving, impatient, and easily angered individuals as ________ personalities.
a. hyperactive
b. stroke-prone
c. ulcer-prone
d. Type A
e. Type B

Stress and the heart, pp. 539-540
Medium, Conceptual/Application, Objective 5, Ans: a

29. Who is the best example of a Type A personality?
a. Philip, a competitive, hard-driving corporation president
b. Kane, a relaxed, easy-going mail carrier
c. Valentin, a self-confident, intelligent journalist
d. Thomas, an introverted, inhibited mental patient

Stress and the heart, pp. 539-540
Medium, Conceptual/Application, Objective 5, Ans: b

30. Who is the best example of a Type B personality?
a. George, a self-confident, time-conscious mail carrier
b. Wang Lung, a relaxed, easy-going dentist
c. Henry, an irritable, impatient college professor
d. Stasio, a fun-loving, hard-driving corporation president

Stress and the heart, pp. 539-540
Medium, Factual/Definitional, Objective 5, Ans: d

31. In their classic nine-year study, Friedman and Rosenman reported that, compared to Type A men, Type B men were ________ susceptible to ________.
a. more; stomach ulcers
b. less; stomach ulcers
c. more; heart attacks
d. less; heart attacks

Stress and the heart, p. 540
Difficult, Factual/Definitional, Objective 5, Ans: d

32. Epinephrine, norepinephrine, and cortisol:
a. are released by the thymus and lymph glands.
b. accelerate the proliferation of lymphocytes.
c. divert blood flow from muscle tissue to the body's internal organs.
d. accelerate the buildup of plaques on artery walls.
e. decrease heart rate and blood pressure.

Stress and the heart, p. 540
Medium, Factual/Definitional, Objective 5, Ans: c

33. Atherosclerosis is most likely to increase one's vulnerability to:
a. stomach ulcers.
b. obesity.
c. high blood pressure.
d. lung cancer.
e. pneumonia.

Stress and the heart, p. 540
Medium, Conceptual/Application, Objective 5, Ans: b

34. Bernard is an ambitious, highly competitive corporation lawyer who recently had a heart attack. He tends to be impatient and a perfectionist, and he gets angry over little things. Research suggests that Bernard's susceptibility to heart attacks may be most closely linked to his:
a. ambition.
b. anger.
c. impatience.
d. perfectionism.
e. competitiveness.

Stress and the heart, p. 541
Medium, Factual/Definitional, Objective 5, Ans: a

35. Type D personalities are:
a. anxious and socially inhibited.
b. competitive and hard-driving.
c. calm and easy-going.
d. anger-prone and time-conscious.

Stress and the heart, pp. 540, 541
Easy, Factual/Definitional, Objective 5, Ans: b

36. Chronic anger ________ the risk of heart disease, and chronic depression ________ the risk of heart disease.
a. increases; decreases
b. increases; increases
c. decreases; decreases
d. has no effect on; increases
e. increases; has no effect on

Stress and susceptibility to disease, p. 541
Easy, Factual/Definitional, Objective 6, Ans: b

37. A psychophysiological illness is a(n):
    a. physical illness that produces a psychological disorder.
    b. illness that is not caused by a physical disorder but instead seems linked to stress.
    c. disease of the central nervous system.
    d. physical or psychological disorder that has a genetic component.

Stress and susceptibility to disease, p. 541
Medium, Conceptual/Application, Objective 6, Ans: d

38. Andrea's physician has suggested that a program of relaxation training would provide the best treatment for her high blood pressure. The physician probably considers Andrea's hypertension to be a ________ illness.
    a. hereditary
    b. hypochondriacal
    c. chronic
    d. psychophysiological
    e. respiratory

Stress and the immune system, p. 542
Easy, Factual/Definitional, Objective 6, Ans: b

39. The macrophage and lymphocytes are major agents of the:
    a. sympathetic nervous system.
    b. immune system.
    c. limbic system.
    d. parasympathetic nervous system.
    e. reticular system.

Stress and the immune system, p. 542
Easy, Factual/Definitional, Objective 6, Ans: d

40. Lymphocytes are:
    a. harmful agents such as chemicals and viruses that cross the placenta from mother to fetus.
    b. stress hormones produced by the sympathetic nervous system.
    c. cancer cells that form in the lymph glands.
    d. white blood cells that are part of the body's immune system.

Stress and the immune system, p. 542
Medium, Conceptual, Objective 6, Ans: a

41. B lymphocytes are to ________ as T lymphocytes are to ________.
    a. bacterial infections; viral infections
    b. sympathetic arousal; parasympathetic inhibition
    c. viruses; cancer cells
    d. alarm reaction; resistance
    e. insulin; glucose

Stress and the immune system, p. 542
Difficult, Factual/Definitional, Objective 6, Ans: c

42. Compared to men, women are immunologically ________ and they are ________ susceptible to lupus and multiple sclerosis.
a. stronger; less
b. weaker; more
c. stronger; more
d. weaker; less

Stress and the immune system, pp. 542-543
Medium, Factual/Definitional, Objective 6, Ans: c

43. Which of the following best explains why stress heightens vulnerability to bacterial and viral infections?
a. Stress hormones accelerate the "hardening" of the arteries.
b. Stress hormones facilitate the depositing of cholesterol and fat around the heart.
c. Stress hormones suppress the production of lymphocytes.
d. Stress hormones trigger the release of digestive acids.

Stress and the immune system, pp. 542-543
Difficult, Conceptual/Application, Objective 6, Ans: a

44. Wild animals placed in zoos sometimes die shortly thereafter. These deaths are likely to result from a(n) ________ in the animals' production of ________.
a. decrease; lymphocytes
b. increase; androgens
c. decrease; cortisol
d. increase; steroids
e. decrease; teratogens

Stress and AIDS, p. 543
Easy, Factual/Definitional, Objective 6, Ans: d

45. The greatest number of deaths in Africa today result from:
a. heart disease.
b. strokes.
c. cancer.
d. AIDS.
e. malaria.

Stress and AIDS, p. 543
Medium, Conceptual, Objective 6, Ans: d

46. The deadly effects of AIDS most clearly result from a decreased production of:
a. epinephrine.
b. acetylcholine.
c. cortisol.
d. lymphocytes.
e. androgens.

Stress and cancer, pp. 542, 543, 544
Easy, Factual/Definitional, Objective 6, Ans: e

47. Stress lowers the body's resistance to:
   a. viral infections.
   b. bacterial infections.
   c. cancer.
   d. heart disease.
   e. all of the above.

Conditioning the immune system, p. 544
Easy, Factual/Definitional, Objective 7, Ans: d

48. Research on taste aversion in rats led to the discovery that suppression of the immune system can be influenced by:
   a. biofeedback.
   b. Type A behaviors.
   c. elevated cholesterol levels.
   d. classical conditioning.
   e. aerobic exercise.

Conditioning the immune system (Figure 14.10), p. 545
Medium, Factual/Definitional, Objective 7, Ans: b

49. In Ader and Cohen's taste aversion experiments with rats, the saccharin-sweetened water was a(n) ________ for ________.
   a. unconditioned stimulus; the release of pain-killing endorphins
   b. conditioned stimulus; the suppression of the immune system
   c. unconditioned response; an overproduction of acetylcholine
   d. conditioned response; a proliferation of lymphocytes

Coping with stress, p. 547
Easy, Factual/Definitional, Objective 8, Ans: b

50. Aerobic exercise has been closely linked to a(n):
   a. decrease in lymphocyte production.
   b. decrease in depression.
   c. increase in blood pressure in reaction to stress.
   d. decrease in the production of endorphins.

Coping with stress, pp. 547-548
Medium, Conceptual/Application, Objective 8, Ans: a

51. Mr. O'Brian is a high school teacher who suffers from hypertension and depression. Research suggests that regular aerobic exercise would ________ his depression and ________ his hypertension.
   a. reduce; reduce
   b. reduce; have no effect on
   c. reduce; increase
   d. have no effect on; reduce
   e. have no effect on; have no effect on

Coping with stress, p. 548
Difficult, Factual/Definitional, Objective 8, Ans: c

52. The best way to increase the production of serotonin is to:
    a. avoid high-carbohydrate foods.
    b. make use of biofeedback.
    c. engage in aerobic exercise.
    d. receive training in meditation.

Coping with stress, pp. 548-549
Medium, Factual/Definitional, Objective 8, Ans: c

53. The results of early research on biofeedback were surprising because they indicated that people could learn to control bodily functions regulated by the:
    a. neurotransmitters.
    b. lymph glands.
    c. autonomic nervous system.
    d. cerebellum.
    e. frontal lobes.

Coping with stress, p. 549
Medium, Conceptual/Application, Objective 8, Ans: a

54. Which of the following is an example of biofeedback?
    a. Milos learns to relax by being provided with information on changes in his heart rate.
    b. Jane decides to quit smoking after seeing a film linking cigarettes with cancer.
    c. Chico learns to lower his blood pressure by meditating twice a day.
    d. Kecia successfully quits smoking after her psychologist has her smoke so rapidly she cannot tolerate another cigarette.

Coping with stress, p. 549
Medium, Factual/Definitional, Objective 8, Ans: c

55. A psychologist would most likely use biofeedback to provide clients with information about their:
    a. cholesterol level.
    b. blood type.
    c. blood pressure.
    d. genetic makeup.
    e. pain tolerance.

Coping with stress, p. 549
Medium, Factual/Definitional, Objective 8, Ans: d

56. The most important benefit of biofeedback is its capacity to:
    a. encourage regular aerobic exercise.
    b. reduce the proliferation of lymphocytes.
    c. elevate blood cortisol levels.
    d. facilitate the relaxation response.

Coping with stress, p. 549
Difficult, Factual/Definitional, Objective 8, Ans: d

57. The relaxation response associated with meditation is most likely to ________ oxygen consumption and ________ finger temperature.
a. decrease; decrease
b. increase; increase
c. increase; decrease
d. decrease; increase

Coping with stress, p. 549
Medium, Conceptual/Application, Objective 8, Ans: c

58. Aviad, a 50-year-old banking executive and Type A personality, recently suffered a serious heart attack. To prevent a recurrence, Aviad would probably benefit most from:
a. acupuncture therapies.
b. early retirement.
c. relaxation training.
d. pain control medication.

Coping with stress, p. 551
Medium, Factual/Definitional, Objective 8, Ans: c

59. When young adults marry, they experience ________ stress and consume ________ alcohol.
a. less; more
b. more; less
c. less; less
d. more; more

Coping with stress, pp. 542, 552
Difficult, Conceptual/Application, Objective 8, Ans: c

60. Confiding one's fears and frustrations to supportive friends is likely to ________ lymphocyte levels and ________ cortisol levels.
a. increase; increase
b. decrease; decrease
c. increase; decrease
d. decrease; increase

Coping with stress, p. 552
Medium, Factual/Definitional, Objective 8, Ans: b

61. College women who had been sexually abused as children were especially likely to report health problems if they had:
a. grown up in a religious family.
b. kept the abuse a secret.
c. been victimized before age 5.
d. been victimized by a stranger rather than by a close relative.

Coping with stress, p. 554
Medium, Factual/Definitional, Objective 8, Ans: d

62. Those who attend religious services regularly are most likely to:
a. have an enlarged adrenal cortex.
b. show a decrease in lymphocyte production.
c. be at increased risk for obesity.
d. experience lower death rates from coronary heart disease.
e. experience numerous colds and flu.

Coping with stress (Figure 14.18), p. 554
Easy, Factual/Definitional, Objective 8, Ans: d

63. A national heath survey indicated that the longest life expectancies were associated with those Americans who attended religious services:
a. less than once a year.
b. less than once a week.
c. once a week.
d. more than once a week.

Alternative medicine (Box), p. 556
Medium, Factual/Definitional, Objective 8, Ans: a

64. Homeopathy and acupuncture are forms of:
a. alternative medicine.
b. biofeedback.
c. psychophysiological illness.
d. aerobic exercise.
e. spontaneous remission.

Alternative medicine (Box), p. 556
Difficult, Conceptual/Application, Objective 8, Ans: d

65. Following each of his acupuncture treatments, Warren has experienced relief from the nerve pain caused by HIV. His pain relief is most likely attributable to:
a. a decrease in lymphocyte production.
b. an increase in heart rate and blood pressure.
c. his Type A personality.
d. the placebo effect.

Smoking, pp. 556-557
Medium, Factual/Definitional, Objective 9, Ans: c

66. In North America, which of the following is most likely to cause premature death?
a. the failure to use automobile seat belts
b. alcohol abuse
c. smoking
d. obesity
e. lack of exercise

Smoking, p. 558
Easy, Factual/Definitional, Objective 9, Ans: c

67. Smoking is especially common among young teens who:
   a. are not very self-conscious about their behavior.
   b. come from wealthy families.
   c. receive low grades in school.
   d. are highly popular among their classmates.

Smoking, p. 558
Medium, Factual/Definitional, Objective 9, Ans: c

68. Which of the following theories offers the best explanation for why adolescents start smoking?
   a. neurobiological
   b. psychoanalytic
   c. social-cognitive
   d. trait

Smoking, p. 558
Easy, Factual/Definitional, Objective 9, Ans: a

69. Young teens are most likely to start smoking in order to:
   a. facilitate their social acceptance.
   b. trigger the release of endorphins.
   c. boost their mental alertness.
   d. diminish their appetite for carbohydrates.
   e. relax their muscles and reduce their blood pressure.

Smoking, p. 559
Medium, Factual/Definitional, Objective 9, Ans: b

70. The most rapid increase in nicotine tolerance occurs among smokers who:
   a. perceive a lack of personal control over their own lives.
   b. feel sick and dizzy the first time they smoke a cigarette.
   c. engage in regular aerobic exercise.
   d. are Type B personalities.

Smoking, p. 559
Medium, Factual/Definitional, Objective 9, Ans: b

71. A rewarding consequence of cigarette smoking is that it reduces:
   a. blood pressure and heart rate.
   b. sensitivity to pain.
   c. mental alertness.
   d. the release of epinephrine into the bloodstream.
   e. all of the above.

Smoking, p. 559
Medium, Factual/Definitional, Objective 9, Ans: d

72. Nicotine triggers a(n) ________ in anxiety and a(n) ________ in mental alertness.
   a. increase; decrease
   b. increase; increase
   c. decrease; decrease
   d. decrease; increase

Smoking, p. 560
Difficult, Factual/Definitional, Objective 9, Ans: a

73. Research on the smoking habits of Canadian adults indicates that since the early 1970s:
 a. a more pronounced decrease in smoking has occurred among men than among women.
 b. smoking is more common among the rich than among the poor.
 c. the percentage of teenage smokers has increased.
 d. the overall percentage of Canadian smokers has remained very nearly the same.

Smoking, p. 561
Medium, Factual/Definitional, Objective 9, Ans: c

74. Researchers had high school students "inoculate" seventh-graders against pressures to smoke by teaching the younger students how to:
 a. practice relaxation techniques that reduce social anxiety.
 b. avoid places where other kids are likely to smoke.
 c. refuse others' persuasive appeals to smoke.
 d. use a nicotine patch to satisfy their drug cravings.

Nutrition, p. 562
Medium, Conceptual/Application, Objective 10, Ans: b

75. Justin wants to avoid feeling sleepy during his early afternoon psychology class. He would be best advised to avoid eating ________ for lunch.
 a. chicken
 b. spaghetti
 c. vegetable soup
 d. a lettuce salad

Nutrition, p. 562
Difficult, Factual/Definitional, Objective 10, Ans: a

76. The level of serotonin in the brain is ________ by a diet high in ________.
 a. increased; carbohydrates
 b. decreased; salt
 c. increased; protein
 d. decreased; sugar

Nutrition, p. 562
Medium, Factual/Definitional, Objective 10, Ans: b

77. Researchers express the most doubt about there being a true link between ________ and a diet high in ________.
 a. hypertension; salt
 b. hyperactivity; sugar
 c. heart disease; cholesterol
 d. cancer; fat

Nutrition, p. 563
Difficult, Factual/Definitional, Objective 10, Ans: a

78. Hypertensive people have ________-than-normal salt intake and ________-than-normal calcium intake.
 a. higher; lower
 b. lower; higher
 c. higher; higher
 d. lower; lower

Obesity and weight control, p. 564
Medium, Factual/Definitional, Objective 10, Ans: c

79. When people's images on a video monitor are widened to make them look fatter, observers perceive them as ________ sincere and ________ friendly.
    a. more; more
    b. more; less
    c. less; less
    d. less; more

The physiology of obesity, p. 565
Medium, Factual/Definitional, Objective 10, Ans: d

80. Research on obesity and weight control indicates that:
    a. when an obese person has lost weight, a diet and exercise program are no longer necessary for maintaining the lower weight.
    b. lean tissue is maintained by fewer calories than is fat tissue.
    c. overweight people typically suffer from a lack of willpower and self-discipline.
    d. no matter how carefully people diet, they can never lose fat cells.

The physiology of obesity, p. 565
Easy, Factual/Definitional, Objective 10, Ans: b

81. When an organism's weight falls below its set point, the organism is likely to experience a(n) ________ in hunger and a(n) ________ in its metabolic rate.
    a. increase; increase
    b. increase; decrease
    c. decrease; decrease
    d. decrease; increase

The physiology of obesity, p. 566
Difficult, Conceptual/Application, Objective 10, Ans: d

82. By dramatically reducing her daily caloric intake, Marilyn plans to reduce her normal body weight by 10 to 15 percent. Research suggests that after three or four weeks of sustained dieting, Marilyn will:
    a. have a lower fat cell count.
    b. feel an increase in pep and physical energy.
    c. experience a decrease in her feelings of hunger.
    d. have a lower resting metabolic rate.
    e. have a lower set point for body weight.

The physiology of obesity, p. 566
Difficult, Conceptual/Application, Objective 10, Ans: d

83. Although John has been obese for as long as he can remember, he is determined to lose excess weight with a special low-calorie diet. John is likely to have difficulty losing weight while dieting because:
    a. fat cells can be lost only with vigorous exercise.
    b. his resting metabolic rate will increase and prompt him to overeat.
    c. he has an unusually low set point for body weight.
    d. fat tissue can be maintained by fewer calories than can other body tissues.
    e. the number of calories a person consumes daily has no effect on body weight.

The physiology of obesity, p. 566
Easy, Factual/Definitional, Objective 10, Ans: b

84. People tend to ________ their daily caloric intake and ________ their daily physical activity.
a. overestimate; underestimate
b. underestimate; overestimate
c. overestimate; overestimate
d. underestimate; underestimate

The physiology of obesity, p. 567
Difficult, Factual/Definitional, Objective 10, Ans: c

85. Obesity in mice has been traced to a gene for producing:
a. serotonin.
b. epinephrine.
c. leptin.
d. estrogen.
e. cortisol.

The physiology of obesity, p. 567
Difficult, Factual/Definitional, Objective 10, Ans: d

86. Evidence that obesity is influenced by factors in addition to genetics includes the fact that:
a. obesity is less common among Americans today than in 1900.
b. weight resemblance is greater among identical twin women than among identical twin men.
c. the fatness of adopted people is positively correlated with the fatness of their adoptive parents.
d. obesity is currently more common among American lower-class women than among American upper-class women.

The physiology of obesity, p. 568
Medium, Factual/Definitional, Objective 10, Ans: b

87. Compared to their counterparts of 40 years ago, today's average American woman weighs ________ and today's average Miss America contestant weighs ________.
a. less; more
b. more; less
c. less; less
d. more; more

The physiology of obesity, p. 568
Easy, Factual/Definitional, Objective 10, Ans: b

88. Studies of those who have lost weight on weight-loss programs indicate that most:
a. males and females manage to maintain their weight loss.
b. males and females eventually gain all their weight back.
c. females regain their weight, whereas most males maintain their weight loss.
d. males regain their weight, whereas most females maintain their weight loss.

Helpful hints for losing weight (Close-up), p. 570
Medium, Factual/Definitional, Objective 10, Ans: d

89. Which of the following suggestions would be the *worst* advice for a dieter?
    a. "Minimize your exposure to tempting foods."
    b. "Be sure to accompany your diet with a sustained exercise program."
    c. "Avoid consumption of soft drinks and alcoholic beverages."
    d. "Avoid eating during the day so you can enjoy a big meal in the evening."
    e. "Reduce your weight gradually over a period of many months."

Essay Questions

1. There's a dramatic increase in the likelihood of a person becoming ill or dying during a brief period following the death of a spouse. Describe some of the specific biological and psychological processes that may contribute to this effect.

2. A classmate argues that "the best way to handle stress is to work harder and meet life's challenges head-on." Evaluate both the strengths and the weaknesses of your classmate's position.

3. Trevor, a college student, has tried to quit smoking on two different occasions. In each case, however, he relapsed into his old habit during the last few weeks of the school year. Explain the possible reasons for this relapse pattern and describe what Trevor can do to avoid repeated failure in his efforts to stop smoking.

4. Kate, who is 50 pounds overweight, has tried a variety of diets. Although she often loses some weight under each diet, she eventually gains it all back. Explain why Kate most likely has difficulty maintaining her weight losses. What are the advantages and disadvantages of her continued efforts to lose weight?

Web Quiz 1

Ans: c

1. A health psychologist would be most likely to conduct research assessing the relationship between:
   a. lung disease and life expectancy.
   b. prenatal hormones and brain development.
   c. unprotected sex and sexually transmitted diseases.
   d. inherited genes and cardiovascular health.

Ans: c

2. An elevated heart rate is to a difficult final exam as ________ is to _______.
   a. behavioral medicine; health psychology
   b. coronary heart disease; hypertension
   c. stress reaction; stressor
   d. macrophage; lymphocyte
   e. Type A personality; Type B personality

Ans: d

3. Walter Cannon confirmed that the fight-or-flight response was associated with the release of ________ into the bloodstream.
   a. acetylcholine
   b. uric acid
   c. lymphocytes
   d. epinephrine
   e. teratogens

Ans: b

4. If they live in a community with _______ income inequality, people at _______ income level are at a greater risk of death.
   a. high; only a low
   b. high; every
   c. low; only a low
   d. low; every

Ans: a

5. As Type A tax accountants worked to finish their clients' tax returns before the April 15 filing deadline, they experienced a(n) ________ in blood cholesterol levels and a(n) ________ in blood clotting speed.
   a. increase; increase
   b. decrease; increase
   c. increase; decrease
   d. decrease; decrease

Ans: d

6. Type A is to Type B as ________ is to _______.
   a. epinephrine; norepinephrine
   b. obesity; cancer
   c. time-conscious; competitive
   d. irritable; calm

Ans: e

7. T lymphocytes are formed in the:
   a. thyroid.
   b. adrenal cortex.
   c. thalamus.
   d. pancreas.
   e. thymus.

Ans: c

8. Compared with monkeys left in stable groups, those who were housed with three or four new roommates each month were more likely to experience:
   a. shrinkage of the adrenal cortex.
   b. reduction of blood cholesterol levels.
   c. suppressed production of lymphocytes.
   d. reduced build-up of plaques on artery walls.

Ans: d

9. An overreactive immune system is to ________ as an underreactive immune system is to ________.
   a. AIDS; multiple sclerosis
   b. multiple sclerosis; lupus
   c. lupus; arthritis
   d. arthritis: AIDS

Ans: b

10. Aerobic exercise ________ the body's production of serotonin and ________ its production of endorphine.
    a. decreases; decreases
    b. increases; increases
    c. decreases; increases
    d. increases; decreases

Ans: e

11. In the late 1960s, experiments indicated that rats could learn to slow their heartbeat if given pleasurable brain stimulation when their heartbeat decreased. This research most clearly demonstrated the potential utility of:
    a. spontaneous remission.
    b. acupuncture therapies.
    c. the general adaptation syndrome.
    d. the placebo effect.
    e. biofeedback.

Ans: a

12. Which of the following is the most noticeable nicotine withdrawal symptom?
    a. insomnia
    b. atherosclerosis
    c. increased serotonin levels
    d. a reduced appetite for carbohydrates

Ans: b

13. Helping people to stop smoking by having them rapidly smoke cigarette after cigarette until they become sick illustrates:
    a. acupuncture therapy.
    b. aversive conditioning.
    c. biofeedback.
    d. cognitive therapy.

Ans: a

14. Eating a lot of bread and potatoes is most likely to increase the level of:
    a. serotonin in the brain.
    b. epinephrine in the bloodstream.
    c. dopamine in the brain.
    d. lymphocytes in the bloodstream.

Ans: c

15. In a classic experiment, obese patients whose daily caloric intake was dramatically reduced lost only 6 percent of their weight. This limited weight loss was due, at least in part, to the fact that their dietary restriction led to:
    a. a proliferation of their lymphocytes.
    b. the inhibition of their dopamine reuptake.
    c. a sharp decrease in their metabolic rates.
    d. a dramatic surge in their cholesterol levels.

Web Quiz 2

Ans: c

1. Professor Dockery is a psychologist who conducts research to assess whether government-sponsored educational programs that encourage people to practice effective dental hygiene have any effect on rates of gum disease. His research best illustrates the field of:
   a. holistic medicine.
   b. complementary medicine.
   c. behavioral medicine.
   d. alternative medicine.
   e. psychopharmacology.

Ans: c

2. One person, alone in a house, dismisses its creaking sounds and experiences no stress; someone else suspects an intruder and becomes alarmed. These different reactions illustrate the importance of:
   a. biofeedback.
   b. lymphocytes.
   c. stress appraisal.
   d. spontaneous remission.
   e. the general adaptation syndrome.

Ans: a

3. The second phase of the general adaptation syndrome is characterized by:
   a. resistance.
   b. bleeding ulcers.
   c. spontaneous remission.
   d. an alarm reaction.
   e. low blood pressure.

Ans: d

4. Workers who select and arrange their own office furnishings are less likely to experience job-related stress. This best illustrates the value of:
   a. aerobic exercise.
   b. biofeedback.
   c. Type B personalities.
   d. perceived control.
   e. the general adaptation syndrome.

Ans: d

5. Who is the best example of a Type A personality?
   a. Bonnie, a relaxed, fun-loving professor
   b. Susan, a brilliant, self-confident accountant
   c. Clay, a reflective, open-minded artist
   d. Andre, a competitive, easily-angered journalist

Ans: b

6. Compared to Type B personalities, Type A people are more likely to experience:
   a. enlargement of the thymus gland.
   b. atherosclerosis.
   c. reduced cortisol levels.
   d. proliferation of lymphocytes.

Ans: d

7. Highly fearful and inhibited individuals have been described as ________ personalities.
   a. Type A
   b. Type B
   c. Type C
   d. Type D

Ans: e

8. Kelsey's painful symptoms of indigestion and heartburn were effectively reduced when her parents and teachers showed support for her decision not to go to college. Kelsey's symptoms of distress best illustrate:
   a. atherosclerosis.
   b. hypertension.
   c. a Type A personality.
   d. hypochondriasis.
   e. a psychophysiological illness.

Ans: b

9. The white blood cells that fight bacterial infections are formed in the:
   a. pancreas.
   b. bone marrow.
   c. limbic system.
   d. adrenal gland.
   e. liver.

Ans: c

10. A hay fever sufferer sees a flower on a restaurant table and, not realizing it is plastic, experiences a rapidly accelerating heartbeat and profuse perspiration. This most clearly illustrates that stress reactions can result from:
   a. hypertension.
   b. atherosclerosis
   c. classical conditioning.
   d. the proliferation of lymphocytes.
   e. biofeedback.

Ans: e

11. Psychologists would most likely use biofeedback to provide clients with information about their:
   a. hunger.
   b. fat cell count.
   c. nicotine tolerance.
   d. estrogen levels.
   e. muscle tension.

Ans: b

12. Which of the following factors is most likely to have contributed to the fact that bloodletting once seemed to be an effective medical remedy of people's ailments?
    a. behavioral medicine
    b. spontaneous remission
    c. the general adaptation syndrome
    d. acupuncture
    e. biofeedback

Ans: a

13. Smoking triggers ________ levels of epinephrine in the blood and ________ levels of dopamine in the synapses.
    a. increased; increased
    b. decreased; decreased
    d. increased; decreased
    e. decreased; increased

Ans: d

14. Those who experience nicotine withdrawal symptoms often snack on ________ foods for a mood lift.
    a. high-sodium
    b. high-protein
    c. low-calcium
    d. high-carbohydrate

Ans: b

15. Which of the following would be the best advice or encouragement to offer someone who wants to lose excess weight?
    a. Avoid complex carbohydrates like potatoes and pasta.
    b. Try to reduce your weight gradually over a period of several months.
    c. Your self-esteem will increase dramatically if you can successfully lose weight.
    d. Once you lose your excess weight, you will experience a big reduction in your appetite for food.

Study Guide Questions

Ans: d, p. 531

1. The field of health psychology is concerned with:
   a. the prevention of illness.
   b. the promotion of health.
   c. the treatment of illness.
   d. all of the above.

Ans: a, p. 531

2. Dr. Williams, who conducts smoking cessation clinics, explains to his clients that smoking is best understood as an interaction of psychological, biological, and social influences. Dr. Williams is working within the ________ perspective.
   a. behavioral medicine
   b. behavioral
   c. general adaptation syndrome
   d. psychophysiological

Ans: d, p. 531

3. According to the text, one-half of all deaths from the 10 leading causes of death in the United States can be attributed to:
   a. stress.
   b. obesity.
   c. nutrition.
   d. behavior.

Ans: c, p. 531

4. Behavioral and medical knowledge about factors influencing health form the basis of the field of:
   a. health psychology.
   b. holistic medicine.
   c. behavioral medicine.
   d. osteopathic medicine.

Ans: c, p. 532

5. *Stress* is defined as:
   a. unpleasant or aversive events that cannot be controlled.
   b. situations that threaten health.
   c. the process by which we perceive and respond to challenging or threatening events.
   d. anything that decreases immune responses.

Ans: b, p. 533

6. Connie complains to the campus psychologist that she has too much stress in her life. The psychologist tells her that the level of stress people experience depends primarily on:
   a. how many activities they are trying to do at the same time.
   b. how they appraise the events of life.
   c. their physical hardiness.
   d. how predictable stressful events are.

Ans: c, pp. 533-534

7. The stress hormones epinephrine and norepinephrine are released by the ________ gland in response to stimulation by the ________ branch of the nervous system.
   a. pituitary; sympathetic
   b. pituitary; parasympathetic
   c. adrenal; sympathetic
   d. adrenal; parasympathetic

Ans: a, p. 534

8. In order, the sequence of stages in the general adaptation syndrome is:
   a. alarm reaction, stage of resistance, stage of exhaustion.
   b. stage of resistance, alarm reaction, stage of exhaustion.
   c. stage of exhaustion, stage of resistance, alarm reaction.
   d. alarm reaction, stage of exhaustion, stage of resistance.

Ans: c, p. 534

9. During which stage of the general adaptation syndrome is a person especially vulnerable to disease?
   a. alarm reaction
   b. stage of resistance
   c. stage of exhaustion
   d. stage of adaptation

Ans: c, p. 534

10. "Tend and befriend" refers to:
   a. the final stage of the general adaptation syndrome.
   b. the health-promoting impact of having a strong system of social support.
   c. an alternative to the "fight-or-flight" response that may be more common in women.
   d. the fact that spiritual people typically are not socially isolated.

Ans: c, p. 534

11. Each semester, Bob does not start studying until just before midterms. Then he is forced to work around the clock until after final exams, which makes him sick, probably because he is in the ________ phase of the ________.
   a. alarm; post-traumatic stress syndrome
   b. resistance; general adaptation syndrome
   c. exhaustion; general adaptation syndrome
   d. depletion; post-traumatic stress syndrome

Ans: d, p. 535

12. Research studies demonstrate that after a catastrophe, rates of ________ often increase.
   a. depression
   b. anxiety
   c. stress related illnesses
   d. all of the above
   e. none of the above

Ans: b, p. 535

13. Karen and Kyumi are taking the same course with different instructors. Karen's instructor schedules quizzes every Friday, while Kyumi's instructor gives the same number of quizzes on an unpredictable schedule. Assuming that their instructors are equally difficult, which student is probably under more stress?
a. Karen
b. Kyumi
c. There should be no difference in their levels of stress.
d. It is impossible to predict stress levels in this situation.

Ans: d, pp. 535-538

14. You have just transferred to a new campus and find yourself in a potentially stressful environment. According to the text, which of the following would help you cope with the stress?
a. believing that you have some control over your environment
b. being able to predict when stressful events will occur
c. feeling optimistic that you will eventually adjust to your new surroundings
d. All of the above would help.

Ans: d, p. 537

15. In one experiment, both "executive" rats and "subordinate" rats received identical electric shocks, the only difference being whether the shocks could be:
a. predicted.
b. weakened.
c. shortened.
d. controlled.

Ans: c, pp. 537-539

16. Which of the following would be the *best* piece of advice to offer a person who is trying to minimize the adverse effects of stress on his or her health?
a. "Avoid challenging situations that may prove stressful."
b. "Learn to play as hard as you work."
c. "Maintain a sense of control and a positive approach to life."
d. "Keep your emotional responses in check by keeping your feelings to yourself."

Ans: b, p. 539

17. Jill is an easygoing, noncompetitive person who is happy in her job and enjoys her leisure time. She would *probably* be classified as:
a. Type A.
b. Type B.
c. Type C.
d. Type D.

Ans: b, p. 539

18. In response to uncontrollable shock, levels of stress hormones ________ and immune responses are ________.
a. decrease; suppressed
b. increase; suppressed
c. decrease; increased
d. increase; increased

Ans: c, p. 539

19. The leading cause of death in North America is:
    a. lung cancer.
    b. AIDS.
    c. coronary heart disease.
    d. alcohol-related accidents.
    e. accidents.

Ans: c, p. 539

20. Researchers Friedman and Rosenman refer to individuals who are very time-conscious, supermotivated, verbally aggressive, and easily angered as:
    a. ulcer-prone personalities.
    b. cancer-prone personalities.
    c. Type A.
    d. Type B.

Ans: b, p. 540

21. Which of the following statements concerning Type A and B persons is true?
    a. Even when relaxed, Type A persons have higher blood pressure than Type B persons.
    b. When stressed, Type A persons show greater output of stress hormones than Type B persons.
    c. Type B persons tend to suppress anger more than Type A persons.
    d. Type A persons tend to sleep more than Type B persons.
    e. Type A persons tend to drink fewer caffeinated drinks than Type B persons.

Ans: e, p. 540

22. The component of Type A behavior that is the most predictive of coronary disease is:
    a. time urgency.
    b. competitiveness.
    c. high motivation.
    d. impatience.
    e. anger.

Ans: b, p. 540

23. One effect of stress hormones is to:
    a. lower the level of cholesterol in the blood.
    b. promote the buildup of plaques on the artery walls.
    c. divert blood away from the muscles of the body.
    d. reduce stress.
    e. decrease the amount of fat stored in the body.

Ans: a, p. 541

24. Genuine illnesses that are caused by stress are called ________ illnesses.
    a. psychophysiological
    b. hypochondriacal
    c. psychogenic
    d. psychotropic

Ans: d, p. 541

25. Randy's score on a recent personality test marked him as "Type D." This means that he is probably marked by:
    a. negative emotions.
    b. social inhibition.
    c. high risk of heart disease.
    d. all of the above.
    e. none of the above.

Ans: c, p. 541

26. Philip's physician prescribes a stress management program to help Philip control his headaches. The physician has apparently diagnosed Philip's condition as a ________ illness, rather than a physical disorder.
    a. psychogenic
    b. hypochondriac
    c. psychophysiological
    d. biofeedback

Ans: e, p. 542

27. Stress has been demonstrated to place a person at increased risk of:
    a. cancer.
    b. progressing from HIV infection to AIDS.
    c. bacterial infections.
    d. viral infections.
    e. all of the above.

Ans: a, p. 542

28. Allergic reactions and arthritis are caused by:
    a. an overreactive immune system.
    b. an underreactive immune system.
    c. the presence of B lymphocytes.
    d. the presence of T lymphocytes.

Ans: c, p. 542

29. The disease- and infection-fighting cells of the immune system are:
    a. B lymphocytes.
    b. T lymphocytes.
    c. both a. and b.
    d. antigens.

Ans: e, p. 542

30. Compared to men, women:
    a. have stronger immune systems.
    b. are less susceptible to infections.
    c. are more susceptible to self-attacking diseases such as multiple sclerosis.
    d. have none of the above characteristics.
    e. have all of the characteristics described in a., b., and c.

Ans: c, p. 542

31. A white blood cell that is formed in the thymus and that attacks cancer cells is:
    a. a macrophage.
    b. a B lymphocyte.
    c. a T lymphocyte.
    d. any of the above.

Ans: b, p. 542

32. When would you expect that your immune responses would be *weakest*?
    a. during summer vacation
    b. during exam weeks
    c. just after receiving good news
    d. Immune activity would probably remain constant during these times.

Ans: a, pp. 542-543

33. One effect of stress on the body is to:
    a. suppress the immune system.
    b. facilitate the immune system response.
    c. increase disease resistance.
    d. increase the growth of B and T lymphocytes.

Ans: c, p. 543

34. AIDS is a disorder that causes a breakdown in the body's:
    a. endocrine system.
    b. circulatory system.
    c. immune system.
    d. respiratory system.

Ans: c, p. 543

35. The AIDS virus is transmitted primarily by:
    a. airborne transmission of HIV.
    b. physical touching.
    c. an exchange of blood or semen.
    d. insect bites.

Ans: d, pp. 543-544

36. Research on cancer patients reveals that:
    a. stress affects the growth of cancer cells by weakening the body's natural resources.
    b. patients' attitudes can influence their rate of recovery.
    c. cancer occurs slightly more often than usual among those widowed, divorced, or separated.
    d. all of the above are true.

Ans: b, p. 544

37. In one study, laboratory rats drank sweetened water with a drug that causes immune suppression. After repeated pairings of the taste with the drug:
    a. the animals developed tolerance for the drug and immune responses returned to normal.
    b. sweet water alone triggered immune suppression.
    c. dependency on the drug developed and withdrawal symptoms appeared when the drug was withheld.
    d. many of the animals died.

Ans: d, pp. 547-548

38. Which of the following was *not* mentioned in the text as a potential health benefit of exercise?
    a. Exercise can increase ability to cope with stress.
    b. Exercise can lower blood pressure.
    c. Exercise can reduce stress, depression, and anxiety.
    d. Exercise improves functioning of the immune system.

Ans: d, pp. 548-549

39. During biofeedback training:
    a. a subject is given sensory feedback for a subtle body response.
    b. biological functions controlled by the autonomic nervous system may come under conscious control.
    c. the accompanying relaxation is much the same as that produced by other, simpler methods of relaxation.
    d. all of the above occur.

Ans: b, p. 551

40. Social support ________ our ability to cope with stressful events.
    a. has no effect on
    b. usually increases
    c. usually decreases
    d. has an unpredictable effect on

Ans: c, p. 552

41. A study in which people were asked to confide troubling feelings to an experimenter found that subjects typically:
    a. did not truthfully report feelings and events.
    b. experienced a sustained increase in blood pressure until the experiment was finished.
    c. became physiologically more relaxed after confiding their problem.
    d. denied having any problems.

Ans: d, pp. 553-555

42. Concluding her presentation on spirituality and health, Maja notes that:
    a. historically, religion and medicine joined hands in caring for the sick.
    b. most Americans believe that spirituality and religion are related to health.
    c. people who attend religious services weekly have healthier life-styles.
    d. all of the above are true.

Ans: d, pp. 553-554

43. Which of the following was *not* suggested as a possible explanation of the "faith factor" in health?
    a. Having a coherent worldview is a buffer against stress.
    b. Religious people tend to have healthier life-styles.
    c. Those who are religious have stronger networks of social support.
    d. Because they are more affluent, religiously active people receive better health care.

Ans: d, p. 554

44. Research has demonstrated that as a predictor of health and longevity, religious involvement:
    a. has a small, insignificant effect.
    b. is more accurate for women than men.
    c. is more accurate for men than women.
    d. rivals nonsmoking and exercise.

Ans: b, p. 556

45. Acupuncture, aromatherapy, and homeopathy are forms of:
    a. psychophysiological medicine.
    b. complementary and alternative medicine.
    c. Chi therapy.
    d. psychosomatic medicine.

Ans: a, p. 556

46. Andrew, who is convinced that an expensive herbal remedy "cured" his arthritis, has decided to turn to homeopathy and herbal medicine for all of his health care. You caution him by pointing out that:
    a. arthritis is a cyclical disease that often improves on its own.
    b. botanical herbs have never been proven effective in controlled experiments.
    c. alternative medicine is a recent fad in this country that has few proponents in other parts of the world.
    d. All of the above are true.

Ans: b, pp. 558-559

47. Research suggests that ________ influences often lead a person to start smoking, whereas ________ influences become important in explaining why people continue to smoke.
    a. biological; social
    b. social; biological
    c. biological; cognitive
    d. cognitive; biological

Ans: c, p. 559

48. Malcolm's report on the effects of nicotine mentions each of the following *except*:
    a. increased heart rate.
    b. appetite suppression.
    c. increased circulation to extremities.
    d. release of endorphins triggered by nicotine.

Ans: c, p. 559

49. I am a widely abused drug that has a calming effect by stimulating the release of dopamine in the central nervous system. What am I?
    a. caffeine
    b. alcohol
    c. nicotine
    d. cocaine

Ans: b, p. 559

50. Which of the following was offered in the text as a reason people continue to smoke?
  a. Social pressure from peers is strong.
  b. Cigarettes serve as powerful reinforcers.
  c. Regular use of nicotine impairs the brain's ability to produce neurotransmitters such as serotonin.
  d. Most adults who smoke don't really want to quit.

Ans: d, p. 560

51. Which of the following is true concerning smoking treatment programs?
  a. Most are effective in the long run.
  b. Hypnosis is more effective than behavior modification.
  c. Treatment programs are more effective with women than with men.
  d. Most participants eventually resume smoking.

Ans: c, p. 561

52. Camelia is worried that her 12-year-old son might begin smoking because many of his classmates do. According to the text, Camelia can most effectively help her son not begin smoking by:
  a. telling him about the dangers of smoking.
  b. telling him that if he begins smoking she will withhold his allowance.
  c. using role-playing to teach him refusal techniques to counteract peer pressure to smoke.
  d. insisting that he not associate with anyone who smokes.

Ans: a, p. 562

53. Studies have demonstrated that meals that are high in ________ promote relaxation because they raise levels of ________.
  a. carbohydrates; serotonin
  b. carbohydrates; cortisol
  c. protein; serotonin
  d. protein; cortisol

Ans: c, p. 562

54. Ricardo has an important psychology exam in the afternoon. In an effort to improve his concentration and alertness, he orders a lunch that is high in ________ and low in ________.
  a. carbohydrates; protein
  b. carbohydrates; fat
  c. protein; carbohydrates
  d. protein; fat

Ans: b, p. 563

55. The tendency to overeat when food is plentiful:
  a. is a recent phenomenon that is associated with the luxury of having ample food.
  b. emerged in our prehistoric ancestors as an adaptive response to alternating periods of feast and famine.
  c. is greater in developed, than in developing, societies.
  d. is stronger in women than in men.

Ans: b, p. 565

56. Research on obesity indicates that:
  a. pound for pound, fat tissue requires more calories to maintain than lean tissue.
  b. once fat cells are acquired they are never lost, no matter how rigorously one diets.
  c. one pound of weight is lost for every 3500-calorie reduction in diet.
  d. when weight drops below the set point, hunger and metabolism also decrease.

Ans: d, p. 565

57. Which of the following is *not* necessarily a reason that obese people have trouble losing weight?
  a. Fat tissue has a lower metabolic rate than lean tissue.
  b. Once a person has lost weight, it takes fewer calories to maintain his or her current weight.
  c. The tendency toward obesity may be genetically based.
  d. Obese people tend to lack willpower.

Ans: b, p. 565

58. After an initial rapid weight loss, a person on a diet loses weight much more slowly. This slowdown occurs because:
  a. most of the initial weight loss is simply water.
  b. when a person diets, metabolism decreases.
  c. people begin to "cheat" on their diets.
  d. insulin levels tend to increase with reduced food intake.

Ans: d, p. 565

59. The number of fat cells a person has is influenced by:
  a. genetic predisposition.
  b. childhood eating patterns.
  c. adulthood eating patterns.
  d. all of the above.

Ans: c, p. 566

60. Kenny and his brother have nearly identical eating and exercise habits, yet Kenny is obese and his brother is very thin. The most likely explanation for the difference in their body weights is that they differ in:
  a. their set points.
  b. their metabolic rates.
  c. both a. and b.
  d. none of the above.

Ans: a, pp. 566-567

61. Research on genetic influences on obesity reveals that:
  a. the body weight of adoptees correlates with that of their biological parents.
  b. the body weight of adoptees correlates with that of their adoptive parents.
  c. identical twins usually have very different body weights.
  d. the body weights of identical twin women are more similar than those of identical twin men.
  e. none of the above is true.

Ans: a, p. 567

62. In studies of obese mice, researchers have found that some mice:
    a. had a defective gene for producing leptin, a fat-detecting hormone.
    b. had abnormally high levels of insulin, a hunger-triggering hormone.
    c. could be conditioned to avoid fatty foods.
    d. had fewer-than-normal receptor sites for a fat-detecting hormone.
    e. are immune to changes in hormone levels.

Ans: a, p. 570

63. Which of the following would be the *worst* piece of advice to offer to someone trying to lose weight?
    a. "In order to treat yourself to one 'normal' meal each day, eat very little until the evening meal."
    b. "Reduce your consumption of saturated fats."
    c. "Boost your metabolism by exercising regularly."
    d. "Without increasing total caloric intake, increase the relative proportion of carbohydrates in your diet."

CHAPTER 15

Personality

Learning Objectives

Historical Perspectives on Personality (pp. 575-590)

1. Describe what is meant by personality, and explain how Freud's treatment of psychological disorders led to his study of the unconscious.

2. Describe Freud's view of personality structure in terms of the interactions of the id, ego, and superego.

3. Identify Freud's psychosexual stages of development, and describe the effects of fixation on behavior.

4. Discuss how defense mechanisms serve to protect the individual from anxiety.

5. Explain how projective tests are used to assess personality.

6. Discuss the contributions of the neo-Freudians, and describe the shortcomings of Freud's ideas.

7. Describe the humanistic perspective on personality in terms of Maslow's focus on self-actualization and Rogers' emphasis on people's potential for growth.

8. Describe humanistic psychologists' approach to personality assessment, and discuss the criticisms of the humanistic perspective.

Contemporary Research on Personality (pp. 590-616)

9. Discuss psychologists' descriptions of personality types, and describe research efforts to identify fundamental personality traits.

10. Explain how personality inventories are used to assess traits, and identify the Big Five trait dimensions.

11. Discuss research regarding the consistency of behavior over time and across situations.

12. Describe the social-cognitive perspective, and discuss the important consequences of personal control, learned helplessness, and optimism.

13. Describe how social-cognitive researchers assess behavior in realistic situations, and evaluate the social-cognitive perspective on personality.

14. Describe psychology's interest in people's sense of self, and discuss the benefits and liabilities of self-esteem and self-serving pride.

15. Describe the impact of individualism and collectivism on self-identity and social relations.

16. Identify examples of nonconscious information processing highlighted by contemporary research.

Personality, p. 575
Medium, Conceptual, Objective 1, Ans: c

1. The concept of "personality" most clearly embodies the notion of:
a. moral integrity.
b. self-consciousness.
c. temporal consistency.
d. self-actualization.
e. gender identity.

The psychoanalytic perspective, p. 576
Difficult, Factual/Definitional, Objective 1, Ans: d

2. Freud became interested in unconscious personality dynamics when he noticed that certain patients' symptoms:
a. resulted from the physical abuse they received from their parents during childhood.
b. resulted from the loss of an internal locus of control.
c. could not be removed by means of hypnosis.
d. could not be explained readily in terms of neurological impairments.

Exploring the unconscious, pp. 576-577
Medium, Factual/Definitional, Objective 1, Ans: c

3. Freud observed that certain symptoms of illness were relieved when patients talked freely about their past. This led Freud to suspect that these symptoms resulted from:
a. genetic defects.
b. an inferiority complex.
c. psychological processes.
d. an internal locus of control.
e. reciprocal determinism.

Exploring the unconscious, p. 576
Easy, Factual/Definitional, Objective 1, Ans: c

4. The use of free association is central to the process of:
a. identification.
b. self-actualization.
c. psychoanalysis.
d. reciprocal determinism.
e. unconditional positive regard.

Exploring the unconscious, pp. 576, 577
Easy, Conceptual, Objective 1, Ans: d

5. Which of the following techniques would Freud have used to discover the latent content of his patients' dreams?
   a. fixation
   b. factor analysis
   c. projective testing
   d. free association
   e. the Barnum effect

Exploring the unconscious, p. 576
Easy, Conceptual/Application, Objective 1, Ans: b

6. A psychotherapist instructs Dane to relax, close his eyes, and state aloud whatever thoughts come to mind no matter how trivial or absurd. The therapist is using a technique known as:
   a. fixation.
   b. free association.
   c. reaction formation.
   d. hypnosis.
   e. projection.

Exploring the unconscious, pp. 576-577
Easy, Factual/Definitional, Objective 1, Ans: c

7. Forgotten memories that we can easily recall were said by Freud to be:
   a. displaced.
   b. projected.
   c. preconscious.
   d. fixated.
   e. unconscious.

Exploring the unconscious, p. 576
Easy, Factual/Definitional, Objective 1, Ans: b

8. According to Freud, the unconscious is:
   a. the part of human personality that lacks a sense of right and wrong.
   b. the thoughts, wishes, feelings, and memories, of which we are largely unaware.
   c. a set of universal concepts acquired by all humans from our common past.
   d. a reservoir of deeply repressed memories that does not affect behavior.
   e. all of the above.

Exploring the unconscious, p. 577
Medium, Factual/Definitional, Objective 1, Ans: b

9. Freud believed that ________ are the "royal road to the unconscious."
   a. projective tests
   b. dreams
   c. erogenous zones
   d. psychosexual stages
   e. hypnotic trances

The psychoanalytic perspective: personality structure, p. 577
Easy, Factual/Definitional, Objective 2, Ans: a

10. According to psychoanalytic theory, the part of the personality that strives for immediate gratification of basic drives is the:
    a. id.
    b. ego.
    c. superego.
    d. collective unconscious.

The psychoanalytic perspective: personality structure, p. 577
Easy, Conceptual/Application, Objective 2, Ans: d

11. When 2-year-old Matthew was told he would get no dessert until he finished the food on his plate, he threw his plate on the floor in a temper tantrum. Freud would have suggested that Matthew was unable to resist the demands of his:
    a. superego.
    b. collective unconscious.
    c. ego.
    d. id.
    e. Oedipus complex.

The psychoanalytic perspective: personality structure, pp. 577-578
Medium, Conceptual, Objective 2, Ans: d

12. Ego is to id as ________ is to ________.
    a. personality; collective unconscious
    b. morality; biology
    c. life instinct; death instinct
    d. reality principle; pleasure principle
    e. self-esteem; self-serving bias

The psychoanalytic perspective: personality structure, p. 578
Medium, Conceptual/Application, Objective 2, Ans: d

13. When 16-year-old Hafez received a large inheritance from his grandfather, he was tempted to purchase an expensive new car. He decided, instead, to deposit all the money into a savings account for his college education. Hafez shows signs of a:
    a. strong self-serving bias.
    b. weak id.
    c. strong collective unconscious.
    d. strong ego.
    e. strong external locus of control.

The psychoanalytic perspective: personality structure, p. 578
Easy, Factual/Definitional, Objective 2, Ans: e

14. According to Freud, the personality system that represents our sense of right and wrong and our ideal standards is the:
    a. collective unconscious.
    b. ego.
    c. self-concept.
    d. id.
    e. superego.

The psychoanalytic perspective: personality structure, p. 578
Easy, Conceptual/Application, Objective 2, Ans: c

15. Janine experiences feelings of revulsion at the prospect of watching a pornographic video. Freud would have attributed these feelings to Janine's:
    a. ego.
    b. id.
    c. superego.
    d. collective unconscious.

The psychoanalytic perspective: personality structure, p. 578
Medium, Conceptual/Application, Objective 2, Ans: e

16. No matter how long and hard Oprah studies, she always feels she hasn't studied as much as she should have. A Freudian psychologist would suggest that Oprah shows signs of a:
    a. weak id.
    b. weak ego.
    c. weak superego.
    d. strong id.
    e. strong superego.

The psychoanalytic perspective: personality structure, p. 578
Difficult, Conceptual/Application, Objective 2, Ans: e

17. Bruce wants to be a loving husband but at the same time wants to express his disgust for some of his wife's habits. According to Freud, Bruce's ________ might enable him to partially satisfy both desires.
    a. actualized self
    b. collective unconscious
    c. superego
    d. Oedipus complex
    e. ego

The psychoanalytic perspective: personality development, p. 578
Easy, Factual/Definitional, Objective 3, Ans: c

18. During the early psychosexual stages, the id derives pleasure from distinct:
    a. gender identities.
    b. defense mechanisms.
    c. erogenous zones.
    d. identifications.
    e. complexes.

The psychoanalytic perspective: personality development (Table 15.1), p. 578
Difficult, Conceptual/Application, Objective 3, Ans: b

19. Two-year-old Damien frequently refuses to obey his parents because he derives immense pleasure from demonstrating his independence from their control. Freud would have suggested that Damien is going through the ________ stage of development.
    a. phallic
    b. anal
    c. genital
    d. latency
    e. oral

The psychoanalytic perspective: personality development, pp. 578-579
Medium, Factual/Definitional, Objective 3, Ans: b

20. According to Freud, boys are most likely to experience the Oedipus complex during the ________ stage.
a. anal
b. phallic
c. oral
d. latency

The psychoanalytic perspective: personality development, p. 579
Easy, Factual/Definitional, Objective 3, Ans: d

21. According to psychoanalytic theory, boys' fear of castration is most closely associated with:
a. an oral fixation.
b. free association.
c. learned helplessness.
d. the Oedipus complex.
e. the genital stage.

The psychoanalytic perspective: personality development, p. 579
Medium, Conceptual/Application, Objective 3, Ans: d

22. One night after he heard his parents arguing, 4-year-old Wei had a vivid dream in which he saved his mother from being bitten by a large snake. A psychoanalyst would most likely suspect that Wei's dream reflects a(n):
a. oral fixation.
b. reaction formation.
c. self-serving bias.
d. Oedipus complex.
e. external locus of control.

The psychoanalytic perspective: personality development, p. 579
Medium, Factual/Definitional, Objective 3, Ans: c

23. Freud suggested that the process of identification is most directly responsible for the development of:
a. the Oedipus complex.
b. free association.
c. the superego.
d. erogenous zones.
e. an inferiority complex.

The psychoanalytic perspective: personality development, p. 579
Difficult, Conceptual/Application, Objective 3, Ans: d

24. Which theory would most likely predict that boys raised without a father figure will have difficulty developing a strongly masculine gender identity?
a. Allport's trait theory
b. Maslow's humanistic theory
c. Bandura's social-cognitive theory
d. Freud's psychoanalytic theory

The psychoanalytic perspective: personality development, p. 579
Medium, Conceptual/Application, Objective 3, Ans: c

25. Gene spends a good deal of time bragging about his numerous sexual exploits. Freud would have suggested that Gene is fixated at the ________ stage.
a. oral
b. latency
c. phallic
d. anal

The psychoanalytic perspective: personality development, p. 579
Easy, Factual/Definitional, Objective 3, Ans: c

26. Freud referred to a lingering focus of pleasure-seeking energies at an earlier psychosexual stage as:
a. reaction formation.
b. projection.
c. fixation.
d. displacement.
e. repression.

The psychoanalytic perspective: personality development, p. 579
Difficult, Conceptual/Application, Objective 3, Ans: e

27. Saleem seeks sexual pleasure by means of solitary masturbation rather than through sexual interaction with his wife. Freud would have suggested that this illustrates a(n):
a. rationalization.
b. projection.
c. inferiority complex.
d. reaction formation.
e. fixation.

The psychoanalytic perspective: personality development, p. 579
Easy, Factual/Definitional, Objective 3, Ans: a

28. Freud suggested that orally fixated adults are especially likely to exhibit:
a. passive dependence.
b. an inferiority complex.
c. an Electra complex.
d. compulsive neatness.
e. messiness and disorganization.

The psychoanalytic perspective: personality development, p. 579
Difficult, Conceptual/Application, Objective 3, Ans: d

29. Arjean is terribly gullible and accepts as true just about anything she is told. According to the psychoanalytic perspective, Arjean is most likely fixated at the ________ stage.
a. genital
b. phallic
c. anal
d. oral
e. latency

The psychoanalytic perspective: personality development, p. 579
Difficult, Conceptual/Application, Objective 3, Ans: e

30. Mr. Hendriks, a high school teacher, washes the chalkboard and realigns student desks in precise rows before every class. According to the psychoanalytic perspective, Mr. Hendriks is most likely fixated at the ________ stage.
    a. phallic
    b. oral
    c. latency
    d. genital
    e. anal

Defense mechanisms, pp. 579-580
Medium, Factual/Definitional, Objective 4, Ans: b

31. According to Freud, defense mechanisms are used by the:
    a. id to defend against the accusations and guilt feelings produced by the superego.
    b. ego to prevent threatening impulses from being consciously recognized.
    c. superego to prevent expression of sexual and aggressive drives.
    d. id, ego, and superego in a repetitive sequence of internal conflicts.

Defense mechanisms, p. 580
Easy, Conceptual/Application, Objective 4, Ans: a

32. When she was 8 years old, Inge was sexually abused by her uncle. At 14, Inge felt uncomfortable whenever she saw this uncle but was unable to understand why she felt this way. A psychoanalyst would be most likely to suggest that Inge is using the defense mechanism of:
    a. repression.
    b. reaction formation.
    c. rationalization.
    d. regression.
    e. displacement.

Defense mechanisms, p. 580
Easy, Factual/Definitional, Objective 4, Ans: e

33. Freud suggested that slips of the tongue illustrate an incomplete:
    a. fixation.
    b. displacement.
    c. rationalization.
    d. projection.
    e. repression.

Defense mechanisms, p. 580
Difficult, Conceptual, Objective 4, Ans: b

34. An excessive fixation is most likely to contribute to:
    a. reaction formation.
    b. regression.
    c. projection.
    d. an Electra complex.
    e. displacement.

Defense mechanisms, p. 580
Easy, Conceptual/Application, Objective 4, Ans: c

35. Four-year-old Timmy has not wet his bed for over a year. However, he starts bed-wetting again soon after his sister is born. Timmy's behavior best illustrates:
a. reaction formation.
b. projection.
c. regression.
d. displacement.
e. repression.

Defense mechanisms, p. 580
Easy, Factual/Definitional, Objective 4, Ans: b

36. Reaction formation refers to the process by which people:
a. disguise unacceptable unconscious impulses by attributing them to others.
b. consciously express feelings that are the opposite of unacceptable unconscious impulses.
c. retreat to behavior patterns characteristic of an earlier stage of development.
d. offer self-justifying explanations in place of the real but unacceptable unconscious reasons for action.

Defense mechanisms, p. 580
Difficult, Conceptual/Application, Objective 4, Ans: d

37. Parents who disguise hostility toward their children by becoming overly protective of them are very likely using the defense mechanism of:
a. projection.
b. regression.
c. rationalization.
d. reaction formation.
e. displacement.

Defense mechanisms, p. 580
Easy, Factual/Definitional, Objective 4, Ans: a

38. The defense mechanism by which people disguise threatening impulses by attributing them to others is called:
a. projection.
b. displacement.
c. fixation.
d. reaction formation.
e. repression.

Defense mechanisms, p. 580
Medium, Conceptual/Application, Objective 4, Ans: b

39. Abdul mistakenly believes that his classmates at school are unusually hostile. In fact, Abdul is the most quarrelsome and aggressive child in the school. According to psychoanalytic theory, Abdul's belief that his classmates are hostile is a:
a. regression.
b. projection.
c. fixation.
d. reaction formation.

Defense mechanisms, p. 580
Difficult, Conceptual/Application, Objective 4, Ans: c

40. Mrs. Smith, who is White and unconsciously in favor of racial segregation, tells her friends that most Blacks prefer to live in residential neighborhoods inhabited predominantly by Blacks. According to psychoanalytic theory, Mrs. Smith best illustrates:
a. fixation.
b. reaction formation.
c. projection.
d. displacement.
e. regression.

Defense mechanisms, p. 580
Easy, Factual/Definitional, Objective 4, Ans: d

41. The defense mechanism in which self-justifying explanations replace the real, unconscious reasons for actions is:
a. projection.
b. reaction formation.
c. repression.
d. rationalization.
e. displacement.

Defense mechanisms, p. 580
Medium, Conceptual/Application, Objective 4, Ans: c

42. Melissa is unconsciously fearful that her husband is a better cook than she. Recently, she refused his offer to prepare dinner because, said she, "You could better spend the time playing with our kids." Melissa's comment best illustrates:
a. regression.
b. projection.
c. rationalization.
d. displacement.
e. reaction formation.

Defense mechanisms, p. 580
Medium, Conceptual/Application, Objective 4, Ans: c

43. While Professor Gomez was going through a painful divorce, he tended to create unnecessarily difficult tests and gave his students unusually low grades. A psychoanalyst would be most likely to view the professor's treatment of students as an example of:
a. reaction formation.
b. rationalization.
c. displacement.
d. projection.
e. regression.

Assessing the unconscious, p. 581
Easy, Factual/Definitional, Objective 5, Ans: b

44. Projective tests are most closely associated with the ________ perspective.
a. social-cognitive
b. psychoanalytic
c. humanistic
d. trait

Assessing the unconscious, p. 581
Easy, Factual/Definitional, Objective 5, Ans: a

45. Henry Murray found that children's perceptions of photographs were biased by their previous participation in a frightening game. Their perceptual reactions most clearly highlighted the potential value of:
a. projective tests.
b. free association.
c. unconditional positive regard.
d. reciprocal determinism.
e. an internal locus of control.

Assessing the unconscious, p. 581
Medium, Conceptual/Application, Objective 5, Ans: a

46. Mr. Dutoit was asked by his psychotherapist to look at some ambiguous pictures and make up a story about each. Mr. Dutoit was most likely taking the:
a. TAT.
b. Myers-Briggs Type Indicator.
c. MMPI-2.
d. Personal Orientation Inventory.
e. Rorschach test.

Assessing the unconscious, p. 582
Medium, Factual/Definitional, Objective 5, Ans: b

47. The major reason for the unreliability of the Rorschach inkblot test is the fact that:
a. the test inhibits individuals from communicating honestly in clinical interviews.
b. psychologists often do not agree on how to score the results of this test.
c. the test does not discriminate effectively between those who are suicidal and those who are not.
d. the test can be used effectively only with individuals who are severely maladjusted.

Freud's early descendants and dissenters, pp. 582-583
Medium, Factual/Definitional, Objective 6, Ans: b

48. Neo-Freudian personality theorists were most likely to disagree with Freud about the importance of:
a. the unconscious dynamics underlying behavior.
b. childhood sexual instincts.
c. anxiety and defense mechanisms.
d. distinguishing between id, ego, and superego.

Freud's early descendants and dissenters, p. 583
Medium, Conceptual/Application, Objective 6, Ans: d

49. Hasina was an abused child; as an adult, she is homeless and squanders any money she can find on alcohol. Alfred Adler would have suggested that Hasina suffers from:
a. an Electra complex.
b. role confusion.
c. an oral fixation.
d. feelings of inferiority.
e. the Barnum effect.

Freud's early descendants and dissenters, p. 583
Medium, Factual/Definitional, Objective 6, Ans: a

50. Karen Horney, a prominent neo-Freudian, disputed Freud's assumption that women:
   a. have weak superegos.
   b. suffer an Electra complex.
   c. often experience learned helplessness.
   d. have stronger sexual instincts than men.
   e. never experience a phallic stage of development.

Freud's early descendants and dissenters, p. 583
Medium, Factual/Definitional, Objective 6, Ans: a

51. Which neo-Freudian theorist emphasized the influence of the collective unconscious in personality development?
   a. Jung
   b. Adler
   c. Horney
   d. Maslow
   e. Bandura

Freud's early descendants and dissenters, p. 583
Medium, Factual/Definitional, Objective 6, Ans: c

52. Contemporary psychodynamic theorists are most likely to emphasize the importance of:
   a. sexual instincts.
   b. free association.
   c. motivational conflict.
   d. the collective unconscious.

Evaluating the psychoanalytic perspective, p. 584
Easy, Factual/Definitional, Objective 6, Ans: a

53. Contemporary psychologists are least likely to agree with Freud's belief that:
   a. conscience and gender identity form during the process of resolving the Oedipus complex.
   b. conscious awareness of our own mental processes is very limited.
   c. memories are often distorted and incomplete.
   d. defense mechanisms help protect individuals from anxiety.

Evaluating the psychoanalytic perspective, p. 584
Easy, Factual/Definitional, Objective 6, Ans: c

54. Freud emphasized that emotional healing is associated with the:
   a. fixation of repressed sexual desires.
   b. projection of repressed fears.
   c. recovery of repressed memories.
   d. displacement of repressed hostilities.

Evaluating the psychoanalytic perspective, p. 584
Easy, Factual/Definitional, Objective 6, Ans: b

55. Survivors' memories of Nazi death camp experiences most clearly challenge Freud's concept of:
a. fixation.
b. repression.
c. the Oedipus complex.
d. motivational conflict.
e. learned helplessness.

Evaluating the psychoanalytic perspective, p. 585
Difficult, Factual/Definitional, Objective 6, Ans: d

56. Freud's theory of personality has been criticized because it:
a. underestimates the importance of biological contributions to personality development.
b. is contradicted by recent research demonstrating the human capacity for destructive behavior.
c. is overly reliant upon observations derived from Freud's use of projective tests.
d. offers few testable predictions that allow one to determine its validity.

The humanistic perspective, p. 587
Medium, Factual/Definitional, Objective 7, Ans: b

57. The humanistic perspective emphasized the importance of:
a. free association.
b. self-determination.
c. reciprocal determinism.
d. personality inventories.
e. projective tests.

Abraham Maslow's self-actualizing person, p. 587
Easy, Factual/Definitional, Objective 7, Ans: c

58. Abraham Maslow studied the lives of Abraham Lincoln, Thomas Jefferson, and Eleanor Roosevelt in order to understand the nature of:
a. reciprocal determinism.
b. unconditional positive regard.
c. self-actualization.
d. personality traits.

Abraham Maslow's self-actualizing person, p. 587
Medium, Conceptual, Objective 7, Ans: c

59. Self-actualized people, as described by Maslow, are least likely to be highly:
a. compassionate.
b. religious.
c. conforming.
d. self-accepting.

Carl Rogers' person-centered perspective, p. 587
Easy, Factual/Definitional, Objective 7, Ans: c

60. Which theorist emphasized that personal growth is promoted by interactions with others who are genuine, accepting, and empathic?
    a. Allport
    b. Jung
    c. Rogers
    d. Freud
    e. Bandura

Carl Rogers' person-centered perspective, pp. 587-588
Difficult, Conceptual/Application, Objective 7, Ans: d

61. Mrs. Sunstedt believes that parents should accept and try to understand their children's feelings and should honestly disclose their own inner feelings to their children. Her approach to parent-child interaction was most explicitly recommended by:
    a. Bandura.
    b. Allport.
    c. Freud.
    d. Rogers.
    e. Jung.

Carl Rogers' person-centered perspective, p. 588
Easy, Factual/Definitional, Objective 7, Ans: e

62. Carl Rogers suggested that the ________ is a central feature of personality.
    a. collective unconscious
    b. Oedipus complex
    c. inferiority complex
    d. Barnum effect
    e. self-concept

Assessing the self, p. 588
Difficult, Conceptual, Objective 8, Ans: c

63. Carl Rogers would have suggested that many of the defense mechanisms described by Freud are used to minimize the perceived discrepancy between:
    a. individualism and collectivism.
    b. the collective unconscious and the personal unconscious.
    c. the actual self and the ideal self.
    d. an internal locus of control and an external locus of control.

Assessing the self, p. 588
Medium, Factual/Definitional, Objective 8, Ans: d

64. Which psychologists are most likely to criticize standardized personality tests for failing to capture the unique subjective experience of the individual personality?
    a. psychoanalytic theorists
    b. trait theorists
    c. social-cognitive theorists
    d. humanistic theorists

Evaluating the humanistic perspective, p. 589
Medium, Conceptual, Objective 8, Ans: c

65. Humanistic psychologists would most likely be criticized for underestimating the value of:
a. an internal locus of control.
b. self-serving bias.
c. social influence.
d. the spotlight effect.
e. individualism.

Evaluating the humanistic perspective, p. 589
Medium, Factual/Definitional, Objective 8, Ans: a

66. Maslow most clearly interjected his own personal values into his study of self-actualized individuals by:
a. selectively studying people with qualities he admired.
b. interpreting their flattering self-descriptions as a self-serving bias.
c. overemphasizing the value of their loyalty to cultural norms.
d. assuming that self-actualization usually takes priority over all other human motives.

Evaluating the humanistic perspective, p. 589
Medium, Factual/Definitional, Objective 8, Ans: d

67. The humanistic perspective has been criticized for promoting an excessive degree of:
a. sexism.
b. spiritualism.
c. nationalism.
d. individualism.
e. personality testing.

Evaluating the humanistic perspective, p. 589
Easy, Factual/Definitional, Objective 8, Ans: d

68. Humanistic theorists have been criticized for:
a. overestimating the impact of childhood experiences on adult personality.
b. underestimating the inconsistency of behavior from one situation to another.
c. overestimating the degree of similarity among people.
d. underestimating the inherent human capacity for destructive and evil behaviors.

The trait perspective, p. 591
Medium, Conceptual, Objective 9, Ans: c

69. Freud is to the psychoanalytic perspective as Allport is to the ________ perspective.
a. behavioral
b. humanistic
c. trait
d. social-cognitive

The trait perspective, p. 591
Easy, Factual/Definitional, Objective 9, Ans: d

70. Characteristic patterns of behavior and motivation are called:
a. aptitudes.
b. fixations.
c. projections.
d. traits.

The trait perspective, p. 591
Medium, Factual/Definitional, Objective 9, Ans: b

71. Trait theorists are more concerned with ________ personality than ________ it.
    a. predicting; assessing
    b. describing; explaining
    c. changing; analyzing
    d. interpreting; observing

The trait perspective, p. 591
Difficult, Conceptual/Application, Objective 9, Ans: a

72. Santa Claus is to Superman as ________ is to ________.
    a. endomorph; mesomorph
    b. pleasure principle; reality principle
    c. anal fixation; oral fixation
    d. internal locus of control; external locus of control
    e. regression; projection

The trait perspective, pp. 591-592
Difficult, Factual/Definitional, Objective 9, Ans: b

73. The Myers-Briggs Type Indicator classifies people according to personality types identified by:
    a. Gordon Allport.
    b. Carl Jung.
    c. Albert Bandura.
    d. Carl Rogers.
    e. Abraham Maslow.

Exploring traits, p. 592
Easy, Factual/Definitional, Objective 9, Ans: c

74. Factor analysis has been used to identify the most basic:
    a. self-serving biases.
    b. defense mechanisms.
    c. personality traits.
    d. psychosexual stages.

Exploring traits, p. 592
Difficult, Conceptual/Application, Objective 9, Ans: a

75. Coretta is quiet, pessimistic, anxious, and moody. In terms of the Eysencks' basic personality dimensions she would be classified as:
    a. unstable-introverted.
    b. internal-impulsive.
    c. manic-depressive.
    d. external-dependent.
    e. passive-aggressive.

Assessing traits, p. 593
Medium, Factual/Definitional, Objective 10, Ans: e

76. A personality inventory that utilizes only those items that have been shown to differentiate particular groups of people is called a(n) ________ test.
   a. factor analytic
   b. multiphasic
   c. aptitude
   d. projective
   e. empirically derived

Assessing traits, p. 593
Difficult, Factual/Definitional, Objective 10, Ans: c

77. Which of the following tests was empirically derived?
   a. TAT
   b. Rorschach inkblot test
   c. MMPI
   d. Myers-Briggs Type Indicator

Assessing traits, p. 593
Medium, Conceptual/Application, Objective 10, Ans: a

78. Dr. Zytowics wants to assess the extent to which a client is suffering from depression, delusions, and other symptoms of psychological disorder. Which personality inventory would be most helpful for this purpose?
   a. MMPI
   b. Rorschach
   c. TAT
   d. Myers-Briggs Type Indicator

Assessing traits, pp. 593-594
Medium, Factual/Definitional, Objective 10, Ans: d

79. Personality inventories typically gather information by means of:
   a. projection.
   b. factor analysis.
   c. free association.
   d. self-reports.
   e. random selection.

The Big Five factors, p. 595
Medium, Conceptual, Objective 10, Ans: d

80. The Big Five trait dimensions were identified by means of:
   a. the MMPI.
   b. free association.
   c. projective tests.
   d. factor analysis.

The Big Five factors, p. 595
Easy, Factual/Definitional, Objective 10, Ans: e

81. A person who is careless and disorganized most clearly ranks low on the Big Five trait dimension known as:
    a. emotional stability.
    b. extraversion.
    c. openness.
    d. agreeableness.
    e. conscientiousness.

The Big Five factors, p. 595
Medium, Conceptual, Objective 10, Ans: b

82. Which of the following Big Five trait dimensions is most closely related to one's level of creativity?
    a. extraversion
    b. openness
    c. emotional stability
    d. agreeableness

The Big Five factors, p. 595
Difficult, Conceptual/Application, Objective 10, Ans: a

83. Morning types are to evening types as ________ is to ________.
    a. conscientiousness; extraversion
    b. agreeableness; openness
    c. extraversion; conscientiousness
    d. openness; agreeableness

How to be a "successful" astrologer or palm reader (Box), p. 597
Easy, Factual/Definitional, Objective 10, Ans: b

84. The tendency to accept favorable descriptions of one's personality that could really be applied to almost anyone is known as:
    a. the halo effect.
    b. the Barnum effect.
    c. projection.
    d. factor analysis.
    e. unconditional positive regard.

How to be a "successful" astrologer or palm reader (Box), p. 597
Medium, Conceptual/Application, Objective 10, Ans: b

85. Frida was informed by a professional palm reader: "You generally communicate openly with others, but you have certain dark secrets that even your closest friends could never guess." The fact that Frida was impressed by the palm reader's insight into her personality best illustrates:
    a. unconditional positive regard.
    b. the Barnum effect.
    c. the Electra complex.
    d. reciprocal determinism.
    e. attributional style.

Evaluating the trait perspective, p. 598
Easy, Factual/Definitional, Objective 11, Ans: d

86. Which theorists have been most directly criticized for underestimating the variability of behavior from situation to situation?
a. social-cognitive
b. psychoanalytic
c. humanistic
d. trait

Evaluating the trait perspective, p. 598
Medium, Factual/Definitional, Objective 11 , Ans: c

87. Walter Mischel's studies of college students' conscientiousness revealed only a modest relationship between a student being conscientious on one occasion and being similarly conscientious on another occasion. According to Mischel, this should make psychologists more cautious about emphasizing:
a. repression.
b. self-efficacy.
c. personality traits.
d. reciprocal determinism.
e. unconditional positive regard.

Evaluating the trait perspective, p. 598
Difficult, Conceptual/Application, Objective 11, Ans: a

88. Sheen is usually animated and talkative when he is with his girlfriend, but he is often quiet and reserved at home. He actively participates in many classroom discussions but frequently seems reluctant to talk with friends at the campus coffee shop. According to Walter Mischel, Sheen's behavior should lead us to question the importance of:
a. personality traits.
b. unconditional positive regard.
c. reciprocal determinism.
d. defense mechanisms.
e. self-efficacy.

Evaluating the trait perspective, pp. 598-599
Difficult, Factual/Definitional, Objective 11, Ans: a

89. In rejecting claims that personality trait measures fail to predict behavior effectively, Seymour Epstein emphasized the importance of:
a. multiple behavior assessments.
b. reciprocal determinism.
c. factor analysis.
d. projective tests.

Evaluating the trait perspective, pp. 598-599
Difficult, Conceptual/Application, Objective 11, Ans: d

90. People's scores on a test of extraversion are likely to be most strongly correlated with the number of social conversations they initiate during the course of a single:
a. hour.
b. day.
c. week.
d. month.

Evaluating the trait perspective, p. 599
Difficult, Conceptual, Objective 11, Ans: c

91. An individual's responses to a personality inventory would be most useful for accurately predicting that person's behavior ________ that involve(s) highly ________ social expectations or roles.
a. in a single situation; ambiguous
b. in a single situation; unambiguous
c. across a wide variety of situations; ambiguous
d. across a wide variety of situations; unambiguous

The social-cognitive perspective, pp. 587, 600
Easy, Conceptual, Objective 12, Ans: d

92. The humanistic perspective is to Maslow as the social-cognitive perspective is to:
a. Allport.
b. Rogers.
c. Adler.
d. Bandura.
e. Jung.

Reciprocal influences, p. 600
Medium, Factual/Definitional, Objective 12, Ans: c

93. According to Bandura, reciprocal determinism involves multidirectional influences among:
a. mind, body, and behavior.
b. thoughts, emotions, and actions.
c. behaviors, internal personal factors, and environmental events.
d. id, ego, and superego.
e. learned helplessness, locus of control, and optimism.

Reciprocal influences, p. 600
Easy, Conceptual/Application, Objective 12, Ans: d

94. Randy's substandard academic performance is both a result and a cause of his feelings of academic inferiority. This best illustrates the importance of:
a. self-serving bias.
b. an internal locus of control.
c. the Barnum effect.
d. reciprocal determinism.
e. reaction formation.

Reciprocal influences, pp. 600-601
Medium, Conceptual/Application, Objective 12, Ans: e

95. Because Mr. Maloney trusts his employees, he treats them very kindly. His kindness leads them to work diligently on his behalf, which in turn increases his trust in them. This pattern of trust, kindness, diligence, and increasing trust illustrates what is meant by:
a. reaction formation.
b. the spotlight effect.
c. displacement.
d. external locus of control.
e. reciprocal determinism.

Reciprocal influences, pp. 600-601
Difficult, Conceptual/Application, Objective 12, Ans: b

96. Because Greta is extremely extraverted, she frequently goes to parties where she is encouraged to laugh and socialize. Because Jim is extremely introverted, he frequently spends weekends in the library where it's easy to quietly reflect and study. Greta and Jim best illustrate what is meant by:
a. an external locus of control.
b. reciprocal determinism.
c. the self-serving bias.
d. the Barnum effect.
e. reaction formation.

Locus of control, p. 602
Easy, Factual/Definitional, Objective 12, Ans: c

97. The perception that one's fate is determined by luck reflects:
a. reciprocal determinism.
b. self-serving bias.
c. an external locus of control.
d. the pleasure principle.
e. the spotlight effect.

Locus of control, p. 602
Medium, Conceptual/Application, Objective 12, Ans: c

98. Sasha believes that the questions on college tests are so unrelated to course work that studying is useless. Sasha's belief most clearly illustrates:
a. reciprocal determinism.
b. reaction formation.
c. an external locus of control.
d. the Barnum effect.
e. displacement.

Locus of control, p. 602
Difficult, Conceptual/Application, Objective 12, Ans: d

99. Laura fails to recognize any connection between her unsafe sexual practices and the likelihood of contracting a sexually transmitted disease. Laura's lack of perceptiveness best illustrates the dangers of:
a. free association.
b. an Electra complex.
c. the spotlight effect.
d. an external locus of control.
e. unconditional positive regard.

Locus of control, p. 602
Medium, Conceptual/Application, Objective 12, Ans: e

100. Emma believes that she will be highly successful in business if she works hard and carefully manages her time. Her belief most clearly illustrates:
a. reaction formation.
b. reciprocal determinism.
c. unconditional positive regard.
d. an Electra complex.
e. an internal locus of control.

Locus of control, p. 602
Easy, Conceptual, Objective 12, Ans: d

101. Compared to those with an external locus of control, people who perceive an internal locus of control are more likely to:
a. be introverted personalities.
b. give others unconditional positive regard.
c. conform to social pressure.
d. cope effectively with stress.

Locus of control, p. 602
Difficult, Conceptual, Objective 12, Ans: d

102. An individual who perceives an internal locus of control would most likely show signs of a:
a. weak id.
b. strong id.
c. weak ego.
d. strong ego.
e. weak superego.

Learned helplessness versus personal control, p. 602
Medium, Factual/Definitional, Objective 12, Ans: c

103. Learned helplessness is most likely to contribute to:
a. collectivism.
b. a self-serving bias.
c. an external locus of control.
d. unconditional positive regard.
e. an Oedipus complex.

Learned helplessness versus personal control, p. 602
Easy, Factual/Definitional, Objective 12, Ans: c

104. Dogs strapped into a harness and given repeated and unavoidable shocks developed:
a. a fixation.
b. a reaction formation.
c. learned helplessness.
d. a higher threshold of pain.
e. unrealistic optimism.

Learned helplessness versus personal control, p. 602
Medium, Conceptual/Application, Objective 12, Ans: c

105. After experiencing inescapable brutalities as a prisoner in a Nazi concentration camp, Mr. Sternberg became apathetic, stopped eating, and gave up all efforts to physically survive the ordeal. Mr. Sternberg's reaction most clearly illustrates:
a. an inferiority complex.
b. repression.
c. learned helplessness.
d. an internal locus of control.
e. reaction formation.

Optimism, p. 603
Medium, Conceptual, Objective 12, Ans: e

106. Learned helplessness is most likely to promote:
   a. collectivism.
   b. unconditional positive regard.
   c. an internal locus of control.
   d. the spotlight effect.
   e. pessimism.

Optimism, p. 603
Easy, Factual/Definitional, Objective 12, Ans: d

107. The best indicator of a person's level of optimism is his or her:
   a. individualism.
   b. ideal self.
   c. gender identity.
   d. attributional style.
   e. unconditional positive regard.

Optimism, p. 603
Medium, Factual/Definitional, Objective 12, Ans: d

108. Researchers found that new life insurance representatives were less likely to quit during their first year on the job if they demonstrated the trait of:
   a. agreeableness.
   b. openness.
   c. extraversion.
   d. optimism.

Toward a more positive psychology (Close-up), p. 604
Medium, Factual/Definitional, Objective 12, Ans: c

109. Martin Seligman's positive psychology differs from the humanistic perspective in that it:
   a. denies humankind's capacity for evil.
   b. focuses more on a person's interaction with the environment.
   c. involves the scientific study of optimal human functioning.
   d. has greater application in the educational setting.

Optimism, pp. 604, 609
Difficult, Conceptual, Objective 12, Ans: b

110. Unrealistic optimism could best be described as a(n):
   a. Electra complex.
   b. self-serving bias.
   c. reaction formation.
   d. fixation.
   e. external locus of control.

Optimism, p. 605
Easy, Factual/Definitional, Objective 12, Ans: e

111. Sexually active undergraduate women perceive themselves as much less likely to experience an unwanted pregnancy than other women at their university. This best illustrates:
a. an Electra complex.
b. low self-esteem.
c. displacement.
d. the spotlight effect.
e. unrealistic optimism.

Assessing behavior in situations, p. 606
Medium, Conceptual/Application, Objective 13, Ans: d

112. The social-cognitive perspective suggests that the best way to predict a political candidate's performance effectiveness after election is to assess that individual's:
a. current feelings of personal control.
b. specific political goals for the future.
c. general feelings of optimism about the future.
d. past performance in situations involving similar responsibilities.
e. personality traits as revealed by the MMPI-2.

Evaluating the social-cognitive perspective, p. 606
Medium, Factual/Definitional, Objective 13, Ans: a

113. The social-cognitive perspective is least likely to be criticized for neglecting the importance of:
a. environmental influences.
b. unconscious motives.
c. personality traits.
d. genetic influences.

Exploring the self, p. 607
Medium, Conceptual/Application, Objective 14, Ans: d

114. Larry studies diligently because he is haunted by an image of himself being unable to gain employment after his college graduation. Larry's diligence best illustrates the motivational impact of:
a. an internal locus of control.
b. unconditioned positive regard.
c. learned helplessness.
d. possible selves.
e. the spotlight effect.

Exploring the self, p. 608
Easy, Factual/Definitional, Objective 14, Ans: d

115. Overestimating the extent to which others notice and evaluate our appearance and performance is called:
a. external locus of control.
b. self-serving bias.
c. reaction formation.
d. the spotlight effect.
e. fixation.

Exploring the self, p. 608
Easy, Factual/Definitional, Objective 14, Ans: c

116. If we are nervous about our personal appearance after adopting a new hairstyle, we are likely to ________ the extent to which others notice our nervousness and we are likely to ________ the extent to which they notice our new hairstyle.
a. overestimate; underestimate
b. underestimate; overestimate
c. overestimate; overestimate
d. underestimate; underestimate

The benefits of self-esteem, p. 608
Difficult, Conceptual, Objective 14, Ans: a

117. Individuals with high self-esteem are more likely than those with low self-esteem to:
a. have a strong ego.
b. experience an external locus of control.
c. dismiss flattering descriptions of themselves as untrue.
d. underestimate the accuracy of their own beliefs.
e. associate with people whose attitudes and personality are very similar to their own.

The benefits of self-esteem, p. 608
Medium, Factual/Definitional, Objective 14, Ans: c

118. Self-esteem is negatively correlated with:
a. personal control.
b. self-serving bias.
c. depression.
d. individualism.
e. extraversion.

The benefits of self-esteem, p. 609
Medium, Factual/Definitional, Objective 14, Ans: b

119. A person whose self-esteem is momentarily threatened is especially likely to:
a. demonstrate an independence from social pressure to conform.
b. criticize the shortcomings of others.
c. lack a clear sense of gender identity.
d. experience an internal locus of control.
e. be motivated by a desire for self-actualization.

Culture and self-esteem, p. 609
Medium, Factual/Definitional, Objective 14, Ans: c

120. People who are challenged by severe physical disabilities are likely to maintain normal levels of self-esteem by:
a. displacing their feelings of resentment.
b. developing an external locus of control.
c. comparing themselves with others who are similarly disabled.
d. accepting more personal responsibility for their problems than for their accomplishments.

Self-serving bias, p. 609
Easy, Factual/Definitional, Objective 14, Ans: d

121. Athletes often attribute their losses to bad officiating. This best illustrates:
    a. an Electra complex.
    b. learned helplessness.
    c. the spotlight effect.
    d. self-serving bias.
    e. the Barnum effect.

Self-serving bias, p. 610
Medium, Factual/Definitional, Objective 14, Ans: c

122. Research on self-perception indicates that most people:
    a. suffer extensively from feelings of unrealistically low self-esteem.
    b. feel more personally responsible for their failures than for their successes.
    c. view themselves very favorably in comparison to most others.
    d. underestimate the accuracy of their beliefs and judgments.
    e. are unrealistically pessimistic about their personal future.

Self-serving bias, p. 610
Medium, Conceptual/Application, Objective 14, Ans: d

123. Jacinda failed her last history midterm. Which of the following conclusions would be most representative of a self-serving bias on Jacinda's part?
    a. "I really didn't prepare well enough for that test."
    b. "I wasn't concentrating very hard during the test."
    c. "I lack ability in history."
    d. "I think the test questions were ambiguous and confusing."

Self-serving bias, p. 610
Easy, Factual/Definitional, Objective 14, Ans: e

124. In one survey, Americans were more optimistic that they themselves would go to heaven than would either Michael Jordan or Bill Clinton. This best illustrates:
    a. an internal locus of control.
    b. the Barnum effect.
    c. an Electra complex.
    d. the spotlight effect.
    e. self-serving bias.

Self-serving bias, p. 610
Medium, Conceptual/Application, Objective 14, Ans: e

125. Although Rolf frequently cheats on classroom tests, he justifies his behavior by erroneously thinking that most other students cheat even more than he does. His mistaken belief best illustrates:
    a. reciprocal determinism.
    b. the Barnum effect.
    c. reaction formation.
    d. an external locus of control.
    e. self-serving bias.

Self-serving bias, p. 610
Medium, Factual/Definitional, Objective 14, Ans: c

126. Which of the following is most likely to contribute to raising one's self-esteem?
    a. the spotlight effect
    b. an Electra complex
    c. self-serving bias
    d. an external locus of control
    e. the Barnum effect

Culture and the self, pp. 611-612
Easy, Conceptual, Objective 15, Ans: a

127. A collectivist culture is especially likely to emphasize the importance of:
    a. social responsibility.
    b. personal control.
    c. self-actualization.
    d. racial diversity.
    e. free association.

Culture and the self, p. 612
Medium, Conceptual/Application, Objective 15, Ans: a

128. Professor Shankar believes that her students' most important personal characteristics are those that distinguish them as uniquely different from most other people. Her attitude best illustrates one of the consequences of:
    a. individualism.
    b. self-serving bias.
    c. reciprocal determinism.
    d. reaction formation.
    e. the spotlight effect.

Culture and the self, p. 612
Easy, Factual/Definitional, Objective 15, Ans: d

129. Individualism is most likely to be emphasized in:
    a. Africa.
    b. Asia.
    c. India.
    d. North America.

Culture and the self, p. 612
Difficult, Conceptual, Objective 15, Ans: a

130. American university students are more likely than Japanese university students to describe themselves in terms of their:
    a. academic abilities.
    b. university affiliation.
    c. ethnic background.
    d. marital status.
    e. gender.

Culture and the self, p. 612
Medium, Factual/Definitional, Objective 15, Ans: b

131. Japanese students are more likely than American students to describe themselves in terms of their:
a. physical appearance.
b. social identities.
c. political ideology.
d. personality traits.

Culture and the self, pp. 612-613
Medium, Factual/Definitional, Objective 15, Ans: e

132. A willingness to switch jobs and move from one part of the country to another best illustrates one of the consequences of:
a. reciprocal determinism.
b. collectivism.
c. free association.
d. learned helplessness.
e. individualism.

Culture and the self, pp. 612-613
Difficult, Conceptual/Application, Objective 15, Ans: e

133. When Professor Thompson lived overseas for a year, he was very surprised at how much respect he received from people simply because he was a retired college professor. His sense of surprise suggests that he had not previously lived in a culture that valued:
a. social diversity.
b. self-actualization.
c. reciprocal determinism.
d. individualism.
e. collectivism.

Culture and the self, pp. 612-613
Medium, Conceptual, Objective 15, Ans: c

134. Individualism is to collectivism as ________ is to ________.
a. personal control; learned helplessness
b. displacement; sublimation
c. independence; interdependence
d. responsibility; freedom
e. pleasure principle; reality principle

Culture and the self, p. 613
Medium, Factual/Definitional, Objective 15, Ans: d

135. The importance of romance in marriage relationships is most likely to be emphasized in cultures that value:
a. role playing.
b. collectivism.
c. reciprocal determinism.
d. individualism.
e. gender stereotypes.

Culture and the self, p. 613
Medium, Factual/Definitional, Objective 15, Ans: e

136. People living in a culture that promotes individualism are more likely than those in collectivist cultures to experience:
   a. divorce.
   b. loneliness.
   c. homicide.
   d. stress-related diseases.
   e. any of the above.

Culture and the self, p. 613
Difficult, Conceptual, Objective 15, Ans: b

137. Religious and ethnic diversity are most likely to be appreciated in a culture that values:
   a. cooperation.
   b. individualism.
   c. reciprocal determinism.
   d. collectivism.
   e. nationalism.

Culture and the self, p. 613
Medium, Conceptual, Objective 15, Ans: b

138. Parents in collectivist cultures are more likely than parents in individualist cultures to encourage teenage children to:
   a. pick out and purchase their own clothes.
   b. participate in household chores.
   c. publicly protest against repressive government policies.
   d. establish close friendships with ethnically diverse groups of people.

The modern unconscious mind, p. 615
Medium, Conceptual, Objective 16, Ans: b

139. Compared with Freud, contemporary research psychologists are less likely to think of unconscious mental dynamics as involving:
   a. parallel processing.
   b. motivational conflict.
   c. implicit memory.
   d. right hemisphere activity.

The modern unconscious mind, p. 615
Easy, Factual/Definitional, Objective 16, Ans: a

140. According to terror-management theory, anxiety about our own mortality motivates our pursuit of:
   a. self-esteem.
   b. parallel processing.
   c. reciprocal determinism.
   d. the collective unconscious.
   e. an external locus of control.

Essay Questions

1. During a heated argument with his father, 15-year-old Jason developed a paralysis of his right arm. Medical examinations can find no physical cause for the paralysis. Use the psychoanalytic perspective to explain how the paralysis may be Jason's attempt to deal with an unconscious conflict between his id and superego.

2. According to a number of distinguished psychologists, a major purpose of the defense mechanisms described by Freud is the protection of self-esteem. Give an example of how repression, reaction formation, projection, rationalization, and displacement could each be used to protect or even enhance a positive self-image.

3. The behavioral psychologist B. F. Skinner emphasized that people are largely controlled by forces outside themselves. Critique the practical implications of personally accepting Skinner's position in light of contemporary research on locus of control and learned helplessness.

4. Andy, a high school sophomore, lacks self-discipline, fails to plan ahead, and is excessively anxious. He is quickly frustrated by challenging tasks and frequently becomes overly critical of others. Use the psychoanalytic, humanistic, and social-cognitive perspectives to give three contrasting explanations of Andy's behavior.

5. Carl Rogers believes that most people consider themselves worthless and unlovable. Reinhold Niebuhr, on the other hand, claims that most people suffer from excessive self-love and self-pride. What do you consider to be the strengths or weaknesses of each of these contrasting positions? Use psychological research findings to support your arguments.

6. Explain how differences between individualist and collectivist views of self contribute to differences in marital expectations and political views. How do pro-choice and pro-life positions regarding the issue of abortion differ with respect to the ideals of individualism and collectivism?

Web Quiz 1

Ans: c

1. The role of repressed childhood conflicts in personality disorders is most clearly emphasized by the ________ perspective.
   a. trait
   b. social-cognitive
   c. psychoanalytic
   d. humanistic

Ans: d

2. Jaydon lacks any recognition that his alcohol abuse and neglect of his family is leading to the destruction of both family and career. A psychoanalyst would suggest that Jaydon shows signs of a:
   a. strong ego.
   b. weak id.
   c. strong superego.
   d. weak ego.

Ans: b

3. Freud suggested that adults with a passive and submissive personality marked by a childlike dependency demonstrate signs of:
   a. projection.
   b. an oral fixation.
   c. an inferiority complex.
   d. reaction formation.
   e. an Oedipus complex.

Ans: e

4. Bryce often acts so daring and overly confident that few people realize he is actually riddled with unconscious insecurity and self-doubt. Bryce best illustrates the use of a defense mechanism known as:
   a. regression.
   b. projection.
   c. displacement.
   d. rationalization.
   e. reaction formation.

Ans: e

5. In 1921, Hermann Rorschach introduced what has become the most widely used ________ test.
   a. multiple personality
   b. empirically derived
   c. thematic apperception
   d. factor analytic
   e. projective

Ans: d

6. Abraham Maslow suggested that individuals who are open, spontaneous, and not paralyzed by others' opinions illustrate:
   a. reciprocal determinism.
   b. extraverion.
   c. reaction formation.
   d. self-actualization.
   e. an external locus of control.

Ans: d

7. Humanistic psychology has been most closely associated with an emphasis on the importance of:
   a. free association.
   b. empirically derived tests.
   c. reciprocal determinism.
   d. a positive self-concept.
   e. an external locus of control.

Ans: b

8. Which personality test classifies people in terms of the personality dimensions highlighted by Carl Jung?
   a. Thematic Apperception Test
   b. Myers-Briggs Type Indicator
   c. Rorschach inkblot test
   d. Minnesota Multiphasic Personality Inventory

Ans: d

9. One of the Big Five personality factors is:
   a. reciprocal determinism.
   b. self-actualization.
   c. individualism.
   d. agreeableness.
   e. psychoanalysis.

Ans: d

10. During a phone call to the Psychic Network, Mark was told that "you often worry about things much more than you admit, even to your best friends." Mark's amazement at the psychic's apparent understanding of his personality best illustrates:
    a. an internal locus of control.
    b. reaction formation.
    c. reciprocal determinism.
    d. the Barnum effect.
    e. unconditional positive regard.

Ans: b

11. Sarah's optimism is both a contributor to and a product of her successful career accomplishments. This best illustrates:
   a. the Barnum effect.
   b. reciprocal determinism.
   c. unconditional positive regard.
   d. self-actualization.
   e. the spotlight effect.

Ans: e

12. Marcy believes that the outcome of athletic contests depends so much on luck that it hardly pays to put any effort into her own athletic training. Her belief most clearly illustrates:
   a. an Electra complex.
   b. the spotlight effect.
   c. the Barnum effect.
   d. self-serving bias.
   e. an external locus of control.

Ans: d

13. Although she is intelligent and a good athlete, Abigail believes that her low grades in school and losing the quarter-mile racing record are reflections of her own intellectual and athletic incompetence. Her conclusions best illustrate a pessimistic:
   a. projection.
   b. ideal self.
   c. reaction formation.
   d. attributional style.
   e. Electra complex.

Ans: a

14. When Vanessa noticed that she was wearing mismatched socks, she overestimated the extent to which others would also notice. Her reaction best illustrates:
   a. the spotlight effect.
   b. an Electra complex.
   c. reciprocal determinism.
   d. the Barnum effect.
   e. an inferiority complex.

Ans: c

15. Displays of self-effacing humility are most characteristic of those who value:
   a. an internal locus of control.
   b. free association.
   c. collectivism.
   d. self-actualization.
   e. reciprocal determinism.

Web Quiz 2

Ans: b

1. Sigmund Freud emphasized the importance of:
   a. unconditional positive regard.
   b. dream interpretation.
   c. an external locus of control.
   d. factor analysis.
   e. reciprocal determinism.

Ans: d

2. Although Alex has frequently been caught stealing money and other valuables from friends as well as strangers, he does not feel guilty or remorseful about robbing these people. Alex most clearly demonstrates:
   a. an inferiority complex.
   b. an external locus of control.
   c. an Electra complex.
   d. a weak superego.
   e. an oral fixation.

Ans: b

3. According to Freud, fixation refers to a difficulty in the process of:
   a. free association.
   b. psychosexual development.
   c. projective testing.
   d. rationalization.
   e. hypnosis.

Ans: d

4. Bonnie is afraid to express anger at her overbearing and irritating supervisor at work, so she is critical of her children instead. A psychoanalyst would suggest that Bonnie's reaction to her children illustrates:
   a. repression.
   b. identification.
   c. reaction formation.
   d. displacement.
   e. projection.

Ans: e

5. Children who have witnessed a parent's murder report memories that most clearly challenge Freud's concept of:
   a. rationalization.
   b. the Oedipus complex.
   c. reaction formation.
   d. displacement.
   e. repression.

Ans: d

6. According to Abraham Maslow, people are highly motivated to achieve self-actualization ________ they become concerned with their personal safety and ________ they become concerned with achieving self-esteem.
   a. before; after
   b. after; before
   c. before: before
   d. after; after

Ans: d

7 Who emphasized the importance of unconditional positive regard in healthy personality development?
   a. Freud
   b. Allport
   c. Bandura
   d. Rogers
   e. Adler

Ans: b

8. Ectomorph is to endomorph as ________ is to ________.
   a. id; superego
   b. thin; plump
   c. extraversion; introversion
   d. oral stage; phallic stage
   e. external locus of control; internal locus of control

Ans: b

9. A "lie scale" that assesses the extent to which a person is faking to make a good impression is included in the:
   a. TAT.
   b. MMPI.
   c. Rorschach inkblot test.
   d. Myers-Briggs Type Indicator.

Ans: d

10. The temporal stability of personality during adulthood best illustrates the value of the ________ perspective.
   a. humanistic
   b. psychoanalytic
   c. social-cognitive
   d. trait

Ans: d

11. Albert Bandura's social-cognitive perspective highlights the importance of:
   a. the collective unconscious.
   b. free association.
   c. projective tests.
   d. reciprocal determinism.
   e. factor analysis.

Ans: d

12. After experiencing prolonged and seemingly inescapable physical abuse from her husband, Kayla became increasingly depressed and hopelessly resigned to her suffering. Her reaction best illustrates:
    a. a reaction formation.
    b. an Electra complex.
    c. unconditional positive regard.
    d. learned helplessness.
    e. an inferiority complex.

Ans: e

13. Most college students perceive themselves as less likely than their average classmate to develop drinking problems or drop out of school. This best illustrates:
    a. the Barnum effect.
    b. unconditional positive regard.
    c. the spotlight effect.
    d. the false consensus effect.
    e. unrealistic optimism.

Ans: e

14. Card players who attribute their wins to their own skill and their losses to bad luck best illustrate:
    a. the Barnum effect.
    b. an Electra complex.
    c. reciprocal determinism.
    d. the spotlight effect.
    e. self-serving bias.

Ans: e

15. Defining one's identity in terms of one's extended family or work group is most closely associated with:
    a. unconditional positive regard.
    b. an external locus of control.
    c. an inferiority complex.
    d. self-actualization.
    e. collectivism.

Study Guide Questions

Ans: c, pp. 497-587, 613

1. Which of the following was *not* mentioned in the text as a criticism of Freud's theory?
   a. The theory is sexist.
   b. It offers few testable hypotheses.
   c. There is no evidence of anything like an "unconscious."
   d. The theory ignores the fact that human development is lifelong.

Ans: b, p. 575

2. The text defines *personality* as:
   a. the set of personal attitudes that characterizes a person.
   b. an individual's characteristic pattern of thinking, feeling, and acting.
   c. a predictable set of responses to environmental stimuli.
   d. an unpredictable set of responses to environmental stimuli.

Ans: d, p. 576

3. Which of the following places the greatest emphasis on the unconscious mind?
   a. the humanistic perspective
   b. the social-cognitive perspective
   c. the trait perspective
   d. the psychoanalytic perspective

Ans: d, pp. 576, 578, 591

4. A major difference between the psychoanalytic and trait perspectives is that:
   a. trait theory defines personality in terms of behavior; psychoanalytic theory, in terms of its underlying dynamics.
   b. trait theory describes behavior but does not attempt to explain it.
   c. psychoanalytic theory emphasizes the origins of personality in childhood sexuality.
   d. all of the above are differences.

Ans: d, p. 577

5. According to Freud's theory, personality arises in response to conflicts between:
   a. our unacceptable urges and our tendency to become self-actualized.
   b. the process of identification and the ego's defense mechanisms.
   c. the collective unconscious and our individual desires.
   d. our biological impulses and the social restraints against them.

Ans: a, p. 577

6. According to the psychoanalytic perspective, a child who frequently "slips" and calls her teacher "mom" *probably*:
   a. has some unresolved conflicts concerning her mother.
   b. is fixated in the oral stage of development.
   c. did not receive unconditional positive regard from her mother.
   d. can be classified as having a weak sense of personal control.

Ans: b, pp. 577-578

7. Id is to ego as ________ is to ________.
   a. reality principle; pleasure principle
   b. pleasure principle; reality principle
   c. conscious forces; unconscious forces
   d. conscience; “personality executive”

Ans: d, p. 578

8. A psychoanalyst would characterize a person who is impulsive and self-indulgent as possessing a strong ________ and a weak ________.
   a. id and ego; superego
   b. id; ego and superego
   c. ego; superego
   d. id; superego
   e. superego; ego

Ans: a, pp. 578-579

9. Which of the following is the correct order of psychosexual stages proposed by Freud?
   a. oral; anal; phallic; latency; genital
   b. anal; oral; phallic; latency; genital
   c. oral; anal; genital; latency; phallic
   d. anal; oral; genital; latency; phallic
   e. oral; phallic; anal; genital; latency

Ans: c, p. 579

10. According to Freud, ________ is the process by which children incorporate their parents’ values into their ________.
   a. reaction formation; superegos
   b. reaction formation; egos
   c. identification; superegos
   d. identification; egos

Ans: b, p. 579

11. Jill has a biting, sarcastic manner. According to Freud, she is:
   a. projecting her anxiety onto others.
   b. fixated in the oral stage of development.
   c. fixated in the anal stage of development.
   d. displacing her anxiety onto others.

Ans: d, p. 579

12. The Oedipus and Electra complexes have their roots in the:
   a. anal stage.
   b. oral stage.
   c. latency stage.
   d. phallic stage.
   e. genital stage.

Ans: c, p. 580

13. Suzy bought a used, high-mileage automobile because it was all she could afford. Attempting to justify her purchase, she raves to her friends about the car's attractiveness, good acceleration, and stereo. According to Freud, Suzy is using the defense mechanism of:
    a. displacement.
    b. reaction formation.
    c. rationalization.
    d. projection.

Ans: c, p. 580

14. According to Freud, defense mechanisms are methods of reducing:
    a. anger.
    b. fear.
    c. anxiety.
    d. lust.

Ans: e, p. 581

15. The personality test Teresa is taking involves her describing random patterns of dots. What type of test is she taking?
    a. an empirically derived test
    b. the MMPI
    c. a personality inventory
    d. the Myers-Briggs Type Indicator
    e. a projective test

Ans: c, p. 582

16. Projective tests such as the Rorschach inkblot test have been criticized because:
    a. their scoring system is too rigid and leads to unfair labeling.
    b. they were standardized with unrepresentative samples.
    c. they have low reliability and low validity.
    d. it is easy for people to fake answers in order to appear healthy.

Ans: b, p. 582

17. Neo-Freudians such as Adler and Horney believed that:
    a. Freud placed too great an emphasis on the conscious mind.
    b. Freud placed too great an emphasis on sexual and aggressive instincts.
    c. the years of childhood were more important in the formation of personality than Freud had indicated.
    d. Freud's ideas about the id, ego, and superego as personality structures were incorrect.

Ans: a, p. 584

18. Which of Freud's ideas would *not* be accepted by most contemporary psychologists?
    a. Development is essentially fixed in childhood.
    b. Sexuality is a potent drive in humans.
    c. The mind is an iceberg with consciousness being only the tip.
    d. Repression can be the cause of forgetting.

Ans: b, p. 587

19. The humanistic perspective on personality:
   a. emphasizes the driving force of unconscious motivations in personality.
   b. emphasizes the growth potential of "healthy" individuals.
   c. emphasizes the importance of interaction with the environment in shaping personality.
   d. describes personality in terms of scores on various personality scales.

Ans: d, p. 587

20. Andrew's grandfather, who has lived a rich and productive life, is a spontaneous, loving, and self-accepting person. Maslow might say that he:
   a. has an internal locus of control.
   b. is an extravert.
   c. has resolved all the conflicts of the psychosexual stages.
   d. is a self-actualizing person.

Ans: d, pp. 587-588

21. In promoting personality growth, the person-centered perspective emphasizes all but:
   a. empathy.
   b. acceptance.
   c. genuineness.
   d. altruism.

Ans: e, pp. 587-588

22. According to Rogers, three conditions are necessary to promote growth in personality. These are:
   a. honesty, sincerity, and empathy.
   b. high self-esteem, honesty, and empathy.
   c. high self-esteem, genuineness, and acceptance.
   d. high self-esteem, acceptance, and honesty.
   e. genuineness, acceptance, and empathy.

Ans: c, p. 588

23. The school psychologist believes that having a positive self-concept is necessary before students can achieve their potential. Evidently, the school psychologist is working within the ________ perspective.
   a. psychoanalytic
   b. trait
   c. humanistic
   d. social-cognitive

Ans: a, p. 588

24. Wanda wishes to instill in her children an accepting attitude toward other people. Maslow and Rogers would probably recommend that she:
   a. teach her children first to accept themselves.
   b. use discipline sparingly.
   c. be affectionate with her children only when they behave as she wishes.
   d. do all of the above.

Ans: d, p. 588

25. For humanistic psychologists, many of our behaviors and perceptions are ultimately shaped by whether our ________ is ________ or ________.
    a. ego; strong; weak
    b. locus of control; internal; external
    c. personality structure; introverted; extraverted
    d. self-concept; positive; negative

Ans: d, pp. 588-589

26. Which of the following is a common criticism of the humanistic perspective?
    a. Its concepts are vague and subjective.
    b. The emphasis on the self encourages selfishness in individuals.
    c. Humanism fails to appreciate the reality of evil in human behavior.
    d. All of the above are common criticisms.

Ans: b, p. 591

27. Dr. Gonzalez believes that most students can be classified as "Type A" or "Type B" according to the intensities of their personalities and competitiveness. Evidently, Dr. Gonzalez is working within the ________ perspective.
    a. psychoanalytic
    b. trait
    c. humanistic
    d. social-cognitive

Ans: b, p. 591

28. Trait theory attempts to:
    a. show how development of personality is a lifelong process.
    b. describe and classify people in terms of their predispositions to behave in certain ways.
    c. determine which traits are most conducive to individual self-actualization.
    d. explain how behavior is shaped by the interaction between traits, behavior, and the environment.

Ans: b, p. 591

29. Bill is muscular and physically strong. Sheldon would classify him as a(n):
    a. endomorphic type.
    b. mesomorphic type.
    c. ectomorphic type.
    d. dysmorphic type.

Ans: a, pp. 591-592

30. The ________ classifies people according to Carl Jung's personality types.
    a. Myers-Briggs Type Indicator
    b. MMPI
    c. Locus of Control Scale
    d. Kagan Temperament Scale
    e. TAT

Ans: d, p. 592

31. Isaiah is sober and reserved; Rashid is fun-loving and affectionate. The Eysencks would say that Isaiah ________ and Rashid ________.
    a. has an internal locus of control; has an external locus of control
    b. has an external locus of control; has an internal locus of control
    c. is an extravert; is an introvert
    d. is an introvert; is an extravert

Ans: a, p. 592

32. Which two dimensions of personality have the Eysencks emphasized?
    a. extraversion-introversion and emotional stability-instability
    b. internal-external locus of control and extraversion-introversion
    c. internal-external locus of control and emotional stability-instability
    d. melancholic-phlegmatic and choleric-sanguine

Ans: b, p. 592

33. Nadine has a relatively low level of brain arousal. Trait theorists would probably predict that she is:
    a. an extravert.
    b. an introvert.
    c. an unstable person.
    d. both a. and c.

Ans: c, p. 592

34. Because you have a relatively low level of brain arousal, a trait theorist would suggest that you are a(n) ________ who would naturally seek ________.
    a. introvert; stimulation
    b. introvert; isolation
    c. extravert; stimulation
    d. extravert; isolation

Ans: c, p. 593

35. In studying personality, a trait theorist would *most likely*:
    a. use a projective test.
    b. observe a person in a variety of situations.
    c. use a personality inventory.
    d. use the method of free association.

Ans: a, p. 593

36. A psychologist at the campus mental health center administered an empirically derived personality test to diagnose an emotionally troubled student. Which test did the psychologist *most likely* administer?
    a. the MMPI
    b. the TAT
    c. the Rorschach
    d. the Locus of Control Scale

Ans: b, p. 593

37. The Minnesota Multiphasic Personality Inventory (MMPI) is a(n):
   a. projective personality test.
   b. empirically derived and objective personality test.
   c. personality test developed mainly to assess job applicants.
   d. personality test used primarily to assess locus of control.

Ans: d, p. 595

38. The Big Five personality factors are:
   a. emotional stability, openness, introversion, sociability, locus of control.
   b. neuroticism, extraversion, openness, emotional stability, sensitivity.
   c. neuroticism, gregariousness, extraversion, impulsiveness, conscientiousness.
   d. emotional stability, extraversion, openness, agreeableness, conscientiousness.
   e. emotional stability, extraversion, openness, locus of control, sensitivity.

Ans: c, p. 595

39. For his class presentation, Bruce plans to discuss the Big Five personality factors used by people throughout the world to describe others or themselves. Which of the following is *not* a factor that Bruce will discuss?
   a. extraversion
   b. openness
   c. independence
   d. conscientiousness
   e. agreeableness

Ans: a, p. 595

40. Recent research on the Big Five personality factors provides evidence that:
   a. some tendencies decrease during adulthood, while others increase.
   b. these traits only describe personality in Western, individualist cultures.
   c. the heritability of individual differences in these traits generally runs about 25 percent or less.
   d. all of the above are true.

Ans: c, p. 598

41. Dayna is not very consistent in showing up for class and turning in assignments when they are due. Research studies would suggest that Dayna's inconsistent behavior:
   a. indicates that she is emotionally troubled and may need professional counseling.
   b. is a sign of learned helplessness.
   c. is not necessarily unusual.
   d. probably reflects a temporary problem in another area of her life.

Ans: b, p. 598

42. With regard to personality, it appears that:
   a. there is little consistency of behavior from one situation to the next and little consistency of traits over the life span.
   b. there is little consistency of behavior from one situation to the next but significant consistency of traits over the life span.
   c. there is significant consistency of behavior from one situation to the next but little consistency of traits over the life span.
   d. there is significant consistency of behavior from one situation to the next and significant consistency of traits over the life span.

Ans: b, pp. 598-599

43. A major criticism of trait theory is that it:
   a. places too great an emphasis on early childhood experiences.
   b. overestimates the consistency of behavior in different situations.
   c. underestimates the importance of heredity in personality development.
   d. places too great an emphasis on positive traits.

Ans: d, p. 600

44. Today's personality researchers focus their work on:
   a. basic dimensions of personality.
   b. the interaction of persons and environments.
   c. grand theories of behavior.
   d. a. and b.
   e. a., b., and c.

Ans: a, p. 600

45. In high school, Britta and Debbie were best friends. They thought they were a lot alike, as did everyone else who knew them. After high school, they went on to very different colleges, careers, and life courses. Now, at their twenty-fifth reunion, they are shocked at how little they have in common. Bandura would suggest that their differences reflect the interactive effects of environment, personality, and behavior, which he refers to as:
   a. reciprocal determinism.
   b. personal control.
   c. identification.
   d. the self-serving bias.

Ans: d, p. 600

46. Which perspective on personality emphasizes the interaction between the individual and the environment in shaping personality?
   a. psychoanalytic
   b. trait
   c. humanistic
   d. social-cognitive

Ans: d, p. 600

47. Because Ramona identifies with her politically conservative parents, she chose to enroll in a conservative college. After four years in this environment, Ramona's politics have become even more conservative. Which perspective best accounts for the mutual influences of Ramona's upbringing, choice of school, and political viewpoint?
   a. psychoanalytic
   b. trait
   c. humanistic
   d. social-cognitive

Ans: c, p. 602

48. Research on locus of control indicates that internals are ________ than externals.
   a. more dependent
   b. more intelligent
   c. better able to cope with stress
   d. more sociable
   e. more depressed

Ans: a, p. 602

49. With which of the following statements would a social-cognitive psychologist agree?
a. People with an internal locus of control achieve more in school.
b. "Externals" are better able to cope with stress than "internals."
c. "Internals" are less independent than "externals."
d. All of the above are true.

Ans: c, p. 602

50. Seligman has found that humans and animals who are exposed to aversive events they cannot escape may develop:
a. an internal locus of control.
b. a reaction formation.
c. learned helplessness.
d. neurotic anxiety.
e. displacement.

Ans: b, p. 604

51. (Close-Up) During a class discussion, Trevor argues that the recent "positive psychology" is sure to wane in popularity, since it suffers from the same criticisms as humanistic psychology. You counter his argument by pointing out that, unlike humanistic psychology, positive psychology:
a. focuses on advancing human fulfillment.
b. is rooted in science.
c. is not based on the study of individual characteristics.
d. has all of the above characteristics.

Ans: c, p. 605

52. In studying personality, a social-cognitive theorist would *most likely* make use of:
a. personality inventories.
b. projective tests.
c. observing behavior in different situations.
d. factor analyses.

Ans: b, p. 606

53. Which of the following is a major criticism of the social-cognitive perspective?
a. It focuses too much on early childhood experiences.
b. It focuses too little on the inner traits of a person.
c. It provides descriptions but not explanations.
d. It lacks appropriate assessment techniques.

Ans: c, p. 608

54. Which of the following statements about self-esteem is *not* correct?
a. People with low self-esteem tend to be negative about others.
b. People with high self-esteem are less prone to drug addiction.
c. People with low self-esteem tend to be nonconformists.
d. People with high self-esteem suffer less from insomnia.
e. People with high self-esteem are more persistent at difficult tasks.

Ans: c, p. 608

55. The behavior of many people has been described in terms of a "spotlight effect." This means that they:
   a. tend to see themselves as being above average in ability.
   b. perceive that their fate is determined by forces not under their personal control.
   c. overestimate the extent to which other people are noticing them.
   d. do all of the above.

Ans: e, p. 609

56. Which of the following groups tends to suffer from relatively low self-esteem?
   a. women
   b. ethnic minorities
   c. disabled persons
   d. all of the above
   e. none of the above

Ans: a, p. 609

57. Research has shown that individuals who are made to feel insecure are subsequently:
   a. more critical of others.
   b. less critical of others.
   c. more likely to display a self-serving bias.
   d. less likely to display a self-serving bias.

Ans: c, p. 609

58. James attributes his failing grade in chemistry to an unfair final exam. His attitude exemplifies:
   a. internal locus of control.
   b. unconditional positive regard.
   c. the self-serving bias.
   d. reciprocal determinism.

Ans: e, pp. 609-610

59. An example of the self-serving bias described in the text is the tendency of people to:
   a. see themselves as better than average on nearly any desirable dimension.
   b. accept more responsibility for successes than failures.
   c. be overly critical of other people.
   d. be overly sensitive to criticism.
   e. do both a. and b.

Ans: b, pp. 609-610

60. Regarding the self-serving bias, psychologists who study the self have found that self-affirming thinking:
   a. is generally maladaptive to the individual because it distorts reality by overinflating self-esteem.
   b. is generally adaptive to the individual because it maintains self-confidence and minimizes depression.
   c. tends to prevent the individual from viewing others with compassion and understanding.
   d. tends *not* to characterize people who have experienced unconditional positive regard.

Ans: b, pp. 611-614

61. Individualist cultures:
a. value communal solidarity.
b. emphasize personal achievement and identity.
c. are less competitive than collectivist cultures.
d. are characterized by none of the above.
e. are characterized by a., b., and c.

Ans: e, pp. 611-613

62. Collectivist cultures:
a. give priority to the goals of their groups.
b. value the maintenance of social harmony.
c. foster social interdependence.
d. are characterized by none of the above.
e. are characterized by a., b., and c.

Ans: d, pp. 612-613

63. Being fed up with your cultural background, you decide to move to a culture that places greater value on maintaining social harmony and family identity. To which of the following countries should you move?
a. the United States
b. Canada
c. Australia
d. Japan
e. Great Britain

Ans: d, p. 613

64. Compared to those in collectivist cultures, people in individualist cultures:
a. are less geographically bound to elderly parents.
b. tend to be lonelier.
c. are more vulnerable to stress-related disease.
d. have all of the above characteristics.

Ans: a, p. 615

65. Professor Minton believes that people strive to find meaning in life because they are terrified of their own mortality. Evidently, Professor Minton is a proponent of:
a. terror-management theory.
b. psychodynamic theory.
c. the humanistic perspective.
d. the social-cognitive perspective.
e. the trait perspective.

Ans: b, p. 616

66. Recent research has provided more support for defense mechanisms such as ________ than for defense mechanisms such as ________.
a. displacement; reaction formation
b. reaction formation; displacement
c. displacement; regression
d. displacement; projection

CHAPTER **16**

Psychological Disorders

Learning Objectives

Perspectives on Psychological Disorders (pp. 620-626)

1. Identify the criteria for judging whether behavior is psychologically disordered.

2. Describe the medical model of psychological disorders, and discuss the bio-psycho-social perspective offered by critics of this model.

3. Describe the aims of DSM-IV, and discuss the potential dangers associated with the use of diagnostic labels.

Anxiety Disorders (pp. 627-633)

4. Describe the symptoms of generalized anxiety disorders, phobias, and obsessive-compulsive disorders.

5. Explain the development of anxiety disorders from both a learning and a biological perspective.

Mood Disorders (pp. 633-643)

6. Describe major depressive disorder and bipolar disorder.

7. Explain the development of mood disorders, paying special attention to the biological and social-cognitive perspectives.

Thinking Critically About Dissociation and Multiple Personalities (pp. 644-645)

8. Describe the characteristics and possible causes of dissociative identity disorder.

Schizophrenia (pp. 646-653)

9. Describe the various symptoms and subtypes of schizophrenia, and discuss research on its causes.

Personality Disorders (pp. 653-655)

10. Describe the nature of personality disorders, focusing on the characteristics of the antisocial personality disorder.

Rates of Psychological Disorders (pp. 656-657)

11. Describe the prevalence of various disorders and the timing of their onset.

Defining psychological disorders, p. 620
Easy, Factual/Definitional, Objective 1, Ans: d

1. Mental health workers label behavior psychologically disordered when they judge it:
a. prejudicial, unconsciously motivated, ingenuine, and insane.
b. biologically based, unconsciously motivated, aggressive, and difficult to change.
c. selfish, habitual, and avoidable.
d. atypical, disturbing, maladaptive, and unjustifiable.

Defining psychological disorders, p. 620
Medium, Conceptual/Application, Objective 1, Ans: c

2. Savannah often appears nervous and agitated; she frequently talks loudly and laughs almost uncontrollably. Her behavior is most likely to be diagnosed as psychologically disordered if it is:
a. not caused by a biological impairment.
b. difficult for her to discontinue.
c. socially unacceptable and disturbing to others.
d. the product of unconscious motives.

Defining psychological disorders, p. 620
Medium, Conceptual/Application, Objective 1, Ans: b

3. Alexis is socially withdrawn and she fears and distrusts many people. This behavior is most likely to be diagnosed as a symptom of psychological disorder if it is:
a. a long-standing pattern of behavior.
b. rationally unjustifiable.
c. not caused by a biological disorder.
d. a response to a stressful life situation.

Understanding psychological disorders, p. 621
Medium, Conceptual, Objective 2, Ans: c

4. The greatest shortcoming associated with explanations of psychological disorders in terms of demon possession is that these explanations:
a. were relevant only to severe disorders such as schizophrenia.
b. encouraged many to believe there was no such thing as insanity.
c. led to some harsh and ineffective remedial treatments.
d. absolved people of personal responsibility for their own behavior.

Understanding psychological disorders, p. 621
Easy, Factual/Definitional, Objective 2, Ans: a

5. According to the medical model, psychological disorders are:
a. sicknesses that need to be diagnosed and cured.
b. maladaptive responses to a troubling environment.
c. purely imaginary symptoms of distress.
d. learned habits that need to be extinguished.

Understanding psychological disorders, p. 621
Easy, Factual/Definitional, Objective 2, Ans: c

6. The discovery that psychologically disordered behavior could result from syphilis infections facilitated the credibility and acceptance of:
a. trait theory.
b. psychoanalytic theory.
c. the medical model.
d. DSM-IV.
e. the social-cognitive perspective.

Understanding psychological disorders, pp. 621-622
Medium, Conceptual, Objective 2, Ans: c

7. A bio-psycho-social perspective on alcohol abuse would be most likely to emphasize:
a. the distinction between neurotic and psychotic forms of alcoholism.
b. the similarities between alcoholism and personality disorders.
c. the interactive influences of nature and nurture on maladaptive alcohol consumption.
d. that alcoholism is a life-style choice and should not be considered a psychological disorder.

Understanding psychological disorders, pp. 621-622
Difficult, Conceptual, Objective 2, Ans: c

8. Which perspective would have the most difficulty accounting for the fact that anorexia nervosa is mostly a disorder of Western cultures?
a. psychoanalytic perspective
b. cognitive perspective
c. medical perspective
d. behavioral perspective

Classifying psychological disorders, p. 622
Easy, Factual/Definitional, Objective 3, Ans: d

9. DSM-IV is a widely used system for:
a. identifying the causes of psychological abnormality.
b. distinguishing sanity from insanity.
c. treating depression.
d. classifying psychological disorders.
e. doing all of the above.

Classifying psychological disorders, p. 622
Medium, Conceptual/Application, Objective 3, Ans: b

10. DSM-IV would be most useful for deciding whether:
a. Sydney is irrational.
b. Katie is depressed.
c. Kareem is extraverted.
d. Max is insane.

Classifying psychological disorders, p. 623
Difficult, Factual/Definitional, Objective 3, Ans: b

11. The DSM-IV does not:
  a. include a classification for personality disorders.
  b. explain the causes of the various psychological disorders.
  c. include a very broad range of psychological disorders.
  d. provide systematic guidelines for diagnosing psychological disorders.

Classifying psychological disorders, p. 623
Easy, Factual/Definitional, Objective 3, Ans: c

12. The term *psychotic disorders* is most often used as a contrast to the less debilitating ________ disorders.
  a. mood
  b. paranoid
  c. neurotic
  d. borderline personality
  e. catatonic

Classifying psychological disorders, p. 623
Difficult, Factual/Definitional, Objective 3, Ans: a

13. DSM-IV bases diagnoses on observable behavior in order to:
  a. improve the reliability of diagnoses.
  b. shorten the time it takes to make a diagnosis.
  c. avoid invading clients' psychological privacy.
  d. reduce the need for medical terminology in psychological assessments.

Classifying psychological disorders, p. 623
Medium, Factual/Definitional, Objective 3, Ans: b

14. DSM-IV is most likely to be criticized for:
  a. attempting to explain behavior by simply labeling it.
  b. classifying an excessively broad range of human behaviors as psychologically disordered.
  c. failing to base diagnoses on observable behaviors.
  d. inhibiting scientific efforts to discover the underlying causes of psychological disorders.

The "unDSM": A diagnostic manual of human strengths (Close-up), p. 624
Easy, Factual/Definitional, Objective 2, Ans: a

15. The newly developed VIA is designed to aid in the process of:
  a. assessing human strengths.
  b. explaining psychological disorders.
  c. reducing current reliance on the DSM-IV.
  d. shortening the time it takes to classify psychological disorders.

Labeling psychological disorders, p. 623
Easy, Factual/Definitional, Objective 3, Ans: a

16. A fundamental problem with the diagnostic labeling of psychologically disordered behaviors is that the labels often:
  a. bias our perceptions of the labeled person.
  b. represent attempts by psychologists to explain behavior by simply naming it.
  c. interfere with effective research on the causes of these disorders.
  d. interfere with effective treatment of these disorders.

Labeling psychological disorders, p. 623
Medium, Conceptual/Application, Objective 3, Ans: c

17. After George learned that Mrs. Min suffered from schizophrenia, he mistakenly concluded that her tendencies to laugh easily and smile frequently were symptoms of her disorder. This best illustrates the:
a. unreliability of DSM-IV.
b. shortcomings of the medical model.
c. biasing power of diagnostic labels.
d. dangers of the psychoanalytic perspective.
e. impact of expectations on another's behavior.

Labeling psychological disorders, p. 625
Easy, Conceptual, Objective 3, Ans: d

18. When children are told that certain classmates are learning disabled, they may behave in ways that inhibit the success of these students in the classroom. This best illustrates the dangers of:
a. delusions.
b. the medical perspective.
c. linkage analysis.
d. self-fulfilling prophecies.
e. the psychoanalytic perspective.

Insanity and responsibility (Box), p. 626
Easy, Factual/Definitional, Objective 3, Ans: d

19. When John Hinckley shot U.S. President Ronald Reagan, he was sent to a mental hospital rather than to prison because he was judged to be:
a. manic-depressive.
b. dysthymic.
c. catatonic.
d. insane.
e. neurotic.

Insanity and responsibility (Box), p. 626
Medium, Conceptual/Application, Objective 3, Ans: c

20. Jeffrey Dahmer was judged to be legally sane at the time he killed and dismembered 15 individuals. This indicates that the jury believed that Dahmer:
a. suffered from an antisocial personality disorder.
b. experienced a massive dissociation of self from ordinary consciousness.
c. was able to appreciate the wrongfulness of his behavior and control it.
d. had a persistent fear of people that caused him to commit crimes against society.
e. was not abused by his parents during his early childhood.

Generalized anxiety disorder and panic disorder, p. 627
Easy, Factual/Definitional, Objective 4, Ans: b

21. A generalized anxiety disorder is characterized by:
a. offensive and unwanted thoughts that persistently preoccupy a person.
b. a continuous state of tension, apprehension, and autonomic nervous system arousal.
c. hyperactive, wildly optimistic states of emotion.
d. alternations between extreme hopelessness and unrealistic optimism.
e. a chronic lack of guilt feelings.

Generalized anxiety disorder and panic disorder, p. 627
Medium, Conceptual/Application, Objective 4, Ans: c

22. Rishi, a college student, complains that he feels apprehensive and fearful most of the time but doesn't know why. Without warning, his heart begins to pound, his hands get icy, and he breaks out in a cold sweat. Rishi most likely suffers from a(n):
    a. dysthymic disorder.
    b. obsessive-compulsive disorder.
    c. generalized anxiety disorder.
    d. phobia.
    e. dissociative disorder.

Generalized anxiety disorder and panic disorder, p. 627
Easy, Factual/Definitional, Objective 4, Ans: c

23. Freud suggested that for those suffering a generalized anxiety disorder, the anxiety is:
    a. psychotic.
    b. cyclical.
    c. free-floating.
    d. narcissistic.
    e. completely outside of conscious awareness.

Generalized anxiety disorder and panic disorder, p. 627
Medium, Conceptual/Application, Objective 4, Ans: c

24. While he was studying, Matthew was suddenly overwhelmed by feelings of intense apprehension. For several minutes he felt so agitated that he could not catch his breath. Matthew was most likely suffering from a(n):
    a. bipolar disorder.
    b. dissociative disorder.
    c. panic attack.
    d. obsessive-compulsive disorder.
    e. dysthymic disorder.

Generalized anxiety disorder and panic disorder, p. 627
Medium, Factual/Definitional, Objective 4, Ans: d

25. The avoidance of potentially anxiety-arousing situations from which escape might be difficult is indicative of:
    a. an obsessive-compulsive disorder.
    b. a dysthymic disorder.
    c. schizophrenia.
    d. agoraphobia.
    e. bipolar disorder.

Generalized anxiety disorder and panic disorder, p. 627
Difficult, Conceptual/Application, Objective 4, Ans: b

26. Sadie is so fearful of being overwhelmed by anxiety that she rarely steps outside her apartment. The thought of going shopping and getting lost in a crowd terrifies her, so she has her groceries delivered. Because of her fear, she earns her living as a freelance writer, working at home. Sadie's behavior is most characteristic of:
a. dissociative disorder.
b. agoraphobia.
c. catatonia.
d. a dysthymic disorder.
e. an obsessive-compulsive disorder.

Phobias, p. 628
Easy, Factual/Definitional, Objective 4, Ans: b

27. Which of the following is characterized by persistent, irrational fear of a specific object or situation?
a. generalized anxiety disorder
b. phobia
c. dysthymic disorder
d. histrionic personality disorder
e. catatonia

Phobias, p. 628
Easy, Conceptual/Application, Objective 4, Ans: e

28. Kaylee is so alarmed by spiders and insects that she avoids most outdoor activities and even refuses to enter the basement of her own house alone. Kaylee appears to suffer from a(n):
a. obsessive-compulsive disorder.
b. histrionic personality disorder.
c. dissociative disorder.
d. mood disorder.
e. phobia.

Obsessive-compulsive disorder, pp. 628-629
Medium, Conceptual/Application, Objective 4, Ans: d

29. Cecil is preoccupied with thoughts of jumping out the window of his tenth-floor apartment. In order to reduce his anxiety, he frequently counts his heartbeats aloud. Cecil would most likely be diagnosed as experiencing a(n):
a. panic disorder.
b. bipolar disorder.
c. generalized anxiety disorder.
d. obsessive-compulsive disorder.
e. phobia.

Obsessive-compulsive disorder, pp. 628-629
Easy, Factual/Definitional, Objective 4, Ans: e

30. Obsessions are:
a. persistent, irrational fears of specific objects or situations.
b. hyperactive, wildly optimistic states of emotion.
c. false beliefs of persecution or grandeur.
d. periodic episodes of intense dread accompanied by frightening physical sensations.
e. offensive and unwanted thoughts that persistently preoccupy a person.

Obsessive-compulsive disorder, pp. 628-629
Medium, Conceptual/Application, Objective 4, Ans: c

31. Mrs. Swift is alarmed by her own persistent and irrational thoughts of murdering her young children. Her experience best illustrates the agitating effects of a(n):
a. delusion.
b. manic episode.
c. obsession.
d. hallucination.
e. panic attack.

Obsessive-compulsive disorder, pp. 628-629
Difficult, Conceptual/Application, Objective 4, Ans: d

32. Repeatedly washing your hands is to ________ as repeatedly thinking about your own death is to ________.
a. neurosis; schizophrenia
b. mania; depression
c. phobia; delusion
d. compulsion; obsession

Explaining anxiety disorders, p. 629
Medium, Factual/Definitional, Objective 5, Ans: c

33. Learning theorists have suggested that a generalized anxiety disorder results from:
a. repeated misuse of alcohol, heroin, or other addictive drugs.
b. a lack of effective childhood training in impulse control.
c. exposure to unpredictable aversive events.
d. a genetically based predisposition to fear unfamiliar objects or situations.

Explaining anxiety disorders, p. 629
Difficult, Conceptual/Application, Objective 5, Ans: b

34. Melissa is fearful of men and refuses to go out on dates. Her therapist suggests that her fear is a result of the sexual abuse she received from her father when she was young. The therapist's suggestion most clearly reflects a ________ perspective.
a. humanistic
b. learning
c. biological
d. psychoanalytic
e. trait

Explaining anxiety disorders, pp. 629-630
Medium, Conceptual/Application, Objective 5, Ans: a

35. Luke suffers from acrophobia, a fear of high places. Luke's therapist suggests that his reaction to heights is a generalization of the fear triggered by a childhood playground accident in which he fell off a sliding board. The therapist's suggestion reflects a ________ perspective.
a. learning
b. psychoanalytic
c. trait
d. humanistic
e. biological

Explaining anxiety disorders, pp. 629-630
Medium, Conceptual/Application, Objective 5, Ans: c

36. Julius is obsessed with avoiding germs and feels compelled to bathe at least 10 times every day. His therapist suggests that Julius continues his maladaptive bathing because this behavior temporarily reduced his anxiety on many past occasions. The therapist's suggestion most directly reflects a ________ perspective.
a. biological
b. trait
c. learning
d. psychoanalytic
e. humanistic

Post-traumatic stress disorder (Close-up), p. 630
Medium, Factual/Definitional, Objective 4, Ans: d

37. Frequent nightmares, insomnia, and the intrusion of painful memories are symptoms most commonly associated with:
a. bipolar disorder.
b. dissociative disorder.
c. anorexia nervosa.
d. post-traumatic stress disorder.
e. histrionic personality disorder.

Post-traumatic stress disorder (Close-up), p. 630
Difficult, Factual/Definitional, Objective 4, Ans: a

38. Compared with other American Jews, those who survived the Holocaust trauma have been ________ likely to have seen a psychotherapist and ________ likely to have had stable marriages.
a. less; more
b. more; less
c. more; more
d. less; less

Explaining anxiety disorders, p. 631
Medium, Conceptual, Objective 5, Ans: c

39. Obsessive thoughts typically ________ anxiety and compulsive behaviors typically ________ anxiety.
a. increase; increase
b. decrease; decrease
c. increase; decrease
d. decrease; increase

Explaining anxiety disorders, p. 632
Medium, Conceptual/Application, Objective 5, Ans: b

40. We can more easily extinguish a fear of driving a car than a fear of holding snakes. This is best explained from a ________ perspective.
a. learning
b. biological
c. psychoanalytic
d. humanistic

Explaining anxiety disorders, p. 632
Easy, Factual/Definitional, Objective 5, Ans: d

41. It has been suggested that compulsive acts typically exaggerate behaviors that contributed to the survival of the human species. This idea best illustrates the ________ perspective.
    a. humanistic
    b. learning
    c. psychoanalytic
    d. biological

Explaining anxiety disorders, p. 632
Difficult, Factual/Definitional, Objective 5, Ans: b

42. An overarousal of brain areas involved in impulse control and habitual behaviors is most characteristic of:
    a. dissociative identity disorder.
    b. generalized anxiety disorder.
    c. schizophrenia.
    d. major depressive disorder.
    e. antisocial personality disorder.

Major depressive disorder, p. 634
Easy, Factual/Definitional, Objective 6, Ans: e

43. A major depressive disorder is most likely to be characterized by:
    a. delusions of persecution.
    b. a massive dissociation of self from ordinary consciousness.
    c. alternations between extreme hopelessness and unrealistic optimism.
    d. a persistent irrational fear of other people.
    e. feelings of personal worthlessness.

Major depressive disorder, p. 634
Easy, Conceptual/Application, Objective 6, Ans: b

44. For the last month, Gabrielle has felt lethargic and has been unable to get out of bed in the morning. She has withdrawn from friends and family because she feels worthless and unlovable. Gabrielle is most likely suffering from:
    a. agoraphobia.
    b. a mood disorder.
    c. schizophrenia.
    d. an antisocial personality disorder.
    e. anorexia nervosa.

Major depressive disorder, p. 634
Medium, Factual/Definitional, Objective 6, Ans: e

45. A chronic state of low energy and low self-esteem that is a bit less disabling than major depression is called a:
    a. bipolar disorder.
    b. generalized anxiety disorder.
    c. phobia.
    d. dissociative disorder.
    e. dysthymic disorder.

Bipolar disorder, p. 634
Easy, Factual/Definitional, Objective 6, Ans: b

46. In which disorder do people alternate between states of lethargic hopelessness and wild overexcitement?
    a. dissociative identity disorder
    b. bipolar disorder
    c. obsessive-compulsive disorder
    d. schizophrenia

Bipolar disorder, p. 634
Easy, Factual/Definitional, Objective 6, Ans: b

47. A condition in which an individual is overexcited, hyperactive, and wildly optimistic is known as:
    a. paranoia.
    b. a manic episode.
    c. a panic attack.
    d. catatonia.

Bipolar disorder, p. 634
Difficult, Conceptual/Application, Objective 6, Ans: e

48. Elmer, the owner of an auto service station, suddenly began smashing the front fenders and hoods of two customers' cars. When asked why, he excitedly but incoherently explained that he was transforming the cars into "real racing machines." When an employee tried to restrain him, he shouted that everybody was fired and quickly began breaking the car windows. Elmer is exhibiting symptoms of:
    a. a dysthymic disorder.
    b. catatonia.
    c. a panic attack.
    d. a phobia.
    e. mania.

Bipolar disorder, p. 634
Difficult, Factual/Definitional, Objective 6, Ans: a

49. During the manic phase of bipolar disorder, individuals are most likely to experience:
    a. high self-esteem.
    b. delusions of persecution.
    c. uncontrollable grief and despair.
    d. visual or auditory hallucinations.

Bipolar disorder, p. 635
Medium, Factual/Definitional, Objective 6, Ans: d

50. George Fredrick Handel composed his *Messiah* during three weeks of intense, creative energy. Many believe Handel suffered a mild form of:
    a. agoraphobia.
    b. dysthymic disorder.
    c. dissociative disorder.
    d. bipolar disorder.
    e. schizophrenia.

Explaining mood disorders, p. 636
Medium, Factual/Definitional, Objective 7, Ans: d

51. Research regarding depression indicates that:
    a. depression is typically unrelated to stressful life events.
    b. depression is unlikely to be overcome without professional help.
    c. depression is associated with abnormally high levels of the neurotransmitter serotonin.
    d. with each new generation, depression is dramatically increasing in its prevalence.

Explaining mood disorders, p. 637
Medium, Factual/Definitional, Objective 7, Ans: c

52. Which perspective suggests that depression is a reaction to loss and the internalization of unresolved anger toward parents?
    a. social-cognitive
    b. biological
    c. psychoanalytic
    d. learning
    e. humanistic

Explaining mood disorders, p. 637
Medium, Conceptual/Application, Objective 7, Ans: c

53. Laura's husband died three years ago, but she is still depressed. Her therapist suggests that she is really angry at her husband for abandoning her. The therapist's interpretation reflects the ________ perspective.
    a. social-cognitive
    b. humanistic
    c. psychoanalytic
    d. trait
    e. biological

Explaining mood disorders, p. 637
Medium, Factual/Definitional, Objective 7, Ans: b

54. Linkage analysis is of greatest interest to those who attempt to explain mood disorders from a ________ perspective.
    a. psychoanalytic
    b. biological
    c. social-cognitive
    d. humanistic

Suicide (Close-up), p. 638
Difficult, Factual/Definitional, Objective 7, Ans: a

55. Suicide rates in the United States are ________ among Whites than Blacks and ________ among men than women.
    a. higher; higher
    b. lower; lower
    c. higher; lower
    d. lower; higher

Suicide (Close-up), p. 638
Medium, Factual/Definitional, Objective 7, Ans: d

56. People are especially vulnerable to suicide if they suffer from:
    a. a dissociative disorder.
    b. agoraphobia.
    c. panic attacks.
    d. alcoholism.
    e. obsessions.

Suicide (Close-up), p. 639
Medium, Factual/Definitional, Objective 7, Ans: a

57. One of the best warning signs of an attempt at suicide is:
    a. suicidal talk.
    b. hallucinations and delusions.
    c. the use of illegal drugs.
    d. generalized anxiety.
    e. repeated academic failure.

Explaining mood disorders, p. 638
Medium, Factual/Definitional, Objective 7, Ans: c

58. Research suggests that abnormally low levels of the neurotransmitter norepinephrine may contribute to:
    a. panic attacks.
    b. schizophrenia.
    c. depression.
    d. phobias.
    e. dissociative disorders.

Explaining mood disorders, p. 638
Medium, Factual/Definitional, Objective 7, Ans: b

59. Drugs that alleviate mania tend to reduce levels of the neurotransmitter:
    a. acetylcholine.
    b. norepinephrine.
    c. dopamine.
    d. chlorpromazine.

Explaining mood disorders, p. 640
Difficult, Factual/Definitional, Objective 7, Ans: b

60. According to the social-cognitive perspective, women are more vulnerable to depression than men because they are more likely to:
    a. have unrealistically optimistic goals in life.
    b. sense a lack of personal control over their lives.
    c. struggle with unresolved feelings of anger toward their mothers.
    d. experience low levels of norepinephrine.
    e. experience cyclical variations in hormone levels.

Explaining mood disorders, p. 640
Difficult, Factual/Definitional, Objective 7, Ans: c

61. The social-cognitive perspective has emphasized that depression is perpetuated by:
   a. feelings of ambivalence.
   b. the internalization of anger.
   c. self-blaming attributions.
   d. egocentrism.
   e. conscious role playing.

Explaining mood disorders, p. 640
Difficult, Factual/Definitional, Objective 7, Ans: d

62. Which perspective suggests that explaining our own failures in terms that are global, stable, and internal contributes to depression?
   a. psychoanalytic
   b. biological
   c. humanistic
   d. social-cognitive
   e. trait

Explaining mood disorders, p. 640
Medium, Conceptual/Application, Objective 7, Ans: b

63. Inanna suffers from chronic depression. According to the social-cognitive perspective, how is she most likely to respond when told that she performed very poorly on a test she took the previous day?
   a. "The professor in this course is probably one of the poorest teachers I have ever had."
   b. "I'm academically incompetent and always will be."
   c. "Yesterday was just my unlucky day."
   d. "I suspect that none of the students in my class did well on that test."
   e. "Hardly any of the professors in this college are effective classroom teachers."

Explaining mood disorders, p. 640
Difficult, Conceptual/Application, Objective 7, Ans: d

64. A therapist suggests that Margaret is depressed because she attributes her failures to her own incompetence instead of blaming her parents and teachers for the unreasonable demands they place on her. The therapist's interpretation most clearly reflects a ________ perspective.
   a. biological
   b. psychoanalytic
   c. humanistic
   d. social-cognitive
   e. trait

Explaining mood disorders, p. 641
Medium, Factual/Definitional, Objective 7, Ans: c

65. One difficulty with a purely attributional explanation of depression is that negative attributions:
   a. have little effect on people's feelings of self-worth.
   b. are more characteristic of men than of women.
   c. may be a consequence rather than a cause of depression.
   d. do not coincide with actual episodes of depression.
   e. are more clearly associated with mania than with depression.

Explaining mood disorders, p. 641
Medium, Factual/Definitional, Objective 7, Ans: a

66. The vicious cycle of depression is often perpetuated by:
a. social rejection.
b. unrealistic optimism about the future.
c. excessive levels of norepinephrine.
d. a breakdown in selective attention.
e. external attributions of blame.

Explaining mood disorders, pp. 642-643
Difficult, Conceptual, Objective 7, Ans: d

67. In order to break the vicious cycle of depression, the social-cognitive perspective suggests that people should be encouraged to explain their failures in terms that are both ________ and ________.
a. internal; stable
b. external; global
c. internal; global
d. external; unstable

Loneliness (Close-up), p. 643
Medium, Factual/Definitional, Objective 7, Ans: a

68. Chronically lonely people tend to attribute their lack of satisfactory social relationships to:
a. their own personal inadequacies.
b. the individualistic emphasis of contemporary culture.
c. the uncaring behaviors and undesirable characteristics of those around them.
d. the depersonalization associated with a highly mobile society.

Dissociation and multiple personalities (Box), p. 644
Easy, Factual/Definitional, Objective 8, Ans: e

69. Disruptions in conscious awareness and sense of identity are most characteristic of ________ disorders.
a. bipolar
b. obsessive-compulsive
c. personality
d. generalized anxiety
e. dissociative

Dissociation and multiple personalities (Box), p. 644
Medium, Factual/Definitional, Objective 8, Ans: e

70. A sense of being separated from your body and watching yourself with a sense of detachment is a symptom of:
a. bipolar disorder.
b. dysthymic disorder.
c. generalized anxiety.
d. agoraphobia.
e. dissociation.

Dissociation and multiple personalities (Box), p. 644
Difficult, Conceptual/Application, Objective 8, Ans: b

71. William, an airplane pilot, is unable to remember anything of a bombing raid in which his plane was severely damaged and two crew members were killed. Because he himself suffered no physical injuries, psychologists suspect that William probably suffers from a:
   a. panic disorder.
   b. dissociative disorder.
   c. phobia.
   d. generalized anxiety disorder.
   e. bipolar disorder.

Dissociation and multiple personalities (Box), p. 644
Easy, Factual/Definitional, Objective 8, Ans: a

72. The experience of multiple personalities is most likely to be characterized by:
   a. a massive dissociation of self from ordinary consciousness.
   b. offensive and unwanted thoughts that persistently preoccupy a person.
   c. delusions of persecution and grandiosity.
   d. a lack of guilt feelings.
   e. alternations between extreme hopelessness and unrealistic optimism.

Dissociation and multiple personalities (Box), p. 644
Medium, Factual/Definitional, Objective 8, Ans: d

73. College students were asked to pretend that they were accused murderers. Under hypnosis, they typically expressed a second personality when prompted to do so by the examining psychiatrist. This most strongly suggests that dissociative identity disorder may involve:
   a. low self-esteem.
   b. unconscious fear.
   c. internal attributions of blame.
   d. role-playing.
   e. feelings of ambivalence.

Dissociation and multiple personalities (Box), pp. 644-645
Difficult, Conceptual/Application, Objective 8, Ans: c

74. Connie exhibits many symptoms of multiple personality disorder. Evidence that information learned by her secondary personality influence the moods and behaviors of her primary personality would most clearly rule out the contribution of ________ to her symptoms.
   a. role-playing
   b. sexual trauma
   c. dissociation
   d. motivational conflict

Dissociation and multiple personalities (Box), p. 645
Difficult, Conceptual, Objective 8, Ans: d

75. A biological perspective would be least helpful for explaining the:
   a. prevalence of schizophrenia throughout the world.
   b. fluctuations in mood experienced by those suffering a bipolar disorder.
   c. fear of snakes experienced by a high percentage of Americans.
   d. dramatic increase in reported cases of dissociative identity disorder during the past 40 or so years.

Dissociative and multiple personalities (Box), p. 645
Medium, Factual/Definitional, Objective 8, Ans: d

76. Evidence that symptoms of dissociative identity disorder are triggered by the suggestions and leading questions of therapists most clearly points out the importance of ________ in the onset of this disorder.
   a. learned helplessness
   b. repression
   c. childhood sexual trauma
   d. role-playing
   e. motivational conflict

Dissociation and multiple personalities (Box), p. 645
Medium, Conceptual/Application, Objective 8, Ans: d

77. Noah's therapist suggests that Noah developed a dissociative identity disorder in order to misbehave without feeling a strong sense of personal shame. The therapist's suggestion most directly reflects a ________ perspective.
   a. humanistic
   b. social-cognitive
   c. trait
   d. psychoanalytic
   e. biological

Schizophrenia, p. 646
Easy, Factual/Definitional, Objective 9, Ans: b

78. Which of the following is considered to be a psychotic disorder?
   a. antisocial personality disorder
   b. schizophrenia
   c. post-traumatic stress disorder
   d. dissociative identity disorder
   e. obsessive-compulsive disorder

Symptoms of schizophrenia, p. 647
Easy, Conceptual/Application, Objective 9, Ans: b

79. Jabar, a 25-year-old auto mechanic, thinks he is Napoleon. He further believes he is being imprisoned against his will in the mental hospital where his relatives have brought him for treatment. Jabar is most likely suffering from:
   a. an antisocial personality disorder.
   b. schizophrenia.
   c. a panic disorder.
   d. a dissociative identity disorder.
   e. a dysthymic disorder.

Symptoms of schizophrenia, p. 647
Easy, Factual/Definitional, Objective 9, Ans: c

80. In which type of disorder is a person's speech likely to be so full of unrelated words and phrases that it could be characterized as a "word salad"?
   a. dysthymic disorder
   b. obsessive-compulsive disorder
   c. schizophrenia
   d. dissociative disorder
   e. anorexia nervosa

Symptoms of schizophrenia, p. 647
Medium, Factual/Definitional, Objective 9, Ans: e

81. A breakdown in selective attention is most likely to be experienced by those who suffer from:
    a. bipolar disorder.
    b. obsessive-compulsive disorder.
    c. phobias.
    d. generalized anxiety disorders.
    e. schizophrenia.

Symptoms of schizophrenia, p. 647
Medium, Conceptual/Application, Objective 9, Ans: a

82. Mr. Hunt believes that he is the President of the United States and that he will soon become the "King of the Universe." Mr. Hunt is most clearly suffering from:
    a. delusions.
    b. obsessions.
    c. hallucinations.
    d. dissociative identity disorder.

Symptoms of schizophrenia, p. 647
Medium, Conceptual/Application, Objective 9, Ans: e

83. Wilma is extremely agitated because she hears voices that tell her to sexually seduce the male nurses in her hospital ward. Wilma is most clearly suffering from:
    a. a dysthymic disorder.
    b. an obsessive-compulsive disorder.
    c. delusions of grandiosity.
    d. a dissociative disorder.
    e. hallucinations.

Symptoms of schizophrenia, p. 648
Difficult, Conceptual/Application, Objective 9, Ans: e

84. Although Mrs. Petrides usually sits passively in a motionless stupor, she sometimes repetitiously shakes her head or waves her arms. She most likely suffers from:
    a. paranoia.
    b. a bipolar disorder.
    c. major depressive disorder.
    d. an obsessive-compulsive disorder.
    e. catatonia.

Subtypes of schizophrenia, p. 648
Medium, Factual/Definitional, Objective 9, Ans: a

85. One of the negative symptoms of schizophrenia is:
    a. an expressionless face.
    b. loud and meaningless talking.
    c. inappropriate laughter.
    d. uncontrollable temper tantrums.

Subtypes of schizophrenia (Table 16.2), p. 648
Easy, Factual/Definitional, Objective 9, Ans: d

86. Delusions of persecution are most common among those with ________ schizophrenia.
a. catatonic
b. disorganized
c. residual
d. paranoid

Subtypes of schizophrenia, p. 648
Medium, Conceptual, Objective 9, Ans: d

87. Sudden development of symptoms is to gradual development of symptoms as ________ schizophrenia is to ________ schizophrenia.
a. chronic; process
b. acute; reactive
c. chronic; acute
d. reactive; process

Subtypes of schizophrenia, p. 648
Difficult, Factual/Definitional, Objective 9, Ans: a

88. People are more likely to recover from ________ schizophrenia than from ________ schizophrenia.
a. acute; chronic
b. process; reactive
c. reactive; acute
d. chronic; process

Understanding schizophrenia, p. 649
Medium, Factual/Definitional, Objective 9, Ans: b

89. Schizophrenia is associated with an excess of receptors for:
a. norepinephrine.
b. dopamine.
c. serotonin.
d. acetylcholine.

Understanding schizophrenia, p. 649
Difficult, Conceptual, Objective 9, Ans: c

90. Dopamine overactivity appears to be most clearly related to:
a. flat affect.
b. agoraphobia.
c. impaired attention.
d. dysthymic disorder.
e. an expressionless face.

Understanding schizophrenia, p. 649
Medium, Factual/Definitional, Objective 9, Ans: a

91. Among schizophrenia patients, the fluid-filled areas of the brain are abnormally ________ and the thalamus is abnormally ________.
a. large; small
b. small; large
c. small; small
d. large; large

Understanding schizophrenia, p. 649
Medium, Factual/Definitional, Objective 9, Ans: e

92. Low birth weight is a known risk factor for:
 a. antisocial personality disorder.
 b. dissociative identity disorder.
 c. major depressive disorder.
 d. obsessive-compulsive disorder.
 e. schizophrenia.

Understanding schizophrenia, p. 650
Medium, Factual/Definitional, Objective 9, Ans: c

93. Evidence suggests that prenatal viral infections contribute to:
 a. generalized anxiety disorders.
 b. obsessive-compulsive disorder.
 c. schizophrenia.
 d. bipolar disorders.
 e. dissociative disorders.

Understanding schizophrenia, p. 650
Difficult, Factual/Definitional, Objective 9, Ans: a

94. People born in ________ during the month of ________ are at an increased risk for schizophrenia.
 a. North America; February
 b. Asia; September
 c. Australia; February
 d. Europe; September

Understanding schizophrenia, p. 650
Medium, Conceptual/Application, Objective 9, Ans: d

95. Which of the following individuals is most likely to suffer from schizophrenia?
 a. Sylvia, whose older sister was diagnosed as having schizophrenia when Sylvia was 7
 b. Sarkar, whose wife and son were both diagnosed as having schizophrenia when Sarkar was 37
 c. Jason, whose fraternal twin was diagnosed as having schizophrenia when they were 12
 d. Neeltje, whose parents were both diagnosed as having schizophrenia when Neeltje was 18

Understanding schizophrenia, p. 650
Medium, Factual/Definitional, Objective 9, Ans: a

96. Research on the causes of schizophrenia strongly suggests that:
 a. there is a genetic predisposition to schizophrenia.
 b. almost anybody will develop schizophrenia if exposed to extensive environmental stress.
 c. schizophrenia patients suffer from a deficiency of the neurotransmitter serotonin.
 d. all of the above are true.

Personality disorders, p. 653
Medium, Factual/Definitional, Objective 10, Ans: d

97. Those with an avoidant personality disorder are most likely to display:
 a. a lack of guilt feelings.
 b. a sense of self-importance.
 c. shallow, attention-getting emotions.
 d. a fear of social rejection.

Personality disorders, p. 653
Medium, Factual/Definitional, Objective 10, Ans: d

98. Those with a narcissistic personality disorder are likely to be preoccupied with:
   a. an irrational fear of people.
   b. delusions of persecution.
   c. physical symptoms of distress.
   d. their own self-importance.
   e. sexual fantasies.

Personality disorders, p. 654
Easy, Factual/Definitional, Objective 10, Ans: e

99. An antisocial personality disorder is most likely to be characterized by:
   a. delusions of grandeur.
   b. a persistent, irrational fear of people.
   c. episodes of intense autonomic nervous system arousal.
   d. disruptions in conscious awareness and sense of identity.
   e. a lack of guilt feelings.

Personality disorders, p. 654
Medium, Factual/Definitional, Objective 10, Ans: c

100. Which of the following disorders is more common among men than women?
   a. bipolar disorder
   b. obsessive-compulsive disorder
   c. antisocial personality disorder
   d. dissociative identity disorder
   e. schizophrenia

Personality disorders, p. 654
Medium, Conceptual/Application, Objective 10, Ans: d

101. Anthony is 32 years old, well above average in intelligence, and quite charming. He has swindled several elderly people out of their life savings, and he seems to have little feeling for his victims, nor does he fear the consequences of getting caught. His behavior is evidence of:
   a. bipolar disorder.
   b. schizophrenia.
   c. obsessive-compulsive disorder.
   d. a personality disorder.
   e. a dissociative disorder.

Personality disorders, p. 654
Medium, Factual/Definitional, Objective 10, Ans: c

102. There is some evidence that a relatively low level of autonomic nervous system arousal may contribute to:
   a. post-traumatic stress disorder.
   b. phobias.
   c. antisocial personality disorder.
   d. dissociative disorders.
   e. generalized anxiety disorder.

Personality disorders, p. 654
Medium, Factual/Definitional, Objective 10, Ans: a

103. The reduced self-control of impulsive murderers is most closely related to reduced brain activity in their ________ lobes.
a. frontal
b. temporal
c. occipital
d. parietal

Rates of psychological disorders, p. 656
Difficult, Factual/Definitional, Objective 11, Ans: a

104. The symptoms of ________ are likely to appear at an earlier age than the symptoms of ________.
a. antisocial personality; schizophrenia
b. major depression; bipolar disorder
c. obsessive-compulsive disorder; phobic disorder
d. schizophrenia; obsessive-compulsive disorder
e. major depression; alcohol abuse

Essay Questions

1. A newspaper editorialist argues that the use of DSM-IV diagnostic labels is destructively antidemocratic, because it enables an elite corps of mental health professionals to subtly control the values and life-styles of the rest of society. First give reasons supporting this argument, then defend the continued use of diagnostic labels.

2. June is so preoccupied with keeping her house absolutely spotless that she has no time to do anything but clean. After each family meal she not only washes the dishes, she also thoroughly cleans and polishes the kitchen table, chairs, floor, and cupboards. Although these cleaning rituals irritate her family, June is unable to discontinue them without experiencing intense feelings of discomfort. Use the learning and biological perspectives to explain June's behavior.

3. A guest on a TV talk show claims that “major depressive disorder is not a psychological problem; it’s a disease that can be medically treated.” Evaluate the strengths and weaknesses of this claim.

4. Differentiate between antisocial personality disorder, dissociative identity disorder, and schizophrenia. What relationships might exist between each disorder and insanity?

Web Quiz 1

Ans: d

1. At one time, disordered people were simply warehoused in asylums. These have been replaced with psychiatric hospitals in which attempts were made to diagnose and cure those with psychological disorders. This best illustrates one of the beneficial consequences of:
   a. the trait perspective.
   b. the legal insanity defense.
   c. the DSM-IV.
   d. the medical model.
   e. linkage analysis.

Ans: e

2. People around the world may experience the same genetically based disorder quite differently depending on their own personal expectations and the definitions of abnormality common to their unique culture. This best illustrates the need for:
   a. the DSM-IV.
   b. the medical model.
   c. linkage analysis.
   d. the legal insanity defense.
   e. a bio-psycho-social perspective.

Ans: e

3. Lenore is unexplainably and continually tense and is plagued by muscle tension, sleeplessness, and an inability to concentrate. Lenore most likely suffers from a(n):
   a. phobia.
   b. dissociative disorder.
   c. dysthymic disorder.
   d. obsessive-compulsive disorder.
   e. generalized anxiety disorder.

Ans: e

4. The avoidance of situations in which help may not be available when panic strikes is most characteristic of:
   a. dissociative identity disorder.
   b. obsessive-compulsive disorder.
   c. dysthymic disorder.
   d. a manic episode.
   e. agoraphobia.

Ans: c

5. Years after he barely survived a terrorist attack that killed his wife and two children, Mr. Puskari suffers recurring flashbacks and frequent nightmares of the event that render him incapable of holding a steady job. Mr. Puskari is most clearly showing signs of:
   a. obsessive-compulsive disorder.
   b. generalized anxiety disorder.
   c. post-traumatic stress disorder.
   d. dissociative identity disorder.
   e. dysthymic disorder.

Ans: c

6. Andrea experiences extreme anxiety when approaching the shoreline of any lake. Her therapist suggests that her fear results from a traumatic boat accident she experienced as a child. The therapist's suggestion reflects a ________ perspective.
   a. psychoanalytic
   b. biological
   c. learning
   d. humanistic
   e. trait

Ans: d

7. Elaine feels that her life is empty, has lost all interest in her career and hobbies, and wonders if she would be better off dead. She is most likely suffering from:
   a. a dissociative identity disorder.
   b. a generalized anxiety disorder.
   c. an antisocial personality disorder.
   d. a mood disorder.
   e. agoraphobia.

Ans: b

8. An overabundance of the neurotransmitter norepinephrine is most likely to be associated with:
   a. a dissociative disorder.
   b. a manic episode.
   c. schizophrenia.
   d. dysthymic disorder.
   e. antisocial personality disorder.

Ans: a

9. The social-cognitive perspective has linked the experience of depression to:
   a. learned helplessness.
   b. unresolved childhood anger.
   c. external attributions for failure.
   d. disruptions in conscious awareness.
   e. a lack of guilt feelings.

Ans: b

10. A sudden loss of memory is one of the symptoms of a(n):
    a. bipolar disorder.
    b. dissociative disorder.
    c. panic disorder.
    d. obsessive-compulsive disorder.
    e. antisocial personality disorder.

Ans: c

11. Mr. James believes that people are constantly laughing at him and that FBI agents are trying to steal his life savings. Mr. James is most clearly suffering from:
    a. compulsions.
    b. catatonia.
    c. delusions.
    d. hallucinations.
    e. post-traumatic stress disorder.

Ans: a

12. Catatonia is characterized by:
    a. periods of immobility or excessive, purposeless movement.
    b. offensive and unwanted thoughts that persistently preoccupy a person.
    c. a continuous state of tension, apprehension, and autonomic nervous system arousal.
    d. hyperactive, wildly optimistic states of emotion.
    e. delusions of persecution.

Ans: a

13. Therapeutic drugs that block dopamine receptors are most likely to reduce:
    a. hallucinations.
    b. depression.
    c. agoraphobia.
    d. dissociative disorders.
    e. generalized anxiety disorder.

Ans: b

14. The relationship between the season of the year in which people are born and their subsequent risk of schizophrenia best highlights the role of ________ in this disorder.
    a. glutamate receptors
    b. viral infections
    c. oxygen deprivation
    d. learned helplessness

Ans: e

15. Kyle is extremely manipulative and can look anyone in the eye and lie convincingly. His deceit often endangers the safety and well-being of those around him, but he is indifferent to any suffering they might experience as a result of his actions. His behavior best illustrates:
    a. schizophrenia.
    b. dissociative identity disorder.
    c. bipolar disorder.
    d. obsessive-compulsive disorder.
    e. a personality disorder.

Web Quiz 2

Ans: a

1. Janette, a 30-year-old teacher, regularly loses her temper and experiences tension and fatigue. Her behavior is most likely to be diagnosed as psychologically disordered if it is:
   a. personally disabling and a cause of suffering.
   b. a reaction to the stresses of her career.
   c. not caused by a biological impairment.
   d. a symptom of her own unconscious conflicts.
   e. indicative of a life-long personality style.

Ans: b

2. If researchers discovered that genetically influenced abnormalities in brain structure contribute to bipolar disorder, this would most clearly add credibility to:
   a. the DSM-IV.
   b. the medical model.
   c. the social-cognitive perspective.
   d. psychoanalytic theory.
   e. the humanistic perspective.

Ans: d

3. After participants in one study were informed that a videotaped interviewee was a psychiatric patient, they characterized the person with phrases such as "a passive type" and "frightened of his own impulses." This study best illustrated the:
   a. value of a psychoanalytic perspective.
   b. dangers of dissociative identity disorder.
   c. unreliability of the DSM-IV.
   d. biasing power of diagnostic labels.
   e. shortcomings of the social-cognitive perspective.

Ans: b

4. Symptoms that may be misperceived as a heart attack are most characteristic of:
   a. bipolar disorder.
   b. panic disorder.
   c. dysthymic disorder.
   d. catatonia.
   e. obsessive-compulsive disorder.

Ans: c

5. Although Mark realizes that his behavior is unreasonable, he is so alarmed by high bridges or expressway overpasses that he avoids them by taking an unnecessarily lengthy route to and from work each day. Mark appears to suffer from a(n):
   a. obsessive-compulsive disorder.
   b. mood disorder.
   c. phobia.
   d. dissociative disorder.
   e. generalized anxiety disorder.

Ans: b

6. Without success, Maxine spends hours each day trying to suppress intrusive thoughts that she might have forgotten to lock her house when she left for work. Her experience is most symptomatic of:
   a. a panic disorder.
   b. an obsessive-compulsive disorder.
   c. a generalized anxiety disorder.
   d. a dissociative disorder.
   e. a histrionic personality disorder.

Ans: e

7. A dysthymic disorder is most likely to be characterized by:
   a. a hyperactive, wildly optimistic state of emotion.
   b. a continuous state of tension, apprehension, and autonomic nervous system arousal.
   c. alternations between extreme hopelessness and unrealistic optimism.
   d. a persistent irrational fear of other people.
   e. a persistently sad mood and low energy level.

Ans: d

8. Mr. Hoffman has always been cautious with his money, but over the past two weeks he has developed grandiose plans to bet his entire life savings on a single horse race. With unrestrained exuberance he has also been giving everybody he sees unsolicited advice on how to make millions in the stock market. Mr. Hoffman's behavior is most indicative of:
   a. an obsessive-compulsive disorder.
   b. a dysthymic disorder.
   c. an antisocial personality disorder.
   d. a manic episode.
   e. a panic attack.

Ans: d

9. Amanda's therapist suggests that her depression results from mistakenly blaming herself rather than a slumping economy for her recent job loss. Her therapist's suggestion best illustrates a:
   a. DSM-IV diagnosis.
   b. psychoanalytic perspective.
   c. medical model.
   d. social-cognitive perspective.

Ans: e

10. Which of the following disorders is associated with a high level of hypnotizability?
   a. generalized anxiety disorder
   b. schizophrenia
   c. dysthymic disorder
   d. obsessive-compulsive disorder
   e. dissociative identity disorder

Ans: a

11. Which perspective suggests that dissociative identity disorders are created as defenses against the anxiety caused by one's own unacceptable impulses?
a. psychoanalytic
b. social-cognitive
c. humanistic
d. bio-social-psychological

Ans: c

12. Mrs. Higgins believes that aliens from another planet have removed her stomach and are watching her to see how long it takes her to grow another one. Mrs. Higgins is most likely suffering from:
a. agoraphobia.
b. bipolar disorder.
c. schizophrenia.
d. a panic disorder.
e. a dissociative identity disorder.

Ans: d

13. Michael complains that threatening voices are constantly telling him that he is so evil that he should drown himself. Michael is experiencing:
a. a panic attack.
b. catatonia.
c. flat affect.
d. hallucinations.
e. a dissociative disorder.

Ans: c

14. Drugs that block ________ receptors are most likely to reduce the _______ symptoms of schizophrenia.
a. serotonin; positive
b. serotonin; negative
c. dopamine; positive
d. dopamine; negative

Ans: a

15. Low levels of anxiety are most characteristic of:
a. antisocial personality disorder.
b. dissociative identity disorder.
c. obsessive-compulsive disorder.
d. paranoid schizophrenia.
e. agoraphobia.

Study Guide Questions

Ans: a, p. 620

1. Which of the following is true concerning abnormal behavior?
   a. Definitions of abnormal behavior are culture-dependent.
   b. A behavior cannot be defined as abnormal unless it is considered harmful to society.
   c. Abnormal behavior can be defined as any behavior that is atypical.
   d. Definitions of abnormal behavior are based on physiological factors.

Ans: c, p. 620

2. The criteria for classifying behavior as psychologically disordered:
   a. vary from culture to culture.
   b. vary from time to time.
   c. are characterized by both a. and b.
   d. have remained largely unchanged over the course of history.

Ans: e, p. 620

3. Behavior is classified as disordered when it is:
   a. atypical.
   b. maladaptive.
   c. unjustifiable.
   d. disturbing.
   e. all of the above.

Ans: b, p. 621

4. Our early ancestors commonly attributed disordered behavior to:
   a. "bad blood."
   b. evil spirits.
   c. brain injury.
   d. laziness.

Ans: e, p. 621

5. The French reformer who insisted that madness was not demon possession and who called for humane treatment of patients was:
   a. Nadel.
   b. Freud.
   c. Szasz.
   d. Spanos.
   e. Pinel.

Ans: b, p. 621

6. Which of the following is true of the medical model?
   a. In recent years, it has been in large part discredited.
   b. It views psychological disorders as sicknesses that are diagnosable and treatable.
   c. It emphasizes the role of psychological factors in disorders over that of physiological factors.
   d. It focuses on cognitive factors.

Ans: c, p. 621

7. Most mental health workers today take the view that disordered behaviors:
   a. are usually genetically triggered.
   b. are organic diseases.
   c. arise from the interaction of nature and nurture.
   d. are the product of learning.

Ans: b, pp. 621-622

8. The fact that disorders such as schizophrenia are universal and influenced by heredity, whereas other disorders such as anorexia nervosa are culture-bound provides evidence for the ________ model of psychological disorders.
   a. medical
   b. bio-psycho-social
   c. social-cultural
   d. psychoanalytic

Ans: d, p. 622

9. Evidence of environmental effects on psychological disorders is seen in the fact that certain disorders, such as ________, are universal, whereas others, such as ________ are culture-bound.
   a. schizophrenia; depression
   b. depression; schizophrenia
   c. antisocial personality; neurosis
   d. depression; anorexia nervosa

Ans: c, pp. 622-623

10. Many psychologists dislike using DSM-IV because of its:
   a. failure to emphasize observable behaviors in the diagnostic process.
   b. learning theory bias.
   c. medical model bias.
   d. psychoanalytic bias.
   e. social-cultural bias.

Ans: d, p. 623

11. The diagnostic reliability of DSM-IV:
   a. is unknown.
   b. depends on the age of the patient.
   c. is very low.
   d. is relatively high.

Ans: a, pp. 623-625

12. Which of the following statements concerning the labeling of disordered behaviors is *not* true?
   a. Labels interfere with effective treatment of psychological disorders.
   b. Labels promote research studies of psychological disorders.
   c. Labels may create preconceptions that bias people's perceptions.
   d. Labels may influence behavior by creating self-fulfilling prophecies.

Ans: a, p. 626

13. The term *insanity* refers to:
    a. legal definitions.
    b. psychotic disorders only.
    c. personality disorders only.
    d. both psychotic disorders and personality disorders.

Ans: a, p. 627

14. Phobias and obsessive-compulsive behaviors are classified as:
    a. anxiety disorders.
    b. mood disorders.
    c. dissociative disorders.
    d. personality disorders.

Ans: d, p. 627

15. Sharon is continually tense, jittery, and apprehensive for no specific reason. She would probably be diagnosed as suffering a(n):
    a. phobia.
    b. major depressive disorder.
    c. obsessive-compulsive disorder.
    d. generalized anxiety disorder.

Ans: d, p. 627

16. Irene occasionally experiences unpredictable episodes of intense dread accompanied by chest pains and a sensation of smothering. Since her symptoms have no apparent cause, they would probably be classified as indicative of:
    a. schizophrenia.
    b. bipolar disorder.
    c. post-traumatic stress disorder.
    d. panic attack.

Ans: c, p. 628

17. Joe has an intense, irrational fear of snakes. He is suffering from a(n):
    a. generalized anxiety disorder.
    b. obsessive-compulsive disorder.
    c. phobia.
    d. mood disorder.
    e. bipolar disorder.

Ans: d, pp. 628-629

18. Jason is so preoccupied with staying clean that he showers as many as ten times each day. Jason would be diagnosed as suffering from a(n):
    a. dissociative disorder.
    b. generalized anxiety disorder.
    c. personality disorder.
    d. obsessive-compulsive disorder.

Ans: b, p. 629

19. The psychoanalytic perspective would most likely view phobias as:
   a. conditioned fears.
   b. displaced responses to incompletely repressed impulses.
   c. biological predispositions.
   d. manifestations of self-defeating thoughts.

Ans: d, pp. 629-630

20. Julia's psychologist believes that Julia's fear of heights can be traced to a conditioned fear she developed after falling from a ladder. This explanation reflects a ______ perspective.
   a. medical
   b. psychoanalytic
   c. social-cognitive
   d. learning

Ans: d, p. 630

21. Although she escaped from war-torn Bosnia two years ago, Zheina still has haunting memories and nightmares. Because she is also severely depressed, her therapist diagnoses her condition as:
   a. dissociative identity disorder.
   b. bipolar disorder.
   c. schizophrenia.
   d. post-traumatic stress disorder.

Ans: a, p. 631

22. Before he can study, Rashid must arrange his books, pencils, paper, and other items on his desk so that they are "just so." The campus counselor suggests that Rashid's compulsive behavior may help alleviate his anxiety about failing in school, which reinforces the compulsive actions. This explanation of obsessive-compulsive behavior is most consistent with which perspective?
   a. learning
   b. psychoanalytic
   c. humanistic
   d. social-cognitive

Ans: a, p. 632

23. To which of the following is a person *most* likely to acquire a phobia?
   a. heights
   b. being in public
   c. being dirty
   d. All of the above are equally likely.

Ans: c, p. 632

24. After falling from a ladder, Joseph is afraid of airplanes, although he has never flown. This demonstrates that some fears arise from:
   a. observational learning.
   b. reinforcement.
   c. stimulus generalization.
   d. stimulus discrimination.

Ans: d, p. 632

25. Which of the following provides evidence that human fears have been subjected to the evolutionary process?
    a. Compulsive acts typically exaggerate behaviors that contributed to our species' survival.
    b. Most phobias focus on objects that our ancestors also feared.
    c. It is easier to condition some fears than others.
    d. All of the above provide evidence.

Ans: d, p. 632

26. Which of the following was presented in the text as evidence of biological influences on anxiety disorders?
    a. Identical twins often develop similar phobias.
    b. PET scans of persons with obsessive-compulsive disorder reveal unusually high activity in an area of the frontal lobes.
    c. Drugs that dampen fear-circuit activity in the amygdala also alleviate OCD.
    d. All of the above were presented.
    e. None of the above was presented.

Ans: a, p. 634

27. Which of the following is the most pervasive of the psychological disorders?
    a. depression
    b. schizophrenia
    c. bipolar disorder
    d. generalized anxiety disorder

Ans: b, p. 634

28. For the past six months, a woman has complained of feeling isolated from others, dissatisfied with life, and discouraged about the future. This woman could be diagnosed as suffering from:
    a. bipolar disorder.
    b. major depressive disorder.
    c. generalized anxiety disorder.
    d. dissociative disorder.

Ans: a, p. 634

29. On Monday, Matt felt optimistic, energetic, and on top of the world. On Tuesday, he felt hopeless and lethargic, and thought that the future looked very grim. Matt would *most* likely be diagnosed as having:
    a. bipolar disorder.
    b. major depressive disorder.
    c. schizophrenia.
    d. panic disorder.

Ans: b, p. 636

30. In general, women are more vulnerable than men to ________ disorders such as ________.
    a. active; anxiety
    b. passive; depression
    c. active; antisocial conduct
    d. passive; alcohol abuse

Ans: b, p. 636

31. Which of the following is *not* true concerning depression?
    a. Depression is more common in females than in males.
    b. Most depressive episodes appear not to be preceded by any particular factor or event.
    c. Most depressive episodes last less than three months.
    d. Most people recover from depression without professional therapy.

Ans: b, p. 636

32. Gender differences in the prevalence of depression may be partly due to the fact that when stressful experiences occur, women tend to ________ while men tend to ________.
    a. act; think
    b. think; act
    c. distract themselves by drinking; delve into their work
    d. delve into their work; distract themselves by drinking

Ans: d, p. 637

33. Connie's therapist has suggested that her depression stems from unresolved anger toward her parents. Evidently, Connie's therapist is working within the ________ perspective.
    a. learning
    b. social-cognitive
    c. biological
    d. psychoanalytic

Ans: d, p. 637

34. According to psychoanalytic theory, memory of losses, especially in combination with internalized anger, is likely to result in:
    a. learned helplessness.
    b. the self-serving bias.
    c. weak ego defense mechanisms.
    d. depression.

Ans: c, p. 638

35. In treating depression, a psychiatrist would probably prescribe a drug that would:
    a. increase levels of acetylcholine.
    b. decrease levels of dopamine.
    c. increase levels of norepinephrine.
    d. decrease levels of serotonin.

Ans: d, p. 638

36. Which neurotransmitter is present in overabundant amounts during the manic phase of bipolar disorder?
    a. dopamine
    b. serotonin
    c. epinephrine
    d. norepinephrine

Ans: b, p. 638

37. Alicia's doctor, who thinks that Alicia's depression has a biochemical cause, prescribes a drug that:
a. reduces norepinephrine.
b. increases norepinephrine.
c. reduces serotonin.
d. increases acetylcholine.

Ans: d, pp. 640-641

38. According to the social-cognitive perspective, a person who experiences unexpected aversive events may develop helplessness and manifest a(n):
a. obsessive-compulsive disorder.
b. dissociative disorder.
c. personality disorder.
d. mood disorder.

Ans: d, pp. 640-641

39. Social-cognitive theorists contend that depression is linked with:
a. negative moods.
b. maladaptive explanations of failure.
c. self-defeating beliefs.
d. all of the above.

Ans: b, pp. 640-642

40. Ken's therapist suggested that his depression is a result of his self-defeating thoughts and negative assumptions about himself, his situation, and his future. Evidently, Ken's therapist is working within the ________ perspective.
a. learning
b. social-cognitive
c. biological
d. psychoanalytic

Ans: b, p. 643

41. Hussein, who suffers from chronic loneliness, probably attributes his unsatisfactory social relationships to:
a. an inherited trait.
b. his own inadequacies.
c. a cultural norm.
d. the social incompetence of other people.

Ans: b, p. 644

42. Dr. Jekyll, whose second personality was Mr. Hyde, had a(n) ________ disorder.
a. anxiety
b. dissociative
c. mood
d. personality

Ans: c, p. 644

43. As a child, Monica was criticized severely by her mother for not living up to her expectations. This criticism was always followed by a beating with a whip. As an adult, Monica is generally introverted and extremely shy. Sometimes, however, she acts more like a young child, throwing tantrums if she doesn't get her way. At other times, she is a flirting, happy-go-lucky young lady. Most likely, Monica is suffering from:
    a. a phobia.
    b. dissociative schizophrenia.
    c. dissociative identity disorder.
    d. bipolar disorder.

Ans: b, pp. 644-645

44. Nicholas Spanos considers dissociative identity disorder to be:
    a. a genuine disorder.
    b. merely role-playing.
    c. a disorder that cannot be explained according to the learning perspective.
    d. both a. and c.

Ans: b, p. 645

45. Psychoanalytic and learning theorists both agree that dissociative and anxiety disorders are symptoms that represent the person's attempt to deal with:
    a. unconscious conflicts.
    b. anxiety.
    c. unfulfilled wishes.
    d. unpleasant responsibilities.

Ans: a, pp. 646-647

46. Claiming that she heard a voice commanding her to warn other people that eating is harmful, Sandy attempts to convince others in a restaurant not to eat. The psychiatrist to whom she is referred finds that Sandy's thinking and speech are often fragmented and incoherent. In addition, Sandy has an unreasonable fear that someone is "out to get her" and consequently trusts no one. Her condition is most indicative of:
    a. schizophrenia.
    b. generalized anxiety disorder.
    c. a phobia.
    d. obsessive-compulsive disorder.
    e. personality disorder.

Ans: c, pp. 646-647

47. Which of the following is *not* a symptom of schizophrenia?
    a. inappropriate emotions
    b. disturbed perceptions
    c. panic attacks
    d. disorganized thinking

Ans: c, p. 647

48. Most of the hallucinations of schizophrenia patients involve the sense of:
    a. smell.
    b. vision.
    c. hearing.
    d. touch.

Ans: d, p. 647
49. Hearing voices would be a(n) ________; believing that you are Napoleon would be a(n) ________.
a. obsession; compulsion
b. compulsion; obsession
c. delusion; hallucination
d. hallucination; delusion

Ans: a, p. 647
50. Many psychologists believe the disorganized thoughts of people with schizophrenia result from a breakdown in:
a. selective attention.
b. memory storage.
c. motivation.
d. memory retrieval.
e. memory encoding.

Ans: c, p. 648
51. When schizophrenia is slow to develop, called ________ schizophrenia, recovery is ________.
a. reactive; unlikely
b. process; likely
c. process; unlikely
d. reactive; likely

Ans: a, p. 649
52. The effect of drugs that block receptors for dopamine is to:
a. alleviate schizophrenia symptoms.
b. alleviate depression.
c. increase schizophrenia symptoms.
d. increase depression.

Ans: d, p. 649
53. Wayne's doctor attempts to help Wayne by prescribing a drug that blocks receptors for dopamine. Wayne has apparently been diagnosed with:
a. a mood disorder.
b. an anxiety disorder.
c. a personality disorder.
d. schizophrenia.

Ans: c, p. 650
54. Janet, whose class presentation is titled "Current Views on the Causes of Schizophrenia," concludes her talk with the statement:
a. "Schizophrenia is caused by intolerable stress."
b. "Schizophrenia is inherited."
c. "Genes may predispose some people to react to particular experiences by developing schizophrenia."
d. "As of this date, schizophrenia is completely unpredictable and its causes are unknown."

Ans: d, p. 650

55. Among the following, which is generally accepted as a possible cause of schizophrenia?
    a. an excess of endorphins in the brain
    b. being a twin
    c. extensive learned helplessness
    d. a genetic predisposition

Ans: c, p. 650

56. Which of the following is *not* true regarding schizophrenia?
    a. It occurs more frequently in people born in winter and spring months.
    b. It occurs less frequently as infectious disease rates have declined.
    c. It occurs more frequently in lightly populated areas.
    d. It usually appears during adolescence or early adulthood.

Ans: b, p. 650

57. Research evidence links the brain abnormalities of schizophrenia to ________ during prenatal development.
    a. maternal stress
    b. a viral infection contracted
    c. abnormal levels of certain hormones
    d. the weight of the unborn child
    e. alcohol use

Ans: d, p. 652

58. The early warning signs of schizophrenia, based on studies of high-risk children, include all but which of the following?
    a. having a severely schizophrenic mother
    b. having been separated from parents
    c. having a short attention span
    d. having matured physically at a very early age

Ans: d, p. 654

59. Bob has never been able to keep a job. He's been in and out of jail for charges such as theft, sexual assault, and spousal abuse. Bob would most likely be diagnosed as having:
    a. a dissociative identity disorder.
    b. major depressive disorder.
    c. schizophrenia.
    d. an antisocial personality.

Ans: b, p. 654

60. When expecting to be electrically shocked, people with an antisocial disorder, as compared to normal people, show:
    a. less fear and greater arousal of the autonomic nervous system.
    b. less fear and less autonomic arousal.
    c. greater fear and greater autonomic arousal.
    d. greater fear and less autonomic arousal.

CHAPTER 17

Therapy

Learning Objectives

The Psychological Therapies (pp. 660-673)

1. Discuss the aims and methods of psychoanalysis, and explain the critics' concerns with this form of therapy.

2. Identify the basic characteristics of the humanistic therapies as well as the specific goals and techniques of client-centered therapy.

3. Identify the basic assumptions of behavior therapy, and discuss the classical conditioning techniques of systematic desensitization and aversive conditioning.

4. Describe therapeutic applications of operant conditioning principles, and explain the critics' concerns with this behavior modification process.

5. Describe the assumptions and goals of the cognitive therapies and their application to the treatment of depression.

6. Discuss the rationale and benefits of group therapy, including family therapy.

Evaluating Psychotherapies (pp. 674-685)

7. Discuss the findings regarding the effectiveness of the psychotherapies, and explain why ineffective therapies are often mistakenly perceived to be of value.

8. Describe the commonalities among the psychotherapies, and discuss the role of values and cultural differences in the therapeutic process.

The Biomedical Therapies (pp. 685-691)

9. Identify the common forms of drug therapy.

10. Describe the use of electroconvulsive therapy and psychosurgery in the treatment of psychological disorders.

Preventing Psychological Disorders (pp. 692-693)

11. Explain the rationale of preventive mental health programs.

The psychological therapies, p. 660
Easy, Factual/Definitional, Objective 1, Ans: d

1. An eclectic therapist is one who:
   a. prescribes the use of drugs as part of psychotherapy.
   b. emphasizes that active listening is the major technique in all effective therapies.
   c. prefers to engage in therapy in a group setting.
   d. uses a variety of psychological theories and therapeutic approaches.

The psychological therapies, p. 660
Medium, Conceptual/Application, Objective 1, Ans: e

2. Dr. Byrne is a clinical psychologist who often uses operant conditioning techniques to treat her clients. She also encourages them to modify their thought patterns, and on occasion she interprets their transference behaviors. Dr. Byrne's therapeutic approach would best be described as:
   a. client-centered.
   b. meta-analytic.
   c. psychoanalytic.
   d. behavioral.
   e. eclectic.

Psychoanalysis, p. 660
Medium, Conceptual/Application, Objective 1, Ans: c

3. Mr. Choi's therapist wants to help him become aware of his conflicting childhood feelings of love and hate for his parents. The therapist's goal best reflects a primary aim of:
   a. client-centered therapy.
   b. cognitive therapy.
   c. psychoanalysis.
   d. systematic desensitization.
   e. operant conditioning techniques.

Psychoanalysis, p. 661
Easy, Factual/Definitional, Objective 1, Ans: e

4. A central therapeutic technique of psychoanalysis is:
   a. stress inoculation training.
   b. systematic desensitization.
   c. observational learning.
   d. active listening.
   e. free association.

Psychoanalysis, p. 661
Medium, Conceptual/Application, Objective 1, Ans: d

5. When Molly told her therapist about her frightening car accident, the therapist instructed her to close her eyes and verbalize any further thoughts stimulated by this experience, even if they were scary or embarrassing. The therapist was making use of a technique known as:
   a. active listening.
   b. transference.
   c. systematic desensitization.
   d. free association.
   e. aversive conditioning.

Psychoanalysis, p. 661
Easy, Factual/Definitional, Objective 1, Ans: b

6. According to psychoanalysts, resistance refers to the:
   a. expression toward a therapist of feelings linked with earlier relationships.
   b. blocking from consciousness of anxiety-laden material during therapy.
   c. replacement of a genuine concern for others with self-centeredness.
   d. conversion of psychological conflicts into physical and behavioral disorders.

Psychoanalysis, p. 661
Difficult, Conceptual, Objective 1, Ans: b

7. Who would be most likely to anticipate that patients are often motivated to avoid fully complying with specific therapeutic instructions?
   a. a humanistic therapist
   b. a psychoanalyst
   c. a behavior therapist
   d. a cognitive therapist

Psychoanalysis, p. 661
Medium, Conceptual/Application, Objective 1, Ans: e

8. During psychotherapy, Leon would begin to stutter whenever he began discussing personally sensitive thoughts. Sigmund Freud would have been likely to interpret this stuttering as:
   a. meta-analysis.
   b. systematic desensitization.
   c. regression toward the mean.
   d. transference.
   e. resistance.

Psychoanalysis, pp. 661-662
Difficult, Conceptual/Application, Objective 1, Ans: b

9. Psychoanalysts would be most likely to discourage patients from:
   a. experiencing strong positive or negative feelings for their therapist.
   b. discontinuing psychotherapy whenever they felt it was no longer necessary.
   c. talking about anxiety-arousing material during therapy.
   d. taking antianxiety drugs during the course of psychotherapy.

Psychoanalysis, p. 661
Easy, Factual/Definitional, Objective 1, Ans: a

10. Which of the following therapists would most likely try to understand an adult's psychological disorder by exploring that person's childhood experiences?
   a. a psychoanalyst
   b. a behavior therapist
   c. a humanistic therapist
   d. a cognitive therapist

Psychoanalysis, p. 661
Easy, Factual/Definitional, Objective 1, Ans: b

11. Transference refers to a client's:
   a. conversion of psychological conflicts into physical and behavioral disorders.
   b. expression toward a therapist of feelings linked with earlier life relationships.
   c. replacement of self-centeredness with a genuine concern for others.
   d. translation of threatening dream content into nonthreatening manifest symbols.

Psychoanalysis, p. 661
Difficult, Conceptual/Application, Objective 1, Ans: c

12. Lynn has begun to buy small gifts for her therapist, and she feels extremely jealous of the time he spends with his other patients. To a psychoanalyst, this is most indicative of:
    a. unconditional positive regard.
    b. the placebo effect.
    c. transference.
    d. therapeutic touch.
    e. free association.

Psychoanalysis, p. 661
Difficult, Conceptual, Objective 1, Ans: c

13. Psychoanalysts are most likely to view patient transference as:
    a. a form of therapeutic resistance.
    b. a sign of healthy personality development.
    c. a helpful aid to the process of therapy.
    d. evidence that no further therapy is needed.

Psychodynamic therapy, p. 662
Medium, Factual/Definitional, Objective 1, Ans: c

14. A psychodynamic therapist is most likely to:
    a. associate patients' undesirable behaviors with unpleasant consequences.
    b. help patients identify a hierarchy of anxiety-arousing experiences.
    c. suggest interpretive insights regarding patients' difficulties.
    d. recommend the use of antipsychotic drugs during the process of psychotherapy.
    e. encourage depressed patients to take more responsibility for their failures.

Psychodynamic therapy, p. 662
Easy, Conceptual/Application, Objective 1, Ans: b

15. Which form of therapy would most likely try to help depressed patients by teaching them how to resolve disagreements with their friends?
    a. systematic desensitization
    b. interpersonal psychotherapy
    c. humanistic therapy
    d. cognitive therapy
    e. psychoanalysis

Humanistic therapies, p. 663
Difficult, Factual/Definitional, Objective 2, Ans: d

16. Humanistic therapists are likely to teach clients to:
    a. focus more on other people's feelings than on their own.
    b. adapt more readily to social norms and expectations.
    c. imitate the behavior of others who are happy and successful.
    d. take more responsibility for their own feelings and actions.
    e. do all of the above.

Psychoanalytic and humanistic therapies, pp. 661, 663
Medium, Conceptual, Objectives 1 & 2, Ans: c

17. Psychoanalytic therapy is to ________ as humanistic therapy is to ________.
a. feelings; behavior
b. Freud; Wolpe
c. past experience; present experience
d. transference; systematic desensitization
e. personal freedom; personal responsibility

Humanistic therapies, p. 663
Easy, Factual/Definitional, Objective 2, Ans: c

18. Empathic understanding of the patient's subjective experiences is a major goal of a:
a. psychoanalyst.
b. biomedical therapist.
c. client-centered therapist.
d. behavior therapist.

Humanistic therapies, pp. 663-664
Medium, Conceptual, Objective 2, Ans: d

19. Which therapeutic approach relies most heavily on patients discovering their own ways of effectively dealing with their difficulties?
a. psychoanalysis
b. cognitive therapy
c. systematic desensitization
d. client-centered therapy
e. meta-analysis

Humanistic therapies, p. 664
Easy, Factual/Definitional, Objective 2, Ans: e

20. An important feature of client-centered therapy is:
a. interpretation.
b. systematic desensitization.
c. transference.
d. free association.
e. active listening.

Humanistic therapies, p. 664
Medium, Conceptual/Application, Objective 2, Ans: d

21. When Murli told his therapist, "I came to see what you could do for me," the therapist responded, "It sounds like you're feeling you need some help. Am I right?" The therapist's response illustrates the technique of:
a. meta-analysis.
b. transference.
c. free association.
d. active listening.
e. systematic desensitization.

Humanistic therapies, p. 664
Difficult, Conceptual/Application, Objective 2, Ans: e

22. During a marriage counseling session, the therapist suggests to Mr. and Mrs. Gallo that they each restate their spouse's comments before making their own. The therapist was applying a technique most closely associated with:
    a. EMDR.
    b. psychoanalysis.
    c. cognitive-behavior therapy.
    d. systematic desensitization.
    e. client-centered therapy.

Behavior therapies, pp. 664-665
Medium, Conceptual, Objective 3, Ans: c

23. The importance of clarifying and enhancing one's sense of self is *least* likely to be emphasized by ________ therapists.
    a. cognitive
    b. psychoanalytic
    c. behavior
    d. humanistic

Behavior therapies, p. 665
Easy, Factual/Definitional, Objective 3, Ans: b

24. Psychological research on the principles of learning has most directly influenced the development of:
    a. psychoanalysis.
    b. behavior therapy.
    c. humanistic therapy.
    d. psychodynamic therapy.
    e. cognitive therapy.

Classical conditioning techniques, p. 665
Medium, Factual/Definitional, Objective 3, Ans: d

25. In classical conditioning therapies, maladaptive symptoms are usually considered to be:
    a. unconditioned stimuli.
    b. conditioned stimuli.
    c. unconditioned responses.
    d. conditioned responses.

Classical conditioning techniques, p. 665
Medium, Factual/Definitional, Objective 3, Ans: c

26. In one treatment for bed-wetting, the child sleeps on a liquid-sensitive pad that when wet, triggers an alarm and awakens the child. This treatment is a form of:
    a. biomedical therapy.
    b. cognitive therapy.
    c. behavior therapy.
    d. humanistic therapy.
    e. psychodynamic therapy.

Classical conditioning techniques, p. 665
Difficult, Conceptual/Application, Objective 3, Ans: a

27. Benny's mother tries to reduce his fear of sailing by giving the 3-year-old his favorite candy as soon as they board the boat. The mother's strategy best illustrates:
a. counterconditioning.
b. cognitive therapy.
c. transference.
d. aversive conditioning.
e. the placebo effect.

Classical conditioning techniques, p. 665
Easy, Factual/Definitional, Objective 3, Ans: c

28. Systematic desensitization is a form of:
a. psychoanalysis.
b. biomedical therapy.
c. counterconditioning.
d. cognitive therapy.
e. humanistic therapy.

Systematic desensitization, pp. 665, 668
Medium, Conceptual, Objective 3, Ans: a

29. A token economy is to operant conditioning as ________ is to classical conditioning.
a. systematic desensitization
b. group therapy
c. electroconvulsive therapy
d. free association
e. drug therapy

Systematic desensitization, p. 665
Medium, Factual/Definitional, Objective 3, Ans: b

30. In 1924, Mary Cover Jones reported that 3-year-old Peter lost his fear of rabbits when one was repeatedly presented while he was eating a tasty snack. This episode best illustrated the potential usefulness of:
a. stress inoculation training.
b. exposure therapies.
c. aversive conditioning.
d. free association.
e. the placebo effect.

Systematic desensitization, p. 666
Medium, Factual/Definitional, Objective 3, Ans: d

31. The most widely used form of behavior therapy is:
a. active listening.
b. aversive conditioning.
c. the token economy.
d. exposure therapy.
e. stress inoculation training.

Systematic desensitization, p. 666
Medium, Factual/Definitional, Objective 3, Ans: d

32. Which of the following best exemplifies exposure therapy?
a. therapeutic touch
b. family therapy
c. stress inoculation training
d. systematic desensitization
e. repetitive transcranial magnetic stimulation

Systematic desensitization, p. 666
Medium, Factual/Definitional, Objective 3, Ans: d

33. Systematic desensitization involves:
a. depriving a client access to an addictive drug.
b. associating unwanted behaviors with unpleasant experiences.
c. replacing a positive response to a harmful stimulus with a negative response.
d. associating a pleasant relaxed state with anxiety-arousing stimuli.
e. vigorously challenging clients' illogical ways of thinking.

Systematic desensitization, p. 666
Medium, Factual/Definitional, Objective 3, Ans: d

34. Systematic desensitization is based on the idea that ________ facilitates the elimination of fear.
a. the placebo effect
b. movement of the eyes
c. therapeutic touch
d. relaxation
e. active listening

Systematic desensitization, p. 666
Medium, Conceptual/Application, Objective 3, Ans: e

35. Jonathan is afraid to ask a girl for a date, so his therapist instructs him to relax and simply imagine he is telephoning a potential date. The therapist's technique best illustrates the process of:
a. interpersonal therapy.
b. free association.
c. cognitive therapy.
d. aversive conditioning.
e. systematic desensitization.

Systematic desensitization, p. 666
Difficult, Conceptual/Application, Objective 3, Ans: c

36. Which of the following techniques would behavior therapists most likely use to help people overcome a fear of flying?
a. aversive conditioning
b. eclectic therapy
c. systematic desensitization
d. transference
e. a token economy

Systematic desensitization, p. 666
Difficult, Conceptual/Application, Objective 3, Ans: d

37. Gina is so fearful of taking tests for college courses that she experiences mild anxiety when registering for a course, intense anxiety when studying for a test, and extreme anxiety when answering actual test questions. Her greatest fear, however, is experienced while waiting for a professor to hand the tests out to the class. During the process of systematically desensitizing her test anxiety, the therapist is likely to ask Gina first to imagine:
    a. answering questions on a college test.
    b. waiting for a professor to hand a test out to a class.
    c. studying for a test.
    d. registering for a college course.

Systematic desensitization, p. 666
Medium, Factual/Definitional, Objective 3, Ans: d

38. Virtual reality exposure therapy is most similar to:
    a. stress inoculation training.
    b. aversive conditioning.
    c. therapeutic touch.
    d. systematic desensitization.
    e. free association.

Aversive conditioning, p. 667
Easy, Factual/Definitional, Objective 3, Ans: e

39. In which form of therapy is unwanted behavior systematically associated with unpleasant experiences?
    a. electroconvulsive therapy
    b. systematic desensitization
    c. eclectic therapy
    d. cognitive therapy
    e. aversive conditioning

Aversive conditioning, p. 667
Difficult, Conceptual, Objective 3, Ans: c

40. Replacing a negative response with a positive response is to systematic desensitization as replacing a positive response with a negative response is to:
    a. transference.
    b. operant conditioning.
    c. aversive conditioning.
    d. eclectic therapy.
    e. electroconvulsive therapy.

Aversive conditioning, p. 667
Easy, Factual/Definitional, Objective 3, Ans: d

41. In programs to treat alcoholism, clients consume alcohol that contains a nausea-producing drug. The therapist is using a technique known as:
    a. operant conditioning.
    b. free association.
    c. systematic desensitization.
    d. aversive conditioning.
    e. transference.

Aversive conditioning, p. 667
Medium, Conceptual/Application, Objective 3, Ans: a

42. To help Claire quit smoking, a therapist delivers an electric shock to her arm each time she smokes a cigarette. The therapist is using:
    a. aversive conditioning.
    b. systematic desensitization.
    c. electroconvulsive therapy.
    d. cognitive therapy.
    e. EMDR.

Aversive conditioning, p. 667
Difficult, Conceptual/Application, Objective 3, Ans: e

43. Connor is constantly chewing tobacco. In order to reduce his appetite for this product, a behavior therapist would most likely use:
    a. EMDR.
    b. a token economy.
    c. systematic desensitization.
    d. virtual reality exposure therapy.
    e. aversive conditioning.

Operant conditioning, p. 668
Easy, Factual/Definitional, Objective 4, Ans: c

44. Which of the following is the best description of techniques involving behavior modification?
    a. Patients are helped to identify a hierarchy of anxiety-arousing experiences.
    b. Clients' illogical ways of thinking are vigorously challenged.
    c. Patients' actions are influenced by therapeutically controlling the consequences of those actions.
    d. What a client says during the course of therapy is repeated or rephrased.
    e. Attention is focused on clients' positive and negative feelings toward their therapists.

Operant conditioning, p. 668
Difficult, Factual/Definitional, Objective 4, Ans: a

45. The approach that has helped autistic children learn to function successfully in school involves:
    a. operant conditioning.
    b. systematic desensitization.
    c. the double-blind technique.
    d. family therapy.
    e. aversive conditioning.

Operant conditioning, p. 668
Easy, Factual/Definitional, Objective 4, Ans: a

46. A token economy represents an application of the principles of:
    a. operant conditioning.
    b. systematic desensitization.
    c. humanistic therapy.
    d. classical conditioning.
    e. observational learning.

Operant conditioning, p. 668
Easy, Conceptual/Application, Objective 4, Ans: c

47. In order to encourage Mrs. Coleman, a withdrawn schizophrenia patient, to be more socially active, institutional staff members give her small plastic cards whenever she talks to someone. She is allowed to exchange these cards for candy and cigarettes. Staff members are making use of:
a. active listening.
b. systematic desensitization.
c. a token economy.
d. free association.
e. classical conditioning.

Operant conditioning, pp. 665, 668
Medium, Conceptual, Objective 4, Ans: c

48. Systematic desensitization is to classical conditioning as ________ is to operant conditioning.
a. aversive conditioning
b. therapeutic touch
c. a token economy
d. psychosurgery
e. EMDR

Operant conditioning, pp. 668-669
Medium, Conceptual, Objective 4, Ans: e

49. "The technique reduces people to puppets controlled by therapists! It doesn't respect human freedom." This criticism is most likely to be directed at:
a. systematic desensitization.
b. cognitive therapy.
c. EMDR.
d. psychoanalysis.
e. a token economy.

Cognitive therapies (Figure 17.3), p. 669
Medium, Factual/Definitional, Objective 5, Ans: b

50. Faculty members in clinical psychology Ph.D. programs are currently most likely to align themselves with a therapeutic orientation that is:
a. psychoanalytic.
b. cognitive.
c. behavioral.
d. humanistic.

Cognitive therapies, p. 669
Medium, Factual/Definitional, Objective 5, Ans: d

51. Which therapeutic approach emphasizes that people are often disturbed because of their irrational interpretations of events?
a. drug therapy
b. client-centered therapy
c. systematic desensitization
d. cognitive therapy
e. virtual reality exposure therapy

Cognitive therapy for depression, p. 670
Medium, Conceptual/Application, Objective 5, Ans: d

52. Dylan is a college sophomore who feels so personally incompetent that he believes his life is worthless and hopeless. Dylan would profit the most from:
a. psychoanalysis.
b. therapeutic touch.
c. systematic desensitization.
d. cognitive therapy.
e. EMDR.

Cognitive therapy for depression, pp. 670-671
Easy, Factual/Definitional, Objective 5, Ans: d

53. Teaching people to take personal credit for their successes and to blame circumstances when things go wrong has been found to be effective in the treatment of:
a. dissociative disorders.
b. schizophrenia.
c. phobias.
d. depression.

Cognitive therapy for depression, pp. 670-671
Medium, Factual/Definitional, Objective 5, Ans: d

54. Cognitive therapists are most likely to encourage depressed clients to:
a. sense and express their own real moment-to-moment feelings of depression.
b. carefully observe the negative consequences of their depression.
c. take more personal responsibility for their own negative feelings and actions.
d. stop blaming themselves for negative circumstances beyond their control.
e. identify a hierarchy of anxiety-arousing experiences.

Cognitive therapy for depression, pp. 670-671
Medium, Conceptual/Application, Objective 5, Ans: c

55. When Rubin received a well-deserved job promotion, he told his therapist it was just a lucky break. The therapist responded, "Let's work together, Rubin, on helping you see that you deserve some credit for your successes." The approach taken by the therapist is most representative of:
a. client-centered therapy.
b. systematic desensitization.
c. cognitive therapy.
d. psychoanalysis.

Cognitive therapy for depression, pp. 670-671
Difficult, Conceptual/Application, Objective 5, Ans: a

56. Oni, who suffers chronic depression, has just learned that she received a high grade on her chemistry exam. A cognitive therapist would be most likely to encourage Oni to attribute her success to:
a. her effective study skills.
b. her reduced course load, which allowed her a large amount of test-preparation time.
c. a relaxed classroom atmosphere, which effectively reduced her test anxiety.
d. the excellent help she received from a friendly chemistry tutor.

Cognitive therapy for depression, p. 671
Medium, Conceptual/Application, Objective 5, Ans: b

57. Melanie's therapist suggests that when she feels anxious, Melanie should attribute her arousal to her highly reactive nervous system and shift her attention to playing a game with her preschool child. This suggestion best illustrates:
a. systematic desensitization.
b. cognitive-behavior therapy.
c. client-centered therapy.
d. psychodynamic therapy.
e. family therapy.

Group and family therapies, p. 672
Easy, Factual/Definitional, Objective 6, Ans: b

58. Group therapy is typically more effective than individual therapy for:
a. encouraging severely disturbed individuals to quickly regain normal social functioning.
b. enabling people to discover that others have problems similar to their own.
c. ensuring that therapists will become more emotionally involved in clients' real-life problems.
d. eliminating clients' anxiety during the process of therapy.

Group and family therapies, p. 672
Medium, Factual/Definitional, Objective 6, Ans: a

59. AIDS patients are ________ likely to be in support groups than hypertension patients, and breast cancer patients are ________ likely to be in support groups than heart disease patients.
a. more; more
b. less; less
c. more; less
d. less; more

Group and family therapies, p. 672
Easy, Factual/Definitional, Objective 6, Ans: d

60. Which form of therapy is most likely to emphasize the importance of examining a person's role within a social system?
a. systematic desensitization
b. cognitive therapy
c. psychoanalysis
d. family therapy
e. client-centered therapy

Group and family therapies, p. 672
Medium, Conceptual/Application, Objective 6, Ans: b

61. In order to help Mr. Eberstadt overcome his addiction to alcohol, Dr. Savimbi first attempted to discover whether the man's chemical dependency was somehow encouraged by his wife's behavior. Dr. Savimbi's concern is most likely to be characteristic of a:
a. psychoanalyst.
b. family therapist.
c. client-centered therapist.
d. biomedical therapist.
e. cognitive therapist.

Is psychotherapy effective?, p. 675
Medium, Factual/Definitional, Objective 7, Ans: c

62. Clients' perceptions of the effectiveness of psychotherapy are often misleading because clients:
a. typically underestimate how much they have improved as a result of therapy.
b. tend to focus on their behavioral changes rather than on changes in their attitudes and emotions.
c. often need to convince themselves that they didn't waste their money on therapy.
d. are often angry about the time-consuming nature of therapy.

Is psychotherapy effective?, p. 675
Difficult, Factual/Definitional, Objective 7, Ans: d

63. In one massive experiment, potentially delinquent boys were assigned to a five-year treatment program that included professional counseling and family assistance. Many years later, Joan McCord's investigation of this program's effectiveness revealed that:
a. clients who received the special treatment subsequently had fewer incidents of juvenile delinquency.
b. clients typically underestimated the truly positive effects of this program on their own lives.
c. only the therapists who were involved in the program could accurately gauge its effectiveness.
d. clients' accounts of the program's effectiveness were often misleading and overly positive.

"Regressing" from unusual to usual (Box), p. 676
Easy, Factual/Definitional, Objective 7, Ans: c

64. The placebo effect typically leads us to ________ the effectiveness of therapy and regression toward the mean typically leads us to ________ the effectiveness of therapy.
a. overestimate; underestimate
b. underestimate; overestimate
c. overestimate; overestimate
d. underestimate; underestimate

"Regressing" from unusual to usual (Box), p. 676
Difficult, Conceptual/Application, Objective 7, Ans: e

65. Although Shawn felt terribly depressed when he began psychotherapy, he was much happier by the time he had completed therapy. It would be reasonable to attribute some of his improvement to:
a. systematic desensitization.
b. therapeutic touch.
c. the double-blind technique.
d. transference.
e. regression toward the mean.

"Regressing" from unusual to usual (Box), p. 676
Easy, Conceptual/Application, Objective 7, Ans: b

66. Students who receive unusually high scores on their first psychology test can reasonably anticipate ________ scores on their second psychology test.
a. very low
b. somewhat lower
c. equally high
d. even higher

"Regressing" from unusual to usual (Box), p. 676
Easy, Conceptual/Application, Objective 7, Ans: e

67. Colette received an A on her first biology test and a B+ on the second, even though she studied equally for both tests. Which of the following best explains Colette's deteriorating pattern of performance?
   a. the double-blind technique
   b. the placebo effect
   c. systematic desensitization
   d. meta-analysis
   e. regression toward the mean

"Regressing" from unusual to usual (Box), p. 676
Difficult, Factual/Definitional, Objective 7, Ans: d

68. After sports magazines give cover-story attention to the outstanding performance of an athlete, the individual often suffers a real decline in performance. This so-called "*Sports Illustrated* jinx" may be at least partially explained in terms of:
   a. free association.
   b. systematic desensitization.
   c. the placebo effect.
   d. regression toward the mean.
   e. stress inoculation training.

Is psychotherapy effective?, p. 677
Medium, Factual/Definitional, Objective 7, Ans: d

69. In the 1950s, Hans Eysenck challenged the effectiveness of psychotherapy because it appeared to be:
   a. too expensive and time-consuming.
   b. less beneficial than drug therapy.
   c. helpful only for those with relatively mild disorders.
   d. no more beneficial than no treatment at all.

Is psychotherapy effective?, p. 677
Easy, Factual/Definitional, Objective 7, Ans: a

70. Meta-analysis refers to:
   a. a procedure for statistically combining the results of many different studies.
   b. the use of a variety of therapeutic techniques in the treatment of a single client.
   c. counseling and treatment of troubled individuals by friends, family, and other nonprofessional helpers.
   d. a procedure for identifying the common factors that underlie many different disorders.
   e. the technique of simply rephrasing much of what a client says during the course of therapy.

Is psychotherapy effective?, p. 677
Medium, Factual/Definitional, Objective 7, Ans: a

71. After performing a meta-analysis of some 475 psychotherapy outcome studies, Smith and her colleagues reported in 1980 that:
   a. evidence overwhelmingly supports the efficacy of psychotherapy.
   b. psychotherapy is no more effective than talking to a friend.
   c. psychotherapy harms just as many people as it helps.
   d. it is impossible to measure the effectiveness of psychotherapy.

Is psychotherapy effective?, p. 678
Easy, Factual/Definitional, Objective 7, Ans: a

72. Psychotherapy is likely to be most effective when a client's problem is:
 a. clear-cut.
 b. the result of unconscious conflicts.
 c. long-standing and habitual.
 d. a response to a stressful life situation.
 e. self-inflicted.

The relative effectiveness of different therapies, p. 679
Medium, Factual/Definitional, Objective 7, Ans: e

73. Exposure therapy has been found to be most useful for the treatment of:
 a. insomnia.
 b. depression.
 c. bulimia.
 d. alcoholism.
 e. anxiety.

The relative effectiveness of different therapies, p. 679
Medium, Conceptual/Application, Objective 7, Ans: e

74. Ron is a 22-year-old mechanic who suffers from claustrophobia. The most effective way to treat Ron's problem would involve ________ therapy.
 a. cognitive
 b. electroconvulsive
 c. psychoanalytic
 d. client-centered
 e. behavior

Therapeutic touch, p. 680
Easy, Factual/Definitional, Objective 7, Ans: c

75. Inflated estimates of the value of therapeutic touch are largely attributable to:
 a. transference.
 b. systematic desensitization.
 c. the placebo effect.
 d. meta-analysis.
 e. the double-blind technique.

Therapeutic touch, p. 680
Medium, Factual/Definitional, Objective 7, Ans: d

76. In a simple experiment, therapeutic practitioners were asked to use their hands to detect a human energy field. This experiment raised serious doubts about the value of:
 a. exposure therapy.
 b. transference.
 c. the placebo effect.
 d. therapeutic touch.
 e. EMDR.

Eye movement desensitization and reprocessing, p. 680
Easy, Factual/Definitional, Objective 7, Ans: e

77. Rapidly moving one's eyes while recalling traumatic experiences is most descriptive of:
    a. free association.
    b. systematic desensitization.
    c. repetitive magnetic transcranial stimulation.
    d. virtual reality exposure therapy.
    e. EMDR.

Eye movement desensitization and reprocessing, pp. 680-681
Medium, Conceptual/Application, Objective 7, Ans: a

78. Kammy vividly imagines a terrifying childhood experience of being abused by her own mother while her therapist triggers eye movements by waving a finger in front of Kammy's eyes. The therapist is apparently using a technique known as:
    a. EMDR.
    b. therapeutic touch.
    c. animal magnetism.
    d. virtual reality exposure therapy.
    e. systematic desensitization.

Eye movement desensitization and reprocessing, p. 681
Difficult, Factual/Definitional, Objective 7, Ans: d

79. Controlled research studies indicate that the value of EMDR actually results from the effectiveness of:
    a. free association.
    b. active listening.
    c. meta-analysis.
    d. exposure therapy.
    e. the double-blind technique.

Light exposure therapy, p. 681
Easy, Factual/Definitional, Objective 7, Ans: d

80. Light exposure therapy was developed to relieve symptoms of:
    a. insomnia.
    b. anxiety.
    c. bulimia.
    d. depression.
    e. alcoholism.

Light exposure therapy, p. 681
Medium, Factual/Definitional, Objective 7, Ans: a

81. Light exposure therapy has been shown to be most effective if administered during the:
    a. morning.
    b. afternoon.
    c. evening.
    d. night.

Commonalities among psychotherapies, p. 682
Difficult, Factual/Definitional, Objective 8, Ans: d

82. The most common ingredient underlying the success of diverse psychotherapies is the:
 a. professional training and experience of the therapist.
 b. temporary escape from real-life pressures offered by psychotherapy.
 c. length of time the client spends in psychotherapy.
 d. client's expectation that psychotherapy will make things better.

Commonalities among psychotherapies, p. 682
Easy, Factual/Definitional, Objective 8, Ans: d

83. The placebo effect refers to:
 a. relief from symptoms without psychotherapy.
 b. the alleviation of depression and anxiety by means of aerobic exercise.
 c. the use of drugs in the therapeutic treatment of psychological disorders.
 d. the beneficial consequences of merely expecting that a treatment will be effective.
 e. the use of a variety of psychological theories and therapeutic methods.

Commonalities among psychotherapies, p. 682
Medium, Conceptual/Application, Objective 8, Ans: e

84. Because Mr. Gotanda mistakenly believed that completing a routine health-history questionnaire was a therapeutic treatment for his phobia, he immediately experienced considerable relief from his symptoms of anxiety. His reaction best illustrates:
 a. systematic desensitization.
 b. unconditional positive regard.
 c. meta-analysis.
 d. counterconditioning.
 e. the placebo effect.

Culture and values in psychotherapy, pp. 683-684
Difficult, Factual/Definitional, Objective 8, Ans: d

85. Although Albert Ellis and Allen Bergin disagree about the value of self-sacrifice and marital fidelity, as professional therapists they both appear to agree that:
 a. psychotherapists should not reveal their personal values to clients.
 b. personal values do not affect professional assessments of therapeutic outcomes.
 c. psychological research should not be used to inform therapists' values.
 d. psychotherapists' personal values actually influence the process of therapy.

A consumer's guide to psychotherapists (Close-up and Table 17.2), p. 684
Medium, Conceptual, Objective 8, Ans: e

86. A psychiatrist would be more likely than a clinical psychologist to:
 a. vigorously challenge clients' illogical ways of thinking.
 b. systematically associate a client's undesirable behaviors with unpleasant experiences.
 c. emphasize that greater self-awareness is the major goal of therapy.
 d. encourage clients to carefully observe the consequences of their maladaptive behaviors.
 e. prescribe antianxiety drugs for the treatment of phobias.

A consumer's guide to psychotherapists (Close-up and Table 17.2), p. 684
Medium, Conceptual/Application, Objective 8, Ans: d

87. Dr. Miller prescribes drugs for the treatment of chronic depression and she encourages rest and relaxation training for clients suffering from excessive anxiety. It is most likely that Dr. Miller is a:
a. psychoanalyst.
b. interpersonal therapist.
c. cognitive therapist.
d. psychiatrist.
e. client-centered therapist.

Drug therapies, p. 685
Easy, Conceptual/Application, Objective 9, Ans: d

88. Dr. Genscher believes that most psychological disorders result from chemical abnormalities. In her work as a therapist, Dr. Genscher is most likely to make use of:
a. psychosurgery.
b. meta-analysis.
c. systematic desensitization.
d. drug therapies.
e. transference.

Drug therapies, p. 685
Easy, Factual/Definitional, Objective 9, Ans: c

89. Psychopharmacology involves the study of how:
a. diseases influence psychological well-being.
b. exercise alleviates depression.
c. drugs affect mind and behavior.
d. physical relaxation reduces anxiety.
e. psychosurgery and ECT influence emotions.

Drug therapies, p. 685
Easy, Factual/Definitional, Objective 9, Ans: d

90. Which form of therapy has most directly contributed to the sharp reduction in the number of residents in American mental hospitals?
a. psychosurgery
b. cognitive therapy
c. electroconvulsive therapy
d. drug therapy
e. behavior therapy

Drug therapies, p. 686
Medium, Conceptual/Application, Objective 9, Ans: e

91. One group of ocean voyagers is given a new but untested pill for seasickness and a second group is given an inactive pill. Neither the voyagers nor the experimental researchers know which group has received the new pill. In this experiment, the investigators are making use of:
a. systematic desensitization.
b. meta-analysis.
c. counterconditioning.
d. regression toward the mean.
e. the double-blind technique.

Antipsychotic drugs, p. 686
Medium, Conceptual/Application, Objective 9, Ans: d

92. Melissa suffers from auditory hallucinations and falsely believes that her former high school teachers are trying to kill her. Melissa's symptoms are most likely to be relieved by ________ drugs.
   a. antidepressant
   b. antianxiety
   c. antimanic
   d. antipsychotic

Antipsychotic drugs, p. 686
Difficult, Factual/Definitional, Objective 9, Ans: a

93. An effective drug for the treatment of schizophrenia is:
   a. Clozaril.
   b. Prozac.
   c. Xanax.
   d. lithium.

Antipsychotic drugs, p. 686
Medium, Factual/Definitional, Objective 9, Ans: c

94. Which drugs appear to produce therapeutic effects by blocking receptor sites for dopamine?
   a. antianxiety drugs
   b. antidepressant drugs
   c. antipsychotic drugs
   d. antimanic drugs

Antipsychotic drugs, p. 686
Difficult, Factual/Definitional, Objective 9, Ans: b

95. Sluggishness, tremors, and twitches similar to those of Parkinson's disease are most likely to be associated with the excessive use of certain ________ drugs.
   a. antidepressant
   b. antipsychotic
   c. antimanic
   d. antianxiety

Antianxiety drugs, p. 687
Medium, Factual/Definitional, Objective 9, Ans: d

96. Xanax and Valium are ________ drugs.
   a. antidepressant
   b. antipsychotic
   c. antimanic
   d. antianxiety

Antianxiety drugs, p. 687
Difficult, Conceptual/Application, Objective 9, Ans: c

97. Xanax would most likely be prescribed in order to help:
   a. Cynthia give up her irrational belief that her husband is a foreign government spy.
   b. Cassius get rid of his suicidal thoughts and feelings of apathy and hopelessness.
   c. Jerome overcome feelings of nervous apprehension and an inability to relax.
   d. Vladim discontinue his habit of smoking more than three packs of cigarettes a day.

Antidepressant drugs, p. 687
Medium, Factual/Definitional, Objective 9, Ans: a

98. Prozac is an antidepressant drug that partially blocks the reabsorption and removal of:
    a. serotonin.
    b. dopamine.
    c. acetylcholine.
    d. chlorpromazine.

Antidepressant drugs, p. 687
Difficult, Conceptual/Application, Objective 9, Ans: d

99. Which of the following individuals is most likely to benefit from Prozac?
    a. Jack, who has lost his sense of identity and wandered from his home to a distant city
    b. Andrea, who hears imaginary voices telling her that she will suffer a fatal accident
    c. Tami, who is so addicted to cigarettes that she now worries about her health
    d. Shannon, who feels helpless and apathetic and thinks her life is meaningless and worthless

Antidepressant drugs, p. 688
Medium, Factual/Definitional, Objective 9, Ans: d

100. Which of the following is most helpful for avoiding inflated estimates of the effectiveness of antidepressant drugs?
    a. EMDR
    b. active listening
    c. therapeutic touch
    d. the double-blind technique
    e. stress inoculation training

Antidepressant drugs, p. 688
Medium, Factual/Definitional, Objective 9, Ans: a

101. One good alternative to antidepressant drugs is:
    a. aerobic exercise.
    b. therapeutic touch.
    c. virtual reality exposure therapy.
    d. EMDR.
    e. Thorazine.

Antidepressant drugs, p. 689
Difficult, Conceptual/Application, Objective 9, Ans: a

102. Edith, a 45-year-old journalist, alternates between extreme sadness and lethargy and extreme euphoria and overactivity. The drug most likely to prove beneficial to her is:
    a. lithium.
    b. Valium.
    c. Clozaril.
    d. Thorazine.

Electroconvulsive therapy, p. 689
Easy, Factual/Definitional, Objective 10, Ans: d

103. Which of the following procedures is most likely to result in a slight loss of memory?
   a. aversive conditioning
   b. the double-blind technique
   c. systematic desensitization
   d. electroconvulsive therapy
   e. psychopharmacology

Electroconvulsive therapy, p. 689
Easy, Factual/Definitional, Objective 10, Ans: d

104. Electroconvulsive therapy has proven to be effective in the treatment of:
   a. phobias.
   b. dissociative disorders.
   c. schizophrenia.
   d. depression.

Electroconvulsive therapy, p. 689
Medium, Conceptual/Application, Objective 10, Ans: a

105. Adelle's feelings of unhappiness, low self-esteem, and hopelessness have become so extreme that she has attempted suicide. Which of the following treatments is likely to provide her with the quickest relief from her misery?
   a. electroconvulsive therapy
   b. drug therapy
   c. psychoanalysis
   d. systematic desensitization
   e. cognitive therapy

Electroconvulsive therapy, p. 690
Medium, Factual/Definitional, Objective 10, Ans: d

106. Repetitive transcranial magnetic stimulation shows greatest promise for the treatment of:
   a. schizophrenia.
   b. anxiety.
   c. alcoholism.
   d. depression.
   e. bulimia.

Psychosurgery, p. 690
Medium, Factual/Definitional, Objective 10, Ans: c

107. Psychosurgery involves:
   a. passing an electric current through the entire brain.
   b. injecting lithium directly into the limbic system.
   c. removing or destroying brain tissue.
   d. all of the above.

Psychosurgery, p. 690
Medium, Factual/Definitional, Objective 10, Ans: a

108. During the 1940s and 1950s, lobotomies were most likely to be performed on psychologically disordered patients who were:
   a. uncontrollably violent.
   b. hopelessly depressed.
   c. obsessively hypochondriacal.
   d. irreparably amnesic.

Psychosurgery, pp. 668, 690
Medium, Conceptual, Objective 10, Ans: c

109. Behavior therapy is to token economy as psychosurgery is to ________.
   a. aversive conditioning
   b. drug therapy
   c. lobotomy
   d. electroconvulsive therapy

Psychosurgery, pp. 690-691
Easy, Factual/Definitional, Objective 10, Ans: c

110. Which of the following therapeutic treatments is *least* likely to be used today?
   a. aversive conditioning
   b. electroconvulsive therapy
   c. psychosurgery
   d. drug therapy

Preventing psychological disorders, p. 692
Medium, Conceptual/Application, Objective 11, Ans: e

111. Dr. Judd is convinced that psychological disorders result largely from stressful social situations rather than from disturbances within the individual personality. Dr. Judd's belief is most consistent with the assumptions that underlie:
   a. psychoanalysis.
   b. cognitive therapy.
   c. psychosurgery.
   d. drug therapy.
   e. preventive mental health.

Preventing psychological disorders, p. 692
Medium, Factual/Definitional, Objective 11, Ans: c

112. Preventive mental health attempts to reduce the incidence of psychological disorders by:
   a. enabling more people to see professional psychotherapists.
   b. encouraging depressed people to take more personal responsibility for their own problems.
   c. establishing programs to alleviate poverty and other demoralizing situations.
   d. emphasizing the importance of using a wide variety of psychological theories and therapeutic methods.

Essay Questions

1. Geraldo, a college sophomore, is so fearful of asking a woman out that he hasn't had a date in over three years. He has recently contacted a psychotherapist for help in overcoming his fear. Describe how a behavior therapist would treat Geraldo's problem differently from the way a psychoanalyst would.

2. Describe how a therapist might use both aversive conditioning and operant conditioning techniques in order to help a client overcome a compulsive habit of smoking more than three packs of cigarettes a day. Be clear about the exact procedures that would be used.

3. One of your best friends feels that he fails at everything he does and that his life isn't worth living. When you suggest that he talk to a psychotherapist, your friend responds, "Talking won't help. The more I talk about myself, the more I think about my problems. The more I think about my problems, the more depressed I get." Explain why your friend's comment illustrates his need for cognitive therapy. What procedures would a cognitive therapist use to help your friend overcome his negative feelings?

4. Isaiah performed miserably on his first psychology test, even though he had carefully prepared written notes on each assigned chapter of his textbook. In an effort to improve his performance, Isaiah subsequently engaged in daily meditation exercises and discontinued his normal practice of textbook note-taking. To his delight, he performed somewhat better on his second psychology test. Give Isaiah some helpful advice regarding any conclusions he might draw about the reasons for his improved performance on the second test.

5. Mr. Andrews suffers from frequent episodes of extreme depression. When a friend suggests that he might be helped by drug therapy, Mr. Andrews responds, "Drugs are just a crutch for people who lack self-discipline and who want to hide from their problems. Besides, I'm not about to hand over control of my life to some psychiatrist and his magic pills." Explain why Mr. Andrews' ideas about drug therapy are inaccurate.

Web Quiz 1

Ans: e

1. Classical psychoanalysts were especially interested in:
   a. encouraging clients to carefully observe the consequences of their maladaptive behaviors.
   b. minimizing the possibility that clients would experience anxiety during therapy.
   c. discouraging clients from using antianxiety or antidepressant drugs.
   d. establishing an empathic and personal emotional relationship with clients.
   e. interpreting the meaning of clients' resistance to therapeutic procedures.

Ans: c

2. While focusing on several intrusive thoughts that had been bothering her recently, Jenny was instructed by her therapist to report any ideas or memories stimulated by these thoughts. Jenny's therapist was making use of a technique known as:
   a. aversive conditioning.
   b. active listening.
   c. free association.
   d. systematic desensitization.
   e. transference.

Ans: b

3. Who emphasized the importance of active listening in the process of psychotherapy?
   a. Mary Cover Jones
   b. Carl Rogers
   c. Sigmund Freud
   d. Hans Eysenck
   e. Joseph Wolpe

Ans: d

4. A therapist helps Rebecca overcome her fear of water by getting her to swim in the family's backyard pool three times a day for two consecutive weeks. The therapist's approach to helping Rebecca best illustrates:
   a. stress inoculation training.
   b. free association.
   c. aversive conditioning.
   d. exposure therapy.
   e. humanistic therapy.

Ans: b

5. Systematic desensitization is a form of:
   a. aversive conditioning.
   b. exposure therapy.
   c. psychosurgery.
   d. eclectic therapy.
   e. electroconvulsive therapy.

Ans: d

6. In a residential treatment facility for troubled youth, adolescent children receive large colored buttons when they hang up their clothes, make their beds, and come to meals on time. The children return the buttons to staff members in order to receive bedtime snacks or watch TV. This best illustrates an application of:
   a. stress inoculation training.
   b. humanistic therapy.
   c. systematic desensitization.
   d. operant conditioning.
   e. virtual reality exposure therapy.

Ans: c

7. Cognitive therapists are most likely to:
   a. focus special attention on clients' positive and negative feelings about their therapists.
   b. employ personality tests to accurately diagnose their clients' difficulties.
   c. emphasize the importance of clients' personal interpretations of life events.
   d. systematically associate clients' undesirable behaviors with unpleasant experiences.
   e. prescribe antipsychotic drugs for the treatment of phobias.

Ans: d

8. Several years after his wife's death, Mr. Sanchez remains incapacitated by feelings of sadness. In order to reduce Mr. Sanchez's depression, a therapist is actively encouraging him to stop blaming himself for not being able to prevent it. The therapist's approach is most representative of:
   a. therapeutic touch.
   b. systematic desensitization.
   c. psychoanalysis.
   d. cognitive therapy.
   e. client-centered therapy.

Ans: e

9. Which form of therapy is most likely to serve as a preventive mental health strategy?
   a. psychoanalysis
   b. systematic desensitization
   c. virtual reality exposure therapy
   d. psychosurgery
   e. family therapy

Ans: d

10. When people's symptoms of psychological distress are at their worst, whatever they do to try to alleviate the condition is likely to be followed by improvement rather than further deterioration. This is best explained in terms of:
   a. systematic desensitization.
   b. psychopharmacology.
   c. counterconditoning.
   d. regression toward the mean.
   e. virtual reality exposure therapy.

Ans: a

11. The effectiveness of psychotherapy shows little if any connection to:
    a. the level of training and experience of the therapist.
    b. the length of time a client has experienced symptoms of disorder prior to therapy.
    c. the particular disorder experienced by a client.
    d. the extent to which the process depends on changing clients' personalities.

Ans: d

12. Because she mistakenly believes that a new herbal remedy will help her lose weight, Mrs. Redding has begun feeling a considerable reduction in her appetite. This best illustrates:
    a. virtual reality exposure therapy.
    b. systematic desensitization.
    c. stress inoculation training.
    d. the placebo effect.
    e. meta-analysis.

Ans: e

13. The double-blind technique is most likely to be used in evaluating the effectiveness of:
    a. cognitive therapies.
    b. behavior therapies.
    c. humanistic therapies.
    d. psychodynamic therapies.
    e. drug therapies.

Ans: c

14. Which of the following individuals is most likely to benefit from lithium?
    a. Olivia, who experiences delusions and auditory hallucinations
    b. Landon, who experiences a generalized sense of apprehension and anxiety
    c. Miranda, who experiences periods of extreme sadness followed by episodes of optimistic overexcitement
    d. Ivan, who experiences sudden brief episodes of intense dread and panic
    e. Juan, who experiences a persistently depressed mood and low energy level

Ans: a

15. Which of the following is least likely to be effective in the treatment of depression?
    a. EMDR
    b. ECT
    c. SSRIs
    d. rTMS

Web Quiz 2

Ans: e

1. Who emphasized the importance of transference in the therapeutic process?
   a. Hans Eysenck
   b. Joseph Wolpe
   c. Carl Rogers
   d. B. F. Sinner
   e. Sigmund Freud

Ans: d

2. During her weekly therapy sessions, Sabrina will often abruptly shift the focus of her attention and lose her train of thought. A psychoanalyst would suggest that this illustrates:
   a. displacement.
   b. transference.
   c. meta-analysis.
   d. resistance.
   e. spontaneous recovery.

Ans: c

3. Client-centered therapists emphasize the importance of:
   a. exploring clients' childhood relationships with other family members.
   b. interpreting the meaning of clients' nonverbal behaviors.
   c. enabling clients to feel unconditionally accepted.
   d. helping clients identify a hierarchy of anxiety-arousing experiences.
   e. discouraging clients from using antianxiety or antidepressant drugs.

Ans: c

4. Unlike psychoanalytic therapists, humanistic therapists tend to focus on the ________ more than the ________.
   a. present; future
   b. past; present
   c. present; past
   d. past; future
   e. future; present

Ans: d

5. In order to help Adam reduce his fear of dogs, a therapist encourages him to physically relax and then simply imagine that he is walking toward a friendly and harmless little dog. The therapist's technique best illustrates:
   a. psychodynamic therapy.
   b. operant conditioning.
   c. stress inoculation training.
   d. systematic desensitization.
   e. client-centered therapy.

Ans: c

6. In order to help Janet overcome her nearly irresistible craving for chocolate, a therapist provides her with a supply of chocolate candies that contain solidified droplets of a harmless but very bitter-tasting substance. This approach to treatment best illustrates:
a. systematic desensitization.
b. light exposure therapy.
c. aversive conditioning.
d. stress inoculation training.
e. eclectic therapy.

Ans: a

7. Recognizing that depressed people do not exhibit the self-serving bias common in nondepressed people is most helpful for appreciating which therapeutic approach?
a. cognitive therapy
b. client-centered therapy
c. behavior therapy
d. psychodynamic therapy
e. family therapy

Ans: e

8. The goal of stress inoculation training is to reduce incapacitating anxiety by encouraging people to say positive things to themselves during anxiety-producing situations. This best illustrates a form of:
a. light exposure therapy.
b. psychodynamic therapy.
c. aversive conditioning.
d. humanistic therapy.
e. cognitive-behavior therapy.

Ans: b

9. Which form of psychotherapy is least likely to occur in therapist-led small groups?
a. client-centered therapy
b. psychoanalysis
c. systematic desensitization
d. cognitive therapy
e. cognitive-behavior therapy

Ans: b

10. Delinquent boys put through Scared Straight programs said they were now ________ likely to be law-abiding. Compared with delinquent boys not assigned to Scared Straight, they became _______ likely to commit new offenses.
a. more; less
b less; more
c. more; more
d. less; less

Ans: e

11. The placebo effect best illustrates the importance of _______ in therapeutic success.
a. active listening
b. free association
c. psychopharmacology
d. behavior modification
e. cognitive processes

Ans: d

12. For which of the following disorders is psychotherapy most likely to be effective in the long run?
a. generalized anxiety disorder
b. major depressive disorder
c. chronic schizophrenia
d. phobias

Ans: b

13. Which of the following factors is not a therapeutically effective component of eye movement desensitization and reprocessing?
a. reliving traumatic memories
b. rapidly moving one's eyes
c. a relaxing therapeutic environment
d. patients' anticipation that the treatment will work

Ans: b

14. Which of the following is a selective serotonin-reuptake inhibitor?
a. Xanax
b. Prozac
c. Valium
d. Clozaril
e. Thorazine

Ans: a

15. Which of the following drugs is most likely to provide schizophrenia patients with some relief from their auditory hallucinations and paranoia?
a. Thorazine
b. Xanax
c. lithium
d. Valium
e. Prozac

Study Guide Questions

Ans: d, p. 660

1. An eclectic psychotherapist is one who:
   a. takes a nondirective approach in helping clients solve their problems.
   b. views psychological disorders as usually stemming from one cause, such as a biological abnormality.
   c. uses one particular technique, such as psychoanalysis or counterconditioning, in treating disorders.
   d. uses a variety of techniques, depending on the client and the problem.

Ans: c, p. 661

2. The technique in which a person is asked to report everything that comes to his or her mind is called ________; this technique is favored by ________ therapists.
   a. active listening; cognitive
   b. spontaneous remission; humanistic
   c. free association; psychoanalytic
   d. systematic desensitization; behavior

Ans: d, p. 661

3. During a session with his psychoanalyst, Jamal hesitates while describing a highly embarrassing thought. In the psychoanalytic framework, this is an example of:
   a. transference.
   b. insight.
   c. mental repression.
   d. resistance.

Ans: d, p. 661

4. During psychoanalysis, Jane has developed strong feelings of hatred for her therapist. The analyst interprets Jane's behavior in terms of a ________ of her feelings toward her father.
   a. projection
   b. resistance
   c. regression
   d. transference

Ans: d, p. 661

5. Of the following therapists, who would be most likely to interpret a person's psychological problems in terms of repressed impulses?
   a. a behavior therapist
   b. a cognitive therapist
   c. a humanistic therapist
   d. a psychoanalyst

Ans: e, pp. 661, 662

6. Which type(s) of psychotherapy would be most likely to use the interpretation of dreams as a technique for bringing unconscious feelings into awareness?
   a. psychoanalysis
   b. psychodynamic therapy
   c. cognitive therapy
   d. all of the above
   e. both a. and b.

Ans: d, pp. 661-662

7. Which of the following is *not* a common criticism of psychoanalysis?
   a. It emphasizes the existence of repressed memories.
   b. It provides interpretations that are hard to disprove.
   c. It is generally a very expensive process.
   d. It gives therapists too much control over patients.

Ans: c, p. 662

8. Unlike traditional psychoanalytic therapy, interpersonal psychotherapy:
   a. helps people gain insight into the roots of their problems.
   b. offers interpretations of patients' feelings.
   c. focuses on current relationships.
   d. does all of the above.

Ans: b, p. 663

9. Of the following categories of psychotherapy, which is known for its nondirective nature?
   a. psychoanalysis
   b. humanistic therapy
   c. behavior therapy
   d. cognitive therapy

Ans: d, p. 663

10. Given that Jim's therapist attempts to help him by offering genuineness, acceptance, and empathy, she is probably practicing:
   a. psychoanalysis.
   b. behavior therapy.
   c. cognitive therapy.
   d. client-centered therapy.

Ans: c, p. 663

11. Carl Rogers was a ________ therapist who was the creator of ________.
   a. behavior; systematic desensitization
   b. psychoanalytic; insight therapy
   c. humanistic; client-centered therapy
   d. cognitive; cognitive therapy for depression

Ans: c, p. 663

12. Which type of psychotherapy emphasizes the individual's inherent potential for self-fulfillment?
   a. behavior therapy
   b. psychoanalysis
   c. humanistic therapy
   d. biomedical therapy

Ans: a, p. 664

13. The technique in which a therapist echoes and restates what a person says in a nondirective manner is called:
    a. active listening.
    b. free association.
    c. systematic desensitization.
    d. meta-analysis.
    e. interpretation.

Ans: a, p. 665

14. Which type of psychotherapy focuses on changing unwanted behaviors rather than on discovering their underlying causes?
    a. behavior therapy
    b. cognitive therapy
    c. humanistic therapy
    d. psychoanalysis
    e. family therapy

Ans: b, p. 665

15. The techniques of counterconditioning are based on principles of:
    a. observational learning.
    b. classical conditioning.
    c. operant conditioning.
    d. behavior modification.

Ans: a, p. 665

16. Leota is startled when her therapist says that she needs to focus on eliminating her problem behavior rather than gaining insight into its underlying cause. Most likely, Leota has consulted a ________ therapist.
    a. behavior
    b. humanistic
    c. cognitive
    d. psychoanalytic

Ans: b, p. 666

17. The technique of systematic desensitization is based on the premise that maladaptive symptoms are:
    a. a reflection of irrational thinking.
    b. conditioned responses.
    c. expressions of unfulfilled wishes.
    d. all of the above.

Ans: a, p. 666

18. In order to help him overcome his fear of flying, Duane's therapist has him construct a hierarchy of anxiety-triggering stimuli and then learn to associate each with a state of deep relaxation. Duane's therapist is using the technique called:
    a. systematic desensitization.
    b. aversive conditioning.
    c. shaping.
    d. free association.

Ans: d, pp. 666-667

19. In which of the following does the client learn to associate a relaxed state with a hierarchy of anxiety-arousing situations?
   a. cognitive therapy
   b. aversive conditioning
   c. counterconditioning
   d. systematic desensitization

Ans: d, p. 667

20. To help Sam quit smoking, his therapist blew a blast of smoke into Sam's face each time Sam inhaled. Which technique is the therapist using?
   a. exposure therapy
   b. behavior modification
   c. systematic desensitization
   d. aversive conditioning

Ans: a, p. 667

21. Using techniques of classical conditioning to develop an association between unwanted behavior and an unpleasant experience is known as:
   a. aversive conditioning.
   b. systematic desensitization.
   c. transference.
   d. electroconvulsive therapy.
   e. a token economy.

Ans: c, p. 667

22. One reason that aversive conditioning may only be temporarily effective is that:
   a. for ethical reasons, therapists cannot use sufficiently intense unconditioned stimuli to sustain classical conditioning.
   b. patients are often unable to become sufficiently relaxed for conditioning to take place.
   c. patients know that outside the therapist's office they can engage in the undesirable behavior without fear of aversive consequences.
   d. most conditioned responses are elicited by many nonspecific stimuli and it is impossible to countercondition them all.

Ans: b, p. 668

23. A patient in a hospital receives poker chips for making her bed, being punctual at meal times, and maintaining her physical appearance. The poker chips can be exchanged for privileges, such as television viewing, snacks, and magazines. This is an example of the ________ therapy technique called ________.
   a. psychodynamic; systematic desensitization
   b. behavior; token economy
   c. cognitive; token economy
   d. humanistic; systematic desensitization

Ans: e, p. 668

24. Principles of operant conditioning underlie which of the following techniques?
    a. counterconditioning
    b. systematic desensitization
    c. stress inoculation training
    d. aversive conditioning
    e. the token economy

Ans: c, p. 668

25. The operant conditioning technique in which desired behaviors are rewarded with points or poker chips that can later be exchanged for various rewards is called:
    a. counterconditioning.
    b. systematic desensitization.
    c. a token economy.
    d. exposure therapy.

Ans: d, pp. 668-669

26. Which of the following is *not* a common criticism of behavior therapy?
    a. Clients may not develop intrinsic motivation for their new behaviors.
    b. Behavior control is unethical.
    c. Although one symptom may be eliminated, another may replace it unless the underlying problem is treated.
    d. All of the above are criticisms of behavior therapy.

Ans: d, p. 669

27. After Darnel dropped a pass in an important football game, he became depressed and vowed to quit the team because of his athletic incompetence. The campus psychologist challenged his illogical reasoning and pointed out that Darnel's "incompetence" had earned him an athletic scholarship. The psychologist's response was most typical of a ________ therapist.
    a. behavior
    b. psychoanalytic
    c. client-centered
    d. cognitive

Ans: c, p. 669

28. Which type of therapy focuses on eliminating irrational thinking?
    a. EMDR
    b. client-centered therapy
    c. cognitive therapy
    d. behavior therapy

Ans: d, p. 670

29. One variety of ________ therapy is based on the finding that depressed people often attribute their failures to ________.
    a. humanistic; themselves
    b. behavior; external circumstances
    c. cognitive; external circumstances
    d. cognitive; themselves

Ans: c, pp. 670, 679

30. Which form of therapy is *most* likely to be successful in treating depression?
    a. behavior therapy
    b. psychoanalysis
    c. cognitive therapy
    d. humanistic therapy

Ans: c, p. 671

31. Ben is a cognitive-behavior therapist. Compared to Rachel, who is a behavior therapist, Ben is more likely to:
    a. base his therapy on principles of operant conditioning.
    b. base his therapy on principles of classical conditioning.
    c. address clients' attitudes as well as behaviors.
    d. focus on clients' unconscious urges.

Ans: c, p. 671

32. Cognitive-behavior therapy aims to:
    a. alter the way people act.
    b. make people more aware of their irrational negative thinking.
    c. alter the way people think and act.
    d. countercondition anxiety-provoking stimuli.

Ans: a, p. 672

33. Which of the following types of therapy does *not* belong with the others?
    a. cognitive therapy
    b. family therapy
    c. self-help group
    d. support group

Ans: d, pp. 672-673

34. Family therapy differs from other forms of psychotherapy because it focuses on:
    a. using a variety of treatment techniques.
    b. conscious rather than unconscious processes.
    c. the present instead of the past.
    d. how family tensions may cause individual problems.

Ans: c, p. 674

35. Before 1950, the main mental health providers were:
    a. psychologists.
    b. paraprofessionals.
    c. psychiatrists.
    d. the clergy.
    e. social workers.

Ans: b, pp. 674, 677-678

36. The effectiveness of psychotherapy has been assessed both through clients' perspectives and through controlled research studies. What have such assessments found?
    a. Clients' perceptions and controlled studies alike strongly affirm the effectiveness of psychotherapy.
    b. Whereas clients' perceptions strongly affirm the effectiveness of psychotherapy, studies point to more modest results.
    c. Whereas studies strongly affirm the effectiveness of psychotherapy, many clients feel dissatisfied with their progress.
    d. Clients' perceptions and controlled studies alike paint a very mixed picture of the effectiveness of psychotherapy.

Ans: b, p. 675

37. Which of the following best describes the results of the 30-year follow-up study of 500 Massachusetts boys who had been considered predelinquents?
    a. Predelinquent boys who received counseling had fewer problems as adults than untreated predelinquent boys.
    b. Predelinquent boys who did not receive counseling had slightly fewer problems as adults than boys who received counseling.
    c. Predelinquent boys who underwent behavior therapy had fewer problems as adults than boys who underwent psychoanalysis.
    d. Predelinquent boys who underwent psychoanalysis had fewer problems as adults than boys who underwent behavior therapy.

Ans: b, p. 675

38. The following are some of the conclusions drawn in the text regarding the effectiveness of psychotherapy. For which of these conclusions did the Massachusetts study of predelinquent boys provide evidence?
    a. Clients' perceptions of the effectiveness of therapy usually are very accurate.
    b. Clients' perceptions of the effectiveness of therapy differ somewhat from the objective findings.
    c. Individuals who receive treatment do somewhat better than individuals who do not.
    d. Overall, no one type of therapy is a "winner," but certain therapies are more suited to certain problems.

Ans: b, pp. 676, 682

39. A person can derive benefits from psychotherapy simply by believing in it. This illustrates the importance of:
    a. spontaneous remission.
    b. the placebo effect.
    c. the transference effect.
    d. interpretation.

Ans: d, pp. 676, 682-683

40. Nick survived a car accident in which another passenger died. Feeling anxious and guilty, he sought treatment from an alternative therapist, who used eye movement desensitization and reprocessing to help Nick return to his normally upbeat, optimistic frame of mind. After several months of treatment Nick began feeling better. Although Nick is convinced that the alternative therapy was responsible for his improvement, it is also possible that it was the result of:
   a. regression toward the mean.
   b. a placebo effect.
   c. merely seeking treatment from any practitioner who provided an empathic, trusting environment.
   d. all of the above.

Ans: c, p. 678

41. Which of the following is *not* necessarily an advantage of group therapies over individual therapies?
   a. They tend to take less time for the therapist.
   b. They tend to cost less money for the client.
   c. They are more effective.
   d. They allow the client to test new behaviors in a social context.

Ans: e, p. 678

42. A relative wants to know which type of therapy works best. You should tell your relative that:
   a. psychotherapy does not work.
   b. behavior therapy is the most effective.
   c. cognitive therapy is the most effective.
   d. group therapy is best for his problem.
   e. no one type of therapy is consistently the most successful.

Ans: d, pp. 678-679

43. The results of meta-analysis of the effectiveness of different psychotherapies reveals that:
   a. no single type of therapy is consistently superior.
   b. behavior therapies are most effective in treating specific problems, such as phobias.
   c. cognitive therapies are most effective in treating depressed emotions.
   d. all of the above are true.

Ans: c, p. 680

44. In one research study of therapeutic touch, the experimenter placed a hand over one of the practitioner's unseen hands to see if the practitioner could detect the hovering hand's purported energy field. The results demonstrated that the practitioners were able to do so:
   a. 100 percent of the time.
   b. about 75 percent of the time.
   c. less than 50 percent of the time.
   d. only if the experimenter mentally concentrated on which hand was being "stimulated."

Ans: d, p. 681

45. A close friend who for years has suffered from wintertime depression is seeking your advice regarding the effectiveness of light-exposure therapy. What should you tell your friend?
    a. "Don't waste your time and money. It doesn't work."
    b. "A more effective treatment for seasonal affective disorder is eye movement desensitization and reprocessing."
    c. "You'd be better off with a prescription for lithium."
    d. "It might be worth a try. There is some evidence that morning light exposure affects the secretion of melatonin, which helps regulate the body's circadian rhythm."

Ans: b, p. 681

46. Light-exposure therapy has proven useful as a form of treatment for people suffering from:
    a. bulimia.
    b. seasonal affective disorder.
    c. schizophrenia.
    d. dissociative identity disorder.

Ans: d, pp. 682-683

47. Among the common ingredients of the psychotherapies is:
    a. the offer of a therapeutic relationship.
    b. the expectation among clients that the therapy will prove helpful.
    c. the chance to develop a fresh perspective on oneself and the world.
    d. all of the above.

Ans: d, p. 683

48. A meta-analysis of research studies comparing the effectiveness of professional therapists with paraprofessionals found that:
    a. the professionals were much more effective than the paraprofessionals.
    b. the paraprofessionals were much more effective than the professionals.
    c. except in treating depression, the paraprofessionals were about as effective as the professionals.
    d. the paraprofessionals were about as effective as the professionals.

Ans: b, p. 684

49. Seth enters therapy to talk about some issues that have been upsetting him. The therapist prescribes some medication to help him. The therapist is most likely a:
    a. psychologist.
    b. psychiatrist.
    c. psychiatric social worker.
    d. clinical social worker.

Ans: c, p. 685

50. Which biomedical therapy is *most* likely to be practiced today?
    a. psychosurgery
    b. electroconvulsive therapy
    c. drug therapy
    d. counterconditioning
    e. aversive conditioning

Ans: c, p. 686

51. In an experiment testing the effects of a new antipsychotic drug, neither Dr. Cunningham nor her patients know whether the patients are in the experimental or the control group. This is an example of the ________ technique.
a. meta-analysis
b. within-subjects
c. double-blind
d. single-blind

Ans: a, p. 686

52. Linda's doctor prescribes medication that blocks the activity of dopamine in her nervous system. Evidently, Linda is being treated with an ________ drug.
a. antipsychotic
b. antianxiety
c. antidepressant
d. anticonvulsive

Ans: a, p. 686

53. The antipsychotic drugs appear to produce their effects by blocking the receptor sites for:
a. dopamine.
b. epinephrine.
c. norepinephrine.
d. serotonin.

Ans: c, p. 687

54. Abraham's doctor prescribes medication that increases the availability of norepinephrine in his nervous system. Evidently, Abraham is being treated with an ________ drug.
a. antipsychotic
b. antianxiety
c. antidepressant
d. anticonvulsive

Ans: c, p. 687

55. Antidepressant drugs are believed to work by affecting serotonin or:
a. dopamine.
b. lithium.
c. norepinephrine.
d. acetylcholine.

Ans: a, p. 687

56. The type of drugs criticized for reducing symptoms without resolving underlying problems are the:
a. antianxiety drugs.
b. antipsychotic drugs.
c. antidepressant drugs.
d. amphetamines.

Ans: b, p. 689

57. Electroconvulsive therapy is most useful in the treatment of:
   a. schizophrenia.
   b. depression.
   c. personality disorders.
   d. anxiety disorders.
   e. bipolar disorder.

Ans: b, p. 689

58. A psychiatrist has diagnosed a patient as having bipolar disorder. It is likely that she will prescribe:
   a. an antipsychotic drug.
   b. lithium.
   c. an antianxiety drug.
   d. a drug that blocks receptor sites for serotonin.

Ans: d, p. 689

59. Which of the following is the drug most commonly used to treat bipolar disorder?
   a. Valium
   b. chlorpromazine
   c. Xanax
   d. lithium

Ans: c, p. 690

60. In concluding her talk entitled "Psychosurgery Today," Ashley states that:
   a. "Psychosurgery is still widely used throughout the world."
   b. "Electroconvulsive therapy is the only remaining psychosurgical technique that is widely practiced."
   c. "With advances in psychopharmacology, psychosurgery has largely been abandoned."
   d. "Although lobotomies remain popular, other psychosurgical techniques have been abandoned."

Ans: d, pp. 690-691

61. Although Moniz won the Nobel prize for developing the lobotomy procedure, the technique is not widely used today because:
   a. it produces a lethargic, immature personality.
   b. it is irreversible.
   c. calming drugs became available in the 1950s.
   d. of all of the above reasons.

Ans: e, p. 692

62. Psychologists who advocate a ________ approach to mental health contend that many psychological disorders could be prevented by changing the disturbed individual's ________.
   a. biomedical; diet
   b. family; behavior
   c. humanistic; feelings
   d. psychoanalytic; behavior
   e. preventive; environment

Ans: d, p. 692

63. A psychotherapist who believes that the best way to treat psychological disorders is to prevent them from developing would be *most* likely to view disordered behavior as:
a. maladaptive thoughts and actions.
b. expressions of unconscious conflicts.
c. conditioned responses.
d. an understandable response to stressful social conditions.

CHAPTER **18**

Social Psychology

Learning Objectives

Social Thinking (pp. 695-702)

1. Describe the importance of attribution in social behavior and the dangers of the fundamental attribution error.

2. Identify the conditions under which attitudes have a strong impact on actions.

3. Explain the foot-in-the-door phenomenon and the effect of role-playing on attitudes in terms of cognitive dissonance theory.

Social Influence (pp. 702-713)

4. Discuss the results of experiments on conformity, and distinguish between normative and informational social influence.

5. Describe Milgram's controversial experiments on obedience, and discuss their implications for understanding our susceptibility to social influence.

6. Describe conditions in which the presence of others is likely to result in social facilitation, social loafing, or deindividuation.

7. Discuss how group interaction can facilitate group polarization and groupthink, and describe how minority influence illustrates the power of individuals.

Social Relations (pp. 714-741)

8. Describe the social, emotional, and cognitive factors that contribute to the persistence of cultural, ethnic, and gender prejudice and discrimination.

9. Describe the impact of biological factors, aversive events, and learning experiences on aggressive behavior.

10. Discuss the effects of observing pornography and violent video games on social attitudes and behavior.

11. Explain how social traps and mirror-image perceptions fuel social conflict.

12. Describe the influence of proximity, physical attractiveness, and similarity on interpersonal attraction.

13. Explain the impact of physical arousal on passionate love, and discuss how companionate love is nurtured by equity and self-disclosure.

14. Describe and explain the bystander effect, and explain altruistic behavior in terms of social exchange theory and social norms.

15. Discuss effective ways of encouraging peaceful cooperation and reducing social conflict.

Social psychology, p. 695
Easy, Factual/Definitional, Objective 1, Ans: b

1. Which branch of psychology is most directly concerned with the study of how people think about, influence, and relate to one another?
a. developmental psychology
b. social psychology
c. personality psychology
d. experimental psychology
e. clinical psychology

Attributing behavior to persons or to situations, p. 696
Easy, Factual/Definitional, Objective 1, Ans: e

2. Attribution theory was designed to account for:
a. the process of revealing intimate aspects of ourselves to others.
b. the impact of both heredity and environment on social behavior.
c. social facilitation and social loafing.
d. the loss of self-awareness that occurs in group situations.
e. how people explain others' behavior.

Attributing behavior to persons or to situations, p. 696
Easy, Conceptual/Application, Objective 1, Ans: e

3. Ksana insists that her boyfriend's car accident resulted from his carelessness. Her explanation for the accident provides an example of:
a. the bystander effect.
b. deindividuation.
c. ingroup bias.
d. the foot-in-the-door phenomenon.
e. a dispositional attribution.

Attributing behavior to persons or to situations, p. 696
Medium, Factual/Definitional, Objective 1, Ans: d

4. Fritz Heider concluded that people tend to attribute others' behavior either to their ________ or to their ________.
a. heredity; environment
b. biological motives; psychological motives
c. cognitions; emotions
d. dispositions; situations
e. abilities; effort

Attributing behavior to persons or to situations, p. 696
Medium, Factual/Definitional, Objective 1, Ans: d

5. The fundamental attribution error refers to our tendency to underestimate the impact of ________ and to overestimate the impact of ________ in explaining the behavior of others.
   a. normative influences; informational influences
   b. informational influences; normative influences
   c. personal dispositions; situational influences
   d. situational influences; personal dispositions

Attributing behavior to persons or to situations, p. 696
Difficult, Conceptual/Application, Objective 1, Ans: a

6. Freire did very poorly on his last arithmetic test. The tendency to make the fundamental attribution error might lead his sixth-grade teacher to conclude that Freire did poorly because:
   a. he is unmotivated to do well in school.
   b. the test covered material that had not been adequately covered in class.
   c. his parents had an argument the evening before the test.
   d. he was not given enough time to complete the test.

Attributing behavior to persons or to situations, p. 696
Medium, Factual/Definitional, Objective 1, Ans: b

7. An example of the fundamental attribution error is illustrated in our tendency to underestimate the extent to which others' behavior is influenced by:
   a. genetics.
   b. social roles.
   c. their political philosophy.
   d. their level of motivation.
   e. personality traits.

Attributing behavior to persons or to situations, pp. 696-697
Medium, Factual/Definitional, Objective 1, Ans: e

8. We have a tendency to explain the behavior of others in terms of ________ and to explain our own behavior in terms of ________.
   a. informational influence; normative influence
   b. situational constraints; personality traits
   c. environmental influences; hereditary influences
   d. normative influence; informational influence
   e. personality traits; situational constraints

Attributing behavior to persons or to situations, p. 697
Difficult, Conceptual/Application, Objective 1, Ans: c

9. Observing yourself on a videotape is most likely to increase your tendency to attribute your behavior to:
   a. social norms.
   b. role playing.
   c. personality traits.
   d. the mere exposure effect.
   e. any of the above.

The effects of attribution, p. 697
Medium, Conceptual/Application, Objective 1, Ans: d

10. Carol is restless during class because her professor's distressed facial expressions lead her to believe that he dislikes teaching. The professor, on the other hand, is distressed because he sees Carol's restlessness as an indication that she lacks any motivation to learn. At this point, both student and professor should be informed of the dangers of:
a. group polarization.
b. the mere exposure effect.
c. deindividuation.
d. the fundamental attribution error.
e. the foot-in-the-door phenomenon.

The effects of attribution, p. 697
Difficult, Conceptual/Application, Objective 1, Ans: b

11. The fundamental attribution error is likely to lead observers to:
a. show sympathy toward those who are poor and unemployed.
b. praise those who have engaged in acts of heroism.
c. show mercy toward those who have committed criminal acts.
d. do all of the above.

The effects of attribution, p. 697
Difficult, Factual/Definitional, Objective 1, Ans: d

12. Poverty and unemployment are likely to be explained in terms of personal dispositions by ________ and in terms of situational influences by ________.
a. the poor; the rich
b. attribution theory; social exchange theory
c. social psychologists; evolutionary psychologists
d. political conservatives; political liberals

Attitudes and actions, p. 698
Easy, Factual/Definitional, Objective 2, Ans: c

13. Attitudes are ________ that guide behavior.
a. norms and roles
b. superordinate goals
c. beliefs and feelings
d. dispositional attributions

Do our attitudes guide our actions?, p. 698
Easy, Conceptual/Application, Objective 2, Ans: d

14. Politicians who publicly oppose a tax increase that they privately favor best illustrate that:
a. people often fail to notice the influence they exert over others.
b. a pooling of efforts toward a common goal contributes to social loafing.
c. the presence of others interferes with individual performance on difficult tasks.
d. actions may sometimes be inconsistent with attitudes.
e. group discussion enhances a group's prevailing attitudes.

Do our attitudes guide our actions?, p. 698
Medium, Conceptual/Application, Objective 2, Ans: e

15. Political pollsters find that people's attitudes toward the presidential candidates are very accurate predictors of the election outcome. This best illustrates that attitudes guide our actions when the attitude:
a. is a response to informational social influence.
b. is closely related to a more general value.
c. has a strongly emotional component.
d. is forged through life experiences rather than mere hearsay.
e. is specifically relevant to the behavior.

Do our attitudes guide our actions?, pp. 698-699
Difficult, Conceptual/Application, Objective 2, Ans: d

16. Vanna is tempted to shoplift a gold necklace even though she has negative feelings about shoplifting. Vanna is least likely to steal the merchandise if:
a. her negative feelings about shoplifting result from normative social influence.
b. she is suffering the effects of deindividuation.
c. her negative feelings about stealing were developed in her early childhood.
d. she is highly aware of her negative feelings about shoplifting.
e. she has recently shoplifted jewelry from several different stores.

Do our actions affect our attitudes?, p. 699
Easy, Factual/Definitional, Objective 3, Ans: c

17. The impact of our actions on our attitudes is best illustrated by the:
a. bystander effect.
b. fundamental attribution error.
c. foot-in-the-door phenomenon.
d. mere exposure effect.
e. frustration-aggression principle.

Do our actions affect our attitudes?, p. 699
Easy, Factual/Definitional, Objective 3, Ans: c

18. The foot-in-the-door phenomenon refers to the tendency to:
a. neglect critical thinking because of a strong desire for social harmony within a group.
b. perform simple tasks more effectively in the presence of others.
c. comply with a large request if one has previously complied with a small request.
d. lose self-restraint in group situations that foster anonymity.
e. experience an increasing attraction to novel stimuli as they become more familiar.

Do our actions affect our attitudes?, pp. 699-700
Difficult, Conceptual/Application, Objective 3, Ans: d

19. When a salesperson visits your home and asks you to try a free sample of a cleaning fluid, you agree. When he returns the following week and asks you to purchase an assortment of expensive cleaning products, you make the purchase. The salesperson appears to have made effective use of:
a. the bystander effect.
b. the fundamental attribution error.
c. the social responsibility norm.
d. the foot-in-the-door phenomenon.
e. deindividuation.

Do our actions affect our attitudes?, pp. 699-700
Medium, Conceptual/Application, Objective 3, Ans: b

20. Aleksis has recently begun to bully and hurt his younger brother. If this behavior continues, it is likely that Aleksis will:
a. experience a substantial loss of self-esteem.
b. develop an increasing dislike for his brother.
c. experience a sense of deindividuation.
d. develop a great sense of admiration and respect for his brother.

Do our actions affect our attitudes?, p. 700
Medium, Factual/Definitional, Objective 3, Ans: b

21. After they had first agreed to display a 3-inch "Be a Safe Driver" sign, California home owners were highly likely to permit the installation of a very large and unattractive "Drive Carefully" sign in their front yards. This best illustrates:
a. the mere exposure effect.
b. the foot-in-the-door phenomenon.
c. the fundamental attribution error.
d. social facilitation.
e. deindividuation.

Do our actions affect our attitudes?, p. 700
Medium, Factual/Definitional, Objective 3, Ans: d

22. Philip Zimbardo devised a simulated prison and randomly assigned college students to serve as prisoners or guards. This experiment best illustrated the impact of:
a. team membership on social loafing.
b. groupthink on social conflict.
c. frustration on aggression.
d. role-playing on attitudes.
e. deindividuation on the fundamental attribution error.

Do our actions affect our attitudes?, p. 700
Medium, Conceptual/Application, Objective 3, Ans: c

23. After she was promoted to a high-level executive position in the large company for which she worked, Jorana developed more pro-business political attitudes. This best illustrates the impact of:
a. deindividuation.
b. social facilitation.
c. role-playing.
d. mirror-image perceptions.
e. the bystander effect.

Why do our actions affect our attitudes?, p. 701
Easy, Factual/Definitional, Objective 3, Ans: a

24. The discomfort we feel when two thoughts are inconsistent is called:
a. cognitive dissonance.
b. group polarization.
c. deindividuation.
d. the foot-in-the-door phenomenon.
e. the fundamental attribution error.

Why do our actions affect our attitudes?, p. 701
Easy, Factual/Definitional, Objective 3, Ans: c

25. Which theory best explains why our actions can lead us to modify our attitudes?
    a. equity theory
    b. scapegoat theory
    c. cognitive dissonance theory
    d. social exchange theory
    e. the two-factor theory

Why do our actions affect our attitudes?, p. 701
Medium, Factual/Definitional, Objective 3, Ans: c

26. We are most likely to experience cognitive dissonance if we feel _______ sense of responsibility for engaging in behaviors of which we personally _______.
    a. little; disapprove
    b. little; approve
    c. a great; disapprove
    d. a great; approve

Why do our actions affect our attitudes?, p. 701
Medium, Conceptual/Application, Objective 3, Ans: a

27. Fernando's favorable attitude toward capital punishment began to change when he was asked to offer arguments opposing it in a college debate class. His attitude change is best explained by ________ theory.
    a. cognitive dissonance
    b. social exchange
    c. scapegoat
    d. equity
    e. the two-factor

Conformity and obedience, p. 703
Medium, Factual/Definitional, Objective 4, Ans: b

28. The experience of empathy is most directly facilitated by:
    a. the bystander effect.
    b. the chameleon effect.
    c. the mere exposure effect.
    d. mirror-image perceptions.
    e. social facilitation.

Group pressure and conformity, p. 705
Medium, Factual/Definitional, Objective 4, Ans: b

29. Solomon Asch reported that individuals conformed to a group's judgment of the lengths of lines:
    a. only when the group was composed of at least six members.
    b. even when the group judgment was clearly incorrect.
    c. even when the group seemed uncertain and repeatedly altered its judgment.
    d. only when members of the group were of high status.

Conditions that strengthen conformity, p. 705
Medium, Conceptual/Application, Objective 4, Ans: a

30. Professor Jones is a member of the faculty committee on academic standards. He personally disagrees with the other committee members' proposed plan to begin accepting students with below-average high school grades. Professor Jones is most likely, however, to vote in favor of their plan if:
    a. the other committee members are unanimous in their opinion.
    b. he stated his personal opinion early in the committee's discussion.
    c. committee voting is done by private ballot.
    d. he has a high level of self-esteem.
    e. he personally dislikes the other committee members and wishes he were on a more prestigious college committee.

Reasons for conforming, p. 705
Easy, Factual/Definitional, Objective 4, Ans: c

31. Normative social influence results from peoples' desire to:
    a. clarify reality.
    b. maintain personal control.
    c. gain social approval.
    d. demonstrate self-restraint.
    e. avoid deindividuation.

Reasons for conforming, p. 705
Easy, Conceptual/Application, Objective 4, Ans: c

32. Kentaro hates to wear ties but wears one to his sister's wedding to avoid his family's disapproval. Kentaro's behavior exemplifies the importance of:
    a. the mere exposure effect.
    b. informational social influence.
    c. normative social influence.
    d. social facilitation.
    e. the reciprocity norm.

Reasons for conforming, p. 705
Difficult, Conceptual/Application, Objective 4, Ans: b

33. Luella publicly agrees with her seventh-grade classmates that parents should allow 13-year-olds to date. Later that day, she writes in her diary that she actually believes parents should prohibit kids from dating until they are at least 15 years old. Luella's public conformity to her classmates' opinion best illustrates the power of:
    a. deindividuation.
    b. normative social influence.
    c. the mere exposure effect.
    d. informational social influence.
    e. social facilitation.

Reasons for conforming, p. 705
Medium, Conceptual, Objective 4, Ans: c

34. Accepting others' opinions about reality is to ________ as the desire to gain approval is to ________.
    a. deindividuation; social facilitation
    b. social facilitation; deindividuation
    c. informational social influence; normative social influence
    d. normative social influence; informational social influence

Reasons for conforming, p. 705
Easy, Conceptual/Application, Objective 4, Ans: e

35. After hearing respected medical authorities lecture about the value of regular exercise, Raul, who has rarely exercised, begins to jog regularly. The change in Raul's behavior best illustrates the impact of:
    a. normative social influence.
    b. the foot-in-the-door phenomenon.
    c. social facilitation.
    d. the mere exposure effect.
    e. informational social influence.

Reasons for conforming, pp. 705-706
Difficult, Factual/Definitional, Objective 4, Ans: b

36. When the task of correctly identifying an individual in a slide of a four-person lineup was both difficult and important, participants in an experiment were especially likely to conform to others' wrong answers. This best illustrates the impact of:
    a. the fundamental attribution error.
    b. informational social influence.
    c. the mere exposure effect.
    d. normative social influence.
    e. ingroup bias.

Reasons for conforming, p. 706
Easy, Factual/Definitional, Objective 4, Ans: b

37. A culture that promotes individualism is most likely to encourage:
    a. altruism.
    b. nonconformity.
    c. ingroup bias.
    d. groupthink.
    e. superordinate goals.

Obedience, pp. 706-707
Medium, Factual/Definitional, Objective 5, Ans: c

38. Most people are likely to be surprised by the results of Milgram's initial obedience experiment because:
    a. the "learners" made so few learning errors under stressful circumstances.
    b. the "teachers" actually enjoyed shocking another person.
    c. the "teachers" were more obedient than most people would have predicted.
    d. the "learners" obediently accepted painful shocks without any protest.
    e. of all the above reasons.

Obedience, p. 707
Medium, Conceptual, Objective 5, Ans: d

39. The Milgram obedience experiments were controversial because the:
    a. “teachers” actually seemed to enjoy shocking the “learners.”
    b. “learners” received painful electric shocks even if they had heart problems.
    c. experiments were performed despite mass student protests against the research.
    d. “teachers” were deceived and frequently subjected to severe stress.

Obedience, pp. 707-708
Medium, Factual/Definitional, Objective 5, Ans: c

40. In 1942, reserve police officers obeyed orders to kill some 1500 Jews in the village of Jozefow, Poland. This incident illustrated that people are most likely to be destructively obedient when:
    a. they fail to realize their actions are morally wrong.
    b. their victims are distant and depersonalized.
    c. they perceive their orders to come from legitimate authority figures.
    d. they derive personal satisfaction from destructive acts.

Obedience, p. 708
Difficult, Factual/Definitional, Objective 5, Ans: a

41. In Milgram’s obedience experiments, “teachers” were most likely to deliver high levels of shock when:
    a. the experimenter was perceived to be an ordinary college student like themselves.
    b. the victim was placed in a different room from the “teacher.”
    c. they saw that other “learners” disobeyed the experimenter.
    d. they saw how “learners” who disobeyed the experimenter were punished.

Obedience, p. 708
Medium, Factual/Definitional, Objective 5, Ans: a

42. In Milgram’s obedience experiments, “teachers” exhibited a somewhat lower level of compliance with an experimenter’s orders when:
    a. the experiment was not associated with a prestigious institution like Yale University.
    b. the “learner” complained of a slight heart condition just before the experiment began.
    c. the “learner” screamed as the shocks became more punishing.
    d. the “learner” was in another room where his physical well-being couldn’t be observed by the “teacher.”
    e. the “teacher” was instructed to administer the learning test and someone else was asked to shock the “learner.”

Lessons from the conformity and obedience studies, p. 708
Medium, Factual/Definitional, Objective 5, Ans: b

43. According to Milgram, the most fundamental lesson to be learned from his study of obedience is that:
    a. people are naturally predisposed to be hostile and aggressive.
    b. even ordinary people, who are not usually hostile, can become agents of destruction.
    c. the desire to be accepted by others is one of the strongest human motives.
    d. people value their freedom and react negatively when they feel they are being coerced to do something.

Lessons from the conformity and obedience studies, pp. 708-709
Difficult, Factual/Definitional, Objective 5, Ans: d

44. The impact of the foot-in-the-door phenomenon is most clearly illustrated by:
a. the increased number of suicides shortly after Marilyn Monroe's highly publicized death.
b. President John F. Kennedy's ill-fated decision to invade Cuba.
c. the tragic murder of Kitty Genovese just outside her New York apartment.
d. the destructive obedience of participants in the Milgram experiments.

Social facilitation, p. 709
Easy, Factual/Definitional, Objective 6, Ans: b

45. Social facilitation refers to the tendency to:
a. neglect critical thinking because of a strong desire for social harmony within a group.
b. perform well-learned tasks more effectively in the presence of others.
c. experience an increasing attraction to novel stimuli as they become more familiar.
d. lose self-restraint in group situations that foster anonymity.
e. comply with a large request if one has previously complied with a small request.

Social facilitation, p. 709
Easy, Factual/Definitional, Objective 6, Ans: d

46. The presence of others does not always lead to social facilitation because:
a. an increasing familiarity with novel stimuli facilitates liking.
b. the loss of self-restraint often accompanies arousal and anonymity.
c. one's focus of attention shifts when playing the role of actor rather than observer.
d. arousal encourages performance of the most likely response.
e. group discussion enhances whatever attitude is initially dominant in the group.

Social facilitation, p. 709
Easy, Factual/Definitional, Objective 6, Ans: b

47. Expert pool players were observed to make 71 percent of their shots when alone. When four people watched them, they made 80 percent of their shots. This best illustrates:
a. the foot-in-the-door phenomenon.
b. social facilitation.
c. group polarization.
d. the bystander effect.
e. the mere exposure effect.

Social facilitation, p. 709
Medium, Factual/Definitional, Objective 6, Ans: d

48. The presence of others ________ a person's performance on well-learned tasks and ________ a person's performance on unmastered tasks.
a. improves; has no effect on
b. hinders; improves
c. has no effect on; hinders
d. improves; hinders
e. improves; improves

Social facilitation, p. 709
Difficult, Conceptual/Application, Objective 6, Ans: d

49. On which of the following tasks would the presence of others be *most* likely to lead to improved performance?
   a. reciting the months of the year in alphabetical order
   b. solving a crossword puzzle
   c. learning foreign language words
   d. raking up fallen leaves
   e. solving complex mathematical problems

Social loafing, p. 710
Easy, Factual/Definitional, Objective 6, Ans: d

50. The tendency for people to exert less effort when they are pooling their efforts toward a common goal is known as:
   a. deindividuation.
   b. the bystander effect.
   c. group polarization.
   d. social loafing.
   e. the foot-in-the-door phenomenon.

Social loafing, p. 710
Easy, Factual/Definitional, Objective 6, Ans: a

51. University students were observed to pull harder on a rope when they thought they were pulling alone than when they thought three others were pulling with them on the same rope. This best illustrates:
   a. social loafing.
   b. the foot-in-the-door phenomenon.
   c. group polarization.
   d. social facilitation.
   e. deindividuation.

Social loafing, p. 710
Medium, Factual/Definitional, Objective 6, Ans: d

52. Social loafing has been found to be especially noticeable among ________ in cultures that value ________.
   a. women; collectivism
   b. women; individualism
   c. men; collectivism
   d. men; individualism

Social loafing, p. 710
Difficult, Conceptual/Application, Objective 6, Ans: a

53. Social loafing is *most* likely among:
   a. audience members who are asked to applaud after a speaker is introduced.
   b. factory workers paid on the basis of individual level of productivity.
   c. a group of runners competing for first place in a race.
   d. students in a college class who are each assigned a different topic for their course term papers.

Deindividuation, p. 710
Easy, Factual/Definitional, Objective 6, Ans: d

54. Deindividuation refers to:
   a. lack of critical thinking due to a strong desire for social harmony within a group.
   b. the tendency to overestimate the impact of personal dispositions on another's behavior.
   c. the failure to give aid in an emergency situation observed by many onlookers.
   d. a loss of self-awareness and self-restraint in group situations that foster arousal and anonymity.
   e. the enhancement of a group's prevailing attitudes through group discussion.

Deindividuation, p. 710
Medium, Factual/Definitional, Objective 6, Ans: d

55. When college women were dressed in Ku Klux Klan-style hoods, they demonstrated significantly more aggression. This finding is best explained in terms of:
   a. social facilitation.
   b. modeling.
   c. groupthink.
   d. deindividuation.
   e. ingroup bias.

Deindividuation, p. 710
Difficult, Conceptual/Application, Objective 6, Ans: b

56. After an exciting football game in which the home team loses by one point, a crowd of fans throws bottles and begins to tear up the field. This behavior is best understood in terms of:
   a. the just-world phenomenon.
   b. deindividuation.
   c. the bystander effect.
   d. groupthink.
   e. social facilitation.

Group polarization, p. 711
Easy, Factual/Definitional, Objective 7, Ans: b

57. Group polarization is most likely to occur in a group in which:
   a. two subgroups of individuals have opposing opinions.
   b. individuals share a similar opinion.
   c. each individual has a unique perspective.
   d. individuals have not formed any opinion.

Group polarization, p. 711
Medium, Conceptual/Application, Objective 7, Ans: c

58. Nora, Ko, Ian, and May each think that Ms. Akey may be a slightly better teacher than Mr. Schwenke. After discussing why each of them believes this to be so, they all conclude that Ms. Akey is definitely a much better teacher than Mr. Schwenke. This episode provides an example of:
   a. social facilitation.
   b. the fundamental attribution error.
   c. group polarization.
   d. deindividuation.
   e. the mere exposure effect.

Group polarization, p. 711
Difficult, Conceptual/Application, Objective 7, Ans: a

59. Individuals who believe that the death penalty should be abolished meet to discuss the issue. Research on group interaction suggests that after discussion the individuals will be:
    a. even more convinced that the death penalty should be abolished.
    b. convinced that the death penalty should be retained.
    c. sharply divided over whether the death penalty should be abolished.
    d. in favor of a more moderate position on the issue.

Groupthink, p. 712
Medium, Factual/Definitional, Objective 7, Ans: e

60. The ill-fated decision of President John F. Kennedy and his advisors to invade Cuba best illustrates the dangers of:
    a. deindividuation.
    b. the bystander effect.
    c. social facilitation.
    d. the mere exposure effect.
    e. groupthink.

Groupthink, p. 712
Medium, Factual/Definitional, Objective 7, Ans: c

61. Which of the following processes most obviously operates in groupthink?
    a. social facilitation
    b. cognitive dissonance
    c. group polarization
    d. self-disclosure

Groupthink, p. 712
Easy, Conceptual/Application, Objective 7, Ans: b

62. Which of the following comments is most likely to be made in a group characterized by groupthink?
    a. "In order to proceed democratically, we need to know the honest opinions of all group members."
    b. "We all seem to be in basic agreement, so there's no sense in continuing our discussion of this issue."
    c. "Do any of you see any potential problem with our group's position?"
    d. "As a group, we have to think carefully about all the pros and cons surrounding this issue."

The power of individuals, p. 713
Difficult, Conceptual/Application, Objective 7, Ans: a

63. Anton is the only juror to favor acquittal on a murder trial. To influence the majority he should:
    a. unswervingly hold to his position.
    b. express some uncertainty about his position.
    c. be the last member to speak and present his argument as briefly as possible.
    d. address his arguments specifically to the member of the majority who seems most disagreeable.

Prejudice, p. 714
Easy, Factual/Definitional, Objective 8, Ans: c

64. Prejudice is best defined as:
    a. the tendency to favor members of one's own group.
    b. a fearful suspicion of people one has never met.
    c. an unjustifiable attitude toward a group and its members.
    d. a perceived incompatibility of actions or goals.
    e. the belief that victims of misfortune deserve their fate.

Prejudice, p. 714
Medium, Conceptual/Application, Objective 8, Ans: c

65. Which of the following individuals most clearly adheres to a stereotype?
    a. Vladimir, who is especially attracted to Latin-American women
    b. Peter, who feels very uncomfortable interacting with African-Americans
    c. Robin, who is convinced that college professors are usually impractical and forgetful
    d. Cyril, who never hires people over age 50 to work in his restaurant

Prejudice (Figure 18.9), p. 714
Easy, Factual/Definitional, Objective 8, Ans: d

66. On the basis of what Americans say, in the last half-century, prejudice toward women has ________ and prejudice toward African-Americans has ________.
    a. decreased; increased
    b. increased; increased
    c. increased; decreased
    d. decreased; decreased

Prejudice, p. 716
Medium, Factual/Definitional, Objective 8, Ans: c

67. When Americans were surveyed about their gender preferences if they could have only one child, a ________ report having a gender preference. Of those who have a gender preference, the _______ say they would prefer a girl.
    a. majority; majority
    b. minority; minority
    c. majority; minority
    d. minority; majority

Prejudice, p. 716
Medium, Factual/Definitional, Objective 8, Ans: b

68. When shown pictures of men with either a slightly feminized or a slightly masculinized face, women were ________ attracted to slightly masculinized faces and they were ________ likely to perceive a slightly masculinized face as belonging to someone interested in a long-term relationship.
    a. more; more
    b. less; less
    c. more; less
    d. less; more

Social inequalities, p. 716
Easy, Factual/Definitional, Objective 8, Ans: e

69. Prejudice is most likely to develop as a way of justifying:
   a. group polarization.
   b. social traps.
   c. mirror-image perceptions.
   d. superordinate goals.
   e. social inequalities.

Us and them: ingroup and outgroup, p. 717
Medium, Conceptual, Objective 8, Ans: e

70. The tendency to favor members of one's own group is likely when people are formed into distinguishable groups on the basis of:
   a. identical racial backgrounds.
   b. shared religious beliefs.
   c. common occupational concerns.
   d. similar leisure-time hobbies.
   e. any of the above criteria.

Us and them: ingroup and outgroup, p. 717
Easy, Factual/Definitional, Objective 8, Ans: b

71. Most children believe their school is better than the other schools in their town. This best illustrates:
   a. the just-world phenomenon.
   b. ingroup bias.
   c. the fundamental attribution error.
   d. the reciprocity norm.
   e. scapegoating.

Scapegoating, p. 717
Easy, Factual/Definitional, Objective 8, Ans: d

72. According to the scapegoat theory, prejudice is likely to result from:
   a. stereotypes.
   b. the just-world phenomenon.
   c. ingroup bias.
   d. frustration.
   e. self-serving bias.

Scapegoating, p. 717
Medium, Conceptual/Application, Objective 8, Ans: d

73. Montel, a white college student, is on academic probation for poor grades. Ever since he received notice of his probation, Montel has become increasingly hostile toward black students on campus. His increasing hostility can best be explained in terms of:
   a. ingroup bias.
   b. the mere exposure effect.
   c. the just-world phenomenon.
   d. the scapegoat theory.
   e. the reciprocity norm.

Scapegoating, p. 717
Medium, Factual/Definitional, Objective 8, Ans: d

74. Disparaging or belittling a despised outgroup provides people with a heightened sense of their own:
   a. fundamental attribution errors.
   b. deindividuation.
   c. superordinate goals.
   d. self-worth.
   e. social loafing.

Cognitive roots of prejudice: categorization, p. 718
Medium, Factual/Definitional, Objective 8, Ans: b

75. People tend to perceive the members of an outgroup as ________ each other and the members of an ingroup as ________ each other.
   a. different from; similar to
   b. similar to; different from
   c. similar to; similar to
   d. different from; different from

Cognitive roots of prejudice: categorization, p. 718
Difficult, Conceptual/Application, Objective 8, Ans: a

76. The tendency to categorize people on the basis of their sex is most likely to lead Jack to believe that:
   a. women all have pretty much the same attitudes about sex.
   b. women seem to be unpredictable, because no two are alike.
   c. most men tend to be logical and emotionally controlled.
   d. in contrast to women, men have very similar tastes in dress and fashion.

Cognitive roots of prejudice: vivid cases, p. 718
Medium, Conceptual/Application, Objective 8, Ans: e

77. Twenty Wallonians were arrested for nonviolent crimes, whereas 20 Pireaneans were arrested for violent crimes. The tendency to judge that more crimes were committed by Pireaneans than by Wallonians best illustrates the power of:
   a. ingroup bias.
   b. the mere exposure effect.
   c. the just-world phenomenon.
   d. deindividuation.
   e. vivid cases.

The just-world phenomenon, p. 718
Medium, Factual/Definitional, Objective 8, Ans: a

78. In laboratory experiments, merely observing someone receive painful electric shocks leads viewers to think less of the victim. This reaction is best explained in terms of:
   a. the just-world phenomenon.
   b. the bystander effect.
   c. the scapegoat theory.
   d. the mere exposure effect.

The just-world phenomenon, p. 719
Difficult, Conceptual/Application, Objective 8, Ans: d

79. An eagerness to believe that victims of a natural disaster are being punished by God for their sins best illustrates a potential consequence of:
   a. deindividuation.
   b. ingroup bias.
   c. the bystander effect.
   d. the just-world phenomenon.
   e. the mere exposure effect.

The just-world phenomenon, p. 719
Medium, Factual/Definitional, Objective 8, Ans: d

80. Only when experimental participants were informed that a woman was raped did they perceive the woman's behavior as inviting rape. This best illustrates that victim-blaming is fueled by:
   a. the mere exposure effect.
   b. the bystander effect.
   c. the foot-in-the-door-phenomenon.
   d. hindsight bias.
   e. deindividuation.

Aggression, p. 719
Medium, Factual/Definitional, Objective 9, Ans: c

81. According to the text, aggression always involves:
   a. physical damage.
   b. anger and hostility.
   c. the intent to hurt.
   d. a reaction to frustration.
   e. all of the above.

Aggression, p. 719
Medium, Conceptual/Application, Objective 9, Ans: b

82. Which of the following persons is most clearly acting aggressively?
   a. a noisy neighbor who often mows his lawn at 8 o'clock on Saturday mornings
   b. a child who tries to hit another child with a rock
   c. an assertive salesperson who interrupts your evening meal with a telephone sales pitch
   d. a careless motorist who accidentally hits a small child running in the street

The biology of aggression, p. 719
Medium, Conceptual, Objective 9, Ans: c

83. Sigmund Freud would most likely have suggested that wars result from:
   a. deindividuation.
   b. frustration.
   c. human instinct.
   d. the fundamental attribution error.
   e. inequitable relationships.

The biology of aggression, p. 719
Medium, Factual/Definitional, Objective 9, Ans: c

84. The fact that human aggression varies widely from culture to culture most strongly suggests that it is *not*:
    a. a reaction to frustration.
    b. influenced by social norms.
    c. an instinctive behavior.
    d. a product of deindividuation.
    e. a result of group polarization.

The biology of aggression, p. 720
Easy, Factual/Definitional, Objective 9, Ans: a

85. When a mild-mannered woman had an electrode implanted in her amygdala, she:
    a. developed more aggressive tendencies.
    b. acted just as she had before the implantation.
    c. became even milder, unable to even say "no" to anyone's request for help.
    d. lost her ability to remember events that had recently occurred.

The biology of aggression, p. 721
Medium, Factual/Definitional, Objective 9, Ans: b

86. Testosterone levels of male college basketball fans were observed to be the highest just ________ a big game that was ________ by their team.
    a. before; won
    b. after; won
    c. before; lost
    d. after; lost

The biology of aggression, p. 721
Medium, Factual/Definitional, Objective 9, Ans: c

87. Aggressive behavior is most likely to be ________ by injections of testosterone and ________ by consumption of alcohol.
    a. increased; decreased
    b. decreased; increased
    c. increased; increased
    d. decreased; decreased

The psychology of aggression: aversive events, p. 721
Medium, Conceptual/Application, Objective 9, Ans: e

88. After Manny's father refused to let him use the family car on Friday night, Manny let all the air out of the tires. His action is best explained in terms of the:
    a. mere exposure effect.
    b. foot-in-the-door phenomenon.
    c. fundamental attribution error.
    d. bystander effect.
    e. frustration-aggression principle.

Learning to express and inhibit aggression, p. 722
Easy, Factual/Definitional, Objective 9, Ans: d

89. Minimal levels of father care are associated with high levels of:
   a. conformity.
   b. group polarization.
   c. social facilitation.
   d. aggression.

Learning to express and inhibit aggression, p. 723
Difficult, Conceptual/Application, Objective 9, Ans: b

90. Which of the following would be the best advice to give parents who are concerned about the frequent aggressive outbursts of their 6-year-old son?
   a. "Encourage your son to express his anger by slugging a punching bag."
   b. "Make a point of rewarding and praising your son whenever he is socially cooperative and altruistic."
   c. "Be consistent in spanking your child after every outburst so he'll realize that aggression never pays."
   d. "Encourage your son to watch the devastating consequences of violence portrayed on TV."
   e. "Don't be concerned about your child's aggressiveness, unless the behavior pattern continues beyond the fifth grade."

Sexual aggression and the media, pp. 723-724
Easy, Factual/Definitional, Objective 10, Ans: a

91. Violent pornographic movies often perpetuate the myth that:
   a. many women enjoy aggressive sexual encounters.
   b. most rapes are commonly committed by victims' dates or acquaintances.
   c. women are more likely rape victims than are men.
   d. most rapes are never reported to the police.

Sexual aggression and the media, p. 724
Medium, Conceptual/Application, Objective 10, Ans: b

92. After watching a large number of violent pornographic movies, Ollie will probably be:
   a. more likely to believe that such movies should be banned.
   b. less likely to believe that women are seriously harmed by rape.
   c. more likely to favor long prison sentences for convicted rapists.
   d. less likely to believe that women enjoy aggressive sexual treatment from men.

Sexual aggression and the media, p. 724
Difficult, Factual/Definitional, Objective 10, Ans: c

93. After extensive exposure to pornographic films, viewers have been found to see their partners as ________ attractive and to be ________ accepting of short prison sentences for convicted rapists.
   a. more; less
   b. less; less
   c. less; more
   d. more; more

TV violence, pornography, and society, p. 724
Medium, Factual/Definitional, Objective 10, Ans: d

94. A significant danger of media violence is that impressionable viewers are subsequently more likely to enact the _______ provided by the media.
a. superordinate goals
b. social loafing
c. self-disclosure
d. social scripts

Do video games teach or release violence? p. 725
Easy, Factual/Definitional, Objective 10, Ans: a

95. Experimental studies indicate that college males who are randomly assigned to play a violent video game experience ________ levels of arousal and become ________ likely to hurt a fellow student.
a. increasing; increasingly
b. decreasing; decreasingly
c. increasing; decreasingly
d. decreasing; increasingly

Social traps, p. 727
Medium, Factual/Definitional, Objective 11, Ans: c

96. A social trap is a situation in which:
a. there are not enough resources to satisfy the needs of all members of a social group.
b. false stereotypes influence how people interpret the behavior of others.
c. the pursuit of self-interest leads to collective harm.
d. the rich get richer and the poor get poorer.
e. all people in a conflict situation suffer, no matter how cooperatively they behave.

Social traps, p. 727
Easy, Factual/Definitional, Objective 11, Ans: c

97. Continuing to operate a fuel-inefficient car despite warnings about the effect of greenhouse gases best illustrates the dynamics of:
a. the just-world phenomenon.
b. social loafing.
c. a social trap.
d. the fundamental attribution error.
e. the mere exposure effect.

Social traps, p. 727
Difficult, Conceptual/Application, Objective 11, Ans: e

98. Despite government warnings of a severe shortage of heating fuels, most citizens continue to turn up their home thermostats in the belief that their personal fuel consumption will have little effect on the country's total fuel reserves. This reaction best illustrates the dynamics of:
a. the bystander effect.
b. the fundamental attribution error.
c. the foot-in-the-door phenomenon.
d. the just-world phenomenon.
e. a social trap.

Enemy perceptions, p. 728
Easy, Factual/Definitional, Objective 11, Ans: e

99. Two conflicting groups who share the same negative views of one another demonstrate:
   a. the reciprocity norm.
   b. deindividuation.
   c. superordinate goals.
   d. GRIT.
   e. mirror-image perceptions.

Enemy perceptions, p. 728
Difficult, Conceptual/Application, Objective 11, Ans: a

100. Haley thinks Keith's silence indicates that he's angry, so she avoids talking to him. Unfortunately, Keith thinks Haley's quietness signifies that she's angry and wants to be left alone. This situation best illustrates:
   a. mirror-image perceptions.
   b. the reciprocity norm.
   c. superordinate goals.
   d. scapegoating.
   e. deindividuation.

The psychology of attraction: proximity, p. 729
Medium, Conceptual/Application, Objective 12, Ans: d

101. Vince, an extraverted college freshman, has just moved into a college dormitory. Vince is most likely to become friends with:
   a. Alfonse, a junior who is majoring in psychology and lives across the hall.
   b. Mohammed, an introverted student who lives on the next floor and enjoys playing chess.
   c. James, a lonely sophomore who lives down the hall and is undecided about his major.
   d. Bill, his assigned roommate who is majoring in computer science.

The psychology of attraction: proximity, p. 729
Medium, Factual/Definitional, Objective 12, Ans: d

102. The mere exposure effect refers to the fact that people:
   a. perform well-learned tasks more effectively in the presence of others.
   b. become more extreme in their opinions following group discussion.
   c. more readily comply with a large request if they previously complied with a small request.
   d. experience increasing attraction to novel stimuli that become more familiar.
   e. often fail to notice the influence they exert on others.

The psychology of attraction: proximity, p. 729
Medium, Conceptual/Application, Objective 12, Ans: b

103. After three months of riding the 8:30 bus to work, Cindy has actually started to feel affection for the gruff and scowling old bus driver. Cindy's reaction best illustrates:
   a. the fundamental attribution error.
   b. the mere exposure effect.
   c. mirror-image perceptions.
   d. the bystander effect.
   e. the social exchange theory.

The psychology of attraction: proximity, p. 729
Difficult, Factual/Definitional, Objective 12, Ans: d

104. People's preference for mirror-image photographs of themselves illustrates the impact of:
a. reciprocity norms.
b. the bystander effect.
c. deindividuation.
d. the mere exposure effect.
e. cognitive dissonance.

The psychology of attraction: physical attractiveness, p. 730
Medium, Factual/Definitional, Objective 12, Ans: c

105. What determined whether college freshmen who had been randomly paired for a Welcome Week dance liked each other?
a. similarity in attitudes
b. similarity in intelligence
c. physical attractiveness
d. self-disclosure skills
e. all of the above

The psychology of attraction: physical attractiveness, p. 730
Difficult, Factual/Definitional, Objective 12, Ans: b

106. Research on physical attractiveness indicates that women are less likely than men to:
a. express unhappiness with their own physical appearance.
b. verbally attribute their liking for physically attractive dates to good looks.
c. judge members of the opposite sex as more attractive if they have a mature appearance.
d. marry someone who is less physically attractive than they themselves are.
e. be attracted to dating partners whose hips are narrower than their waists.

The psychology of attraction: physical attractiveness, p. 730
Difficult, Conceptual/Application, Objective 12, Ans: a

107. Svetlana, a 20-year-old college sophomore, is beautiful. Research suggests that she is likely to ________ than less attractive college women.
a. be perceived as more socially skilled
b. have a much higher level of self-esteem
c. be perceived as less intelligent
d. date less frequently
e. have more difficulty securing employment

The psychology of attraction: similarity, p. 732
Easy, Factual/Definitional, Objective 12, Ans: b

108. Which of the following proverbs is most clearly supported by research on social attraction?
a. The beautiful are the lonely.
b. Birds of a feather flock together.
c. Familiarity breeds contempt.
d. Absence makes the heart grow fonder.

The psychology of attraction: similarity, p. 732
Medium, Conceptual/Application, Objective 12, Ans: a

109. Felippe, a 19-year-old college freshman, is very talkative, intelligent, assertive, and politically conservative. Research suggests that he would be most likely to develop a close friendship with:
   a. Toren, who is talkative and assertive.
   b. Erez, who is quiet and passive.
   c. Tom, who is intelligent and quiet.
   d. Fabio, who is politically liberal and talkative.

The psychology of attraction, pp. 730, 732, 737
Difficult, Conceptual, Objective 12, Ans: c

110. Our tendency to establish and maintain warm relationships with people if they are physically attractive and similar to us is best explained in terms of:
   a. the bystander effect.
   b. attribution theory.
   c. social exchange theory.
   d. the just-world phenomenon.
   e. the foot-in-the-door phenomenon.

Passionate love, p. 733
Easy, Factual/Definitional, Objective 13, Ans: b

111. The two-factor theory of emotion has been used to explain:
   a. the bystander effect.
   b. passionate love.
   c. social facilitation.
   d. the mere exposure effect.
   e. the just-world phenomenon.

Passionate love, p. 733
Medium, Conceptual/Application, Objective 13, Ans: c

112. Casandra, who is attractive and likable, has just telephoned Mike and asked him for a date. According to the two-factor theory of emotion, Mike is likely to experience the most intense romantic feelings for Casandra during their telephone conversation if he has just:
   a. awakened from a short nap.
   b. finished eating a delicious meal.
   c. completed a series of aerobic exercises.
   d. been studying his history lecture notes.

Passionate love, p. 733
Medium, Factual/Definitional, Objective 13, Ans: d

113. In an experiment by Dutton and Aron, one group of men were asked by an attractive woman to complete a short questionnaire immediately after they had crossed a swaying footbridge suspended 230 feet above the Capilano River. This experiment was designed to study the factors that contribute to:
   a. the bystander effect.
   b. social facilitation.
   c. the mere exposure effect.
   d. passionate love.
   e. the foot-in-the-door phenomenon.

Companionate love, p. 734
Medium, Conceptual/Application, Objective 13, Ans: c

114. Elsworth is unusually attractive and intelligent, and she works hard to please her husband. He displays little affection for her, however, and spends most of the family's resources on his own interests. Elsworth's relationship with her husband is best characterized as:
a. deindividuated.
b. companionate.
c. inequitable.
d. complementary.
e. reciprocal.

Companionate love, p. 734
Easy, Conceptual/Application, Objective 13, Ans: d

115. Natasha and Dimitri have a fulfilling marital relationship because they readily confide their deepest hopes and fears to each other. This best illustrates the value of:
a. passionate love.
b. deindividuation.
c. social facilitation.
d. self-disclosure.
e. the mere exposure effect.

Altruism, p. 735
Medium, Factual/Definitional, Objective 14, Ans: a

116. The tragic murder of Kitty Genovese outside her New York apartment stimulated social psychological research on:
a. altruism.
b. the mere exposure effect.
c. the fundamental attribution error.
d. the foot-in-the-door phenomenon.
e. the effects of exposure to violent pornography.

Bystander intervention, pp. 735-736
Easy, Conceptual/Application, Objective 14, Ans: e

117. When 12-year-old Jamilah saw an old man lying on the sidewalk in apparent discomfort, he prepared to offer help. But when he noticed several adults walk past the man, he concluded that the man did not need any help. His reaction most clearly illustrates one of the dynamics involved in:
a. the mere exposure effect.
b. the fundamental attribution error.
c. social loafing.
d. the foot-in-the-door phenomenon.
e. the bystander effect.

Bystander intervention, pp. 735-736
Difficult, Conceptual, Objective 14, Ans: b

118. The best explanation for the inaction of bystanders during the Kitty Genovese murder is that they failed to:
   a. experience any empathy for a stranger.
   b. assume personal responsibility for helping the victim.
   c. realize that the incident was really an emergency situation.
   d. notice that the incident was taking place.
   e. do any of the above.

Bystander intervention, p. 736
Medium, Factual/Definitional, Objective 14, Ans: d

119. Darley and Latané observed that most university students failed to help a person having an epileptic seizure when they thought there were four other witnesses to the emergency. The students' failure to help is best explained in terms of:
   a. the ingroup bias.
   b. a failure to interpret the incident as an emergency.
   c. indifference and apathy.
   d. their limited feelings of responsibility.
   e. the foot-in-the-door phenomenon.

Bystander intervention, p. 736
Easy, Factual/Definitional, Objective 14, Ans: d

120. The bystander effect refers to the tendency for an observer of an emergency to withhold aid if the:
   a. emergency takes place in a large city.
   b. observer has just endured a frustrating experience.
   c. emergency victim is a member of a different racial group than the observer.
   d. emergency is being observed by a number of other people.
   e. observer has been exposed to many similar emergencies in the past.

Bystander intervention, pp. 736-737
Medium, Conceptual/Application, Objective 14, Ans: b

121. Which of the following people would be most likely to help Gita study for her history exam?
   a. Gita's older brother, who probably has nothing better to do that evening
   b. Gita's mother, who is excited about the unexpected bonus she just received from her employer
   c. Gita's father, who always points out how differently men and women think and act
   d. Gita's younger sister, whose boyfriend just canceled their date for the next evening

The psychology of helping, p. 737
Medium, Factual/Definitional, Objective 14, Ans: a

122. According to social exchange theory, altruistic behavior is guided by:
   a. calculations of costs and benefits.
   b. feelings of social responsibility.
   c. reciprocity norms.
   d. family ties.

The psychology of helping, p. 737
Difficult, Conceptual/Application, Objective 14, Ans: c

123. Two classmates ask you to spend a couple of hours helping them prepare for a chemistry test. According to social exchange theory, you would be most likely to help them if:
a. your parents helped you study for tests when you were younger.
b. your classmates are slow learners who really need your help.
c. you know you would feel terribly guilty for refusing their request.
d. you know that no one else is willing to help them.
e. your classmates cannot afford to pay for a private tutor.

The psychology of helping, p. 737
Medium, Conceptual/Application, Objective 14, Ans: e

124. After she received a free hand-painted Christmas ornament from a religious organization, Mrs. Montevecchi felt obligated to mail a cash donation to the organization. Her response to the free gift best illustrates the impact of:
a. the foot-in-the-door phenomenon.
b. the mere exposure effect.
c. the just-world phenomenon.
d. the fundamental attribution error.
e. the reciprocity norm.

The psychology of helping, p. 737
Medium, Factual/Definitional, Objective 14, Ans: a

125. Gallup surveys indicate that Americans who frequently attend religious services are particularly likely to:
a. report that they are currently aiding the poor and infirm.
b. demonstrate the bystander effect.
c. violate the social responsibility norm.
d. base their altruistic acts on the principle of reciprocity.

Peacemaking, p. 738
Medium, Factual/Definitional, Objective 15, Ans: d

126. Sherif's study of conflict in a Boy Scout camp indicated that conflict between two groups of boys could be reduced most effectively by:
a. bringing the members of both groups into close contact.
b. having one group make conciliatory gestures to the other group.
c. allowing leaders of the two groups to communicate.
d. exposing the groups to tasks that required their joint cooperation.

Peacemaking, p. 738
Difficult, Factual/Definitional, Objective 15, Ans: d

127. Sherif planned a disruption of the water supply in a Boy Scout camp in order to observe how social relationships are influenced by:
a. ingroup bias.
b. social traps.
c. group polarization.
d. superordinate goals.
e. the mere exposure effect.

Peacemaking, p. 738
Medium, Conceptual/Application, Objective 15, Ans: c

128. If one were to generalize from Sherif's study of conflict resolution between two groups of children campers, the best way for the United States and China to improve their relationship would be to:
  a. hold highly publicized athletic contests between the two countries.
  b. minimize their trade and economic exchanges.
  c. conduct a joint space program designed to land humans on Mars.
  d. allow citizens of each country the right to freely immigrate to the other country.

Peacemaking, p. 739
Medium, Conceptual/Application, Objective 15, Ans: d

129. Pablo and Sabina argued bitterly about which of them should have use of the family car that night. Neither realized, however, that Sabina needed the car only in the early evening and that Pablo needed it only in the late evening. Pablo and Sabina's failure to resolve their argument for their mutual benefit best illustrates the dangers of:
  a. superordinate goals.
  b. the mere exposure effect.
  c. ingroup bias.
  d. a win-lose orientation.
  e. GRIT.

Peacemaking, p. 739
Medium, Factual/Definitional, Objective 15, Ans: c

130. GRIT attempts to reduce conflict through:
  a. third-party mediation.
  b. intimidation.
  c. conciliation.
  d. pacifism.

Peacemaking, p. 739
Medium, Conceptual/Application, Objective 15, Ans: b

131. Which of the following would be most consistent with a GRIT strategy?
  a. announcing that even a small attack on an ally will result in a nuclear attack on the enemy
  b. announcing that defense expenditures will be cut by 5 percent and inviting the enemy to do likewise
  c. announcing that one has formed an alliance with several countries encircling the enemy
  d. announcing that the opposing party's invasion of a neutral country will be challenged in an international court of law

Essay Questions

1. David's history teacher asked him why so many German people complied with Hitler's orders to systematically slaughter millions of innocent Jews. David suggested that the atrocities were committed because the Germans had become unusually cruel, sadistic people with abnormal and twisted personalities. Use your knowledge of the fundamental attribution error and Milgram's research on obedience to highlight the weaknesses of David's explanation.

2. Latitia, a college sophomore, reported: "Although I was not at all sure that I really loved my boyfriend, he coaxed me into sleeping with him. After that, I convinced myself that I really did love him." Use your understanding of cognitive dissonance theory to explain why Latitia developed such positive feelings for her boyfriend. What could Latitia do in the future to ensure that her sexual behaviors are guided by her own true attitudes and desires?

3. Jill, a female employee at Acme Industries, recently complained that she had been sexually harassed by one of her male supervisors. Upon hearing of this complaint, Luis, a fellow employee, commented, "If the women around here would stop some of their flirting, they'd be left alone." Jason, another coworker, quickly added, "If the women in this country stopped trying to act like men, they'd all be treated with more respect." Explain how these insensitive remarks illustrate some of the social, emotional, and cognitive roots of prejudice.

4. Research indicates that we often form more positive impressions of beautiful people than of those who are physically unattractive. Explain how advertisements, movies, and children's fairy tales might encourage this tendency. Use your knowledge of the factors that facilitate interpersonal attraction to suggest how people could be influenced to feel more positively about those who are physically unattractive.

5. While walking through a busy city park, Mr. Cruz experiences sharp chest pains that indicate to him the onset of a heart attack. Describe several things Mr. Cruz should do to increase the chances that someone will come to his aid and quickly provide him with appropriate medical attention. Explain the rationale for your advice in light of research on altruism and the decision-making process underlying bystander intervention.

Web Quiz 1

Ans: e

1. Marilyn judges her professor's strict class attendance policy to be an indication of his overcontrolling personality rather than a necessity dictated by the limited number of class sessions in a course that meets only once a week. Her judgment best illustrates:
   a. the mere exposure effect.
   b. group polarization.
   c. deindividuation.
   d. the foot-in-the-door phenomenon.
   e. the fundamental attribution error.

Ans: b

2. Bart complied with his friends' request to join them in smashing decorative pumpkins early one Halloween evening. Later that night he was surprised by his own failure to resist their pressures to throw eggs at passing police cars. Bart's experience best illustrates the:
   a. bystander effect.
   b. foot-in-the-door phenomenon.
   c. fundamental attribution error.
   d. frustration-aggression principle.
   e. just-world phenomenon.

Ans: e

3. Cognitive dissonance theory is most helpful for understanding the impact of:
   a. frustration on aggression.
   b. groupthink on social conflict.
   c. deindividuation on the bystander effect.
   d. team membership on social loafing.
   e. role-playing on attitude change.

Ans: b

4. In making wedding preparations, Jason conforms to the expectations of his future bride's family simply to win their favor. His behavior illustrates the importance of:
   a. social facilitation.
   b. normative social influence.
   c. mirror-image perceptions.
   d. the mere exposure effect.
   e. the bystander effect.

Ans: c

5. The level of obedience in the Milgram experiments was highest when the "teacher" was ________ the experimenter and ________ the "learner."
   a. close to; close to
   b. far from; far from
   c. close to; far from
   d. far from; close to

Ans: d

6. Bonnie pedals an exercise bike at her health club much faster when other patrons happen to be working out on nearby equipment. This best illustrates:
   a. the bystander effect.
   b. the mere exposure effect.
   c. the foot-in-the-door phenomenon.
   d. social facilitation.
   e. group polarization.

Ans: a

7. When a group of high school students who were all prejudiced discussed racial issues, their attitudes became even more prejudiced. This best illustrates:
   a. group polarization.
   b. the bystander effect.
   c. social facilitation.
   d. the mere exposure effect.
   e. social loafing.

Ans: e

8. Kelly, a Republican, and Carlos, a Democrat, both believe that members of their own political party are more fair-minded and trustworthy than members of other parties. Their beliefs best illustrate:
   a. the social responsibility norm.
   b. the just-world phenomenon.
   c. the two-factor theory.
   d. deindividuation.
   e. ingroup bias.

Ans: c

9. When visiting the Bergin-Belsen concentration camp shortly after World War II, one German civilian was said to have remarked, "What terrible criminals these prisoners must have been to receive such treatment." This reaction is best explained in terms of:
   a. the mere exposure effect.
   b. social facilitation.
   c. the just-world phenomenon.
   d. the social responsibility norm.
   e. deindividuation.

Ans: c

10. After extensive exposure to X-rated sexual films, men are subsequently ________ accepting of women's sexual submission to men and _______ likely to perceive a woman's friendliness as sexual interest.
   a. more; less
   b. less; more
   c. more; more
   d. less; less

Ans: d

11. Max fails to recycle his glass, metal, and plastic garbage because he thinks it's personally inconvenient and likely to have minimal impact on the city's already overflowing landfills. His reaction best illustrates the dynamics of:
    a. the mere exposure effect.
    b. the just-world phenomenon.
    c. the fundamental attribution error.
    d. a social trap.
    e. social facilitation.

Ans: b

12. When buying groceries, many shoppers prefer certain products simply because they have a familiar brand name. This preference best illustrates the importance of:
    a. social traps.
    b. the mere exposure effect.
    c. mirror-image perceptions.
    d. the reciprocity norm.
    e. deindividuation.

Ans: c

13. Which theory best explains why the excitement that lingers after a frightening event can facilitate passionate love?
    a. social exchange theory
    b. cognitive dissonance theory
    c. the two-factor theory
    d. the scapegoat theory
    e. equity theory

Ans: c

14. Mr. Hughes heard what sounded like cries for help from a swimmer located 30 yards from the ocean shoreline. He continued walking along the beach, however, because he figured that one of the many swimmers in the vicinity would provide help if it was needed. His reaction best illustrates the dynamics involved in:
    a. the fundamental attribution error.
    b. group polarization.
    c. the bystander effect.
    d. the foot-in-the-door phenomenon.
    e. the mere exposure effect.

Ans: c

15. The hostilities between two racial subgroups of a riverfront community were dramatically reduced when the threat of their river flooding its banks required that they work together to save their town. This best illustrates the impact of:
    a. the mere exposure effect.
    b. groupthink.
    c. superordinate goals.
    d. deindividuation.
    e. the bystander effect.

Web Quiz 2

Ans: d

1. The fundamental attribution error involves:
   a. failing to give aid in an emergency situation involving many onlookers.
   b. becoming more extreme in one's individual opinions following group discussion.
   c. performing a complex task more poorly when in the presence of others.
   d. underestimating situational constraints on another's behavior.
   e. losing self-restraint in group situations that foster anonymity.

Ans: a

2. Professor Stewart wrote a very positive letter of recommendation for a student despite his having doubts about her competence. Which theory best explains why he subsequently began to develop more favorable attitudes about the student's abilities?
   a. cognitive dissonance theory
   b. social exchange theory
   c. two-factor theory
   d. scapegoat theory
   e. equity theory

Ans: b

3. Research participants who worked alongside someone who rubbed his or her face or shook his or her foot were observed to do the same thing themselves. This best illustrated:
   a. the mere exposure effect.
   b. the chameleon effect.
   c. social loafing.
   d. deindividuation.
   e. the bystander effect.

Ans: b

4. Using the Asch procedure, studies reveal that conformity to group judgments is least likely when:
   a. participants announce their own answers only after the other group members have done so.
   b. participants are not observed by other group members when giving their answers.
   c. it is very difficult for anyone to make correct perceptual judgments.
   d. judgments are made in a group that has more than three people.

Ans: c

5. In a study of social loafing, blindfolded students were asked to pull on a rope as hard as they could. The students tugged hardest when they thought:
   a. three others were pulling with them.
   b. three others were pulling against them.
   c. no others were pulling with them.
   d. no one was monitoring how hard they pulled.

Ans: c

6. Although Frieda is typically very reserved, as part of a huge rock concert crowd she lost her inhibitions and behaved in a very sexually provocative way. Frieda's unusual behavior is best understood in terms of:
   a. the bystander effect.
   b. social facilitation.
   c. deindividuation.
   d. the mere exposure effect.
   e. the fundamental attribution error.

Ans: c

7. Groupthink is fueled by a desire for:
   a. conflict.
   b. self-disclosure.
   c. harmony.
   d. passionate love.
   e. cognitive dissonance.

Ans: d

8. Following Germany's defeat in World War I and the economic chaos that followed, many Germans experienced increasing levels of prejudice toward Jews. This surge of hostility can best be explained in terms of the
   a. mere exposure effect.
   b. reciprocity norm.
   c. just-world phenomenon.
   d. scapegoat theory.
   e. bystander effect.

Ans: e

9. Shortly after Alex learned that he had failed to make the high school football team, he vandalized the team's locker room and broke several classroom windows. His behavior is best explained in terms of:
   a. group polarization.
   b. the mere exposure effect.
   c. social loafing.
   d. deindividuation.
   e. the frustration-aggression principle.

Ans: d

10. Although the leaders of two enemy nations admit to a buildup of their own military forces, each sees the other country's actions as unreasonable and motivated by evil intentions. This situation best illustrates:
   a. deindividuation.
   b. the mere exposure effect.
   c. the just-world phenomenon.
   d. mirror-image perceptions.
   e. social facilitation.

Ans: c

11. When asked how much they like various letters of the alphabet, people tend to prefer those that happen to be found in their own names. This best illustrates the impact of:
    a. deindividuation.
    b. social facilitation.
    c. the mere exposure effect.
    d. the fundamental attribution error.
    e. the foot-in-the door phenomenon.

Ans: a

12. Compared to less attractive people, those who are physically attractive are *least* likely to be perceived as very:
    a. honest.
    b. healthy.
    c. socially skilled.
    d. happy.

Ans: a

13. Although Natalie receives somewhat greater rewards from her marriage than does her husband, both are satisfied with the relationship because they each benefit in proportion to what they put into it. This best illustrates the significance of:
    a. equity.
    b. deindividuation.
    c. the bystander effect.
    d. social facilitation.
    e. the mere exposure effect.

Ans: e

14. The neighbors' failure to call the police in time to save the life of Kitty Genovese best illustrated:
    a. group polarization.
    b. the frustration-aggression principle.
    c. the mere exposure effect.
    d. the just-world phenomenon.
    e. the bystander effect.

Ans: b

15. After Mrs. Chanski and her children had helped themselves to free samples of the cookies being promoted in the grocery store, she felt obligated to buy some, even though they seemed unreasonably expensive. Her reaction best illustrates the significance of:
    a. social facilitation.
    b. the reciprocity norm.
    c. the bystander effect.
    d. the just-world phenomenon.
    e. deindividuation.

Study Guide Questions

Ans: d, p. 696

1. Professor Washington's students did very poorly on the last exam. The tendency to make the fundamental attribution error might lead her to conclude that the class did poorly because:
   a. the test was unfair.
   b. not enough time was given for students to complete the test.
   c. students were distracted by some social function on campus.
   d. students were unmotivated.

Ans: d, p. 696

2. Which theory describes how we explain others' behavior as being due to internal dispositions or external situations?
   a. social exchange theory
   b. reward theory
   c. two-factor theory
   d. attribution theory

Ans: c, p. 696

3. When male students in an experiment were told that a woman to whom they would be speaking had been instructed to act in a friendly or unfriendly way, most of them subsequently attributed her behavior to:
   a. the situation.
   b. the situation *and* her personal disposition.
   c. her personal disposition.
   d. their own skill or lack of skill in a social situation.

Ans: d, p. 698

4. Which of the following is true?
   a. Attitudes and actions rarely correspond.
   b. Attitudes predict behavior about half the time.
   c. Attitudes are excellent predictors of behavior.
   d. Attitudes predict behavior under certain conditions.

Ans: b, p. 699

5. Which of the following is an example of the foot-in-the-door phenomenon?
   a. To persuade a customer to buy a product, a store owner offers a small gift.
   b. After agreeing to wear a small "Enforce Recycling" lapel pin, a woman agrees to collect signatures on a petition to make recycling required by law.
   c. After offering to sell a car at a ridiculously low price, a car salesperson is forced to tell the customer the car will cost $1000 more.
   d. All of the above are examples.

Ans: d, p. 701

6. Which of the following situations should produce the *greatest* cognitive dissonance?
   a. A soldier is forced to carry out orders he finds disagreeable.
   b. A student who loves animals has to dissect a cat in order to pass biology.
   c. As part of an experiment, a subject is directed to deliver electric shocks to another person.
   d. A student volunteers to debate an issue, taking the side he personally disagrees with.

Ans: b, p. 701

7. Before she gave a class presentation favoring gun control legislation, Wanda opposed it. Her present attitude favoring such legislation can best be explained by:
   a. attribution theory.
   b. cognitive dissonance theory.
   c. social exchange theory.
   d. evolutionary psychology.
   e. two-factor theory.

Ans: c, p. 701

8. According to cognitive dissonance theory, dissonance is most likely to occur when:
   a. a person's behavior is not based on strongly held attitudes.
   b. two people have conflicting attitudes and find themselves in disagreement.
   c. an individual does something that is personally disagreeable.
   d. an individual is coerced into doing something that he or she does not want to do.

Ans: e, p. 704

9. Conformity increased under which of the following conditions in Asch's studies of conformity?
   a. The group had three or more people.
   b. The group had high status.
   c. Individuals were made to feel insecure.
   d. The group was unanimous.
   e. All of the above increased conformity.

Ans: d, p. 705

10. Subjects in Asch's line-judgment experiment conformed to the group standard when their judgments were observed by others but not when they were made in private. This tendency to conform in public demonstrates:
   a. social facilitation.
   b. overjustification.
   c. informational social influence.
   d. normative social influence.

Ans: a, p. 705

11. Which of the following is important in promoting conformity in individuals?
   a. whether an individual's behavior will be observed by others in the group
   b. whether the individual is male or female
   c. the size of the room in which a group is meeting
   d. the age of the members in a group
   e. whether the individual is of a higher status than other group members

Ans: a, p. 705

12. Maria recently heard a speech calling for a ban on aerosol sprays that endanger the earth's ozone layer. Maria's subsequent decision to stop using aerosol sprays is an example of:
   a. informational social influence.
   b. normative social influence.
   c. deindividuation.
   d. social facilitation.

Ans: c, p. 705

13. José is the one student member on the college board of trustees. At the board's first meeting, José wants to disagree with the others on several issues but in each case decides to say nothing. Studies on conformity suggest all except one of the following are factors in José's not speaking up. Which one is *not* a factor?
   a. The board is a large group.
   b. The board is prestigious and most of its members are well known.
   c. The board members are already aware that José and the student body disagree with them on these issues.
   d. Because this is the first meeting José has attended, he feels insecure and not fully competent.

Ans: d, p. 707

14. In his study of obedience, Stanley Milgram found that the majority of subjects:
   a. refused to shock the learner even once.
   b. complied with the experiment until the "learner" first indicated pain.
   c. complied with the experiment until the "learner" began screaming in agony.
   d. complied with all the demands of the experiment.

Ans: d, p. 708

15. In Milgram's obedience studies, subjects were *less* likely to follow the experimenter's orders when:
   a. they heard the "learner" cry out in pain.
   b. they merely administered the test while someone else delivered the shocks.
   c. the "learner" was an older person or mentioned having some physical problem.
   d. they saw another subject disobey instructions.

Ans: a, p. 708

16. Which of the following conclusions did Milgram derive from his studies of obedience?
   a. Even ordinary people, without any particular hostility, can become agents in a destructive process.
   b. Most people are able, under the proper circumstances, to suppress their natural aggressiveness.
   c. The need to be accepted by others is a powerful motivating force.
   d. All of the above conclusions were reached.

Ans: e, p. 709

17. Which of the following would most likely be subject to social facilitation?
   a. proofreading a page for spelling errors
   b. typing a letter with accuracy
   c. playing a difficult piece on a musical instrument
   d. giving a speech
   e. running quickly around a track

Ans: b, p. 710

18. Which of the following most accurately states the effects of crowding on behavior?
   a. Crowding makes people irritable.
   b. Crowding sometimes intensifies people's reactions.
   c. Crowding promotes altruistic behavior.
   d. Crowding usually weakens the intensity of people's reactions.

Ans: d, p. 710

19. The phenomenon in which individuals lose their identity and relinquish normal restraints when they are part of a group is called:
    a. groupthink.
    b. cognitive dissonance.
    c. empathy.
    d. deindividuation.

Ans: a, p. 711

20. Jane and Sandy were best friends as freshmen. Jane joined a sorority; Sandy didn't. By the end of their senior year, they found that they had less in common with each other than with the other members of their respective circles of friends. Which of the following phenomena most likely explains their feelings?
    a. group polarization
    b. groupthink
    c. deindividuation
    d. social facilitation

Ans: d, p. 711

21. Which of the following statements is true?
    a. Groups are almost never swayed by minority opinions.
    b. Group polarization is most likely to occur when group members frequently disagree with one another.
    c. Groupthink provides the consensus needed for effective decision making.
    d. A group that is like-minded will probably not change its opinions through discussion.

Ans: d, p. 712

22. Which of the following is most likely to promote groupthink?
    a. The group's leader fails to take a firm stance on an issue.
    b. A minority faction holds to its position.
    c. The group consults with various experts.
    d. Group polarization is evident.

Ans: d, p. 712

23. Which of the following best summarizes the relative importance of personal control and social control of our behavior?
    a. Situational influences on behavior generally are much greater than personal influences.
    b. Situational influences on behavior generally are slightly greater than personal influences.
    c. Personal influences on behavior generally are much greater than situational influences.
    d. Situational and personal influences interact in determining our behavior.

Ans: b, p. 713

24. Research has found that for a minority to succeed in swaying a majority, the minority must:
    a. make up a sizable portion of the group.
    b. express its position as consistently as possible.
    c. express its position in the most extreme terms possible.
    d. be able to convince a key leader of the majority.

Ans: c, p. 716

25. Alexis believes that all male athletes are self-centered and sexist. Her beliefs are an example of:
    a. ingroup bias.
    b. groupthink.
    c. stereotypes.
    d. the fundamental attribution error.

Ans: a, p. 716

26. People with power and status may become prejudiced because:
    a. they tend to justify the social inequalities between themselves and others.
    b. those with less status and power tend to resent them.
    c. those with less status and power appear less capable.
    d. they feel proud and are boastful of their achievements.

Ans: a, p. 717

27. Students at State University are convinced that their school is better than any other; this most directly illustrates:
    a. an ingroup bias.
    b. prejudice and discrimination.
    c. the scapegoat effect.
    d. the just-world phenomenon.
    e. mirror-image perceptions.

Ans: c, p. 717

28. Ever since their cabin lost the camp softball competition, the campers have become increasingly hostile toward one camper in their cabin, blaming her for every problem in the cabin. This behavior is best explained in terms of:
    a. the ingroup bias.
    b. prejudice.
    c. the scapegoat theory.
    d. the reciprocity norm.
    e. mirror-image perceptions.

Ans: c, p. 718

29. Given the tendency of people to categorize information according to preformed schemas, which of the following stereotypes would Juan, a 65-year-old political liberal and fitness enthusiast, be most likely to have?
    a. "People who exercise regularly are very extraverted."
    b. "All political liberals are advocates of a reduced defense budget."
    c. "Young people today have no sense of responsibility."
    d. "Older people are lazy."

Ans: b, p. 718

30. We tend to perceive the members of an ingroup as ________ and the members of an outgroup as ________.
    a. similar to one another; different from one another
    b. different from one another; similar to one another
    c. above average in ability; below average in ability
    d. below average in ability; above average in ability

Ans: b, pp. 718-719

31. Which of the following was *not* mentioned in the text discussion of the roots of prejudice?
    a. people's tendency to overestimate the similarity of people within groups
    b. people's tendency to assume that exceptional, or especially memorable, individuals are unlike the majority of members of a group
    c. people's tendency to assume that the world is just and that people get what they deserve
    d. people's tendency to discriminate against those they view as "outsiders"

Ans: a, pp. 718-719

32. The belief that those who suffer deserve their fate is expressed in the:
    a. just-world phenomenon.
    b. phenomenon of ingroup bias.
    c. fundamental attribution error.
    d. mirror-image perception principle.

Ans: b, p. 719

33. Which theorist argued that aggression was a manifestation of a person's "death instinct" redirected toward another person?
    a. Milgram
    b. Freud
    c. Lorenz
    d. Janis
    e. Asch

Ans: b, p. 719

34. *Aggression* is defined as behavior that:
    a. hurts another person.
    b. is intended to hurt another person.
    c. is hostile, passionate, and produces physical injury.
    d. has all of the above characteristics.

Ans: a, p. 719

35. Which of the following is true about aggression?
    a. It varies too much to be instinctive in humans.
    b. It is just one instinct among many.
    c. It is instinctive but shaped by learning.
    d. It is the most important human instinct.

Ans: d, p. 720

36. Research studies have found a positive correlation between aggressive tendencies in animals and levels of the hormone:
    a. estrogen.
    b. adrenaline.
    c. noradrenaline.
    d. testosterone.
    e. epinephrine.

Ans: c, p. 721

37. Regarding the influence of alcohol and testosterone on aggressive behavior, which of the following is true?
    a. Consumption of alcohol increases aggressive behavior; injections of testosterone reduce aggressive behavior.
    b. Consumption of alcohol reduces aggressive behavior; injections of testosterone increase aggressive behavior.
    c. Consumption of alcohol and injections of testosterone both promote aggressive behavior.
    d. Consumption of alcohol and injections of testosterone both reduce aggressive behavior.

Ans: d, p. 721

38. After waiting in line for an hour to buy concert tickets, Teresa is told that the concert is sold out. In her anger she pounds her fist on the ticket counter, frightening the clerk. Teresa's behavior is best explained by:
    a. evolutionary psychology.
    b. the reciprocity norm.
    c. social exchange theory.
    d. the frustration-aggression principle.

Ans: d, pp. 723-724

39. Research studies have shown that frequent exposure to sexually explicit films:
    a. may promote increased acceptance of promiscuity.
    b. diminishes the attitude that rape is a serious crime.
    c. may lead individuals to devalue their partners.
    d. may produce all of the above effects.

Ans: a, pp. 723-724

40. Research studies have indicated that the tendency of viewers to misperceive normal sexuality, devalue their partners, and trivialize rape is:
    a. increased by exposure to pornography.
    b. not changed after exposure to pornography.
    c. decreased in men by exposure to pornography.
    d. decreased in both men and women by exposure to pornography.

Ans: a, p. 724

41. Most researchers agree that:
    a. media violence is a factor in aggressive behavior.
    b. there is a negative correlation between media violence and aggressiveness.
    c. paradoxically, watching excessive pornography ultimately diminishes an individual's aggressive tendencies.
    d. media violence is too unreal to promote aggression in viewers.

Ans: c, p. 727

42. Social traps are situations in which:
    a. conflicting parties realize that they have shared goals, the attainment of which requires their mutual cooperation.
    b. conflicting parties have similar, and generally negative, views of one another.
    c. conflicting parties each pursue their self-interests and become caught in mutually destructive behavior.
    d. two conflicting groups meet face-to-face in an effort to resolve their differences.

Ans: d, p. 728

43. Mr. and Mrs. Samuels are constantly fighting, and each perceives the other as hard-headed and insensitive. Their conflict is being fueled by:
   a. self-disclosure.
   b. stereotypes.
   c. a social trap.
   d. mirror-image perceptions.

Ans: d, p. 728

44. Two neighboring nations are each stockpiling weapons. Each sees its neighbor's actions as an act of aggression and its own actions as self-defense. Evidently, these nations are victims of:
   a. the self-fulfilling prophecy.
   b. groupthink.
   c. the self-serving bias.
   d. the fundamental attribution error.

Ans: c, p. 729

45. Most people prefer mirror-image photographs of their faces. This is best explained by:
   a. the principle of equity.
   b. the principle of self-disclosure.
   c. the mere exposure effect.
   d. mirror-image perceptions.
   e. deindividuation.

Ans: d, p. 729

46. Which of the following factors is the *most* powerful predictor of friendship?
   a. similarity in age
   b. common racial and religious background
   c. similarity in physical attractiveness
   d. physical proximity

Ans: d, p. 729

47. The mere exposure effect demonstrates that:
   a. familiarity breeds contempt.
   b. opposites attract.
   c. birds of a feather flock together.
   d. familiarity breeds fondness.

Ans: d, p. 730

48. Ahmed and Monique are on a blind date. Which of the following will probably be *most* influential in determining whether they like each other?
   a. their personalities
   b. their beliefs
   c. their social skills
   d. their physical attractiveness

Ans: a, p. 732

49. Having read the chapter, which of the following is best borne out by research on attraction?
    a. Birds of a feather flock together.
    b. Opposites attract.
    c. Familiarity breeds contempt.
    d. Absence makes the heart grow fonder.

Ans: a, p. 733

50. Opening her mail, Joan discovers a romantic greeting card from her boyfriend. According to the two-factor theory, she is likely to feel the most intense romantic feelings if, prior to reading the card, she has just:
    a. completed her daily run.
    b. finished reading a chapter in her psychology textbook.
    c. awakened from a nap.
    d. finished eating lunch.
    e. been listening to a tape of love songs.

Ans: a, p. 733

51. In one experiment, college men were physically aroused and then introduced to an attractive woman. Compared to men who had not been aroused, these men:
    a. reported more positive feelings toward the woman.
    b. reported more negative feelings toward the woman.
    c. were ambiguous about their feelings toward the woman.
    d. were more likely to feel that the woman was "out of their league" in terms of attractiveness.
    e. focused more on the woman's attractiveness and less on her intelligence and personality.

Ans: c, pp. 733-734

52. The deep affection that is felt in long-lasting relationships is called ________ love; this feeling is fostered in relationships in which ________.
    a. passionate; there is equity between the partners
    b. passionate; traditional roles are maintained
    c. companionate; there is equity between the partners
    d. companionate; traditional roles are maintained

Ans: d, p. 735

53. Research studies indicate that in an emergency situation the presence of others often:
    a. prevents people from even noticing the situation.
    b. prevents people from interpreting an unusual event as an emergency.
    c. prevents people from assuming responsibility for assisting.
    d. leads to all of the above.

Ans: d, p. 736

54. Increasing the number of people that are present during an emergency tends to:
    a. increase the likelihood that people will cooperate in rendering assistance.
    b. decrease the empathy that people feel for the victim.
    c. increase the role that social norms governing helping will play.
    d. decrease the likelihood that anyone will help.

Ans: a, pp. 736-737

55. Which of the following is associated with an increased tendency on the part of a bystander to offer help in an emergency situation?
   a. being in a good mood
   b. having recently needed help and not received it
   c. observing someone as he or she refuses to offer help
   d. being a female

Ans: b, p. 737

56. According to social exchange theory, a person's tendency toward altruistic behavior is based on:
   a. a determination of the relatedness of those who will be affected.
   b. a cost-benefit analysis of any action.
   c. social norms.
   d. all of the above.

Ans: d, p. 737

57. After Sandy helped Jack move into his new apartment, Jack felt obligated to help Sandy when she moved. Jack's sense of responsibility can best be explained by:
   a. evolutionary psychology.
   b. two-factor theory.
   c. the social responsibility norm.
   d. the reciprocity norm.

Ans: a, p. 737

58. Driving home from work, Althea saw a car run off the road and burst into flames. Althea stopped her car, ran to the burning vehicle, and managed to pull the elderly driver to safety before the car exploded. Althea's behavior can best be explained by:
   a. the social responsibility norm.
   b. the reciprocity norm.
   c. two-factor theory.
   d. reward theory.

Ans: e, p. 738

59. Which of the following strategies would be *most* likely to foster positive feelings between two conflicting groups?
   a. Take steps to reduce the likelihood of social traps.
   b. Separate the groups so that tensions diminish.
   c. Have one representative from each group visit the other and field questions.
   d. Increase the amount of contact between the two conflicting groups.
   e. Have the groups work on a superordinate goal.

Ans: b, p. 739

60. Which of the following best describes how GRIT works?
   a. The fact that two sides in a conflict have great respect for the other's strengths prevents further escalation of the problem.
   b. The two sides engage in a series of reciprocated conciliatory acts.
   c. The two sides agree to have their differences settled by a neutral, third-party mediator.
   d. The two sides engage in cooperation in those areas in which shared goals are possible.